The Recovery Book

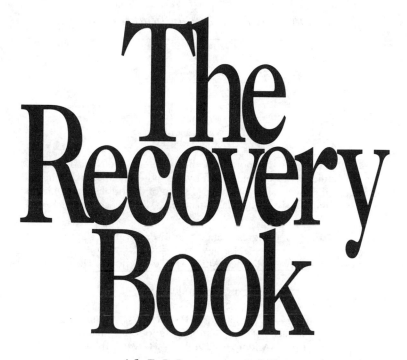

The Recovery Book

Al J. Mooney, M.D.
Arlene Eisenberg
Howard Eisenberg

❖ ❖ ❖ ❖

With a Foreword by Stanley E. Gitlow, M.D.,
Clinical Professor of Medicine,
Mt. Sinai School of Medicine,
New York, NY

WORKMAN PUBLISHING, NEW YORK

Dedication
To Dot and Dr. John, without whom...

 Published simultaneously in Canada by Thomas Allen & Son Limited.

Library of Congress Cataloging-in-Publication Data
Mooney, Al, Dr.
The recovery book / by Al Mooney, M.D., Arlene Eisenberg, Howard Eisenberg
p. cm.
Includes index.
ISBN 1-56305-084-6 (pbk.)
1. Alcoholics—Rehabilitation—Handbooks, manuals, etc.
2. Narcotic addicts—Rehabilitation—Handbooks, manuals, etc.
I. Eisenberg, Arlene. II. Eisenberg, Howard. III. Title.
HV5275.M56 1992 362.29'128—dc 92-50284
CIP

Cover illustration: Nikki Middendorf

Workman Publishing Company, Inc.
708 Broadway New York, NY 10003

Manufactured in the United States of America
First printing November 1992
10 9 8 7

Many Thanks

As anyone who has ever tried to kick an addiction knows, recovery is a lot easier when you have a good support group. When writing a book on recovery, you need a good support group, too. We had the best. And our heartfelt thanks go to:

The Mooney family—first and foremost. Dr. John and Dot Mooney, Carol Lind, Jimmy, and Bobby (now Dr. Robert) dedicated the lives they recovered to tossing life preservers to anyone willing to open his or her hands and hold on. Their wisdom and insights, built on years of drinking and using followed by even more years of sobriety, have immeasurably enriched this book.

The great greater Willingway family—staff, patients, and friends who shared their insights and experiences during interviews early on and those who later read and commented on the rough manuscript. (We loved when they said, "This is great! Get it published quick so we can use it." But we appreciated, too, "This section is a little off. What it ought to say is . . .") Special thanks to Ida and C.D. Collins; Susan Pajari and Roger Pajari, PhD; Lonnie Simmons, CAC; Sarah Todd, CAC; Eddie and Linda Byrd; Casey King, CAC; Martha Jones, CAC; Betty and Herb Cody; Rex Mock, CAC; Louie Glisson, CAC; Bert McVay, CAC; Geno Hampton; Tracie Smith, TRS; Janice Blakely; Pam Mosley, LMSW; Chris Marsh; Beth Tarpley; Beth Holloway; Jenny Lynn Anderson; Les Cradit; Ann Lewis; Lynn Lanier; Peggy Taylor; Terry Odom; Michelle Hodges; Desiree Llaneza; Shirley and Joe Wallace, MD; Roy Stump; Carolyn Martin, PhD; David Ruffin, PhD; Dallas Cason, RN; Honey Bowen; Maryanna Hite; Sarah "Aunt Tatey" Riggs; and posthumously, Uncle Bill.

And of course, to Willingway's superb medical staff, past and present: Charles Morgan, MD; David Morris, MD; Melissa Lee Warner, MD; Robert Bryan, MD; Julie Cowart, Director of Nursing; Malinda Jackson, RN; Kay Bowen, RN; Dena Hattaway, RN; and Faye Hill, LUN.

The greatest greater Workman family. For people who knew little about recovery, they sure got into it with a full heart. Thanks to Peter Workman for being Peter Workman; to Kathie Ness for dotting our i's and crossing our t's so skillfully; to art director Ira Teichberg for his imaginative cover and crisp layouts; to Nikki Mittendorf for the cover illustration; to David Schiller for the snappy cover copy; to Shannon Ryan for, as always, doing her job with competence and good humor; and, of course, to the best editor anywhere, Suzanne Rafer. Tough as forged steel nails. Good as 25-karat gold.

The experts. The physicians, nurses, lawyers, psychologists, clerics, and other professionals whose generously (and patiently) given expertise was invaluable: Andrea Barthwell, MD; LeClair Bissel, MD; Burns Brady, MD; David Conney, MD; George DeLeon, PhD; Stan Gitlow, MD; Jim Graham, MD; Ron M. Kirsner, MD; Steve Mersky, MD; Ron Moody, MD; Tony Radcliffe, MD; Mindy Seidlin, MD; Michael Smith, MD (ACU); Walter Wahl, MD; Jim West, MD; Thomas White, MD; Joe Frawley, MD. And Nancy Waters, RN; Ann Hardin, RN; Roger Cadwalter, PhD; Rabbi Jim Goodman; David Evans, Esq; Barry Kantrowitz, Esq; Nancy Paull; Kallia Bokser; EAP consultants Claire Fleming, CEAP, Don Sandin, CEAP, and Walter Scanlon, CEAP; Velane White and Nancy Stremmel; David Grant; Charles Jurgensen; Miriam Pollack and Michael Rehmar, MD; Tom Perrin; and Lois Trimpey.

The other experts. The patients of Willingway and the hundreds of other anonymous AA members whose concerns and questions, agony and euphoria at the meetings we attended were the rock on which we built *The Recovery Book*.

The good friends and associates. Eddie Fisher, Eve Coulson, Chris Coulson, and Joan Coulson offered sound advice and much appreciated suggestions. Niurka Zumeta, the all-round assistant at Writing Associates, without whom nothing would ever get copied or filed. Elise and Arnold Goodman, our agents and friends, for their support every step of the way.

Our own families. Jane, John, and Rachel, whose patience and understanding far exceeded the call of duty. And Heidi and Sandee who graciously (if not patiently) waited for us to finish this book so their co-author could get on with the next.

Since this project has been going on for more than three years, bouncing from New York to Statesboro, Georgia, and back, we are pretty certain that we have omitted some important names from this list. If we've forgotten you, we apologize and offer our gratitude.

Al J. Mooney, MD
Arlene Eisenberg
Howard Eisenberg

Contents

PART 1

Getting Sober: If You're Not Sober Yet, Start Here

PART II

PHASE ONE: SAVING YOUR LIFE

PART III

MOVING INTO PHASE TWO: REPAIRING AND ENJOYING YOUR LIFE

PART V

CHEMICAL DEPENDENCY: A FAMILY DISEASE—WHAT EVERY FAMILY MEMBER SHOULD KNOW

PART VI

THE REST OF YOUR LIFE IN RECOVERY: MAKING THE MOST OF YOUR CHEMICAL-FREE LIFE

PART VII

FOR YOUR INFORMATION

FOREWORD

Shortly after Bill W. and Dr. Bob founded the major self-help group of this century (Alcoholics Anonymous, 1935), it became apparent that written explanations of the recovery process were needed for explanation, understanding, and ongoing consistency of the program. The "Big Book" and other elements essential to the program followed.

It fell to the first woman in AA, Marty Mann, to write what became the standard-bearing beginner's text on this illness, *The Primer on Alcoholism*. Its question-and-answer format saw it through numerous printings in many languages, while its author proceeded to found The National Council on Alcoholism and lead the long battle for acceptance by the public of this addiction as an illness. Until now, I had not read a text that in any way could be compared with the "Primer." Finally *The Recovery Book* has arrived and can rightfully accept the mantle of Marty Mann's ground-breaking book.

To be of ultimate use to the individual whose drinking or other drug abuse has become a problem—whether just to his or herself, or to his or her family, employer, employee, judicial system, physician, or others—a book must deal first and foremost with the likelihood that its readers possess a firm belief in their "uniqueness" and cling desperately to the illusion that their private fears and public rationalizations bear little resemblance to those of "drunks and addicts." Only when you've heard *all* the denials, as Al Mooney has, can you deal constructively with the troubled questions, drug-numbed feelings, drink-deadened belief systems, and dead-end attitudes that obstruct recovery.

Be you male, female, young, old, Caucasian, Black, Hispanic, Christian, Jew, Atheist, gay, straight, single, married, divorced, mother, father, employer, employee, retiree, wealthy, impoverished, with or without complicating illness—if you are touched by alcoholism or other addictions this book has been written for you.

For the patient: it will guide you through the difficult early days and years of recovery soundly and expertly, expressing almost every imaginable thought or fear, conscious or otherwise. Every issue is addressed, always with hope and understanding, and often with direct suggestions promising relief and improvement.

For physicians and other helping professionals: You will understand your addicted patients and clients as never before.

For the oft-times despairing members of Al-Anon: replace the literature you have planted about the house with *The Recovery Book*. Nothing could be better.

—Stanley E. Gitlow, M.D.
Clinical Professor of Medicine
Mt. Sinai School of Medicine
New York, NY

INTRODUCTION

REACHING FOR LIFE PRESERVERS

My name is Al Mooney, and I'm not an alcoholic or a drug addict—yet.* But everyone else in my family is—my parents, my brothers, Jimmy and Bobby, and our kid sister, Carol Lind. So drinking and drugging are more than just a challenging clinical problem to me. They're personal. Very personal.

When one of my patients says, "Well, gosh, we never drink around the kids, so they couldn't possibly be affected by our drinking," I feel a sudden twist in my gut. Children are affected by everything that goes on in the home. I know I was. True, I rarely saw my parents drink and never saw them take drugs. But a lot of confusing things happened, and no one ever explained what was going on. How could they? Much of the time, they didn't know what was going on either.

*I say "yet" because the biological markers are there, and some of the character traits are too. I've carefully avoided testing the heredity theory by shunning alcohol and mood-altering drugs.

My father was a wonderful physician—so good that one of his former patients once told me, "I'd rather have had John Mooney operate on me drunk than any other doctor in town sober." And because he didn't want to treat anybody when he'd been drinking, my dad broke out his bottle only at night. For office hours he switched to pills, alternating uppers and downers to meet his needs of the moment in what he whimsically referred to in AA talks years later as "the balanced life."

But he was playing with pharmaceutical fire, and one night in our living room he went into a convulsion from an overdose that sent him to the first of a long series of psychiatric hospitals for "drying out." When he disappeared for a week or a month, my mother would tell us, "Daddy's off learning to be a better doctor." (Which, since it's tough to be a doctor when you're under the influence, wasn't altogether a lie.) When he came home, he'd bring us a bunch of toys he'd built in occupational therapy shops—which I guess was one way he'd convince himself that in spite of everything, he was still a good father. Once he brought us a wooden toy chest he'd made, and I remember wondering what in the world they did at those medical meetings.

His patients got the same stories we did. My father would put a notice in the newspaper that he was going to California for a four-week graduate course in, say, orthopedic surgery. It happened so often that his patients either figured out what was going on or concluded he was the best-trained doctor in the state of Georgia.

My mother, Dot Mooney, was doing her level best to be a good mom, too, but as she admitted much later, she never let that get in the way of her drinking and drugging. No matter how hung over she was, she conscientiously drove us to Sunday School. Then she scrunched down in the back of the classroom with her hands covering her mouth, so no one could smell the liquor on her breath.

With an M.D. for a husband, it wasn't hard for my mother to get hold of all the drug samples she wanted. She popped codeine for her hangover headaches, tranquilizers for depression, barbiturates so she could sleep, and Demerol for back pain. One night she gave herself a 2 c.c. shot of Demerol fifteen times between midnight and daylight, from a vial she'd filched from my father's bag. Eventually her mind got so foggy that she was afraid to take us anywhere—especially after she dropped my little brother Jimmy at the library and forgot to pick him up.

In a crazy sort of way I began to feel responsible for what was going on. I didn't have a choice. Like so many other eldest children of alcoholic/addict parents, I knew I had to take charge—to poke my mother awake every time she fell asleep at the wheel and to tell her where to turn so she wouldn't keep driving till she ran out of gas. Relatives and family friends complimented me on being "the little man in the family" in that and dozens of other out-of-control situations, and I acquired a lot of self-confidence running rescue operations anytime the Mooney family train ran off the tracks. But at the age of ten, I shouldn't have been the engineer. I should have been just a kid playing in the backyard.

It all finally turned around when my father, who'd written himself hundreds of phony narcotics prescriptions, was sentenced by Judge Renfrow to six months at the federal facility in Lexington, Kentucky in lieu of a two-year state felony sentence (fortunately the judge didn't want to see the career of one of the best doctors in town destroyed).

It was there one day, on the wrong side of the bars, that he looked out and saw a herd of Angus cattle grazing peacefully in a meadow and thought, "Those ignorant cows out there are running free, and here's Mooney, with all his college degrees and medical school education, locked up in a federal prison." There was only one possible conclusion, and he reached it: "If it hadn't been for all my drinking and doping, I could be out there just as happy-go-lucky as those cows."

A local AA member came to visit my father during his first week in Lexington. Sick on the inside and shaking on the outside, dad turned to his visitor and said wearily, "Houston, if I could just find out what in the world is causing me to get drunk, I believe I could straighten out." His visitor said quietly, "John, did it ever occur to you that the only thing causing you to get drunk is the whiskey?" For the first time, instead of trying to figure out what was causing him to drink (at various times he'd blamed it on stress and overwork, the lack of a hobby, abscessed teeth and the nagging of his first wife), my father began to look at what his drinking was causing.

John Mooney emerged from Lexington ready for sobriety. He understood finally that he'd been looking for God in the bottle, and that it was the last place in the world that God could be found.

Back in Statesboro, my father cheerfully reopened his medical office. A few days later he was forced to close it down. He was summoned to appear before the state medical board and told that his license had been revoked, but that—no guarantees—he could apply for reinstatement in six months. It was a shattering blow. But AA had taught him that there's good in whatever happens to you, no matter how bad it looks at first—you just don't see it yet. The good thing, it turned out, was that now he couldn't busy himself treating other people's problems. He'd felt cocky and cured and had planned to be so busy rebuilding his practice that he'd maybe go to AA meetings once a month. Now, with nothing else to do, he resigned himself to doing ninety meetings in ninety days, driving with an old drinking buddy, C.D., and C.D.'s wife, Ida, all over the state of Georgia to attend them.

My mother, who was such a mess she needed to drink three beers to work up the courage to take us to church, still wouldn't admit to being an alcoholic, but she was so sick of the life she'd been leading that she went along "for the ride." At the end of six months, the medical board reinstated my father's license. Then an interesting thing happened. As his doctor friends began to believe that maybe this time John Mooney was on the wagon to stay, they asked him to help them counsel their alcoholic patients. And Mom, who by now had 'fessed up and sworn off anything stronger than coffee, helped with the women.

My dad outfitted two rooms in his office as bedrooms for detox. But that wasn't nearly enough, so he began checking them into Bulloch County Hospital. As his reputation for sobering up alcoholics grew and patients began coming to him from all over the Southeast, filling beds his colleagues needed for their local patients' appendectomies and herniorraphies, they finally said enough was enough and set strict limits on out-of-towners. With no place else to put them, my folks started bringing their drunks home.

In the five years that followed, 583 patients were detoxed and treated in our big old house on Lee Street, often as many as 22 at a time. Three beds were set up in the dining room. Jimmy and I were at college, so our bedrooms became dorms. Temporarily evicted from their rooms, Bobby slept in a log cabin in the backyard; Carol Lind, age seven, shared a walk-in closet with an alcoholic teenage girl.

At first my parents charged no fees. But at income tax time, my father's accountant, Earl Dabbs, became concerned. "Look here, John," he said, "you're spending all this money on food and medical supplies. You're cutting into your office time. This thing could break you." So my dad started charging $5 a day "to cover costs." And gradually billing became more realistic—$600 for four weeks, then $800 when we put on a night shift. That seemed like a good idea after my mother, in her nightgown, broke her toe tackling a big guy in his pajamas as he dashed out the kitchen door, trying his darnedest to outrun the DT's.

When my parents applied for a building permit to add a five-bedroom wing to the house so their children could sleep in their own beds again, our long-suffering neighbors petitioned the city. Permit denied. But Earl solved the problem. He introduced the Mooneys to Ed Tingle, head of the Small Business Administration in Atlanta. Result: a low-interest loan and the construction of a twenty-nine-bed hospital (it's forty beds now) right there in Statesboro. My mother named it: Willingway.

You'd think that, seeing the mess alcohol and drugs had made of their parents' lives, the Mooney kids would be little angels, fearing to tread in their parents' footsteps. No such luck. One by one, the little angels fell. All those meetings our parents went to every night, often leaving him on his own, may have contributed a bit to Jimmy's problem. Bobby says his drinking with his buddies began around the time he started resenting "all those drunks hanging out at my house, and no place for me or my friends." And my sister went to so many meetings with my mother that on the first day in second grade, when the teacher went around the room asking the children to identify themselves, she announced, "My name is Carol Lind, and I'm an alcoholic." But the main reason they got to drinking and drugging was simpler than that: Alcoholism is a disease that runs in families, probably for both genetic and environmental reasons.

Like many firstborn children of alcoholics/addicts, I went to great lengths to avoid alcohol and mood-changing drugs. Maybe first children are most likely to remain abstinent because we're responsible for taking care of everybody else, and we're older and more involved in the anguish of it all than our siblings are. On that score, Alateen helped me a whole lot. It was a real comfort to learn that we weren't the only family going through these things.

I knew I wanted to be a doctor like my dad, but I wasn't at all sure I wanted to work with addicts and alcoholics. I felt like I'd seen too much of them already. So though my medical training was a hard grind it was also a great escape—and alcoholism was nowhere to be found in the curriculum.

There was a lot of "common knowledge" about it, though, and I began to hear things that I knew weren't true, all adding up to a consensus that "alcoholics aren't treatable." A senior resident told us that we needed to learn to diagnose all the alcoholics in our care (I perked up—at last some common sense). "Once you've identified them," he continued, "just ignore them and concentrate on all the other patients you can help."

I knew better. But still I leaned away from treating alcoholics. In training, I thrilled to the quick fixes of surgery. Even when all I did was scrub and close, helping to perform surgical miracles did wonders for the ego. But to my surprise, surgical rotation quickly convinced me that I could do a lot more good in my father's size 11's than in the operating suite.

What opened my eyes were my nostrils. It didn't matter whether the broken and bleeding teenager or middle-aged trauma patient laid bare on the table was there because of a stabbing, a motorcycle accident, a gunshot wound, or family violence. Time after time, when we opened them up, a sour bouquet of brewery and barroom suddenly permeated the operating room. I found myself wondering why medicine didn't choose a better way; preventing alcoholic/addicted patients from coming apart instead of belatedly sewing them back together.

I still had a lot to learn, but one thing I knew for sure. I wanted no further part in the kind of solutions I'd been a reluctant party to in the OR—like the surgery on a stubborn alcoholic who suffered terribly painful pancreatitis anytime he drank. Our team's quick fix was to remove 95 percent of his pancreas, "curing" his pancreatitis and allowing him to drink himself to death.

Like most drinkers, my father was a heavy smoker. Although he finally quit when he was in his sixties, progressive chronic lung disease slowed him down a lot and took him from us when he was in his early seventies. By the time he died, he knew that what he'd started wouldn't die with him. Everyone in the family who needed to be was in recovery. My mother was the head women's counselor at Willingway. Jimmy had studied business administration and become our administrator. Bobby had finished medical school, enrolled in a psychiatry residency, and looked forward to joining our medical staff. Carol Lind was a crackerjack women's counselor, had decided to go to law school, and planned to come back to help people in the fight for their legal right to the "pursuit of happiness" through sobriety and recovery. And I was medical director.

Most of what I know is in this book, and I learned it from John Mooney (or "Dr. 58520," as he wryly referred to himself after his stay at Lexington), a man I'll always remember not as a hopeless drunk but as a wise teacher and wonderful father. Like me, he always wanted to find a practical recovery book to send his patients home with: a whole-family life preserver to keep them clean, sober and afloat when our staff was no longer around to hug, love and counsel them.

I believe Dr. John would feel that this is that book. I (and my co-authors) hope that you will, too.

—Al J. Mooney, M.D.
Statesboro, Georgia

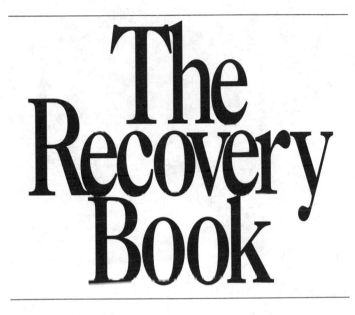

The Recovery Book

1

RECOVERY ROAD MAP

Like traffic on the Oregon Trail 150 years ago, traffic on Recovery Road is pretty heavy these days. That's good. But as they did heading west, a lot of people are getting lost or falling by the wayside. That's not good.

Part of the problem is that there has been no truly comprehensive road map to recovery—something that could show people what to expect along the way. Recovery, it seemed to us (one of us being a rehab hospital medical director with a desperate need for an A-to-Z book that departing patients could take with them), was even less well charted than the Old West. That's why we've written this book.

We've tried hard to take into account individual differences and reactions—the fact that although all are going in the same direction, the road isn't the same for every traveler.

This introductory chapter lays out your itinerary, tells how to avoid getting stuck in the mud of apathy, describes what you can expect in recovery, and walks you through the three distinct phases leading from the slavery of addiction to the freedom of sobriety.

Get started. The first steps are the hardest. After that, it's going to get better and better.

UNDERSTANDING RECOVERY

Recovery is no horizon-to-horizon superhighway. There are lots of tricky detours. Lots of ruts and bumps. Lots of flat tires—and flat moods. Lots of running out of gas. The good thing is that you don't have to ride it in a covered wagon. And you don't have to pioneer it. Hundreds of thousands of once "hopeless drunks" and "depraved addicts" have followed this road before you. Instead of dying of cancer or cirrhosis of the liver, they've survived to tell their tales—to share with you the

Guide Lines

❖ Alcoholism/addiction is a disease.

❖ This disease strikes all kinds of people—young and old, rich and poor, educated and illiterate.

❖ Having the disease does not mean you are immoral or weak-willed.

❖ Recovery from alcoholism/addiction, like recovery from most diseases, is gradual.

❖ Swearing off alcohol and drugs is the easy part of recovery. The hard part is living happily ever after. Abstention will not automatically make your life better; a better life will come only with time, patience, and hard work.

❖ Although this book can guide you through the maze of recovery, it is highly unlikely that you can have a successful recovery without additional support. A lot of that support will come from other recovering alcoholics and addicts, but the help of a trained professional may also be needed.

lessons of their setbacks and successes.

It's all here—the experiences and wisdom of thousands of good people victimized by addictive disease, distilled into practical advice that takes you step by step along Recovery Road, from the moment you decide on sobriety through the weeks, months, and strength-gathering years that follow.

THE WAY TO GO

Becoming clean and sober is important—no question about that. The operative definition of sober is "abstaining from alcohol and drugs," and if you want to save your life, clearly that's the first change you'll need to make. But who, other than a funeral director, would want to live the other definition of sober: "serious, solemn, grave"?

No, recovery isn't about becoming clean, sober, and solemn. It's about living a better life—about loving relationships, satisfying work, invigorating play, about good health and good spirits. Of course you can't build this better life without getting sober. But it's equally true that you can't stay sober without building a better life. You can't, experience shows, have one without the other.

Treatment for the disease of alcoholism/addiction is, in fact, unique in that it not only eliminates the symptoms of the illness but has the potential to make life better than it has ever been before.

It takes time, patience, and hard work. But with a solid recovery, you can:

❖ Regain the freedom to make choices.

❖ Begin to find pleasure in friends, family, nature, art, music, work.

❖ Rediscover peace of mind—or discover it for the first time.

❖ Escape from fears—of people, of new experiences, and of financial insecurity.

❖ Benefit from a new honesty in your relationships.

❖ Stop pitying yourself and start caring about others.

❖ Achieve liberation by giving up your need to control people, events, everything in your life.

❖ Become comfortable with yourself and with others; feel loving and lovable.

❖ Learn to solve life's problems with thoughtful actions instead of blotting them out with chemicals.

❖ And (possibly most important of all) learn how to break the cycle of addictive behavior handed down from parent to child so that your children, or the children you hope to have in the future, or the grandchildren you already have, will not have to suffer as you've suffered.

These are the goals of recovery, and of this book. You can't achieve them by waving a magic wand, by popping a magic pill, or even by reading this book from cover to cover. If you're accustomed to immediate gratification, the slow process of recovery may at first be difficult to comprehend. But if you think about it, you will remember that you didn't get into trouble with alcohol and/or drugs overnight. And you can't put the pieces of your life back together between sundown and sunup either.

Step by step, *The Recovery Book* will guide you on the rocky route through recovery, with each section of the book taking you a giant step farther.

"I'm glad I'm an alcoholic. It's given me what little wisdom, compassion, and understanding of other folks I have. In order to know what it feels like to be hit by a hammer, you have to ask another nail."

Getting Sober

The desire to become sober and the willingness to stop using all mind-altering chemical substances are the first essential steps on the road through recovery. If you haven't yet made a commitment to sobriety, read Chapter 2. Once you have made that commitment, you'll need to examine the various pathways to sobriety in Chapter 3 (from going it alone to intensive inpatient treatment) so you can decide which suits you best. If you

WHERE ARE YOU NOW?

We don't know whose hands are holding this book, whose eyes are reading this page. Because we wanted to be all things to all alcoholics and addicts, we've arranged things on these pages so that no matter where you are on Recovery Road, you'll be able to find your place quickly. (And, a bit more slowly, your way.) This book is for those just starting out—who swore off ten minutes ago or plan to swear off twenty minutes from now. It's for those in their first months or year of recovery—still uncertain, still feeling lost, still not sure they're going to get there.

It's also for those who've been clean and sober for years but still feel as though something's missing, as though a piece here and a piece there in the puzzle of sobriety have somehow been misplaced. And it's for those who've made false starts in the past, taken wrong turns, gotten stuck in mental cul-de-sacs, or been mugged by "just one drink" or a seductive "one little hit" along the way.

A DRUG BY ANY NAME

It doesn't matter whether your drug of choice has been alcohol, cocaine, Valium, or another mood-altering substance. The problems you face in recovery will, for the most part, be the same. To bring this fact home, we refer throughout this book to the disease of "alcoholism/addiction" and to anyone afflicted with it as an "alcoholic/addict." We occasionally use "mood-altering chemical," "chemical substance," or just plain "drugs" to mean all drugs, including alcohol. Alcohol, of course, is a drug. But since so many people tend to separate it out—probably because it is legal and so widely used—and so that alcoholics won't feel ignored, we most often specify "alcohol and drugs." Though some of the questions and concerns raised by people in recovery throughout this book refer to one or another type of drug, the answers are generally relevant to everyone. When we mention AA, we mean it to represent all the Twelve-Step substance-abuse fellowships (Narcotics Anonymous, Pills Anonymous, Cocaine Anonymous, and so on), unless otherwise noted.

Keep in mind that if you have had a problem with one or more of these substances, switching to another in recovery—from alcohol to pot, for example, or from pills to booze—will intensify, not cure, your problem. If you have trouble with one mind-altering substance, you will have trouble with all of them.

choose the inpatient route, Chapter 4 will tell you what you can expect. If you aren't yet sober, the next step will be to safely withdraw from your drug (or drugs) of choice. What this will be like—and how the discomfort of detox can be minimized—is outlined in Chapter 5.

Experience has shown that after withdrawal, recovery falls into three phases, each lasting a year or more.

Phase One: Saving Your Life

In this stage, which starts with a rude awakening more often than a spiritual one, your chief concern is survival. You may seem self-centered to family and friends, focusing all your energies on yourself and your recovery (just as you focused them on your addiction). But that's the way early recovery has to be. Push the hold button for everything else while you concentrate on finding out what recovery is about, how a mutual support group like Alcoholics Anonymous (AA) can help you move into it successfully, how to get the most out of such a group, and how to deal with your family, friends, and job during this time. Your body will probably complain bitterly, with new symptoms related to recovery and old ones you never noticed when your brain was anesthetized. Your head will probably be shrouded in fog, and your emotions will flip-flop frequently. You'll need to learn how to cope with body, mind, and moods without chemical support. Chapters 6 to 15 will help get you through this often difficult, sometimes painful, but ultimately rewarding adjustment period. If you're a teenager, Chapter 16 will get you started on your road to recovery.

Phase Two: Enjoying Your Life

With the craving for alcohol or drugs diminishing and your recovery on track, you can switch gears from saving your life to making it more fulfilling. Work at rebuilding old relationships and beginning new ones; look for new educational opportunities and job challenges; and explore hobbies and leisure activities. With a smog-free head and more stable emotions, you can begin to have fun. Chapters 17 to 21 will guide you along this rosy path, which is not without the occasional thorn.

Phase Three: Extending Your Life

Somewhere in the third or fourth year of sobriety (a little earlier for some, a little later for others), the focus switches again. Once you've saved your life and learned to enjoy it, it's time to consider how you can best extend it. Chapters 22 to 25 explain how to do this with the help of a sensible diet, a realistic exercise program, and other preventive health measures. This phase is also the time to continue to reach out to help others.

A Family Disease

Those around the addict/alcoholic are like dolphins helplessly trapped in a tuna net. To help you help your family and other loved ones escape from the net your addiction has cast, Chapter 26 provides guidelines for raising children who won't follow in your footsteps, and Chapters 27 and 28 are addressed directly to your significant others. These chapters are meant to help them better understand the disease, what you are going through, and their own feelings. It will also give them the freedom to stop trying to control you, teaching them that each of us is responsible only for our own life.

PARDON THE JARGON

We've tried hard to avoid it, but nevertheless there may be times when words or phrases pop up that are unfamiliar to you if you are new to recovery. Should you come across such verbal obstacles, turn to the glossary in the back of the book.

The Rest of Your Life in Recovery

Of special concern to everyone in recovery is the possibility of relapse. Roughly half of all first-time recoverees slip back into drinking or using. Chapter 29 shows how to side-step relapses, how to recognize one heading your way, and how to use a slip to strengthen your recovery.

Making a Difference

Your recovery can make a difference not only in your own life and in the lives of those you care about, but also in the life of the community at large.

YOU DON'T HAVE TO BE AN ALCOHOLIC OR AN ADDICT

You don't have to be an alcoholic/addict to benefit from reading this book. If someone you care about has a problem, it can help you understand what he or she is going through in recovery, and what you can do to help. "Chemical Dependency: A Family Disease," beginning on page 467, was written for you. This book can also be helpful to the professional (counselor, physician, Employee Assistance Program) who works with alcoholics/addicts and to employers who deal with them on the job. Special messages are addressed to physicians and employers in "For Your Information" in the back of the book.

Alcohol and drugs are a factor in the majority of auto accidents, drownings, and violent and nonviolent crimes. They contribute to child and spouse abuse, broken families, and broken lives. The illness and other mayhem they cause is responsible for the drain of billions of dollars of public funds, funds that could be put to better use. What you can do to turn this situation around is spelled out in Chapter 30.

Some people succeed in getting sober but spend the rest of their lives being miserable. This book can help you avoid their mistakes. We don't promise that it will make your life perfect—nobody's life is. You'll still have problems—everybody does. But following the basic tenets of recovery can improve the way you cope. And, that, ultimately, can bring happiness to you and to those you love.

PART I

GETTING SOBER

If You're Not Sober Yet, Start Here

The ten-second radio and TV "public service" spots on sports shows make it sound so easy: "Just say no to drugs!" If you're wondering why the announcer doesn't add, ". . . and alcohol," the series of lucrative beer commercials minutes later tells you why.

In fact, as every alcoholic/addict knows, the decision to say no to chemicals isn't easy at all—but it is the vital first step on the journey to recovery. The decision is less difficult for some (when health, a marriage, or a job is on the line), far tougher for others, particularly experts in denial ("stop bugging me—I can handle it!"). Self examination and seeing your excuses and rationalizations slowly fall away one by one can help speed decision making.

The second step—actually quitting—is harder still. Many people swear to quit over and over again, but they never do. Others just don't care anymore. They don't believe they can go home again. But sometimes the inertia is the result of lack of information. Befuddled and bewildered, they don't know what their options are or how to go about choosing among them. They're afraid of the unknown: What will detox be like? Or AA? Or treatment? Or sobriety? Knowing the answers will make taking this step easier.

2

THE FIRST STEP: DECIDING TO QUIT

If you've already decided to call it quits, go on to Chapter 3, which will help you carry out your decision. If you're uncertain, vacillating, inventing more excuses than Edison had patents, this chapter is for you. If you've already chosen sobriety but some "buts" and "maybe nots" still linger, then you, too should read this chapter.

To your doctor and your family, one thing is sure: Continue to drink and/or use drugs, and you will reduce both the quality and the length of your life. But *you* have to believe that. Your spouse may be after you to quit drinking. Or your supervisor may have put you on warning: "If you can't stop snorting coke, we don't want you around here anymore." Maybe your exasperated parents have sent you packing, with an admonition not to come home again until you stop drinking and drugging. Or your four-year-old has pleaded, "Please, don't drink anymore! Please, daddy (or mommy)!" Or your physician has warned that if you keep abusing your body, you're headed straight for a headstone with your name on it. All to no avail.

Nothing anyone else does or says is going to get you clean and sober. The choice between life and premature death is yours alone, and you have to want to choose life. To someone who isn't an alcoholic or addict, the choice seems obvious. But it may not be so obvious to you. You may have a lot of questions about what making that choice will mean. This chapter will attempt to answer them. As you read it, contemplate the words of a seventeen-year-old to her dead mother: "You didn't have to die, but you preferred your friends, drugs, the streets, over me." You don't have to die either.

Guide Lines

❖ Denial—the lies you tell yourself to justify continuing to use alcohol or drugs—is a common symptom of alcoholism/addiction (as it is of many other diseases).

❖ You don't have to hit bottom on Skid Row to stop drinking. You only have to realize that alcohol or drugs are having an increasingly negative impact on your life.

❖ Becoming sober doesn't mean giving up the good life (assuming you think your life is good now) in return for a dull one. The idea is to make life in sobriety better than it ever was before.

❖ Even if you don't think you have a drinking or drug problem, you have nothing to lose and a lot to gain if you try sobriety—one day at a time.

❖ Deciding to give up mind-altering chemicals is only the first stride on the road to recovery.

❖ Most people are afraid of what's ahead when they decide to become clean and sober. This fear is normal; there are ways of dealing with it.

WHAT'S ON YOUR MIND?

FEARS ABOUT LIVING SOBER

"I know that drinking and using have messed up my life. But the thought of life without my 'best friends' scares me."

You've leaned on chemical crutches for a long time now, not just to enjoy life but to help you cope with it—to "solve" your problems, endure your job, cheer you up, calm you down, alter your thinking, help you forget what a mess your life has become. In short, to survive. They're as much a habit as putting your left foot after your right. You're afraid that existence without them could be as painful as a double amputation.

Furthermore, you don't know what to expect in sobriety. How will you talk to your spouse, unfortified by your favorite substance? Cope with your boss's demands? Survive an all-day conference? Or even have fun? Life may be hell right now, but it's a familiar hell. The unknown, the darkness out there, is a lot scarier.

What will help is flooding that darkness with light—the goal of this book. Knowing what to expect in the difficult months ahead will make it easier to take those first faltering one-at-a-time steps into the unknown. It will also help if you don't take those steps alone, but with a qualified counselor in an inpatient or outpatient treatment setting, or with others in a mutual-help group, like AA, who've been there before you.

It won't be enough for you to simply stop drinking and drugging. You will need to develop skills for dealing with your spouse, your family, your job, your social life, without chemical assistance—and a structured program based on the successful experiences of others can help you do this best. In the end, you will be surprised to see how, as the darkness dissipates, the world out there becomes brighter than it ever was when you were "looking for God in a bottle."

DO I REALLY HAVE A PROBLEM?

"Okay, I agree that I drink a lot. But I function okay. I take good care of my family and my home. I'm not a falling-down drunk. Don't you have to hit bottom before you need to go on the wagon?"

Each person's "bottom" is different. Some people recognize they are in trouble early. When they don't feel in control of their drinking anymore. When they lose a promotion or mess up a deal. When the bedroom becomes a nightly battleground. When they're booked for driving while intoxicated. Or when their kids start having problems in school because nobody's paying attention to them at home.

Others wait until they lose their jobs or their families, until they hurt someone in a traffic accident, until a child runs away from home, or until liver disease lands them in the hospital. Still others stubbornly hold out for a bottom that lands them in jail or on the street: penniless, homeless, jobless, friendless. Some, of course, like the woman who ignores the lump in her breast or the smoker who scoffs at the signs of lung cancer, never stop denying until they are undeniably dead.

What you need to ask yourself is, "How far down do I want to go before I make an effort to come back up? How much am I willing to risk the possibility that I'll never make it back up?"

"When I was an inpatient, my doctor puzzled me. First day after detox when we talked, I told him what a miserable creature I'd become and what a mess my life was. I said, 'I've got financial problems.' He said, 'That's good!' I said, 'My wife wants to divorce me.' He said, 'That's good!' I said 'And they've taken away my medical license.' He said, 'That's good, too! It's going to make you clean and sober. It's going to save your life.' Then I wasn't puzzled anymore."

"My husband keeps bugging me and saying I'm a drug addict. That's ridiculous. I only pop a Valium once or twice a week, plus maybe a couple of Nembutals and Xanax. Sure, I drink most days. But not a lot. So I think I'm okay."

Your husband is probably right. The drugs you're taking—Valium, which is a benzodiazepine, Nembutal, which is a barbiturate, Xanax, one of the newer benzodiazepines, and alcohol—are all sedatives or central nervous system depressants (see pages 278 and 293 for a more complete list of sedatives). Though they are all slightly different, their effects are similar enough that your body can't distinguish between them. When you start to get withdrawal symptoms from any one of them, taking any other one wards off these symptoms. Which means you're dependent on sedative drugs.

See a physician qualified in addiction medicine (see page 46) or seek other professional treatment for help in

YOU DON'T HAVE TO BE OUT OF CONTROL

Your drinking doesn't have to be out of control to damage your body and your mind. Since alcohol use affects every cell in the human organism, there is virtually no part of you that won't suffer if you overindulge. More than 350 separate illnesses have been linked to alcohol consumption. If you're a male, more than two drinks a day (1 drink equals 1½ ounces of 80- to 100-proof distilled spirits, 5 ounces of wine, or 16 ounces of 5-percent beer) can eventually damage your liver, nervous system, brain, reproductive system, muscles, heart, blood pressure. If you're a female, because of smaller size and insufficient levels of an enzyme needed to process the alcohol efficiently, you may start to damage your body with more than one drink daily. Heavy drinking is also related to the development of several types of cancers. If you regularly exceed two drinks a day, or just occasionally binge on six drinks or more, you need to do something about your drinking—even if you're supremely confident that it's "totally under control."

ridding yourself of your pill-popping habit. And do it before it starts seriously interfering with your life, before your husband stops talking and starts walking.

"I'm willing to quit drinking, even though I'm sure I'm not an alcoholic. I may have some problems with booze, but I'm not like those other people."

Most people who have a drinking problem are sure they aren't that terrible "A" word: alcoholics. A majority of drug users don't think they are addicts. They're all sure they're not like "those other people"—the stinking wino dozing in a doorway, the red-eyed drunk charged with driving under the influence and waiting behind bars for someone in the family to bail him out, the desperate woman swapping sex for drugs on street corners. "Terminal uniqueness" is a major symptom of the disease called alcoholism/addiction. Not me, think the afflicted. Not yet, they need to be reminded. It doesn't matter who you are or where you came from. Chemicals of abuse don't play favorites; addiction is the great equalizer. The Ph.D. and the school dropout, the loving mother and the self-hating streetwalker, the Wall Street prince and the back-street pauper can all end up on slabs at the morgue years ahead of schedule if they don't stop drinking and drugging. It's the similarities you share with these people (on careful examination, you'll find more of them than you would have believed possible), not the differences, that are significant. And it's these similarities that you'll be forced to confront on your road to recovery.

If you're doing a fair amount of drinking, your mind isn't working on all cylinders—though it isn't likely that you realize it. It may take months, or even a year or more, for the fog to clear and for you to look back at your behavior and evaluate it objectively.

Meanwhile, don't let terminology get in the way of getting help. You don't have to be an alcoholic to quit drinking, or a drug addict to stop using. You only have to want to quit. Maybe just to be able to say goodbye to hangovers forever. To learn to fly an airplane or climb mountains. To protect your health. Or so you can drive home from a party just once without someone saying, "Uh, maybe *I* ought to take the wheel."

"My friends and family think I have an alcohol and drug problem, and they're after me to quit. Sometimes I think they're right. But other times I think, 'Hey, if they're wrong, I'll be giving up the stuff for nothing.' "

Maybe you have a problem, and maybe you don't. If you do, the odds are good that you're denying it, at least most of the time. Self-deception is a front-line symptom of the disease of alcoholism/addiction. It helps the drinker/user escape from unpleasant reality and is rarely a conscious lie.

There are some good ways to find out whether or not a problem exists—none of which require your going dry until you're ready:

❖ Get a copy of the Alcoholic Anonymous Big Book (see page 101) and read it. Do you see yourself in any of the life histories? Remember, focus on the similarities you share with these people, not the differences.

❖ Go to a few open AA meetings (see page 102 for how to do this). Do you see yourself in any of the speakers?

❖ Write a mini life history, with special reference to activities that include, or are affected by, your drinking or drug use. Be as honest as you can, and focus not on the quantity and frequency, but on how the quality of your life is affected. Note opportunities missed, money spent, impact on your family, job, friendships, and other aspects of your life. Denial often keeps alcoholics/addicts from seeing the problems their abuse is causing, so you should probably talk candidly and patiently to some of those around you in order to see yourself as others see you.

❖ Do a family alcoholism or drug abuse history. Have any other members of your family had trouble with alcohol or drugs? Since some types of alcoholism/addiction seem to be inherited, the fact that there are relatives with the problem may suggest that you have it, too.

❖ Ask yourself the questions on pages 16 and 17.

And remember, you don't have to be

THE DENIAL DILEMMA

Why do people with certain illnesses—cancer and alcoholism/addiction, for example—practice denial? It's not because they are bad or stupid or just plain pig-headed. They deny they are ill—to themselves as well as everyone else—in order to protect themselves from facing a fearsome reality. The cancer patient doesn't want to know out of fear of the unpleasant treatments that might be needed and an even greater fear of the consequences should treatment fail. The alcoholic/addict doesn't want to know because of the fear of being branded with the stigma attached to the diagnosis and an even greater fear of having to give up his trusty chemical life supports.

Denial is what is known in psychiatric jargon as a defense mechanism. It is a primitive mechanism—a self-deception useful for a short time but destructive over the long term. For both the cancer patient and the alcoholic/addict, stubborn denial can be fatal.

Learning about alcoholism/addiction and the hope that treatment provides—by reading this book and other recovery materials and by going to AA meetings—can help overcome denial and open the door to recovery.

MINI-GUIDE

Self-Diagnosis: Critical Questions to Ponder

If you find the answer is "yes" to even two or three of these questions, you should seriously consider the possibility that your alcohol or drug use is a problem. If there are more than a few "yes" answers, you should seek help now.

❖ Have you ever felt you should cut down on, or tried to control (successfully or un-), your drinking or drug use?

❖ Have you ever felt bad or guilty about your drinking or drug use?

❖ Do you ever take a morning eye-opener to steady your nerves or get rid of a hangover? Do you use drugs daily or weekly? Do you use prescription drugs more often than prescribed? Have you ever asked more than one doctor to prescribe a drug for you?

❖ Are alcohol or drugs sometimes more important than other things in your life—your family, your job, your school, your values? Is drinking with your buddies more important than seeing your child in a school play? Is snorting coke more important than visiting your mom on her birthday? Is smoking pot all weekend more important than taking the make-up course you need to graduate?

❖ Do you find yourself lying to your spouse, your kids, your friends, your employer, to cover up your drinking or drug use—though you really don't like lying?

❖ Have you ever switched from one kind of drink to another in the hope that this would keep you from getting drunk? Or from one drug to another to prove you're not addicted?

❖ Have you had problems connected with drinking or drug use during the past year (DUI's,* lost work or school days, missed appointments, failed exams, financial problems, auto or other accidents with or without injury)?

❖ Has your substance use caused trouble at home or work? Are those around you annoyed by or concerned about it? Are you annoyed by their concern? Do you become defensive?

*Driving Under the Influence (DUI); in some states the term Driving While Intoxicated (DWI) is used.

100 percent convinced you're an alcoholic or addict to quit drinking or using, to go to AA, or to get treatment. If your drinking or drugging is causing difficulties in your life, or if someone who cares about you believes that it is, it could be time to give sobriety a try.

"Ever since I was a child I remember alcohol being a part of our family life. A lot of dishes were cooked with it. It was used when someone in the house was sick and for babies who were teething or cried a lot. It's hard for me to believe that it can really be harmful and that I have a problem."

Alcohol is harmful enough to kill more than 100,000 people in this country every year, either by damaging the body (it is linked to more than 350 medical problems, from cancer to brain damage) or causing an accident. The medicinal benefits are

❖ Have you gone to work or driven a car while intoxicated, high, or in a drug-induced haze?

❖ Have you been drunk or high more than four times in the past year? Do you sometimes stay drunk for days at a time?

❖ Do you need to resort to chemical assistance in order to do something (start the day, work, have sex, socialize, for example) or to change how you feel (sad, scared, anxious, or angry), to banish shyness or bolster confidence?

❖ Do you notice you need more alcohol or more of your drug of choice in order to get a reaction? Can you handle more than before? More than most people? Or do you suddenly find you can't drink or drug as much?

❖ Do you panic when you have to be somewhere where no booze or drugs will be available? Do you scrounge for extra drinks at parties because you feel you aren't getting enough? Do you keep going when everyone else has had enough?

❖ Do you create situations where you can drink—like inviting friends over for a drink or arranging a meeting at a bar?

❖ Do you panic when your bottle of pills gets low?

❖ Do you sometimes carry booze or drugs around with you?

❖ Do you tell yourself you can stop drinking or using drugs any time you want to, but find you keep getting drunk or high when you don't mean to?

❖ Do you wake up the morning after with no memory of the night before? Have these blackouts—periods of which you have absolutely no memory—become more frequent?

❖ Do the people you spend most of your time with drink too much or take drugs? Do you try to avoid other friends and family when you're drinking?

❖ Do you do things while under the influence that you wouldn't do otherwise? Do you find yourself regretting them later?

❖ Have you ever thought that your life might be better if you didn't drink or take drugs, or that life as it is just isn't worth living?

❖ Has a doctor found signs of alcohol damage and warned you to stop drinking?

❖ Are you taking illegal drugs?

almost non-existent.* Still many alcoholics/addicts who come from backgrounds such as yours prefer to accept the myth that alcohol can be good for you. It makes denying they have a problem easier.

If you answer yes to some of the questions above, then it's time to stop denying and start taking action.

*There are some who claim that a small amount of red wine may help prevent heart attacks (see page 269).

"I've been feeling for a while that I may have a drinking problem. Most of the time I can control it, but then every once in a while I go off the deep end. I've discussed my feelings with my wife and my parents, and they all think that I'm exaggerating the problem. Who's crazy?"

When friends and family suggest someone has a drinking problem, they're probably right.

When they discount the possibility of a problem, they're almost certainly practicing denial—which is almost as common among those around alcoholics as among alcoholics themselves. (In some cases, the denial is rooted in the family member's also having an unacknowledged problem.) Your family is probably trying to block out the unpleasant reality that you could have a problem. Luckily, you seem ready to confront that reality.

Right now there is no blood test or biopsy that detects early alcoholism (though in the later stages, liver damage and other physical symptoms appear). If you believe your drinking might be out of control, don't allow yourself to be talked out of your concerns. Read this chapter, ask yourself the questions on pages 16 and 17, go to several open AA meetings as an observer. It may be that you've recognized your disease early in its progression, which means you can treat it before the more serious consequences begin to occur, and before everyone you know recognizes you have a problem. Don't ignore your own feelings, and don't let anyone talk you out of them.

"My wife wants me to go to AA, and I think that's ridiculous. I never take a drink during the week, and on the weekends I drink nothing but beer—and only after 4 P.M. Maybe I do get a little soused, but it's only a couple of nights a week."

Anyone who gets drunk periodically, whether it's once a week or once a month, has an alcohol problem. That you can go for days, weeks, or even months between drunks doesn't prove a thing. The question is, when you do drink, do you lose control? If you're getting drunk, then it seems you are.

Nor does the substance you get drunk on or the time at which you start drinking mean anything. You can have an alcohol problem drinking distilled spirits (scotch, vodka, gin, whiskey), beer, wine, Kahlua, amaretto, wine coolers, rubbing alcohol, cough medicine, or vanilla extract. And you can start drinking first thing in the morning, never touch a drop until late in the day, or get drunk only on the second Saturday night of every month and still be an alcoholic.

If you're drinking enough to become intoxicated, you're drinking enough to damage your health. You could try limiting your weekend imbibing to a couple of beers a night. If this doesn't work, you have nothing to lose (except maybe those morning-after hangovers) and everything to gain by going to a few AA meetings and learning about chemical dependency and the disease of alcoholism.

"I always laugh when anyone calls alcoholics 'weak-willed.' I would have stepped on the neck of anyone who stood between me and a drink. I'd put my hand in boiling water for a drink."

"I don't believe I have an alcohol problem, but my employer says that if I don't get treatment, I'm out. This seems very unjust."

It's a lot less unjust than an employer telling you you're out, period. If you're resisting treatment, you need to ask yourself some questions. How much do you like or need your job? Are you willing to give it up for the privilege of drinking? If you are, you're saying that drinking is more important than your job—which, like your denial, is a classic sign of alcoholism/addiction. Anyone who ranks drinking or drug use above the things he believes he values most in life—marriage, career, parents, children, or even the weekly basketball game with the guys—has a problem, whether he owns up to it or not.

Even if you can't be convinced you have a problem, you have little to lose by going into treatment, and a lot to gain, including your job.

WHO'S TO BLAME?

"If only my husband didn't work such long hours, if only he had time for me, if only I had help with the kids, if only. . . I know I would behave differently, I wouldn't have a problem."

Most people with substance-abuse problems feel just the way you do. It's a spouse's fault. Or a parent's. Or a boss's. But they're wrong. They have problems with alcohol or drugs because they're doing the wrong thing, not because someone else is. You're the one who brings the double Bloody Mary to your lips or the cocaine to your nose, or who swallows the pills. You may be unable to change what a neglectful spouse does. Or a harsh parent. Or an unfair boss. All the wishing (or drinking or drugging) in the world won't make them live up to your high hopes and wistful expectations. But you can change what *you* do. And that's what recovery is all about.

Oddly enough, when you change your behavior in sobriety, your feelings will improve even if your spouse doesn't. You will feel better about yourself. And when you do, your spouse may change his behavior. Either way, your involvement in a recovery program can help you deal with the relationship in a much more rational way.

FIXING UNDERLYING PROBLEMS

"Our marriage is a mess. My husband says it's because of my drinking. I think if we just get some marriage counseling, everything will be okay. He thinks I've got to stop drinking first."

The person with a serious infection may find temporary relief from the pain and fever with the use of aspirin, but unless the underlying infection is treated, she could die. It's the same in your situation. You might ease some of your marital problems by seeing a counselor (and maybe you should), but unless you deal with the underlying alcohol problem, you will still be at risk: a clear-cut case of curing the symptom while the patient dies of the disease.

It doesn't make much sense, after all, to try to solve a problem of communication, which is at the core of many troubled marriages, when your mind is so anesthetized that you can't communicate. So treat your alcoholism first, and then start treating your marriage. See the sections on relationships in Chapters 27 and 28 for tips on rebuilding your marriage in sobriety. And be sure that any professional you see for marital counseling is also experienced at treating drug and alcohol problems.

"We recently discovered that our son has been drinking heavily. We think it's because he's been depressed about his grades nose-diving and being dropped from the soccer team. Shouldn't he see a psychiatrist?"

Not yet. Alcoholism as well as other addictions can mimic or produce psychiatric symptoms—such as depression, anxiety or panic attacks, hallucinations, mood swings, sleep problems, impulsive behavior, and low self-esteem—which are usually difficult to deal with until the addiction is treated. Even suicide attempts, which we generally associate with severe emotional distress, are frequently provoked by substance abuse. The numbers are cause for alarm: Alcoholism and drug dependence trigger 25 percent of completed suicides.

So rather than thinking about psychiatric treatment at this point, get your son into a good alcohol treatment program (see the options in Chapter 3) as soon as possible. If, after he's been sober for about three months, his grades don't pick up and he continues to be depressed, then a consultation with a psychiatrist or other mental health professional is in order.

Be sure, too, that others in the family who are drinking excessively, popping pills, or using illegal drugs also seek treatment. Substance abuse is a family disease, and youngsters with a problem often mirror parental behavior.*

GOOD REASONS FOR DRINKING AND DRUGGING

"We lost our child in a freak accident. That's when I started drinking and taking pills. I don't think I can live without something to keep me from thinking about that horrible moment."

You've got a better alibi for abusing drugs than most people. But (and this isn't meant to sound cruel) it's still only an alibi. Many people have gone through equally life-shattering experiences without getting drunk or taking drugs. Only someone with this disease called alcoholism/addiction copes with life's problems—big and small—by turning to chemical substances.

But it is true that you now have two problems to deal with. One is your disease and the other is the devastation you feel about losing your child. Treating the disease—and quitting those chemicals—has to come first. Not until your mind is clear can you be helped to work out your feelings about your terrible loss, face what happened, and learn to go on. Professional grief counseling is probably a good route to healing, augmented by participation in a self-help group for parents who, like you, have lost a child.** The ache in your heart will probably never completely go away. But it will get duller, especially if, instead of numbing your brain, you give yourself a chance to mourn. You wouldn't want to deaden or lose those memories completely. Alcoholics/addicts often drink and drug as though their principal goal in life is to get rid of feelings. But feelings, glad and sad, are what make us human. They are also the way we learn and grow.

"I started drinking when my husband left me and my whole life went wrong. What good will quitting do? My life will still be miserable."

Ask yourself, "Has drinking made my life better?" Or has it only compounded your problems? Sure, you don't feel the misery as much when you're smashed, but it's there just the same, growing like an insidious tumor. And it won't go away until you start calling the shots, instead of letting alcohol call them. It will fester and grow until you look at the breakup of your marriage honestly, mourn it, and finally get past it.

*Heredity, of course, can also be a factor; see page 474.

**Ask your doctor or call a local hospital and ask them if they can recommend such a group.

About one in ten people respond to a life crisis (loss through separation, divorce, death; disappointment with school or job; serious injury or illness in themselves or loved ones) by drowning their sorrows in drink or smothering them in drugs. It's not that their problems are worse than everybody else's, just that they turn to chemical substances instead of employing the more effective coping mechanisms used by the other nine.

One in ten is also the estimated proportion of alcoholics in the adult population. If they didn't have a real crisis in their lives, they would create one. Deep down, they don't really want things to get better, because then they would lose their reason for drinking. When a marriage breaks up, they are more likely to blame the spouse than the drinking. If they move into other relationships and continue drinking, predictably they will fail again—unless, as sometimes happens, they find a drinking-buddy partner, in which case they may get along fine all the way to the cemetery.

Get help for your drinking through AA or another traditional route (see Chapter 3). If that doesn't help the misery diminish, then get some additional counseling from a professional who is certified in alcoholism/addiction and is familiar with grief counseling.

"I've tried to get sober before, but every time I do I just want to kill myself. My father did terrible things to me when I lived at home, things I don't want to think about."

Most people can get clean or sober and do just fine without psychotherapy. But some can't stay both sober *and* alive unless they face the deep-seated problems in their past (or present) lives. So while it's crucial for you to get treated for your addiction, you must also deal with the demons inside. The ideal treatment for you is probably the kind offered in a program designed to help people whose illness coexists with other psychological problems. Do seek help immediately. You *can* live sober, but not without skilled professional treatment.

EMBARRASSMENT

"As a black woman with a strict Baptist upbringing I'm embarrassed about my drinking. I can't stop, but I just don't know how I can go to a stranger for help."

A lot of people feel just the way you do. Maybe because they were brought up to believe that you don't hang out the family's business like the wash for everyone to see. Or maybe it's that they can't trust the "establishment" structures set up to provide help, whether they are medical, educational, social services, or drug rehab. People fear that going for help will expose them to the risk of police harassment or even arrest, of having their kids taken away or of losing their homes. Or they are ashamed to admit to drinking or using drugs because it goes against what they were taught in church or by their parents. It's no wonder that they are, like you, uneasy about going for help.

But if you don't get help, the alternatives are even worse than all your fears. Your drinking will hurt those you love and eventually kill you. The longer you wait to get help with a medical problem (whether it's cancer or alcoholism/addiction) the worse your chances of beating it are.

Of course, it may not be so easy to get help. There aren't enough alcohol and drug treatment programs to meet the needs of chemically dependent people in this country, and many people can't afford the programs that are available.

The best thing for you to do is to go to someone you do trust—a minister, a friend who you know goes to AA or is in recovery, a doctor you feel comfortable with, an attorney (legal aid, if money is a problem) you've worked with, a social worker. Anyone with contacts with the establishment who you feel you can talk to openly. They should be able to assist you in finding help.

"I've got a long-term problem with alcohol and pills, but I'm so embarrassed about this kind of thing at my age—I'm past sixty—that I can't even talk to my doctor about it. I want to stop on my own, but I can't seem to."

Like the woman who finds a breast lump and is too embarrassed to get it examined by her doctor, your attitude is suicidal. So get help before it's too late. No professional is going to blink an eye at seeing an older person with an addiction problem. There are literally hundreds of thousands of you.

If you shrink at the idea of bringing your problem to your own doctor, check with the local medical society for the name of an addiction specialist (see page 45). Discuss the problem with such a doctor and work out a plan for treating your illness. If you do go to a treatment program, try to find one that specializes in older patients, or that at least treats many of them. In some cases, a program that treats elderly people with a variety of problems (including addictions) may work better than a drug rehab program for people of all ages. In others, getting help in a mixed age program may be more beneficial, as long as your living space gives you the privacy required to meet any special needs you may have.

When you look for an AA group, you will also want one that includes some other seniors. You and they can serve as good role models for younger alcoholics/addicts. Instead of spending your time alone drinking and looking forward to nothing but empty days and nights, you can find new hope and purpose in life by helping others.

WORK-RELATED ISSUES

"The doctor says my liver is acting up and I've got to give up drinking. There is no way I can do that in my business. Drinking is part of the courting of clients."

If you were a longshoreman and had a heart attack and the doctor said you had to give up lifting heavy loads, would you say, "No way?" Your condition is every bit as life-threatening as a bad heart and may similarly require lifestyle modifications. Fortunately for you and others who have to give up alcohol, there's a changing community attitude and a recognition that drinking is an option, not an obligation. More and more people are finding that it is socially acceptable to order sparkling water, iced tea, or other nonalcoholic beverages, even at high-powered business meals. Perhaps you've been too busy stirring your drink—or too brainwashed by the ads on billboards and in magazines that are meant to help you justify your drinking—to notice this.

Yours isn't an unusual situation. All kinds of people connect drinking or drugs with their work: those rock musicians who are convinced they can play only when high on drugs ("It's what makes me creative"); assembly-line workers certain they'll be bored

"A friend of mine said, 'Every alcoholic stops drinking. It's nice to be alive when you do.' That did it for me."

stiff if they have to work without having a drink first ("If my mind were clear, I wouldn't be able to stand doing this stuff any more"); salesmen who fear they won't be able to make deals if they're sober ("I need a belt under my belt to make a sales pitch"). Such fears are understandable. If you've been doing something for a long while with what you believe is the friendly support of chemical substances, then it's only natural to worry about functioning without them.

The fact is that there are fine musicians who say "no" to drugs, factory workers who are teetotalers, and salesmen who can sell snowballs in Siberia with nothing stronger than caffeine-free cola in their glasses. You can do your job sober, too—probably a lot better than you're doing it now. But you may need some support and retraining to help you get started (see page 232 for tips on going back to work sober).

"My husband and other family members have persuaded me to get help for my drinking. But I'm not sure whether I should just quietly sign up for treatment somewhere, or admit to the people at our Employees Assistance Program that I've got an alcohol problem."

The recovering alcoholic (or addict) needs all the help she can get. Employees Assistance Programs (EAP's), developed by larger companies to deal with problems adversely affecting the work of employees (such as child care and elder care, single parenting, financial problems, and so on, in addition to substance abuse), generally offer a lot of it. They can arrange for treatment at a program they know has a good success record (precertifying you for treatment if that is necessary under your health provider's policy), then help devise a quality continuing care program. Often you can utilize insurance benefits for your alcoholism/addiction only if you go through the EAP, and the EAP may arrange to pick up costs not picked up by insurance. So unless you're independently wealthy, going through the EAP may be an absolute necessity.

Once you are back on the job, the EAP can help you arrange your work schedule to enhance your recovery, and will keep tabs on you to be sure life's little (or big) problems aren't driving you up a barroom wall. EAP's can help you locate any additional support services you may need, such as child care, marital counseling, or treatment for the physical effects of substance abuse. They may even help other family members deal with their own abuse problems, if any. Perhaps most important, they help newly recovering employees to understand that as helpful as treatment is, it's not the real world, and that adjusting once they are back on the job won't be easy. Some EAP's offer a weekly meeting—usually at lunch hour—where recoverees can discuss readjustment issues.

EAP's, although paid for by the employer, are designed to be advocates for the employee. They often work together with unions and other employee representatives to develop the best possible programs for workers at all levels in a company. The company doesn't pay for this out of the goodness of its stockholders' hearts, but rather with the goal of increasing productivity. Effective EAP's are not arms of the personnel or security departments (at least, the vast majority are not) and do not hire and fire. If you come in to talk about a problem—any problem—the subject you discuss should remain confidential. (If a company's EAP policy is discontinued, a responsible EAP department chief is almost obligated ethically to destroy confidential files as he exits.)

If you are still nervous about presenting yourself to an EAP staffer, check around with others who have turned to the EAP for help. If they seem satisfied with the treatment they got, then you should feel safe doing likewise. You can also check credentials—most EAP personnel are certified, either as employee assistance professionals (CEAP) or addiction counselors (NCAC). Of course, if for any reason you find yourself uncomfortable with the EAP staff, it may be best to turn elsewhere for help.

If you want to get as much information as possible before making any admissions, try the old "I've got a friend who..." routine. This generally works, and most EAP's will respect your privacy and not pry further. Or telephone anonymously and ask all your questions: How do I know I have a problem? What can I do about it? How can the EAP help me? Once you've established rapport, you can make an appointment to go in and see the EAP counselor.

In most cases, only larger businesses can afford an EAP, but smaller employers sometimes sign up with a group program that services several firms.

While you can feel free to contact an EAP, going to the personnel department (or what is often euphemistically called "human resources") about a drug or alcohol problem is not a good idea. Some human resources departments have been known to be less than humane. You're better off going elsewhere for help, and not divulging your problem until you're sober. Once you are sober, it is actually illegal—thanks to the Americans for Disabilities Act—for you to be dismissed on the basis of your alcoholism or drug addiction.

"I thought I never had a hangover. When I stopped drinking, I realized I had lived in a hangover."

Should you relapse, of course, that protection becomes void.

TIMING

"I agree that I need to get treated for my problem, but I can't spare the time now. I've got a big deal pending."

What about the next big deal? And the next? And the one after that? One of them is going to be your last if you don't get serious about getting treatment. If your doctor diagnosed early colon cancer and said you needed immediate surgery or the disease would kill you, what would you do? Very likely, you would have the surgery. It makes sense to give the same kind of attention to your addiction, which is as dangerous to your health as any malignancy.

If, as is likely, this is a deal that can wait, that someone else can handle, or that doesn't make much difference one way or the other, then drop it or hand it over to a colleague and get help immediately. Though your productivity may suffer in the short run, in the long run it can only benefit from your sobriety.

If not completing this big deal will sink your business, leave your family destitute, or otherwise wreak havoc in your life, then by all means take care of it—assuming you're sober enough to see it through safely. You may think you are, but even small amounts of alcohol have a detrimental effect on your thought processes, and thus on your business dealings.

But set a definite date for going sober, put down a deposit for treatment, and start attending AA meetings now as an interim measure. You will be welcome even if you haven't yet gone dry or stopped using.

Beware, however, if every time you consider sobriety there's another big deal or crisis to hold you back. Either you're creating these diversions to avoid facing your problems or you've got too much cooking on your stove. Either way, you've got to put everything else on the back burner and turn up the flame under recovery.

"I've promised my family and my employer that I will check into an alcohol and drug treatment center next week. They want me to get clean and sober now in preparation. I say, 'No way.' "

For once *you're* right. It usually isn't a good idea for someone to try to get sober before going into treatment, for a couple of reasons. One is that once sober you may feel, "Hey, I don't need treatment. I've quit on my own." And celebrate your self-control by getting high as a kite. Another is that cold sober you may not have the courage to turn up for treatment. Few patients arrive at a treatment facility with a completely clear head, and a lot of folks are seen draining the last dregs from a bottle as they come through the admitting-room door. And they do okay—as long as some one else drove them there.

Perhaps most important, complications from abrupt withdrawal can in some cases be life-threatening. When there is cross-addiction, withdrawal presents complex problems even for the trained professional. You're doing well if you agree to treatment; don't push your luck by playing doctor (even if you are one).

SPECIAL ISSUES

"I'm black and the inpatient rehab program my boss wants to send me to doesn't have any black counselors and probably won't have any other black patients while I'm there. Is this a good idea?"

That's the wrong question. The question is: Do you have any other options? If you explain your concern, will your boss be willing to send you to an integrated program? (If management balks, ask them if they would be comfortable in an all-black program as white participants, where not just the skin color, but the culture, the talk, and maybe even the food were not what they were used to.) If the answer is still no, do you have the resources to pay for treatment elsewhere on your own? If you don't, then you have no choice but to accept your boss's choice, even if it's not ideal.

It will then be up to you to make the best of the situation. Following the tips on page 72 will help. You might also recommend to your counselor a booklet for those who work with black patients: *Chemical Dependency and the African-American* by Peter Bell. Try to push aside any cultural differences that pop up and concentrate on the things you have in common with your counselors and the other patients. The experience could very well turn out to be good for you and consciousness-raising for the others.

"My company is willing to send me for inpatient treatment for my drug problem. How can I make sure that the place I go will be one where I can feel comfortable talking about my being a lesbian and where my lover will be accepted as 'family'?"

The only way to find out is to ask. Call the places you are considering and ask them these questions: Are you comfortable with patients who are homosexual? Will I be able to speak freely about my sexual orientation and my relationships? Will my lover be able to participate as my family? Are there any homosexual people on staff? If the answer to each of these questions is an unconditional yes (you may have to judge from the tone of voice whether there are conditions), then all else being equal, you have found your treatment program.

"I'm a Native American and my liver is going bad. I've been thinking seriously about getting treatment for my drinking. But my friends all laugh at me."

You'll have the last laugh when you regain your health and they are the ones with problems. Don't delay getting help. But unless you can find a Native American counselor or treatment program, expect that some of it may seem very alien to your way of thinking. When you were young you may have learned that it is ill mannered for someone to tell you what to do, feel, or think. You may automatically reject such interference in your life. Instead, try to look at it as a medical treatment (which it is) that you have to submit to in order to save your life.

Getting adjusted to AA meetings won't be easy either. Give yourself time to adjust. You can't attend for two weeks and think "I've got it." Like assimilating any culture, getting into sobriety takes a while.

It may also be a good idea for you to discuss with your doctor the option of taking Antabuse—a medicine that makes you feel sick if you take even a tiny amount of alcohol. That way it will be easier for you to turn down your buddies when they pass the bottle.

And keep in mind that going into recovery with a casual attitude ("I'll attend counseling sessions and AA meetings when I feel like it) won't work. If you truly want to get better, you have to attend regularly (at least weekly) with a full heart, and get a sponsor you can confide in.

If you live on a reservation, you should talk to those in charge about establishing activity centers that provide competitive sports, employment training, and so on, to help replace drinking.

"I live on an Indian reservation. I recently got married and think I may be pregnant. But I can't seem to stop drinking. Where can I get help before I hurt my baby?"

Contact the alcohol and substance-abuse coordinator at the Indian Health Service office nearest your home. This professional should be able to give you information on Native American alcoholism and addiction counselors, on AA groups run by Native Americans, and on culturally sensitive in- or outpatient treatment, if you need it. Also contact the maternal/child service department or a local obstetrician. But move quickly. Your baby's future depends on your becoming sober now.

If you're like most Native American women, especially those from matriarchal tribes, you may feel more comfortable seeking help from a woman with a background like your own. With the right connection, you will quickly find that you've become both willing and able to seek out the social supports you need.

"I'm retired and I started drinking heavily when my wife died. My son has persuaded me that it's getting out of hand and that I ought to get treatment, but will Medicare pay for it?"

Possibly. It depends on the treatment center and the type of program. Medicare does pay for alcohol and drug rehab at psychiatric facilities (particularly if a diagnosis such as depression is used to justify admission), but at a rate much lower than many programs charge.

But inpatient treatment may not be necessary. If you've been drinking heavily for only a short time, you may be able to get sober by attending Alcoholics Anonymous meetings near your home. If you would like to take this route, be sure to get a complete physical first from a doctor who knows about your drinking and knows what to look for (see page 45). If no problems are uncovered, then it's likely you'll get the go-ahead to go to AA.

If AA isn't adequate, outpatient treatment—from an experienced physician or therapist, or as part of a group program—may do the trick.

On the other hand, if you've been drinking heavily enough to cause blackouts, tremors, and memory loss, and experience withdrawal symptoms when you abstain for a few hours, you will require careful supervision of your withdrawal in a medical facility. Ideally, a doctor experienced in treating the elderly (a gerontologist) should be present along with an addiction specialist. Clearing the chemicals from your system may take longer than it would for younger addicts, especially if you've also been taking a variety of medications, prescribed or bought over-the-counter.

If inpatient treatment is necessary following withdrawal, look for a place that will accept Medicare reimbursement. You may be able to complete the program in several weeks; but it's also possible that your head won't even start to clear until that point and that you will have to remain in treatment for two or three months. The good news is that you have a better chance of benefiting from treatment than a younger alcoholic.

Once you are out of treatment, your continuing care will be particularly important. Unlike younger people with stronger support systems, you may find yourself floundering unless you immediately link up with a continuing care program and an AA group. They will not only help to keep you sober, but will become an important part of your life.

If you adhere to a recovery program, your chances of living out your life normally are very good. If you botch it, the chances that you won't have to worry about anything at all (except, perhaps, who's going to pay for your funeral) are even better.

"I'm a widower with no family nearby. I have nothing and nobody. My drinking is all I have left. Now my doctor tells me I have to give it up."

Certainly your loneliness is real. The problems of aging are all real. But alcohol doesn't make them go away—it only masks them. In many cases it even makes them worse, exacerbating hypertension, heart problems, diabetes, osteoporosis, and other ailments and increasing the risk of injury from falls, auto accidents, and fire. If you're taking medication (as about 25 percent of older people are), the alcohol can interact badly with it.

Still, you may feel as though your doctor is asking too much of you. But that isn't really true. The prospect of giving up alcohol may seem unsettling (it seems that way to anyone who depends on it for solace), but there is another way to look at becoming sober. It can open up whole new vistas. Many older people who give up alcohol do so by going to Alcoholics Anonymous. At AA they find what they were seeking but not getting from alcohol—friendship, support, unconditional love, something constructive to do, and people to do it with. You can, too.

"I knew if I didn't quit, I'd die. I can still taste the shotgun I put in my mouth. And the fear. Fear is a really good motivator."

"I know I drink too much. But I think it's because I've been engaging in homosexual behavior since I was a teen. If I got my sexual orientation straightened out I think I could stop getting drunk."

Gays and lesbians often start drinking in the difficult teen years, when they use chemicals to mask the loneliness and isolation they feel in being different from their peers. They often believe that only drugs or drink can keep them from falling apart completely. Surveys suggest that chemical dependency is higher in the homosexual than in the heterosexual community, though just how much higher isn't clear. Certainly the stress of living "in the closet" contributes to the problem. So does a lifestyle that is often built around bars and drinking parties.

But the idea that changing your sexual orientation will eradicate the need to drink is a delusion. Your sexual orientation is something you're born with, your drinking is something you can control. If you work at your sobriety, not only won't you fall apart, you will feel whole for the first time in your life. But you may also need to work at accepting who you are, so consider getting counseling from a therapist who understands both alcoholism and homosexuality.

CRACKING CRACK

"Yeah, I'd like to get this monkey off my back before it kills me. But the monkey I got is crack—and everybody knows you can't kick the crack habit."

When crack, the poor man's cocaine, came on the scene in the early 1980s, smoking it quickly wrecked so many lives that there was absolutely no doubt—as there sometimes is with a new drug—that it was dangerous and addictive. And the word on the street was that once hooked on this drug, the only escape was the morgue.

Actual experience, however, has taught us that in some ways crack, for all the devastation it has wrought and the speed with which it addicts, is a lamb as compared to the tiger that is alcohol. And according to at least one study, addiction to it is no harder to kick than addiction to alcohol, though it may take a little longer.

TIME WILL TELL: ALCOHOL AND COCAINE

They say that alcohol kills by inches, cocaine by yards, crack by miles. The alcoholic may take twenty years to reach the point where life is a mess and help is desperately needed. The cocaine addict may arrive there in a few years. The crack addict in a few months.

Because of differences in experience, there may be differences in behavior during early recovery. Alcoholics, burned out after the long, gradual spiral downhill, are often ready to change their lives—but they may have difficulty because their behavior is so deeply ingrained. Crack or cocaine addicts are usually younger, less mature, and usually have plunged from the first high to the bottom in a brief span of time. Because their usage is of shorter duration, they may be less persuaded of the seriousness of their situation and less ready to open their minds to what they need to know to get well. If they do, however, their chances of success are good.

So you can get well, but you need to give yourself enough time. Leave treatment prematurely or ignore your continuing-care plan (see page 71), and the odds of relapse will skyrocket.

CONFIDENTIALITY

"Lord knows I need help. But I'm worried that everyone I know will find out that I have a problem if I go for treatment."

You're almost certainly kidding yourself if you think that your colleagues, employer, family, and friends don't already know you have a problem. Even the most discreet of heavy drinkers or users transmits a steady stream of unmistakable signals of addiction.

Still, if you want to keep your recovery private, you have that right. Strict federal laws protect the confidentiality of any professional treatment you receive. And for some people, keeping the initial phase of recovery under wraps—for either professional or personal reasons—makes sense. If you're planning on inpatient treatment, you can do this by selecting a program in another state or even another part of the country and taking off on "a long overdue vacation." That way you can immerse yourself in recovery without embarrassment or the fear of being "discovered." If you fear being recognized, you may want to use an assumed name when registering. At home you can see an addiction specialist, who will certainly respect your privacy.

AA (Alcoholics *Anonymous*) pioneered in making anonymity possible for all its members. It does this, first of all, by the use of first names only at meetings ("Hello, I'm Jan, and I'm an alcoholic"). And AA tradition insists that who's seen or what's heard at an AA meeting is never to go beyond the meeting-hall doors. Other Twelve-Step programs are equally anonymous. If you're still uncomfortable about the possibility of bumping into an acquaintance at a meeting, it's possible to explore AA undetected by attending meetings in neighborhoods or neighboring towns where you are unknown. Remember, if you do bump into an acquaintance at a meeting, he or she will be every bit as eager to keep the encounter quiet as you are.

"I like to talk out my problems at meetings. There's no cross-talk, no interruptions at AA. I can say what I want. I can't do that at home."

Wanting to protect your privacy while building up a good sobriety track record is understandable, but keeping your recovery permanently "top secret" may be damaging in the long run. It's an established fact that people with good recoveries share, rather than hide, their problem. An important part of getting better is the willingness to help others who are ill—by talking about one's own experiences.

That seems to be true also of people with other serious health problems, from heart surgery and breast cancer to mental illness. Talking about the experience builds a bridge of empathy that helps both the talker and the listener deal with the problem more successfully.

"I've got a good job and I'm afraid I'll blow it if I go into treatment and the boss finds out. He's sure to fire me."

If your boss doesn't already know you have a problem, he's sleeping on the job. In any case, he will before long. Alcoholism/addiction is a progressive disease. If you don't get better, it will get worse. Eventually there will be no way in the world you will be able to cover it up.

Still, you're wise to be wary about telling your boss outright that you're going in for treatment. Society is, unfortunately, not uniformly accepting of those with chemical dependency problems (or with AIDS or even cancer or mental illness, for that matter). Not every employer is understanding; some may see this as a moral issue or have their feelings or thinking colored by personal alcohol or drug problems or those of family members. Some may tolerate an employee who drinks a lot or is being treated with tranquilizers, but not one who openly admits to alcoholism or illicit drug use.

If you work for a large company, you can find out what the response will be to your going for treatment by having your doctor, lawyer, a friend, or counselor call the personnel manager, the employee assistance program counselor, or whoever is in charge of policy and ask some questions anonymously. This person can say, "I have a patient [or client, or friend] who works for you and who's interested in getting help, but who is unsure how you will look at this. What's your company policy on alcoholism/addiction?" (Most companies now have one.) "Do you have an employee assistance program? Will you pay for treatment? Will the employee have to pay a portion out-of-pocket? Will your knowledge of this person's disease prevent future advancement? Or will this knowledge mean immediate dismissal?" Then the caller can request a copy of the company policy on the subject.

Most of the time, the response will be, "We like to keep our employees on and will do anything we can to help." Enlightened companies have learned that—at least with employees who possess special skills or expertise—it costs more time, money, and effort to fire and replace than to rehabilitate the alcoholic/addict. Employees who are unskilled and/or recently hired are less likely to get support from their employers and may even be dismissed. When the work involves public health or safety (pilots, bus drivers, railway workers, doctors, and so on), there may be stipulations that require regular drug testing, mandatory treatment, or immediate dismissal if drugs are found.

If you work for a small company, you may be able to obtain support and encouragement from a boss, supervisor, or colleague just by acknowledging your problem and seeking help. It's ideal if you can share your situation with one or two trusted coworkers, so that they will feel like partners in your decision and can help others understand it. But even if you can't, and even if you have no sense of what the response to your going for treatment might be, you should not let uncertainties be barriers to getting help. Get it and then worry about the consequences. In the long run, recovery always returns many times more benefits than it takes away.

The fear of losing your job if your dependency is disclosed may deepen your sense of Catch-22 despair and make you want to pour yourself another drink, but there's a positive flip side. Working for someone who doesn't understand—and doesn't want to understand—anything about the disease you're battling won't help you in the long run. You'll probably be better off finding new employment after treatment. (For tips on how, see page 238.)

Be sure, however, that in your anxiety you don't misinterpret the reaction you get at work. When your boss says, "It's okay—take all the time you need," he's not saying, "Don't bother coming back—we don't want you anymore."

An employer who would like to learn more about the disease and the ramifications of employees getting treatment should read page 580.

"My husband is being treated for alcohol and drug abuse. He was in such a bad way that we just rushed him to the rehab hospital. What do I tell his boss?"

That depends on the situation. If his problem was known—it usually is if it's as advanced as this—then say he's finally getting treated, which should make his boss happy. If you're uncertain how the news will sit with the super-powers that be, you or the doctor can call and say that your husband has taken ill, is in the hospital, and that you will keep them posted on his condition. Be vague about the reason for the hospitalization ("The doctor will know more when tests are completed" or "It's something my husband will want to discuss with you himself when he's up to it.")

Unless he's got an awful lot of vacation time coming, no employee can disappear for a month or more without a good reason, so sooner or later, a full account will be imperative. In your present stressed condition, you'd clearly like it to be later. For now, avoid embarrassing questions when you make that call by getting off the phone as fast as decently possible.

TELLING THE FAMILY

"I'm on warning from my employer: either go into a residential treatment program or get fired. I don't know how to tell my wife and kids about this."

Probably no one will be happier than your family to know that you're finally going to do something about your problem. First tell your wife. It's unlikely she'll be surprised. Unless she's your drinking buddy, she certainly knows you need help. (If she *is* your drinking or drugging buddy, she needs help, too; see page 33.) She may be upset that you're going to have to be away from home or that you will be devoting so much time to recovery, but she'll be happy you're trying to get well.

Tell her how important her support is going to be, that you realize now that alcoholism/addiction is a disease that affects the whole family, and that though recovery is something you've got to do yourself, you're going to need all the family support you can get. Have her read Chapters 27 and 28, and urge her to begin attending Al-Anon* meetings while you're in treatment. She will probably be invited to attend individual and family sessions toward the end of your inpatient stay.

She needs to know that the transition to sobriety will not be easy for you or for the rest of the family, but that the better you all understand the disease and the recovery process, the better your chances will be of making recovery work.

Tell your children as soon as possible. Whether they are toddlers or teens, they will sense something is going on—especially if you go away for treatment, but even if you only go as an outpatient or attend AA meetings every evening. Telling them the truth will be less shattering than what they imagine may be going on. Children sheltered from the truth often blame themselves for the bickering and other family problems they see or sense. This, in turn, sets them up for another generation of family dysfunction. (For ways of trying to keep your children clean and sober, see Chapter 26.)

The best way to tell the kids is at a family conference. If you're not used to holding such meetings, now is a good time to start. They're a great way to foster intrafamily communication, which is going to be very important in your lives from now on. Explain to them that you are sick, that it is the

*Al-Anon is the Twelve-Step program for those who live with an alcoholic (see page 515).

RECOVERY ECONOMIC INCENTIVE PLAN

You're worried about the high cost of treating your alcohol or drug habit? Flip the coin over: Think about how much money you're going to save by staying sober. Carefully calculate the amount you spent on alcohol and/or drugs each week, and then add on the legal fees you incurred, the speeding fines you paid periodically, the penalties for missed mortgage payments, the late charges and interest on credit cards, the cost of lost promotions, alimony, clothes you ruined and valuables you absent-mindedly lost or left behind, and any other user-related expenses. Total it all up, and you have the financial cost of your drinking or drugging.

As you can see, even if you opt for inpatient treatment, sobriety will reimburse you in a fairly short time. Once the bills are paid, open up a special bank account and each week squirrel away just half of what you would have spent on booze or drugs. Before you know it, you'll have money for something special—a subscription to the theater, golf or tennis lessons, or even, if you were a big spender, a European vacation, a Caribbean cruise, or a spanking new car.

Another approach to socking away savings is to put a coin in a piggy bank or an oversized jar (a small one may fill up too quickly) every time you feel a craving. Every month, move the accumulated coins to your bank account. You could be rich by the end of the first year of recovery. By the second year, you may find your piggy bank remaining empty for weeks on end. But that's not so bad either.

drugs or alcohol you are using that have made you sick, and that you are going to a hospital that teaches people how to stop using them.

Tell them that you haven't been drinking or taking drugs because you want to, but because you had to—that you couldn't stop yourself any more than the Cookie Monster can resist stealing from the cookie jar. Explain that the problem is that alcohol and other drugs are more dangerous than cookies. And that you are getting help because you don't want to be a slave to these substances anymore. Make it clear that they are not responsible for your problem (and never have been), but that you will need their help to get better. And explain that their going to Alateen (the Twelve-Step program for teenaged children of alcoholics) or Alatot (if this program for younger children is available in your area) will help you as well as them.

Finally, explain that if you all work hard at recovery, it will soon be easier for the family to talk to one another, to understand one another, and to show love to one another. It's going to be difficult for a while, but the result—a happier family—will be worth waiting for. (Chapters 10 and 19 will help you work toward this goal once you are out of treatment.)

TELLING FRIENDS

"I've been drinking after work with the guys for fifteen years. How can I tell them I can't drink anymore? They're going be wondering what kind of man can't hold his liquor."

A man with the disease known as alcoholism. That means all kinds of men: weight-lifters and bookworms, shortstops and longshoremen, farmers and accountants. But, because of the attitudes of our society—that men are supposed to be tough, never cry, refuse to be defeated, and always be in control—it is often hard for them to admit they have a problem.

It's sometimes easier to tell the guys you can't drink anymore if you have a better-understood condition—heart disease, for example. But even then, some men won't admit they have to give up the booze and continue to drink themselves to death.

You have that option. Or you can be a real man, and acknowledge that you're an alcoholic. It takes strength to stand up and be counted, even more strength to lick alcoholism. Following your recovery program will make you a winner, not a wimp. Don't let any beer-bellied clown tell you differently.

DOUBLE DEPENDENCY

"After years of getting drunk, my husband and I have finally opened our red-rimmed eyes and realized that we both have an alcohol problem. What now?"

Double trouble in a family isn't unusual, though it is less common for both partners to admit the problem and be willing to do something about it at the same time. There are several ways to go:

Outpatient or AA/Al-Anon treatment for both. In many cases, both partners do well on nothing more than outpatient treatment or a 90-AA-meetings-in-90-days approach. If you both meet the criteria for an AA-only recovery (see page 44), you could start right in with meetings. If at all possible, select different meetings for your home groups; going to the same meetings could stifle your freedom of expression, at least at first. Later, when you are well along in recovery and have begun to share your deeper feelings with one another, you can go to some meetings together and others separately. You may find that the ones you attend as a couple will turn out to be more social than therapeutic, but that's okay.

If you have no young children at home, or if a daily sitter is easily available, you can go to different meetings at the same time and perhaps meet afterwards for coffee with friends. If not, stagger meetings and, if you have them, counseling sessions—one of you going to an earlier meeting, the other to a later one. You may want to alternate early and late shifts. Of course, if there is only one meeting a day in town or one outpatient counseling session, this will be impossible. In such a situation, do the best you can. For example, your partner goes to meetings on Monday, Wednesday, and Friday. You go on Tuesday, Thursday, and Saturday. And you go together on Sunday.

Joint treatment. There are some advantages to joint treatment, especially if you're very supportive of each other. You will have the opportunity to build on the principles of the same program and get to work with the same professionals. These professionals will know you even better because they'll get to know the person you live with. But joint treatment doesn't always work. Your relationship may be strong enough to strengthen any denial either of you is harboring, and may help

"AA is a selfish program. You are there for yourself. When my wife is having a problem, I don't make suggestions. I say, 'I think you'd better call your sponsor.' It's better for her because advice is more helpful when it comes out of someone else's mouth than mine."

parry verbal punches from the counselor or others in the group that should be allowed to hit their marks. It may also be difficult to be totally honest in group discussions with your spouse present. (For some people this kind of airing is beneficial, and at some point in your recovery you'll need to achieve complete honesty with your spouse. But you may need to bounce your feelings off others before you can do so with him.) If for any reason your relationship seems to be undermining treatment, the counselor will probably recommend that one of you transfer to another facility.

Separate inpatient treatment. This is recommended when one (or both) of you is overly dependent on the other or when your relationship is shaky. The separation will allow each of you to look at yourself, each other, and your relationship in as objective a way as possible. Avoid telephone chats during treatment—you should be getting counseling from your counselor or from your AA group, rather than from each other—but feel free to write to each other if you wish. Be sure beforehand that both treatment facilities have similar approaches to alcoholism/addiction, and that your respective counselors are willing to maintain frequent contact. That way you won't come home filled with conflicting ideas, which could start recovery at home off on the wrong foot.

Inpatient treatment for one, outpatient or AA and Al-Anon for the other. In many cases, only one partner requires inpatient treatment. In such a situation, the other partner can remain at home, going to outpatient treatment and/or Alcoholics Anonymous and Al-Anon. Again, there should be contact between the counselors treating the spouses. If, as sometimes happens, the burden of keeping the home fires stoked becomes unbearable for the stay-at-home partner, child care or other assistance should be sought. Early recovery is not the time for anyone to try to don a Super-Mom or Super-Dad cape.

Consecutive treatment. If family responsibilities are heavy and one partner is well enough to wait for treatment, consecutive treatment may be the answer. While the sicker partner is being treated, the other spouse should be attending AA and Al-Anon, and if necessary seeing a counselor. When the first course of treatment ends, the partners change places. If possible, treatment for each should take place in the same facility, so that counselors can deal with family relationships as well as individuals.

WHO WILL MIND THE KIDS?

"God knows I need treatment. Alcohol has totally ruined my life. But I have two kids and nobody to take care of them."

For women—and sometimes also for single fathers—what happens to the children while they undergo treatment is a significant concern. The kids have usually suffered a lot already, and the parent is loath to expose them to more trauma. Still, a less-than-perfect care situation for the short term may be less traumatic than continuing to live with a parent who is an alcoholic or addict. Or losing an only parent to the disease. Sometimes compromises have to be made in order for the family to become whole.

There are several options to explore:

The other parent. Sometimes a parent who has left the home because of his spouse's drinking will be willing to return—at least temporarily—to care for the children while the custodial parent undergoes treatment. Or the children can be moved for the duration to his home. Of course this isn't an option when the absent father is also addicted or is abusive, irresponsible, or otherwise untrustworthy.

The grandparents. No one, other than the parents themselves, can give children the kind of love and attention they can get from grandparents. Though many in the older generation might not be able to handle children on a permanent basis, most can do the job very well for the short haul. When they can't, it is sometimes possible for them to do so with some minimal help (a teenager to come in and do the extra laundry and food preparation, for example, and take the youngsters to the playground).

Other relatives or close friends. When it comes to child care, next best to parents or grandparents are other relatives or family friends who know the children well. Of course, you have to feel confident that the person you select will be able to provide a safe environment for your children and isn't a substance abuser too. Someone from your religious community, if you belong to one, is often a good choice.

A combination solution. When there are several children and none of the above options will work for them all, it may be possible to combine two or more. For example, the grandparents and other relatives or friends may alternate child care. Or an older child may stay with elderly grandparents while a younger one lives with friends. Or daycare can be arranged, with family members taking over after work. With a little creative thinking, a satisfactory solution can usually be arrived at.

A residential treatment program with child care. A few treatment programs provide child care for patients. Ask the counselor or physician who is advising you about this possibility.

Outpatient treatment. It's possible that you can be treated on an outpatient basis, spending most of the day in a treatment program and evenings at home with your family. If your children aren't already in school or daycare and the program doesn't provide child care, your counselor may be able to help you find a temporary daytime place for them. Outpatient treatment probably won't work if you have already tried to get sober several times and failed, or if your problem is an overwhelming one (see page 50).

Foster care. Sometimes you have no option but to allow the state to take custody of your child until you are well. Check the child protective services policy in your state, so that you will understand how you can best safeguard your children and your own rights as a parent. Consult a legal aid lawyer if you are confused about what the policy means.

In almost all cases, child protection personnel prefer to return children to their homes and to improve family functioning rather than break families up. So they will assist in every way possible to make your treatment and child care arrangements successful. Though foster care isn't ideal, if you take your treatment seriously, the separation should be brief.

Arranging supervision by a counselor or physician and agreeing to a structured aftercare program after treatment may allow you to get your children back sooner. Or you might be able to get into an extended-treatment facility or halfway house with facilities for children.

ACCIDENTAL CONCEPTION

"I just agreed to go for treatment for drug dependency. Then I found out I was pregnant. I don't know what to do."

WOMEN AND SUBSTANCE ABUSE

Sure, women are different from men. But not as different as our cultural traditions tell us—even in our earliest nursery rhymes. ("What are little girls made of? Sugar and spice and everything nice. What are little boys made of? Snips and snails and puppy dogs' tails.")

The fact is that although there are some innate differences between boys and girls, the female of the species is not one whit kinder than the male. Girls, like boys, feel anger and malevolent urges. But while boys are expected to act out their impulses and feelings, girls are expected to lock them in; in fact, they often get the message that having feelings at all is unnatural.

That goes, too, for getting drunk or high. Parents may shake their heads (hiding a bemused smile) when a teenaged son comes home drunk for the first time but be horrified when their daughter does the same thing.

It's not surprising, then, that when a girl or young woman has feelings that she's been told are "not ladylike," she fears there is something innately wrong with her. Her self-esteem plummets. She may try to hide all such feelings and be a Goody-Two-Shoes. Or she may say, "I'm not like other girls. I'm bad. And I'll be as bad as I can be."

Both those who try to live up to the ladylike role and those who reject it are particularly subject to the temptations of alcohol and drug abuse. The former because they are trying to drown their unnatural feelings; the latter because they are trying to prove they're as bad as the boys.

But women get caught up in using chemicals (they favor sedatives, amphetamines, and tranquilizers more often than men do) for other reasons too. Some trace a drinking habit back to being given alcohol as a treatment for menstrual cramps. Others link their substance abuse to a particularly traumatic event, such as childhood sexual abuse. A background of sexual abuse is, in fact, more than twice as common in addicted women as in women with no substance abuse problems, and it's estimated that as many as 70 percent of chemically dependent women have suffered this kind of trauma. The experience often leads to lowered self-esteem and increased depression, to feeling different and associating with others who are also different.

Women alcoholics/addicts also are much more likely than male alcoholics/addicts to experience problems with food (bulimia, anorexia). For recovery to succeed, these underlying problems have to be addressed. Otherwise a woman is left with the notion that she doesn't deserve to get well.

The first thing you should do is commit yourself to getting treatment. No matter what decision you make about your pregnancy, getting clean has to be your number one priority.

As far as your pregnancy goes, there are several factors to consider:

❖ How far along is your pregnancy? If it's been less than six weeks since you conceived, the chances are that if any serious damage was done to the developing embryo, you will lose the pregnancy through miscarriage. If you don't miscarry, then get sober, and stay that way; chances are good that the baby will be okay. If it's two or three months since you conceived and you used or drank heavily during that time,

If they live with a heavy drinking (or drug-using) partner, women are likely to drink heavily (or use drugs) themselves. They are more likely to drink when the nest is empty than when it's full. And while a wife is likely to stay with an alcoholic husband, the alcoholic woman is generally deserted by her spouse.

If they work and travel in a man's world, professional women may be eager to show that they can keep up with their male colleagues—all the way to the hotel cocktail lounge. And for women, whose capacity for alcohol and other drugs is about half that of men, this can lead to trouble. It's double trouble because not only do they get drunk faster (because of their generally smaller size and the fact that they metabolize these chemicals differently), they also develop serious abuse problems faster and sustain physical damage sooner.

Women tend to develop alcohol or drug problems later in life than men do, which means it's necessary for them to be alert to the possibility and to practice prevention well into their golden years. Although the patterns change with age, women are more likely to be substance abusers if they are single, separated or divorced, unemployed, have no children, or have children who have flown the nest. They are more likely to abuse prescribed drugs or alcohol than illegal drugs.

As attitudes toward women change, however, and society becomes more open, it appears that the patterns of abuse are also changing. The way drugs are used and abused by teenage girls is becoming more and more similar to that of boys. It can probably be expected that unless massive efforts are made at education and prevention, this will continue, and more and more women will develop problems.

But the narrowing of the gap between men and women has its positive side, too. In the past, because of the stigma attached to women drinking or using drugs, neither the abusing woman nor those who cared about her were ready to admit that a problem existed (erratic behavior could be attributed to the premenstrual syndrome, menopause, or other "female" problems), and so treatment was rarely sought. Now, with the growing recognition that men and women are more alike than different in their recreational use of chemicals, more women are beginning to come out in the open and get treated. However, they are more often motivated by the fact that their abuse is hurting their health or their families than are men, who tend to be spurred on by a threat to their job or a legal threat (from DUI's, for example).

As a woman with a substance abuse problem, you have a better chance than ever before of getting help and controlling your disease.

it's still likely that your baby could be born okay if you become sober immediately. Every day of sobriety you add to your pregnancy increases the odds of having a healthy baby. Each day you continue to drink or use drugs decreases these odds.

❖ What are the odds if you quit now? This will depend on the types of drugs you've been using, and how long and how heavily you've used them. Prenatal diagnostic tests may be able to provide some information. If it's not clear what the chances of a healthy baby are, or you're not sure how to evaluate information you've been given, ask for a consultation with a doctor, preferably one certified by the American Society of Addiction Medicine, or with a

METHADONE MAINTENANCE FOR TWO

Until recently, methadone maintenance was the preferred way to withdraw pregnant women from heroin and other narcotics. But although mothers treated this way did produce healthier babies than addicted mothers, the babies still had many serious problems, including addiction to methadone. Today there is a shift toward weaning the pregnant addict from drugs entirely, and using methadone (or sometimes clonidine) in decreasing doses only for that purpose. Treatment is best carried out in an inpatient medical facility that can provide good prenatal care along with intensive attention to the addiction. For the good of both mother and baby, a structured continuing-care program (see page 71) is essential after treatment.

genetic counselor familiar with the latest information on pregnancy and addiction. A genetic counselor can tell you what the odds are of your baby being healthy, and then can help you understand their implications.

❖ What are your feelings about having a baby now? Are you married? Is there a father around to support you—emotionally and financially? If you're alone, do you have a way of supporting yourself and a child?

❖ How will your having a child now affect others? The father? Your parents? Any other children?

❖ What is your attitude toward elective abortion? If the father is a factor in this equation, what is his attitude?

❖ Does the treatment program you've been considering accept pregnant women? Most do not. If you intend to continue your pregnancy, call the NIDA Treatment Referral Hotline: (800) 662-4357.

If a genetic counselor determines that you are no more (or only slightly more) likely to have a damaged baby than other women, if you feel comfortable about caring for the baby, and feel you can give it a good home, and if you are confident that you'll have enough support to be able to handle both a new baby and a new recovery, then you may decide to continue the pregnancy.

If there is reason to believe that the developing embryo has already been hurt by your drug abuse, and if neither you nor the father (if one is involved) object to abortion, then you may decide in favor of terminating this pregnancy in the hope that a future pregnancy can start off under much better circumstances.

Often the answers aren't clear-cut. If the baby has a fifty-fifty chance of being damaged, if you are unclear about your feelings on abortion, if your parents' feelings or the father's are contrary to yours, if having a baby now would be an overwhelming financial problem, discuss all these factors with a trusted counselor at your treatment center before making a decision.

Once you make your decision, no matter what it is, accept it and learn to live with it. You did the best you could under the circumstances.

3

Roads to Clean and Sober

What do you do when you decide to stop drinking or using? Do you wake up one day and just tell yourself, "Okay, this is it—I'm clean and sober from now on?" Do you go to AA and say, "Hello, I'm Sam, and I'm an alcoholic and an addict"? Do you head for your family doctor or to the couch of an empathetic psychiatrist? Do you check into a treatment facility and put yourself in expert hands?

This chapter describes the most common paths to recovery, beginning with the least intensive. It's meant to help you decide which one (or which combination) is most likely to get you there safe, sound, clean, and sober.

The route you take depends on you, your addiction, and your history. You may make the decision yourself, or you may need help from your family and/or a professional. If the first street you take to sobriety doesn't get you there, don't give up—try another. It doesn't mean you're a hopeless case, just that you'll probably have to try a more intensive pathway.

If you're already sober, but periodically feel the ground tremble beneath your feet, you may want to explore the options in this chapter in your search for ways and means to strengthen your recovery.

A Guide to Choosing the Best Treatment

Going It on Your Own

Every study shows that this is the rockiest road. Occasionally someone does decide to "just say no," and it works. But there's more to sobriety than abstaining from chemicals. If you've been drinking or using for years, you need to learn new ways to cope with life, and that won't be easy on your own. If you're physically addicted, you may need medical attention in coming off, or withdrawing from, your drug (or drugs) of choice—what is commonly

Guide Lines

❖ The recovery program you select should be geared to your individual needs. No one program is right for every alcoholic/addict.

❖ The psychiatrists, other physicians, therapists, and counselors you entrust your treatment to should be professionally certified.

❖ No treatment program, no Twelve-Step fellowship, will keep you clean and sober. Only *you* can keep you sober.

❖ Because your mind is clouded by chemical abuse, you may not be in a position to clearly evaluate all the possible paths to sobriety. If reading about the following choices makes your head swim, consult with your doctor, a knowledgeable clergyperson, a trusted family member or friend, or an AA member you know and respect before you make your decision.

❖ Treatment may be difficult or impossible in an atmosphere that does not accept and respect all patients equally while still understanding the particular needs of those belonging to special populations.

called detoxification, or detox. Going into withdrawal solo could be risky.

If you live in an environment that encourages your addiction (three-martini lunches, routine beer bashes after work, a mate who drinks or uses and encourages you to do the same, pushers on every corner, a social group contemptuous of sobriety), trying to go sober at home could range from difficult to impossible. If you're used to drinking or drugging with friends, you're likely to find working on sobriety on your own a lonesome business. As with dieting, most people have a better chance of succeeding in a compatible peer group.

Many of those who do manage to become sober on their own later find that their recovery is shaky and that being dry is not enough. The wise ones head over to Alcoholics Anonymous (or another Twelve-Step program) for additional support or sign up for inpatient or outpatient treatment.

Before you decide to do it yourself, read the alternatives mapped out in this chapter. And then, even if you're still intent on a lone wolf approach, don't slam the doors to other paths of support in the future.

*ALCOHOLICS ANONYMOUS AND OTHER MUTUAL-HELP GROUPS**

One way or another, Alcoholics Anonymous (AA) or a similar Twelve-Step program is an integral part of almost all successful recoveries from alcohol or drug abuse. In fact, it is widely believed that not including a Twelve-Step program in a treatment plan can put a recovering addict on the road to relapse. For some people, regular participation in

*To make the text less cumbersome, we use the term AA or Alcoholics Anonymous to mean any of the Twelve-Step programs that might be appropriate for dealing with addiction, including Narcotics Anonymous, Cocaine Anonymous, Pills Anonymous, and so on. You will need to find the group in your area that works best for you. See the Appendix for a listing of the major Twelve-Step groups.

†If you use both alcohol and drugs, you will need to want to stop using both. If you use drugs and choose to attend NA, CA, PA, or another Twelve-Step program, you will find the single requirement for membership is the desire to stop using.

such a mutual self-help group is all that is needed to become and remain sober.

Alcoholics Anonymous, the granddaddy of the mutual self-help movement, is a nonsectarian, nondenominational, nonpolitical, loosely set up organization that is more fellowship than organization. AA looks upon alcoholism/addiction as a disease, a physical allergy of sorts coupled with a mental obsession, that can be treated into remission but never cured. Once an alcoholic or an addict, says AA, always an alcoholic or addict. The heart of AA's control program is total lifetime abstinence from alcohol and other drugs—one day at a time.

Even before research showed it to be the most effective approach to recovery, Alcoholics Anonymous had spawned many parallel groups (including Narcotics Anonymous, Cocaine Anonymous, Pills Anonymous, Overeaters Anonymous, Gamblers Anonymous, and Smokers Anonymous) that operate on the same principles and use the Twelve Steps, but deal with specific addiction problems. The only requirement for membership in AA is a desire to stop drinking.

Some studies show that those who join AA rather than try to go it alone are most likely to be middle-class, are more sociable and more likely to be "joiners" (though "loners" who come to learn about their disease rather than socialize also turn up at AA), are more likely to feel guilty over past behavior, usually prefer to rely on external structure, and like simple answers. Their substance-abuse problems are often more chronic and severe than those of go-it-aloners, but in recovery they tend to be physically healthier and more socially stable.

The dropout rate is rather high, although many return to try again. Half attend meetings for three months or less—which speaks to the importance of motivation. Just how many of these dropouts remain sober and how many relapse isn't known. Still, AA alone does work for some people.

"When my father was sick and in an ICU, I had a serious drug problem, and I went to him for money for drugs. I knew how that hurt him. I thought, well, if I could get sober that would make him better. But at first I wasn't really interested in getting sober. So I thought, if I could die, that would help. But it wouldn't, because it would kill Daddy. Then I thought maybe it would be better for him to die so he wouldn't see all this. It wasn't until I went to AA that I realized I couldn't make him better, but I could make me better. And that was a start."

The basic therapy in AA is group "sharing." Members share their past experiences with alcohol and drugs, their present fears, and hopes for the future. The concept began in 1935 with the original members of AA, who were amazed to discover that after sharing their stories and feelings with one another, they experienced relief from previously insatiable compulsions to drink. AA members—each of whom also works through the Twelve Steps (see page 108) at his or her own pace—have been making the same discovery ever since. As members often chant hopefully and optimistically at the close of AA meetings: "Keep coming back! It works if you work it."

For more about how AA functions, see Chapters 6 and 7.

MINI-GUIDE

Nonspiritual Alternatives: Rational Recovery and Secular Organizations for Sobriety

Alcoholics Anonymous is far and away the most popular mutual-help recovery organization in this country and the world. But it isn't the only one. Alcoholics and addicts who failed to find a comfortable home in AA but were nevertheless determined to become sober have founded at least two other major organizations to help others become clean and sober. These groups—Rational Recovery (RR)* and Secular Organizations for Sobriety (SOS)—reject the "spiritual" approach of AA.

RATIONAL RECOVERY. In some important ways RR and AA are similar. Both set a goal of total abstinence for their members. And both recognize that life isn't perfect and isn't always fair, but that the destructive consequences of alcohol and drug abuse are eminently avoidable with sobriety. And both specify that what happens at meetings is to be kept confidential.

But in most ways, Rational Recovery is the very opposite of Alcoholics Anonymous. RR rejects the notion that alcoholics and addicts are powerless to stop their addictions, suggesting instead that until now they simply have not chosen to do so. Instead of reliance on a Higher Power (which RR considers just another dependency), RR members are urged to build on strengths within themselves; the movement inspires independence whenever humanly possible. A constant theme is "Think yourself sober." (For more on what is meant by a Higher Power, see page 130.)

Nor are there steps, sponsors, or moral inventories. RR asks that members learn to accept themselves as they are, to love themselves, drunk or sober, no matter what they do. There is no effort to try to become a better person; the goal is to stop ruining your life because you are already worthwhile. Giving up alcohol and drugs may indeed be difficult, says RR, but in the end, it will make life better.

There is no making amends to others or even caring about what others think of you. According to Rational Emotive Therapy, on which RR is based, human beings should feel good about themselves because they are human beings and not because others think well of them. What others think is irrelevant.

The concept of staying sober one day at a time is rejected in favor of a decision to never drink or use again, period. Sobriety is not supposed to become the cornerstone of one's life, only to give one back one's normal life. The goal is for members to wean themselves from dependency on alcohol, then from dependency on people, and finally from dependency on the group. Meetings take place only twice a week, and most people attend for only one year, after which they may be pronounced "recovered." They can, however, return to meetings whenever the need arises. Discus-

*Rational Recovery and Rational Recovery Systems are not connected to Rational Recovery Services in California, to Rational Recovery, Inc., of Florida, or to the Institutes for Rational Recovery in various states.

sions at meetings focus on the here and now rather than past history, and cross-discussion is encouraged. Like AA, the hat is usually passed at meetings to cover local costs. No money, except that raised from the sale of literature, goes to the national Rational Recovery Systems, which is a nonprofit organization.

Whereas AA relies totally on nonprofessionals helping one another, RR is run by professional coordinators, and each group has volunteer professional advisors available for advice and input. This is necessary because, unlike AA, there are no old-timers around to help newcomers. Advisers attend meetings only occasionally. Rational Recovery, like AA, offers written materials, the core of which is *Rational Recovery from Alcoholism: The Small Book* (meant to contrast with the Big Book of AA).

RR spurns the concept of outside influences on individuals (a Higher Power, the group, family, friends, or even alcohol or drugs) playing a major role. We may claim that we are angry or sad or irresponsible or drunk because of others (a boss, a spouse, a child, a parent), but this thinking is irrational. In reality we are the only ones responsible for the way we feel and the way we behave. We have a choice to drink or not to drink, and we are competent to make that choice (an idea not foreign to AA).

RR suggests instead that we look within ourselves for strength and direction. We all have within us an inner voice, says RR, that challenges us to go wrong. It's this voice, nicknamed "Beast," that urges you to drink or use drugs, that takes over during blackouts and gets you to do terrible things, and that speaks louder than your own rational self. It's the voice that tells you things like, "You can stop anytime (but not now)" or "You're not really addicted (you just like the taste)," and that tears angrily into those who criticize or try to help you.

An acronym, based on the word "beast," is used to help RR members avoid taking another drink or drug:

B is for Boozing Opportunities (weddings, parties, trips, and so on). RR says you need to be aware of the pitfalls but do not need to avoid such events. You are not powerless in the face of temptation, and can choose not to succumb.

E is for Enemy Recognition. You need to distinguish those thoughts coming from the Enemy (Beast) that are positive about booze or drugs.

A is for Accuse the Beast of Malice. You can be angry at the Beast for its evil deeds (trying to tempt you) or you can laugh at it. Either way you need to make clear to the Beast that you have the upper hand and you won't relinquish it.

S is for Self-Control and Self-Worth Reminders. You must find ways of showing the Beast that you have self-control (like moving your hands in front of your face and holding them there, totally in your control, until Beast backs down); you must also find ways of telling yourself that you are a worthwhile person. You then choose not to drink for the same reason you drank: to feel good about yourself.

T is for Treasuring Your Sobriety. This means focusing on the pleasures of life that are attainable only in sobriety (a concept similar to that in AA).

Those preferring AA may question the RR philosophy, just as RR enthusiasts find flaws in AA. Many

(continued on next page)

MINI-GUIDE

(continued from previous page)

RR members first become sober in AA and then, not wholly satisfied, move over to the newer organization—often carrying some AA thinking with them. But some are also apt to indulge in AA-bashing.

Alcoholics Anonymous has proven itself over the years by helping millions to sobriety. Its basic tenets have held up under scientific scrutiny, and it has earned the backing of physicians and therapists who work with alcoholics/addicts. Rational Recovery, founded in 1986, on the concept of rational-emotive therapy pioneered by Albert Ellis and the foundation for RR, has groups in hundreds of cities. Although it has yet to gain wide support in the medical community, a few treatment programs do offer an RR option. Whether or not RR will prove itself over time is not yet clear; two major studies are presently being done to evaluate its effectiveness. Certainly it is likely that, in the spirit of "different strokes for different folks," there's more than one road to sobriety. Whether RR is one of them, only time and further research will tell.

SECULAR ORGANIZATIONS FOR SOBRIETY. Secular Organizations for Sobriety (SOS) is also of recent vintage and offers another nonspiritual alternative to AA. Like both the other organizations, SOS preaches total abstinence. It is nonprofessional and nonprofit, and more closely mirrors AA (without the spiritual element) than does RR. SOS is not antagonistic toward AA, has adopted the one-day-at-a-time philosophy, and doesn't discourage AA attendance. In fact, some SOS members also attend AA. Instead of Twelve Steps, SOS is based on six suggested guidelines:

1. To break the cycle of denial and achieve sobriety, we first acknowledge that we *are* alcoholics.
2. We reaffirm this truth daily and accept without reservation—one day at a time—the fact that, as clean and sober individuals, we cannot and do not drink or use, *no matter what.*
3. Since drinking/using is not an option for us, we take whatever steps are necessary to continue our sobriety priority lifelong.
4. A high quality of life—the good life—can be achieved. However, life is also filled with uncertainties; therefore, we do not drink/use regardless of feelings, circumstances, or conflicts.
5. We share in confidence with each other our thoughts and feelings as sober, clean individuals.
6. Sobriety is our priority, and we are each individually responsible for our lives and our sobriety.

Cost of AA

With no dues or membership fees, not-for-profit AA is far and away the least expensive treatment option. At most meetings the hat is passed for contributions to cover rent, coffee, cookies, and incidentals. Members and guests drop in what they can, if they can.

Who Can Benefit from AA Alone?

It's estimated that three out of five alcoholics and addicts can recover with no treatment other than regular attendance at Alcoholics Anonymous or another Twelve-Step program. This may be all you need if:

❖ You do not need medical supervision of your withdrawal (see page 78).

❖ You are a social being, used to spending a lot of time with your drinking or drugging buddies. You'll find the same friendly folks at AA, the difference being that now they socialize without chemical lubrication.

❖ You are well disciplined and self-motivated (you'll have to talk yourself out of your excuses and into attending meetings every day for at least three months).

❖ You have a good support system at home—family members active in Al-Anon or who have been in AA for a long period of time.

In some cases, those without insurance or access to free treatment, who cannot afford to pay for a residential or outpatient program themselves, may have no recourse but AA, even if they don't meet the above criteria. And it's certainly better than doing nothing.

Selecting the Right AA Group

No two groups are exactly alike. Each has its own personality, a composite of the attributes, attitudes, and histories of its members. To find the home group most comfortable for you, you'll have to do some research. Which groups are mostly male or mostly female? Which are smoking or nonsmoking? Which welcome babies or young children? Which are made up mostly of professionals, or working people, or homemakers? Which tend to be rather religious, which more agnostic? Attend several different meetings before deciding where to hang your hat and coat. (For more about finding a group, see page 102.)

Meetings of your home group probably won't be the only ones you attend. Most groups don't meet often enough to fulfill the needs of those in early recovery: ninety AA meetings in ninety days. You may want to attend lunchtime meetings on Tuesday and Thursday near your shop or office, and your home group on Monday, Wednesday, and Friday evenings, with yet a third group on weekends. Or if your home group meets only on weekends, you may want to find another group for weeknights.

Concerns about AA

Many people who could benefit from Alcoholics Anonymous don't because they imagine meetings to be very different than they actually are. If you hesitate to turn up at an AA meeting because you fear it will resemble the drunk tank at a county jail (it's as civilized as a PTA meeting) or you're afraid you'll be pressured into talking about yourself (you won't be) or you fear it's too religious for you (it's not a religious organization) or for any other reason, read Chapters 6 and 7 to find out what AA is really like. You can also read *Alcoholics Anonymous* (also known as the Big Book), the *Little Red Book*, and *As Bill Sees It* or get a copy of the AA video (see "For Your Information"), which helps acquaint newcomers with AA.

AA philosophy urges newcomers to stick with the winners—people who are clean and sober long-term. Among mutual-help groups, AA is the runaway winner.

OUTPATIENT TREATMENT BY A PHYSICIAN OR AN ADDICTION SPECIALIST

Seeing a doctor for addiction problems is essentially going the outpatient route, with the doctor as the counselor or part of the treatment team. As with any outpatient program, patients are generally urged to go to Alcoholics Anonymous. If the thought of attending AA makes you break out in a rash, your doctor may ask you to build your recovery around some similar elements: things like regular counseling, group meetings, personal inventories, meditation, reflection, and changing your ways. Treatment "technology" has become so sophisticated that it's possible to develop a successful treatment plan for every addicted person.

Who Can Benefit from Physician Treatment?

Essentially the same people who are good candidates for other kinds of outpatient treatment (see page 49). It is, of course, necessary to have access to a skilled, well-qualified physician.

Cost of Physician Treatment

Costs will vary depending upon the physician's fees (which differ from one part of the country to another), the number of visits scheduled, and how long this phase of treatment lasts. In most cases, the cost will be less than residential treatment, and possibly less than a more complex outpatient program. Though physician treatment may be less costly, it is also less intensive.

Selecting the Right Physician

Forty years ago, when John Mooney, the founder of Willingway, first became a family doctor in Statesboro, he would have been of little help to a Georgian with a drinking or drug problem. Today most doctors still have very little knowledge or experience in the area of addiction. But more and more are becoming familiar with the subject, either through residency programs like the one at Willingway or through special courses sponsored by the American Society of Addiction Medicine (ASAM) or the American Academy of Psychiatrists in Alcoholism and Addiction (AAPAA).

A doctor certified by either of these organizations will probably be able, and will certainly be willing, to work with you on your alcohol or drug problem. If not, he can help you evaluate your options. Also a good prospect is a doctor—even without certification—who is recommended by old-timers in AA. Such a doctor may be recovering. Whatever you do, avoid a physician who doesn't know how to end a visit without writing a prescription (see page 243). Also avoid a physician (or any other professional, for that matter) who assures you with a parting slap on the back that you can learn to drink safely. There is absolutely no credible evidence that alcoholics or drug addicts can do this.

OUTPATIENT TREATMENT BY A PSYCHIATRIST

Assuming the psychiatrist is trained in the treatment of alcoholism/addiction, the treatment will be very similar to that given by other savvy physicians. The primary goal will be to help you achieve abstinence from drugs and alcohol. In general, you'll be asked to go to AA and to follow the basic precepts of AA in becoming sober. Once you are solidly sober, the therapist will then start looking at personality traits that need fine-tuning, help you build self-esteem, and work with you on such troubling feelings as rage, shame, depression, aggression, anxiety, helplessness, powerlessness. The issue of self-care (if you don't take care of yourself, who will?) may also be addressed.

If psychiatric problems—such as deep depression—are interfering with treatment for alcoholism/addiction or put the patient or others at risk, then they will be treated immediately, along with the addiction.

If you do choose psychiatric treatment, don't con yourself into believing that once your psychiatric problems are solved you will be able to drink or use drugs again. That would be a major mistake.

Who Can Benefit from Psychiatric Treatment?

Usually, alcoholics/addicts with serious coexisting mental illness require the care of a psychiatrist qualified to provide treatment for both the illness and the addiction. This is particularly important when the condition is life-threatening—when, for example, patients are dangerous to themselves or to others. Or when they are unable to benefit from treatment for addiction because their mind is so muddled by the disorganization of schizophrenia or mania, or so numbed by depression, that concentration is impossible.

If you have troubling symptoms but are uncertain whether psychiatric treatment would be best for you, have your condition evaluated by a qualified addiction specialist, who can make a recommendation. If you are functioning well enough to get sober first, it may be a good idea to wait three to six months after withdrawal to see if psychiatric symptoms still exist. In many cases, they will have disappeared along with the bottle in your hip pocket or the packet of cocaine in your purse. Once you're sober, however, if you are still suffering from deep depression, serious mania (a wildly happy but unproductive high), or schizophrenic symptoms, consulting a qualified psychiatrist (see below) is a must. You should also see a psychiatrist or an experienced therapist if you are troubled by the effects of sexual or other kinds of abuse or serious trauma or loss in your life.

Cost of Psychiatric Treatment

The cost of psychiatric treatment depends on the hourly charge of the therapist (anywhere from $50 to $150) and on the number of hours the therapy continues. In most cases, the total cost of treatment for the addiction itself will be about the same as treatment by any addiction specialist. Of course, if treatment is needed for mental illness as well, the cost could be considerably higher. This additional cost, however, will often be covered by insurance. Often even the treatment for addiction will be covered when a psychiatrist provides the care. That's because the psychiatrist can use a dual diagnosis (specifying that mental illness coexists with the addiction) on insurance claims. If psychiatric treatment is dispensed in an inpatient facility, the costs will be similar to other inpatient facilities.

"Hey, I'm not so bad. All I ever did was some drinking. I never did drugs."

Selecting the Right Psychiatrist

Like most physicians in the country, the majority of psychiatrists, particularly older ones, have not been trained to treat drug and alcohol abuse problems, or even to identify them. Those trained in the last few years are more likely to be knowledgeable, but for the most expert treatment look for accreditation by the American Academy of Psychiatrists in Alcoholism and Addictions (AAPAA) or the American Society of Addiction Medicine (ASAM), for considerable hands-on experience in treating substance abuse. Ideally, get a recommendation from someone in AA or from a physician or counselor with experience in addiction.

Psychiatrists familiar with the treatment of alcoholism/addiction recognize that it can masquerade as one or a combination of mental illnesses. They do not routinely use mood-altering medication to treat addicted people once withdrawal is completed, unless serious mental illness or a life-threatening situation exists. And they are strongly supportive of Alcoholics Anonymous, or at least of the principles of recovery it espouses.

OUTPATIENT COUNSELING BY A PSYCHOLOGIST, SOCIAL WORKER, COUNSELOR, OR OTHER THERAPIST

Thousands of counselors and therapists are presently treating chemically dependent people. Their approach usually does not differ very much from that offered by other professionals and will usually include individual and group therapy as well as referral to AA. How effective the treatment is depends upon the training, skill, and orientation of the counselor.

Cost of Treatment by Counselor or Therapist

Like other outpatient treatment, this is less expensive than an inpatient program. Non-M.D. therapists are usually somewhat less expensive per session than M.D.s. How the costs compare long-term depends on how long the therapy runs.

Choosing the Right Counselor or Therapist

An unqualified professional can do more harm than good, especially if he or she fails to focus on the alcoholism/addiction issue from the first. Counselors who are in recovery themselves rarely make this error. They usually have a good grasp of the problems in recovery and can identify with their clients. But this isn't enough. To ensure that your therapist is qualified and will tackle addiction issues first, be sure he or she has met the standards for a Certified Addiction Counselor or Credentialed Alcoholism Counselor. The most beneficial additional training or experience depends on your needs. If your job is your biggest problem, a social worker familiar with career counseling may be most helpful; if it's your marriage, a marriage counselor; if incest or child abuse is part of your background, a psychologist or psychiatrist familiar with these problems.

AN OUTPATIENT TREATMENT PROGRAM

Outpatient programs vary widely, but in general they are less intensive than inpatient programs. Because patients are not kept overnight, a substantial reduction in cost is possible. And for those who can benefit from it, there is the advantage (risky though it may be) of learning to stay sober in the real world rather than in the sheltered world of an inpatient facility.

Outpatient treatment may be started when the patient is already clean and sober, or it may be preceded by carefully supervised withdrawal on an inpatient or outpatient basis. Outpatient treatment programs usually consist of many, sometimes all, of the following: evaluation and assessment interview, family history, employer interview (with the patient's consent); physical exam (including a urine drug screen, liver function tests, and a red blood count) and periodic physician reassessments and drug-use monitoring (urine screens, family and work confirmations, signatures to show attendance at AA meetings and counseling sessions, and so on); daily Antabuse (a drug that makes an individual unable to tolerate alcohol), if needed; individual, group, and family therapy; audiovisuals and reading material; an introduction to AA (including what's in the Big Book, an explanation of the ninety-meetings-in-ninety-days program, what the reason behind the signed AA log is, why you are assigned a sponsor, and so on); and special individual and/or group sessions and Al-Anon for the family. Some programs require an hour-a-day attendance, others several hours, some even full-time. Because there are usually fewer hours of therapy daily, outpatient programs run for months, or even a year or more, rather than the four to six weeks common for inpatient programs.

For some particularly shaky people, outpatient programs can be risky. Dredging up deep feelings could lead to dropping into a bar after a session, or to dropping out of the program entirely. (At an inpatient program, it's not easy to pick up and leave. And there's time to give those feelings a decent burial before you are sent out into the hard cruel world.) It may also be difficult for some people to concentrate on recovery issues while work, family, and other outside environmental factors continue to tug their emotional strings.

In choosing treatment, the quality of a program and whether or not it fits you well is more important than whether it is inpatient or out. A good outpatient program can do more for the motivated patient than a poor inpatient one. Some experts, in fact, endorse lower-cost outpatient treatment as a good alternative to residential programs for certain patients.

Outpatient and inpatient treatment aren't mutually exclusive. You can choose outpatient, find it isn't intensive enough to keep you clean and sober, and later decide to try an inpatient facility. At that point, what you learned in the outpatient experience will have prepared you to get more from an inpatient experience. Or you could start with an inpatient program, find yourself still in need of help on discharge, and opt to continue with outpatient treatment back home. Again, the one-two punch may be better than either alone.

Who Can Benefit from an Outpatient Treatment Program?

You are a good candidate for outpatient treatment if most of the following are true:

❖ You've been having problems with alcohol and/or drugs for only a short time and have decided to take action before your life is a total mess.

❖ You are already sober, or your physician has determined that the risk of serious problems with withdrawal is not great, or the plan is for you to go through detox as an inpatient and then move into an outpatient program.

❖ You have completed an inpatient program but feel too shaky about your recovery to go into a traditional, less intensive continuing-care (or aftercare) program.

❖ Your physician has determined that you have no serious medical problems that could put your health at risk if you attempt recovery as an outpatient.

❖ You are not seriously depressed, manic, or psychotic, and haven't been thinking about—or attempted—suicide.

❖ It would be extremely difficult for you to leave your job and/or family at this time.

❖ You have a relatively stable and supportive home environment, and are confident that your treatment won't be sabotaged by family or friends. Your family is receptive to attending Al-Anon and open AA meetings.

❖ You don't feel residential treatment is necessary (see page 50 for the list of reasons inpatient treatment might be needed), but believe you need a program more structured than AA alone.

❖ You admit to your addiction, are motivated (by your own feelings or by external factors, such as the risk of losing your job) to do something about it, and are open-minded about following professional recommendations. Without adequate motivation, you could just fail to show up on a day when you don't feel well, then start missing sessions regularly, and finally drop out entirely. You are a less captive audience than in inpatient treatment.

❖ You are receptive to intensive involvement in AA.

❖ You tend to put more effort into something you (or your employer) pay for (in which case, cost-free AA might not work).

Selecting the Right Outpatient Program

There are good and bad programs, and quality is largely unrelated to cost. Most of the same features that make for a good inpatient program (see page 52) also make for a good outpatient one. Try to meet the staff of a prospective outpatient program before making a final decision; be sure they are people you feel you can trust and will listen to. You don't have to feel comfortable, however, about everything they are going to ask you to do. Feeling uncomfortable is the route to an eventually comfortable recovery.

Outpatient programs have multiplied since insurers and employers became cost conscious, but there are still many communities without a good program, or without any program. If you live in such a community, it may be necessary to work out your own program with a counselor or therapist—one that includes group and individual counseling plus daily AA meetings.

Cost of Outpatient Treatment

Outpatient programs cost about half as much as inpatient treatment. Presently they range from about $3,000 to $12,000, depending on the part of the country, how much treatment is needed, and the length and type of program. The tab has been picked up by employers more and more frequently in recent years, and some large companies—in order to control both costs and effectiveness of treatment—have set up their own outpatient programs. Although medical insurance does not always cover all of outpatient treatment, it frequently covers some portion of the psychotherapy component. How the provider fills out the paperwork can affect the benefits you receive from your insurer. Some insurance providers, for example, will say no to "counseling" and yes to "psychotherapy." So be sure that your provider is familiar with your coverage. In some cases you may have to pay some part of your treatment out of your own pocket. In the long run, it will be a lot less expensive than the cost of abusing alcohol and drugs.

AN INPATIENT TREATMENT PROGRAM

Inpatient treatment is the most expensive, most intensive, most structured, and most immediately time-consuming approach to getting well. But it is also, for many people, the surest method of successfully getting sober and staying that way. Inpatient programs, in which alcoholics and/or addicts live together in a therapeutic environment, totally immersed in learning about their disease and developing coping skills for their return home, traditionally last four to five weeks for alcoholics and six or more weeks for those who are either on other drugs or cross-addicted. Treatment may sometimes be condensed into a two- or three-week period because of cutbacks in funding by health plans.

In quiet, comfortable surroundings, patients usually have opportunities for both individual and group therapy and are encouraged to look at themselves in the mirror, warts and all. With few distractions and plenty of time for introspection and interaction, they end up with answers to questions they didn't even know they should ask. Before patients come in for treatment, they have no choice but to continue their self-destructive tailspins; the goal of treatment is to give them back the choice to live sober. It's a choice all alcoholics/addicts have to make every day for the rest of their lives.

Some inpatient treatment programs have their own detoxification facilities; others will detox you elsewhere before admitting you.

Who Can Benefit from Inpatient Treatment?

Not everybody needs inpatient treatment. You should seriously consider it, however, if:

❖ You've had severe withdrawal symptoms when going without your drug of choice before, or fear you may have a hard time withdrawing (see page 78).

❖ You've relapsed after failing to stick to a less intense plan.

❖ You have either rejected AA or it hasn't worked for you, and outpatient treatment is not available.

❖ You've failed to stay sober after previous out- or inpatient treatment.

❖ You have medical problems (such as liver disease, lung disease, AIDS, heart disease) that could possibly complicate recovery.

❖ You have serious psychological, behavioral, or emotional problems—such as depression, manic-depression, schizophrenia, or thoughts of suicide—that could possibly complicate recovery.

❖ You are in a safety-sensitive or highly responsible field of work (such as airline, railroad, or trucking employee, physician or nurse, nuclear or other power plant worker, or police officer), making the consequences of a relapse particularly costly to the public and coworkers as well as to yourself.

❖ You have a particularly stressful or drug-oriented environment to return to. The distance may not only help you focus on recovery, but also help you consider an alternative place to live.

❖ You are, or may be, addicted to both alcohol and other drugs, or to more than one drug.

❖ You are still in denial about your disease and are unable to look at yourself honestly (you may not be able to decide this for yourself).

❖ You are still in your teens and need to work out a lot of typical adolescent problems before you are ready to accept the responsibility for continuing your recovery on your own.

❖ You feel total immersion in a controlled environment would give you the best start on the road to recovery.

❖ You have a desire to understand completely the nature of your disease.

❖ You're just plain scared that if you don't do something drastic soon you're a dead duck.

Cost of Treatment

Treatment at an adequate inpatient program can cost anywhere from $7,000 to $35,000 for a four-week stay, and quality is not necessarily related to cost. Some of the best programs have endowments that help keep costs down. Others keep costs down by not providing medical services and by sending patients with medical problems or detoxification needs elsewhere. Some very expensive programs provide country club accommodations, which in no way improve treatment outcomes but can raise costs by 50 percent or more. Costs may be higher in some parts of the country—New York or California, for example. Some states fund their own inpatient programs for those who are unable to pay for private treatment; costs may vary depending upon ability to pay.

Anything more than $25,000 all-inclusive for six weeks of treatment is probably a rip-off. On the other hand, an unusually low price quote can also be a signal to be wary. Though there is a truth-in-lending law, there is no similar law governing billing of health care. A low quote (as when you're pricing a car) may just mean that many items have been left out of the estimate but will be added to your bill when you leave. Be sure that fees for detoxification, laboratory tests, psychologist, physician, and other professional fees, intensive medical evaluation, x-rays, participation of spouse, parent, or significant other, and continuing care are all included in the price that's quoted when you are comparing programs. Remember, too, to factor in the cost of round-trip transportation for yourself as well as anyone else who may plan to visit and/or participate in the program.

Whether or not the program qualifies for reimbursement under your health insurance policy or your company's Employee Assistance Program may be a major factor to consider. In many cases, insurance will cover treatment, though what kind of treatment and to what extent will vary from policy to policy. Some policies will pay for medical or psychiatric treatment but not for "counseling." Health Maintenance Organizations (HMOs) generally provide little or no coverage for substance abuse treatment. Some policies with mental health coverage will pay for treatment of the symptoms of substance abuse (depression, for example) but not for the underlying addiction. Some will pay for two weeks of inpatient treatment, others for four or more. Others will fund inpatient treatment under specific circumstances only. Get advice from your treatment center as well as your employer's benefits counselor (if there is one) before applying for insurance benefits. In some instances, you may have to pay a part of the fee out of your own pocket.

It may be possible to persuade an employer that it is penny-wise and dollar-foolish to refuse to pay for or skimp on treatment. Billions of dollars are lost annually by business and industry because of alcohol and drug abuse by employees, and billions more are spent to pay for the one in three hospital admissions caused directly or indirectly by the effects of substance abuse. These could be greatly reduced by providing effective treatment at the start. Your employer might better appreciate this by reading page 580.

Selecting the Right Treatment Center

A quality program is important not only because it will increase your chances of successfully becoming sober, but because a poor one may sour you on treatment permanently. It isn't easy to determine quality, but an in-person visit or interviews with former patients can help. Recommendations from local AA members or a physician or counselor who works with recovering people may also be valuable.

There are no industry-wide quality standards, and no two alcohol/drug treatment programs are exactly alike. In general, however, the best programs share the following qualities:

A philosophy that puts patients and their sobriety first, ahead of staff convenience or financial considerations. You can probably determine this only from someone who has already been through the program; ask around at AA meetings or check with your counselor or knowledgeable Employee Assistance Program personnel at work about the quality of a program you are considering.

A medical approach to alcoholism/addiction. Alcoholism/addiction is viewed as a disease. Alcoholics/addicts are treated as sick people come to get well, not crazy people who need to get sane or bad people who need to reform.

TREATMENT PROGRAM APGAR

When a baby is born, doctors do a quick assessment of its condition by using what is known as an APGAR score. You can do a quick screening of treatment programs using *this* APGAR. Once you've found some that pass the test, you can go on and do the more detailed examination described throughout this chapter.

This system rates a treatment program on a scale of 0 to 10 on the basis of whether or not the most critical components are present. You can obtain the information you need by asking a program physician, counselor, or admissions coordinator the following questions. Award 1 point for each positive response. Unknown, ambivalent, and negative responses are all scored 0.

Alcoholism as a primary disease:
___1. Does written program material state that the staff believe that addictive illness is a primary disease?
___2. During the program, is a patient required to complete a written life history?
Professional qualifications:
___3. Are at least half the physicians on the attending medical staff certified by the American Society of Addiction Medicine?
___4. Are at least half the counselors in the program certified as addiction counselors?
Groups specially designed for addiction treatment:
___5. Does the program have group meetings to discuss the application of the steps of Alcoholics Anonymous?
___6. Does the program have group meetings for families and to meet other special needs of addictive patients?
Abstinence orientation of the program:
___7. Are more than 90 percent of patients discharged abstinent from all mood-altering drugs and medications?
___8. Is there a hospital policy that clinical staff remain abstinent from alcohol and other mind-altering drugs?
Recovery priority of the program:
___9. Are more than one third of the clinical staff recovering from alcohol or drug problems themselves?
___10. Are patients given the opportunity to attend and join Alcoholics Anonymous during treatment?

A detox facility, if you need one. It makes sense to go through detox and treatment in the same facility—not just because you could get derailed between detox and treatment at the first saloon you pass, but because it will mean better care. There won't be any conflicting philosophies to confuse you, any prolonged medical effects of withdrawal will be dealt with more easily, and those who are treating you will be more familiar with your case from the start.

Strong AA involvement. That doesn't mean AA runs the program, just that the staff introduces patients to what AA is and what it does. It's best if patients have the opportunity to leave the treatment center (with counselors and others in their program) to attend real community AA meetings, so they will be less hesitant to attend them when they get back home. Next best is having AA meetings at the facility, to which those in the local area are invited. Any treatment program that doesn't heartily endorse AA should be heartily avoided.

Adequate treatment time. A minimum stay of four weeks for alcoholics and six weeks or longer for those addicted to drugs or who are poly-

MULTIDISCIPLINARY TREATMENT

Some treatment programs employ a variety of experts (addictionist, psychiatrist, psychologist, social worker, and possibly other professionals). This can work splendidly or terribly, depending on the approach. If it is *inter*disciplinary, with all the professionals working together using a single therapeutic approach based on the idea that alcoholism/addiction is a disease, it can work well, giving the patient the benefit of a wide range of expertise. If, on the other hand, it is *multi*disciplinary, with each expert thinking he or she can solve your problem best, you may be more confused and worse off than before.

addicted has been traditional for many years. More recently, however, there has been a trend toward shorter inpatient programs coupled with intensive outpatient continuing care. This has been motivated by insurers and employers trying to contain spiraling medical costs. How this will work over the long haul is not yet clear. If you can swing the longer stay, then go for it.

A professional environment. While a relaxed, homelike atmosphere is good, too informal or too posh a setting could undermine treatment. You should feel as though you are a patient at a medical facility, not a guest at a resort. Features such as TV and videos, tennis, golf, and boutique shopping may sound appealing, but they are also distracting and can sabotage therapy.

An educational program. The better you understand alcoholism/addiction, the better you can fight it. The curriculum should include such topics as the disease concept of addiction; history and statistics on the drug epidemic; how it's possible to break through denial (or self-deception); information on tolerance, dependence, and withdrawal symptoms; the pharmacology of drugs and cross-addiction; the possible medical complications in recovery; how alcoholic/addict families work and what kinds of family complications can be expected in recovery; how to prevent relapse; and how to immunize your children against addiction. These subjects are best taught through a combination of lectures, audiotapes, videotapes, and movies. Tapes and books should be available for patients to check out for use during leisure time as reinforcement for what is learned in the group.

Quality staffing. A mix between academically trained professionals and recovering alcoholics/addicts is preferable. Be wary of a treatment program run entirely, or almost entirely, by recovering people without a staff of professionals. Or, conversely, one that has few recovering people on staff. Counselors should be certified by the NADAAC (National Association of Drug Abuse and Alcoholism Counselors) or an affiliate and routinely assigned to patients of the same sex. Staff physicians should be certified by ASAM or AAPAA. Such specialists are equipped to handle most medical as well as behavioral complications of chemical dependency. A big-name hospital with a lot of subspecialists may seem appealing, but if there are too many chiefs and not enough staff communication, patients—and sometimes even their families—may be able to manipulate the staff, playing one against the other, telling one story to A and another to B, and derail their own treatment.

Adequate staffing. There should be at least one counselor for every seven patients. The best programs will have some counselors with special expertise who can deal with specific issues, such as marital and family problems, women and addiction, ethnic issues, homosexuality, AIDs, and adolescence.

Full-time staffing. Even the best of staffs can't do the best of jobs if they are available only from nine to five. There should be qualified people for patients to talk to whenever the need arises, day or night, weekdays and weekends. Visit or call a prospective facility after hours or on the weekend, and ask to speak to a qualified counselor. If you are put off until the next morning, reconsider. At the very least, counselors should be available until 11 P.M. or midnight seven days a week, with other support staff on hand around the clock.

A sound policy toward the use of medication in treatment. The use of medication to ease the symptoms of withdrawal is proper procedure, but continuing to use drugs during treatment, except in rare cases, places time bombs on the road to recovery. Ask what percentage of patients receive mind-altering drugs after detox. Any facility that continues to medicate more than 5 percent of patients is probably not the best place for first-time treatment, except for individuals with severe mental illness.*

A self-discovery approach. Patients should have the chance to really look at themselves, preferably by writing a life history and confiding as much as they wish of it to a counselor. You should not be required to show this life history to anyone, and it should be routine policy that it be burned or otherwise destroyed after you've discussed its implications with your counselor. Steer clear of programs that fail to offer a structured opportunity for this kind of valuable honest introspection, or that mandate reading life histories to a group or insist on saving them to be read in the months or years ahead.

Adequate group sessions. There should be at least three daily patient group meetings, led by a professional. There should be more group meetings if there is not a lot of one-on-one work being done. Some meetings should be educational (nutrition, health, pharmacology), others therapeutic (discussions of feelings, experiences, and so on). There may also be special meetings for women, families, adolescents, repeaters, or other specific groups. Group sizes should range from six to ten for counseling sessions, twenty-five to fifty for educational lectures and AA-type meetings. Group meetings that run from sunup to bedtime are a red flag—they may leave no time for introspection or informal "sharing" with other patients.

One-on-one therapy. There should be scheduled time with a counselor at least twice a week.

A comfortable schedule—one that is designed for the benefit of patients, not staff. The philosophy of some programs is to maintain a very rigid schedule so that patients are roused at an early hour, then heavily programmed for the entire day. Others prefer a looser schedule, placing more responsibility on patients to get out of bed, get to meals, and get to meetings. This allows counselors to identify (and give extra help to) those who have trouble scheduling their own time, while not penalizing those who can handle these small responsibilities. This probably more closely simulates the real world of recovery back home, where you will have to get up on your own, get to meetings on your own, and so on. Looser scheduling also allows more time for patients to discuss and digest what went on in meetings, to learn to engage each other in casual conversa-

*The rate of medicating will be probably be higher at psychiatric facilities, which usually treat individuals with coexisting psychiatric problems, who may indeed need to be treated with medication.

MINI-GUIDE

The Right Treatment Program for You

Some discomfort is necessary during drug or alcohol treatment for progress to be made. If you don't experience any, then you aren't spilling out your innermost feelings, and probably aren't being honest with yourself or anyone else. But discomfort when you feel you are among people very different from yourself can hinder progress. So in choosing an in- or outpatient program, be sure there are others like yourself, not only in treatment, but serving as counselors.

If you come from a rural area or are a sophisticated suburbanite, an inner-city program may not work for you. If you are black, an all-white program may increase discomfort. On the other hand, a program where everyone else is just like you may not be the best choice either; you may end up focusing on your subgroup problems rather than your recovery needs. In most cases, a program that serves a mixed population but is attentive to minority differences is the ideal.

When you choose a program, be sure your final selection gives you a good comfort zone in all the following areas. If you're in no condition to determine the answers to these questions, trust a sober friend or relative to help.

SOCIOECONOMIC LEVEL. Are most of the patients poor, working class, middle class, wealthy? What is the background typical of most counselors? Will you feel comfortable with the mix?

MALE-FEMALE RATIO. Are there enough patients and counselors who are the same sex as you?

AGE. Are there at least several other patients in your age bracket? Are counselors experienced in dealing with your age group?

LANGUAGE. If you aren't fluent in English, is there someone on the staff who speaks your native tongue? Are there other patients who do?

ETHNIC BACKGROUND. Are there others on the staff and in the patient population whose backgrounds are similar to yours?

SEXUAL ORIENTATION. Are there people on the staff and/or in the patient pool who share yours, be it homosexual, heterosexual, or bisexual?

COMMUNITY BACKGROUND. Are people from similar circumstances (city, inner city, suburban, rural) or with similar lifestyles involved in the program?

SPECIAL NEEDS. If you are handicapped, multi-addicted, or have any other special requirements, will those be met ungrudgingly?

ATTITUDE. Do you get the feeling from talking to representatives of the treatment program that differences are respected, that you won't be treated as a second-class patient because you are poor, African-American, Hispanic, Jewish, Native American, homosexual, bisexual, old, young, female, or just from a different part of the country? Does it seem that counselors are willing to deal compassionately with possible side issues—such as self-hate, low self-esteem, and bias toward your group, for example?

tion, to do some self-evaluation and study in their rooms, and to seek help when they feel they need it.

Treatment centers usually have a set bedtime so that patients get into a normal day/night pattern. Some, however, allow patients who are unable to sleep to seek out a staff member to talk to after lights out.

An intergenerational patient and staff mix. Sharing with others in different age groups can improve communications skills, open up solutions to emotional problems, foster empathy for others, and initiate resolution of family problems. Older patients and staff bring their experience and wisdom to the treatment environment and young people bring vitality and optimism. Together they create a surrogate family atmosphere in the therapeutic environment.

Family involvement. A good program will emphasize the importance of "significant others" in the recovery process. It will urge these family members or friends to attend Al-Anon meetings during the treatment period and to continue attendance following it. It will also invite them to participate in the treatment program itself, usually toward the end, with individual, couples, and family counseling. This helps the worried folks at home more fully understand the process of recovery and gives them the opportunity to have their own questions answered (they're bound to have a lot of them). The best programs will arrange additional support through contacts with patients and families in their own community who are doing well in recovery.

Recreational therapy. It's not enough for a treatment center to tell patients not to use drugs; it should also teach them the importance of learning new things to do with their time (other than go to AA meetings). Recreation preparation can include art, music, exercise, indoor or outdoor games, arts and crafts, hobbies. A good recreational therapist helps patients understand that—surprise!—they can have fun while sober and begins teaching them how.

Physical activity is important for everyone, in recovery or not. But in recovery, exercise programs should be custom-tailored. Most patients in early recovery are not ready for a strenuous program that includes high-stress aerobics or jogging, because of a combination of inactivity during active addiction and damage to muscles, nerves, and bone by alcohol and other drugs. Walking, swimming, and water aerobics are usually safe and effective for most recoverees at this stage.

Question the validity of a program that overemphasizes exercise or other recreational activities that can distract from treatment.

Confidentiality assurance. The center should agree not to give out any information—including the fact that you are a patient there—to anyone except those people you have specifically okayed. Patients should also be cautioned not to pry into each other's full names or backgrounds (though they may be free to divulge them if they wish) and not to take photographs or identify other patients when communicating with family or friends on the outside.

A passing grade on the Kleenex test. Boxes of tissues strategically placed throughout counseling areas and in sleeping quarters tell you that patients are expected to do a lot of crying. The "good cry" is an important part of emotional recovery.

Snack stations. Since recovering alcoholics and addicts are subject to snack attacks, such stations (preferably offering such healthy choices as fruit, peanuts, and pretzels, as well as noncaffeinated beverages) are another sign of a place that cares.

Healthful foods. Good nutrition is imperative in recovery, so many programs now provide healthy meals designed by a knowledgeable nutritionist. They also provide nutritional advice and, sometimes, even recipes for patients to use on returning home. The daily diet should emphasize whole grains and plenty of fresh fruits and vegetables, while limiting fat, sodium, refined foods, and sugar.

A good referral network. A good program should be able to give you the names of satisfied graduates as well as professionals in your geographic area who can vouch for its work. Beware of programs that advertise heavily; such advertising jacks up the cost of treatment. It could also indicate that the program is having trouble filling beds through professional referral channels, either because it's ineffective or because it's overpriced.

A continuing-care (or aftercare) program. Treatment is not only the end of a life of alcohol and drugs, but the beginning of a new drug-free life. To continue the process begun in treatment, it's vital to follow through with an ongoing program of support, meetings, and, if necessary, counseling or even outpatient treatment when you get back home. The treatment center should be prepared to arrange a continuing care program for you.

Convenient location. The quality of a program is more important than its location, but location is a factor to consider. Sometimes being far from home can be a real advantage and may even improve the chances of successful treatment. Out of your usual milieu, it will be easier to focus on changing your lifestyle. Distractions and temptations will be fewer; there won't be any sudden impulses to leave and drop in at the office or see your family.

On the other hand, you may be uncomfortable in surroundings that are foreign to your accustomed way of life, and the expense of transporting several family members to a distant treatment program may be prohibitive. So whether the program that's right for you is near or far is a personal decision.

Wherever you go, you should be plugged in to a continuing-care program in your own community once treatment is over. That kind of cross-pollination—going to one program for treatment and then to another for continuing care, being exposed to different mentors with different backgrounds—may also turn out to be beneficial.

THE THERAPEUTIC COMMUNITY (TC)

What Is a TC Like?

Therapeutic communities are a unique form of treatment center originally developed by groups like Synanon to treat the inner core of hard-core drug addicts. Though Synanon's rise, development into a religious cult, and subsequent fall gave a black eye to the TC movement in the U.S., the movement has fully recovered. Today there are about 500 community-style anti-substance-abuse programs in the country, and any resemblances to the original Synanon are purely evolutionary.

Because professionals knew little about the treatment of drug abuse when TCs first developed, these programs were generally run entirely by recovering people. This is still true today, but most TCs also have a staff of professionals (who may or may not be recovering). The primary "therapist" is the community itself, which includes both staff and other residents. Therapy is based on peer pressure and finding one's own strength in the group. The central therapeutic tool is often "the game," a free-for-all encounter group facilitated by a staff member, in which patients can shout, rail, talk, and cry at and with each other. The group tears down denial, then helps build from there. Since most of those in TCs have not developed conventional lifestyles or mainstream values, they may need 'habilitation' (learning how to live) rather than rehabilitation (*re*learning how to live). The goal is to change the negative patterns of behavior, thinking, and feeling that predispose to drug use and to replace them with the values (honesty, responsibility, accountability, social concern, community involvement) that constitute a responsible drug-free lifestyle.

Detox is not usually part of the TC program. Most residents are detoxed before admission or are admitted and then sent to a medical detox facility.

In order to help residents understand that behaviors have consequences, they may be expected to live up to a "contract," with infractions resulting in extra chores or a reduction in privileges. Most TCs also incorporate the Twelve Steps, psychotherapy, and more traditional counseling in their programs. The therapeutic community offers a supportive but demanding surrogate family in a tightly structured environment. Sometimes the inpatient programs are located in rural areas, with the outpatient and continuing-care parts of the program back in the neighborhoods from which clients came.

To prepare residents to return to society, most TCs provide extensive job training, vocational guidance and help finding employment. Those programs geared to teens and young adults also provide ongoing education during treatment, and may even offer experiences in the arts and organized sports. Many also provide for extensive family involvement in the rehabilitation process.

Traditionally TCs required a fifteen- to twenty-four month commitment, sometimes more. Today, most offer several options, including long- or short-term treatment, outpatient or day treatment. Length of stay, however, appears to be the single greatest predictor of successful recovery in a TC, with a longer stay predicting a more stable recovery. Random drug testing is used by most TCs to be sure residents are living up to their commitments.

Some programs are especially geared to adolescents, particularly those who are having behavior problems in addition to their drug abuse.

Who Can Benefit from Treatment in a TC?

Many see TCs as an alternative to the criminal justice system, a way for those otherwise doomed to revolving-door jail terms to learn discipline, gain self-respect, develop a notion of right and wrong, and build productive lives. Originally designed to help the most alienated members of society, TCs are now serving more and more of society's mainstream. The majority of patients are white, though blacks and Hispanics are well represented. TCs are especially useful for young people who are out of control, and are not being helped elsewhere.

Cost of Treatment in a TC

TC treatment is highly cost effective, averaging about $13,000 to $20,000 a year, less than the cost of the usual four week stay at most traditional inpatient treatment programs. A few programs are as low as $9,000 for the year. Fees are usually based on a sliding scale according to the ability to pay; insurance may in some cases cover all or a portion of the tab. SSI, welfare, food stamp programs and Medicaid will also help subsidize the treatment. Part of the cost of running the programs may be defrayed by donations, part by state and local funds, and part by income from TC-owned businesses used for vocational training.

Selecting the Right Therapeutic Community

Recommendation—from alumni of a TC you're considering or from a professional who has worked with graduates—is important. No reputable TC allows drinking or use of marijuana or condones physical or other brutal punishment. Avoid any program that does. Also look for at least some medical personnel and other trained professionals on the staff; they can be recovering addicts, but they should also have the necessary credentials (see page 46). A day-long visit is one way to get a good sense of the atmosphere and the people at a TC.

MISCELLANEOUS APPROACHES TO TREATMENT

Each of these approaches, because they offer alternatives to mood-altering medications for the management of the physical and emotional symptoms so common in recovery, plays a minor role in the treatment of addictive disease. It may turn out that one of them may be helpful to you. But beware of depending on any single "panacea" to turn your life around. One or another specific technique may help initially to keep you from drinking or using drugs, but unless you follow a complete recovery program, it won't keep you clean and sober. Indeed, if you're not careful, it's possible that you might attempt to use acupuncture or hypnosis as you used chemicals—to avoid acknowledging your feelings and problems.

Behavior Modification

This technique takes aim at the patient's current behavior pattern and attempts to alter it for the better. In a sense, the traditional AA approach to alcoholism/addiction is a form of behavior modification because its goal is to change the way you've been doing things, the way you've been living your life. Most good treatment plans include all or most of the various types of behavior modification, including:

❖ **Talk therapy.** Not psychoanalysis (which delves into the subconscious), but the kind of counseling and/or psychotherapy (solo and/or group) consciously aimed at changing behavior.

❖ **Contingency management.** A system of rewards for desirable behavior and disagreeable consequences for undesirable behavior that provides incentive for patients to change for the better. For example, every time you take a drink you lose privileges, such as watching television or socializing with friends (a form of aversion therapy). Or as a reward for abstinence or going to meetings, you receive money (or tokens to use as money), increased responsibility, or increased freedom. This method works well with adolescents, who may not appreciate that abstinence is its own reward. Chart systems with merits and demerits, stars, or a color code may also be effective.

❖ **Conditioning therapy.** Systematic controlled exposure to alcohol- or drug-related stimuli in the absence of the substance itself is used to reduce or erase withdrawal symptoms or drug craving. For example, drug paraphernalia (without the drug) may be displayed at specific intervals in front of a cocaine addict, with a counselor present to discuss the individual's feelings and response.

❖ **Skills development.** This involves the teaching of specific cognitive and social skills (for example, decision making, assertiveness, relaxation techniques, stress management), the absence of which may have contributed to the patient's problems with alcohol and drugs.

❖ **Peer support self-help groups**—which, like AA, help change behavior through various means such as sharing, support, and example.

Aversion Therapy

This approach is aimed at converting the alcoholic/addict's pleasant memories of alcohol or another drug to unpleasant memories. This is typically done by administering the drug and then causing vomiting, applying a mild electric shock to the arm, or showing nauseating or unpleasant scenes that, through suggestion, cause nausea or disgust. Used as part of a total treatment program, aversion therapy has been shown to improve the chances of long-term sobriety in patients with an otherwise poor prognosis (the frequent relapsers). Chemically induced aversion is unsafe for people with certain digestive-tract and cardiovascular problems, so a complete medical exam is necessary beforehand. The mild shock therapy, on the other hand, is safe enough to be used even on pregnant women and patients with pacemakers. If your physician recommends aversion therapy, it's worth a try. But don't kid yourself—it's not a cure-all. You will still have to do all the other work of recovery.

Hypnosis

Hypnosis isn't a panacea that can sober up alcoholics/addicts and keep them that way, but it can be a handy tool in the recovery process. Used by a well-trained professional who has taken a mental health history of the patient and understands the possible risks, hypnosis can help overcome barriers to treatment, such as denial, making the patient more receptive. Used as relaxation therapy, it can remove physical barriers to recovery, such as the musculoskeletal symptoms of withdrawal, muscle tension and spasm, and pain. Hypnosis can also help reinforce a commitment to sobriety, persuade a patient itching to leave treatment against medical advice to complete the program, and assist patients in recovery to wait out or even abort compulsions. It is also a useful drug-free way to deal with pain and other symptoms of both withdrawal and recovery, as well as with discomfort that may have been at the root of an addiction to pain medication. Drawbacks: It takes a lot of costly professional time, and it doesn't work for everybody.

Acupuncture

Needles have long been used to deliver mind-altering drugs. Is it possible that needles inserted in the earlobes and elsewhere can reduce the desire for drugs and alcohol? The answer appears to be yes. Recent research has shown that the ancient Asian art of acupuncture can facilitate withdrawal from alcohol and other drugs (including cocaine and crack cocaine, opiates, and phencyclidine), and for many alcoholics/addicts reduces craving. The treatment is simple, inexpensive, painless, and—as long as the needles are properly sterilized—safe. Hospitals using it generally provide a daily forty-five minute treatment over a two-week period, asking patients for a daily urine screen to see if they are remaining drug-free. If they are, treatment is tapered off gradually. If the urine screens are positive, treatment is begun all over again.

The needles are usually applied to the earlobes of patients in a group setting so that nervous newcomers to the program can see that the treatment doesn't hurt. Because acupuncture can reduce or eliminate the need for medication during detox, it is particularly safe for pregnant women. No electrical stimulation is used. Along with the acupuncture, patients receive counseling and help in reintegrating socially, and are expected to participate in traditional Twelve-Step programs. Drug testing is used to monitor patients. The few studies that have been done have been very positive.

While acupuncture may not be a panacea for drug abuse, it is clearly becoming a useful tool. If it is to be used in your treatment, be sure the personnel administering it are properly trained and that sterilization techniques are meticulous.

4

An Inside Look at Inpatient Treatment

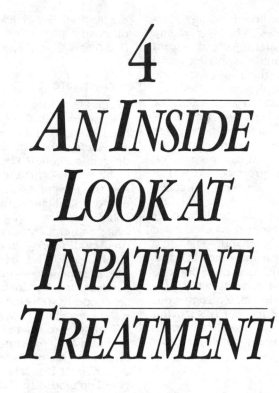

Of all the routes to treatment, inpatient programs are the most daunting. The alcoholic/addict going that route is a lot like Columbus when he set sail in the *Santa Maria*. He had only a vague idea of what was ahead, and the ideas he did have were largely wrongheaded.

These days, anyone sailing to the New World embarks equipped with maps, books, and endless information. You need to be equally well prepared to set out on the emotionally stormy seas of inpatient treatment on your way (if you have the courage to sail on) to a New World of your own.

Inpatient treatment is not only for those who are attempting to become sober. It can also help strengthen those already well into recovery. If you've been sober for a while, but do not seem to be feeling any better, a short stint at a good treatment facility may be just the booster shot you need.

For some people, a course of inpatient treatment isn't enough and they need to go to a halfway house or extended care program to solidify their recoveries before returning home. Everyone leaving treatment needs a continuing-care plan to guide them when they are are back on their own.

Guide Lines

❖ No one who goes into an inpatient treatment program for the first time knows what to expect. But you'll be in that boat with plenty of company.

❖ Successful recovery will depend more on you than on anyone else.

❖ There may be many times during treatment when you'll feel like checking out—either because you are angry and uncomfortable or because you feel so good that you decide you've already licked your problem. Stick with it. Both feelings will pass.

❖ Though an inpatient program will give you plenty of opportunity for looking at yourself and your life without distractions, it isn't the real world. You will have to use the tools you are given in the program to learn to live outside of it.

❖ Treatment—inpatient or out—is only the beginning of a recovery program. A continuing-care plan is a must for every recoveree.

WHAT'S ON YOUR MIND?

WHAT WILL TREATMENT BE LIKE?

"I know I'm lucky that my boss is willing to foot the bill for four weeks of treatment at a very reputable rehab hospital, but I feel like I'm headed into the unknown. It's very scary."

Feeling scared is normal. Ease your anxiety by learning as much as you can about the rehab program you're headed for. They can probably send you literature in advance, and possibly even some videos. The following outline, based on what it's like at Willingway, may also be helpful. Though treatment is a little different in each rehab center, the basic thrust is usually the same. You can ask the center you choose how their procedures differ, so you'll know what to expect when the door closes behind you, leaving your checkered past outside.

A friendly hello. You will be greeted by a staff member. From the first, every attempt will be made to support your decision to get help. An on-the-spot evaluation will determine if there is any need for emergency treatment for withdrawal or overdose. If such treatment is necessary, most of the rest of the procedure will wait until these immediate needs have been taken care of. If you have to go through detoxification first, you won't be wholly integrated into the program until withdrawal is completed.

Getting to know you. Once you're feeling comfortable, and assuming you're not heavily intoxicated or in the midst of withdrawal, there will be a fairly exhaustive admissions interview with you and, if they're present, with any family members. Taking care of the paperwork early will avoid inconvenience and distraction during the treatment period. The interview will include questions about your alcohol and drug usage. Dishonest answers, for whatever reasons you might be tempted to give them, will only complicate and prolong treatment. If you'd rather that those who've accompanied you not hear the gory details, this part of the admissions process can be private. Often pride, embarrassment, or memory lapses keep patients from being totally open. Aware that the disease is often still in charge of your tongue at this stage, admissions personnel try to make the interview as relaxed and informal as possible.

Family orientation. Your family will get a tour of the facility if they're not already familiar with it. They need to be satisfied that you're in good hands.

A luggage search. Does that sound as though the staff doesn't trust you? To answer a question with a question: Do you trust yourself? The search is done for your protection and to preserve a drug- and alcohol-free environment—the only environment that's safe for you and your fellow patients right now. It's not a strip search, but it's thorough. Staff members have seen it all—cocaine in talc containers, pills buried deep down in toothpaste tubes, alcohol in deodorant bottles. It isn't likely that a new patient will put anything over on them. If you do, you're the one who will be hurt most.

Settling in. Next you will be taken to your room by a staff member (you may have a private room or a share, depending on the facility and your arrangement) and given time to unpack and settle in. You will probably want to rest at least briefly.

Assessment. Laboratory tests will be performed, and you will be examined and extensively interviewed. Your condition will be evaluated from many angles: psychiatric (is there depression, anger, grief that hasn't been expressed?), social (are you concerned about children, parents, your marriage, not being married, other relationships?), medical (is there a physical disability that could interfere with treatment or an illness that needs therapy?), spiritual (are you unhappy about being alienated from your religious background?), and intellectual (do you understand the disease nature of addiction?). This initial assessment is then discussed and evaluated by the staff, and a treatment plan is developed that best fits your individual needs.

Orientation. If you have to go through detox, orientation will usually wait until that phase is past and you're a little better able to understand what is going on. If you arrived in a blackout and suddenly awaken to find yourself in a treatment facility, don't be afraid to ask questions about where you are and what is happening. Even if you don't ask, you can expect to get a lot of answers from nurses, counselors, and others about what you can expect during the next few days. In fact, you'll get them over and over again, just to be sure you *really* understand.

Schedule and rules. Every facility sets schedules and rules. At some, your calendar allows virtually no free time; at others, patients who appear able to use it constructively are allowed more freedom during the day. There may or may not be a designated wake-up hour in the morning; there almost certainly will be a lights-out time. The daily schedule will include meals, several group meetings, individual counseling sessions, and probably some time to spend familiarizing yourself with recovery—through reading, audio tapes, and videos. There will probably also be time for physical exercise.

Rules vary. Phone calls, visitors, casual reading matter, work, television, and excursions off the grounds (except group trips to AA meetings) may be limited or banned entirely. You may be expected to take care of your room, do your laundry, and take on other minor chores—setting the table, for example.

Whatever the rules, they will apply to everyone alike—the millionaire movie star, the successful attorney, the truck driver, and the mother on welfare. This tends to reawaken a sense of humility.

Meetings, lectures, and counseling sessions. These will be the heart of your treatment. You will listen to lectures on a variety of topics, including the nature of the disease of alcoholism/addiction and the dangers of using any mind-altering substances in recovery. You will also attend numerous group meetings where patients share their thoughts, feelings, and experiences, past and present. Though the idea of speaking at a group meeting may be unnerving, you will have plenty of time to become adjusted to it. You will probably be given a chance to talk about yourself one-on-one with your counselor, then in small groups, finally in a larger group. Most people are able to "share" by the time they are ready to leave treatment (see page 126).

A life history. At some point, you will probably be asked to write a life history or autobiographical essay, which will require you to dig deeply and honestly into your past (see page 105). You may be asked to share some parts of the history at a sharing meeting. And finally, you may ceremoniously burn the history—and symbolically with it the ignominious part of your past.

Introduction to Alcoholics Anonymous. You will have a chance to learn about AA as well as to become familiar with its meeting formats. You will probably go to meetings in the facility, and possibly outside in the community as well.

The family visit. Since alcoholism/addiction is a family disease, your treatment won't be complete unless it also includes one or more of the significant others in your life: spouse, child, parents, lover, or close friend. These visitors will be exposed to information on the disease and Al-Anon, and will be expected to attend individual, couple, and group therapy sessions.

Continuing-care conference. At this session, which may continue over several days, you and your counselor will make plans for your continuing recovery when you return home (see page 71). This is a critical part of your treatment.

Final counselor and physician conferences. This is the time to bring up any unanswered questions, to raise any unsettling concerns.

Thank you and goodbye. One way you will be able to say thank-you to those who have helped you during treatment is by sharing your experiences with the newcomers, who are as nervous as you once were, during your first days in residence.

Although you may feel apprehensive when you arrive at the treatment facility, you will probably be even more apprehensive about leaving what will most likely have turned out to be a warm and loving environment. Be sure you share these apprehensions with your counselor and deal with them in your continuing-care plan.

BEING "LOCKED UP" IN A REHAB FACILITY

"I've agreed to go to an alcohol treatment center, but the whole idea is driving me to drink even more. Being away from my family, unable to work, spending all my savings, and, worst of all, being locked up like a criminal—I can't deal with it."

If you'd had a stroke and had to go to a rehabilitation hospital, the conditions would be pretty much the same. You'd have the same worries—about leaving your family, not working, spending your savings, and being in an institution—but you'd go because the alternative might be death.

Well, your situation is just as serious. Sure, it's worrisome. Sure, you don't know what's going to happen. Sure, you'd rather spend your money on a new car or your time vacationing in the tropics. But you don't have a choice. If you continue drinking you will become (if you aren't already) a hostage to alcohol and maybe to drugs. Isn't it worth the short-term loss of liberty to gain lifelong freedom from dependency on chemical substances?

Think about it. What's the worst thing that can happen if you go into treatment? You'll be lonesome? You'll fall behind on your work? You'll end up broke? Everyone will know you're an alcoholic? You'll end up sober?

On the other hand, what's the worst thing that can happen if you don't go for treatment? You could be permanently lonely, losing your family for good. You could do worse than fall behind on your work—you could be out of a job entirely. You could do more than lose your savings—you could lose your home, your car, everything you have. Not only will friends know you're an alcoholic, they'll know you are an alcoholic who hasn't done anything to help himself. And, instead of sober, you could end up dead.

An honest appraisal generally leaves little question as to the rational path to take. Going off to treatment may be easier, however, if you prepare for it beforehand, assuming you're in a condition to do so.

"Much too quickly I was saying, 'It's time for me to leave. I've done everything you told me to and now I've got to get out and start planning my daughter's wedding.' Thank goodness no one took me seriously."

Accept your fears as normal. Everyone has some fears when going into a hospital—for any reason. That's compounded right now by many other fears: fear of withdrawal. Fear of being with all those alcoholics and addicts. Fear of becoming sober, of losing your escape valve, of being cut off from your source. Fear of losing your friends and your lifestyle. Fear that you'll never be able to have fun again. Fear of learning about yourself, and of having that self exposed to others. Fear of discovering that you have brain and liver damage, or other addiction-generated health problems. Fear of embarrassment once the word is out. And vague nonspecific fear—a common symptom of addiction. You may even have a fear of getting well; many people do.

Though these fears are understandable, they are based on an unrealistic view of your life and your situation. Most of them will dissolve as treatment progresses and as you learn more about yourself, your disease, and the real world that you've been avoiding all these years.

Get a preview. Ask for information, a video if one's available, about the program you will be entering. What's a typical day going to be like? What will be expected of you? (You may find it's a lot more appealing than you think.) What can you expect from others? Some people look back upon their stay as a peak life experience.

Express your fears. Of dying. Of getting sober. Of being with strangers. Of leaving home. A counselor at the treatment center should be available for you to talk to before you take the plunge.

Keep the home fires glowing. You'll feel better leaving if you know that your family or significant others are behind you and are getting help themselves. So be sure to urge them to attend Al-Anon or Alateen, as appropriate. It will give them something to do while you are away, something that will help them understand your problem as well as support your efforts at recovery. They will probably be more concerned about you than about themselves, so it will help for you to write to them with encouragement and specific suggestions that will be supplied by the staff or your counselor.

Talk to your boss or colleagues. You'll have one less thing to worry about if you feel squared away at work—although in some situations this may not be practical (see page 18).

Check payment options. If money is a problem, and it is for most people, talk to the treatment center about possible ways of covering the costs (see page 51). Sometimes people consider paying for treatment themselves when confidentiality is a serious concern.

DISCOMFORT WITH COUNSELORS

"A lot of people in the recovery business seem afflicted with homophobia. As part of my treatment I wrote up my checkered history—a marriage, kids, divorce, seven years with a lover, physical fights, a split with my lover. When my counselor read it, he asked, 'Well, do you think your wife would take you back?' Like my homosexuality was some sort of aberration and now that I was sober I should be able to go 'straight.'"

Unfortunately, sensitivity toward and understanding of homosexual behavior is still lacking—not just in the recovery community but in society at large. What you experienced is just a reflection of that. Of course the fact that it's common doesn't make it right, nor does it make it easier or more comfortable to deal with.

It's also common, when you care about someone, to want for them what you would want for yourself. And your counselor was also reflecting that sentiment. It's tougher (ask any parent) to want for your friend or loved one what they want for themselves. Ideally that's what an unbiased counselor should want, but not everyone can live up to that ideal.

Someday, perhaps, as more gay men and lesbian women live their lives openly, the negative attitudes will change. In the meantime, don't let your counselor's lack of sensitivity blind you to whatever valuable advice he has to impart. Most of what is important about recovery for chemically dependent straight people holds equally for you. Get the added help you need from a gay and lesbian AA group or from like-minded individuals.

"I felt so sick and miserable when I came in and I feel so great now, how could I possibly still be sick? You convinced me. After hearing everything you all told me, I'll never drink or drug again. I have sure learned my lesson."

THE QUICK CURE

"I've been in this treatment center for nearly a week. I feel great. I'm cured. Why can't I leave now?"

Because the euphoria you are feeling now won't last. You're no more cured than the strep throat patient who feels better after taking an antibiotic for two days. If he stops the medication the moment the pain goes away instead of completing the prescribed ten-day course, he is almost sure to find that the throat is worse than ever a couple of days later—and the infection may even be complicated by rheumatic fever. The addiction patient who wants to cut treatment short takes a similar risk. Those who leave early usually relapse.

Feeling ready to lick the world after a few days of treatment is not at all unusual. It's like the rosy glow of a honeymoon, and even less likely to last. Besides, moods in recovery are mercurial—you may feel deliriously joyous today and mightily miserable tomorrow. You also may be a poor judge of just what "feeling great" is. It's been a long time, after all, since you achieved that sensation without the use of chemicals. You may be willing to accept not feeling miserable as being as good as it gets. Alcoholics/addicts usually fall short of their own goals early in life and compensate by lowering their standards. Now is the time to start raising yours.

Wanting to leave treatment early is often just a compulsion to drink or use in disguise. So stick with the recommendations of the professionals treating you. They've been down this river before. They know where the rapids are and how to help you steer through them. Get used to accepting constructive guidance from others—you will be needing more of it in the future. And it's a great way to grow and to learn. Dispose of the typical addict behavior of dropping out as a way of avoiding failure. Now you have a chance to succeed. Take it.

A LOSS OF CONTROL

"I know I need treatment, but just thinking about having someone else control every aspect of my life is driving me crazy."

Many people going into treatment feel just the way you do. What they forget is that they've been controlled for years by alcohol and/or drugs. Relax, and recognize that sometimes someone else has to do the driving. That isn't a sign of weakness. The willingness to trust others and accept help may, in fact, be the surest sign of inner strength. Admitting you can't control your life now will, in the end, put you back in the driver's seat.

FEAR OF RETURNING TO "THE REAL WORLD"

"I really didn't want to go into treatment—my wife pushed me into it. But it turned out to be great for me. Now I'm worried about going home."

A little trepidation at this stage is a good thing and probably means you've learned your lessons well. It's very much to your advantage to leave your treatment program with a healthy fear of the powerful disease of addiction and a concern about what's to come in the crucial next phase of your life. It's overconfidence that's dangerous. The person who feels sure of himself on discharge is usually the one who refuses to live what was learned in treatment, skips AA meetings, spurns advice from sponsors, and is most likely to fall off the wagon with a resounding crash.

Of course, excessive apprehension could paralyze you, even drive you back to drinking and drugging. There's no reason to panic. Take a good look at yourself and you'll realize that you aren't the same person you were when you entered treatment. First of all, you've been clean and sober for several weeks. Second, you've acquired valuable new skills that will help you not only to stay away from alcohol and drugs, but to cope with the every-day problems of life. Third, you're probably leaving treatment with a thoughtfully detailed let's-anticipate-everything continuing-care plan that will help see you through the rough days—of which there will be more than a few. (If you don't have such a plan, see page 71.) Finally, you are going to take life just one day at a time. And one day, no matter how difficult, isn't more than you can handle.

"I am about to get out of treatment. This is my second time around, and I'm worried about what's going to happen when I get back to my neighborhood, where it's easier to get coke than Coca-Cola."

Going back home may not be ideal for you. An inner-city neighborhood where drug dealers are not only socially acceptable, but at the top of the social ladder, and where law enforcers are the enemy, is no environment for staying clean and sober. At least not until you have at least six months of solid sobriety to your credit.

Many who return to drug-drenched areas after treatment find that dealers are waiting for them with open arms—and open hands: "Here, try this stuff. You never had anything like it. It's on me." Friends, lovers, casual acquaintances are often enlisted to lure former drug customers back, either through the direct approach ("Just this once won't hurt!") or the indirect ("Honey, I just have to have some stuff. Can you get it for me, please?"). Even with your good intentions, these may be just the cues that trigger a relapse.

If it's at all possible, it would be better to arrange to go to a halfway house or to enroll in an extended-care program where you can spend several months solidifying your sobriety in a controlled and safe environment. When you do go back to your community, you should be sure to have several AA, church, or other sober contacts to build your new life around. If you're lucky, you may even be able to wangle a room in a halfway house that is part of a program to help integrate recoverees back into their communities.

You may face a lot of hostility from former buddies, maybe even from some family members. Staying clean and sober won't be easy, but if you want it badly enough, you can do it. If you're going to deal successfully with hostility, it's important to make clear through your behavior that your sobriety is the most important thing in your life. Forget that even for a moment, or let others forget it, and your recovery is in big trouble. When, after a hard day at a legitimate job, you feel outclassed by the user-dealer driving a Mercedes and wearing designer duds, remind yourself that there's a good chance he'll be dead or in jail within a couple of years. Remind yourself, too, that he's enslaving and killing those around you—even if he has never pulled a trigger or used a knife. And that you—by going back to your community, staying straight, and setting a visible example for young people—can save a lot of lives.

You can prepare yourself for that return by thinking ahead and planning every aspect of your life. How will you get to meetings? Whom will you turn to when you're upset, lonely, tempted? What other kinds of problems are you likely to encounter? Think of each possibility (running into your former dealer; being offered a hit; having a friend ask you to pick up some coke), and plan exactly how you'll respond to it. Rehearse what you will do and say with a counselor, an AA sponsor, or a friend. That way you'll know what to do when your moment of truth comes along.

Plan too how you'll handle your money. Carrying a lot of cash, or even a checkbook, could lead you into temptation. So consider putting every paycheck right into the bank. It's even better if your company direct-deposits it for you in the bank of your choice (as many will do on request). An added advantage: it usually is credited to your account a day or two sooner. Make it a savings account and draw out money only as you need it. Use bank checks or money orders to pay your bills. If you feel shaky about taking this much financial responsibility immediately, a trusted friend or family member can handle your funds for you, doling out what you need for legitimate purposes. Of course this approach isn't a long-term solution, but it can be helpful during early recovery if your environment is less than the best. You can't afford to let down your guard. If you do, someone will be poised to jab you, probably with one of the substances you have been trying so hard to avoid.

But drugs and booze won't be your only concerns. You will also have to be wary of casual and unprotected sex. HIV infection (and the AIDS it causes) is running wild, and poorer communities are particularly at risk. You will have to take precautions to be sure you don't recover from one disease only to fall victim to another. Read the material that begins on page 306 for ways to protect yourself.

Your most important protection against drugs, alcohol, and AIDS will be a change in lifestyle. That means replacing your old ways of life and your old values with newer and healthier ones—as recommended throughout this book.

"I was born and grew up in a drug jungle. I got sent to a rehab program instead of jail. I'm clean now, but, hell, what does it matter? There's nothing I have to look forward to anyway."

The typical middle-class person who gives up booze or drugs has a lot to gain. Clean and sober, he or she will usually (though not always) be welcomed back into the community by friends, family, employers, and so on. However, if you live in a community where using or dealing drugs seems to offer the only escape route from being poor (dealers drive the biggest cars and flash the fattest rolls of cash), where kids see using alcohol and other drugs, getting into crime, or getting pregnant (rather than graduation from high-school, going to college, getting a job, getting married) as signs of growing up, it may be hard to see any reason for getting clean and sober and staying that way. Not only is it possible that you won't be welcomed home and that old friends who are still pushing or using will turn their backs on you, but it is likely that you won't have a job waiting.

If that's your situation, you need to plan ahead. Start thinking now about the rewards you want in recovery and how you plan to earn them. It may be a good idea to start over after treatment in a new community where drugs and alcohol aren't an accepted part of the lifestyle. Or to begin the first months of your sobriety in a halfway house or other sheltered environment where you can nurture your recovery and chart your new life. If you've been involved with gangs and possibly even criminal behavior, a good therapeutic community may be the answer (see page 58).

Even once you are out of treatment, you should consider participating for at least a year, maybe two, in some kind of outpatient program where you can see a counselor every week or so for a good eyeball-to-eyeball talk. The more you build safeguards like these into your recovery, the better your chances of staying clean and sober.

Don't despair if you find sobriety difficult and the possible rewards very distant. If you are like most alcoholics/addicts, you may never have learned non-chemical ways of coping with stress or life's problems. You may be accustomed to thinking in terms of short term goals (living from pay check to pay check, for example) and wanting to see results in a hurry. You've got to separate yourself from such thinking, and recognize that becoming sober is hard but staying that way is even harder. It requires learning new living skills and new ways of thinking (all of which are discussed throughout this book). But in the long run, it will improve not only your own life but those of the people you care about most.

Ideally, you should try to find a sponsor or an AA friend who is from a background like yours but who has moved out of the cycle of poverty and depression and into a life that is not only clean and sober but successful. Such a person can serve as an example of what you too can do, and can also give you a lot of guidance as to how to do it. Unfortunately, many of those who have managed to pull themselves out of addiction and poverty also pull themselves out of the community they came from as well. So you may have to do some looking to find the right role model.

CONTINUING CARE

"I'm finishing up my residential treatment in a week. I know I have to go to Alcoholics Anonymous when I graduate. Is there anything else I need to do?"

Plenty. No responsible treatment program, inpatient or out, will get you clean and sober and then send you packing without a continuing-care plan (sometimes called an aftercare plan). Recovering is not a process that takes place in four or six weeks spent at a treatment program. To some extent it will continue for the rest of your life. What you do during the first year following treatment—particularly in those early months—can make a difference between staying sober permanently and relapsing back into an ever-downward spiral of alcoholism/addiction.

An individually tailored continuing-care plan that wraps around every part of your life should be worked out by you and your counselor before discharge. How complex the plan will be depends on your needs and the kind of home and community to which you are returning. At the very least, it should include the name of an individual back home who can act as your temporary sponsor. This should be someone known to, and respected by, your counselor—possibly a past patient with several years of sobriety or a long-time AA member. Ideally, you should call the contact to set up a first meeting before discharge from the hospital, just in case your feet get cold when they touch down on familiar turf, either because you're embarrassed or because you feel so great that you talk yourself into believing you no longer need hands-on help.

You should also be linked to an addiction professional, if one is available in your town, so that you have somewhere to turn in case of an emergency. In addition, you should be able to contact the counselor you were closest to and others you've worked with at your treatment program by mail or phone if you have questions or concerns over the next year or two. And there should be a carefully mapped retreat path—one that will take you back to some kind of treatment without much effort on your part in case your recovery should falter.

"You're such a good counselor and you've done such a good job with me that in just two weeks you got me completely well. I don't need to be here any longer."

MINI-GUIDE

Treatment Success

Treatment for alcoholism/addiction is not something someone does to you. It's something you do for yourself. Even the best of programs won't succeed if you don't practice HOW: honesty, openness, willingness. Treatment succeeds only when both you and your program live up to your respective responsibilities. You'll help yourself if you:

DO SOME SOUL-SEARCHING. If you want to come out of treatment successfully sober, you have to face your past instead of going into your habitual I-don't-want-to-talk-about-it denial dance. That means taking a hard look at your life up until now. Amassing a dirty-laundry list of episodes and incidents to talk about with your counselor will help you get started. Be ready to sit down in a quiet corner and write a life history starting with "I was born . . ." No one else has to see that history (unless you choose to share it with a counselor). If you're totally honest, this panoramic view of your past will probably be filled with revealing surprises. It should also help you discover where you got lost and how you can find your way back. When you've finished the history, thoroughly analyzed it, and if you wish, shared it (with your counselor, sponsor, or another trusted person), it's a good idea to burn it and, symbolically, your past. See page 105 for more on writing your history.

LISTEN AND OBSERVE. And let it all soak in. Consider each person you meet and each situation you face as an addiction experiment in progress, one from which you can extract valuable information about your disease. Even when the subject doesn't seem relevant (you're a lesbian and a woman is discussing her problems with her husband, or you're an alcoholic and the topic is

In some cases, it may be decided that you need or want more intensive continuing professional care. This may include individual and group sessions two or three times a week at first, tapering down to once a week in the second half of the year. Or it may consist of just one counseling session a week for the full year. These sessions usually deal with the transition back to Planet Earth and other topics relating to early sobriety: how to find a comfortable AA home group, how to cope with your job and your family in the early weeks, and so on.*

Continuing-care therapy may be provided by a physician, counselor, or therapist trained in addiction or by the continuing-care arm of a local treatment program. This linkage of treatment to long-term recovery should be set up before you leave your inpatient (or outpatient) program and not left to chance. (You remember where chance leads.) Newly recovering people are more likely to continue attendance at such sessions if they are prodded or reminded regularly by a professional in the program.

If you're an alcoholic for whom Antabuse seems advisable (see page 154), a physician who can administer it back home should be contacted and the procedure for fitting it into your routine should be activated.

Your continuing-care plan should

*These sessions differ from outpatient treatment in that they don't deal with crises or new issues.

methamphetamines), listen and learn. You never know when or from whom the bytes of wisdom that can turn your life around will come.

SHARE YOUR THOUGHTS, FEELINGS, AND EXPERIENCES. Though some are eager for the catharsis that comes with opening up to others, others are reluctant and uncomfortable sharers. But everyone benefits from the exercise. There's been ample evidence since Bill W. and Dr. Bob had their first meeting of what later became AA that, in some miraculous way, sharing the experience helps relieve the addict of the compulsion to drink or use drugs. Start talking in small groups, and one day you'll be amazed to find yourself addressing packed meeting halls without your palms so much as sweating.

BE HONEST. Honesty is the foundation of every good recovery (see page 202). If you share only half truths, or worse yet, untruths, you will surely sabotage your recovery efforts.

COMMIT YOURSELF TO A TWELVE-STEP PROGRAM. No matter where you begin your recovery (on your own, or through in- or outpatient treatment), you should expect to continue it in AA or another mutual-help program.

BE PATIENT. You didn't become an alcoholic or addict yesterday, and you won't feel wonderful the day after tomorrow. It will take a lot of time and effort before you feel like a new man or woman. Judge your progress one day at a time. If you feel better today than yesterday, or last week, or last month, then you are headed in the right direction. But never forget that nobody—addict or not—feels great all the time.

also include information on an AA group in your home town. If there is none (a town without an AA group is rarer than one without a Burger King), the continuing-care counselor may suggest ways of organizing a new group there. (Groups from surrounding communities are usually happy to help.) If that's not feasible, or if it's decided that would be too stressful a task for you so early in recovery, it may be wise to temporarily delay the trip home and participate in an extended-care or halfway-house program (see page 74).

The continuing-care counselor should also make certain that you have a family doctor or internist to go home to, and may even make an appointment for you before discharge. If you have no doctor, the counselor will probably recommend one with addiction experience. You may also be provided with a listing of medications that, if not avoided, could cause problems for you in recovery. If not, see Chapter 13 for tips on safe healthcare.

The written continuing-care document that you negotiate with your counselor should be a complete battle plan, specifying the things you need to do and not do back home in order to stay clean and sober. It should include the number of AA meetings you'll attend weekly (anywhere from three to seven or more, depending on the situation), how you will deal with your family and your job to keep stress at a minimum, and how you'll spend the newly available spare time you used to spend drinking or drugging.

In drawing up this plan, you should try to identify areas of anxiety ("I'm scared to death that when I'm home and Saturday night rolls around, I'm gonna be tempted to go out and party with my friends" or "What do I do when my husband starts trying to get me to do coke with him?"). Then you and your counselor can work out a practical response, rehearsing the scene until you've got your lines down pat. Maybe you'll decide to make plans in advance for Saturday evening, designating it "movie night" or AA dance night. Or conclude it would be best to live apart from your drug-using spouse. If marital counseling, therapy to deal with sexual or other abuse in childhood, or another type of therapy is needed, it should be arranged in advance.

"It took me four times through treatment before I realized that what I had to do was take the cotton out of my ears and put it in my mouth."

The idea of a continuing-care plan is to help you build your own supportive social structure in your home town rather than permit an existing destructive one to entrap you. Your campaign plan should be mapped out several days before you're ready to go home, so that there is some time for second thoughts. When both you and your counselor are sure the plan is as complete and practical as possible, you will probably be asked to sign it. It's a lot like signing a check. If you haven't put the money in the bank, and don't intend to, it could bounce you right back into trouble.

Continuing care may be included in the treatment tuition, or there may be an extra charge, depending on the policy of your treatment program. In some cases, you will have to pay a fee directly to the continuing-care or outpatient program you attend back home. If you aren't offered a plan, ask for one. It's risky to return home without this insurance policy in hand.

But having a continuing-care plan isn't enough. You have to follow it faithfully. People who stick with their plans greatly enhance their chances of a successful recovery.

EXTENDED CARE

"One of the other women in treatment with me is supposed to get out next week. They are recommending that instead of going home she go into an 'extended-care' program. What is that and why would she need this?"

Many people feel shaky as the formal course of inpatient treatment is about to end. A little reassurance and a good continuing-care program will send most of them happily packing. But a small percentage—although they no longer need the intensive expensive treatment environment—are probably not yet ready to return home. Either they don't have supportive surroundings to go home to, or they need to do more work on building recovery skills. These people need something in between. The something that works best is usually extended-care or halfway-house living. Treatment gives people the tools for sober living; extended care allows them to practice using those tools in a secure and supportive setting under professional guidance.

At the moment, though programs are sprouting like summer dandelions, there are no universally accepted standards for extended care. Generally, extended-care patients live in a home-like, carefully supervised environment

A DOZEN SURE-FIRE WAYS TO FLUNK TREATMENT

Just as there are some basic steps you can take to improve your chances of a successful recovery, there are some you can take to ensure that you will fail:

❖ Concentrate your time and effort on playing solitaire and Scrabble, watching TV, and exercising to get back into shape.

❖ Insist you have to make several business calls a day or your company will go belly up.

❖ Repeatedly threaten to jump ship; actually leave before the course of treatment is completed.

❖ Sleep late, then sack out again after breakfast. Skip meetings and counseling sessions. Think up good excuses (like a blinding migraine) to explain your absences.

❖ Go through the motions to appease your counselor; pretend you're together and paying attention when you're really not.

❖ B.S. everybody; say you'll do what you should, but then conveniently forget. Lie to yourself and to everyone else. After all, who will know?

❖ Stubbornly resent the fact that "they" have taken away your freedom, that you're cut off from the love of your life and your bosom buddies—and show that resentment by fighting treatment every step of the way.

❖ Wallow in self-pity—what AA people sometimes call "sitting on the pity pot": "Poor me, nothing ever goes right for me. So treatment won't work either. I only drink [or drug] because of all my problems, and my problems won't go away." Ignore these important truths: You drink or take drugs because you have a disease called addiction; everybody has problems, some even worse than yours; not everybody turns to chemicals to deal (or escape dealing) with them.

❖ Be a know-it-all patient. "What do counselors know anyway? They're alcoholics, too. Besides, I'm smarter than all these other addicts. I don't need a string of clichés to live my life by, or a sponsor to tell me what to do; I can take care of myself. I'm not a puppet whose strings they can pull." Forget about who—or what—was pulling the strings when you were drinking or drugging.

❖ Act dumb, so nothing will be expected from you. Nothing is just what you'll get out of treatment.

❖ Romance the drink—or the drug. Talk about all the good things you felt or that happened when you were using alcohol or other drugs. Daydream a lot about drug paraphernalia and culture.

❖ Keep compatible company. Spend all the time you can with people doing the things listed above.

where, if they slip by succumbing to the temptation to drink or use drugs again, people they trust can help get them back on their feet. They have access to counseling and to a house manager who is either an empathetic ex-patient, a sympathetic professional, or both. They also have each other around the clock—for support, group meetings, exchanging hopes, fears, and feelings, and working out problems together. As part of their retraining-for-reentry residents are usually expected to share the chores (taking care of the house and grounds, buying and preparing the food, doing laundry), to go to meetings regularly, and, when ready, to work in the community—usually at a low-pressure or volunteer job. Any women who don't plan on a job outside the home are encouraged to learn how to live in and maintain a household and to socialize without chemical support. (A modest goal, but no small thing for an addict.) Cars are usually prohibited—it's too easy to look for trouble in them—and residents walk, bike, or take public transportation to get to work, the store, or the movies.

The families of those in a good extended-care program are not forgotten. They receive encouragement and support to construct their own recovery programs (see Chapter 28). Once patient and family are on their individual roads to solid recovery, attention is turned to a happy intersection. Family visits with the patient and patient visits home—along with joint counseling sessions, workshops, and similar activities—begin the healing process and improve the odds of ultimately restoring healthy family function.

While the lengthy separation of extended care often ultimately strengthens family bonds, personal and financial stresses are generated that tend to strain them. Additional therapy may be needed when the family is once more together to reopen communications, bury hatchets, and rebuild burned bridges. (Read about relationships in Phase One, Chapter 10, and Phase Two, Chapter 19; have family members read Chapters 27 and 28.) Dating and the forming of new relationships is usually forbidden during extended care.

"Living in that halfway house I met a lot of people, all recovering. I did ordinary things like vacuuming the floor and doing the laundry. We did a lot of things together. We went to an amusement park, and rowing on a lake, and just walking. It was the first time I had fun without being high or drunk."

Because they aren't as profitable as treatment centers, and insurance does not usually help with costs, extended care programs are not as available as they should be. The better ones are run as a nonprofit service, making extended care no more expensive than living independently would be. The costs are shared by everyone in the house, and usually run about $1,000 to $1,700 a month per person, including rent, utilities, food, and professional fees. There is some control over personal finances. Recoverees in extended care are generally not permitted to have credit cards, take out bank loans, or otherwise heighten stress by encumbering themselves financially.

When extended care isn't possible, those who need extra support on leaving treatment can benefit from a very strong continuing-care (page 71) or outpatient program near home (page 45).

5
GOING THROUGH DETOX

Deciding to become sober was your first major decision on the road to recovery. Withdrawal from your chemicals will be the first major hurdle. Knowing what's ahead won't make the experience easy, but it can make it safer and more comfortable. Most important to understand: the kind of help you may need; when it's imperative to withdraw in a hospital setting; why you need a sitter if you elect to do detox at home and what the sitter should do; the kinds of symptoms to expect and for how long; and what can be done to make withdrawal less of an ordeal. The same information will also be valuable to anyone who is helping a friend or loved one through detox.

If you've already gone through withdrawal, you may find that this chapter will heighten your understanding of the experience, and help you to recognize that what you went through was normal and expected. But you may prefer to move directly on to Phase One (page 95).

A GUIDE TO WITHDRAWAL AND DETOX

WHAT IS WITHDRAWAL?

At least in part, the symptoms experienced during withdrawal are believed to be a direct response to your body's desperate efforts to remain in *stasis,* or healthy balance, in spite of the health-wrecking alcohol or drugs it's been fed.

In general, when you take a drug that numbs or slows down your body and mind (as alcohol or sedatives do), your body counters by speeding up. Take a drug that speeds it up (such as amphetamines or cocaine), and your body tries to slam on the brakes and slow down. In each case, even as the effects of the drug wear off, the body continues to overcompensate—by sprinting or foot-dragging—as it struggles valiantly to return to its normal physiologic baseline. This makes you edgy and uncomfortable, so you respond by taking more of the drug. You feel a

Guide Lines

❖ Certain types of withdrawal are extremely dangerous and should be attempted only under medical supervision. Medication may be needed to reduce the most severe symptoms.

❖ Withdrawal symptoms can range from slightly uncomfortable to downright miserable. But all will disappear, most sooner rather than later.

❖ How difficult withdrawal is depends on the chemical you are withdrawing from, how long and how often you used it, and on your own makeup.

❖ Some drugs (such as alcohol) clear from the body rather rapidly; others (such as diazepam and other benzodiazepines) can take considerably longer.

temporary rush of relief, but then the new dose forces your body to struggle even harder to return to normal.

As the tug of war continues, you find you require larger doses of the drug to overcome your body's stubborn resistance. Drug "tolerance" has developed. Ironically, the chemical substance that caused your internal physiological warfare is the only thing that can establish a shaky truce. So now your body craves it continuously. You are physically addicted.

When the supply of the chemical is cut off completely, the body is confused. Uncertain how to handle this new situation, it continues its overcompensation in the expectation that its archenemy (the drug) will arrive at any moment. This confusion produces a variety of unpleasant physical and psychological effects known as withdrawal symptoms.

As you continue moving through withdrawal, your body will *seem* to resist your good intentions, seem to be pleading for more drugs to relieve its acute distress. That really isn't what it's saying. A more accurate translation would be: "Please help me get back to normal—even if it hurts."

The goal of withdrawal is to detoxify your body and clear your mind. Once it's completed, you'll be ready to begin the real work of recovery and your new drug-free life.

HOME OR HOSPITAL?

As thousands of alcoholics/addicts can testify, withdrawing from alcohol or other drugs is a stressful experience. It can also be dangerous. That's why, for most people, it's best to be withdrawn from chemicals in a hospital or treatment center detox unit. A well-run detox unit will not only make detox safer, it can make you more comfortable.

Occasionally detox can be successful in an extremely supportive home environment buttressed by frequent visits to the doctor (or visits *from* the doctor if necessary), carefully allotted medication, and round-the-clock sitters (see facing page and page 80). If you opt for such outpatient detox, you have to be punctilious about making your doctor visits and taking your medication *only* as directed. Be prepared to switch to inpatient detox if your withdrawal symptoms become difficult to tolerate or you find yourself overwhelmed by your craving for drugs or alcohol. If you experience any of the symptoms in the box on page 82, get emergency medical help immediately.

Choose inpatient detox in a medical facility right from the start if:

❖ You experience withdrawal symptoms, such as extreme nervousness, tremors, hallucinations (you see or hear things: bugs, pictures, snakes, geese, squirrels, elephants of any color), when you need a drink or a fix—a sign that you are physically addicted. (If you are only psychologically dependent on the drug, you may be upset but you won't have physical symptoms.)

❖ You're middle-aged or older and have been drinking heavily for many years.

❖ You have health problems other than your addiction.

❖ You are severely depressed.

❖ You feel life is not worth living, have a history of suicide attempts, or have been having self-destructive thoughts.

❖ You've had episodes of violent behavior while intoxicated or during withdrawal.

❖ You've had seizures, or convulsions, previously.

❖ You have had a recent head injury or have been hurt in an accident and suffered injuries that have not been evaluated.

❖ You're afraid of doing it alone or have been unsuccessful at previous do-it-alone attempts.

❖ You have been regularly abusing any one of the following drugs: Placidyl (ethchlorvynol); Miltown, Deprol, Equagesic, Equanil, Meprospan, PMB (meprobamate); Alurate (aprobarbital); B-A-C (butalbital); Butisol Sodium (butabarbital sodium); Mebaral (mephobarbital); Nembutal (pentobarbital); Pentothal (thiopental sodium); phenobarbital; or any other barbiturate.

Of course some alcoholics and addicts who fit one or more of the above categories have elected to go through withdrawal on their own without medical supervision. This has worked best for those who were not yet physically dependent on their drug, and thus did not experience serious side effects on its withdrawal. But it's risky to try (and *should not be tried at all*) if you take any of the drugs listed above, or if you've experienced severe withdrawal symptoms when you've needed a drink or a fix. It's probably also unwise if you've been using alcohol, benzodiazepines (Librium, Valium, Xanax, etc.), or stimulants (cocaine, etc.) *daily*.

WHAT WITHDRAWAL IS LIKE

You'll feel worse before you feel better. But you *will* feel better eventually. Each person experiences withdrawal differently. Just which symptoms you have will depend on the drug (or drugs) you've been taking, how long you've been taking it, and on your own body's re-

(continued on page 82)

A DETOX MUST: A SITTER

Though you may under certain circumstances be able to safely detox at home, you should under no circumstances detox alone. Someone should be with you around the clock until all signs of withdrawal have passed. The sitter should be either an AA or Al-Anon member (those doing Twelfth-Step work are usually happy to help) or a friend or relative who is not a drinking or drugging buddy. The sitter should read the Mini-Guide on page 80 carefully before withdrawal begins.

MINI-GUIDE

Home Detox: What the Sitter Must Know

Sitting with an alcoholic or addict going through withdrawal is a major responsibility and a difficult task. These tips should be useful in helping someone safely to the other side of addiction—toward sobriety.

❖ Prepare yourself by reading the pertinent parts of this chapter, so that you will know what to expect and what you will need to do.

❖ The patient should be examined by and supervised by a physician familiar with addiction and withdrawal, preferably certified by ASAM or AAPAA (see page 46). The physician should be willing to make home visits, if necessary. In some communities, an experienced visiting nurse may be available; check with the physician or look in the Yellow Pages.

❖ Prepare in advance a list of emergency numbers and post them near the phone. They should include numbers for the police, the closest hospital emergency room, the doctor handling the case, and if possible one or more strong neighbors who have agreed to be available to give you assistance if your charge should become violent.

❖ Make sure the environment in which the withdrawal will take place is "clean": search it thoroughly for hidden drugs or alcohol. Check not just the medicine chest and the bar, but kitchen cabinets (for vanilla extract or other high-alcohol flavorings), the first aid kit (for rubbing alcohol—which alcoholics will drink if sufficiently desperate), under beds, inside drawers, deep in laundry hampers, behind books, under sofa cushions, in toilet tanks, pockets, handbags, luggage, and so on. Be suspicious of everything. Overlook nothing.

❖ Restrict visits from anyone not connected to and supportive of the recovery plan. One well-meaning but ill-advised visitor at a critical point could take your charge from almost there to nowhere.

❖ Administer no mind-altering drug or medication without an order from the supervising physician.

❖ Be sure that your charge is never left alone until all severe withdrawal symptoms are gone. Share the "watch" with other sitters; shifts can be twelve hours long, eight hours long, or even shorter if there are several sitters.

❖ The atmosphere should be calm. Lights should be on, but not too bright. Soft music and conversation are good; loud or abrupt noises are not. There should be a comfortable chair for the patient, as well as a low bed for resting and sleeping (a restless sleeper could fall from a high bed and be injured).

❖ Remember the therapeutic value of touch. Handle your charge gently, and "lay on hands" (pat shoulders or arms, hold hands) to calm anxiety, and reassure the patient that he or she is not alone.

❖ Take any mention of suicide (see page 93) seriously and get professional advice for dealing with it; have an emergency number ready to call in case the subject is raised.* If your charge begins to cheer up after talking about suicide, this is *not* a good sign. More people commit suicide emerging from depression than in it.

❖ Give the patient unconditional love and care. Forget about lectures and sermons. It's important that he or she feels worthy of your efforts and attention.

❖ Encourage your charge to talk about his or her feelings. Be a good listener, but don't try to give a lot of advice. Do give direct accurate answers to the best of your ability, and don't be evasive. Be careful not to act as though you don't believe or trust your patient.

❖ Recognize that any anger or hostility aimed your way is not meant personally. It's just part of the withdrawal syndrome. But if violence seems about to erupt, get help immediately. Often a strong neighbor or friend or two can help to restrain the violence (by holding the patient's arms and legs), but if this doesn't work, be prepared to call the police to protect both your own safety and that of the patient.

❖ If your charge seems to be afraid of you, try to be reassuring; use a soothing tone of voice and calming words. Again, this is nothing personal, just another reaction to the withdrawal of drugs. If you're afraid, try not to project your fear, because people in withdrawal tend to pick up their feelings from those around them. Ideally, act as you would like your charge to: calm, relaxed, positive, optimistic.

❖ Hallucinations (seeing or hearing things that aren't there) are common. The patient may not tell you about the hallucinations in so many words; you may have to deduce their existence from your own observations. The most common tip-offs are glancing looks or other inappropriate eye movements (aimed seemingly at nothing), incongruous actions or words (directed at empty space), and picking at the skin (as if to remove insects).

Hallucinations are very real to the person experiencing them and often very frightening. If your charge has them, your laughing at them or denying they exist could be interpreted as a lack of support or concern. Challenging the patient in the hope that the visions will disappear may only make things worse. Instead, acknowledge that they exist in your charge's mind and try to calm him or her with reassurances that they can't do any harm and will soon go away.

Although the hallucinations are not harmful in themselves, you should report them to the physician supervising the withdrawal. Later, it's important to be sure that the patient understands that the hallucinations were not real.

❖ Let your charge drink all the fluids he or she desires. Provide high-carbohydrate (fruit, pretzels, muffins, crackers) and high-protein snacks (nuts, cheese and crackers, yogurt, peanut butter sandwiches), which may relieve the compulsion to use alcohol or drugs. If sleep is a problem, warm milk may help. Honey and lemon juice may soothe a cough. And a heating pad will make physical aches and pains more tolerable.

❖ Call for emergency medical help if your charge shows any of the symptoms listed on page 82.

*Many communities have a suicide hotline. If there is none listed in your local telephone directory, look under "Mental health services." If there is no suicide line, call the mental health service before withdrawal begins, and ask for a number to call if someone is threatening suicide. Keep this number readily available during the entire detox period.

(continued from page 79)
sponse to what's going on inside. So, though a whole list of common withdrawal symptoms may have been reported for the drug you've been taking, you may experience only one or a few of them. Or you may have some less common symptoms.

Medical approaches to detoxification from alcohol or other drugs may also differ in different situations. Frequently, medication and nutritional supplements will be given to prevent the most serious symptoms of withdrawal and to ease the psychological pain. (Intravenous fluids, such as glucose and electrolytes in water, used to be administered routinely, but these are avoided now since they can increase the fluid level of the brain and precipitate seizures, delirium, even death.)

The person supervising your withdrawal from alcohol or drugs may question you about suicidal thoughts. Such thoughts are very common in alcoholics and drug addicts. If you have them, don't be afraid to talk about them. It's understandable that you don't like yourself or the way your life has been going. You feel desperate to change it at all costs—even your life. But if you stick with your treatment plan, you'll find there's a better way to change.

In some cases, withdrawal may feel like a roller-coaster ride as you soar from the low of withdrawal up to a giddy high and plunge down again, though you haven't been anywhere near your chemical of choice. That high isn't a hallucination; it's the true intoxication that occurs when the drug you've been using is released from storage in your fat cells during withdrawal. With luck and plenty of pluck,

THE HOME DETOX: WHEN EMERGENCY HELP IS NEEDED

When an alcoholic/addict goes into withdrawal at home (intentionally or otherwise), a sitter or family member should call 911 or the local emergency number or get the patient to an emergency room at once if any of the following occur:

❖ Vomiting that doesn't let up, or any vomiting of blood.

❖ A fever that is higher than 102°F on an oral thermometer.

❖ Difficulty breathing, shortness of breath, or very rapid breathing. (The respiration rate can be determined by counting the number of times the chest rises in a one-minute period; more than twenty-five respirations a minute is too fast.)

❖ Pulse rate that is more than 120 beats per minute, even after you have tried to calm the patient down.

❖ Sudden chest pain or severe abdominal pain.

❖ A seizure (a spastic convulsion of the body) from which the patient doesn't awaken within fifteen minutes—or a second seizure.

❖ Shaking chills.

❖ Unconsciousness (you can't rouse the patient).

❖ Recurring hallucinations.

❖ Severe agitation, even after you've tried to talk the patient down.

❖ Delirium (the DT's).

❖ Violent behavior or the threat of violent behavior.

it will be your last chemically induced high.

ALCOHOL WITHDRAWAL

Alcohol is a central nervous system depressant and the most abused drug in the U.S. Because it affects virtually every cell in the body, withdrawal can be very complicated.

When Do Symptoms Begin?

Usually six to twelve hours after the last drink; they can begin even while significant concentrations of alcohol remain in your blood.

What Are They Like?

Alcohol withdrawal is usually divided into four stages; the goal of treatment is to prevent progression to the perilous later stages.

Stage I: Your mind and body will race in response to the withdrawal of the depressant alcohol. An early manifestation of this hyperactivity will be tremors, commonly known as the "shakes" or "jitters." They may be so bad you can't function, or no more than a faint fluttering inside. Loss of appetite, nausea, and vomiting are also common. You may have noticed these symptoms before when you urgently needed a drink, particularly first thing in the morning. Though you may feel unusually alert, you may also be irritable, a bit disoriented, and easily startled.

You may be agitated, restless, and unable to sleep while at the same time, paradoxically, desperately craving rest and sleep. Your face may be flushed, your body sweaty, your pulse racing, your blood pressure high, and your manners not at their best. Most of these symptoms—the shakes and loss of appetite, for example—will subside within a few days. Others, such as sleeplessness, may take weeks to improve (see Chapter 13). You may not feel completely "normal" for a year or more.

ARE YOU WITHDRAWING FOR TWO?

If you have any suspicion that you might be pregnant, ask for a pregnancy test before you go through withdrawal. Some of the drugs routinely used during this phase can be harmful to an unborn child.

Stage II: Usually between twenty-four and forty-eight hours after the last drink, about one in four alcoholics, in addition to continuing Stage I symptoms, sees or hears (or sometimes smells or feels) things that aren't there and/or complains of bad dreams or nightmarish episodes. The hallucinations, which are usually more vivid and intense at night, are most often of people, animals, or insects—frequently enlarged, shrunken, or gruesomely distorted. Snakes, roaches, and rats may swarm in the windows. Pink or polka-dot elephants may dance on the walls. Friends or foes may throng ceaselessly around the room. The air may be filled with disembodied voices, haunting music, or bloodcurdling screams and sounds.

Though often terrifying, both to the person experiencing them and to inexperienced bystanders, the shakes and hallucinations are not serious in themselves. But if you have them, they should be reported to the doctor supervising your home withdrawal, or to the attendant or nurse at your hospital or clinic detox unit.

Stage III: Usually during the second day, but as early as six or as late as

WHAT ABOUT RESTRAINTS?

About one in a hundred patients becomes agitated enough during withdrawal to require physical restraints. They sound medieval, but as long as they're used in a loving and supportive environment, they can provide a welcome sense of security to patients unsettled by the feeling of being out of control. And of course restraints protect violent or self-destructive patients from harming themselves or others. Usually leather straps are used to restrain arms and legs. Sometimes just one arm restraint will do the job, reminding a patient to remain in bed. Restraints should never be used as a substitute for attention from the staff.

If at any time during your withdrawal you feel as though you are about to lose control, you should tell the nurse or attendant on duty. It's possible that restraints might make you feel safer. And if you do feel violent, don't be afraid that this is "the real you" emerging. Such Mr. Hyde feelings are simply an aspect of withdrawal. Like Dr. Jekyll's, they will pass.

seventy-two hours after the last drink, some alcoholics experience seizures, or convulsions ("rum fits"). These don't usually recur and are rarely life-threatening. They can almost always be prevented in a good medically monitored withdrawal program.

Stage IV: The DT's (more elegantly referred to in Latin as *delirium tremens*) usually occur two to three days after the last drink but may appear as late as the second week, especially when there is cross-addiction to other drugs. With the DT's, Stage I symptoms become more severe and Stage II hallucinations more graphically intense. There is usually severe shaking, sweating, paranoid delusions ("Everyone's trying to get me!"), inability to sleep, irritability, and increased blood pressure, pulse, and temperature. The DT's generally follow, but they can usually be prevented by early medical treatment.

It's at this point that withdrawal in a controlled environment becomes particularly important. The patient may lose touch with reality, begin to perceive helpers as enemies, fight to escape caretakers, even become violent. When severe, the DT's can be fatal. Just why isn't certain. It's suspected that the dehydration, shock, and heart irregularities induced by an extra heavy adrenaline flow and the super stimulation of the nervous system in withdrawal are generally responsible.

Often the hallucinations experienced during a severe withdrawal may be remembered as vividly as if they were real. It's possible to believe that the doctor, nurse, sponsor, or other person who attended you during that period was trying to kill or hurt you. If you have such hallucinations, you may have to be "debriefed" later, retracing your experience so that you can replace the distorted images with reality in your memory. Otherwise, you may go through life believing your delusions were real. If you are in any way confused or worried about what happened during withdrawal hallucinations or the DT's—and it would be surprising if you weren't—talk about your feelings with the professional caring for you.

If you experience unusually severe withdrawal symptoms, your doctor should check to be sure there are no other underlying causes, such as an undiagnosed illness or injury.

Treatment of Alcohol Withdrawal

The lurid motion picture scene of the alcoholic trembling violently through the DT's, strapped to his bed to prevent his harming himself or others, is not at all the way drying out has to be. Carefully supervised medical withdrawal can head off the worst symptoms, making you more comfortable and putting you at virtually no risk.

It's likely that you'll be given medication—often phenobarbital or another sedative replacement drug in decreasing doses for six days, to ease the symptoms of alcohol withdrawal. You'll probably also be given magnesium sulfate, thiamine (100 mg), folate (1 mg), and perhaps a multiple vitamin supplement, which also reduce the risks of seizures and the DT's. Some physicians prescribe benadryl (diphenhydramine), with or without ascorbic acid (vitamin C), to improve sleep, or L-tryptophan and a variety of other over-the-counter medications (antidiarrheals, antacids, acetaminophen, skin ointments) to ease symptoms. Sometimes they are necessary, but in general the sooner a chemically dependent person comes to recognize that popping a pill isn't the way to deal with every little discomfort, the better. And detox isn't too soon to start.

In some cases, particularly during an outpatient detox, the doctor may elect to administer disulfiram (Antabuse), usually 250 mg daily. Because it inhibits a specific enzyme (aldehyde dehydrogenase) in the alcoholic's system, taking disulfiram results in abnormally high levels of acetaldehyde when alcohol is consumed. As a result you pay a high price for even one drink: flushing, headaches, palpitations, sweating, and chest pain. These unpleasant symptoms provide a strong motivation to avoid alcohol. Research is in progress on other drugs—such as angiotensin converting enzyme (ACE) inhibitors—that can similarly discourage drinking.

"This is a nice place, but I'm not ready to get sober yet."

How Long Does Withdrawal Last?

The shakes are usually at their uncomfortable worst on the third or fourth day, but they can continue for a few weeks. After day four, the risk of seizures diminishes considerably. The onset of the DT's can occur as late as the tenth day, and in the heavy-duty alcoholic they can continue for two weeks and (very rarely) even longer.

After Withdrawal

The alcohol you've flooded your system with for years has overpowered your body's metabolism, but with withdrawal there will be a rebound. In the early weeks of sobriety, your long-abused body works hard to repair the damage. Liver swelling will go down, muscle tissue will come back, bone marrow will improve its performance in your immune system, kidneys will release excess fluids (increasing your visits to the john). Most of this repair work will be completed by the end of four weeks, although some damage may be permanent. While you were drinking, brain cells may have died, your liver may have become scarred (cirrhosis), and heart muscle may have been damaged. Now only long-term abstinence can supply the resources to compensate for such changes. (See Chapters 13, 14, and 21 for more on the physical symptoms experienced during recovery.)

Mood swings, often with severe depression, may continue for months, or occasionally for as long as two years. It is rarely necessary, and usually unwise, to treat these symptoms with medication. Such treatment can reactivate the entire addictive process and put you back at square one.

WITHDRAWAL FROM OTHER CENTRAL NERVOUS SYSTEM DEPRESSANTS

Central nervous system (CNS) depressants—including barbiturates (Nembutal, Pentobarbital, Phenobarbital, Pentothal), meprobamate (Miltown, Equanil), glutethimide (Doriden), benzodiazepines (Ativan, Librium, Valium), and several other tranquilizers, sedatives, and hypnotics—are cross-reactive with each other and with alcohol. That is, the withdrawal symptoms of one of these drugs can be eased by any other one. As a result, many addicts routinely use them interchangeably to ward off withdrawal and often mistakenly believe they're not addicted to any of them.

When Do Symptoms Begin?

Anywhere from twelve to twenty-four hours after the last drug dose, or as long as several days, depending on the amount of the drug used and its half-life.*

What Are They Like?

Every act of courage has its price, and flushing your last vial of sedatives down the toilet is no exception. The withdrawal that follows is similar to that of alcoholics. Because these drugs are less acutely intoxicating than alcohol, their withdrawal tends to be less severe (at least to observers). But because their effects are longer-lasting, the symptoms produced in withdrawal can continue for a much longer time.

Barbiturate withdrawal can lead to very serious medical complications

"I spent my whole life building up that business of mine, and now my wife is trying to take it away from me. She put me in here just to destroy my reputation. If my children don't get me out of here by tomorrow morning, I'm gonna cut every last one of them out of my will."

and is *not* for do-it-yourselfers. Without medical supervision, it can be fatal. Beginning eight to twelve hours after the last dose, patients can expect nervousness, tremor, and general hyperactivity of the nervous system and of the deep tendon reflexes (muscles may seem to jerk or jump). They may also experience fever; nausea and vomiting, loss of appetite, and abdominal cramps; sweating (particularly at night); and generalized aches, pains, and muscle cramps. Between the second and fourth day after the last dose, or as late as six or seven days after, one or more seizures (similar to the "rum fits" of alcoholics), usually with a loss of consciousness, may occur. Sometimes the seizures are localized, affecting only one part of the addict's body. These seizures may recur periodically for months following cessation of the drug. Delusions and hallucinations, or even full-blown psychotic delirium resembling the DT's, sometimes also develop.

With benzodiazepines, the pattern is somewhat different. Since they have a long half-life and linger in the body, it's not necessary to use them daily to produce physical dependence and withdrawal symptoms. So even casual users of benzodiazepines—even those who've used the drugs for as little as two or three weeks—can experience

*The half-life of a drug is the amount of time it takes for half the drug to leave the body. Half-life is used as a gauge of how long symptoms associated with the drug and with its withdrawal can be expected to last. The longer the half-life, the longer the symptoms persist.

withdrawal symptoms. These vary, and can include anxiety, panic attacks, depression, and distorted sensory perception. In the past, such symptoms were frequently mistaken for some new or reemerging emotional problem, but they are now recognized as a normal manifestation of withdrawal. As withdrawal progresses, patients often describe alternating good and bad days, with good days eventually beginning to outnumber the bad ones.

Treatment of Withdrawal from CNS Depressants

Generally, another drug in the same class is administered in decreasing doses to minimize the effects of withdrawal. For sedatives, barbiturates or benzodiazepines are usually used. With drugs that have a long half-life and therefore hang on in the body for a very long time, such as the benzodiazepines, diminishing medication therapy may have to be continued for weeks or even months. In inpatient detox, the sedatives used for withdrawal are gradually tapered off over a period of two weeks and then stopped. In outpatient management the usual procedure is to go to alternate days, then twice a week, then weekly, sometimes taking as long as three months to complete the process. At the point the process is completed, the drug can be stopped with minimal side effects.

How Long Does Withdrawal Last?

Because central nervous system depressants, particularly benzodiazepines, have such a long half-life, withdrawal symptoms persist longer than they do with most other drugs. With benzodiazepines, symptoms peak in three or four weeks but can last to some degree for months. Effects may still be noticed over a year after drug use is discontinued. But the severity does lessen with time, and eventually all symptoms disappear.

WITHDRAWAL FROM COCAINE AND CRACK

Cocaine is an expensive and in some ways flamboyant drug that has gotten a lot of media attention. Long snorted in powder form, it has become popular to smoke the paste form, as crack, which allows the absorption of larger doses of the drug at a lower cost. It isn't unusual for those addicted to cocaine to deny that they are also dependent on alcohol or sedative drugs, setting the stage for severe or fatal withdrawal complications if the detox plan doesn't strictly prohibit the use of these drugs along with that of cocaine.

When Do Symptoms Begin?

What is often called "post-cocaine crash" begins about nine hours after the drug is last taken.

What Are They Like?

Abstinence from cocaine causes profound depression and deep unhappiness—the "cocaine blues." The earliest symptoms are agitation, depression, loss of appetite, and strong craving for another hit. In the next day or so, depression continues, fatigue replaces agitation, insomnia becomes a problem even though there is great sleepiness, and craving diminishes. About three or four days into withdrawal, the patient is exhausted, drowsy, sleeps a lot, and notices no craving. By the end of the first week, sleep patterns are normalized, mood levels off, anxiety is reduced, and there is a gradual return of craving, which after several weeks becomes very strong. There is then a period of several weeks during which the ordinary pleasures of life (food, sex, friends) don't seem very pleasant, when doing anything at all seems difficult to impossible, and when anxiety begins to build. Suspiciousness, even actual paranoia, can persist for weeks.

Treatment of Cocaine or Crack Withdrawal

Most important is round-the-clock support, preferably from people in long-term recovery. Symptoms can also be eased by keeping the patient comfortable during the first few days, and providing individual and group therapy as soon as the patient is able to benefit. The amino acids tyrosine and tryptophan, which are needed for the body to produce norepinephrine and serotonin (chemicals that regulate mood), are often given during this time. Some studies have shown that antidepressants, bromocriptine, or amantadine, can reduce cravings. But if not handled cautiously, such medicating, in addition to causing its own unpleasant side effects, risks continuing the drug use cycle. It says to the patient that the way to deal with a problem, even a drug problem, is to use a drug.

How Long Does Withdrawal Take?

By the end of ten weeks of abstention, most people start to enjoy life again and have more energy. But periodic craving—sometimes out of the blue and sometimes triggered by specific cues—is still a problem. Because memories of the adverse effects of cocaine use often dim with time, the craving can provoke a relapse.

WITHDRAWAL FROM OTHER STIMULANTS

Once amphetamines were the primary stimulant of abuse. Now, in addition to cocaine, a long list of other stimulants have joined them, including phenmetrazine (Preludin), methylphenidate (Ritalin), and phentermine (Fastin), and the made-in-the-U.S.A. designer drugs, such as methamphetamine ("ice" and "crank").

When Do Symptoms Begin?

Usually about twenty-four to thirty-six hours after the last drug was taken.

What Are They Like?

Withdrawal from stimulants is less clearly defined than withdrawal from depressants or narcotics. Usually it leaves you feeling depressed, moody, fatigued, slowed physically and mentally, and very sleepy. Appetite, impeded by the drug, rebounds considerably when it is discontinued. But because the gastrointestinal tract has also slowed down, indigestion and bloating are common as normal eating resumes. At a time when you need the support of others the most, stimulant withdrawal may leave you feeling suspicious of everyone, even paranoid. Stimulants deplete the natural supplies of norepinephrine (a chemical necessary for normal brain function) in the brain. Deprived of home-grown norepinephrine, you may experience strong, periodic compulsions to take more of the drug—which acts as a replacement for these chemicals.

Withdrawal from stimulants is not often life-threatening in itself, but attempting withdrawal without medical help isn't wise. That's because without close supervision, a strong craving could lead to violent or reckless behavior in an effort to satisfy it. And that could threaten not just the patient's life but the lives of others as well.

Treatment of Stimulant Withdrawal

Stimulants are not cross-tolerant with either depressants or narcotics, so sedatives can't be used to counteract a stimulant's effects or to treat withdrawal—though antidepressants may be helpful in calming a patient in withdrawal. In most cases, supportive treatment and efforts to deal with the underlying addiction are all that is necessary in helping the patient through detox. If he or she is also addicted to alcohol or mixed drugs (this is common because abusers of "uppers" use depressants to bring themselves down), many addiction specialists will supplement the stimulant detox regimen with a sedative drug.

How Long Does Withdrawal Last?

It's deceptive. Patients appear to recover very quickly. After a few days, appetite, sleep patterns, and sex drive all return to normal, producing a false sense of security. But the most dangerous withdrawal symptom—a nagging craving for more of the drug—continues for many months. The danger is that the recovering addict feels so good, he or she begins to wonder, "Why not give in to that craving?" See Chapter 9 for how to deal with temptations.

WITHDRAWAL FROM OPIATES/NARCOTICS

The opiates fall into three subgroups. There are the natural opiates, morphine and codeine, which are derived from the opium poppy. The synthetic or semisynthetics include heroin, meperidine (Demerol), methadone (Dolophine), hydromorphone (Dilaudid), and fentanyl (Innovar, Sublimaze). Then there are the newer opiates, created by pharmaceutical companies in the legitimate pursuit of disease treatment and profit, but abused by users in the pursuit of a high. These include propoxyphene (Darvon), pentazocine (Talwin), nalbuphine (Nubain), and butorphanol (Stadol). Withdrawal from all these drugs is similar.

When Do Symptoms Begin?

Grade 0 symptoms (see below) usually begin eight to sixteen hours following the last dose, and Grade 3 symptoms begin about thirty-six hours into withdrawal. But symptoms begin earlier when the drug being withdrawn is a short-acting one (like fentanyl), which leaves the body in a hurry. And they may be delayed in the case of long-acting narcotics (such as methadone).

What Are They Like?

Patients being withdrawn from narcotics are likely to try to manipulate, wheedle, demand, and plead for another dose of the drug. They may pretend to have symptoms or greatly exaggerate them. But trained medical personnel have seen the game played before and aren't taken in by this behavior.

The symptoms of opiate/narcotic withdrawal are characterized by the disruption of the autonomic nervous system (the one that carries on the day-to-day functions of life that we don't consciously think about, like breathing). They are often classified according to severity, from 0 to 3, with 3 the most severe response:

Grade 0: Anxiety; drug craving; drug-seeking behavior.
Grade 1: Yawning; sweating; tearing of the eyes (lacrimation); runny nose (rhinorrhea); restless, broken sleep.
Grade 2: Dilation of pupils (mydriasis); goose flesh (piloerection); muscle twitches; leg cramps; anorexia; irritability.
Grade 3: Weakness; insomnia; low-grade fever (under 100°F); increased respiratory rate; increased blood pressure; restlessness; abdominal cramps, nausea, vomiting, diarrhea; weight loss.

Treatment of Opiate/Narcotic Withdrawal

In the past, slowly tapered doses of the addictive methadone were used to wean addicts off their opiate/narcotic of choice (much as sedatives are used to wean addicts from sedative drugs). Today, clonidine (Catapres), which blocks many of the withdrawal symptoms, is much more likely to be used. It is usually administered (via a skin

COLD TURKEY COULD MEAN DEAD TURKEY

As dangerous as it is to start taking drugs without medical supervision, it may be even more dangerous to stop them on your own. Be careful to read this chapter and follow its recommendations—including the need for medical advice—before going through withdrawal.

patch or orally) for four to six days—often longer for patients who have used longer-acting narcotics. Since it can cause the blood pressure to drop to below-normal levels, blood pressure is usually carefully monitored when clonidine is given.

When the patient is pregnant, some physicians prefer to use tapered doses of methadone or another substitute narcotic, believing that the safety of clonidine for the fetus has not been shown; others believe that clonidine works better than methadone and is safer for the fetus. More research will undoubtedly show which route is better. In either case, the fetus is monitored via ultrasound to detect fetal distress resulting from the medication or the withdrawal.*

How Long Does Withdrawal Take?

Symptoms become more and more pronounced, peaking at about forty-eight to seventy-two hours after the last drug dose, and then gradually begin to decline. Most symptoms are completely gone in seven to ten days, but you may experience some sleeplessness, anxiety, a feeling of weakness, and muscle aches for several weeks. Periods of craving for the drug may continue for months.

*The babies of women who are weaned off drugs entirely tend to do much better than those of women who are maintained on methadone throughout their pregnancy. Getting off the drug also gives mothers a better chance of being able to keep their babies, or to have earlier access to them, because they are drug-free. It's yet another important reason for expectant mothers to get clean and sober as soon as possible.

WITHDRAWAL FROM MARIJUANA AND OTHER HALLUCINOGENS

These distorters of reality include marijuana (cannabis), PCP (phencyclidine), LSD (lysergic acid diethylamide), mescaline (from the peyote cactus), and psilocybin (found in several species of mushrooms).

When Do Symptoms Begin?

This varies, depending on how quickly the drug in question acts in the body and how quickly it leaves.

What Are They Like?

Marijuana's long half-life makes it a tenant not easily evicted from the system, so users tend to be fairly lethargic and unmotivated during the early days of withdrawal. They may even be too apathetic to crave more of the drug. Anxiety, confusion, depression, and irrational behavior are common, but sometimes the only personality changes obvious to others during the first two weeks are self-centeredness and a slowing of the thinking process. After two to three weeks of abstinence, the daily user in withdrawal becomes restless, starts acting out, and begins to crave the drug once more.

There are no serious effects from the withdrawal of LSD, but flashbacks (hallucinations that appear out of the blue when the drug has not been taken) are quite common. With PCP there can be very dramatic effects from intoxication, but there seems to be no special withdrawal syndrome. The panic, anxiety, violence, and behavior changes (occasionally permanent) seen during withdrawal are a continuation of the effects of the drug as it wears off.

Treatment of Withdrawal from Marijuana and Hallucinogens

Physical rest, emotional support, good nutrition, and adequate fluid intake are all basic to the treatment of marijuana withdrawal. Since the process is not life-threatening, medication isn't absolutely necessary. But in many cases a sedative schedule similar to that given in alcohol withdrawal may be given to alleviate symptoms.

Withdrawal from LSD or PCP doesn't usually require medication, but the lingering symptoms of intoxication may require medical care in a very supportive environment. The hallucinations associated with these drugs can be disorienting and anxiety-provoking; the medical staff usually has to use visual and auditory cues to keep prompting the patient to remember who he is, where he comes from, where he is, and why he's there. Concentrating on this interaction helps to dampen the overwhelming hallucinogenic effect. Without this kind of support, patients might believe that they really can fly, a belief that could have fairly serious consequences. Sedation may also be needed. A tube that runs through the nose and down into the stomach, or medication to acidify the urine, may be used to speed the removal of the drugs from the body.

"Why'd you take my pills away? I'm here to get off alcohol, not medicine. My doctor prescribed those pills for me. If you're taking them away, I better leave this place, because goddamnit, you people don't know what the hell you're doin'."

How Long Does Withdrawal Take?

Although it enters the body quickly, marijuana is stored in fat tissue and leaves slowly. Energy doesn't begin to replace apathy until the end of the first two or three weeks. Once high energy levels return and the patient becomes more active and attentive, a craving for marijuana may also return.

How quickly PCP and LSD leave the body depends on not just the dose of the drug taken, but also on the level of stress and the fluid balance in the body. For reasons that are not clearly understood, although half the dose of either of these drugs is usually out of the body in three days, their effects persist—the song is over, but the malady lingers on—often for months, even for a year or more. And some personality changes may be permanent.

WITHDRAWAL FROM ANTIDEPRESSANTS AND ANTIPSYCHOTICS

Antidepressants (such as Elavil, Limbitrol, Prozac) and antipsychotic drugs (Compazine, Haldol, Mellaril, Thorazine) play a very important role in the treatment of some kinds of depression and other thought disorders. They are not useful for treating such symptoms when they are caused by alcohol or drug addiction, and in fact can only make matters worse. Withdrawing the drugs enhances the recovery process.*

*If you are on such medications and are being treated for other types of addiction (to alcohol or other drugs), then it is likely that these drugs, too, should be withdrawn—but only under close medical supervision.

When Do Withdrawal Symptoms Begin?

This varies with the drug.

What Are They Like?

There is some disagreement among experts as to whether there actually are withdrawal symptoms when antidepressants or antipsychotic drugs are discontinued. But experience has shown that the initial period after discontinuance can be as difficult to handle as any other drug withdrawal. Almost all the behavioral and musculoskeletal symptoms that occur with withdrawal of other drugs are possible, though their physiological origin isn't always clear.

Treatment of Withdrawal from Antidepressants and Antipsychotics

Withdrawal isn't life-threatening. Emotional support, physical rest, quality nutrition, and adequate fluid intake are often all that is needed during the initial withdrawal period. Sometimes, however, sedatives may be used to reduce symptoms. This is particularly useful if other drugs have been taken by the patient, whether or not addiction to them is admitted.

How Long Does Withdrawal Take?

This will vary depending upon the drug, its half-life, the usual daily dose, and other factors. But generally symptoms are gone in a matter of weeks.

MAKING IT THROUGH WITHDRAWAL

During withdrawal, you may feel the compulsion to leave treatment, to use more drugs, or to escape the therapeutic process in some way. These feelings are normal. Painful and difficult as it may seem at the moment, just hang in there—things will get better a minute, an hour, a day at a time. Meanwhile, there are things you can do to make the process a little easier.

❖ Be sure you are not alone. At a medical detox facility, a supportive, caring staff is crucial. If you are at home or elsewhere, you should have an experienced sitter with you (see page 80).

❖ Talk with others who are further along in the process than you are, or who have gone through it before you. It's good to know that you're not the only one who has ever felt so awful and out of control, and that others have survived the ordeal intact (and in fact now feel better than ever).

❖ Stop resisting and relax. Temporarily try to give up control so you will ultimately be a better manager of your life. This may not seem to make sense now, but hundreds of thousands of other addicts have found that "letting go" is helpful during this extremely difficult period.

❖ Make certain that you are in a calm and comfortable environment. Hub-

STAYING WITH WITHDRAWAL

Getting stuck with needles may not be your idea of heaven, but many alcoholics/addicts who have been treated with acupuncture during detox have found that it makes the experience much less of a hell. Why it works isn't clear, but this traditional Asian medicine seems to reduce or eliminate withdrawal symptoms and reduce craving in many people.

bub, noise, people who upset you, will all make withdrawal more difficult.

SELF-DESTRUCTIVE FEELINGS

There are two mind sets that make withdrawal an especially high-risk period for the alcoholic/addict. One is "I'm scared that I'm slowly killing myself with chemicals, but it all seems so hopeless. I might as well just die now instead of on the installment plan." The other is "I'm so afraid of life without drugs. I'd rather be dead than sober." Both of these are conscious feelings, brought about by depression and despair. During withdrawal they are often easier to hear than the subconscious survival instinct that exists in all of us: "I want to live, and I know that to live I need to change."

If, in fact, you find that self-destructive thoughts are outshouting your wish to live, even fleetingly, talk about them. Talk to a doctor, nurse, or attendant if you are at a medical detox facility, or to the friend or relative who is helping you through withdrawal at home or elsewhere. Don't let shame or guilt about these feelings (neither of which is warranted) stand in the way of unburdening yourself.

Fortunately, these feelings usually begin to lessen as the initial withdrawal period ends. When you begin to feel better (no matter how you measure this) for several days in a row, you've probably passed the period of greatest danger. Depression and despondency may recur periodically for a while, but the "down" periods should become fewer and further apart as the months roll by. If at any point self-destructive feelings return, discuss them immediately with your sponsor, counselor, or doctor. Or call your local suicide Hotline.

FEELINGS OF POWER AND SUCCESS

At some point during withdrawal, you may begin to feel really good. (Just when this happens will depend on the drug from which you're withdrawing.) This can be dangerous if you then conclude, "Great, I've licked my addiction. Now it's back to business as usual." Well, the truth is that now that you're detoxed, you're just beginning to deal with your problem. For at least the next year, the business of recovery will have to be the focus of your existence. Business as usual will have to wait.

PART II

PHASE ONE

Saving Your Life

Phase One recovery, which begins the moment you give up alcohol and/or other drugs, is the most intense of the three phases. As you struggle to save your life, you're required to selfishly put all else aside. You have to concentrate every ounce of your physical and mental energy on getting well, almost to the exclusion of everyone (even loved ones) and everything (even job and community responsibilities) else. This phase begins in the first days of sobriety and usually ends about a year—sometimes, two—later, when the mental fog lifts.

Phase One is a time of learning. Learning about yourself—about who you really are, what you really want, what you can really do. Learning about your disease—what it's done to you, what it can do to you, how it can be controlled. Learning about recovery support groups in your community (such as Alcoholics Anonymous) and how they can help you. Learning about sobriety—how to maintain it and how to live comfortably with it. Learning how to function sober, how to cope with your problems without chemical assistance.

It's also a time when you are likely to experience a wide range of physical, emotional, and intellectual symptoms, related both to your addiction and to your withdrawal from it, symptoms that may confuse or frighten you if you aren't prepared for them and don't know how to deal with them. For many people this is the toughest phase of recovery, but it's also the phase during which you will see the most dramatic changes.

6

GETTING TO KNOW ALCOHOLICS ANONYMOUS

Joining a support group is the first step in the first phase of recovery for most people seeking sobriety. A support group doesn't guarantee a successful recovery, but it sure improves the odds. Alcoholics Anonymous (AA) is the major support group for more than 2 million alcoholics in the U.S.A. and 114 other countries. Other important Twelve-Step groups for addicts include Narcotics Anonymous, Cocaine Anonymous, and Pills Anonymous, all similar in structure, and certainly in objectives, to AA, the granddaddy of them all.

A GUIDE TO TWELVE-STEP AND OTHER SUPPORT GROUPS

Why do you need a support group to make a good recovery? Nobody knows for sure. Partly it's for the same reasons that mastectomy patients, stroke victims, diabetics, and grieving or single parents all do better when they participate in support groups. You know you're not alone, and you can learn from others who have been through it before you. It may be that humans are tribal beings—genetically programmed to live in groups, to feel better when sharing their lives with others, helping and being helped by them.

Guide Lines

❖ Virtually everyone in recovery does better when involved with a support group.

❖ AA is the support group with the longest and most successful track record. But no one shoe fits all. Those who find Twelve-Step programs like AA genuinely unpalatable may be able to find help in other support groups. (But for your own sake, give the Twelve-Steppers a fair and patient trial first.)

❖ The only requirement for membership in AA is a desire to stop drinking. Requirements for membership in other Twelve-Step programs are equally simple—usually the desire to give up a particular behavior or chemical.

❖ AA meetings provide a caring, supportive, nonjudgmental atmosphere for aiding recovery. Still, many people approach their first meeting with apprehension.

❖ The most successful recoverees participate fully in AA, working the Twelve Steps and confiding in a sponsor, right from the start.

❖ Although most people reduce the number of meetings they attend as they move into Phases Two and Three of recovery, withdrawing totally from AA tends to increase the risk of relapse down the road.

❖ AA is not a religious organization, so those from all backgrounds (Christian, Jewish, Muslim, agnostic, atheist, whatever) can find a comfortable niche there.

❖ In recovery, alcoholics/addicts have more in common with one another than they do with the specific population groups they belong to. Nevertheless, some aspects of subgroup cultures play a role in the recovery process.

But partly it's for a reason unique to alcoholics/addicts. A support group replaces the negative drinking or drugging social group they formerly bonded with, and serves as a positive substitute for some of the dependency needs the old group filled. Recoverees share a bomb-shelter camaraderie: alone you die, united you live. And the early fixed structure of Twelve-Step programs and their later open-endedness allow for maximum growth.

So if you've been in in- or outpatient treatment, or have been seeing a doctor or therapist about your addiction, it's very likely you will also be urged to participate in a support group. Studies have shown that the best treatment is apt to unravel if it's not followed up by participation in such a group.

WHAT IS AN AA GROUP?

Most people who've never been to an AA meeting have a somewhat distorted view of Alcoholics Anonymous. They've seen movies, perhaps, or just imagined what it might be like. They picture a lot of skid-row drunks in frayed trousers sitting around, sipping black coffee, announcing "I'm Joe, and I'm an alcoholic," and exchanging maudlin stories. Here's what an AA group really is:

❖ A place where a wide range of people (many with backgrounds similar to yours, others from very different backgrounds, but all of whom suffer from the same disease) meet to share their problems and help each other, to form no-strings friendships in a patient, nonjudgmental atmosphere. For many it's a second family; for others it's the only real family, or at least the only supportive family, they've ever known.

❖ A place to develop and practice basic living skills, the kinds of skills that many alcoholics/addicts never learned (responsibility, communication, empathy, assertiveness).

❖ A place to socialize and interact with others without the crutch of toxic chemicals.

❖ A place to try-try-try again in your quest for recovery, without fear of rejection or recrimination if at first you don't succeed.

❖ A place to begin to be honest with yourself and with others, in an atmosphere of trust.

❖ A place to learn from other people's mistakes, and to let others learn from yours. It's a mirror, where by looking at others you see yourself. And you find out you're not so bad, after all.

❖ A place for picking up information about recovery and for making contacts for help and support on your own. The AA clubhouse and community can be a base camp, where coffee and advice are dispensed almost around the clock.

❖ A security blanket for recovering people, where they know that at certain times, weekly or daily, or even several times a day, they can turn for help and encouragement. Members feel secure just knowing it's there for a lift when they're low.

❖ A place where, ultimately, sobriety is contagious, just as drinking is contagious in a bar or at a party.

❖ A place where you can be as anonymous as you wish. Though individual groups may keep lists of members so they can be informed of special meetings and called for help when needed, no one is ever listed without his or her okay. Names are kept absolutely confidential; there is no registration, no forms to fill out.

HOW DO AA GROUPS WORK?

Bill W. (Bill Wilson, founder of AA) really started something—a not-for-profit fellowship that gives a lot, asks for little in return, and whose only requirement for membership is a desire to stop drinking. You don't have to be an alcoholic or drug addict. There are no dues. The hat is passed at each meeting, and contributions are welcome but never mandatory. Most people drop in a dollar or two (not bad for an evening's therapy and spiritual refreshment). No one is permitted to contribute an amount so large that it might give him or her undue influence over group policy. The funds are used for rent, coffee, literature, and support of the central office.

Groups meet in churches or synagogues, union halls, schools, hospitals, community centers, homes—virtually anywhere adequate inexpensive meeting space can be found. The Traditions prohibit AA groups from owning property, so they can't institutionalize themselves by purchasing their own meeting halls or clubhouses. (Sometimes, however, a group of appreciative recoverees will get together to buy a particularly suitable property through a private nonprofit corporation and then rent the space back to the group.)

Each AA group is autonomous and is organized in its own way, guided by the Twelve Traditions (see page 115). Leadership roles rotate. In most groups there is a chairperson, a secretary, a treasurer, and a general service representative (GSR) to the national headquarters of Alcoholics Anonymous

"This is what I told myself when I started going to AA: 'I'm going to do what they recommend, no matter what, for a year. That doesn't mean I have to do it gracefully, because I don't. I don't have to like it. But I'm going to do it. If they tell me to take off my tight clothes, I'm going to do it. If they tell me to wear a bra, I'm going to do it. I don't know why. It doesn't make sense. But I'll do it anyway. I'll try it for a year. And if I don't like it—well, they're not going to quit making drugs or booze.'"

World Services. There may also be a steering committee, made up of people with long-standing sobriety; and large groups may set up hospitality and other subcommittees. The steering committee chooses a chair, or leader, for each meeting. The chair runs the meeting, and if it's a speaker meeting, invites specific members to speak. Holding a position is not a sign of honor or authority, but of service to the group.

Members come from every walk of life and every level of society, from every religious persuasion and every race. Millionaire executives and out-of-work laborers, teenage dropouts and retired grandpas, scholarly professors and illiterate dishwashers are equal in the life of AA. Possibly in no other setting are differences erased as completely as at an AA meeting.

Better than one in three AA members is a woman, about one in five is under thirty, and 3 percent are under twenty-one. At the other end of the age spectrum are the nearly 25 percent over fifty and almost 8 percent who are retired senior citizens. Nearly half of all AA members are addicted to drugs as well as alcohol; that percentage almost doubles among eighteen-year-olds and is significantly higher among women than men. More than a third of AA members were recommended by other members, while a growing percentage (now about 40 percent) were recommended by counselors or rehab programs. Still, more than one in four come to AA on their own.

Wherever there are people, there are people addicted to alcohol and other drugs. And where there are alcoholics, there is Alcoholics Anonymous. There are AA groups in every city in the country and in most major population centers around the world. That means that AA members can find support everywhere they wander.

WHAT'S AN AA MEETING LIKE?

Whatever you think about your first Alcoholics Anonymous meeting, you won't be bored. The atmosphere is that of an informal social group, though less raucous (nothing stronger than coffee is served) and more interesting. Real people tell real stories, stories very much like your own, stories probably more emotionally gripping and sometimes funnier (fun poked at the speakers by themselves) than anything you've ever seen on TV or in the movies. Since people are not judged by what they say, most feel free to speak up, under the guise of anonymity if they wish. Others prefer to remain silent, at least at first. No one participates at any meeting except voluntarily. Nor is anyone present pressured to admit

AA FOUNDATION STONES

THE TWELVE STEPS. These form the basis of recovery in AA, each step taking members a little further along in the struggle to turn their lives around (see page 110).

THE TWELVE TRADITIONS. The Traditions, covering group organization, function, funding, anonymity, and relationships within and without the group, are the cornerstone on which AA groups from the local to the international level are built (see page 115).

THE SERENITY PRAYER. A nondenominational affirmation that has helped millions, both within AA and outside of it, to cope with their problems realistically (see page 102).

THE BIG BOOK. Officially titled *Alcoholics Anonymous,* the Big Book is the basic text for AA. The forty-four diverse life histories chronicled in its pages show how alcoholics from all walks of life, from the time of the founding of AA until today, have benefited from the program. First published in 1939, it was most recently revised in 1976.

to a drinking or drug problem.

Most meetings start on time, so people often arrive early to chat with friends. Meetings generally open with one or more readings (of the Twelve Steps, the Twelve Traditions, the Serenity Prayer, or some other AA material). Then there may be one or more speakers and/or open discussion, or "sharing," on a topic usually chosen beforehand by the chair. Some meetings are expressly for newcomers; others focus on one of the Twelve Steps or on a chapter in the Big Book. Open meetings welcome visitors and guests who are not alcoholics, or who are not sure they are. Attending one of these is a good nonthreatening information-gathering way to see what AA is like.

Closed meetings are more intense gatherings of people with one common bond—they want to stop drinking. Many have reached the point where they proudly identify themselves as AA members. Meeting formats are scheduled well in advance, usually by the steering committee, so each individual can choose the one that best fits his or her needs of the moment. In the past, because it's always been so difficult for alcoholics/addicts to break their nicotine addiction, many a clubhouse was referred to as "the Smoke House." Smoking is still tough to shake, but more people are shaking it, and these days nonsmoking meetings are increasingly common.

Most meetings last about an hour—sixty minutes crowded with emotional recollections of personal struggles, revealing insights, practical suggestions, and a lot of tears and laughter. Surprised flashes of "Well, at least I'm not the only one!" are common, as listeners appreciatively identify with speakers they recognize as co-tenants of what they'd thought was their own private hell. Some groups don't mind running long, some stop exactly on time. Many close with a recitation, such as the Serenity Prayer or the Lord's Prayer, followed by coffee, tea, and conversation. Sometimes refreshments are served at the beginning or in mid-meeting. Group size varies from a handful to a hundred, with occasional regional meetings attended by thousands. Each type of meeting serves a different purpose; all can be helpful.

Contrary to common belief, AA meetings bear no resemblance to religious revival meetings. Alcoholics Anonymous is neither sectarian nor religious. Members from all religious backgrounds, including Catholic, Protestant, Jewish, and Muslim, as well as from the ranks of agnostics and atheists, can find a comfortable niche in AA. Of course every group reflects its members, and each recoveree needs to find a group that's compatible. And for more about the term Higher Power, see page 130.)

HOW DO YOU TRACK DOWN A MEETING?

If your counselor, physician, or treatment center doesn't refer you to a specific AA contact or group, you can get the name of a group near your home from a friend in AA, or by checking your local phone directory under AA or Alcoholics Anonymous. Look under NA or Narcotics Anonymous if your problem is solely narcotics, or CA or Cocaine Anonymous if it's cocaine. What's at the other end of the line will vary from city to city and town to town. In a major metropolis, a paid secretary may answer; in other places you may hear a recorded message listing daily meetings; in still others an AA volunteer may respond, often from home. Sometimes the number is that of an AA clubhouse and anyone who is there will pick up; sometimes the phone is unattended or busy, and you may have to call again. Keep trying.

THE SERENITY PRAYER

Grant me the serenity
To accept the things I cannot change;
Courage to change the things I can;
And wisdom to know the difference.

"I was embarrassed about going to AA, so I drove forty miles to the next town to go to a meeting there. I needn't have bothered. A big part of that group were folks from my home town. They'd also gone that far so they wouldn't be recognized."

In some communities a printed booklet listing regular meetings is available free of charge. Listings include locations and times (morning, noon, night, and in-between) and specify whether meetings are "open" or "closed," discussion or speaker, whether special topics are on the agenda, and whether smoking is permitted. Listings may even specify which meetings are accessible to the physically disabled and which provide interpreters for the hearing impaired.

YOUR FIRST MEETING

There will be many choices for your first meeting if you live in a large city, fewer if you live in a small town. Where available, a Beginners Meeting gives you a chance to meet with other newcomers and ask questions of an AA veteran. Where no Beginners Meeting exists, select an Open Meeting, preferably an Open Speaker Meeting. With a speaker (an AA member celebrating a sobriety anniversary, for example), it's easy to drift in or out, and there is no expectation of participation. If you're not uncomfortable about participating in a discussion your first time, or won't feel uncomfortable if others participate while you remain silent, you can elect to attend an Open Discussion Meeting.

If the thought of attending your first meeting makes you sweat as much as an invitation to an IRS audit, try to find someone to go with you—an AA member you know, your spouse, a parent, or a friend.* If you're embarrassed to tell anyone at the meeting about your drinking or drug problem, use that old tried-and-true standby: "I need to find out about AA for a friend." Or call the AA phone number and ask if they could suggest an AA veteran willing to meet you somewhere before the meeting and accompany you there.

"The first year I just stood in the doorway at meetings, afraid to involve myself completely. Then one day this little old white lady came over and said, 'I'm gonna be your sponsor.' Fifteen years later, she still is."

If you're interested in meeting people, come fifteen minutes early or plan on staying for coffee afterward. If you'd rather not talk to anyone, arrive five minutes after the listed starting time and take a seat in the back.

At the meeting you needn't do anything but listen. If you're asked to identify yourself, you can give your first name, simply say "I pass," or if even that makes you uncomfortable, make up a name. Do, however, pick up the pamphlets that are displayed for newcomers, including one, if available, that lists all meetings scheduled in your area. It's also a good idea to purchase a copy of the Big Book if you don't already have one. (In paperback it sells practically at cost, for less than $5.) Keep in mind as you look around that you're surrounded by people very much like you. Before it wrecked (or almost wrecked) their lives, they got their kicks drinking or drugging. Now they'll cheerfully assure you (if their recovery is well along its way) that they have even more fun sober.

*If the person who accompanies you is not an alcoholic/addict, be sure to choose an Open Meeting.

GETTING INTO A HOME GROUP

Once you decide you want to be part of AA (that's all you need to do to become a "member"), you will be warmly welcomed at AA meetings, open or closed, anywhere in the world. (Of course not everybody in every group is going to greet you like a long-lost brother or sister. Don't let the occasional grouch or grinch turn you away.) But unless you live in a one-meeting town, you will still want to shop for a group you can call home.

The first group you visit may not be a perfect fit for you—or even the second. Groups have different kinds of memberships—some primarily young, others older; some middle class, others working class; some more religious, some agnostic or humanist; some composed primarily of doctors, or lawyers, or businesspeople, or students, or mothers, or people in the entertainment world. There are men's groups and women's, gay groups, groups for young mothers, and groups with easy access for handicapped people.

The home group you choose will also depend on your drug or drugs of abuse. If you're an alcoholic, the choice is pretty clear: Alcoholics Anonymous. AA may also be the choice if you've abused both alcohol and other drugs. But although some AA groups welcome those with drug problems other than alcohol, others are less re-

FITTING IN UNDER THE RECOVERY UMBRELLA

As anyone who has ever been to an AA meeting knows, individual differences fade next to the power of the one common tie: alcoholism/ addiction. An Hispanic laborer speaks and a white, obviously well-to-do professional responds warmly, "I really identify with what you said." Alcoholics and addicts—whether male or female, young or old, black or white, rich or poor, Native American or Asian, homosexual or heterosexual, fully able or disabled, no matter what their religious background—have much in common. They share a disease, have similar symptoms, require the same basic treatment.

Nevertheless, some people belonging to minority subgroups feel (or fear they will feel) out of place at recovery meetings. They have questions pertaining to their backgrounds, to issues that are raised by who they are or where they are from or related to the common traits and experiences with that subgroup.

In dealing with your addiction, you need to understand not only the issues addressed in this book that apply to you as one of the millions of alcoholics/addicts in this country, but also those that relate to you as a member of a subgroup. The goal: to overcome your addiction without losing what is precious to your culture or identity. Also: to deal forthrightly with issues specific to your group rather than use them as a cop-out for avoiding treatment. Sharing your recovery with others from a similar background will help make this easier.

ceptive, and a few ban drug addicts entirely. Heroin addicts often do well at Narcotics Anonymous meetings, and those addicted to pills at Pills Anonymous. Cocaine Anonymous may seem the natural choice for cocaine addicts, but this isn't always the case. Sometimes they find their craving is set off by hearing others at CA meetings romancing the drug; these individuals often do better at AA, especially since they need to avoid alcohol (a gateway drug for them) as assiduously as cocaine. For some alcoholics/addicts, Overeaters Anonymous (OA) or Smokers Anonymous is more congenial and works even better than the alcohol- or drug-directed programs.

Factors to look for in finding a group that feels like a comfortable home include:

❖ *The type of Twelve-Step program.* Is it AA, or NA, or CA, or Pills Anonymous, or some other group that will most enhance your recovery?

❖ *Location.* If the meetings are too far from where you live, you may not go when you need it most—when you're feeling tired, lazy, resentful, self-pitying, depressed.

❖ *Meeting times.* If they don't coincide with your schedule, you'll miss meetings you should be attending.

❖ *Compatibility.* If you're a young single nonsmoking male, you're going to feel out of place at a group made up mostly of middle-aged women who chain-smoke.

❖ *Comfort level.* Do you feel at home with the people, the meeting formats, the programs?

Though you'll be most closely associated with your home group, you should still continue to go to other meetings, especially if your home group doesn't meet daily and you need a meeting every day. Attending a variety of meetings will broaden your perspective on recovery and will help you grow.

HOW MUCH IS ENOUGH?

The slogan "Ninety meetings in ninety days" works for many people in early recovery. A meeting every day for three months makes sobriety a habit, provides momentum, keeps them on track, reminds them of the universality of their problem and of the things they need to focus on, and supplies daily booster shots of support. But some people can't manage a meeting every day, either because of other life stresses or because they just can't handle so many meetings.* For them, fewer may be better. For others, one a day is too few—they may go to a meeting before work, brown-bag a second at lunch hour, and do a third in the evening.

Less important than the number of meetings you attend is your attitude at the meetings, and how seriously you follow the prescription for recovery set down by your counselor, physician, other professional, or by AA between meetings. You can go to two or three meetings a day and still get drunk. You can go to two or three a week and stay sober.

Ideally, attend as many meetings as you can on a regular schedule. It's not a good idea to adjust the frequency of meetings to the way you feel. The time you don't feel like going to a meeting is probably the time you need one most.

"I called my sponsor and said stuff like, 'I want to go to the grocery store, but I don't know if I can or not. Do you think I'll get drunk if I walk past the beer?' I called about the dumbest things."

WRITING YOUR LIFE HISTORY

You probably haven't written a life history since you were in fourth grade and pasted photos of your mom and dad, your siblings, and yourself as a baby on colored construction paper. When you did it then it was an important learning experience. Doing it now, at the beginning of your recovery, is an even more important learning experience. The Fourth Step in AA is making a searching and fearless moral inventory of oneself; it's even better to go further and do a complete-as-you-can-make-it life history.

Start with the day you were born and go on from there. Don't worry about what you don't remember, but include everything you can recall. The day you first talked back to your mom, when you got your first dog, the first time you saw anyone drink alcohol, the first time you took a drink or a drug. Try to dredge up things you haven't thought about for years.

Include everything you've done that relates to your drinking or drug use—speeding fines, child abuse, auto accidents, embarrassing moments, jobs lost, and so on—as well as how much money you spent on your chemical routes to getting high. Don't freeze up because you're afraid you won't do a professional job. You're not aiming for the Nobel Prize in literature. Style, penmanship, spelling, grammar, and neatness don't count. You don't even have to use complete sentences. Use symbols, shorthand, even stick figures—anything that you can decipher. If you don't know how to start, just begin by using the tips on page

*Be wary, however. Feeling that you're getting too much AA is sometimes a sign that you're not getting enough.

DRESSING FOR RECOVERY SUCCESS

"A recovery dress code? Come on! What difference could it possibly make what I wear to an AA meeting?" A reasonable question. But think about it. The way you dress is part of your lifestyle. If you want to change your lifestyle—which you clearly do—it makes sense to change your wardrobe. Say you're a student, wearing jeans and plaid flannel shirts day in and day out. When you get a job in a law firm, you start wearing suits. Or dresses. If you frequent discos, you dress differently than if you spend your leisure hours at a country club or camping.

Even in rags, you'll be accepted at an AA meeting. It's what's inside that counts. But you will probably make better progress if you dress for recovery success. It will signal to yourself and to others that you're serious about getting well. Examine what you normally wear. Does it reflect your drinking and drugging past? If it does, then you'll continue to attract people who dress as you do, and who drink or drug as you did.

How to dress for recovery success? Cleanliness is a good start: nails clean, hair neatly groomed, clothing fresh. Alcoholics/addicts tend to be considerably less than meticulous about their personal grooming, and you should remedy that now if you haven't already. Next, avoid distractingly provocative clothing. If you're a female, that means wearing a bra, underwear, and socks or stockings, and abandoning micro-miniskirts, clinging clothes, tank tops, see-through sheers, and eye-catching strapless styles. (Catching eyes is not what you're going to AA for. Catching sobriety is.) In the same way, tank tops, tight pants, and shirts open to the navel, along with a gold chain collection worthy of a Tiffany window, may send the wrong message when worn by a man.

Certain items will act as dangerous reminders of your drinking or drugging life: a hat you always wore to parties, boots that were part of your disco uniform, dark glasses you wore day and night to mask bloodshot eyes or dilated pupils, the long-sleeved shirts that concealed the tracks on your arms. Pack such articles up and give them away to charity. (When the sun's bright, you should still wear protective lenses. But get yourself a new starting-life-over pair.)

It isn't practical, of course, to go out and buy a whole new wardrobe, but sift through what you have for clothes that aren't come-ons or overly revealing. Wear loose sweaters over shirts that might look too seductive. Avoid flashy jewelry and extreme hair styles. You don't have to be a fashion plate; just dress neatly, simply, and conservatively. When you find an AA or other support group you like, dress to fit comfortably into that group.

107. If you have a lot of difficulty writing, try speaking your history into a tape recorder. Since this works less well than actually seeing your life in writing in front of you, you might want to then transcribe your spoken words onto paper.

Give yourself plenty of time—at least a week. You can't finish the story of your life in one sitting. (If you think you can, you're not really willing to look deeply enough and need some help dealing with this denial.) Your finished history should fill at least ten pages, but ideally should be much longer. Be so candid that you will want no one else ever to see your recollections. (No one will, unless you want them to.) To be sure no one sees your work accidentally while it's in progress, and so you won't be inhibited in your writing by the fear that someone will, keep it in a totally safe place (maybe on your person). If you don't carry it around with you, do carry a small notebook so that you can jot down thoughts as they occur.

When you finish, try to analyze your story as you would someone else's. Look for insights into what brought you to where you are today. Try to track the development of your disease from your first exposure. It's also a good idea to share your history with somebody—your sponsor; a minister, priest, or rabbi; the physician or therapist who has been treating you; or some other person who can view it objectively. *Don't* show it to your parents, your spouse, your children, or anyone else who is emotionally involved in your illness. You can be sure that your sponsor and any professional you are working with will not be surprised by or judgmental about anything you've written. They've seen it all before, and probably worse. After reviewing your life history, go through the ritual of burning it. Think of it as symbolically incinerating the garbage of your past life.

If you can't seem to write your life history at all, it may be a sign that your recovery is in trouble and that you need professional help. If there are some events in your life that you haven't been able to put on paper, this could also indicate the need for help. But that's okay. Some things (incest, abuse, violence) are just too difficult and dangerous to deal with without professional support.

Tips for Writing Your Life History

When you write your life history, answer these questions, always being sure to describe your feelings as well as the facts:

❖ When and where were you born?

❖ Who are/were your parents? Where were they from and what do/did they do to earn a living? What are/were they like as people? How did they influence your life?

❖ Do you have any siblings? When was each of them born? What did you think of each one as a child? As an adult?

❖ What was it like growing up? Do you remember your childhood as happy or unhappy? Why? Give specific recollections: About how you felt you were treated by others. About how family members communicated with one another. About family relationships. Friends. Important people in your life.

❖ How did you feel about school? Were there any teachers who had a particularly strong influence on you?

❖ Did you have any pets? If so, what part did they play in your life?

❖ Were you ever abused as a child—emotionally, physically, sexually? (If the answer is yes, see page 21.)

❖ How many years of school did you complete? Did you go as far as you would have liked? Did you get out of it all you wanted?

❖ What do you remember about the first time you noticed alcohol being used in your home? Outside of it? How did you feel about this? What did you think when you first saw a drunk? What can you recall about your parents' drinking habits or their use of drugs? Did siblings use drugs while you were growing up? How did alcohol or drugs affect your life when you were growing up?

❖ How and when did you have your first drink? Use your first illicit drug? How did you feel about these experiences?

❖ When did your drinking or drug use first get you in trouble?

❖ Do you remember any other examples of problems caused by your sub-

PRACTICE MAKES PERFECT

While you're thinking about getting rid of your faults and flaws, you should also be concentrating on developing positive traits. And the way to make them a part of you is to practice them. Smile at the check-out clerk at the supermarket; say "Good morning" to the bus driver or the car-park attendant; try not to explode when one of your children drags mud in on the newly cleaned carpet; greet your late-arriving spouse with a joke rather than a nasty epithet. The more you try to be pleasant, the more you think positively rather than negatively, the more you turn to humor instead of anger, the more natural such behavior will become. If you continue to act like a really nice person, before you know it you will be one.

stance abuse? DUI's? Fights? Absenteeism? Problems at school or work? Missed appointments? Accidents? Spouse or child abuse? Parental abuse? Stealing? Lying?

❖ Did your drinking or drug use ever hurt others? Anyone you care about?

❖ Have you ever done something you were ashamed of while under the influence?

❖ How did your drinking or drug use affect your love life, relationships, marriage, family?

❖ What about your social life? With whom did you usually spend your time? Where did you spend most of your time? Who was the most important constructive influence in your life? The most destructive?

❖ What kind of work do you do? Do you enjoy it? How was it affected by your substance abuse?

❖ Have you ever tried to or actually become clean and sober and then relapsed? Describe the experience and what you think triggered the relapse. Describe your previous treatment experiences, if any.

When you think you're finished, go over what you've written and be sure no major events and no time spans have been left out. Also be sure you've described your feelings in each case. If there are any glaring gaps, this could indicate a problem area that needs a closer look.

YOUR DAILY INVENTORY

Burning your life history doesn't mean you stop looking at yourself and your life. Step Ten in AA says that you should continue to take a personal inventory daily. This kind of honest tally of events and feelings allows you to analyze your actions after the emotions of the moment have subside, but before they've slipped away entirely.

You can do a daily inventory during a meditation period or in a conversation with your sponsor, or it can be jotted down in a journal. The last is ideal for high-risk people, those who've had a relapse, those who have trouble being honest with themselves (it's harder to fib on paper), or those who want to be very thorough. A written journal also has the advantage of allowing you to review your progress since yesterday, last week, last year, and the advantage of letting you see where you came from and where you are now.

"I woke my sponsor in the middle of the night. I was having a compulsion to drink real, real bad. She said to take a hot bath and some lemonade. So I did that, and sat there and thought this is pretty weird. She called me the next day, and she said, 'Did I tell you to get in the tub and drink lemonade?' I said, 'Yes.' She said, 'I'm sorry. I wasn't really awake when you phoned.' But you know, it worked."

If you decide on a journal, buy an inexpensive notebook, tie a pen to its spiral binding, and keep the book next to your bed, near the kitchen table, or anywhere else you will be able to spend some time with it daily. At the end of each day, jot down the date, then enter your activities, people you've seen, things you've accomplished, meetings you've attended: "I was on the phone all morning.... Had lunch with Jamie.... The afternoon meeting with Mr. Davidson went well." Be specific about things that may have some importance: "This morning, I got up late and was late for work." Try to jot down feelings as well as activities: "I handed in my report two days early, and I was really angry at my boss for not even saying 'Thank you.'" Record good feelings as well as bad ones: "I was scared to death before I gave my first talk at AA, but afterward I was on cloud nine."

The next morning, during your meditation period or whenever the dust of the previous day has settled, look over your entry and see if anything in it tells you how you are doing. Look for patterns over the previous days or weeks, and for changes from last month or the month before. Look for the character defects you listed in your inventory, and for signs that you're still in their grip. Your diary can tell you that your recovery is doing well, or that your attitudes need some correcting.

It may also be helpful to go over your journal periodically with another person—your sponsor, counselor, physician—to see if they pick up something that you've missed. It's possible to lie to yourself, even on paper.

Tips for Taking a Daily Inventory

Ask yourself the following questions as you look back on each day:

❖ Did I have a plan for the day, and did I follow it?

❖ With whom did I spend most of my time?

❖ Where did I spend most of my time?

❖ What was the quality of the judgments I made today?

❖ Did anything threaten my sobriety today? What?

❖ What specific work did I do on my AA program (attending meetings, doing meditations, reading AA material or listening to it on audio tapes, etc.)?

❖ Did I feel my attitude toward recovery was constructive today?

❖ Was I honest in all my dealings?

❖ Have I been fair in all my interaction with others? Were there situations today where I was wrong or unreasonable? Did I make amends?

❖ What good things happened? How did I react to them?

❖ Did any bad things happen? What were they? How did I react?

❖ What do I feel I have accomplished this day? What would I have liked to have done that I didn't do? What would I have done differently?

MINI-GUIDE

The Twelve Steps*

STEP ONE: *We admitted we were powerless over alcohol—that our lives had become unmanageable.*

STEP TWO: *Came to believe that a Power greater than ourselves could restore us to sanity.*

STEP THREE: *Made a decision to turn our will and lives over to the care of God* as we understood him.

STEP FOUR: *Made a searching and fearless moral inventory of ourselves.*

STEP FIVE: *Admitted to God, to ourselves, and to another human being the exact nature of our wrongs.*

STEP SIX: *Were entirely ready to have God remove all these defects of character.*

STEP SEVEN: *Humbly asked Him to remove our shortcomings.*

STEP EIGHT: *Made a list of all persons we had harmed, and became willing to make amends to them all.*

STEP NINE: *Made direct amends to such people wherever possible, except when to do so would injure them or others.*

STEP TEN: *Continued to take personal inventory and when we were wrong promptly admitted it.*

STEP ELEVEN: *Sought through prayer and meditation to improve our conscious contact with God* as we understood him, *praying only for knowledge of His will for us and the power to carry that out.*

STEP TWELVE: *Having had a spiritual awakening as the result of these steps, we tried to carry this message to alcoholics, and to practice these principles in all our affairs.*

...And How They Can Help You

Newcomers often observe that AA members seem to put the Twelve Steps right up there with the Ten Commandments. What gives the Steps the power they seem to have? The answer is simple. Like the Ten Commandments, they work. That's the best recommendation any set of rules can have.

The Twelve Steps date back to the early days of what later became known as Alcoholics Anonymous.

In searching for ways to deal with their compulsion to drink, the founding members realized that shifting their obsession to drink to an obsession to tell others about their passion for alcohol—and its consequences in their lives—relieved them of the need to drink again. Sharing, they found, was truly "the fuel of sobriety." The stresses of day-to-day living depleted this fuel rapidly and AA members quickly learned that continued sharing of experience, strength, and hope was needed to ward off the need to drink.

They knew that what they were

*Reprinted with permission of Alcoholics Anonymous World Services, Inc. See copyright page for full credit line.

doing was working. But how could they pass it on to others? They couldn't say, "Hey, just watch us. Do what we do." So they dissected the process of their recovery and codified it into Twelve Steps. At first some believed they ought to impose these Steps as "commandments" for AA newcomers to follow. But wiser heads prevailed, and instead of being a list of "thou shalts," the Twelve Steps were written down as a simple history of how these recovery pioneers succeeded at remaining sober: "*We* admitted *we* were powerless over alcohol . . ." and so on. The Steps became a "suggested" part of the recovery program for each arrival into the fellowship. Most AA old-timers, as well as experts in the recovery field, agree that side-stepping them is a sure routc to disaster.

When you first go to AA you will hear about the Steps, see literature on them, possibly see them posted. Your sponsor (see page 114) will talk to you about them. But nobody will "push" them. These explanations of the Twelve Steps are a blend of some common views of these valuable recovery tools. But they arcn't the only way to view them. Each individual interprets and uses the Twelve Steps in the way that is most helpful personally. Study them. Think about them. Make them your own. But most important of all, follow them. They have worked for millions of others. They can work for you.

STEP ONE: It's no fun to admit to being powerless. The more you see your world unraveling around you, the more unmanageable your life becomes, the more frightening is the prospect of surrendering what little control you have left. But, as those early AA members learned, the urge to control is just another obsession, and this loudly proclaimed dominance over drinking behavior ("Hey, I can handle it!") inevitably succumbs to the biological drive to drink. They found that admitting they couldn't control their drinking allowed them to go on to address the problem in a way they couldn't when they were still wrestling for control. And, as a dividend, it enabled them to develop humility—which not only aided the recovery process but made them better human beings.

STEP TWO: If you take the first step and accept that you can't control your drinking, what next? You can either give up entirely or you can make the leap of faith that says there is hope, that you need not continue living with the insanity that is alcoholism (or addiction). You're hoping, praying (or just plain betting), there is some power out there—it may be God, or your AA group, a counselor or sponsor, or just some unnamed entity—that can help restore you to sanity.

STEP THREE: Admitting you can't control your addiction and believing there is help somewhere are not enough. You have to follow this up with a decision to take action, to actually relinquish control to some Higher Power (see page 130 for more on how different people view this concept). Turning the reins over won't be easy. You'll find yourself chafing at the bit every time you want to take one road and your Higher Power directs you down another. Learn to relax and let things happen. You'll find you'll get to where you really want to go in the end. The first three steps are sometimes paraphrased: "I can't. He can. Let Him."

(continued on next page)

MINI-GUIDE

The Twelve Steps, *continued*

STEP FOUR: Another action step. Honesty is the major distinction between those who recover and those who don't. Step Four calls for an honest and thorough appraisal of your life. The alcoholic's investment in dishonesty makes this step toward sobriety painful, but to avoid it sweeps garbage under the carpet that is likely to smell later. Ideally, this inventory should be written as a life history (see page 105 for how to go about this process). If you're as searching as you are fearless, you will be rewarded with knowledge of the good things you have done as well as the bad, your character strengths as well as your defects. Many behavior patterns, both healthy and destructive, will become evident. External influences that had not previously been observed will also become apparent.

This is a step many people find themselves returning to over and over again, as their lives change or they find themselves in difficulty. A self-reexamination at times of crisis can be a guide to the best ways to maximize your talents and minimize your weaknesses.

STEP FIVE: Early AA groups learned and psychotherapists now know that talking about the problems in our lives gives us insight into our lives and problems and makes us feel better. Talking the crippling past "off our chests" gets us out of its control and helps us move into the future with a clear mind and a clean slate. So share your story with your Higher Power and an objective person, such as your sponsor.

STEP SIX: You've seen your flaws and faults. Now you have to be willing to relinquish them. For the nonalcoholic, this may seem obvious and simple; but it's difficult when emotions, personality traits, preferences, and values have evolved over a lifetime (even generations) to justify the urge to drink. But you must be willing if you're going to be ready for the next step, and for a life that doesn't need alcohol or drugs.

STEP SEVEN: Now that you're willing, you can make it happen. Through prayer, meditation, shouting into a canyon or from the top of a building, walking in the park or hiking in the woods, or however you best relate to that force greater than yourself. How do you know if it's working, if those defects are peeling away? You'll get feedback assuring you that those negative traits are loosening their hold and that you are coming closer to being the person you want to be through your experiences with others (at home, work, meetings, during casual interactions and more formal counseling), through comparing yourself with life histories and other examples in AA literature, and through keeping and regularly evaluating a journal (see page 108). You won't see results immediately, but consistent improvement over time should be encouraging, especially if you reflect on what you've done so far.

STEP EIGHT: If Step Four is fresh in your mind, it will be easy to draw up the list. If not, another inventory may be in order first. Be thorough; try not to let any name slip by. Resist the temptation to justify your conduct, and don't worry about how you will make amends. Just get every name down, and be willing to make up for your past actions.

This is another step you may return to again and again. As your self-centeredness diminishes and your perspective broadens, new names will pop up that you had forgotten about previously.

STEP NINE: Now comes making those amends, correcting the wreckage of the past without regard to what it does to you. And there are probably as many ways of going about this as there are people you've hurt. For help on how to go about making amends constructively, see page 372. Guidance from other AA members and your sponsor will be essential. Adherence to this step molds the alcoholic into a tool for good, just as addiction molded him or her into a tool for destruction.

STEP TEN: Steps Four and Five revisited! Thoroughness prior to Step Ten pays off here. Hard work there clears the slate so day-to-day life can be analyzed and improved upon. A regular schedule and honest review (through daily meditation, talks with a sponsor or counselor, or keeping a journal; see page 108) helps keep character defects from sneaking back into thoughts and behavior. We will all make mistakes, and negative traits will always exist, but if you follow Step Ten faithfully, these traits won't sneak up on you. You will know about and be able to deal with them. Keeping a journal will also help you to see how much progress you've made, week to week, month to month, year to year.

STEP ELEVEN: In Step Three you turned your life over to your Higher Power. It might be easy to assume that now you can just take back the reins and head off on your own. But the alcoholic (or addict) within you is waiting patiently to reappear. The honesty, insight, and selflessness of your recovery have starved the alcoholic and nourished the real you, but the illness is part of you and will always be there. Alcoholism's destructive power can work only if you allow it to have control over your life, so delegating your life direction to a Higher Power of your choosing holds the addictive forces at bay.

STEP TWELVE: This Step takes you full circle, meaningfully consolidating the work of the previous Steps. Spreading the word will not only help others deal with their addictions but will help you to keep your recovery strong. Just how you will "carry the message" will depend on your own strengths and inclinations. You may want to work directly with other alcoholics (or addicts), become active in the AA fellowship, volunteer to speak at schools, or try to influence public opinion and press for needed legislation. For ways of helping others, see Chapter 30.

SUMMARY. If a year or two down the road you feel that you have worked hard on these Steps yet find you still don't have a fulfilling life, it will probably be because you have left out some important element. To avoid this, be sure you don't allow your denial (page 15) to hoodwink you into skipping one or more Steps or attending to them halfheartedly. Don't allow shame or guilt (page 150) to freeze your feelings and make you unable to look at yourself as the Steps require. And be sure you don't try so desperately to overcompensate for past wrongs (you now want to be the best employee, best spouse, best parent, best child in the world) that you leave yourself no time to work on your recovery.

ALL ABOUT SPONSORS

Who Needs a Sponsor?

The answer, simply, is every recovering alcoholic/addict. For the shaky newcomer to AA, a sponsor is a reassuring lifeline to sobriety. For those who have gone through treatment, a sponsor is an introduction to AA and a mirror in which to try out their new reflection in the real world. And for those with many years of sobriety, a sponsor is a friend who knows them better than anyone else in the world, who is both a sounding board and a security blanket, in good times and bad.

Nevertheless, the idea that you, a mature person, need to lean on a stranger may make you very uncomfortable—especially when you learn you will probably be referred to as a "sponsee" or "pigeon."* In our society, where independence is so valued (probably misguidedly so), leaning on another person is considered a weakness. But for the alcoholic, it can prove to be a strength.

The alcoholic/addict has been likened to two personalities wrestling for control within one body. In early recovery there's a struggle to keep your addicted half from subduing your still fragile better half and regaining the upper hand. When you relinquish major decisions to your sponsor—someone with your well-being and recovery in mind, who knows you and your disease well—you deny power to the addict inside you. Starved for control, the addict struggles at first, then hibernates, waiting for the next opportunity to stage a coup.

Millions before you have found that leaning on a wise sponsor can help overcome this self-destructive aspect of the disease and can be your key to a successful recovery. Working with a sponsor now will allow you one day, in the not so distant future, to take another important step on the road to recovery: sponsoring someone who, just as you are now, is beginning a recovery.

Choosing a sponsor

Selecting a sponsor is a significant step in the recovery process. It's your sponsor you will turn to when a crisis—big or small—arises. Because the sponsor is well along in his or her own recovery process, and gets to know your situation but is not emotionally involved in your life, the opinions and advice he or she offers are often more valuable than what your own not-yet-entirely-reliable emotions will tell you.

Like selecting a spouse, selecting a sponsor is very personal. The sponsor

"I picked somebody who had what I wanted, who lived the kind of life, had the kind of program I wanted. Somebody who would not tell me what I wanted to hear, but what I needed to hear ('You're real sick; you're selfish; you have a big ego . . .'). I needed somebody to be hard on me, but who could also love me when I was down on myself."

*Sponsee is to sponsor as employee is to employer. AA archivists believe that Ben Franklin may have been the first to use the word "pigeon" to refer to a drunk, but distinguished journalist and saloon habitué H. L. Mencken apparently popularized that usage by describing heavy drinkers as "pigeon-eyed." Devoted Mencken reader and AA founder Dr. Bill Wilson, adapting the word fondly, used to tell fellow AA members, "There's a new pigeon coming to tonight's meeting." Hence: sponsor/pigeon.

THE TWELVE TRADITIONS OF ALCOHOLICS ANONYMOUS

1. Our common welfare should come first; personal recovery depends upon AA unity.

2. For our group purpose there is but one ultimate authority—a loving God as He may express Himself in our group conscience. Our leaders are but trusted servants; they do not govern.

3. The only requirement for AA membership is a desire to stop drinking.

4. Each group should be autonomous except in matters affecting other groups or AA as a whole.

5. Each group has but one primary purpose—to carry its message to the alcoholic who still suffers.

6. An AA group ought never endorse, finance, or lend the AA name to any related facility or outside enterprise, lest problems of money, property, and prestige divert us from our primary purpose.

7. Every AA group ought to be fully self-supporting, declining outside contributions.

8. Alcoholics Anonymous should remain forever nonprofessional, but our service centers may employ special workers.

9. AA, as such, ought never be organized; but we may create service boards or committees directly responsible to those they serve.

10. Alcoholics Anonymous has no opinion on outside issues; hence the AA name ought never be drawn into public controversy.

11. Our public relations policy is based on attraction rather than promotion; we need always maintain personal anonymity at the level of press, radio and films.

12. Anonymity is the spiritual foundation of all our Traditions, ever reminding us to place principles before personalities.

who is right for you might be all wrong for someone else. Still, good sponsors have certain qualities in common:

❖ *Same gender as the sponsee.* Crossing gender lines for your sponsor is not a good idea. If you are gay or a lesbian, see page 119.

❖ *Long sobriety.* If you select someone who is not much further along in sobriety than you, the relationship could be a disaster for you both. It's generally best if a sponsor has at least three or four years of sobriety, although some people turn out to be good at the job after just two years of solid recovery.

❖ *Quality sobriety.* You can judge this from talking to and listening to prospective sponsors at meetings. Look for someone who seems happy with sobriety and life in general and who is respected by the group, as a speaker and as a sponsor. While a good personality is a plus, more important is solid sobriety and a strong foundation in AA and the AA program.

❖ *Broad AA interests.* The sponsor who is active in AA outside of your home group—locally, regionally, or nationally—can introduce you to a broader AA program, including interesting meetings at other groups, inspirational regional and national conventions, relaxing and renewing weekend retreats, and so on.

❖ *A record of successes.* Generally you want someone who has already had success in helping other sponsees. But of course, for every sponsor there's a first time.

❖ *Congeniality.* A sponsor should be easy to talk and listen to—someone you immediately feel comfortable with and have confidence in. This is a subjective judgment only you can make.

❖ *Trustworthiness.* You won't want to share your deepest and most intimate feelings and problems with someone you don't trust completely.

❖ *Objectivity.* Your sponsor should not be someone who is emotionally involved in your life, except as it relates to your recovery. A spouse, a live-in lover, a friend, might seem appealing but in no way would be an appropriate sponsor.

❖ *Availability.* Your sponsor should live within a short distance of your home so that one-on-one meetings are easy to arrange. But you can choose a supplementary sponsor (one who can serve as support in areas in which your local sponsor lacks the necessary background or expertise) who lives at a distance.

❖ *Toughness.* You don't want a sponsor who is a yes-man (or yes-woman), but rather one who tells it like it is, even if (or especially if) you don't want to hear it that way. Look for a person who you think will be willing to confront you if are headed for another fix or another drink—someone who won't wait until it happens.

❖ *Compassion.* While it's important to have a tough sponsor who can point out mistakes and weaknesses, it is also important, especially if your sense of self is poor, to have one who will point out your good points and help you build up your feelings of self-worth.

❖ *Compatible lifestyle and family.* If you have a couple of kids, a sponsor with a family may be perfect, allowing you to share many activities. If you're young and single, a sponsor who is a peer will be more likely to understand what you're thinking and feeling and will be able to participate in nonmeeting social activities with you. (Of course, if you're attracted to someone "older and wiser," that's okay too.) Some people find that sponsors who are in the same field of work, come from the same part of the country, share a similar lifestyle and ethnic and religious background, are the most compatible since they can understand specific problems. For others, someone with an entirely different background may work better, since they can singlemindedly focus on the only thing they have in common: their addiction. They can also avoid the intellectual jousting or professional competitiveness that can come with sharing other interests.

"My sponsor is Louie. I needed somebody tough and thorough, who would see right through me. I'm a conner. And he's not going to give me any breaks."

Having Multiple Sponsors

For quality recovery, everyone needs at least one sponsor. But some people need more than one. Consider multiple sponsors if:

❖ You have multiple problems that are more than one sponsor can handle. For example, you've used both drugs and alcohol, have a couple of children, and are divorced. You may not find a sponsor who is comfortable dealing with all of these issues. In such a case, co-sponsors work well.

❖ You have specific needs that require expertise—you're a recovering lawyer or doctor, for example, who needs advice on when and how to regain a suspended professional license.

❖ You are a young person who would like to have a sponsor close to your own age but would also benefit from an older, more experienced advisor.

❖ Your chief sponsor travels a lot or has a demanding schedule that limits his or her availability. In this case, you might want someone who is around all the time and will be available to provide extra help when you need it.

"I needed a loving sponsor. I have a big ego, but I was so hard on myself that it was holding back my recovery. C. D. was my sponsor in the lodge. We would meet for breakfast and he figured me out the very first morning. 'Let's keep talking every day,' he said, 'and I'll tell you when you need to beat up on yourself.' It must be working. I'm beginning to like myself now."

❖ Someone you admire is too busy to take you on but is willing to be "on call" once in a while when you feel you need extra help or guidance. This person can serve as a second sponsor as needed.

Even if one sponsor is enough, you should have another friend—or preferably several—in AA with whom you build a strong relationship. Call them occasionally. Have a meal with them. Go to a meeting with them. That way, if your sponsor should be ill, out of town, or otherwise unable to help, you have somewhere to turn. You should, in fact, have at least half a dozen (make that a dozen) office and home numbers of AA friends with you at all times, just in case you urgently need to talk to someone but hit a wall of no-answers, answering machines, or busy signals.

Rejection by a Sponsor

Sometimes an eager newcomer, after careful deliberation, asks a respected and admired AA member to serve as sponsor and is turned down. If that happens to you, don't take it as a personal rejection. It's likely that either the potential sponsor is so well thought of that he or she already has as many sponsees as can comfortably be handled, or has decided, probably wisely, that the two of you are not an appropriate match. In either case, the rejection is really for the best. Look elsewhere for your sponsor, but do keep in mind that you can call upon many people in the group for advice and encouragement—including this unavailable first choice. Of course, if the response you get feels like a brusque or disinterested rejection, consider yourself lucky. You don't want a sponsor who makes you feel ill at ease. In most cases, the person who turns you down will suggest a couple of other potential sponsors.

One caution: Sometimes newcomers are so afraid of rejection that they hesitate to approach anyone. Fear not. Being a sponsor, as part of working the Twelfth Step, is a piece of everyone's recovery. You'll be helping your sponsor while your sponsor helps you.

"Using" Your Sponsor

Choosing a sponsor is important, but how you use this person in your recovery will be even more important. Don't just leave contacts to chance. In addition to seeing each other at AA meetings, have a regular time to speak to your sponsor daily—at least until you've been clean and sober for four months. Confer wherever and whenever it's most convenient—at a coffee shop breakfast, on the commuter train en route to work, in the car on the way to a meeting, on the telephone just before lunch or at the end of the day.

Call, too, when you have a particular problem or a decision to make. If you have automatic dialing, program your phone so that you can push just one number to get your sponsor in an emergency. You can talk to your sponsor as you talk to no one else, because a sponsor's only interest in your life is your sobriety. For example, you may have trouble telling your wife, who's worried about money and has a stake in what you do, that you're afraid to ask for a raise. You fear she will call you yellow and tell you to "be a man."* A sponsor, on the other hand, will probably respond sympathetically ("I've felt the same way. It's normal") and offer some constructive advice about how to boost your courage without turning to the bottle. Or you may find yourself attracted to another man, and you know you can't discuss these still undeveloped feelings with your live-in boyfriend. Your sponsor will hear you out without judging you, and will suggest safe ways of dealing with what might potentially be a fatal attraction.

When you do your Fourth Step moral inventory or your life history (if you haven't already done it in treatment) and want to share it, it's your sponsor you should show it to and discuss it with.

Your sponsor may occasionally make a suggestion that you don't think makes sense. You needn't just swallow it blindly. Be honest, and raise your questions or objections. Your sponsor will then be able to explain the reason for the suggestion, giving you further information on which to base a final decision, which is yours alone. Sometimes it may help to talk to a cosponsor or other respected AA friends to get additional input. Before you resolve the issue, however, consider that your judgment may be flawed. Your sponsor, with a clearer mind and more experience in sobriety, is more likely to be right than you are. But remember, too, that nobody's perfect. Not even a sponsor.

"The first time I called my sponsor in the middle of the night, he came right on over to my house and sat with me and we talked and talked. The next time, he said, 'Now pick up your Big Book and look at pages so-and-so, and you will get your answer.' Well, I did. And I got through the night. Alone. That was the best gift my sponsor could give me."

It's critically important for your sponsor to be able to recognize behavior that can lead you into temptation, so tell him or her just which situations have been triggers for you in the past (going out of town, feeling depressed, seeing old friends). Keep your sponsor posted on what's happening in your life (troubling physical symptoms; new relationships; job concerns; difficulties with your marriage, children, parents). And don't make any decisions that could affect your recovery (from taking a cold tablet to changing your job) without consulting your sponsor. If you're experiencing cravings, aren't working your program, or sense that you are headed for a slip, call your sponsor immediately. If you are scheduled to undergo a dental or medical procedure requiring medications, ask your sponsor to accompany you.

*Later, your spouse may become your confidante. But early in recovery, when so much dirty water has already flowed under the bridge, you're not likely to feel comfortable confiding. You may be afraid of betraying yourself, fearful of erecting new barriers before you're able to demolish the old.

In the end, your sponsor will be only as good as your willingness to take full advantage of the relationship.

Imposing on Your Sponsor

The addict who smokes pot at 2 A.M. because she is embarrassed to call her sponsor in the middle of the night to deal with her "puny problem"—a compulsion to use—may believe she is acting with both humility and consideration. Actually, she is being arrogant and thoughtless. Arrogant to assume she can handle the problem on her own. And thoughtless to assume that her sponsor valued her own sleep more than her sponsee's recovery.

Your sponsor has been through it all, has probably awakened her sponsor many a night herself. She wants you to call when you're in need—helping you helps her. So don't hesitate to contact your sponsor if you need to talk, particularly if you have a compulsion to drink or use. If your sponsor doesn't seem to appreciate such calls, then switch sponsors (see below). And

SPONSORS FOR GAYS AND LESBIANS

If you're gay or lesbian, should your sponsor be the same sex as you or the opposite, homosexual or heterosexual? There are differing points of view on this and all have some validity. You can evaluate the various positions and make your own decision, with the help of the professional, if any, you are working with. The obvious options:

❖ A heterosexual of the same sex to whom you feel no physical attraction. Such a sponsor would have the advantage of keeping your priorities where they belong: on your recovery rather than on relationships. The fact that you are homosexual should not be a major issue in early recovery, except as it relates to your substance abuse. Still it is important that the person you choose be someone who accepts your sexual orientation and who does not appear to be uncomfortable with it. Of course, neither of you may be aware of any deep-seated prejudices at first. If they do surface, you should switch. Just don't use prejudices—yours or anyone else's—as an excuse to squirm out of your recovery responsibilities.

❖ A homosexual of the opposite sex. Such a sponsor would offer empathy without physical attraction or sexual game playing. This could work well as long as the focus of early recovery remains where it should be, on getting better.

❖ A sponsor team made up of a heterosexual to deal with recovery issues and a homosexual to deal with issues related to your sexual orientation.

❖ A same-sex homosexual. Such a sponsor will, in most cases, be most able to understand your feelings and your needs. But choosing a same-sex homosexual sponsor could open the same Pandora's box the heterosexual unlocks when choosing an opposite-sex sponsor: Sexual game playing and manipulation may hamper the growth of an honest relationship. Be alert to such goings-on. If they occur and neither of you seems to be able to prevent them (through honest discussion and hard work), then you should probably switch sponsors.

In the end, your sponsor's sexual preference is far less important than whether the two of you have a true sponsor-sponsee relationship. You will have to be honest with yourself about this one.

when your turn comes to play sponsor, be sure you have a phone at your bedside; you're certain to be getting some middle-of-the-night calls.

Switching Sponsors

Most of us spend a lot of time choosing our spouses, yet some of us find out later that we've made the wrong choice. It's the same with sponsors. If you find as you work with your sponsor that the relationship isn't right for you, don't be embarrassed to switch—but not until you've given the decision some thoughtful consideration. Don't announce a switch when you're angry, or on the basis of unsubtantiated rumors. (If your sponsor slips, you will have to make a change, at least temporarily.)

There are several ways to go about switching sponsors. Possible steps to take include:

❖ Call some old-timers in your group and ask them how they'd go about making a switch.

❖ Pick someone to be a co-sponsor and call upon that person more often. That way you won't have to fire your first sponsor, but you can get the support you need. If you feel it's necessary, you can gradually switch over entirely.

❖ Explain to your sponsor that you seem to have outgrown each other, and you feel it's time for a change. Or you feel that at this stage of recovery someone else can help you more. This kind of honesty should come more easily as you progress in your recovery.

Just don't let the situation fester. If you don't either make the break or work things out one-on-one, you may hurt yourself. You may even find yourself ducking meetings just to duck your sponsor.

When a Sponsor Slips

Relapse isn't as certain as death and taxes, but it does happen—sometimes even to those with a solid period of quality sobriety. Still, it can bring on a cold sweat when the person who slips is your sponsor. Your first thought: "It can happen to me." And that's true. It can happen to anyone—anyone who isn't living the AA principles of recovery 100 percent. And though it may not have seemed that way, that had to be true for your sponsor.

To protect your own sobriety when your sponsor slips, immediately hook up with a temporary substitute. It will be a while at least until your previous sponsor will be able to help you—he or she has to focus on self-help for now. And the worst thing you can do is drift like a boat whose anchor line has parted. A co-sponsor or someone else in AA you've turned to for support before would make a perfect fill-in.

You may be tempted to try to help your sponsor as he or she's helped you. But without guidance from someone who has been around AA a lot longer, this could be very risky. If you fail, you could even end up going out and getting despondently drunk yourself. But don't completely stifle that instinct to help. Pay a supportive visit, but make it with someone else with long-term sobriety, possibly your fill-in sponsor. Do a lot of listening, and have a good long talk with your new sponsor soon after, to try to understand how and where your mentor went wrong. Every relapse is a lesson, and the more who learn from it the better.

Incidentally, if you notice that you have developed a pattern of picking sponsors with questionable sobriety, look at yourself as well as at them. Are you still being attracted to the wrong people?

7

AA: The Facts and Your Feelings

Many people suffer from *AA-phobia*, dreading the idea of affiliating with Alcoholics Anonymous or any other Twelve-Step support group. Their reasons are many and varied: Attendance admits something they've been denying for years. They fear the stigma of being labeled an "alcoholic." They are put off by AA's "spirituality," "sharing," and what they see as a kind of public confession. They may worry, too, about bumping into someone they know at a meeting. Or being bored or feeling out of place.

Whatever the reasons, not going to AA because of fears or discomfort is about as sensible as a person with pneumonia refusing to go to the doctor for a penicillin shot because he is afraid of the hypodermic needle, or uncomfortable about having to expose his bottom. You need AA the way a sick person needs an antibiotic. Knowing what AA is like in advance (read the previous chapter as well as this one) will allay your worries and make taking this very necessary medicine much easier.

WHAT'S ON YOUR MIND?

SENSORY OVERLOAD

"I went to my first AA meeting and I was overwhelmed. All that talk about Steps and Traditions and sponsors and stuff. My head is still spinning."

The spinning will stop, if you give it a chance. In the meantime, don't let the fact that you can't seem to think straight and have a lot to learn about AA keep you from going to meetings.

Reading Chapters Six and Seven in this book—especially the "boiled down" principles on page 124—will give you a crash course in AA. But if your mind is as foggy as most people's in early recovery, you may have to reread the material several times before it begins to sink in. If you're hearing a lot of terms you don't understand,

Guide Lines

❖ Few people feel calm and serene when crossing the threshold into their first AA meeting. Most are pleasantly surprised to find themselves very much at home.

❖ Though "sharing" of thoughts and feelings is an integral part of AA, no one is ever pressured to speak up at a meeting. Personal secrets need never be divulged. Everything said is held confidential.

❖ Initially, AA seems to take away one's freedom and independence; in the end, members have more freedom than ever before.

❖ The term "Higher Power" is interpreted in different ways by different members of AA; not all interpretations relate to religion.

check the glossary starting on page 574. But don't worry if it all seems to elude you for a while.

Right now, there are just two things that you have to focus on: One, staying clean and sober, one day at a time. And two, going to a meeting every day.

The rest will come with time.

NO AA MEETING NEARBY

"I stopped drinking two weeks ago. I'm climbing the walls. My brother who lives in Denver says I need to go to AA every day for ninety days. But I'm a rancher and there isn't a town—much less a meeting—in easy driving distance."

Your brother is right about your needing AA, but it's obviously not particularly practical for you to spend the next ninety days in your car. Still, you do need help. And you can get it if you're creative. Here are some possible options. Decide which combination of them will work best for you—then go for it.

❖ Get a course of inpatient treatment. At a good rehab program you will get the tools necessary for rebuilding your life sober. You will also establish contacts who can help you when the going gets tough.

❖ Take some time off—two or three months if that's possible—and move in with your brother or get a sublet in the city. Get in at least a meeting a day during the visit; hook up with a temporary sponsor and utilize him to the fullest. Getting some outpatient counseling during this time may also be beneficial.

❖ Work out a way of getting to an AA meeting at least once a week—even if it means a couple of hours driving each way. Listening to AA tapes going and coming or making the trip with another local recoveree will make the time go faster. It will also get you in the mood for the meeting en route and maintain the meeting high all the way home.

❖ Select a sponsor and have daily contact with him, by telephone if necessary. If you can find one who lives fairly close to you, so much the better, since that would allow for more frequent face-to-face meetings.

❖ Try to find some other folks who are recovering in your area and see if you can set up your own local AA group. All it takes is two interested

"My daily routine hasn't changed since I came out of treatment. First thing in the morning, I ask God to keep me sober and help me with my shortcomings. Then I read One Day at a Time *and* 24 Hours a Day. *This puts focus in my life, in my day. I do my worldly things. Then in the evening there's the meeting. I don't run around like I used to. About 10 P.M. I zone out in front of the TV. Then I get ready to go to bed about 11. I'm in touch with things. I can meditate for about ten minutes and pray."*

people and a coffee pot. You could then combine local meetings with long-distance ones.

❖ On days when you can't get to a meeting, devote at least an hour to recovery tapes and written AA material (see page 568). If you can get your hands on taped AA speaker meetings, listen to one. If you can't, it's possible that the AA group in the nearest town would be willing to tape an occasional meeting for you.

If all else fails, you may have to spend the next ninety days in your car. But that sure beats spending them under the table.

"The town I live in doesn't have any public transportation and I don't know how I'm going to get to AA meetings without a car."

Did you manage to get to places to drink or take drugs before you got sober? You can also find a way to get to AA meetings—people who are serious about staying clean and sober do. Hitch rides with other AA members, for example, or get a bike or consider walking. You can probably use the exercise. Plan ahead. Always know how you are getting to each meeting beforehand. Don't just wait for things to happen, or they won't. And don't expect others to arrange your transportation. Like a lot of other things in your new life, it's your responsibility.

FEELING UNCOMFORTABLE AT AA

"I've gone to a couple of AA meetings and felt very uncomfortable. I really don't think it's the place for me."

There are a number of possible reasons for your thinking that. First of all, it's a new situation. Most people feel awkward when starting a new job or beginning a new relationship. It takes time *and willingness to try* to begin to feel at ease. And a couple of meetings isn't enough time. Go to meetings daily for a month before passing judgment.

Second, as an alcoholic/addict, going to an AA meeting doesn't seem natural to you. AA is the antithesis of what has been the center of your life for a long time: drinking and/or drugging. Its very success may threaten the emotional bonds that tie you to your chemical crutch. Again, time and learning about your disease will shift your center—if you let them.

Third, maybe the meeting you picked was not the right one for you. If other meetings are available in your area, try them. Look for one that's a better match with your background

AA FOR BEGINNERS

Early in recovery, before the fog lifts, many people find it difficult to grasp what is going on at Alcoholics Anonymous meetings. Twelve Steps seem too many—and too complicated—to handle. It may help at first to think in terms of just six basic AA principles:

1. You admit you're in trouble and can't get out of it on your own.

2. You recognize there's some Power—God, your AA group, whatever—greater than you are and turn to that Power.

3. You start telling yourself the truth.

4. You talk about your problem with others who've gone through it before you.

5. You think about those you've harmed and try to make amends.

6. Once you are on the road to getting better, you start helping others as you've been helped—both for your good and for theirs.

and interests. But don't wander indefinitely, looking for Nirvana. AA is a support group, not a new drug. It doesn't have to give you a high. You get out of it what you put in.

Fourth, AA, with its Twelve Steps, Twelve Traditions, and Serenity Prayer, may seem a little simplistic to you. It *is* simple, but those who have lived with it—including professors, scientists, doctors, lawyers, and a lot of other highly intelligent people—know it's not simplistic. And, above all, they know it works.

Finally, your feelings may have nothing to do with AA and everything to do with your own attitude. Your rejection of AA may be part of your disease—just another form of denial.

Whatever your reasons, the fact remains that research and experience show that those who participate in AA or one of the other Twelve-Step programs adjust to sobriety more easily and completely than those who don't. And—not unimportant—are more likely to stay sober.

At this point, you have four options:

❖ You can continue to go to AA even if you are uncomfortable. Treatment for disease is not always pleasant, but you could die without it. With time, your comfort level is sure to rise.

❖ You can attend another AA group that seems more your cup of coffee. Or, failing that, try another recovery fellowship, such as the newer Rational Recovery or Secular Organizations for Sobriety (see page 42), to see if it's more compatible philosophically.

❖ You can seek treatment as an outpatient, inpatient, or with a qualified physician or counselor. (Eventually, most will urge you to join AA or at least to follow its principles. But by then you may find that the boot no longer pinches.)

"I know now I can't help how I feel, that there's no such thing as right and wrong feelings. But if I can be honest and admit and talk about how I feel, I'm more likely to be able to change my behavior. And if I change my behavior, I'm going to feel better."

❖ Or you can try to stay sober on your own. This is the most difficult and least promising path to take. Recovery is not about abstention from one's chemical of choice; it's about rebuilding your life in such a way that the chemicals you once thought you couldn't live without become unnecessary. This is tough to do without others who've gone before to show you the way. Still, if this is your choice, it will work best if you borrow successful AA principles for the underpinnings of your recovery (the Twelve Steps, the daily discipline, and the use of a sponsor), as embodied in the Big Book and other AA literature, even if you don't go to meetings. But you should always be ready, if you begin to falter, to turn to more traditional paths for help.

"I've gone to a dozen AA meetings, and the more I hear, the more I'm turned off. Spirituality isn't my thing. Maybe I should drop out now and continue on my own."

Before you lock the door to AA and throw away what could be the key to your recovery, be sure you've given it, and yourself, a fair chance. First, have you tried several different groups to see if one is more comfortable for you than the others? Each AA group is, after all, a reflection of its members, and some have a more worldly bent. Next, are you aware that "spirituality" is wide open to individual interpretation, that many people do not view it in a religious sense at all? (If not, see the discussion of spirituality on page 333.) Finally, examine your motivation for rejecting AA. Is this program really incompatible with your thinking? Or is it merely incompatible with your drugging and drinking?

If after honest self-examination you still sincerely believe that AA won't work for you, but you're dead serious about your recovery, look for another mutual-help group in your area, such as Rational Recovery. You can check your phone book or inquire at a local treatment center. Though it's true that millions have climbed the Twelve Steps and found what they needed at the summit, many others have walked out the clubhouse door and never returned.

"Some days I believe in God and some days I don't. But every day I know there's a power greater than I am. Most days, it's the Twelve Steps."

Whether you choose AA or another support group, you won't succeed unless you commit yourself to getting well, to abstaining from mind-altering substances, and to developing a coherent recovery philosophy—whether it's AA- or RR-based.

"I have been going to Rational Recovery meetings and find them more helpful than AA. Your book seems to be built around AA, so I'm not sure it can be useful to me."

To ignore AA's contributions to recovery would be like dismissing Einstein's to quantum physics or Babe Ruth's to baseball. Yes, it's true that this book focuses heavily on Twelve-Step philosophy. But the major portion of it—particularly the material on withdrawal, health, relationships, and work—is valid for everyone in recovery, whether they go to AA, go to another group, or go it alone. Different cloaks for different folks. As children, we learn from our mothers, our fathers, our teachers, our friends, sometimes from our worst enemies. Whatever the source—and some have found Rational

Recovery a worthwhile one—if it strengthens your recovery, great! Apply it in your new clean and sober life. But don't ignore solid advice from other sources.

DISCOMFORT WITH "SHARING"

"I didn't like the touchy-feely stuff that went on in the Sixties, and I still don't like it. Words like 'sharing' irritate me. That's why the idea of getting involved in AA just turns me off."

You're not the only one. Out of "sophistication," shyness, shame, repressive upbringing, or because "touchy-feely stuff" seems distastefully 1960s, many people feel as you do. They don't like the idea of sitting around with a bunch of strangers and sharing (yep, it's a tired word, but nobody's come up with a better one) their most private thoughts. Still, most of them eventually come to terms with the need to talk the past out of their systems, especially when they realize that there's no obligation to share intimate details. Those are usually reserved for a sponsor. Yours can be, too.

Start by going to a few open meetings. Just sit in the back and take it all in. At some point you may feel the urge to say something yourself. If you don't, don't. Once you've heard the stories of others and find that most of these people are very much like you, it should be easier to tell your own. Many people find that this story-swapping helps reduce their "nobody hurts like I hurt" self-centeredness. And when you feel there's no way out of the stygian blackness of your tunnel, it helps to meet people who've already seen the light at the end of theirs.

The desire, or ability, to unload some of the burden you've carried so long may not come immediately. Never mind. A nod of your head, a smile, or a chuckle at a meeting is a basic form of showing your feelings. Once you've tried that, verbal interaction is just a baby step away. One-on-one conversations with others, particularly with the person you choose for a sponsor, should also be helpful. And suddenly one fine day you'll hear yourself speaking at a meeting, even if it's just to say, "I'm really impressed with everyone here." Of course, if you're still not convinced you have a problem, you could just say, "I don't think I'm an alcoholic. I am a little worried that I may be on the way to becoming one."

You don't have to "spill your guts" in public unless and until you're ready. If you do, you can be sure that no one will judge or condemn you (crosstalk is strongly discouraged), and no matter what you say, no one will be surprised or shocked. You'll be accepted as you are—fears, doubts, warts and all. There aren't many places where that's so.

"I could not admit and talk about a lot of the feelings that I had because I had been brought up not to air dirty linen in public. I had to overcome that, and when I did, I got better."

It's important to keep in mind that the sharing that goes on at AA meetings isn't exhibitionism. It's a necessary part of the recovery process—and, like other forms of group therapy, it works. Recent research suggests it may be because it actually triggers mood-lifting brain chemicals. People who talk about their experiences with alcohol and/or drugs, and who describe the ravages and wreckage these substances caused in their lives, find relief from the wounds of pain, guilt, and anger and the beginning of freedom from the need for mood-altering chemicals.

If you find it impossible to open up at AA meetings, or even to go to them, you might consider seeking professional help from a qualified physician, psychiatrist, or counselor (see the information beginning on page 45). Sometimes denial, resentment, and other emotional factors become barriers to your participation in what AA has to offer.

"I've started going to AA meetings and I don't like all this unloading of personal stuff. I hardly know these people; how am I supposed to trust them?"

Trust is a major problem for a lot of people in early recovery. Many alcoholics/addicts (especially those who grew up in an inner-city neighborhood, a poor rural town, a reservation, or who were separated in some other way from mainstream America) feel reluctant to trust others—whether they are counselors or AA members, doctors or social workers. Not surprisingly, they've built a defensive wall against what they view as a hostile environment.

It will take time for you to feel less threatened, to believe that people in the recovery business want to help you, not get you in trouble. Give yourself a chance; try to do your sharing one on one or in small groups at first. AA is a friendly and welcoming environment and if you open yourself up even a little bit you will eventually learn to feel safe in it.

"At meetings I always looked for people I thought would understand how I felt, and talked to them about my real feelings. They didn't reject me. They really understood."

"My family originally came from Puerto Rico and I find the idea of AA strange. I can't believe the way people talk about their personal lives. I could never do that in front of strangers. But alcohol is messing up my family—I have to do something."

If you don't do something, you'll continue to mess up your family. If the AA meetings you went to put you off, you might try some other ways of getting and staying sober:

❖ Go for family alcoholism/addiction counseling or outpatient treatment if you can afford it, or if your company or insurance will pay for it. The counselor should be someone who is trained and certified to treat alcoholics and drug addicts, and should also be someone you feel comfortable with and can trust. It will be even better if this person speaks Spanish, so that if it's more comfortable for you, your sessions can be in your native language. Unfortunately, there aren't enough well-trained multi-lingual counselors to go around.

❖ Go for inpatient treatment. Try to find a rehab program that has at least one or two counselors from a background similar to yours. Once you get out, you will need to continue some kind of support group, such as AA, but you should find it more comfortable once you've been exposed to treatment.

❖ Check the churches in your neighborhood for a Spanish-speaking AA group or locate one by calling the AA number in the telephone directory white pages. Because many of the members will probably feel the way you do, there may be less of the kind of talk that makes you feel uncomfortable. And because the others will seem less like "strangers," you will probably find it easier to open up yourself.

❖ Continue attending AA meetings as a "listener." No one will ever force you to say anything that you don't want to say, but you will still be able to learn a lot from others.

❖ Start a mini support group. Whether or not you go for family counseling or attend AA as a listener, you also need a small group of people you can talk to about your problems. Find a few people whom you feel you can trust and who are trying, like you, to stay sober. Meet two or three times a week, and talk about your feelings and problems. At first it may be hard to do. But if you keep trying, it will get easier.*

It should help you to know that once the barrier of denial is broken and patient and family are helped to understand the nature of the disease and what needs to be done about it, those from Latino backgrounds tend to do very well in recovery.

"I'm African-American and I've been going to a mixed AA group but I haven't opened my mouth yet. I just don't like telling everything to people I don't even know, especially when a lot of them are white."

Many newcomers to AA don't want to talk about their experiences and feelings in front of others. And African-Americans often feel even more strongly about this—because they aren't ready to trust their feelings to whites. One reason is that they fear rejection. A lot of them—probably you included—have experienced enough prejudice to justify concern. But the fact is that talking about your life is the way you get better when you have this disease of alcoholism/addiction. It's like taking strong medicine: It may not taste good, and it may even have some unpleasant side effects, but it makes you feel better.

It will probably take you a while to get over your uneasiness in a large mixed AA group. So why don't you get together with a half dozen or so black members of your group and meet separately a few times (but don't stop going to your regular meetings), so that you can start learning to share in a more comfortable environment. Once you've done it among friends, it will be easier in the larger group.

What you will probably find in the end is that there are few other places where race is less important than at an AA meeting. The similarities shared by alcoholics/addicts are more important than the differences between those of different races.

If you continue to feel uncomfortable in a mainly white AA group, just work on enlarging your own little group—and make it an official AA group (see page 417).

"I haven't shared the fact that I'm a lesbian with anyone but my lover and a few others. I don't think I'm ready to talk about my personal life publicly at an AA meeting."

Coming out is a personal process, and both the speed and the extent to which it occurs are up to you. You will have to decide how open to be with your group. It may help to test the waters with a sympathetic person—your sponsor, for example.

---

*For more information on substance abuse in the Hispanic community, contact: the National Coalition of Hispanic Health & Human Services Organization (COSSMHO), 1030 15th Street N.W., Suite 1053, Washington, DC 20005; (202) 371-2100, or the National Hispanic Family Against Drug Abuse (NHFADA), 1511 K Street, Suite 1029, Washington, DC 20005; (202) 393-5136.

You can also ask other gay AA members what their experience has been. In the end, you will have to decide what you can live with, whether to be totally open, just a little open, or not open at all. (You are expected to tell your story at AA in a general way; it's not necessary to paint intimate details.)

Hopefully you will find a group with which you can be completely honest, at least as honest as any person can be. You deserve that opportunity and it is important for a healthy recovery. When (and if) you feel the time is right, you might choose to take that opportunity in a gay/lesbian AA group, of which there are many.

Above all, do what is right for your sobriety, which is your number one priority. If you stay sober, any other issues will eventually fall into place, or the answers or help that you need to resolve them will become available to you. If you're not sober, you won't be able to resolve anything else.

BEING HONEST ABOUT FEELINGS

"I don't understand how anyone can get up in front of a group like AA and do an emotional striptease."

People may strip away a lot of barriers when they get up and talk at AA, and it often gets emotional, but there's nothing of the tease in it. Decades of experience have shown that those who honestly disclose their personal stories in a general way to others greatly improve their chances of long-term sobriety. Self-deception—lying to the most important person in your world—is dishonesty at its most foolish and dangerous, breeding attitudes that lead inevitably to drug and alcohol relapse. As is the case in many other spiritual movements, including most religious ones, self-examination followed by confession to others nurtures healthy emotional growth. This cleansing process is particularly essential in addiction recovery. Since what's said at meetings is held in strictest confidence, participants can share without fear of having their stories leave the meeting room. Everyone, after all, has a stake in maintaining privacy at a support group.

Still, opening up a wriggling personal can of worms in public isn't easy for alcoholics/addicts. They have more trouble being honest about their feelings than most people. They're used to smothering feelings with chemicals and have turned self-deception into an art form. But part of recovery is learning to recognize and express your feelings. Feelings, you will learn in recovery, are okay. Even negative ones. Everybody has them. It's only actions that can be right or wrong.

At first you may not even realize that the feelings are there. They've been frozen for so long they'll take a while to thaw. Once they do, try to learn to accept them. And then to share them.

The goal of sharing feelings is not simply to confess and thus unburden yourself. That's a big step. But the next step is steeper: going on to change

"My friend talked me into volunteering to make coffee when I first started going to AA. I made lousy coffee. I still do. But knowing I had that responsibility kept me going to all the meetings—I couldn't beg off on a small pretense. Doing that little job made me feel good, made me feel needed, made me feel a part of the group."

your behavior. Some people get stuck at the level of sharing feelings and never move on to the taking-action phase. If they continue on this emotional binge, they can go from the emotional starvation they experienced during addiction to emotional overdose—and be only slightly better off than when they started.

"The things I did while I was using drugs were unbelievably awful. Do I have to tell all at AA?"

Absolutely not. First, you'll want to omit the name of anyone who might be damaged in any way by your account, and events that could identify and put others in harm's way. Second, you need only talk about your history generally ("I still can't believe the things I did when I was living on the streets") rather than specifically ("I sold my body for drugs, I slept with any kind of low life just to get a fix"). Many speakers do get into specifics, but how much you open up will depend on your own feelings and on your AA group. It's a good idea to discuss these issues with your sponsor before you plan a talk.

If there are feelings or experiences you need to talk about but don't want to discuss publicly, your sponsor, therapist, or counselor can serve as a discreet, understanding, and nonjudgmental sounding board.

LOSS OF INDEPENDENCE

"I'm a single guy trying to establish my independence, and what I dislike most about AA is that if I really get into it, I'll lose all control over my life."

Funny you should feel that way. You've just been through a lengthy period of your life in which you did lose all control—to a chemical substance. Getting involved in AA, though it may seem at first to be taking away your freedom and independence, will actually give it back to you as you learn how to make your life more manageable.

In the meantime, remember that being able to turn to someone else for help is not a sign of weakness, but a sign of strength. The weak person hesitates to ask for help because he fears others will find out about his inner weakness. The strong person has inner confidence and doesn't worry about what others may think.

DISCOMFORT WITH THE IDEA OF A HIGHER POWER

"I want to go to AA, but I can't swallow all this stuff about a Higher Power."

As long as you don't swallow any alcohol, no one will care whether or not you swallow the idea of a Higher Power. Many people in AA think of the Higher Power as God, though there may be as many interpretations of just what is or who God is as there are AA members. Others accept that some power out there—maybe it's God and maybe not—that is stronger than they are can help them lick their alcoholism/addiction. Still others consider the AA group or the Twelve Steps to be their Higher Power. Whatever the form of their belief, believing that some power outside of themselves can help them change their destructive behavior seems to be important to the recovery of many with drug and alcohol problems.* There is, however,

*The founders of Alcoholics Anonymous were so concerned that nonbelievers not feel excluded from the fellowship that they devoted an entire chapter in the Big Book to talking about the approximately 50% of the original group that felt as you do. Read that chapter ("We Agnostics") and see if it offers some help.

some potential danger in the concept of turning one's life over. Some folks rely so heavily on this Higher Power, that they forget that it's necessary to work with it to become co-creators in reshaping their lives.

FEELING OUT OF PLACE

"I'm black and my local AA group is all white. I've gone a couple of times and have felt totally out of place."

Most people, no matter what their background, feel out of place at their first couple of AA meetings. It's even more uncomfortable being a minority of one. But don't automatically assume that the color of your skin makes a difference to anyone else. Although it's certainly possible to find bigots at AA, to most AA members, a drunk is a drunk, whether he is black or white, whether he sees pink elephants or gray ones.

Your discomfort may be more in your head than in theirs. Still, it's real. So try to find an integrated or all-black group to go to at first, even if that means extra travel and effort. Attending such a group will allow you to get used to participating at AA meetings in a non-threatening atmosphere. (If the group invites a white guest speaker occasionally this will help increase the comfort level with whites.) Once you feel comfortable with recovering black alcoholics/addicts, you may find that you can fit in even at all-white meetings. Fill in with these when an all-black or mixed meeting is not available.

If there is no integrated meeting you can get to, try various all-white groups to see if you are more comfortable with one than with others. If you aren't, maybe you need some support. Ask a couple of friends to go with you to the meeting that seems least awkward. It could be drinking/drugging friends who want to get sober too, or just a couple of friends who want to help you out. You will feel less intimidated and able to participate more freely.

Another alternative is to try to set up a new group in a local church. More and more black churches are recognizing the importance of Twelve-Step groups and are cooperating in getting them going. These groups talk AA, but they often discuss community issues as well and are becoming an important community force.

Whatever you do, don't use the fact that the only AA group available to you is white as an excuse not to stay sober. The fact is that AA people, no matter what their skin color, may understand you better than anyone else. Maybe better than you think.

"I'm black and I've been going to an almost all white AA group. It's been okay. People are pretty accepting and I'm pretty comfortable. But it's the social stuff that I seem to get left out of—like when everybody goes out for coffee after meetings."

That is a major problem for a lot of people who attend groups where they feel like outsiders. And though it may seem that it's okay just to go to meetings and go back home alone, you really do miss out on an important part of the camaraderie of AA. This isn't just a social issue; it's also a recovery issue. Part of a good recovery is building social relationships with other recoverees. To remedy the situation, there are several things you can try:

❖ Become more active in the group. Arrive early and help set up chairs. Offer to make coffee or pick up cookies or take care of other responsibilities. The more you are part of the group, the more people will forget that their skin color is different from yours.

❖ Try taking the initiative and inviting a couple of people you're friendly with at meetings out to coffee after a meeting. If they accept, you will have broken the ice; maybe next time they will ask you along. If not, try some others.

❖ If you have friends in other AA groups, ask them to come to yours or start attending theirs—at least some of the time. That will give you some ready-made friendships. Or spend time socially with them at times when you don't have meetings.

❖ Find some friends—of any race—who you think could benefit from AA and invite them to your group. If they stick with it, not only will you have helped them, you will have helped yourself.

❖ Try some other AA groups. Each one has its own personality and membership; you may find one that's more friendly and less uptight about interracial socializing.

❖ If all else fails, try starting your own group with a few friends (see page 417).

"I'm supposed to go to an NA meeting every night. But the group in my neighborhood meets only three times week. The only other meetings that are near enough for me to get to are in a neighborhood with a lot of people better off than I am. I'm going to feel like I don't belong."

If you qualify for NA (or AA or another support group), you belong, no matter what kind of people are in the group. Of course telling you that may not change the way you feel or make you less uncomfortable. Still, there's no escaping the fact that you need those daily meetings. So what can you do?

First of all, double check to see if there are any other options. Maybe there's a more mixed group near where you work that meets before or after work, or at lunch time. Or maybe you can get together with a few members of your home group to meet every day for a while. If you can't work that out, you're going to have to give in and try the meetings in the other neighborhood.

"I do my daily inventory when I'm in bed at night. I think of all the things I've done during the day and evaluate them. This goes in the good column, that in the not so good, the other in the bad. Next day, I try to rectify the bad."

Plan to do most of your participating in your home group at first. At the new one, just show up and listen for a while. As you become more comfortable in your own group and start to feel like an NA oldtimer, you'll find yourself increasingly at ease in the other group. Faces will become familiar and so will stories. You'll find that you have comments to make and things to add from your own experience—which, because your background is different, will be of special interest to the others. You'll find, too, that although these people have more money than you, their problems with drugs are very much the same.

Don't dread these meetings. See them as an opportunity, a way of getting to know people from different backgrounds, in a comfortable situation where, for all the differences, everyone has a lot in common. If you can learn to be comfortable in mixed company, doors may begin to open—not

FRIENDS OF BILL W.

If you're chatting with a new acquaintance or business associate and you suspect from the way the conversation is going that this person may be a member of Alcoholics Anonymous, but are embarrassed to ask, try this question instead: Are you a friend of Bill W.? Anyone who is familiar with AA will also know its respected founder Bill Wilson and should respond accordingly. If you get a puzzled nod, you know you guessed wrong.

just to AA meetings but to jobs and other opportunities as well.

"I've been through a treatment program for alcohol and drug addiction and I've been told that I will have to attend Alcoholics Anonymous meetings as part of my aftercare program. This worries me since I'm Jewish and AA is a Christian-oriented organization."

Although founded by Christians, Alcoholics Anonymous is not a Christian organization; it isn't even a religious organization. It's a fellowship of men and women of all faiths and of no particular faith who have joined together with a common goal: sobriety. If you want to become sober, then AA is the place for you.

You can get further support in your recovery from JACS (Jewish Alcoholics, Chemically Dependent Persons, and Significant Others Foundation). JACS supports existing Twelve-Step programs (such as AA and NA) and is not a substitute for them. It is intended to give additional help to addicted Jews and their families, helping them to integrate Jewish traditions and heritage into their recovery programs. It also is meant to serve as a resource center for information exchange and to provide community outreach and education through lectures, holiday programs, and retreats.

In some communities Jewish support groups, or havurot (with names like "Klean and Kosher"), have sprung up to give additional help to those in traditional Twelve-Step programs. You can find out about these programs from your rabbi or by calling your local Federation of Jewish Philanthropies.

"I'm a Jewish alcoholic. I went to my first AA meeting, and I was really uncomfortable. The way they talked about spirituality somehow seemed un-Jewish to me. Then they read the Twelve Steps, which are so Christian, and ended with the Lord's Prayer. I'm not sure I should go back."

Many Jews (as well as atheists and other non-Christians) feel uncomfortable with the idea of becoming active in AA because of the inclusion of one or more prayers at meetings and because they sense there is a Christian theme behind the Twelve Steps. However, many Jewish experts on the subject, from all branches of Judaism, have pointed out that neither the Twelve Steps nor the most commonly recited AA prayers should make Jewish recoverees uncomfortable.

The Twelve Steps, for example, do not run counter to Jewish thinking at all. There are parallels for each of them in rabbinic Judaism. The twenty steps in Rabbenu Yonah of Gerona's *The Gates of Repentance,* for example, are full of similar ideas. So is the service for the Day of Atonement, with its vocal public confession. In fact, the more familiar Jews become with the Twelve Steps, the more they recognize the repeated echoes of Jewish thinking in them.*

"I was so estranged from God and my religion that I never even thought about whether or not I believed. Then I became involved in a Twelve-Step program and found God. This led me to becoming active in my faith for the first time."

The Lord's Prayer, sometimes recited at the close of AA meetings, appeared in the New Testament and has over years of usage among Christians certainly taken on a Christian image. But its foundations are thoroughly Jewish, with almost every phrase finding a direct parallel in the Kaddish, the Eighteen Benedictions, or in one or another of the rabbinic writings. If the prayer nevertheless is one you do not want to say, look for a group in your area that uses the Serenity Prayer instead or is willing to substitute the Twenty-Third Psalm, or another verse from the Book of Psalms. If you can find no such group, simply remain silent, or repeat the psalm or any other Jewish prayer you feel is appropriate. You certainly are not required to participate in the recitation. The Lord's Prayer is not an official prayer of AA; even Bill W. couldn't recall how the custom of reciting it started. Just don't let the recitation of a single prayer keep you from getting the help you need.

The Serenity Prayer (see page 102), frequently recited or quoted at AA meetings and in AA literature, was indeed written by a modern Christian clergyman, but it is by no means exclusively Christian. Its theme is universal and universally useful.

However, many rabbis have pointed out that even if one had to recite the Lord's Prayer at an AA meeting in order to participate in the program, it would be within Jewish law to do so. It is simply a matter of "saving a life," which outweighs all other laws.

As for spirituality, there are numerous threads in Judaism, but many modern Jews are unaware of them. There is, of course, the spirituality of the Kaballah and the Mystics. But spirituality is also a factor in modern Judaism. It's been said that "The spiritual Jew is the ideal embodiment of Judaism."

Far from rending Jews from their roots, the search for spirituality that Jewish recoverees make in AA has brought many of them back to those roots, strengthening their faith and their belief in God.

"I got caught by a drug screen in the navy. I'm sure my 'Higher Power' had a hand in it. I would have kept using anyway, but the medical board sent me to a treatment center. It was horrible. But if you want to be sober, you go to any length. I saw how powerless I was, that I couldn't do it without help from this 'force.' If you truly believe, it does get better."

**Twelve Jewish Steps to Recovery,* written jointly by a rabbi (Kerry M. Olitzky) and an addiction specialist (Stewart A. Copans, M.D.), clearly spells out the way that the Twelve Steps can be used by Jews.

If in spite of this reassurance you are still uncomfortable with the idea of AA, consider whether your discomfort is a form of denial, and actually part of your disease. Are you really worried that AA is not Jewish enough, or are you looking for a way to avoid dealing with your alcoholism?

"My doctor recently told me to stop drinking because of my health and suggested I start going to AA meetings. I feel funny about that because I've got a feeling that I'm going to be the only senior citizen there."

It's true that as the population ages, there seem to be fewer and fewer alcoholics/addicts. There are several possible reasons. One, of course, is the shorter lifespan of substance abusers; many die before they reach sixty, direct or indirect victims of their addictions. Another is the fact that many older people have medical problems that require that they give up drinking. Still another is the wisdom that comes with age, which often leads to a new sobriety.

But there are many seniors in AA—nearly 10 percent of all members are over sixty. Most of them have long years of sobriety behind them. But many entered AA or treatment programs more recently. These folks either became problem drinkers late in life or are among the lucky few to have survived through years of self-abuse. Some lifelong moderate drinkers suddenly have a problem handling their alcohol, not because of increased drinking but because of an increase in the use of prescribed or over-the-counter medications. Or because their aging bodies can no longer handle the alcohol as efficiently as previously.*

*Because it takes older people longer to eliminate drugs from their bodies, withdrawal is usually prolonged. This should be taken into account during detox.

Those who start problem drinking later in life (estimated to be about a third of all older alcoholics) may have previously been light drinkers or occasional bingers or even abstainers. They usually turn to alcohol for a variety of reasons: increased isolation and loneliness; loss of spouse, job, friends, family members; reduced status, self-esteem, and sense of usefulness; declining financial resources; excessive leisure time and boredom; poor health, physical disabilities, and pain; sleep problems; thoughts about mortality; depression and suicidal feelings. Whatever the reasons, the number of drinkers in the sixty-five-plus bracket is growing; it was estimated to be about 3.7 million in 1991.

So you most likely will not be the only senior at your AA meetings. At most meetings you will find a good mix, with members in every age bracket from late teens to late seventies. Many seniors enjoy this mix both because they can learn about recovery from younger members and because they get a chance to spend some quality time with young people, something that for many in this isolated world is a real treat.

"I'm gay and very comfortable about it. But the first AA meeting I went to I was totally turned off. One young woman was whining about a boyfriend who abused her. A guy was complaining about his wife not understanding him. It was so hetero, there was no way I could talk about the problems I'm having with my lover."

There are two issues here. One, did you come to the meeting in the right frame of mind? And two, was this the right meeting for you?

As to the first, it may be that you were so focused on what made you different from these other folks (your sexual orientation) that you were ignoring what made you the same (your chemical dependency). The fact is that there may have been little difference between the roots of the problems the others were having and your own problems—if you would only open up your mind and listen. It may be tough to do this because your brain persists in picking out the differences, but it's necessary.

As to the second issue, there's no question that most gays and lesbians feel initial discomfort at a meeting that is primarily made up of heterosexuals. For this reason, it makes sense to try to find a meeting specifically for gays and/or lesbians that can become your home group. Most big cities have such meetings, and you can obtain the location of one by calling Alcoholics Anonymous or the local gay hotline or healthline listed in the White Pages of your phone directory (or call 1-800-4GAYNET).

"I was sure there wasn't any power greater than my own will. Then I looked at my life. There I was, doing drugs even though it was destroying my work, my family, everything. I wasn't doing drugs because I wanted to. There had to be some power out there stronger than I was, controlling me."

If there is no gay/lesbian AA meeting in your area and if your recovery is solid and you have support from either the AA group you're in now or your sponsor (or both), look into the possibility of setting one up. You may find other gay AA members in neighboring communities who are willing to help get your group started. The tips on getting a new AA group going on page 417 will also help, but there will be special issues that you will have to address in setting up your group. Unless you have been openly out for a long time, you may initially feel uncomfortable announcing the meetings or being identified as an officer. You may be disappointed if other gays and lesbians would rather remain closeted and don't flock to your first meeting. If you do decide to go ahead, be prepared to put in a lot of time and to keep trying until you succeed—which may take several months or more.

In spite of the effort required, or maybe because of it, setting up your own AA group can be a very valuable growing experience. And the good feelings that come out of helping other gay alcoholics are unequaled. When starting a group, also be aware that many gay/lesbian groups choose to practice "double anonymity," which means that neither the gay status nor the alcoholic/addict status of members can be revealed outside meetings.

Most gay and lesbian alcoholics find that once they become comfortable at their own meetings, they are able to attend and benefit from other meetings—although they may confine talk about sexuality issues to their own groups. It's always possible, even likely, that you will run into some homophobia at general AA meetings. AA members are human and have their faults and prejudices just like everyone else.

You may not be able to organize a gay and lesbian AA group. You may not find a general meeting where you feel free to come out. Life, as you well know, isn't fair. Go to AA anyway. Don't let anybody's homophobia (not an AA group's or a counselor's) or your own discomfort keep you out of AA. If you're not comfortable coming out, then don't. But do get sober, no matter what.

"I grew up on a reservation where everybody drank alcohol. I moved to the city, but I still drink a lot. A friend said I should try AA, but the only AA meeting I ever went to was very foreign and uncomfortable."

Your reaction isn't unusual. Many Native Americans have the same problem with their first AA encounter. The trick is to shop around for the right meeting. In areas with a large Native American population, there are usually one or more AA groups that are run by and for Native Americans, and are tied closely to the Indian heritage. As at other AA meetings, spirituality is an important element, but at these groups, Great Spirit and God are used synonymously with Higher Power. The thrust is toward recovery at several levels, beginning with the inner self, moving on to the family, then the ancestors, and finally Holy Beings. Sharing may be done in the traditional "talking circle," particularly in the Southwest. With nearly 400 different Indian nations, each with its own language and customs, it's not surprising that a wide variety of traditions have grown up at Indian AA meetings in different parts of the country. As at other AA meetings, there is no judging, no feedback other than supportive remarks like, "You're an okay person."

Sometimes the circle takes place in a sweat lodge, a bark structure filled with steam from hot rocks doused with water, in the belief that you are more aware of your body if you're sweating. Sometimes an Indian prayer may be substituted for the Serenity Prayer usually recited at the close of AA meetings.

"I wish somebody had told me that the essence of recovery in AA was not the fellowship (as helpful as that is), but the daily discipline of working the steps and collaborating with your sponsor."

If there is no Native American oriented AA group, there are some steps you can take to make yourself more comfortable at another group.

❖ If you live in a town with several AA groups, visit them all. Look for a group that does not play up Christian thinking if such thinking makes you uncomfortable.

HANG TOUGH

People at Twelve-Step meetings are like people everywhere. They have their weaknesses and their prejudices. Though it's true that people in recovery tend to be more accepting of differences than most, it's possible to run into a meeting (or, more likely an individual or two, at a meeting) where intolerance rears its ugly head—against blacks, Jews, women, homosexuals, or anyone else who is different. If you find yourself the object of such intolerance, look for another meeting. If that's not possible, try to hang in there anyway. Don't let the ignorance of others stand in the way of your recovery. If the actual cruelty is interfering with your attendance at meetings, turn to an understanding counselor or sponsor for advice and support.

FOR WOMEN ONLY

Because many women have found that traditional AA groups do not meet all their needs, women-only groups have sprung up around the country. Some are AA-affiliated, others independent. Some are part of a relatively new network of support groups for women called Women for Sobriety (WFS). Based on thirteen positive-thinking "statements of acceptance" (see page 570), the program emphasizes that women are capable, competent, confident, caring, and compassionate. At meetings, women introduce themselves with "My name is ________, and I am a competent woman." Instead of focusing on past miseries, discussion centers on present concerns and questions as well as successes. The emphasis is on building self-esteem. The great majority of women in WFS are also AA members. For information on WFS, write to Box 618, Quakertown, PA 18951, or call (215) 536-8026.

Women in Recovery, also for women only, is an annual conference that deals with issues of specific interest to women, including sexual abuse, incest, and child battering, issues that are rarely discussed openly at AA.

❖ If you're the lone Native American showing up at AA, you may feel more comfortable taking a friend along.

❖ Use some mind control. If you can't find the perfect AA group, settle for what you can get. If there's a lot of talk about God and Christianity, then try substituting the "Creator" or the "Great Spirit" in your mind.

❖ Get additional preparation for recovery. A good way to do this is by getting inpatient or outpatient treatment, which will make you feel more at ease in AA-type groups. The ideal program will have at least some Native American counselors, but such programs are rare. Next best are programs that are low-pressure, since they are most compatible with the noncompetitive contemplative Indian style you are probably used to. See the Indian Health Service or another Indian program in your area for information.

❖ Learn about your roots. It's a fact that people with a sense of their own culture have an easier time in recovery.

❖ Remember that—in spite of what you may have learned as a child—it's okay to ask for help. In the wider community, it's not an insult to others to do so.

Many Native Americans are discovering that AA and its spirituality, far from being foreign, can become very comfortable—especially when intertwined with old traditions. And making a decision to become sober will give you freedom you probably never had.

DISCOMFORT WITH HUGGING

"I just went to my first AA meeting and everybody was hugging. Even strangers. That was really weird."

Touching is one of the most important ways human beings communicate. A pat on the shoulder or a hug can show caring without a word being spoken. But, because they come from families that don't touch a lot, many people feel as you do that hugging is "weird." Don't feel you have to join in the hugging if it makes you uncomfortable, but be open to learning about it. It would be a valuable communication skill for you to learn, to enrich your own life and to pass along in time to your children. So relax and let the hugging happen. Eventually it could become such an important part of your life that you won't want to live without it.

EMBARRASSMENT

"I went through detox in a jail cell. They told me that I can be on probation if I start going to a Twelve-Step program, but I can't walk in there and face all those people. I've been living on the street, selling my body for nickel bags. I'm so ashamed."

You have a disease, a disease that makes people do things they may later feel terrible about. But so do all those other people at Alcoholics Anonymous, Narcotics Anonymous, Cocaine Anonymous, and other support groups for chemically dependent people. Most of these people also felt ashamed about their behavior under the influence when they become sober.

If you walk into a meeting you may look around and think, "Hey, these people look pretty good. They can't have done the things I've done." But that isn't true. They only look good because they've been in recovery for a while. If you had known them while they were using, you probably wouldn't recognize them now. Listen to their stories, and you will hear many that sound much like your own.

When you've been around a bit yourself and it comes your turn to speak, remember that you don't have to go into any gory details that make you uncomfortable.

If it makes you feel more comfortable to start with, try to find a friend who is clean and sober or who would like to get that way to go with you to your first few meetings.

"For me to meditate, I have to be alone. I don't want anyone around me. I get up real early in the morning and go down to to the office before anybody is there and do my meditation for half an hour. Then I'm ready to put in a sixteen-hour day."

Keep at it, and one of these days you will be one of those sober oldtimers that newcomers think "look pretty good."

SPECIAL NEEDS

"Because I've got cerebral palsy, I'm pretty much a loner—which is probably why I developed a drinking problem. I think I can stop drinking on my own, but my doctor says that I have to go to AA meetings. I dread it."

Not long ago a young woman finished a 26.2-mile marathon in 3 hours and 31 minutes. Pretty good for anyone—but she was paralyzed from the waist down and completed the course in a wheelchair. The 1988 Alpine Skier of the Year shussed down the slopes on one leg. A man with no hands shot a respectable 85 for 18 holes in a golf tournament. Blind people become doctors; the hearing impaired, teachers; those with cerebral palsy, lawyers.

Everywhere, people with physical disabilities are showing that they are just like everyone else. And just like everyone else they are susceptible to alcoholism/addiction. In fact, their ranks are often swelled by substance abusers who've become handicapped through the use of alcohol or drugs—usually through accidents, but sometimes through the toxic effect of their chemicals of choice.

For many people with disabilities, AA is a haven where they can meet friends, talk about their fears and concerns, and be treated like one of the gang. In many towns, meetings with handicapped access are available for those who are in wheelchairs or on crutches.

No one should presume to tell you it will be easy to face strangers. Still, if you have to meet new people there probably aren't any anywhere who will be more accepting than those at an AA meeting. After all, most of these folks have learned to look at their alcoholism/addiction as a disability. They are (or at least they should be) the last people to look at others in a disparaging way.

Check in advance to be sure that there is handicapped access to any meeting you are planning to attend. If you can't find a meeting with easy access, see if special arrangements can be made with the steering committee of a nearby group to make it possible for you to attend AA meetings.

"I've been deaf since an infection in infancy, and an alcoholic since I was 12. I've been reading AA literature, and would like to go to meetings. Are there any where there is simultaneous signing?"

If you live in a large city, the answer is almost certainly yes. To find a meeting with an interpreter for the deaf, have someone call the central AA number in your city. If you live in a small town or rural area, far from a major population center, finding such a meeting will be more difficult. Alcoholics Anonymous World Services can provide a list of groups or helpful contacts for the hearing impaired. They can also send you the Twelve Steps translated into sign language. Write AA General Service, Box 459, Grand Central Station, New York, NY 10163 or call (212) 870-3199 (TDD).

If there is no meeting with signing available near your home, there is no reason why you can't bring your own interpreter to any meeting you go to—or even find a meeting you like and ask if a regular interpreter can be arranged. By doing this, you may be helping others who, like yourself, can't hear what's going on at a meeting without simultaneous translation.

AA SPEAKS MANY TONGUES

Since Alcoholics Anonymous is an international fellowship, the Big Book and many other publications are available in a wide range of languages. If you're interested obtaining a copy of the Big Book in Afrikaans, Dutch, Finnish, Flemish, French, German, Icelandic, Italian, Japanese, Korean, Norwegian, Portuguese, Spanish, or Swedish, write to the General Service Office (GSO) of Alcoholics Anonymous, Box 459, Grand Central Station, New York, NY 10163. GSO can give you information on how to obtain a wide range of other AA materials in Spanish. Some pamphlets are available in Arabic, Chinese, Korean, Russian, and Vietnamese. Some Al-Anon materials, too, are available in Spanish and other languages.*

*A computer program, Spanish Assistant, is available that translates materials into Spanish. It is also available in German and French.

LANGUAGE DIFFICULTIES

"My first language is Spanish and I feel very uncomfortable at an English-speaking AA meeting."

Most people who learned a language other than English in the cradle—even those who speak English well now—feel uneasy when they are at an AA meeting or a counseling session where English is spoken.

Speaking from the heart about fears, problems, or experiences is easiest in your mother tongue. It's also easier when at least some of those you are sharing your thoughts with come from the same kind of culture and can understand what your family life is like, what things are important to you, what kinds of problems you have in trying to deal with those outside the community.

So if you are a native Spanish speaker, look for a group that speaks your language.*

GIVING A TALK OR "LEAD"

"I've been asked to speak at our AA group and I'm scared to death. What if I blank out up there? Anyway, my life story is boring compared to most of those I've heard. I might put everybody to sleep."

Like a lawyer making his first jury summation or a freshman senator in her maiden speech, almost everyone feels their pulse pounding like a pneumatic drill the first few times they speak in front of others. Few ever die doing it and those relaxed eloquent AA speakers who now command your rapt attention once felt just the way you do. When they dove in, they found that the water was fine. To their surprise and profound relief, they realized that they had a lot more to say than they'd imagined—things they'd been unable to articulate for years just came pouring out—and in AA's safe and accepting environment everything was easier to say than they'd believed possible. They felt great accepting hugs and congratulations afterward.

Think about it. Your topic is one on which you are the world's greatest authority: your life. You won't have to do a lot of research or memorize a lot of boring statistics. All you'll have to do is tell it as you lived it. As it was and is.

Before you give your first talk, get some practice speaking about feelings and experiences during discussion meetings or in informal one on one give-and-take conversations with other AA members ("The one thing I find hardest to deal with is the loneliness. What do you do about that?") or with your sponsor. Then move on to a slightly larger audience of two to four people, and continue increasing the group size until you are comfortable in any group ready for national TV.

Ease pre-talk jitters with careful preparation. Ready a memory-jogging key-phrases outline to speak from (page 142), or even write out your story in advance. This does several things. It gives you an insurance policy against "blanking out," assures you of plenty to say, and guarantees (as you're almost sure to find when you reread it) that you won't put everyone to sleep. The process is also certain to give you new insights, helpful to you and to the group. Some people find that once they've done this pen and spade work, they can speak—whether in a chair or on their feet—without notes. Others feel more comfortable with a backup in hand—an outline, or notes on handy index cards. Still others prefer to read

*The same suggestions apply to anyone whose first language is not English. If you live in a large city, you may be able to find a group that speaks your language, or you may be able to start one. Phone your city's central AA number, or contact AA World Services.

their story word for word. Do whatever sends your butterflies off to a happy landing.

If they keep flapping their wings, there's another way to build your confidence before you go. Rehearse a time or two in front of a mirror, a friend, or a family member. Or—with the added advantage of a playback—into a tape recorder or even a video camera.

AA TIME COMMITMENT

"From what I've been hearing, I've got to devote my life to AA in order to recover. How can I do that when I have a family to support, community responsibilities, and a busy social life?"

That's an interesting question, one that is raised by many newly sober people. But let's answer it with another question. How much time did you devote to drinking and drugging? Probably a lot—maybe almost all your time. All you're being asked to do is to put the same time and energy you put into getting high (or thinking about it) into getting well.

Basically, you have two choices: devoting a lot of time to AA in order to get well or skimping on AA time, relapsing, and not being able to take care of family, job, or any other responsibilities. Good sense strongly recommends the first choice. That doesn't mean letting your life go to rack and ruin. Just strip your life down to the essentials, the way you would if you were recuperating from a heart attack. Go to work, of course, but don't work longer hours than are absolutely necessary. Spend some time with your family. But drop all other extraneous activities—hobbies, organization, church, synagogue, or community work, heavy socializing, home improvement projects, sports—until your recovery is on solid ground, probably after the first year or so. If you try to do everything now, ignoring the need for a solid foundation for recovery, your new world will collapse like a house of cards.

OUTLINING YOUR AA TALK

The purpose of your AA talk is to help yourself. Helping others is just the candle on the cake. So be totally honest. Drunks like to make good stories better with a series of half-truth embellishments and exaggerations. Scrub that. If you're alive and sober, your true story will be strong enough. Focus on what you've done, not on what others have done to you. Your talk shouldn't be a "poor me" story. Nor, if a good recovery is your goal, should it be a drunkalog or a just-for-laughs comedy routine.

When you sit down to plan your first talk, answer these questions:

1. What was your life like before sobriety?

2. What happened to open your mind to recovery?

3. What is your life like now?

Try to weave into your talk how AA principles (the Twelve Steps, for example) tie in to your life then and now ("In those days, the more I tried to take control of my life, the more I drank. Now, the more completely I turn my life over to my Higher Power, the easier it is to stay sober."). This will make your talk more valuable to listeners and to you. As you move along in your recovery, you'll find the focus of your talks changing from "what was then" to "what is now." That's normal and healthy.

MINI-GUIDE

Working Your Program

Many people new to AA wonder just what everyone means when they talk about "working the program." For each person it may mean something slightly different, but basically, working the program is the AA way to a successful recovery. That means including all of the following in your life:

❖ Working the Twelve Steps (see page 110).

❖ Having frequent and regular contact with your sponsor.

❖ Meditating and/or praying daily (see page 320).

❖ Attending meetings regularly.

❖ Reading and/or listening to AA material (see page 568) regularly.

A LIFETIME SENTENCE

"When can I stop going to AA?"

You can stop tomorrow. But as long as it's today, you need to go. That's AA's one-day-at-a-time philosophy, which urges people to think only about today. Staying sober today. Going to a meeting today. Tomorrow will take care of itself. Of course, for some of us that's a difficult philosophy. We've been trained to worry about tomorrow.

It's clear that many people gradually reduce the number of meetings they attend over the years. Many go to meetings for the rest of their lives. Some eventually stop, but their recoveries almost always suffer if they don't continue to live the AA principles—meditating, doing daily inventories, listening to tapes, reading AA literature, talking to and socializing with AA friends, persuading other alcoholics or addicts to get help. Once AA thinking and behavior become ingrained, the structure of regular meetings may not be required. Still, there's solid evidence that people who stop going to meetings are at higher risk of relapse than those who continue.

AA is like an insurance policy. You may never need it, but it's good to know you have it going for you—just in case. At high risk periods in your life you may want to increase your coverage (and your AA attendance). And you have to keep in mind that like any insurance policy, its protective benefits run out if they aren't renewed.

8

MAINTAINING SOBRIETY IN PHASE ONE

Getting clean and sober is easy compared to staying that way—especially in the first weeks and months of recovery. But if you know what kinds of problems to expect and how to deal with them, you can remain chemical-free. You can start to turn your life around. You can begin to exorcise your alcoholic/addictive thinking and exercise a clean and sober (but not somber) lifestyle.

WHAT'S ON YOUR MIND?

SETTING PRIORITIES

"I've been sober for six weeks and I feel as though I'm being pulled in four directions at once—family, work, church, AA. I don't know what to do first."

All day, every day, we make choices. And we make those choices, or should make them, based on our value systems. But alcoholics and drug addicts turn their value systems upside down. For example:

❖ A doctor who has always put his career right up there after God and family suddenly finds that whiskey is the most important thing in his life. More important than getting home for dinner with his family or taking them to church on Sunday. More important than his patients.

❖ A teenager who has dreamed of being a teacher and a mother does cocaine on a dare or for the thrill of it. Soon she's so obsessed with the drug that she drops out of school, abandons her hopes of going to college, sells her body for drug money, and exposes herself to diseases that could cripple her chances of having children.

Guide Lines

❖ While you're not responsible for your disease, you are responsible for your recovery. Once you recognize that you are an alcoholic/addict, it is your responsibility to become sober and stay that way.

❖ Fear, anxiety, insecurity, uncertainty, and confusion are just some of the feelings that you can expect to experience in recovery. Through a good recovery program you can learn to deal with them sober.

❖ Unless you change the way you live your life and learn to confront your problems instead of using a chemical eraser on them, your sobriety will always be at high risk.

❖ What you have to do to make a successful recovery from any disease (cancer, heart disease, alcoholism/addiction) is usually not fun, but it is often necessary for survival.

❖ In Phase One it's imperative to focus on getting better and not to allow yourself to be sidetracked by issues related to the ethnic or other group to which you belong. In Phase Two you can begin to pay attention to those issues.

❖ A mother who truly loves her family spends most of her household money on vodka. Her kids wear outgrown shoes, don't get enough nutritious food, and are emotionally deprived.

Values—and lives—turned upside down.

Once your drug of choice was the most important thing in your life, too. Now getting well has to be number one. More important than your job, your family, your hobbies, more important than anything else. That would be pretty obvious to you and those around you if you'd suffered a heart attack. It may be less obvious to you and to them if you're recovering from alcohol or drug addiction. But for now, nothing should come before your AA group, aftercare meetings, meditation periods, and if you're having them, your counseling sessions.

"I had to learn to make sobriety my number-one priority. That meant learning that no matter what happened—say, I flunked out, or I got in trouble with mom and dad—as long as I didn't take a drink, I'd be okay."

The choices you'll face won't be easy. It will be time for your AA meeting and the World Series or the Miss America pageant will be on TV. What do you do? Go to the meeting. (But tape the show if you have a VCR.) Not that entertainment and relaxation are bad for you, but right now anything that scrambles your priorities jeopardizes your recovery.

Other priorities will also have to take a back seat. You'll be tempted to plunge enthusiastically back into your old life and make up for lost time. Don't. If you can afford to work part-time or at a stress-free job for a while, that would be ideal. Transforming yourself from a drugaholic into a workaholic would not be. At least try to avoid twelve-hour days and sixty-hour weeks. See Chapter 12 for tips on organizing your work life during early recovery.

If you're not already in a love relationship, this is not the time to begin one. Relationships that develop during early recovery are almost always disastrous. You may believe yours will be an exception—everyone does—but read page 214 to see why postponing love makes sense now. If you do have a spouse or special person in your life, that relationship is probably pretty sick, thanks to your destructive past behavior. It isn't going to get miraculously better instantly, and in fact will take considerable effort to resuscitate. Meanwhile, your special person will have to be a paragon of patience because you won't be able to put much of that effort in until your recovery is on a sounder footing. Happily, your drug and alcohol recovery will eventually help your relationship recover.

If you're a parent, you won't even be able to spend much extra time with your children, making up for missed moments and lost opportunities during your years of addiction. That, too, will

"I wanted to be a good father, husband, churchman, attorney, citizen, and drink whiskey—in that order. Or so I thought. I wouldn't believe that whiskey was the most important priority in my life—until I lost everything to it. My wife, my right to practice law, my religious life, even my freedom."

THE SUPERWOMAN SYNDROME

You've seen her. You may even *be* her. She gets up before dawn to do a load of laundry, press a dress for work, pack the kids' lunch boxes, and maybe squeeze in a meditation. Then it's getting the kids off to school, husband off to work, the dishes in the dishwasher, and she's off to her job. She is a workaholic all morning (to prove she is no longer the other kind of "holic"), then slips off during lunch to buy a birthday present for the party her daughter is going to and to pick up a new tie for that important business meeting her spouse has scheduled.

She's exhausted, but her day has only just begun. There is the afternoon at work, ferrying children when she gets home, cleaning (her house can pass the white-glove test any hour of any day of any week), cooking (Julia Child would be impressed), mothering (her kids are at the top of the class). She pushes on, trying to do it all, putting her health and her recovery at risk.

No one can do it all without paying too high a price. Exhaustion, remember, is a risk factor for relapse. It interferes with good judgment and rational behavior. And Superwoman is exhausted most of the time.

To avoid falling into this trap, set your priorities and limit your commitments. Use shortcuts when you can (disposable plates, ready-to-serve foods, frozen vegetables, broilable meats and fish). Learn to ignore the dust balls under the sofa and the drip marks on the kitchen cabinets. Remove them once a week instead of daily. Hire a baby sitter occasionally, or exchange sitting with a neighbor or friend. And get your spouse, if you have one, to get involved. *Wife* should not be synonymous with *slave*.

have to be put on hold. But don't worry about losing your loved ones while you recover. What they want and need more than anything else is for you to be sober for good. And they will understand that if they read Chapter 27, which is addressed to them, and especially if they become involved in Al-Anon or Alateen.

STAYING CLEAN AND SOBER

"I've just gotten back home after four weeks of inpatient treatment. But I'm nervous. I've tried to go on the wagon before and never succeeded. I don't know if I can this time, either."

At your next AA meeting, look around you. Multiply the people in the room, all or most of whom have succeeded in remaining sober, by 68,000 AA groups around the world. You don't have to be a great mathematician to realize that literally millions of people have managed to stay sober through AA. And you can join the crowd. The trick is to use the tools you were given in treatment. Neglect or forget them, and you will almost certainly fail.

To improve your chances of making it, do what those who have been most successful do: immerse yourself in Alcoholics Anonymous or another Twelve-Step program, attend meetings more than once a week, participate in the group, work all the Steps (not just the first three), take a sponsor,* and later, sponsor others. Right now that may seem like a tall order. It is. But it works.

In fact, the success rate in treating alcoholism this way (assuming patients strictly adhere to their programs) is a lot better over the long haul than the success physicians have treating diabetes with insulin, cardiovascular disease with bypass surgery, or cancer with chemotherapy.

If you don't follow the recommendations for dealing with your alcoholism (or your addiction) given to you during treatment or at AA, then your odds of long-term survival are about as poor as those of the diabetic who dumps half the sugar bowl in his morning coffee, the coronary patient who insists on bacon and eggs for breakfast every day, or the cancer victim who fails to show up for her course of chemotherapy. Those odds, as you know, aren't very good.

In bed tonight, just before you fall asleep (the hardest time for most of us to lie to ourselves), ask yourself, "How much do I want to stay clean and sober?" If you tell yourself, "More than anything in the world. I'll do anything to get myself straight!" you've got a good chance of making it. If you hesitate, if you're not ready to make a total commitment to the effort, you've probably already lost the game.

Remember, you're a person who, when you wanted booze or drugs, did whatever you had to do to get it. You let nothing stand in your way. Transfer this same determination and creativity to your recovery, and you'll be picking up clean-and-sober anniversary chips at AA meetings from here to eternity.

FEAR OF FAILURE

"I really want to stay sober, but I keep worrying that I'm going to slip and blow it."

If you're worried, you're in good shape. It's the folks who *don't* worry who are more likely to relapse. Working your program religiously, heeding the suggestions of your counselors, sponsor, and other

*You'll see a lot of references to your "sponsor" throughout this book. See page 114 for a complete explanation of how the sponsor system works in Twelve-Step programs.

advisors, and following the recommendations in this book will help to keep you on your feet. Still, you never know when a banana peel will suddenly appear in your path. It's estimated that about half of all recoverees will have at least one slip or relapse.

If at any point you feel shaky and fear a slip is imminent, see the tips for forestalling relapse on page 549. If, in spite of all your efforts, you do relapse, don't feel it's the end of your world. Like most negative experiences in life, relapse can have its positive side if you look for it. By examining your slip and what led up to it, you have the power to take what looks like failure and transform it into success: a more solid recovery next time.

KEEPING YOUR SECRET

"I've been on the wagon for six weeks, going faithfully to AA. But I haven't told any of my friends about this—it's very embarrassing."

Some people are embarrassed to talk about having a depressive illness or getting a divorce or being put on restricted activity because of a heart condition. It's natural. Nobody likes to be different. Most people don't like to be pitied. But as millions of people have learned in all kinds of support groups, talking about our problems rather than burying them really helps.

The word "anonymous" is used so much in alcoholism circles—Alcoholics Anonymous is after all the center of the world for most recovering people—that those in recovery sometimes take this to mean that they should keep it all a deep dark secret.

In fact, the anonymity in AA applies only to those members who speak out in the media—the press, radio, TV, and films—where full names are not to be divulged. During meetings members use just first names to introduce themselves ("I'm Leslie, and I'm an alcoholic"), but most share their identities as well as their problems fully and openly with other members.

Actually, it's important to your recovery for others outside of AA to know about it. If, for example, your drinking buddies don't know you've given up alcohol, they may lead you into temptation without intending to. Telling them you are sober will give them a choice: They can either support your efforts or bow out of your life.

But being open about recovery is not significant just for you. When you let it be known at a party that you don't drink, or talk openly about going to AA meetings, you offer support and encouragement to others who are contemplating sobriety but are afraid of venturing into the unknown. After years of being under the influence, you can become a good influence.

LITERACY PROBLEMS

"I met this guy at an AA meeting who, when I suggested he take some booklets and pick up a copy of the Big Book, admitted he can't read. Without that kind of support, how is he going to stay sober?"

Your friend is not alone. Many people on alcohol and drugs do not read well. But they can and do get sober if they're willing to try. Assure your friend that he can, too.

The first thing he needs to do is to be sure that he goes to a Twelve-Step meeting every day—twice a day when he can. What he can't get out of books, he can get at meetings.

Second, he should get hold of AA tapes. Much AA material—including the Twelve Steps, many books, and some great talks—is on tape. Other recovery books and materials are also available on tape at local bookstores as well as through mail order (see page 568). Tuning in every morning and evening will help strengthen your friend's recovery.

Third, he should be sure to select an experienced sponsor and use him as a resource. Working his program will build your friend's confidence and positive feelings about himself. He can put his life history and moral inventory on tape rather than on paper. Illiteracy shouldn't be a bar to his succeeding at recovery.

Fourth, he should ask his sponsor or counselor about finding a literacy class. Almost every city and town has such classes for adults. Improving his reading skills will improve his chances of making a new and better life for himself, and thus his chances of staying sober.

FEELING MISERABLE

"I haven't had a drink in two months. I should be happy as a June bug; everything should be great. So why do I feel miserable? Why is my life such a mess?"

Coming to grips with the idea that sobriety is not instant heaven is an important step in your recovery. No matter how much they may be warned, most alcoholics/addicts expect their upside-down world to turn immediately right side up. Instead, for a while it may spin like a top.

That really shouldn't be surprising. There you are out in the world without your "best friend"—no drinking buddies, no ego, no self, no nothing. You feel like a black hole in outer space. You've surrendered your habitual way of coping with life, and now you have to find new ways—without your chemistry set. At the same time you have to start mopping up the mess you made of your life. All this won't happen while you count to ten. Don't expect too much too soon.

In the meantime, don't cry over spilt gin. You'll have plenty of time later to make amends. And don't worry about the future—how you will get through the year, or even the month, or the week. If you can make it through until it's time to put on your pajamas, that's all you need. Just get better one day at a time. Use any or all of the tools available to you: a Twelve-Step program like Alcoholics Anonymous; a continuing-care program, if one was developed for you during inpatient treatment; an outpatient program; your sponsor, your counselor, physician, or psychiatrist; others further along in recovery than you; the Big Book and other AA materials; and books like this one.

Right now it may seem an impossible dream, but you will get better *if you work at it*. However, and this is an important however, you won't always be happy. Nobody is. You've been anesthetized by chemicals for so long that you've probably forgotten that crucial fact. Life is full of highs and lows, which you are just beginning to feel again. For a while during recovery, they are going to be exaggerated—you'll feel *very* up or *very* down. But that will change. As you learn to cope with ordinary feelings and everyday problems, your moods will moderate.

You may find that part of your discontent is linked to the work of recovery. You may not find it jolly good fun to attend seemingly infinite numbers of aftercare and AA meetings, or to study the Big Book, or to meditate. And you may find working your steps the hardest work you've ever done. But the diabetic doesn't think it's fun to self-inflict insulin wounds every day. Nor does the average kidney patient look forward to his regular dialysis appointment. They accept these uncomfortable treatments in order to save their lives. And that's exactly why you should faithfully follow your recovery program.

For more on dealing with depression, see page 326. If nothing seems to help and you aren't finding good days among the bad, get professional help from a therapist certified in the treatment of alcoholism/addiction.

FEELING GUILTY

"Ever since I started drinking, my father's been telling me that I was bad. Now that I'm sober, I know he was right. How could I have ever done the things that I did? To my family? To myself?"

Father doesn't always know best. The fact that you did some bad things—even a lot of them—while you were drinking doesn't mean *you* are bad. The generalized accusation that drinkers or addicts are bad people just isn't true, yet many recoverees accept it and drown themselves in guilt instead of chemicals. The alcoholic/addict is no more evil than the asthmatic or the person with allergies. All are victims of a disease.

To understand why alcoholics do things when they are high that they would never do sober, you (and your father) have to understand the way alcohol affects the brain. Alcohol is an anesthetic to the central nervous system, which includes the brain. Even small amounts of alcohol can turn off activity in the cerebral cortex, the most sophisticated part of our brain. Long before alcohol causes us to stagger or slur our speech, it has numbed the part of the brain that we use for judgment and that controls our value system, our memory, and some of our feelings and emotions. Some drugs, such as those that depress the central nervous system (sedatives, for example) work in a similar way, others somewhat differently. But all affect the brain and, thus, behavior.

With even a little alcohol or a single dose of a drug, we are ready to flout the law, ignore the difference between right and wrong, and behave in ways totally contrary to our sober concepts of good and evil. What tends to come out are more primitive emotions, the kinds associated with survival: inappropriate sexual feelings and urges, the fight or flight response to a perceived threat, aggression. Don't expect to see it in the tens of thousands of beer commercials, but studies have shown that most crime in this country, particularly violent crime, is committed under the influence of alcohol and other drugs. Not because everyone who drinks or uses drugs is bad, but because their controls, moral and otherwise, are temporarily turned off.

So honor thy father, but respectfully reject his idea that you are inherently evil for drinking. Do examine your life for the things you've done that you aren't proud of, that have caused others pain. As you move forward along the steps in recovery, do what you can to make amends. To be sure that you avoid causing pain in the future, never again take that first drink or drug. That's the one that will get you into trouble.

"My husband has been very forgiving about the things I did while I was drinking. But I don't think I can forgive myself."

It's easy to accept the notion that nobody is perfect, but many alcoholics/addicts find it difficult to apply it to themselves. Without self-forgiveness, however, recovery isn't possible. When under the influence, everyone does things they later wish they hadn't. That doesn't make them right, but it does make them forgivable. Perhaps you should even be grateful for some of that terrible behavior. In the end, it's probably what made you realize you had a problem. So forgive yourself, and start to make behavior consistent with your value system—behavior you can be proud of—part of your everyday life.

Working on a recovery program that

includes the Twelve Steps will also help you learn to forgive yourself. Some people find the Fourth Step particularly helpful (see page 111).

POWERLESSNESS AND CONTROL

"I'm totally confused. How can admitting I'm powerless and turning control of my life over to a Higher Power, as AA tells me I should, help me to control my drinking?"

Sometimes the laws of nature don't work the way we think they should. For example, we all have a natural instinct to avoid falling, and most of the time this makes sense. But one of the first things an instructor teaches the student learning to fly a small plane is to dramatically modify this reaction. If the plane stalls and goes into a tailspin, you have to ignore the instinct that screams to yank back on the stick and slow the fall. In fact, you need to do just the opposite: Push forward on the stick to accelerate your plane's deadly plunge toward the earth far below. Surrendering control—in this case to natural law and the greater power of gravity—increases the speed that is absolutely essential if you are to regain power and altitude, avoid a fatal crash, and soar happily and safely off.

When life dives out of control, the instinct is to exert more control to level it off. This works for most people. But it's different for those with the disease of alcoholism/addiction. In the struggle against the compulsion to use alcohol and other drugs, this instinctive reaction only makes things worse—much as it does in a plummeting plane. Paradoxically, people with the greatest self control often have the most difficult time with alcohol and drug habits. The more control they exert, the greater their compulsion to use. With more use, more bad things happen, which encourages more attempts at control, which . . . and the cycle continues. The need to control often spills over into other aspects of life—family, work, recreation—and fosters a false sense of also controlling one's drinking or drug use. But no matter how much control is exerted, the compulsion to use doesn't go away. In fact, with each renewed effort at control, it grows and again overwhelms.

Just as it takes doing the opposite of what instinct tells us when a plane stalls, so it takes doing the opposite when our lives become unmanageable because of alcohol or other drugs. Instead of attempting to seize more control, we must completely abandon consciously trying to dominate the compulsion. What happens? Paradoxically, with no tug-of-war over control, the compulsion diminishes. As they say in AA, "The surrender stops the battle."

Surrendering control of your life, your drinking, those around you—isn't easy for the alcoholic/addict. For most, running the show (usually into the ground) has become a way of life. But it is necessary. And in the end, it will make your life more manageable.

"I can't convince my husband to go to Al-Anon. He just doesn't seem to want to get involved in my recovery."

Just as you have to stop trying to control your drinking, you have to stop thinking it's your job to control those around you. You can't change everybody else—only *you.* You can't force others to do what you want them to do; you can only get *you* to do what you want. So let it go.

Your husband will eventually notice that you're no longer trying to control him, and he may even come to recognize that he is as responsible for his behavior as you are for yours. At that point he just might volunteer to go to Al-Anon.

Of course you can gently (without nagging) suggest that he go to Al-Anon. You can drop a few appropriate folders on the kitchen table. Even leave this book open at Chapter 27. Maybe he will get the message, maybe he won't. If he doesn't, don't let that lead you off on a distracting emotional side trip. Accept it, and focus on yourself.

It may take those around you a while to forget how you used to try to pull their strings, to forgive you for the chaos you wrought in their lives. Once they begin to see that you've really changed, they may be ready to change themselves.

FEELING GREAT

"Since I got out of treatment, I feel like I could lick the world. I can't believe how good I feel."

You'd be smart not to believe it because, alas, it's unlikely to last. Today you may be on top of the world, tomorrow in the pits. Some recovering people enjoy more good days than bad, some more bad than good, but virtually all have Death Valleys between their Pikes Peaks.

It's not uncommon for recoverees to feel reborn and omnipotent after a week or ten days of sobriety—like you, ready to take on the world. If they're in treatment, they decide it's time to go home. If they've been going to AA, they're ready to taper off. If they're in outpatient treatment, they start missing appointments.

Some manage to stay sober while the good feelings last. Then the moment a dark mood engulfs them, they tumble off the wagon. Others, lulled by feelings of euphoria, conclude there's been some mistake and they were never addicted at all. They blithely return to their old ways, and to the downward spiral of their lives. Still others manage to stay sober for a while, but swiftly resuming their overcommitted lives, neglect their recoveries and end up "losing it."

So it's okay to appreciate feeling good, but it's a bad idea to read too much into it or to expect it to last forever. No one is happy *all* the time. Faithfully and patiently follow your program as if you were feeling awful, force yourself to keep a lid on your activities and emotions, and give yourself time to heal. You will.

COERCED SOBRIETY

"I was pushed into treatment and now I'm going to AA—all against my will."

You're not alone. A lot of people come into treatment with footprints on their backsides and a fifth in their hands. It may be the footprint of their boss, a spouse who issued an ultimatum, the sheriff who picked them up for DUI, the doctor who gave fair warning, or some life crisis of middling to serious intensity.

Many of these people aren't as honest as you are about their feelings. They don't own up to the fact that it's "against their will," that they don't really want to change their way of living, that they bitterly resent being forced to bring the good drinking times to a dead end. They just go through the motions, pretending to be interested in sobriety.

But that doesn't doom them—or you—to failure. It's said that "if you bring the body, the mind will follow." All that's necessary is to be open to change. The odds are that down deep somewhere that's what you want, or you wouldn't have gotten involved in recovery no matter what the pressures.

You've come this far. Give sobriety a

chance. Life down the road could turn out to be a lot more enjoyable sober. Give it your best shot by working your program faithfully. And give it some time. Enough time so that you're over the initial discomforts and your head has cleared. Usually this takes about a year—though it may seem like ten. Then evaluate the situation, using your own judgment and the impressions of those around you. Is life more satisfying? Are you feeling better? Have your relationships improved? Are you doing your job better? One thing is sure: Your health will be better.

In the meantime, keep in mind that the drinking you enjoyed so much was slowly but surely terminating you (that's true of heavy drinking even if it's not out of control). And that sobriety, like any treatment for a disease, isn't fun and games. How many heart attack victims do you know who were thrilled to give up their T-bone steaks?

CONTROLLED DRINKING?

"My husband says that he's heard that instead of abstaining completely, it's possible for an alcoholic to return to controlled drinking after a while."

File this one under "Impossible Dreams." Unfortunately for those alcoholics who are fatally attracted to the idea of "controlled drinking," there isn't much evidence to support it. There's been some suggestion that a small number of young problem drinkers who imbibe fewer than 48½ drinks a week (we didn't make up the number—it came from a study) can return to controlled drinking after a period of abstention. Even if this is so, it would be impossible to predict just which drinkers could safely try controlled drinking, and picking the wrong ones could be a fatal mistake.

At any rate, long-term studies don't hold out much hope. The original research that claimed it was possible for alcoholics to return to controlled drinking was less than reliable. In fact, it was tainted by charges of fraud, with most of the purportedly successful study subjects later hospitalized, in prison, or dead. What may have been only a matter of flawed technique for the researchers may well have been, in its imprudent encouragement of controlled drinking, a matter of life and death for some unlucky alcoholics.

The fact is, it's extremely rare for a person with a long-term problem to be able to switch permanently to controlled drinking. The first drink tends

ONE DAY AT A TIME

You'll hear a lot of one-day-at-a-time talk in Alcoholics Anonymous and among recovering alcoholics. It makes sense. It works. And it bears a comfortably familiar resemblance to your old drinking and drugging lifestyle. Think about it. One day at a time is the way you lived day after miserable day: "I'll drink today and quit tomorrow." "Just one last snort today, then never again." "Where am I going to get a hit today?" All your energy, all your efforts, all your imagination and creativity aimed straight as a laser at getting today's supply, at getting through the day. But that was then. Now all you have to do is worry about getting through one more day *without* your favorite substances. Tomorrow will take care of itself. Or rather, you'll take care of it when it becomes today.

A PILL FOR ALCOHOLICS

When dealing with alcoholism/ addiction, it's usually preferable not to fight fire with fire—a drug with a drug. But sometimes there's no other way. The one and only way that's been found to stop some really hard-core alcoholics from drinking is to give them a drug that will make them terribly sick if they imbibe even a swallow of booze. That vile but vital medication is disulfiram, or Antabuse, administered as a white tablet that looks like an oversize aspirin.

Antabuse blocks the enzyme that breaks down acetaldehyde (the by-product of alcohol metabolism) in the blood. It leaves a metallic or garlicky taste in the mouth and may trigger drowsiness, fatigue, and headaches. But it does much worse to the poor soul who takes it and then dares to drink. Since further metabolism is blocked, acetaldehyde (its closest cousin is embalming fluid) builds up in the blood. The face flushes, the skin gets red, the heart begins to pound; there is nausea, vomiting, headache, shortness of breath, and rapid heartbeat. It's reportedly like being seasick and having a migraine headache, an asthma attack, and a coronary simultaneously.

Antabuse is not usually given during treatment, or to a person who hasn't been sober for at least twenty-four hours. It's generally doled out daily in a doctor's office, at a clinic, or through an outpatient program. To ensure that it is taken, it's crushed (wily alcoholics have been known to tuck a whole pill into a cheek to be spat out later) and mixed with water. The slurry is downed in full view of a watchful doctor or other medical personnel. This daily dose is usually continued for several months. Once a pattern of sobriety is established, a double dose given three times a week is normally satisfactory.

Antabuse use should be individually tailored. For some recoverees, it is only necessary during the transition to sobriety and can be gradually tapered off. For those with a history of repeated relapse, it may need to be continued for a year or even two. If

to be like the first salted peanut. Some drinkers are able to control their consumption for a while—trying to do so is, in fact, a sign of the disease. They take just one drink a day for a few weeks and persuade themselves that they don't have a drinking problem. The next step is to say, "Okay, I've proved I'm not an alcoholic. I can control my drinking if I want to. I just don't happen to want to right now." Pretty soon Mr. Overconfident goes out on the town, gets plastered, and is right back where he started.

Asking to be allowed to try controlled drinking makes about as much sense as someone allergic to penicillin demanding to be put on a regimen of "controlled" penicillin. Besides, if someone has already run amok on alcohol or drugs, why would he insist on keeping it a part of his life unless he felt he couldn't live without it? If that's not an out-of-control addiction, what is?

WHEN THE EUPHORIA WANES

"I felt so good for the first month, so proud of myself for not drinking. Now suddenly the thrill is gone. I'm so depressed."

You're right on schedule. If you kept feeling great, that would probably interfere with your re-after two years a patient still feels unable to cope without Antabuse, his or her recovery program needs evaluation.

Taking Antabuse is another way of learning to be accountable to someone, since you're expected to show up every day at the same time, same place. It also switches your focus from drinking to not drinking, and requires you to make a conscious decision each day to abstain.

But Antabuse isn't for everybody. It doesn't work for any drug except alcohol. And it's not given to pregnant women, or to anyone with cardiovascular disease or severe liver disease. Good candidates are recovering alcoholics who:

❖ drink on impulse and are likely to find themselves drinking before they realize what they are doing (this teaches them the hard way to "think before you drink");

❖ are young healthy beginners and can benefit from the education—they must learn to read labels for hidden alcohol, and to be up front about their problem to waiters, pushy party hostesses, and old drinking buddies;

❖ need to assure their employers they aren't drinking (sometimes it's a required part of an employee rehab program); or

❖ are going through a particularly stressful or high-risk period.

In the rare person, Antabuse causes no significant reaction and so is ineffective in the usual doses. Strongly motivated patients may agree to have the dosage increased. Also rarely, the drug may cause or exacerbate medical problems, particularly those that affect the heart or respiratory system. If you are on Antabuse and do ingest alcohol, either intentionally or inadvertently, go to the nearest emergency room or call your doctor immediately. To ensure that you are properly treated if you are in a medical emergency and lose consciousness, carry an Antabuse ID card. Also be sure to inform family and friends, as well as hosts, waiters, and anyone else serving you food or drink that you can have *absolutely no alcohol.*

covery, and keep you from looking at yourself and working your program. A real recovery goes beyond the first pink clouds and the novelty of being sober. Reality, where you'll be best off living, has its ups and downs, and as you get well it's normal to feel its variations. We all do.

Being depressed, anxious, or confused at this stage serves as a reminder that you still have a way to go in recovery. Such feelings should help to point you in the right direction—toward, for example, a couple of extra AA meetings—for further growth in sobriety. The "down" of depression is really where the no-pain/no-gain part of your recovery begins. Now it's time for the hard work.

SUBSTITUTE COMPULSIONS

"I haven't had a drink in two months. It doesn't even seem to bother me much anymore. But I seem to be going for food with the same urgency that I went for booze."

Alcoholics and drug addicts are compulsive. Their addictions are obsessive attempts to help them get rid of bad feelings, to help them feel good inside by changing the world around them. Where other people can resign themselves to occasional bad

LEST YOU FORGET: THE BAD OLD DAYS

We humans have a wonderful ability to block out bad memories. That ability allows a mom who has endured a grueling forty-hour labor to cheerfully return to the delivery room two years later, ready to go through the same harrowing experience again. It allows a person who has had a disastrous marriage to try again. And again. And unfortunately, it allows alcoholics and addicts to forget how bloody awful things were when they were drinking or using, and to jump-start the whole process for the umpteenth time.

The advice to "remember your last drunk [or high]" is valuable, but it's difficult to do. So that your bad memories will remain forever an incentive to remain sober, capture them in words, pictures, or both. While the images are still vivid in your mind, write yourself a letter describing the degradation and misery of your life before you became sober. Don't spare a single squalid detail. If you have any photographs to document your words, attach them to the letter.

A photo of you looking like a Bowery wino or a degenerate junkie sleeping in the streets would be a fine addition. Or one of the car you totaled. Or the couch you vomited on. Or of the wife or child you battered. If you have a video camera, you can tell your story and show close-ups of your photos on tape. Those gory details may someday save your life.

If you feel you might shrink from looking at this incriminating evidence on your own, entrust it to your sponsor or a friend with orders to show it to you when, nostalgic about "the good old days," you seem on the brink of a drink or a drug.

If you ever forget your last drunk, you probably haven't had it.

---

feelings (sorrow, anger, disappointment, insecurity, pain), alcoholics/addicts try to rinse them away with chemicals. When the chemical option is removed during recovery, they turn to other "highs." A hot fudge sundae, a new dress, a new set of golf clubs, a new sweetheart, cleaning the house that's already spic and span from top to bottom. The problem is that the good feeling thus gained quickly fades, and then they need to compulsively repeat their actions.

Substitute compulsions often lead right back to the original one: drinking or drugging. Or ultimately they become self-destructive themselves. Potentially hazardous compulsions include overeating, smoking, gambling, excessive spending, promiscuous or inappropriate sex (adultery, incest, pedophilia), and overworking (the classic workaholic). See the facing page for ways of dealing with compulsions.

It would be nice to eliminate all destructive obsessions—to change the alcoholic/addict's pattern of thinking, to help them acknowledge and accept bad feelings as normal. But this can be difficult. And often, once treatment is over and outside controls relax, recoverees lapse into their old obsessive ways.

Substituting a positive compulsion can often have a more favorable impact on recovery than fruitless attempts at uprooting compulsive behavior down to the last twitch. Going to AA meetings and working the program is one such positive compulsion. (Even if it becomes an addiction, at least it will save your life rather than take it.) Exercise is another. But don't let jogging, swimming, or biking grow into an obsession that takes over your life and distracts you from the more vital work of recovery.

If you find yourself hobbling along on the crutch of a substitute compulsion in early recovery, ask yourself if, in the long run, you wouldn't be a lot better off learning to deal with your inner feelings rather than compulsively covering them up. Get some help from your sponsor in deciding which behaviors can stay and which must go.

CONTROLLING NONCONSTRUCTIVE COMPULSIONS

Wanting a drink or a drug may not be the only compulsion you experience in recovery. There may be a whole range of substitute compulsions that fill your life. If you're prepared for them, you have a better chance of handling them. Here are compulsion-banishing techniques that other recoverees have used successfully.

THE RANDOM COMPULSION: You wake up one fine Monday morning and feel a sudden burst of inspiration. You know exactly what you need to make your life complete: a motorcycle. A white one. A BMW. By the time the sleep is out of your eyes, you're phoning around town to price one. If you're not careful, you could own one before noon. Instead, give your compulsion some rope. Wait until Thursday and see if the need is still pressing. (It's not likely to be.) If it is, then start making those phone calls. But find out not only what it will cost, but what the monthly payments are, where you would keep it, how you would learn to drive it, what the risks are, and so on. Don't take any final action for at least two weeks. By then, you'll probably have lost interest.

If it's a small thing you just must have or die, simply postpone the gratification for a few hours. If, for example, at 11 A.M. you feel a burning compulsion to buy another bangle bracelet (although you're well aware you have six you haven't even worn yet), plan not to make your purchase until 3 P.M. In the meantime, find someone to lunch with to take your mind off the glittering prize. By 3, the odds are excellent that the compulsion will have passed.

THE REPEATED COMPULSION: You are becoming as addicted to food or to work or to playing the horses or to sex or to bags of Snickers as you once were to drugs or alcohol. It's all you think about, and it's interfering with your getting on with a normal life. Such a compulsion is dealt with in much the same way as your chemical addiction. Recognize that you have no control or power over these habits and seek help to deal with them—from your Higher Power, your sponsor, your counselor. Try meditation, apply the first three Steps to your problem, or recite the Serenity Prayer. Find and join a Twelve-Step program geared to your compulsion (Overeaters Anonymous, Gamblers Anonymous, Sex Anonymous, etc.). If necessary, start one (see page 417). But remember, your compulsive behavior is probably telling you something—that you have not yet applied yourself completely and earnestly to recovery.

THE DANGEROUS COMPULSION: If your compulsion is hurting you or someone else (food binges or purging, sexual acting out, violent behavior, gambling, for example), you need, and should seek, professional help immediately.

"I started watching TV compulsively when I was using cocaine. Now that I'm in recovery I still spend nearly every waking hour at home in front of the box. My husband is about to pull the plug."

Disconnecting the TV might be the best thing that could happen to you. The role of couch potato is not conducive to a healthy recovery. In fact, because of the association with using cocaine, excessive TV viewing now could lead to a compulsion to use again.

Like you, many recoverees feel powerless to get up and turn off the TV. (They're not the only ones in our society, of course.) The inertia becomes self-perpetuating. The longer they sit and watch, the more passive they become, and the less likely they are to summon up the energy to push the Off button.

Many claim they watch TV to help them relax. But studies show that people are less relaxed following a session in front of the TV than they are following a session of exercise or other leisure activities.

Compulsive or excessive viewers tend to be more irritable, tense, and sad than the rest of us. They often feel that they aren't in control of their lives. (Controlling the channels may, in fact, be a kind of power trip for them.) And they are much more likely to switch on the set when they are sad, lonely, anxious, or angry, or when they are seeking to distract themselves from their worries or their ennui.

So maybe you should cancel your cable subscription or stuff your TV deep into the hall closet for a while. Find other, more constructive activities, particularly out of the the house, to fill your time. Go to more AA meetings. Try museums, concerts, the theater, sober parties (where nobody drinks). Start an exercise program. Take up reading, petit point, woodworking, drawing, or the guitar. If you crave watching figures interacting on a screen, catch a movie now and then. Because it runs for under two hours and you share it with a live audience that laughs and cries with you, it tends to be a less passive activity than TV watching.

If you still have trouble shaking those bad feelings, don't rebury yourself in TV-land. Seek professional counseling instead.

COMPULSIVE BUSYNESS

"My sponsor thinks I need to slow down. I admit I have a pretty hectic schedule, but there's nothing I can cut out. Everything I do is top priority."

Only one thing can be "top priority" right now: your recovery. Keeping busy is okay, and may even be helpful. But there's a difference between choosing to occupy yourself with a lot of healthy activities and keeping busy out of compulsive need. With the first, you're in control; in the second, compulsive behaviors control you. If you find that the list of things you *absolutely must* do is endless, which is what it sounds like, you're probably under the thumb of your compulsions. This can be somewhat risky even if your pursuits are all worthwhile (AA-, family-, or work-related, for example), but it's particularly dangerous if they aren't. Turn to your counselor, your sponsor, or your doctor for guidance.

CONTINUED CRAVINGS FOR DRUGS OR ALCOHOL

"I haven't had a drink in two months. But a day doesn't go by that I don't think, 'God, I want a drink.' When will the craving go?"

Hard to say. It's different for each recovering person. Some people claim their cravings ceased virtually the moment they quit—almost miraculously. But for most people, the compulsion to drink or drug gradually loosens its bulldog-grip day by day during the first year. In the beginning, there may be a constant gnawing. Then cravings pop up only several times a day. Suddenly you realize you haven't had a craving in a week, or a month. Nobody continues to crave chemicals forever.

If cravings continue after a year of sobriety, it's time to get some extra help from an addiction counselor or from a physician with ASAM or AAPAA accreditation (see page 45). You may even need to consider in- or outpatient treatment if you've never had any, or a brief booster visit if you have. Living with frequent or constant cravings over a long period of time can be pretty miserable and could hinder your recovery. Worse, it could cause you to stumble down the rocky road to relapse. See page 162 for tips on what to do when a craving strikes.

SEXUAL COMPULSIONS

"While I was using drugs, sex was no big deal. It was a way to get drugs. Now suddenly I want to go to bed with every guy I meet."

You've probably substituted one compulsion (sex) for another (drugs). This isn't a healthy substitution—especially with AIDS, syphilis, and gonorrhea rampant among the chemically addicted. But it is a very common one. People afflicted with the disease of addiction often have difficulty with relationships. They seem unable to achieve true intimacy, to communicate with loved ones much beyond a superficial level. Drugs or alcohol can camouflage this inadequacy. When these chemical cover-ups are removed, the need for intimacy resurfaces. Confusing intimacy with intimate acts, compulsives try to satisfy their hunger for love and intimacy through sex—with different partners, over and over again. But no matter how they tally up the score, it's never fulfilling because they never achieve the personal rewards of a genuinely loving and mutually responsive relationship.

"The first thing I wanted to do when I got rejected by my first-choice college was to start using again. The second thing was to kill myself. But I went to a meeting and talked about it, and I survived. And it turns out my second-choice school isn't half bad."

The compulsion may lead beyond promiscuous sex to bizarre and reckless sex, possibly even including pedophilia, rape, incest, adultery. The individual wants to believe that (like the lines of coke of yesteryear) the pleasures of sexual conquest will conquer inner discontent. But shortly after orgasm, the feelings of worthlessness, regret, even shame, are likely to return. In the end, the bad feelings are even worse.

When recovery is well under way, and especially when relations with one's own partner improve or when an enduring new relationship develops, these compulsions tend to fade. If they don't, a Twelve-Step program (Sex Anonymous) may be helpful. In extreme cases, especially if the behavior could be risky, professional help should be sought.

Acting on your compulsions could sabotage your recovery. Talk to your counselor or sponsor about your feelings. You may hesitate because you feel embarrassed or awkward discussing something so personal, but an inability to open up about real feelings is a major reason you have this problem in the first place. Talking about it may help unblock the channels of communication and lead to your being able to enjoy what you really crave: a truly loving relationship.

SWITCHING POISONS

"I drank for years and never had a problem with alcohol. But six months of cocaine got me in terrible trouble. Now that I'm over the coke, shouldn't I be able to drink again?"

If wishes were horses, you could mount, ride to the nearest saloon, and drink to your heart's content. You're not the first recovering addict who hoped the answer to that question would be yes. It's not.

Doubters who test the theory discover that for themselves—painfully. And before they know it, they find themselves back on their drugs, worse off than when they quit. Or they suddenly have a new problem: alcohol. Some can manage controlled drinking for a while, but never for long. You've escaped the fire. Why jump into the frying pan?

Kitty Dukakis, the wife of the 1988 Democratic presidential nominee, can tell you from personal experience what many have learned the hard way before and since: Switching poisons can be lethal for addicted people.

Even seemingly innocuous medications (over-the-counter antihistamines, for example) can trigger relapse. If you're addicted to alcohol or other drugs and value your sobriety, stay away from any mood-altering substance except in life-or-death situations (see page 246).

DISAPPOINTMENT

"I've never been so disappointed in my life as when I failed to get the job I've always wanted. I feel like giving up."

Disappointment is tough to handle. Its sting is especially painful to anyone accustomed to dissolving sorrows chemically. But it can be done. You just need to know how. Don't bury your disappointment inside. Talk about it—to your sponsor, to AA friends, at an AA meeting, to an understanding spouse or friend. As you share your disappointments, others will be moved to share theirs, often adding postscripts on how things turned out for the best in the end. Think about your situation. Maybe that wasn't really the right job. Something even better may be just around the corner.

With time, you will feel the sorrow of disappointment lift and see it replaced by optimism for tomorrow. Maybe you didn't get the job, but you're still sober, you're alive and getting well, and the future looks a whole lot better than it once did.

One of the many lessons of sobriety is that we need to stop dreaming about greener pastures and start enjoying our own, even if they are still a little brown around the edges.

IMPATIENCE

"After seven weeks of sobriety I still feel rotten. I can't sleep, I'm depressed half the time, and I can't think straight all the time. When is it going to get better?"

Your alcohol or drug addiction didn't develop like an instant snapshot, and you won't get better instantly. For addicts, who tend to be impatient people anyway, progress often seems agonizingly slow and unsteady. But you should be feeling better now than you did during and right after detox. And each week should be a little bit better than the week before, with an occasional minor regression. Don't expect perfection. Instead, expect progress in the right direction.

Progress is usually slower for those on cocaine or long-lasting drugs, like the benzodiazepines. But everyone who sticks with a recovery program makes progress. There will come a time in your recovery when you'll feel good more often than blah. What's out there won't change, but you will. You'll be able to cope better, your head will be clearer, you'll sleep through the night more regularly. It won't happen tomorrow. It may not even happen next month or next year. It may take several years, but one day at a time, it will happen.

That's not what you want to hear. You want recovery *now.* Instant gratification is what most alcoholics/addicts are accustomed to—with a sniff, a swallow, or a shot. Waiting to feel better is not part of their philosophy. But patience is a skill that can be learned. It's like working out in the gym. Initially you feel sore all over, and when you look in the mirror, your abdomen is as flabby as ever. But keep working at it and eventually you'll look like an advertisement for the health club.

Train yourself to be patient by practicing postponed gratification. Say, for example, you feel a compulsion to have a chocolate sundae with lunch. Put off giving in to that compulsion until midafternoon, or even the next day. You're eager to see a new movie that's just come to town? Instead of rushing off the minute the title appears on the marquee, wait a couple of days to plunk down your money for tickets. The more you discipline yourself to delay gratification (and learn that a reward is sweeter when you've waited for it), the more easily patience will come to you. That will make it easier to wait to feel better in recovery. And it will make all of living easier as well.

THE OTHER GUY'S RECOVERY

"My wife and I are both in recovery. She isn't going to meetings as often as she should, or working the Steps. What should I do?"

What you should do is look after your own recovery. That may seem like a selfish response, but it's what you need to do. Taking someone else's inventory rather than your own is a common error in early recovery. It sometimes means that you are seeing your own behavior problems in others. Worry about yourself. Your spouse's recovery isn't your responsibility. Your recovery is.

If upon further reflection, you're still sure your wife is taking a wrong turn, mention it to her sponsor or counselor and let them take it from there. Later on, when you are both much further along and have learned to communicate better, you will probably be able to confront her in such a situation—not in order to control her or to take charge of her recovery, only to let her know what you see. Then the ball will be in her court.

THE DRY DRUNK

"I heard a couple of people talking about a guy being in a dry drunk. What did they mean?"

Now that you're in recovery, "dry drunk" is a term you will probably hear fairly often. Just what the term means depends on who is using it, but there are at least two interpretations. One is fairly obvious: the

(continued on page 164)

MINI-GUIDE

Controlling Cravings

To resist cravings, it helps to consider why you feel them. A craving for alcohol or drugs comes on for either negative or positive reasons. You may fear the withdrawal symptoms that you know will come with abstention. Or you may longingly recall the rush or the glow you associate with a favorite chemical. Cravings are irrational and can be bathed in such a rosy incandescence that, unless dealt with quickly, they are powerful enough to overcome rational memory of the havoc your use of drugs and/or alcohol has wrought. Cravings eventually diminish in frequency and intensity, and for most people finally disappear entirely.

In the meantime, you can reduce the number of cravings you experience by learning to thwart temptation (Chapter 9) and by keeping your lifestyle in balance. But there is no way to completely wipe out the last vestige of desire for your drug of choice—at least not immediately. Rare is the person who quits drinking or using drugs and never again feels a compulsion—a need, a craving, an insatiable hunger, an uncontrollable thirst—to drink or use.

Feeling a compulsion, however, doesn't mean you have to give in to it. You can, like others who experience an overwhelming compulsion, fight it off. Over a period of time, people in successful recovery develop their own strategies for dealing with compulsions. Early in recovery, however, it's often helpful to know what the options are. You may find some of these work for you, or you may find other ways of coping that work better. The moment you feel—even fleetingly—that you would like to drink or use, resort to them. And remember, a craving does *not* have to end in drinking or using drugs.

❖ Call your sponsor, your counselor, your doctor, your treatment center. If the first person you call isn't available, try calling ten or twelve other AA people, whose phone numbers should be in your pocket or purse at all times for just such an emergency. (Even if you don't reach anyone, by the time you've finished dialing the craving will have diminished or disappeared.)

❖ Find someone—a friend or your spouse—to talk to. Share how you feel if you can, but talk about anything if you can't. Ask them not to leave you alone.

❖ Distract yourself with something else at home—playing catch or Jeopardy with the kids, washing the dishes or the car, taking a shower or a leisurely bath, cleaning out a closet or mowing the lawn, watching a video, reading a gripping book, making love. Or leave the house and go somewhere where neither drugs nor booze is available—a drive in the country, a movie, a museum, a concert. By the time you're ready to return home, the craving should have passed.

❖ Find an AA meeting that is about to begin and head directly for it.

❖ Remind yourself that you are helpless against drugs (the First Step). That once you start, you can't stop. This could scare off your craving.

❖ Try to stay sober for one minute at a time. Start doing something (polishing shoes, ironing a shirt), and set your alarm for five minutes. When you've managed to get through the first five minutes, try for ten. Keep increasing the time. Tell yourself you only don't have to drink right now, today.

❖ Do push-ups or other calisthenics, head for the gym, or go jogging or for a brisk walk—but not in the direction of the liquor store, a bar, or your old pusher.

❖ Pray. Ask your Higher Power to remove your craving. Recite the Serenity Prayer or another comforting prayer. Many successful recoverees, crisis or no crisis, each morning ask their Higher Power to relieve them of this compulsion, and each night say a thank-you for having gotten through the day without drinking or using.

❖ Meditate (see page 320).

❖ Read the Big Book or other AA materials; read the Bible, if that helps you. Watch your favorite recovery video or listen to a tape.

❖ Keep in mind that, for you, alcohol or drugs are not viable options. Your disease has progressed to the point at which a drink or a drug means instant pain and illness. Remind yourself that this disease of alcoholism/addiction is a fatal one.

❖ Remember the bad old days. Pull out the letter (or video) in which you described them. Read (or view) it. Or simply think about those days—the DUI's, the near misses, the DT's, the degradation, the black abyss. Remember, just one drink or drug and you'll be headed right down that tube again—only further. The pain and the consequences of drinking or drugging are worse than anything you can be feeling now.

❖ Remind yourself about the good things in your life. Look at a picture of someone you love. Think about your job. Recall how far you've come in your recovery. Feel that AA attendance chip in your pocket.

❖ Have a snack—preferably one that is low in sugar (see page 427). Include a sugar-free beverage, such as juice, soda (without caffeine), water, milk, decaffeinated coffee. If that doesn't work, forget the calories—better to blow your diet than your sobriety. Eat anything that satisfies you.

❖ Take the money you are thinking of spending on alcohol or drugs and spend it on an on-the-spot treat for yourself, or put it in a piggy bank for a future treat.

❖ Instead of thinking about drinking or drugging, think about *not* drinking or drugging. Think about the things you can do sober.

❖ If you want to drink or use because you're depressed or anxious, see page 328 for tips on dealing with these emotions. If your compulsion was triggered by a problem in your life, try to deal with it honestly instead of shoveling pills or powder onto it.

❖ If you're out of town when a compulsion strikes, look up AA in the local telephone directory and call immediately. Find a meeting or someone to talk to.

❖ Remember, cravings too shall pass.

(continued from page 161)

person who acts intoxicated—giggly, hysterical, uncontrollable—without having used a drug or had a drop to drink. The second type of dry drunk is the person who behaves like an active addict—resentful, inconsiderate, not attending meetings, denying his addiction, neglecting family responsibilities—while remaining sober. He only needs alcohol or drugs to make his life complete, and if his attitude doesn't improve, they'll be back in his life very soon.

If you ever find yourself in a dry drunk, immediately take steps to temporarily rev up your recovery. Double up on meetings, share your feelings at them, talk to your sponsor, pray for relief. If you have gone through similar episodes in the past, remind yourself that you survived.

If you experience frequent emotional dry benders, then examine your recovery program. Are you doing all the things recommended in Phase One? Are you going to meetings, working the Twelve Steps, taking a daily inventory? The odds are that you are slipping up somewhere, and that's the reason for your behavior. Another possibility: Something is going on at home or at work that is chronically souring your mood. If so, family or other counseling may be urgently needed in addition to your recovery work.

If you experience a dry drunk later on, say in Phase Two or Three, then you may need to move back to Phase One, at least for a while, to solidify your recovery.

They say in AA:
"I came [to AA] . . . I came to [my senses] . . . I came to believe [that I could remain sober]."

DRUNK DREAMS/ USER DREAMS

"I woke up in a cold sweat in the middle of the night after dreaming I took a drink at a party. It was so real, I could taste it."

Like the faithful dieter who dreams she nuked her diet with a hot fudge sundae, the alcoholic/addict often dreams about blowing sobriety. People often smell and taste their drugs of choice in such dreams, and translate this into a sign of repressed desire. But probably even Sigmund Freud would agree it's more likely to be the fear of a misstep.

"The week I got out of treatment, I had to pay my drug dealer the $8,000 I owed him. When I laid it on the counter, he said: 'I got some Peruvian flake. The best. On the house.'
'Thanks,' I told him, 'but not right now.' I just couldn't close the door. He was the most important man in my life for so long."

Because such dreams are so vivid, they usually have substantial emotional impact. Sometimes they stimulate panic and fear, including palpitations and sweating, or they may provoke a craving. The best way to respond is to change the subject. Steer your mind in a different direction. Get out of bed and do push-ups, pad into the kitchen for cookies and milk, turn on the TV and watch a late movie, wake up your spouse and talk. Don't lie in bed obsessing about the dream. If you think about anything, think about what a mess your life used to be when you were using or drinking. The next day, share your dream at an AA meeting. Happily, for most people such dreams fade away after the first few months of sobriety.

If your using dream doesn't scare you; if in fact you feel it let you beat the system by getting a free high without the consequences, beware. You're not taking your disease seriously enough.

SLIPPING UP

"I went to my cousin's birthday party and though I tried hard to stay away from the bar, I finally succumbed and told myself I could have just one drink. Of course, I didn't have just one drink. I got stinking drunk. I'm so ashamed to have blown my recovery that way."

Some recovering alcoholics/addicts stop drinking or using, period. They never have another drink or use another drug. But many have at least one slip. A slip doesn't necessarily doom you to a swift downhill slide back to your pre-recovery life. In the one-day-at-a-time philosophy, slipping today doesn't automatically mean forfeiting tomorrow. Most people are resilient enough to clamber back on the wagon. But many may need a leg up getting there—outpatient or inpatient treatment, for example.

SLIP has become an acronym meaning "Sobriety Lost Its Priority," and generally that's exactly why a slip occurs. Either you stopped giving adequate attention to the needs of your recovery, or you were never serious about quitting in the first place.

Though anyone can slip anytime (even twenty-five years into sobriety), slips appear to be most common in the early months of recovery. Cravings become fewer and interest in the "old scene" lessens as the months roll by. If, in the future, you sense that old feeling coming on again and you fear a slip, see the tips on dealing with cravings on page 162. For more information on dealing with your slip, see Chapter 29.

MANUFACTURING ESCAPE HATCHES

"A speaker at last night's meeting referred to 'escape hatches.' What did she mean?"

The jet pilot likes to be sure that he can safely eject if his engine should malfunction. The consumer making a mail-order purchase likes to know there is a return policy in case the shoes are tight when she tries them on. And the alcoholic/addict, too, likes to know there's a way out if sobriety pinches him unduly. That's why many create "escape hatches" that will allow them to return to their chemicals "just in case."

But this kind of thinking, like going into marriage figuring you can always get a divorce if it doesn't work, indicates a pretty flabby commitment. It should be viewed as a red flag warning of the fragility of your desire to stay clean and sober. Should you find yourself cunningly leaving open escape routes back to your past, consciously or unconsciously, reevaluate your recovery and talk to your sponsor about what you can do to strengthen it.

The kinds of escape hatches that signal trouble ahead include:

❖ Keeping a stash of money or credit secret from your family—just in case you decide you need to use again.

❖ Failing to firmly notify your dealer that you are absolutely not interested in further purchases. Saying, "Well, not right now" is a way of leaving the door ajar, and a cue he's sure to pick up and translate as "Try me again next month."

❖ Refusing to allow anyone else to remove liquor, drugs, and pills from your house while you're in treatment. Being embarrassed or not wanting to ask favors is a feeble excuse for your reluctance to cancel your "insurance policy."

❖ Allowing liquor to remain in your home because your spouse or someone else drinks. Ask yourself: "Am I worried about *their* not being able to take a drink—or *my* being unable to have one?"

❖ Accepting gifts of liquor from friends who are unaware of your problem.

❖ Not informing the family doctor who prescribed the pills you abused about your addiction and recovery—just in case you need to go back to the well again.

"Going to an AA meeting when I've got a problem in my life is an act of faith. My mind asks what in the hell good that will do, especially if it's a legal matter or work-related. But my program tells me go. So I go. I may talk about the problem or not. But just going always helps."

❖ Planning an out-of-town trip alone or with colleagues who don't know you're recovering without making an AA contact at your destination—just in case you get thirsty away from home.

❖ Insisting on attending a party, wedding, or other event at which you know there will be drinking—though you barely know the people involved.

❖ Keeping, or discreetly acquiring, a hideaway that people who are aware you're in recovery don't know about.

❖ Not cutting off an extramarital affair or a special friendship in which drinking or drug use played a major role.

HANDLING RESPONSIBILITIES

"My wife always said that I was irresponsible when I was drinking. I really didn't think I was that bad—I kept a job and was a pretty good father and husband. But now I notice that a lot of responsibilities I wasn't aware of before keep cropping up."

Reality dawns. When an alcoholic/addict's life isn't in a shambles, it's occasionally because he's managed through superhuman effort to remain responsible even at the most difficult moments. But more often it's because many or most of his neglected responsibilities were picked up and handled by someone else: a secretary who concocted brilliant excuses for missed meetings, an assistant who finished reports or a coworker who completed jobs, a nurse who fibbed to patients about "emergencies" when the doctor didn't show up for appointments, a spouse who took over all child-care duties, bill paying, and planning (and canceling) of social engagements.

Now that you're well, it's likely that many of these people have stopped filling in for you. Suddenly the list of responsibilities looms large, maybe too large for someone in early recovery. This is not the time for you to skipper the fleet. A reduced schedule at work and at home is a good idea while you get your sea legs. That means, when possible, fewer business meetings, letting someone else continue finishing reports or completing jobs (and getting full credit for them), a reduced patient or client load, and leaving most (but not all) family responsibilities in your spouse's hands. It also means learning to say no. Otherwise you and your recovery could capsize when seas get rough.

Gradually, as your recovery becomes more secure, you can resume a full measure of responsibility—responsibly (see page 192).

HANDLING LIFE'S PROBLEMS

"Every time I mention to my sponsor that I have a problem at home or at work, she tells me to go to an AA meeting. That seems like a crazy way to handle a problem."

Was drinking or taking a drug a saner way? That was almost certainly your old method of handling disappointments, frustrations, or anger, and almost anything would be better than that. But though more than a few AA members initially thought that going to an AA meeting was "a crazy way to handle a problem," most of them have found that, through some mysterious mood-changing alchemy, it works. What else can you do? Here are a few suggestions:

❖ Identify the problem that's troubling you. Be honest. Whether it's back taxes, a court date, a botched project at work, or a relative you're not on speaking terms with, don't ignore it, define it. Putting it down in writing may help. When you look at it in black and white, it may not seem as bad as it seemed swirling around inside your head.

❖ Talk about it. Problems that we keep to ourselves seem to get bigger and more out of our control, and often eventually cause an explosion. Those that we talk about become smaller and easier to get a handle on and conquer, and the talking safely relieves the pressure that's building up inside. You're also likely to get some new ideas, sound advice, and a new perspective

DON'T BE A GUINEA PIG

One way to think of the journey to recovery is as a research project in which you learn to understand yourself and your disease. Absorbing case studies—other people's lives and experiences—are all around you. You can study them at AA meetings, on tapes and videos, and in books and pamphlets.

Almost anything that you might contemplate doing—controlled drinking, having an affair, cheating on your drug screen, going to a wild disco, smoking marijuana—someone else has done before you. As an interested researcher, you can look at these case studies and see what the results were. Did the controlled drinker live happily ever after or finally die of liver failure? Did the friend who was fooling around improve her marriage or end up divorced and miserable? Did the colleague switching urine samples fool only himself, cracking up his car when high on crack?

Most of the time, the answers are clear-cut and tell you what you need to do to protect your own sobriety. If any answer is ambiguous, you'd be wise to steer away from the action—unless you enjoy playing the role of the guinea pig experimenting with his own life.

SAND IN THE ENGINES OF RECOVERY

Be on the lookout for any of the following feelings and attitudes, which can sometimes be as destructive to sobriety as booze or drugs. If you notice one or more of them trickling sand in the engines of your recovery, do something about it before your motor conks out completely. You can find out more about dealing with each of these qualities on the pages noted in parentheses.

FEAR. A little fear is not only normal but healthy. Too much fear can be debilitating (see page 147).

GUILT. While guilt that leads you to make amends is useful, guilt that hampers you from getting better is not (see page 150).

UNREALISTIC EXPECTATIONS. Dreams and hopes are what keep us going, but expecting the impossible can leave us chronically dissatisfied (see page 315).

RESENTMENTS. Clinging to anger against others for past or recent hurts doesn't harm those you feel have trespassed against you, but it can hurt you and your recovery. You have to learn to forgive and forget (see page 329).

LOW SELF-ESTEEM. If you don't feel good about yourself, if you don't feel you deserve the joy of recovery, you are sure to "punish" yourself and slip back into alcoholism/addiction (see page 316).

PROCRASTINATION. If you don't deal with problems promptly, they'll grow such hard shells that you may decide you need alcohol to dissolve them (see page 167).

DISHONESTY. Lying to yourself and to others usually becomes a habit in addiction. You lie about your drinking—how much, when, where, why; about where you've been and with whom; about why you haven't met responsibilities; about your feelings and values. Dishonesty may be protective in active addiction, but it's downright harmful in recovery (see page 202).

on what works and what doesn't from others who have been there before you and really do know how you feel.

❖ Decide how you want to deal with the problem. But before you do, collect all the information you can on the subject (from both your own experience and outside sources); sort out the information; outline your options, listing the risks and benefits of each, and how they will affect you and others; discuss the options with your sponsor and other trusted advisors; pick an option to follow, based on the information you've collected as well as your values and goals; carry out the decision; and finally accept responsibility for it. (For more on decision-making, see page 193).

❖ Don't procrastinate. Deal with problems as they arise instead of keeping them on the back burner until they burn the pot. This doesn't mean handling them on impulse—that's as bad as procrastinating. As has long been the case, "Think before you act" is a good motto to live by.

❖ Use stress-reduction techniques—such as exercise, meditation, yoga (see Chapter 15)—to help you function more effectively.

In sum, though taking your problems or a blue mood to an AA meeting may at first seem irrational to you, it's like the cowardly lion taking his quest for courage to the Wizard: Acts of faith can work as well in the real world as they did in the fantasy world of Oz. And they'll help you grow and recover.

HAVING AN ALCOHOLIC PARENT

"As an adult child of an alcoholic who is also recovering, I am not sure exactly where to start and where I belong—AA, Al-Anon, or ACOA."

First things first. You need to deal with your addiction. So like any other alcoholic, you need to start with a good recovery plan (see Chapter 3). You also need to start going to Alcoholics Anonymous to support your sobriety.

As an adult child of an alcoholic, you will very probably need more. Many adult children find that Al-Anon meetings are an important supplement to AA involvement. At AA they hear stories that arouse anger and resentment: the father who beat his kids when he was drunk, the mother who neglected them. At Al-Anon, they meet the victims of such abuse, people they can readily identify with. These people sometimes become a substitute family, and hearing and discussing each other's histories often helps to dissipate the anger.

Adult Children of Alcoholics (ACOA) groups may also be valuable. Again they offer the opportunity to swap stories and compare feelings with others in the same psychologically leaky boat, and a chance to learn how they've managed to remain afloat emotionally in spite of their stormy pasts.

Of course, sometimes the sign on the door may be less important than the makeup of the group. In some cases, a very nurturing AA group may provide all the support you need.

But if you have experienced abuse (sexual, physical, emotional) from your alcoholic parent, or if you are suffering from guilt, deep-seated anger, or disabling depression or anxiety, even a combination of AA, Al-Anon, and ACOA may not be enough. Discussing these issues in a self-help group can be tricky and can sometimes backfire. They are best dealt with by a professional therapist.

"For me any place I used to drink is immediate death. A smoke-filled bar with leather banquettes, an easy comfortable atmosphere, and a nice-looking lady—no way I could stay dry. So I stay away."

THE SIX-MONTH SNARE

"I picked up my six-month chip last night and I feel like a million!"

Picking up that six-month chip is a significant "I did it!" point. It *is* an important achievement—something to be rightfully proud of. But it's no time for overconfidence. There is growing evidence that you have to work just as hard over the next six months to solidify your recovery. Those who relapse before they pick up their one-year chips usually are the cocky ones who ease up on their programs—reduce attendance at meetings, stop working their Steps, or kiss their sponsors goodbye. If you continue to work hard at your recovery during the second six months, you tremendously improve your chances of long-term sobriety. So, congratulations—but keep up the good work!

MAKING CHANGES

"When I mentioned to my sponsor that I was looking for a new job, he suggested waiting a while before I switch positions."

That's good advice. Decisions made during the first year of recovery are often regretted in the second. With your mind still muddy, you're more likely to act on impulse now than on careful consideration. Even if you're capable of giving adequate thought to a life change, doing so would take time and energy from your number one priority: recovery. You may be eager to start fresh, but achieving sobriety is no small task. It will take round-the-clock energy and focus.

Not only is this not a good time to change jobs, it's also not the time to make any other major changes in your life—getting married, getting divorced, starting a new relationship, buying a new car, or getting engrossed in a new hobby, for example.

*"I have a little wooden box that I keep on the mantel. And when something is bothering me I write it down on a slip of paper, fold it up, and tuck it into my God Box. And sure enough, I feel better. Pretty soon, I know what I have to do."**

And it's definitely not the time for the monumental distractions of having a baby. Keep this in mind when you slip between the sheets and switch off the lights, because without all those poisons flowing through your veins, you're likely to suddenly be very fertile.

*Ready-to-use "God Boxes" are available in stores that cater to recoverees. Some of them are cans labeled "When I can't, God Can."

9

THWARTING TEMPTATION

Ever since the serpent conned Eve and her agreeable spouse, Adam, into sinking their teeth into the first juicy McIntosh, humans have been succumbing to temptation. Usually, as the tenants who broke their lease in the Garden of Eden discovered, much to their discomfiture. So it is with those in recovery.

There are serpents bearing apples everywhere. The only way to avoid falling victim to their wiles is to be able to see through their disguises, to avoid them when possible, and to know how to confront their seductive come-ons. It's also important to identify the kinds of feelings that leave you open to temptation and to learn how to outmaneuver them.

HOW TO RESIST TEMPTATION

CHANGING CUES

As far back as the first Greek drama production, cues have been used to prompt an actor who has lost his place in the script. You don't always consciously recognize them, but your daily life also presents any number of "cues"—a favorite disco, a glass-top table, a twinge of back pain, the baseball park, a certain song, or a satisfying meal—that prompt your memory and trigger a yearning for a drink or a drug. The point of recovery is to revise the script and change any negative cues. Among them:

Playgrounds

Most habits are associated with specific settings. You don't whip out your toothbrush in the car on your way home, but walking into the bathroom at bedtime, you automatically reach for the brush. You pull out a cigarette in the kitchen at breakfast, but you wouldn't think of it in the bus on the way to work. You have no trouble putting alcohol out of your mind all morning in the office, but the moment you step out to lunch and pass your favorite saloon, you thirst for a drink. Or, drowning yourself in your work, you manage to avoid looking for another hit of cocaine for a day and a half; then

Guide Lines

❖ It takes constant vigilance to neutralize the cues (things you see, hear, smell, taste, feel) that trigger the craving to use or the compulsion to drink.

❖ Changing "playmates, playgrounds, and playthings" is virtually indispensable if you are to avoid chemical seduction.

❖ You will be most susceptible to temptations of any kind when you are hungry, angry, lonely, or tired (HALT in AA); bored, sad, worried, nervous, or depressed; or physically unwell.

you go to a rock concert and find the craving irresistible.

That's why recovering alcoholics/addicts are urged to change the scenes in which their lives are played, particularly in early recovery. Not only do familiar locales in themselves trigger cravings, but in some people, old haunts can trigger psychological reactions that in turn stimulate I-need-a-chemical reactions. These range from troubled (tension, anxiety, and what appear to be withdrawal symptoms) to titillating (pleasant expectancy, with salivation, giddiness, and an imagined inner warmth.)

So it's vital to avoid the settings where you played out your drinking or drugging scenes—the bars, the clubs, the dances, the parties, the rock concerts, the liquor stores where you're known by your first name, the restaurants (choose those without liquor licenses, or at least without bars), the sports events (unless there's a no-alcohol area), and memorable street corners. Drive or walk a few blocks out of your way to avoid these dangerous intersections. If you're not clear where your quicksand lies, do a special personal inventory (see page 108) to remind yourself—even if you've done one before.

If you drank or used in places you can't avoid—at home, at work—use some of that old addict ingenuity to erase the danger signs. Get rid of the living-room bar as well as the liquor, the table you prepared your cocaine on as well as the paraphernalia. Dump your pills down the toilet, but don't stop there. If you always popped them in the bathroom, get rid of the familiar bathroom water glass and rinse your mouth in the kitchen. If you always drank beer when you watched football on the living-room TV, watch it with a pitcher of lemonade in the bedroom.

Spend a lot of time in places where it's impossible, or at least difficult, to drink or use drugs: Museums. Stores. The gym or health club. AA meetings. The theater. Your workplace (unless you're a rock musician or a bartender, in which case changing your line of work is worth considering). The ski slopes (unless a fully stocked Saint Bernard patrols them). Churches and synagogues (but be sure there is—or offer to supply—a grape juice option for communion, or for the kiddush that concludes the Sabbath service).

If you spend time in places where drinking or drug use is optional, plan ahead to avoid peer pressure to be "one of the guys [or gals]." At the theater or a concert, for example, bring your own soft drink for intermission, so you can't touch the bar with a ten-foot pole. When you schedule your day or your week, recheck to be sure you aren't setting yourself up for a fall overboard from the good ship *Clean & Sober* by choosing destinations that are the chemical equivalent of the Bermuda Triangle.

Playmates

Just as specific settings can turn on your cravings, so can a specific cast of characters: the folks you always drank or used with. Stop seeing them for now. You may feel the urge to visit with them, telling yourself "They're good friends. We had great times together. I miss them." But you're just kidding yourself. What you miss most is what you did with them. If there is an old friend you really yearn to see, arrange to meet in a coffee shop or at your home along with your AA sponsor or another successfully recovering AA buddy. A true friend will be happy to see you getting better and won't object to your chaperone.

Renew old friendships with people who don't drink or use, the ones you stopped seeing when you started getting heavily into your habit. You may find there are more of them than you thought, and that you really enjoy their company. And make new friends. You'll find a host of great candidates at AA meetings—people like you, no matter what you're like. Gregarious people who've learned how to party without chemicals. Calm, serene people comfortable with themselves and with others now that they are sober.

Playthings: Déjà Vu Dangers

It won't be enough to change the scenery and the cast of characters. You will have to be wary of the props that surround you as well. In our society, we are constantly bombarded by images of alcohol and drugs. Any of these—visual, psychological, even olfactory (related to smell)—can bring on signs of physical craving, with sweaty palms, fast pulse, and agitation. You'll have to be constantly on the alert for such cues. If the first few times you are exposed to them, they trigger fear rather than craving, don't be tricked into believing you're forever safe. This fear reaction is common in early recovery, but repeated exposure to the same cue can dilute and finally wash away the fear. So learn to recognize and avoid them completely. Watch out for:

❖ *TV ads for beer or wine.* It may mean a lot of exercise, but get up and leave the room when they come on during a sports event or a show you're watching. Such commercials are most dangerous when they show drinking scenes that dredge up pleasant memories. Romantic moments highlighted by candlelight and bubbling wine; exhilarating moments sailing on a sunlit bay with glasses raised; exciting moments celebrating the home team's victory with a frosty beer at a ball game. (The ads never show the drinkers weaving drunkenly home, being pulled over for DUI, puking on the carpet before making it to the bathroom, or blearily waking up with head pounding and breath foul the morning after).

❖ *Ubiquitous liquor ads.* Cravings may also be triggered by alluring posters in subways and buses, by roadside and bus-stop billboards, and by glossy pages in magazines depicting gloriously happy people building enduring friendships, improving their already enviable sex lives, and generally having a wonderful time thanks to booze. So change your seat, avert thine eyes, or turn the page in a hurry.*

❖ *TV shows or movies in which the drink's the thing.* It would be wise to deny your patronage to films or shows featuring casual drug use, unless the unromantic consequences are also shown. And as entertaining as it might

*Though brewers and distillers are reluctant to admit it, liquor ads are targeted directly at you, a longtime heavy consumer who now has reason to stop consuming. Subtle, sophisticated socio-psychological warfare techniques firing invisible marketing bullets will seek to convince you it's okay, even beneficial, to drink again. Because about 10 percent of Americans consume more than half of the liquor in the country, the alcohol industry is as addicted to alcoholics as alcoholics are to the toxic fluids it bottles.

be, a sitcom set in a bar would probably be one to avoid, as would be one in which one or more characters intermittently moan, "Boy, do I need a drink!" Novels in which drinking (or drug use) is important (many by mucho macho Ernest Hemingway, for example) could also trigger a problem and are best shelved right now.

❖ *Loose sugar, baking soda, cornstarch.* All of these, when spread on a table or a dish, are uncomfortably reminiscent of cocaine. So whoever does the cooking in your house should avoid leaving any of these items lying around, and should supply sugar in packets rather than in a bowl. Fun is fun, but don't dump any of these substances on the table and play at cutting them. If you use them for cooking, they should go directly from the container into the food you're preparing. Is that being too careful? In recovery, you can never be too careful.

❖ *Windex and similar glass-cleaning preparations.* These have an odor strikingly similar to cocaine. Let your windows and mirrors grow whiskers, or use old newspapers (their newsprint contains a cleansing chemical) to rub them clean.

❖ *Drug paraphernalia.* The very sight of it has been known to trigger a relapse. Dump all of yours and maintain a safe distance from anyone else's. Don't pass paraphernalia on to a friend, for your sake as well as theirs—you might be tempted to borrow it back. You may not consider a mirror to be drug paraphernalia, but if you prepared your cocaine on one, that's what it was. Banish mirrored trays or other horizontal mirrored surfaces from your decor.

❖ *Your favorite liquor store or bar.* Try to avoid passing it, even if it means sailing around the Horn. If beer, wine, or liquor is sold in your supermarket, make a wide detour around that section when you do your shopping.

❖ *Your old drug dealer.* If you have to pay an old debt, ask a friend to do it for you. More than one recovering addict has been rehooked in the process of getting off the hook—especially when the dealer, eager to win back a lost client, made an offer he couldn't refuse, like, "Hey, this stuff is on me. Just for old times' sake."

❖ *Hot-weather activities.* Fishing, boating, barbecues, even mowing the lawn, can summon up drinking memories for some people. Avoid them if they do for you, or engage in them only in a controlled situation where booze would be out of the question—with another AA member, for example.

❖ *The end of your work day.* If this was when your drinking day began, you urgently need to change your after-work routine. Maybe go straight to an AA meeting before going home, or jog, or go to the gym to work up a sweat instead of a thirst.

❖ *The corner where you used to make drug buys.* Your old pusher will be only too glad to see you, but don't go within shooting distance of the spot. If there's no way to get around it, avoid being "cornered" by sailing through under escort with an AA buddy.

❖ *Nostalgic music.* Rock music, dance music, or a song you associate with drugs or alcohol could blast you into

"My hometown is sixty miles from here, and I can't go back there, even after three years' sobriety, without every street triggering drug memories. The only way I could safely visit my parents is by parachute, straight down into their backyard."

ROMANCING THE DRINK OR THE DRUG

Recovering surgery patients like to talk about their operations. Recovering alcoholics/addicts often like to talk about their drinking and drugging days. But while reminiscing is harmless for bypass patients (who remember the fear, the pain, the physical discomfort), it could be fatal for recovering people, who tend to remember the good stuff (what cold frosty beer tastes like, rather than the hangover, the dent in the car the next morning, and the sudden fear—"Did I hurt someone in my blackout last night?").

Fantasizing about drinking and drugging, sometimes called "romancing the drug [or the drink]," is dangerous because it can change your focus from sobriety (where it should be) to using (where it shouldn't). "Romancing" can lead, like other visual and psychological temptations, to cravings. And it's a short distance from the craving to the bar or the dealer. When you hear such conversations starting, leave in a hurry. Don't worry about being rude, just about staying alive. Conversations should focus on living, not drinking; on answers, not problems.

Sometimes during recovery, however, your mind focuses on drinking or drugging whether you want it to or not—in dreams. To learn what these dreams mean, see page 164.

orbit. If that's the case, steer clear of such music entirely until your sobriety is well established, and even then do your listening in safe surroundings. For now, substitute an AA tape or some Mozart in your Walkman, stereo, or boom box. (See page 180 for party-going tips.)

❖ *Romantic dinners.* If a dinner without wine seems as unromantic as a traffic jam, try substituting candlelight and soft music, poetry and flowers. When dining out, seek restaurants that lack a liquor license. If you find yourself in a restaurant that serves alcohol, ask the waiter not to leave a wine list at your table and to remove any wine glasses. If there's a bar, ask to be seated far, far away. (Maybe someday restaurants will provide "no drinking" sections, too.)

❖ *Stimulating situations.* Situations as diverse as sky diving, playing poker, and trying to con someone can all trigger a rush of adrenaline, which can in turn trigger a craving for cocaine. Exercise can also trigger adrenaline flow, but it doesn't cause a problem because the adrenaline is utilized during the physical activity.

❖ *Pharmacological perils.* If cough medicines or other over-the-counter preparations were among your drugs of last resort, stay away from the aisles in which they're found at your pharmacy and supermarket. If a bottle of vanilla extract turns you on, steer clear of the spice section at the grocer's. Find this difficult? Shop with a buddy.

❖ *Pain and other medical ills.* A backache, a splitting head, a runny nose, can send you to the pharmacist for what seems a good reason. And before you know it, you don't even remember the reason why you're reaching for the medicine. Instead, learn how to prevent the ailments that bushwhack you most, and how to treat them without drugs when prevention fails (see Chapter 13 for specific tips on doing this).

❖ *Any other cues that trigger your cravings.* You know better than anyone what they are. List them in your Inventory or Life History (page 105), and steer away from them as the prudent helmsman does the jagged reef.

While doing your best to avoid these dangerous old cues, you need to begin to establish new cues and rituals for recovery. Plan as you would for a war: the battle to salvage the rest of your life. Create a set of new cues that remind you to remain sober as powerfully as the old cues led you to drink and use. Use recovery tapes, books, videos, your sponsor and other AA friends, meditation, prayer, the sight of your loved ones, your sober image in the mirror, a good job evaluation, possessions you've obtained since sobriety (a car, house, or stereo, for example). Associate finishing dinner with going to a meeting rather than with drinking yourself under the table.

> *"My wife wants to empty our liquor cabinet into the garbage. I say that wouldn't be fair to her or our guests. I'm in control now, and I won't have a problem with the bar being stocked."*

HANDLING EMOTIONAL CUES

Certain feelings can be as hazardous to recovery as bumping into your drug dealer on a street corner. Knowing what they are and how to handle them can prevent their triggering cravings or weakening your defenses against other time-for-a-hit cues.

Good Feelings

In early recovery, even a little fun may seem out of sight. But eventually (sooner for some, later for others), a pleasant experience will make you feel wonderful and give you an emotional high—possibly the first in many years enjoyed without benefit of chemicals. Great! But be wary. Your still-befuddled brain may confuse that unexpected high with a drug-induced one, and start craving the drug.

The process is a physiological one. When you engage in an activity that leads to an emotional high, your body's internal feedback-and-reward system is activated. You get a rush, a feeling of pleasure. This is probably a part of our primitive survival mechanism. Something feels good (love, sex, eating, inventing the wheel). So we repeat it. This is good for our survival, or for the survival of our species.

Drugs like cocaine also activate the reward centers of the brain, producing a similar rush and feelings of pleasure. But they confound the system: You get the reward without engaging in an activity related to survival, or in fact any activity at all (except taking the drug). Instant gratification. No effort. Ultimately, no survival.

Many alcoholics/addicts are people who fail to get that good feeling in the normal ways. Either they are unsuccessful at finding love, in winning at tennis, or in running a profitable business or they succeed outwardly but get no pleasure from their success and still don't feel good inside. So when they find they can get that feel-good high from a drug on demand—without working or playing hard or giving anything emotionally—they quickly become stuck on it. Unfortunately, now they never have to develop the skills that will help them to earn these good feelings naturally.

If we understand the similarity between what happens in our brain when we have a pleasurable experience and when we take a drug, we can understand that pleasurable experiences during recovery (falling in love, finishing a project, winning at bowling, getting straight A's at school) can remind the brain's reward center of the drug we used to take and, like any other cue, trigger a craving.

That doesn't mean you have to go through the rest of your life wearing a perpetual frown or avoiding happiness at all costs.*

Just be aware that feeling good *can* masquerade as a drug high. Don't let it charm you into seeking more of the same the "easy" way. Your sponsor should be able to help you recognize the unreal thing when you're too hog-happy to see it.

Bad Feelings

Sometimes rage or resentment can also cause a rush reminiscent of a cocaine rush. Try to avoid such feelings, and if you have them, learn to purge yourself of them. (See page 329 for tips on handling anger and resentment.)

Distress, depression, shakiness, apprehension, jumpiness, a knot in the stomach, fear of dying, and a feeling of sickness or of being out of control are also associated with strong craving. Tension, unease, irritability, restlessness, insecurity, self-disgust, vague guilt, and annoyance are associated with mild craving—which may be only an elbow's-length away from strong craving.

That's why pure white-knuckle abstention is rarely enough to maintain sobriety. Just as important is a solid recovery program that helps you both to feel good about yourself and to deal with emotions quickly and effectively. Chapter 15 will help you with these troublemaker feelings.

Defense-Lowering Feelings

In addition to triggering cravings, feelings can lower our defenses against the other "oh-hell-why-not?" cues that assault us daily. We are most susceptible to temptations when we are hungry, angry, lonely, or tired (again the acronym reminder is HALT), or bored, sad, worried, nervous, or depressed. This is particularly true in recovery. Try to avoid those mental states as much as you can (for more on anxiety and depression, see page 323; on anger, page 329). Keep busy, but not so busy that you are always exhausted. Get adequate rest and relaxation. Eat regularly and wisely (see Chapter 23). Learn to deal with resentments and anxieties, possibly using stress-reduction techniques (page 320). And do things that make you smile a lot.

*Though falling in love isn't recommended in early recovery (see on page 214), it can be wonderful in Phase Two.

THWARTING HOME-SWEET-HOME TEMPTATIONS

The Liquor Cabinet

There's no simple answer to the question of whether or not recovering alcoholics/addicts should ban all alcohol from their homes. But in most cases there are sound reasons for keeping the temptations away. It's like stashing a gallon of chocolate-chocolate-chip ice cream in the freezer when you're trying to diet. Every time you open the door to pluck out a couple of ice cubes for your diet soda, temptation winks.

Then there are the cravings that pop up periodically. If, when suddenly assaulted by the "I've gotta have a drink" blues, you have to get in the car and go to the liquor store or bar to fulfill the craving, time and distance are on your side. The desire may pass before you've buckled your seat belt and turned on the ignition. If, on the other hand, the object of your affection is in the next room, your romance could be back on in a half-dozen compulsive steps.

If you're willing, and especially if you're eager, to keep alcohol in your home, you're not as free of your compulsion as you'd like to think. You're trying to keep an escape hatch open, to stash some booze—just in case.

If your family is accustomed to wine at dinner parties and the prospect of a table full of soda bottles and lemonade pitchers sounds depressing, invite a few AA friends to your first alcohol-free party. That way you'll be able to discover that you can have a good party—even a great one—without alcoholic beverages. Your non-AA friends (if they're real friends and don't have drinking problems of their own) will also respect your new lifestyle and will be able to enjoy dinner at your home without wine, parties without cocktails, picnics without beer. If they don't act as cues to you, you might use elegant goblets for the lemonade and handsome mugs for the soft drinks to brighten things up.

The Medicine Cabinet

It's also probably not a good idea to keep mood-altering medications (such as tranquilizers, antidepressants, stimulants) in the house. If a family member needs to take them, it might be better if they were kept elsewhere (at the office, for example). Unless the individual is suffering from a major psychiatric illness, these medications should be prescribed for short periods of time only; that will keep the supply small enough so that the purloining of pills will be easily detected. A medication should be discarded when the condition it was intended for abates. If it recurs, the patient can see the doctor again and obtain a new one-time-only prescription.

Making mood-altering drugs less accessible will benefit everyone by providing a little extra incentive for the whole family to develop a lifestyle that doesn't rely on drugs. This approach will also unify and focus the family's attention on its primary problem. A casual approach toward medication could, on the other hand, undermine your newfound recovery.

FOILING AWAY-FROM-HOME TEMPTATIONS

On the Road

Though some people are more susceptible to slip-ups in old familiar playgrounds, others are more likely to be tempted while anonymously exploring new worlds. On a business trip or vacation, you become the Invisible Man—or Woman. "No one knows me. No one will know if I take one little drink or one little toke." Far from your usual support group, the restraints you feel in your hometown peel away as easily as a banana skin. To avoid turning a business or pleasure excursion into a bad trip, plan ahead.

Early in recovery, the safest vacations are AA group weekends or retreats to attractive locations. An important spin-off of attending AA conventions and retreats is that you'll meet people from all over the country. Then when you travel, no matter what your destination, you'll probably already have a friend in sobriety there. More and more travel agencies now feature nonalcoholic package tours. Don't be shy about inquiring about "sober travel" (see page 210). The more people do, the more interesting vacation options will become available.

On other kinds of trips you should, whenever possible, travel with an AA

"I banged my elbow on the corner of the cabinet I used to keep the liquor in. It hurt like hell. Without thinking, I started rummaging through the cabinet for some relief, at the same time muttering, 'Thank God there's nothing here.' "

buddy or a friend or family member who doesn't drink or do drugs. (At least one recovering alcoholic, fearing the worst, resorted to hiring an investigator to keep a private eye on him during a trip.) If that's impractical and you don't already have an AA friend in the town you're headed for, check around to get the names of some AA people or groups there (they meet virtually worldwide, and even abroad someone is sure to speak your language). If you can't get this information in advance, check the local phone book under Alcoholics Anonymous the moment you arrive in a town. (You'll also find a listing under AA.) In small towns, it's sometimes the very first number in the book. In larger cities, your call may be answered by a recorded announcement that lists available meetings. Waste no time. Doff your cloak of invisibility and attend a meeting your first evening. That way, whether in London, England, or New London, Connecticut, you'll find yourself feeling at home and among friends.

If you're attending a business or professional convention or conference out of town, it's very possible that AA meetings are already scheduled daily right on-site. Check with the convention organizers. If no meeting has been arranged, try to set one up. One way to do this is to post or make an announcement, saying: "Are there any friends of Bill W. here?" or "Open Twelve-Step Meeting at . . ." You'll be amazed at the turnout you'll get.

When planning a vacation, inquire in advance to make certain that activities at your destination don't orbit around drinking, and that nonalcoholic beverages (hot chocolate, mulled cider, or other refreshers for après ski, for example) will be readily available.

In the Air

Flying is one of the most difficult times for some recovering people, especially those who used to overcome their fear of flying by drinking. Planes don't have a "No Alcohol" section, so it's very possible that the passenger in the next seat will order something alcoholic. What do you do?

Ideally, fly with someone you know, someone who knows you have a drinking problem and will avoid drinking during the trip.

If you're flying alone, explain your situation to the flight attendant. Ask if he or she can help you change your seat if anyone seated beside you orders anything stronger than tomato juice. Even on a crowded plane, where there is good will there is a way, and swapping seats is almost always feasible. If you do get stuck next to a drinker, close your eyes and meditate.

If possible, carry on a bottle of soda or juice or a container of coffee so that you have something to sip even before beverages are offered. If you can't manage that, order your beverage as early in the flight as possible. Also bring along some AA literature to read and an earphone-equipped cassette player and AA tapes. A long flight is a perfect time to catch up on material you haven't had a chance to read or listen to yet, or that you would like to go over again.

Another suggestion: Have someone put you on the plane and meet you at your destination, so that you can't stop at one of the bars generously sprinkled throughout airport terminals. It doesn't have to be a friend; it can be the driver who takes you to the airport or picks you up.

"I just hosted a Christmas party. Someone brought a packet wrapped like cocaine. I saw it, and I froze for five seconds. And I've been clean for three years."

MINI-GUIDE

Socializing Sober

How do you handle parties, business lunches, and other occasions where you previously imbibed, and where just about everyone else still does? Ideally, just boycott them early in your recovery. Sometimes, of course, that's impossible. You may have no choice but to attend your brother's wedding, a business convention, or your boss's twenty-fifth anniversary party. If that's the case, these tips will help you get home suitably sober.

EVALUATE YOUR MOTIVATION. Why do you want to go? The experienced alcoholic usually has a credible motive or two up his or her sleeve: I love to dance. Or these people will be insulted if I don't show up. Or it's important for me to be there for business reasons. Evaluate those reasons. Are they honest? Or deep down do you still fantasize about the good old lifestyle, still long for the good old drinking/drugging days?

Alcoholics often insist that the only reason they go to clubs is because they love to mambo. But once there, they seem to be epoxied to the bar stool. So forget the rationalizations, and avoid wet events unless you have strong reasons that have nothing to do with drinking.

EVALUATE YOUR FEELINGS. Are you nervous as a cat at a dog show when alcohol in any form is around? That's an okay feeling, and if you are, maybe you should beg off all wet parties. But be even more wary if yours is still the bravado of the alcoholic. "Hey, I can handle that!" are famous last sober words. They're also a sign that you haven't conquered the addict's reckless need to construct straw villains to combat and conquer. You're safest accepting an invitation if you retain just a modicum of hesitancy.

FOREWARN YOUR HOST OR HOSTESS. If they're not already aware, let them know in advance that you don't drink alcoholic beverages. That way you can be reasonably sure there will be some risk-free alternatives. It's unwise to attend any party or event at which there are no options other than alcohol or water.* Even your own wedding.

FOREARM YOURSELF. Decide in advance that there's no way in the world that you will drink or use drugs at the event. Ask for help from your Higher Power, because you may need it. Know and rehearse exactly what you will say if someone asks, "Would you like a drink?"

DON'T GO IT ALONE. Think of yourself as swimming in deep swift waters, and take an AA buddy along. If you can't take a buddy, take someone at the party into your confidence (the host, a good friend, even a waiter), keeping in mind that candor will serve you better than pride, embarrassment, or guilt. Tell them that you can't drink, and enlist them as bodyguard. It will make the event easier for you, and will keep you from winding up behind the highball.

*Nonalcoholic beers and wines are not completely alcohol-free (see page 183) and are not a safe substitute for someone in recovery.

DON'T GO LATE. You're safest arriving early, before everyone is cheerfully high or roaring drunk and you're sucked into the maelstrom.

SERVE YOURSELF. When you arrive, walk straight to the liquid refreshments and help yourself to juice or a soft drink. (If you choose a Virgin Mary or rumless piña colada, examine your motives. Is this your choice because it's alcohol-free or because it's the closest thing to a familiar friend? It's safer to switch to something without even a faint resemblance to your old "usual.") Keep that beverage in your hand for the rest of your time at the party (refilling it when necessary). That way you won't have to keep turning down offers of something to drink. If you set your drink down while you're dancing or when you step into the powder room, get a new one when you return. Don't take a chance on anyone having accidentally switched drinks or good-naturedly "topped" yours off.

If you can't serve yourself, just make it clear that you want a soft drink or juice. Nine out of ten people will serve you without blinking. The tenth person, of course, will be one with a problem of his or her own. Move on with a "No, thank you" when you hear, "Oh, come on. Just one. To drink to the . . ." If you do drink a toast, you can drink it every bit as sincerely with juice or a soft drink.

TRY CAMOUFLAGE. To ward off pressure to drink, order something that looks like it might contain alcohol: spicy tomato juice with a celery stick; club soda with a dash of cola; seltzer, sparkling water, or ginger ale with a twist; a Coke with lemon; orange juice; ginger ale in a champagne glass (again, unless your usual).

DON'T BE A BARFLY. Once you have your beverage, put some space between you and the bar. Dance, circulate, sit and chat. But keep a safe distance from the source. Give your sobriety some elbow room.

CURB RESENTMENT. You're almost sure to run into someone who'll say with a superior smile, "Do you mind if *I* have a drink?" Your automatic answer will most likely be "Oh, no, I don't mind." The truth is you probably do resent it. You're as good as the other guy. If he can drink, why can't you? (Maybe he's got genes that allow him to drink and you don't, a small point it would be rash to ignore.) If you feel resentment building, make your excuses and find your buddy, slip out to a meeting, or head for a phone booth and call your sponsor.

BE READY TO LEAVE. Keep your car keys or carfare in your pocket. Should drugs appear, or should you suddenly feel overwhelmed by temptation, leave immediately. Don't wait to test yourself. It's too soon, and your arm's too short to box with drugs or alcohol.

BEWARE OF HIDDEN TROUBLE. If food is served, be sure it won't sabotage your recovery (see page 182).

DON'T LINGER. Let the hostess know that you have to leave early, and that you can't stay longer than half an hour or so. The more tired you are, the more vulnerable you become. (Once you're more secure in your sobriety, you won't have to check out that fast.)

THWARTING HIDDEN TEMPTATION

Alcohol doesn't come only in a glass or a bottle. It can come in bowls and plates, too. And what you don't know *can* hurt you. One reason, of course, is that even a small amount of alcohol can trigger a relapse. Another is a psychological risk: the taste plus the "thrill" of knowing that you're consuming alcohol could turn on a compulsion to drink. So to be sober rather than sorry, always be sure that your food has been prepared completely without wine or spirits.

At home, that should be easy. In other people's homes or in restaurants, it doesn't have to be much harder. There's no need to go into any long explanations—just say that you are not allowed to have anything with alcohol in it. To be sure your hostess or waiter takes you seriously, you can add, "My doctor's given me strict orders." Of course when you're a guest in someone else's home, this information should be passed along when you accept the invitation. If you save it for the moment you sit down at the dinner table, your announcement could cause your proud hosts consternation.

Be very careful of the following:

Foods cooked in wine or other spirits. The old wisdom that if wine or liquor is simmered for five minutes or more, the alcohol cooks out has been scientifically debunked. Even an hour or more of cooking will not eliminate all the booze. So avoid any dish that includes alcohol, even minute amounts, as an ingredient. Spurn it even more stubbornly when you're the one doing the cooking, whether it's for yourself or when hosting company. With a chef's hat on your head and a bottle in your hand, that old one-for-me-one-for-the-pot feeling is sure to reappear.

Some dishes announce their alcohol content loud and clear: Salmon with Madeira Sauce, Beef Bourguignon, Turkey with Grand Marnier Apricot Stuffing, Coq au Vin, Prune and Armagnac Purée, Fettuccine with Vodka Cream Sauce, and Rum Pecan Pie, for example. Others are standard recipes that you can be pretty sure are made with alcohol: Sauce Chasseur (Hunter's Sauce), Cumberland Sauce, Sole Véronique, Cheese Fondue, Welsh Rarebit. And of course, Irish coffee and all the other national permutations (Jamaican, Mexican) whose claims to fame rest on firm alcoholic foundations. But a good many more dishes are made with spirits, and only the cook knows for sure. To play safe, always ask whether soups, sauces, marinades, or salad dressings are made with wine, beer, whiskey, liquor, or other alcohol-based beverages.

Uncooked foods flavored with alcohol. Of course alcohol can be hiding in a great many dishes where it hasn't been cooked at all, and is as powerful as it was in the bottle. For example, dips can be spiked with brandy or other spirits. So can desserts, such as Rum-Raisin Ice Cream, Holiday Fruitcake, Hard Sauce, Zabaglione, Baba au Rhum, or Berries Romanoff. Ask before plunging in.

Flaming dishes. Both main courses and desserts that are served flaming (flambé) use alcohol to fuel their flames.

Extracts and flavorings. When cooking at home, try to use vanilla and other extracts that are prepared without alcohol (at 40 percent alcohol, it's like holding a hand grenade without the pin). They may be hard to find, but they are available. You needn't worry about eating commercial ice creams or baked goods flavored with vanilla, almond, or other nonalcoholic flavorings, or similar items prepared by friends. The amount of alcohol will be

FLEETING THOUGHTS

A fleeting thought about "the good times" may seem innocent, but here's what often happens: The thought leads to fantasizing (a more organized, scripted mental picture of a longed-for event). The fantasy becomes a preoccupation (a focused pattern of thought about the event). The preoccupation becomes an obsession (the thought develops a self-fulfilling control over the person). Now the not-so-innocuous, not-so-fleeting thought is in charge and converts the obsession into a compulsion and the need to take action. It's not far from the compulsion to the nearest bar. So, the moment it surfaces, banish that fleeting thought.

negligible in a single serving and the taste will not be apparent at all. But avoid such foods with rum or other spirit flavors, whether or not they actually contain alcohol (many fancy cakes and gourmet ice creams do)—the flavor alone can trigger a craving.

Wine vinegars. There is no alcohol in commercial vinegars—so don't worry about salad dressings in restaurants or in other people's homes, unless the vinegar is homemade. Don't keep wine vinegar at home, however, because just the look and smell of it could conjure up old feelings and lead to craving.

Nonalcoholic beverages. It seemed to be a boon to the recovery community when counterfeit wines and beers came on the market. But they are less boon than booby trap. "Nonalcoholic" does not mean 0 percent alcohol, but rather no more than 0.5 percent. That doesn't sound like much, but it may be enough to trigger a craving for more. Pseudo-beers and wines that say "contain no alcohol" should be alcohol-free. But even these present a problem. Here it's the psychological feeling of drinking, of participating in a drinking lifestyle, that could put your recovery at risk. So school yourself to avoid them, particularly early in recovery.

Foods you associate with drinking. If you always drank beer with your pizza, bypass the pizzeria for a while. Do the same with any other foods that you always ordered a drink with. They are as likely to trigger a craving psychologically as the first sip of alcohol does physiologically.

Nonstick vegetable sprays. Some of these contain alcohol as a propellant, but the chemical evaporates as soon as it hits the air. Still, if just knowing there's alcohol in the can makes you edgy, look for an alcohol-free brand.

10 YOUR RELATIONSHIPS AND SOCIAL LIFE

If you're like most alcoholics/addicts, you've left a trail of maimed relationships behind you. Early recovery may seem like the ideal time to pick up the pieces. It's not. It's the time to concentrate on your recovery and nothing else. Starting new relationships and mending old ones will have to wait. Still, you can hardly live in this world without relating to others. How do you do that now? How do you keep old relationships from souring further and avoid starting distracting new ones?

WHAT'S ON YOUR MIND?

PERSUADING OTHERS YOU'RE SERIOUS

"I've gone to several AA meetings and haven't had a drink in three weeks. My wife says I'll soon be back on the sauce again, just like every other time I quit. How can I persuade her that this time I mean it?"

You can't do it with words. Only with actions. You've lost her trust and you're not going to regain it with a kiss and a promise.

You can tell her that you finally realize what alcohol has done to you, to her, and to the family, and that you're trying to do something to end the devastation. Ask her to judge you one day at a time. Invite her to come to an open AA meeting with you. Urge her to go

Guide Lines

❖ Phase One recovery is not the time to attempt to heal crippled relationships.

❖ Starting a new relationship in Phase One can be hazardous to recovery.

❖ The only way you can prove yourself to friends and family right now is by staying sober and working your program.

❖ You can't change other people, but you can change yourself.

❖ Though a lot of your fence mending will take place in Phase Two, you can begin improving relationships now by making honesty a priority.

to Al-Anon and to read the chapter for spouses in the Big Book and Chapters 27 and 28 in this book. She needs as much support as you do right now because she's been through so much, heard so many promises, had her high hopes dashed so many times, and been so thoroughly betrayed and confused by your addictive behavior that she may think *she's* the one who's crazy.

But an important lesson of recovery is to understand that you can't change other people, or the way they think and feel. You can only change yourself. So don't focus on trying to change her attitudes. Work on changing your own. Don't be controlling or overbearing, hostile or aggressive; don't attempt a hard sell. Give your spouse time, distance, and space. Let her decide for herself whether this time is really different.

Whether it will be will depend on you. The AA program comes with unconditional love, but no unconditional guarantees. If you're honest, open-minded, and willing to do whatever is necessary to get well, you can greatly improve the odds of success.

"How can I let my friends know that this time I'm sober for good? I know they're sick and tired of hearing me say that I'm going on the wagon."

And probably even more tired of seeing you fall off. This time, don't bother to announce your intentions. Just change your behavior, and pretty soon they'll notice that staying sober is as much a way of life with you as staying drunk was. But trust isn't built in a day, so although they're rooting for you, it may take a while for them to believe you're serious.

If they ask you what's happening, tell them that you're sober today, and that you're determined to stay that way a day at a time. Be honest—that's part of your recovery—but don't preach or promise the world. And make it clear that though they should no longer consider you an empty shot glass that constantly needs refilling, they needn't handle you like a Ming vase, either. You won't break if someone says the wrong thing.

You're the one who has to set the tone for your relationships, and it shouldn't be a somber one. It's not only okay to joke about your situation, humor is the best approach to take: "Hey, sorry I can't go to see *Star Wars 14* with you. I'm on my way to the longest running show in town—my AA meeting."

Some friends will ask a lot of questions and want to know all about your alcoholism/addiction. Be candid with them. Invite them to accompany you to an open meeting to see for themselves. It could do them some good, too, either personally (after all, better than one person in ten has a problem) or in dealing with a family member (one in three has a close relative who is chemically dependent). For those who have little interest in the details, tell them only as much as they want to hear. In most cases, it's enough to say that you've turned over a new leaf, and that you're going to do your darndest to see that this one doesn't dry up and blow away.

You may also feel bad about the way you've treated your friends in the past. But that past behavior is fixed as permanently as history now. Expending the effort necessary to rewrite history in this phase of recovery may weaken the effort required to live successfully in the here and now. There'll be time enough to do this later in Phase Two (see page 372). In the meantime, good friends will forgive you; with the others you'll have to earn your wings and halo gradually.

THE RUMOR MILL

"Hardly a day goes by that one good friend or another doesn't tell me some wild story he heard about me. How can I close down the rumor mill?"

You can't. If some of the stories are true, you can't change the facts. If some aren't true, they aren't worth your attention. If someone called you a donkey, would you order straw for dinner?

What you can do is act in a way that will force the rumor mill to close for repairs. If you're sober and going to meetings and acting responsibly, what can they say about you? "That guy is nuts—he goes to an AA meeting every night." You could do a lot worse.

If the rumors continue, you can ask friends who report them to you to help set the record straight. Have them calmly and politely tell the story-teller that you were a mess for a long time and you know it, but that now you'd be grateful for their helping you earn a second chance. Have them explain that all you're asking is for them to forget the way you were and bury the past.

Still, there may be some people who will continue to pass stories. They will be the ones who are still drinking or using drugs and don't want to see you go straight. Ignore them.

"While I was drinking I had an affair with my secretary. I love my wife and I really regret it. Some people at the office knew about it, and I'm afraid my wife will find out."

Sometimes, even a long while after someone has become sober, ugly stories surface from the past. When they do, it's important to be honest about them, but it's also important to show that you have changed. Turn a negative into a positive. Make it clear that the person who committed those indiscretions, crimes, or whatever, wasn't "you." When you drank your judgment was anesthetized. You had to be drunk to sleep with the other woman; your wife you love sober. If your commitment to your marriage is genuine, your future actions, far more than your words, will reassure her that she is indeed your one-and-only.

"Early in recovery I kept thinking, 'I'm doing pretty good, but my wife is sick.' She would say, 'You forgot to close the screen door,' and my reaction would be angry; 'Don't tell me, just close it yourself.' It was rough for both of us."

THE ULTIMATE TEST

If you are a recovering spouse and come home late from work, you can expect doubt, dirty looks, and nasty comments. Better than inviting a suspicious mate to smell your breath ("Sure, you've switched to vodka!") is to pull out a nifty little dipstick called Alco-Screen, available by calling 1-800-348-5174. The pad on the dipstick is treated with an enzyme that changes color on exposure to ethyl alcohol. Just dip the stick in your saliva, and have your spouse compare it to the color codes on the back of the package. If you haven't been drinking, you're safe. The test doesn't show any false positives.

You may resent having to prove you're clean, but you have to remember how many times you've angered and disappointed your spouse in the past. Until doubt moves out and trust moves back in, that little stick could be your best ally. (And think how nice it'll be to have it on *your* side for a change.)

If your wife is so upset at hearing of your past infidelities that she isn't willing to judge you on your present behavior, suggest the possibility of marital counseling.

UNCOOPERATIVE FAMILY

"I came home from treatment and started to clean out all the liquor from the house. My husband had a fit. He said just because I'm a drunk, that doesn't mean he can't have a drink when he gets home."

There's a bigger problem in your family than whether or not to have alcohol in the house. When a spouse (or another family member or lover), though well aware of the risks, adamantly refuses to allow liquor to be banished from the house of an alcoholic, it's a pretty good bet that the anti-prohibitionist has an alcohol problem, too. But he obviously isn't admitting it, and his problem could be a bigger problem for you. Like the wife who insists on keeping a cat even though its dander is making her husband's allergies go haywire, your husband's need for alcohol certainly sounds compulsive.

When one person in a family is fighting to stay sober and the other is fighting for the right to drink, they are on a collision course. Try to persuade your spouse to go to Al-Anon, if not AA. If he absolutely refuses, talk to your sponsor, your counselor, or your physician about how to maintain your sobriety under these conditions. (Also see page 195.)

Occasionally a spouse refuses to dump the liquor in the house not because he has a problem but out of resentment: "For twenty years I had to change my lifestyle to suit yours; now I have to do it again? Well, I won't." In such a situation Al-Anon can be helpful; if it isn't, then professional counseling should be sought.

AL-ANON FOR EVERYONE

"Now that I'm going to AA, I thought it would be helpful for my lover to go to Al-Anon. Are there groups for gays and lesbians?"

There are in some areas. Ask around at your own AA meeting or check your local Al-Anon listings. Obviously a gay/lesbian Al-Anon

SAYS WHO?

Your perceptions of what you put your family (or other loved ones) through may be very different from theirs. So when the time does come to make amends, you can't base your actions on your views alone. You need to reestablish communications, discuss each individual's perceptions, and reconcile the differences before you can begin to make up for the hurt you've caused. For example, maybe you feel guilty about all the lost weekends that you spent soused or hung over, all the chances for family outings and togetherness you missed. You want to begin making up for these omissions by scheduling an outing every weekend. But maybe outings are not what your family missed. Maybe it was just your love and care and attention that they yearned for. Taking control and forcing outings on them may, even with good intentions, seem selfish, reinforcing their old resentments and creating anew the impression that you don't care enough about their feelings to consult them.

would be best, but relationship issues are pretty much the same whether you are gay or straight. Also have your partner read Chapters 27 and 28, which are for the significant others in the lives of recoverees. Although we generally use pronouns that indicate heterosexual relationships, the advice is equally appropriate for homosexuals.

GUILT: FEELING BAD ABOUT HURTING OTHERS

"I hurt so many people—my husband, my parents, my friends, my boss—while I was using cocaine that I don't know how I can ever make it up to them."

First things first. In this case, your recovery comes first. Initially this may seem selfish and self-centered, both to you and to those around you. But this is a different kind of self-centeredness than the destructive brand you exhibited while devoting yourself singlemindedly to the pursuit of self-gratification. In the long run, it will benefit not just you but everyone you know.

Ask—implore, if necessary—the people in your life to be patient a little longer. There'll be plenty of time to make full amends later (see page 372). Right now, the most valuable thing you can do is to concentrate on your recovery. It's like triage in a hospital emergency room: If the patient bleeds to death, it won't matter how well the legs are set. So they stop the bleeding before they attend to the broken limbs. In your case, stem your addiction now; attend to the other damage later.

In the meantime, watch out that your guilt over past behavior doesn't sabotage your recovery by making you feel unworthy of the benefits it yields. Everyone who works at recovery is worthy of them. That includes you.

"Some of the things I did when I was using drugs will haunt me all my life. The worst was this little kid getting killed. My friend was driving, but we were both high as kites. He was arrested, but I wasn't. Still I feel guilty."

Nothing you do will bring that little boy back. Nothing you say is likely to make his parents feel any better. The important thing now is that you concentrate on your recovery. That way you can ensure that you, at least, will never again be a party to such a tragedy.

When your recovery becomes more solid and you are ready to make amends (see page 372), you can help prevent others from repeating your mistakes. Probably the best way is by telling your story, completely and honestly. You can tell it to schoolchildren, AA groups, drivers ed classes, programs sponsored by MADD (Mothers Against Drunk Driving) or SADD (Students Against Drunk Driving). When they've heard what it feels like to erase another human being, how it feels to live with it for the rest of your life, they may think twice before they drink or drug and drive. A school counselor, alcohol or drug counselor, or a representative of an anti-drunk driving organization can help you arrange such talks.

No, you can't bring that child back. But you can dedicate yourself to seeing that other lives not be heedlessly and needlessly lost because of alcohol or other drugs.

TELLING ALL

"While I was drinking and using I did some things that were so bad even I don't want to think about them. But now I'm trying to be real honest with my folks. Should I tell them?"

Do you think they really want to know about what you did? If it hurts you to think about it, just imagine how they'd feel hearing about it. What you fertilize grows. The more you talk about and dwell on the past, the more it is likely to grow in your mind. So, for their peace of mind as well as your own, accentuate the positive present, not the negative past.

However, don't minimize or ignore past behavior when the subject comes up. While their feelings might be a reason to avoid confessing all, your own embarrassment or shame is not. Your sponsor and AA group can help you steer between these rocks. You can bet that at one time or another they've all been in the very same boat.

If your parents should find out things you'd rather they hadn't heard—and that sometimes happens—consider that to be for the best. But it will be easier for them to deal with the gory details if they become regular Al-Anon members. Hearing other parents' stories, they will come to realize that what you did was part of your disease and not a reflection of the kind of person you are or can be. Knowing about your past may also help them to understand what you've been through and better equip them to help you in your recovery.

WHAT HAPPENED DURING BLACKOUTS

"The things I remember doing during the last few years are bad enough. I'm afraid that what I did during blackouts may have been even worse. Should I try to find out now so I can start to make amends?"

For the present, don't ask questions about these blank spaces in your life. It's possible that people aren't meant to know what they did at such times. If you did find out, you might not be able to handle it right now. In time you may begin to hear about some of those things, but by then you should be far enough along in recovery to be able to deal with them. In Phase Two you may want to carefully solicit information about what happened during blackouts from family and friends. This will not only help fill in the blanks, but may also help you to rebuild your relationships.

Right now, however, there's no reason to spend a lot of time dwelling morbidly or sorrowfully on the past. Instead what you need to concentrate on is making sure that you never live like that again.

"I'm so ashamed of what happened when I was drinking. I would proposition perfect strangers at parties; I had a crush on my boss. And that's just what I remember—God knows what I did during blackouts. I keep wondering if I should tell my husband about all this now."

Honesty is important in any relationship—as long as it doesn't hurt someone. Opening the closet to show your husband the skeletons will hurt him, and rattling all those old bones won't help your marriage. Odds are he has suspicions but doesn't really want to know any more. So bury the messy minutiae of your past life; burn them with your life history. Instead concentrate on your recovery, and tell your husband how he can help you through it.

Not talking about past mistakes doesn't absolve you from responsibility for them. As you move on in recovery, into Phase Two, it's important to work the Ninth Step and make amends when possible (see page 372).

If you had sexual relations with someone other than your spouse while you were drinking, you do have to be concerned with the possibility of having contracted a sexually transmitted disease. Talk to your doctor about getting tested (see page 310). If you get a clean bill of health, then you can forget about telling your spouse. If, on the other hand, you have picked up something, it will be important to get yourself treated and your spouse checked. See page 308 for how to deal with such a troubling situation.

ANGER TOWARD OTHERS

"I know you're supposed to get rid of your anger in recovery. But after what my parents put me through—the physical and emotional abuse from the earliest time I can remember—I don't know if I ever can."

Getting rid of anger in recovery isn't something you do for someone else. It's something you do for yourself. Continuously simmering anger is incompatible with recovery. It can easily boil over into relapse.

That doesn't mean that your anger isn't justified. Anyone who is mistreated should feel angry. But you don't have to feel angry forever. You can learn, if not to forgive and forget, to accept what happened and move on. There are several ways in which you can do this:

❖ Express your anger; talk about your hurt. You may not yet be ready to talk to your parents about it, but you can discuss it with your counselor or your sponsor. It may help, too, to write a letter to your mother and dad, explaining your feelings.

❖ Examine your anger. Are you really angry at your parents? Or are you angry at yourself for triggering their mistreatment? Many abused children feel they deserve what they get. If you blame yourself, you need to recognize that no child ever deserves to be abused. You also need to build your own sense of self-worth, which is a major goal of recovery.

❖ Try meditating as a way to banish your anger. Or ask your Higher Power to release you from it. Remember, as long as you retain the anger, your parents' abuse is continuing to hurt you.

❖ Make an attempt to understand your parents' behavior. Was there so much hate and anger between them that there was no room in the house for love? Could the abuse directed at you have largely, or at least in part, ricocheted from their own wretched relationship? When spouses constantly pot-shot at one another, stray bullets of hostility or self-hatred often strike unintended targets. Or perhaps alcohol or drugs were a factor in the abuse you suffered. Knowing the reason doesn't make the abuse okay, but it should help you to understand that you were not responsible for it.

Once your recovery becomes more solid and you enter Phase Two, you'll need to reevaluate your relationship. After what your parents did to you, regardless of their reasons, you may never be able to love them with enthusiasm again. But you may feel better if you can manage to forge some kind of permanent peace.

YOUR ROLE IN THE FAMILY

"I'm sober now. Why can't my family just accept that, and let me take back my rightful role as head of the family?"

For years your family has been tiptoeing around you. Now you're the one who has to tread lightly. That's not easy. The urge to control flourishes in people in active addiction. Since they find it difficult to control their use of chemical substances, alcoholics/addicts attempt to control everything else in their lives—including their families. In sobriety, that urge to control often remains strong.

But control is just as unrealistic now as it was when you were drinking or using. You can't suddenly walk in and announce to your family that from now on you're in charge, that this, this, and this is how things are going to be run. They've adjusted over time to doing remarkably well without you, and they will resist your interference—sometimes fiercely. Understandably, they are too angry and resentful to welcome you back as dictator. After all that has happened, it's hard enough to open their arms and welcome you back at all.

You're going to have to earn your reinstatement in those arms with a long period of sobriety, and by regaining the trust of your spouse and your kids. That means that you can't tell your spouse how money or time should be spent, how the household should be organized, who should be in charge of what. Nor can you dictate to your children what your relationship to them should be, who they can pal around with, or how much time they should spend at home or with you.

The alienation that came about because of your drinking or drug abuse isn't going to go away just because you're sober. Things will get better, but it won't be as easy as walking into a room and switching on the lights. It will be more like waiting patiently for the sun to rise in the final hours of darkness just before the dawn. Even if you work hard at recovery, earning back your family's respect is going to take time. In fact, much as you'd like to rush it, the major part of your effort at rebuilding your relationships won't come until Phase Two of recovery.

In the meantime, you can take some positive steps to win back your family. Staying sober will be the most important, but not the only one. The other steps are the same ones needed in nourishing any relationship: honesty, respect, consideration, love. As an alcoholic/addict, these may not come easily at first because it's likely that suppressing your emotions and relating to others in unhealthy ways (cheating, deceiving, exploiting, being unreliable and inconsiderate) have been second nature to you for so long. You need to relearn, or perhaps learn for the first time, how healthy human beings relate to each other within a family and how a healthy family functions as a democratic (not a totalitarian) unit. Working your AA program and using this book will help.

So will showing interest in your family and spending time with them. But don't dictate, invite. Ask your spouse to see a movie with you, or surprise her with tickets to a concert. Invite your kids to go fishing, see a ballgame, do some shopping—whatever it is you think they might enjoy doing with you. But don't be resentful if they turn you down. Just give them more time, and try again.

REASSIGNING FAMILY RESPONSIBILITIES

"I understand why my husband took over handling the family finances, organizing our children's lives, and controlling the direction the family was going while I was out of it—taking pills all the time. But I'm sober now, and I don't know why I can't take those jobs back."

That may sound reasonable. But it isn't. Not yet. First of all, you need to concentrate on recovery, not on trying to juggle a lot of additional, often stressful, responsibilities. You have meetings to go to, meditations and reading to do, sessions with a sponsor and possibly a therapist—enough to fill most, if not all, of your spare time. For now, consider yourself lucky that your spouse has taken over most family responsibilities; that will help speed your recovery.

Second, before you regain the right to participate in running your family you have to regain trust. Each day you need to prove in little ways that you are ready for added responsibility. You can do that by staying sober, working on your recovery, and fulfilling whatever responsibilities you still have (everyone has some things they must get done), whether it's making sure the beds are made and dishes washed or just getting out of bed, to and from work, and home to dinner on time. Many people in early recovery find this is about all they can handle anyway.

Finally, early recovery is delicate, and some people do have slips. If you had one after taking back these responsibilities, you could seriously damage the family's finances, mess up the kids' lives, take the family in the wrong direction.

So don't struggle to regain any major responsibilities until you are farther along in recovery. Then you and your spouse can begin to reexamine the functioning of the family as a joint responsibility, and can negotiate the redivision of labor. At that point, he'll no longer feel the need to handle everything to keep the family from falling apart, and will probably be only too happy to make you an equal partner again.

"I've been clean and sober for nearly two months. I live at home and my parents are now dumping all kinds of family responsibilities on me. Drive my brother here. Take my sister there. Babysit for both of them. I feel so overloaded I want to scream—or worse."

You haven't had a drink or a drug in two months. You're acting pretty much like a normal person. Why shouldn't you start participating in family life like a normal person? That's the way your parents—and many others who live with people in recovery—see it.

What they clearly don't recognize is that this is a period of recuperation. Like recovery from the flu or any other illness, getting back into full activity too soon often leads to relapse. The less stress in your life in the months ahead, the better your chances of successful recovery. Explain that to your parents, and ask them to read Chapters 27 and 28. Also have your counselor, if you have one, or your sponsor discuss the situation with them. This should help them understand and take some of the pressure off of you.

That doesn't mean you shouldn't be contributing anything at home. Taking responsibility for certain family chores—laundering your own clothes, keeping your room neat and not adding to the clutter around the rest of the house, doing the dishes after you return from evening meetings (it's a great time to think about and evaluate your day)—will give you a sense of accomplishment as well as help ease family tension.

In the hierarchy of your life right now, of course, AA and your recovery have to come first. But these family responsibilities should come ahead of any outside commitments (such as sports, clubs, youth groups, socializing with friends), all of which may have to be put on hold for a least a year.

FAMILY COMMUNICATIONS AND DECISION-MAKING

"Every time we have to make a decision in our family, there's a major blowup."

It's typical for families in early recovery to have difficulty communicating and making decisions. For years there has been little constructive communication. Decisions were usually made in one of two ways: by fiat (handed down by either the addicted person or the spouse or other family member desperately struggling to maintain a measure of control) or by default (no one was in any condition to make a choice, so things just happened). There was probably an ongoing struggle for control, with power, physical size, and dishonesty dominating, while positive values like caring, helping, and honesty were trampled underfoot.

Sobriety alone won't alter these family dynamics; you'll have to work consciously at changing them if you want your children to learn that there's a better, more rational way. If you fail to change the rules, they'll continue to dominate your life—and those of your children.

How do you change? For starters, try introducing some democracy. Suggest that decisions affecting all the family be resolved at family councils. Call such councils or meetings regularly, with everyone in the household included. Don't wait for a crisis, or even the need for a decision. At least weekly, sit down and discuss how things are going. Include on the agenda not just minor problems or major gripes that have cropped up since the last gathering, but compliments for jobs well done and for kindness or thoughtfulness. Be sure to set ground rules for the discussion:

❖ Each speaker, no matter what his or her age, will be listened to with respect.

❖ Everyone has a right to voice an opinion, but not to judge anyone else.

❖ No one should be criticized for an opinion or a feeling expressed.

❖ Everyone has the right to bring up items for discussion, and to air problems or grievances. But personal attacks ("His breath stinks 'cause he never cleans his teeth!") are taboo.

When a decision has to be made, follow the steps for good decision-making on page 358. Allow children, even young ones, to voice opinions and cast votes. The rule needn't always be one person, one vote. The person who is most affected by a particular issue should carry more weight. For example, if you are deciding about a new washing machine and the oldest child is in charge of the laundry, then his or her well-reasoned campaign for a particular model washer should be respected. Health, safety, cost, family values, and the impact on recovery should all be subjects for discussion and be weighed in coming to a decision. Ideally, you should try to reach a consensus. When there is a split vote (even when it isn't split down the middle), the issue should be resolved through negotiation if possible.

If you repeatedly find yourselves battling like jackals over a lion's leftovers, it's time to consider family counseling.

PRIORITIES WITHIN THE FAMILY

"I was on my way out the door to an AA meeting when I knocked over a pot of coffee as I reached for my handbag. There were coffee, grinds, and glass splinters all over the kitchen floor. I didn't know whether to just walk out and go to my meeting or to clean up the mess. Instead of deciding, I just sat down and cried."

That was a lot better than reaching for a tranquilizer or a drink, but it wasn't the best of all possible responses. If you're going to make recovery your number one priority, you have to keep it at the top of your priority list all the time. A more constructive way to deal with a messy situation like this would have been to close the kitchen door (or blockade the entrance) so no barefoot boy or girl could walk in and get hurt, and explain to your spouse or babysitter that you simply had to get to your meeting and would clean up the shambles when you returned.

One way to avoid this kind of dilemma—and avoid the cliff-hanging you've probably specialized in for years—is to cultivate the art of thinking ahead. For example, plan on leaving for AA meetings twenty minutes early. Then, confronted by a snag that could delay you, you can attend to it without worrying about being late. If there's no snag, getting to the meeting early gives you time to chat with other members and to help set up chairs and the coffee pot—which is an excellent way to get to know people and to feel part of the group.

THE STRAIN OF SOBRIETY ON RELATIONSHIPS

"If I had known what a strain sobriety would be on my marriage, I'm not sure I'd have quit drinking. My husband and I have been fighting more than ever."

All the alcoholic or addicted spouse needs to do is quit drinking and the couple will live happily every after. That's what virtually every family with a drinking or drug problem wishfully thinks. But it's as farfetched as a Grimm's fairy tale. In the old days, whether you seemed to be getting along fairly well (usually an illusion fostered by a sick interdependence) or your marriage was clearly foundering, there certainly were deep-seated problems that can't now be cured just by erasing whiskey and pill bottles from the family portrait. Added to the previous problems is a new one: Husbands and wives become different people when chemical dependency drops out of their lives. They have to get to know one another all over again.

That's why, for almost all relationships, the first year of sobriety can be painful; for some, it can be fatal. In most cases, the best preventive medicine is Alcoholics Anonymous for the newly sober partner and Al-Anon for the codependents. If the problems are severe, family workshops or family therapy with a certified addiction counselor or other qualified person may also be needed. Treatment at a family-centered rehab program may also help get the family out of the quicksand and back on solid ground.

"When I got sober, we'd been married for seven years and had two kids. When I got out of treatment, it was like I didn't even know her. And I'm sure she didn't know me. We had to build a relationship from scratch. We just celebrated our tenth anniversary, and it was really like our third for the people we are now."

Remember, the goal is to get closer, to share with each other. It isn't to prove who's right and who's wrong. Don't keep rehashing old or new problems. Rehashed problems just grow ever more impenetrable crusts. Instead, discuss an issue once—if necessary, twice—and then move on. Secrets, too, are a block to understanding. When you start telling each other the truth (though not truth that hurts your partner), a light goes on as though Diogenes finally found that honest man. Trust and new hope naturally follow.

Even if the marriage seems to be in terrible trouble during early recovery (and it often does), it's a bad idea for either partner to rush off to see a lawyer unless abuse, active addiction, or other serious problems exist. Like any other major change in one's life, it's best to put on hold any decision to break up a marriage until sobriety is well established—usually by the end of the first year. If marital stress is interfering with recovery, an amicably agreed-upon temporary separation could be the way to go.

That fairy tale ending is still possible. But you're going to have to do more than just kiss your frog to turn him into a prince. Most of that work, however, will have to wait until Phase Two.

A SPOUSE WHO IS STILL USING

"I've been clean for three months. I thought my husband was, too. I got a real shock this morning when doing the laundry I found a packet of coke in the jeans he'd just worn. If I hadn't had the presence of mind to flush it down the toilet, I don't know what would have happened. But what do I do now?"

You get help. Immediately. Call someone you trust (physician, counselor, sponsor) and explain your situation. It's important that you not stay in your home as long as your husband is there. Seek shelter with family or friends until the issue of your husband's using drugs is resolved.

Once you're in safe living quarters, talk with a professional (someone who has been treating you or someone recommended by your sponsor or physician) about arranging an intervention for your husband. (See page 508 for step-by-step directions.) The primary goal will be to try to get your husband into treatment for his drug problem. If that's unsuccessful, the secondary goal will be to let him know that you can't live with him under the circumstances and that a separation will be necessary. It may be a good idea to have a lawyer or divorce mediator present to work out the details on the spot.

If you value your recovery, don't agree to meet with your husband alone or to move back in with him under any circumstances. If you love him, set a good example and continue to try to

MINI-GUIDE

Whiting Out the Holiday Blues

For recovering people (and for millions of others whose lives are out of sync), holidays are often times of tension, sadness, and depression. They are also a time when temptations to jump off the wagon mushroom and multiply. Some of the following tips may help you beat back the blues:

❖ Keep your expectations realistic, so you don't set yourself up for a downer. Just because you're sober doesn't mean life will suddenly become a bowl of Bing cherries. Other people in your life probably haven't changed, and many of the conflicts and rivalries that customarily crop up at family reunions will doubtless crop up again. Accept that this is so, roll with the punches (and away from the rum punch), and rein in the urge to manipulate everything and everyone. It will be enough for you to just take care of and control yourself.

❖ Limit the amount of time you spend with relatives who make you crazy. If all of the clan is gathering for the holiday, including your brother, who drinks like a school of fish, plan on an overlap of just a day or two while he's there. (If he's arriving on Christmas Day and staying the week, you can arrive a couple of days before Christmas, help your parents prepare, enjoy a quiet Christmas Eve, and then leave the next morning.)

❖ If the holidays mean being away from home and your home AA group, be sure to attend meetings wherever you are. This will give you the booster support shot you'll almost certainly need at this difficult time—the chance to say, "Sure, I love my family, but sometimes they drive me up the wall," or to talk about whatever else it is that almost drives you to drink at the old homestead.

get him to help himself. But remember, you can't do it for him. And don't feel guilty if he doesn't. This kind of undeserved guilt can undermine your own recovery. To help you cope better with a chemically dependent spouse, go to Al-Anon meetings as well as continuing your AA or CA meetings, and read Chapters 27 and 28.

A SPOUSE WHO IS ALSO NEWLY SOBER

"My wife and I have both recently become sober through AA. It sort of puts us in a funny position. Are we supposed to play both roles—both recovering alcoholic and recovering spouse?"

In a sense, yes. You should both continue your AA affiliation—most of the time going to different meetings, if that's possible, and occasionally going together for a more social time. You should probably also go to some Al-Anon meetings, separately, to gain a better understanding of the spousal role in the disease of addiction.

Being in recovery together gives you the advantage of each being able to understand what the other has been through. But there is a disadvantage. If one of you slips, the other might fall. Or if you're having to deal with heavy financial or other problems and you both begin to think about the "good old days," you could become victims of romancing the drink. So be particularly careful to remember that the good old days were really pretty bad, proba-

❖ Plan activities other than just sitting around and gabbing—which in many families means sitting around and drinking. Movies, museums, special holiday concerts, skating, long walks, sledding with the kids, snowball fights, participatory or spectator sports, religious services, can all help fill the time pleasantly and limit stress. If the weather keeps you indoors and you want to keep the conversation from getting out of hand, suggest such activities as singing (carols, holiday oldies, whatever), games (Monopoly, Jeopardy, Scrabble), or old-favorite video viewing (Clarence earning his angel wings with Jimmy Stewart could make a marble statue feel *It's a Wonderful Life*).

❖ If the holidays mean visiting your old hometown, take time to see old friends you enjoy; avoid those you used to drink or drug with.

❖ Get plenty of rest, watch what you eat, get your usual exercise, and take time for meditation.

❖ If the holiday celebration includes the use of alcoholic beverages (such as wine at Passover), make sure in advance that there is an adequate supply of a substitute (such as grape juice) for you and anyone else who doesn't want to drink the harder stuff.

❖ If you aren't going home for the holidays, plan to celebrate with AA friends. If you haven't been invited, do the inviting yourself. Follow old family traditions or start some of your own.

❖ Particularly during winter holidays, be sure there is plenty of light in your life. Keep the lights bright at home, try to get out when the sun is shining, light a cheery fire in the fireplace. Winter solstice darkness and drabness can be psychologically (and physiologically) depressing.

bly awful (see page 156 for tips on how to keep them fresh in your memory). And spend a lot of time in social situations with recovery-oriented friends.

WHAT TO TELL YOUR KIDS

"I've been going to AA and haven't had a drink in six weeks. My kids should be glad, but they keep treating me like an ax murderer. At the same time they keep complaining that I never have time for them."

Some of the anger and confusion your children are expressing is probably related to your inattention now, but a lot of it is held over from when you were drinking. Youngsters generally don't let you in on all they're really thinking. This is especially true in alcoholic/addict families. Your children developed many of their personality traits by adapting to and imitating yours. Dishonesty and deceit is something they've both experienced and been forced to practice. But "stuffing" or disguising all those feelings takes its toll, and the result in many children is anger, either expressed or thinly concealed.

As with everyone else in your life, earning back the respect of your kids is going to take time and plenty of good behavior. In the meantime, you do have to give your children, even very young ones, some explanation of what is happening.

Exactly what you say (and how) will

depend on their ages. A very young child needs not much more than a brief explanation; a teenager can probably read this entire book, or at least Chapters 27 and 28 which are designed for family members.

Whatever you say, above all be honest. You can't make promises (you made and broke too many of those while you were drinking and drugging), and you can't make demands (you haven't earned that right). The thrust of your message should be:

❖ Your drinking or drug use wasn't their fault. When something is wrong in a family, children tend to blame themselves: "If only I were better behaved, or smarter, or..." Make it clear to your children that nothing they did was responsible for your alcoholism/addiction, or the things you did because of it.

❖ Alcoholism/addiction in a family member is not something to be embarrassed by or ashamed of. It's an illness, like any other illness. People stricken by it drink liquor or take pills or other drugs instead of doing things their families need or want. These chemicals mix up their thinking, make them fight or forget promises, even say mean and hurtful things. The only way they can get better is by not drinking alcohol or taking other drugs. If someone they know has a chronic condition requiring continuing care and treatment to keep it from flaring up, you can point to it as a way of explaining your own.

❖ It's normal to feel scared, confused, embarrassed, ashamed, angry, or guilty when a parent has this disease of alcoholism/addiction. The anger and disappointment they feel about you as a parent (because of broken promises, physical or emotional abuse, or... you fill in the crime) is absolutely justified. Assure them they are not "bad" because they are angry at (or even feel they hate) a parent who has treated them and the family as you have. Tell them it's not only okay to have these feelings, it's important to get them out in the open—to talk about them with you, with an Alateen sponsor, or with a counselor who is helping them. (For your own information, repressing that anger is classic behavior of children in a family with an addiction problem.)

❖ For a while, recovery has to be the number one priority for your family. You are sick and you have to do a lot of things to get well, like going to AA. Ask them to understand. Tell them you hate to miss doing things with the family, going to Little League or a school play or even a movie together. When they see you going to AA meetings instead of going out with them, they need to remember it's as if you were going to the doctor's office to get treatment for an illness. And it won't be forever—just until your sobriety is firmly established. In the meantime, you'll try hard to be easier to live with than you used to be.

❖ You want them to continue asking you to do things with them, and you will try hard to do them when you can.

❖ You want them to tell you how they feel—even if they feel angry. You'll do your best not to lose your temper, to give them support, and to stop and think before you react. (This is something you will have to stick to if you ever want to regain their trust.)

❖ If you should ever start drinking or using drugs again it won't be their fault—no matter what you may say under the influence. If you do (and you hope you never will), they shouldn't feel as though they have to fib or cover up for you to keep you out of trouble. That will only make it easier for you to keep on drinking and drugging.

❖ Because they are your children they may also have this disease. To be sure that they don't get into trouble with it, they need to avoid alcohol and other drugs just the way you must.

❖ If everyone tries very hard, you can

get to understand and know each other better than ever before, and the love you have can become stronger and stronger. Things won't get better overnight, but they will get better.

Don't say "I know a lot of people who got better and are now able to do more things with their kids. Pretty soon we can do that, too." Though this may seem like a good approach, it sounds too much like a drinking promise, the kind you've made but never kept before.

And don't fall into the trap of trying to buy forgiveness and acceptance with gifts. Material handouts may assuage your guilt, but they'll also act as a smoke screen to cover up the real issues that need to be addressed. (And they'll probably remind your kids of many another expensive guilt offering from your uncaring past.)

Make a special effort to do at least some little things that are important and age-appropriate to your children. Come back from your AA meeting with a quart of double chocolate almond crunch ice cream, play softball or Clue together, or watch a favorite TV show. Set a time every week for doing something with the family. These little things can mean a lot.

Don't just try to make yourself part of your children's lives again. Try to make them a part of your new life, too. Invite them to open AA meetings and other AA activities, especially those designed for families. Introduce them to the new people in your life and to the children of these new friends. Plan outings with them; invite them to your home. That way your children will begin to feel comfortable about your rushing off to meetings every evening. Instead of feeling threatened by all this activity, they'll feel part of it. Equally important, they'll begin to understand that there are a lot of other families who have gone through what they have suffered, that this really is a disease that you have, and that drinking was not something you did to punish them. It will make it easier for them to separate you from your disease and begin to believe that you can get better.

Not that it will be easy. Your children have been disappointed too many times in the past to have much confidence in your words. But your actions will speak loudly. Your children may not say much, but gradually, as you prove yourself not by telling but by showing, they'll notice that your priorities have changed—that where booze or drugs used to take precedence, now recovery and family are number one.

If you're consistent in your behavior and love, and stay sober, they'll come around soon enough. Children learn to trust again more quickly than grown-ups; they are also more forgiving. And they want to be able to love you.

"I don't see any reason to tell my six- and ten-year-olds about my having been in treatment—they think I was on a business trip. I was very discreet about my drinking, and I'm sure they aren't aware of it. It will only upset and embarrass them. And now I'm sober, anyway."

You may be sober, but you're thinking like an alcoholic. You're not being honest, to them or to yourself. And you're trying to cover up feelings—yours and theirs.

Even if your children were not aware that you were drinking (which is about as unlikely as a Shetland pony winning the Kentucky Derby), they've known for a long time that something's been seriously upsetting family tranquility. Now is the time to explain to them what the problem has been, and what you've done to correct it. Explain what liquor did to you and why you're not going to have it any more. (See the previous question for tips on explaining your condition.) If you don't give them an explanation, their fantasies about what's wrong (all kids have them in these kinds of situations) will continue to worry them and to interfere with their lives.

Being straight with your children now is important not just for present family harmony, but for your children's future. Since alcoholism has a strong genetic component, they are at high risk for following in your footsteps, right to the corner liquor store. If you teach them the importance of honesty, encourage them to be open with their feelings, and describe to them how the disease works,* you'll help them turn toward sobriety in their own lives (see Chapter 26 for more on prevention).

PARENTAL RESISTANCE

"My parents have been giving me a hard time ever since I started going to AA. They're embarrassed that their sweet* little *daughter (I'm 32) says she's an alcoholic and an addict. It can't, according to them, possibly be true. They were the best enablers in the world when I was drinking and using—but they are lousy at enabling me to stay sober. Should I just ignore them?"

It may sound cruel, but the answer for now may have to be "yes." They love you but they also see you as an extension of themselves and have trouble dealing with the fact that this extension isn't perfect. So they prefer to deny the existence of your problem rather than acknowledge it. They aren't unusual. Most people in our society don't understand the disease of alcoholism/addiction. They see it as a moral failing, something to be ashamed of. They will only start to see it in its true light when they talk to other parents going through the same thing—preferably at Al-Anon. Since their self-worth depends on your remaining messed up so they can be your caretaker, getting them involved won't be easy.

You might try staging a "reverse intervention." Just as families often confront the alcoholic/addict in order to get her to recognize she has a problem, so you may be able to confront your parents. To do this you should:

❖ Gather together a group of people, preferably the kind your parents will respect. You might include a clergyperson familiar with alcoholism/addiction, a doctor or counselor trained in the addictions, any relatives who are supporting your recovery, and several parents who are active in Al-Anon.

❖ Select a site for the intervention in which your parents will be comfortable. It could be their home if you live with them, or your apartment if you don't. Or it could be neutral ground, such as your house of worship or family doctor's office.

❖ Ask each professional who is going to attend to be ready to present a few words about alcoholism/addiction as a disease not a moral weakness. Ask the Al-Anon contingent to be ready to talk about their own feelings on hearing of their child's problems and how sharing their concerns with other parents at Al-Anon has been helpful.

❖ Prepare a list yourself of the kinds of things that you were doing that convinced you that you had a problem. You needn't include any specifics you would rather not talk about now, but do be honest.

❖ Invite your parents, telling them there are some people you'd like them to meet. If they balk, you may have to spring the intervention on them as a surprise. (You can invite them to your house for coffee and dessert, or get your minister to call and invite them for tea at the church vestry, or have your counselor suggest a meeting.)

*Some valuable books for children are listed on page 573.

❖ At the intervention, ask one of the professionals present to moderate, so that this won't be a direct confrontation between you and your folks.

Your efforts may succeed at getting your parents to understand your illness better and to recognize the benefits of their getting support through Al-Anon. But then again they may prefer to continue in their denial. If they do, you will have to steer clear of frequent contacts because the stress they generate could be hazardous to your recovery. If you live at home, you might consider getting your own place or moving in with an AA friend for a while—especially if your parents' denial includes a refusal to get rid of alcohol and/or pills that may be around the house. If you already live on your own, you should be the one to set the ground rules for seeing your parents: No booze. No arguments. No rehashing past history. Try to meet in safe surroundings—go to a concert together, or a tennis match, or bowling, anything you all enjoy as long as it won't endanger your recovery or give you too much time for confrontation.

"My parents are still reeling. In one week they found out that I was both a drug and alcohol addict and gay. Thank God they haven't rejected me, but I don't think they've stopped crying since they heard the news."

Your parents, like the parents of any other person in recovery, need help as much as you do. The best way for them to get this help is through attendance at meetings of gay Al-Anon. These groups help parents of gays and lesbians to understand their children's lives as well as the disease of alcoholism/addiction. They also help families deal with their own feelings of confusion, disappointment, failure, and betrayal. Also helpful is the organization called Parents and Friends of Lesbians and Gays (PFLAG). Chapters in major cities are listed in the telephone directory.

If there is no such group available to them, or if they are totally unwilling to attend such a group, discuss the possibility of private counseling. The counselor, of course, should be qualified in alcoholism/addiction and should also understand homosexuality. It would be a good idea, if possible, for you to visit the counselor first to be sure that he or she won't actually make matters worse. Or contact the National Association of Lesbian and Gay Addiction Professionals (NALGAP) for a list of qualified counselors.

But more than that will be needed. You, too, will have to make an effort to improve communications and build trust. This will be difficult and may take time (even years), since trust has not been a part of your relationship for a long time. And communication has probably been almost totally disrupted—or at least reached a level so superficial as to be meaningless. Read about rebuilding relationships in Chapter 19 (which applies to all chemically dependent people, no matter what their sexual orientation). Be patient with your family, if you can. They will be dealing with many of the issues that you are struggling with or have already put behind you.

Many religious parents are deeply troubled by alcoholism/addiction and homosexuality. Whether they can get help from their present spiritual advisors or not depends on their affiliation and the individual clergyperson. In general, the More Light Presbyterian Churches (Protestant), Dignity (Catholic), and Reformed and Reconstructionist rabbis and organizations can offer the most support.

Remember that your family does not have to accept or condone your way of life for you to stay sober or be happy—although it would be nice if they did. AA will provide you with the support, the steps, and the tools to be okay no matter what your family does. You need to make amends for the *effects* of your alcoholism/addiction and the hurt that resulted, but you do not have to apologize for the illness itself. You didn't cause it. As for your sexual orientation, apologizing for it is not only unnecessary, it is inappropriate.

DISHONESTY

"Everybody at AA meetings keeps talking about the importance of honesty in all our relationships. Boy, I don't know where to begin. It's been so long since I told the truth."

Dishonesty becomes a way of life for most alcoholics/addicts. They lie to themselves and they lie to others. About feelings. About substance use. About money. About where they've been and what they've done. Partly it's a way of protecting their drinking or drug use, and partly it's because their minds are so addled and emotions so muddled they can't really discern the difference between truth and fiction.

As you've discovered, the tendency to be untruthful doesn't just disappear when you swear off booze and drugs. Dishonesty is a longstanding practice that has to be unlearned. And the fear that the consequences of telling the truth (to an employer, for example, or a spouse or even friends) will be disastrous has to be overcome. Neither of these challenges is easily met. But you can't have a good recovery without meeting them.

You probably slipped into your dishonest ways in active addiction gradually. You will probably only learn to become honest gradually. But remembering the following will help speed and ease the process:

❖ The first person you have to start telling the truth to is yourself. If you don't level with yourself, you can't level with anyone else. You took the first steps in the right direction when you admitted you had a chemical dependency problem and wrote a life history and/or made a searching personal inventory. Being honest with yourself means acknowledging your good qualities as well as the not-so-good ones. That may be harder than you think. You may be so used to beating up on yourself that you've come to believe you have no good character traits.

❖ No one can be perfectly honest all the time. Honesty is the absence of intention to deceive—but sometimes we deceive ourselves or others about our feelings or intentions without realizing that it's out of a desire to please. We can forgive ourselves for that. But we can also learn to be smarter about evaluating ourselves, others, and situations so we can avoid unintentional deception in the future.

❖ Honesty to the point of hurting others is as wrong as direct lying. "Brutal honesty" is more brutal than honest, and the motivation is often more to hurt than to tell the truth.

❖ Telling the truth seems harder at first, especially when you aren't used to it, but in the long run it is easier. You don't have to keep tabs on what story you told to whom. You are released from worrying about being "caught" and from the guilt of knowingly misleading someone.

❖ The fear of telling the truth about oneself is almost always unfounded. Most people will appreciate hearing the truth. The few who do not probably have problems of their own that they aren't facing. You may be uncomfortable with a negative reaction to the truth, but that's better than not knowing how the other person feels, or assuming their reaction will be worse than it is.

❖ When you lie to others, you lose their trust, but you also lose their help. And without the trust and help of others the world is a very lonely place.

❖ At first others may not be ready to accept your word as gospel. Accepting that you are dishonest is as much habit to them as being dishonest is to you. It will take long-term honesty in your relationships before it is accepted as the norm.

❖ A successful recovery is impossible without honesty. Since lying is one of the trappings of alcoholism/addiction, continuing to make it a way of life is very likely to lead you right back to the well.

If staying honest continues to be uncomfortable in spite of trying what is recommended above, you may want to reexamine your behavior. Alcoholics tend to live lives glued together with deceit. Often they continue living that way into early recovery. Are you? Do you still have a lot to hide? Your goal should be to live the kind of life that would leave you feeling at ease even plastered across the front page of your local newspaper.

INCEST AND ABUSE

"While I was drinking I did some appalling things to my little girl. Now that I'm sober, I find that she comes up to me and wants me to hold her and . . . Could she really want me to touch her again?"

Like a lot of other people in this world, your little girl has confused sexual feelings with love and intimacy. Your attention to her, as terrible as it was, was attention. It may have been the only way that she felt loved and wanted by you. She thinks it's normal. She doesn't know it was sick behavior and that's not the way other daddies behave. Both you and your child need long-term professional therapy to deal with what has gone on in the past.

Family therapy will also be necessary, since incest and other parental abusive behavior, like alcoholism/addiction, affects everyone in the household. If you don't get help, problems could begin all over again, even if you remain sober. Or the guilt and anxiety could drive you back to drink. If your child doesn't get help, she may carry the scars of those early encounters for the rest of her life. She may never be able to have a normal relationship with a man, may never understand what real love and intimacy are about, and may end up looking for the same pattern in later life, marrying a man who drinks and abuses her sexually. All too often, addictive disease dominoes other self-destructive cycles, which become disasters on their own.

"I tried to explain to my 14-year old daughter that now that I'm sober I won't touch her again. But she won't talk to me, won't even stay in the same room with me alone, and stays away from home as much as she can, especially when her mother is out."

The legendary eloquence of Demosthenes couldn't persuade your daughter that the abuse has ended. You will have to prove it over a long period of time through your behavior towards her. This won't be easy. She is old enough to know that what you did was wrong, bad, sick. But her feelings are very confused. Maybe she hated what you did and hated you for doing it. But maybe she also needed that love and attention from you. She may be staying away from you as much because of her own mixed feelings as out of fear.

There's often a tremendous sense of inertia in a family when it's time to

INCEST KNOWS NO BOUNDS

Though we often think of incest in terms of fathers abusing daughters, there are many other family relationships that are tainted by incest. Father-son, mother-son, brother-sister, uncle-niece, and so on. *Any* incest needs immediate attention and professional treatment for the entire family. Sobriety itself is only the first, small (though clearly essential) step in wiping out the effects of this kind of damaging behavior done under the influence.

come to grips with incest. But it cannot and should not be ignored. Dealing with incest is beyond the scope of self-help groups such as AA (though the group therapy of special AA meetings organized in some communities for that purpose may be a useful part of a total treatment plan). Both you and your child need *professional* help right away to keep from damaging your relationship further, to help you understand what you did and how to prevent your behavior from recurring, and to help her overcome the harm done in the past and develop a healthy way of looking at love, sexuality, and intimacy. You will both have to learn how to relate to each other in normal and healthy ways, as father and daughter. Your wife, too, needs to be involved in therapy, since she's been a party to the incest—either by closing her eyes to what was going on, or by being so detached from her family that she failed to notice it. You will both have to work on your relationship and learn to fulfill each other's emotional and physical needs, so that neither of you has to turn elsewhere.

They say in AA:
"AA can help you either solve your relationship problems or learn to live with them."

Also post the number of the local Child Abuse hotline near your phone. Your wife and your child should both be aware of the number and why it is there—and should feel free to call it should the need arise.

STARTING A NEW RELATIONSHIP

"I feel like I'm starting a new life now, and I want to find someone nice to share it with, to support me in my sobriety. Should I start looking around?"

That wouldn't be quite as risky as looking around for your old drug dealer, but it's still a bad idea. It's usually recommended (and for very good reasons) that you begin no new romantic relationship in the first year of recovery. So resist early emotional entanglements as you would an alluring cocktail lounge. And keep the following in mind:

❖ At this point in recovery, people are so needy that they're likely to feel that *anyone* who smiles at them is Ms. or Mr. Right. Your judgment right now is not reliable enough to use it to make important decisions. Later, when your mind clears and you look back at those who seem attractive to you now, you'll probably bless this go-slow advice.

❖ Developing a new relationship takes

time and energy, both of which you should be devoting to staying sober.

❖ Sobriety is still very fragile during the first year, and most people are better off without the stress involved in weathering the disappointments and disagreements that go hand-in-hand with relationship-building.

❖ Because of the way addiction freezes personality development, if you started drinking or using in your teens, no matter what your chronological age, you are probably socially and emotionally still a teenager. You should be spending the first year of recovery maturing and advancing your interpersonal skills before you try to build a serious relationship.

❖ People who are involved in trying to find or develop a new relationship tend to don masks in order to gain attention and affection. If they find that others react well to the false face, they think, "Well, I guess that's who I really am or ought to be." And they continue the masquerade. During recovery, when finding the human being beneath the addiction is so important, this kind of thinking is counterproductive, even dangerous.

❖ There is a tendency in any relationship to lean on the other person. This can give you a false sense of strength, which at this early stage could be a fatal weakness. What you need in recovery is not strength, but vulnerability. The minute alcoholics/addicts feel powerful, they feel that alcohol and drugs can't get them into trouble. Poof! The genie of denial pops out of the bottle, and takes charge. This illusory strength will keep you from developing the deep inner emotional muscle needed to nurture your recovery.

❖ You'll be a poor partner in any relationship until you feel good about yourself. Don't plan to play duets until you're a polished soloist.

❖ Though we don't usually notice it at the time, many relationships during early recovery are largely selfish. Deprived of our chemicals, we are looking for substitute ways to feel good or worthy, and the applause and bouquets of a playmate superficially provide that. But as with drugs, this kind of dependent relationship can backfire. It transmits the message: "You are incompetent, incapable of feeling good or worthy on your own. Someone else must run your life for you." It's just exchanging one kind of bondage for another.

❖ Any heavy relationship in early recovery—even a platonic, nonsexual one—in which you let your security become bound up in another individual can put your recovery at risk. Should the other person flounder or fail in some way, you may, too.

All this doesn't mean you're doomed to a year of monkish solitude. There's a relationship continuum that starts with shy glances and ends in commitment. Until your recovery is more established, you've got to stop somewhere in the middle. Start getting to know new people. Spending some time talking at meetings or over coffee is okay. Going out in groups is, too. But there's an invisible line (which you can usually sense) past which a relationship turns more intimate and more dependent, and that's where it can ultimately become destructive.

There are some red flags that should tell you to hit the brakes on a budding relationship: You're spending more time with this person than with anyone else. You begin to experience sexual fantasies about him or her. You place this person on an emotional pedestal. Gifts or favors are given or exchanged. The relationship lures you away from recovery activities. The relationship becomes a substitute compulsion.

Many people assume that although other liaisons are taboo, an AA relationship is a good bet. But it's a better bet that you'll focus your energies and attention on the object of your affection rather than on the objectives of AA. You will look at the other person rather than at yourself. Still, if you must have a relationship at this stage, someone in AA is usually safer than someone outside.

Of course, it's possible you will meet someone and, without trying, believe you've fallen in love. You can't change the way you feel. But you don't have to *act* on those feelings. Don't trade short-term good feelings, as you have in the past, for long-term serenity and happiness. If this is the real thing, it will still be real after you've collected your one-year chip and are ready for it. In the meantime, keep the object of your interest at arm's length.

"After the mess I've made in picking boyfriends, I feel like I should just give up trying. I always pick the wrong guy."

Though this phase of recovery is not the time to be selecting a new partner, it is a good time to give some thought to just what kind of person you'd like that partner to be. Evaluate what was wrong with previous attachments and think about what you want now. You can do this just the way you do your daily inventory, listing the things you want (compatibility in education, religion, hobbies, lifestyles, goals, values) and don't want (things that irritate you or that you don't respect) in a mate. You don't necessarily want someone just like yourself, but maybe someone whose personality complements or completes yours (he's great in the kitchen, you're terrific handling money), someone whose interests can enrich your life (and vice versa). The ideal person doesn't have to be an AA member, but he should be willing to learn about AA and to become involved in it as a way of supporting you.

The composite picture you sketch now is only preliminary. As you mature in recovery, you may find your vision of the Ideal Mate gradually altering. As you get to know yourself better, you'll have a clearer image of the kind of person you want to spend the rest of your life with. By the time you're ready to move into Phase Two, it's likely you'll have a pretty accurate portrait of that person. And it's likely, too, that you'll be ready to meet him.

BREAKING UP

"I've been in a relationship for the last several years. But now that I'm sober, this guy doesn't seem right for me. Should I stay put?"

No. If a relationship has gone sour, you don't have to hang in there, even during early recovery. Get out, and quickly. Otherwise, you may find that the tension of living in an unhappy situation will jeopardize your recovery.

If you aren't living together, breaking up will be relatively easy. If it's the kind of relationship where you feel you can explain that it's over and that will be that, do so. If it isn't, force yourself to be unkind. Write a "Dear John" letter. Don't return phone calls. Turn down engagements. Refuse to be civil. That may seem cruel, but it will probably end the affair more quickly and more permanently than kindness would. If he's offended, so be it. That way he'll never bother you again.

In a live-in situation, cutting the cord may be more complicated. If it's your house, serve notice that if he doesn't move by a certain date, you will put all his things out on the sidewalk. If he threatens you, tell him you'll call the police. If it's his place or you share it, you'll have to pick up and leave. If there are a lot of jointly owned possessions (furniture, pictures, dishes, and so on), try to work out an agreement on who gets what. If this is impossible, just take what you feel is rightfully yours, and go. If things get really nasty, you may be best off leaving pronto with your clothes and other personal belongings, thereby avoiding a really unpleasant and possibly physically harmful hassle.

"I'm torn between going back to my wife and staying with my girlfriend. I don't know what to do."

For now, it may be a good idea to separate from them both. The seesaw emotions this situation presents can't be good for your recovery. Try the bachelor life for a while. Concentrate on staying sober and learning more about who you are and what you want out of life. As you become more self-aware, you'll be better able to judge whether one or the other, or neither, of these women is right for you.

If, however, you think you'd like to move back home (assuming your wife will have you) and you believe home will be a relatively supportive environment for your recovery, say goodbye to your lover (see above) and give your marriage another try. But get some marital counseling to improve the odds of a successful reconciliation.

DATING JITTERS

"I'm nearly thirty years old, but whenever I have to even talk to a woman I get all tongue-tied, my hands get clammy, and I practically start to shake. I don't understand it—I've been going out with girls since I was about 15, when I started using. One thing about being high—I was a lot smoother."

That wasn't you being smooth—it was your chemical lubrication. When you started using, you stopped developing skills for relating to people, including those of the opposite sex. You felt you were a smooth operator, but in reality the person beneath the drugs wasn't operating at all. Now what you have to do is to start right back there where you were when you were 15, learning to become a mature human being. Honesty, consideration, reliability, are all traits that take time to ripen, and all will be important to you as you struggle a little belatedly to become an adult. They will help you feel better about yourself and make you a much more appealing date.

In the meantime, don't rush into a relationship but do spend some time talking to women at meetings and social events. As your recovery strengthens and your confidence builds, your tongue will untie, your hands will dry, and it will get easier and easier.

You missed a lot of life while you used. You're being given a second chance to enjoy it.

"I can't tell you how many guys I was with before, when I was drinking. Now when a guy just approaches me, I get so nervous I think I'm going to faint. What's wrong with me?"

Like the young man in the question above, whose tongue turns to stone when he has to talk to a woman, your social and emotional development halted when you started drinking. You may have an adult body, but crouched inside you is a self-conscious teenager. Give that person inside you a little time and plenty of sobriety, and she'll catch up. By the time you're ready for a real relationship—not in Phase One—she'll be ready, too.

Working at your recovery is the best preparation. Going to AA meetings, conventions, and retreats, learning to talk easily to the many different men and women you meet at these programs, will help build the social skills you'll need later. So will learning to feel good about yourself, recognizing your worth, and building your confidence.

It may seem difficult to believe now, but you will be able to face men again without your knees turning to rubber, *and* without the false bravado provided by alcohol. You will be able to have a relationship that is far richer than any you've known in the past.

"I haven't been with a man since I became sober nearly a year ago. I always needed a few drinks to get into the mood. I don't think that I can feel sexy without booze."

This is a very common fear in recovery (it's more common among women, though men also experience it), but it's an unnecessary one. Although you may have convinced yourself that you needed alcohol (or drugs) in order to enjoy sex or may have used it to lessen your inhibitions, the fact is that alcohol actually interferes with orgasm, arousal, and other aspects of sexual performance.

Give yourself a little more time. A year of sobriety is usually recommended before entering into a new romantic relationship. Then, when you meet a man you really like and respect, who really likes and respects you, let the relationship develop in other ways before bringing sex into it. Reading about sexuality in recovery in Chapter 11 will help you to better understand yourself and your feelings and prepare you for a new intimate relationship.

You will find that not only will you be able to enjoy sex again, it will be a more fulfilling experience than ever before. The sexual encounters so common during the abuse of alcohol and drugs pale when compared to the deeper and more meaningful relationships that can develop during recovery.

GENDER PREFERENCE CONFUSION

"I've been living with other guys for the last six years, since I was seventeen, so I've assumed that I'm gay. But sometimes I also feel attracted to women."

If you feel some confusion about your sexual orientation, don't panic. And don't try to start any new relationships—homosexual or heterosexual—during this first year. Focus on your recovery program, doing what you must to get better. When you can, spend time in social situations with both heterosexuals and homosexuals, and see if you find yourself moving in one direction or the other. If you do, and if you feel comfortable about that direction, stay with it. If you don't, or if you still feel uncomfortable when you are about eighteen months into recovery, seek qualified professional help, preferably from someone who has experience both with addiction and homosexuality.

SAME SEX FRIENDSHIPS

"Everyone says that since I'm female, I should have a female sponsor and counselor, and that I should do most of my socializing with women. But I get along better with men than with women. So why can't I hang out with them?"

Chemistry. Most of us get a good feeling when we're with those of the opposite sex. But it's a dangerous feeling for you right now because it's based on chemistry and not on real communication. With gender opposites, there's often more coquetry than candor. You feel more in charge, and are more likely to be able to manipulate the other person, to con him into telling you what you want to hear. You are more likely to see yourself as you'd like to be seen than as you really are, which makes it hard to engage in the self-examination that leads to growth in recovery.

Serious discussions with sponsors, counselors, and other recovery friends during early sobriety must be totally honest, with no fences up and no holds barred. For that reason these confidantes should be of your own sex. Recovery depends on your hearing it like it is, with no chance to flirt your way out of it.

HAVING FUN SOBER

"I'm just twenty-one and fresh out of treatment after eight years of drinking and playing around with drugs. I'm glad I'm sober, but I'm pretty depressed, too, when I think that there's gonna be no more laughing, no more fun, no more parties in my life."

It's true that something will be missing from your life during recovery. But contrary to what almost every alcoholic/addict believes, it won't be the "fun." It will be the DUI convictions. The hangovers, cold sweats, blackouts, DT's. Kneeling at the porcelain altar to spill your guts. Gone will be the failing grades and creditor-docked pay checks, the desperate midnight drives trying to make a drug buy or find an open liquor store.

And there will be plenty of opportunities for fun down the road, with different playmates in different playgrounds. It may not seem that way at first, as you struggle with staying sober. But it will happen. Many people, in fact, report that their social lives really don't take off *until* they get sober.

Remember, most people in this world do not abuse alcohol or take drugs. And most of them have plenty of fun. You may be surprised to discover this, but the local bar or club is not the good-time center of the universe.

For now, most of your fun will have to come at AA meetings and activities. You've probably already noticed that folks solidly into recovery at these meetings seem to be having a wonderful time. If you think about it, it may strike you that they aren't very different from your old drugging and drinking pals. And you'd be right. They are, in fact, the same people (or at least the same kinds of people) gone sober. (Sober meaning "abstemious," not grave or solemn.) They are people just like you, who've given up their booze and their booze-guzzling buddies for coffee and coffee-drinking buddies. At first, most of the time they used to spend drinking and drugging, they spent at AA. But they soon began to add other activities. In time, you'll do the same.

The fact is that there are a lot more fun things you can do when you're sober than when you're not. Most people who drink and take drugs spend all their free time feeding their habits, with little time for anything else. True, you remember the good times rolling at parties, discos, clubs, and bars (though it's likely you blocked out what really happened at, and after, those events). But do you remember doing anything else?

Now there's a whole new world of activities to enjoy. You can still have your dances and parties, your clubs and discos. The difference is that you'll choose those at which no alcohol is served or drugs dispensed, and you won't wake up with foul breath, soiled clothing, and your head pounding. And, too, there'll be extra added attractions—things you may not have had the patience for, like movies, concerts, the golf course, and the beach. As your recovery becomes stronger, there will be things you didn't have the stamina or coordination for: tennis, swimming, jogging, softball, basketball, cross-country skiing, ice-skating, bicycling, camping. And things you couldn't sit still for: reading, board games (including some developed to help strengthen your recovery while you play*), jigsaw or crossword puzzles, needlepoint or sewing, drawing and painting, playing a musical instrument. You can do all the things normal people do. And you'll do them sober, just like normal people.

Later, in Phase Two of recovery, with sobriety well established, you'll be able to expand your recreational opportunities. You'll be free to do things that would have been dangerous (okay, downright crazy) when you weren't sober—flying, water- and downhill skiing, gymnastics, ice hockey, horseback riding, white-water rafting, skydiving.** And you'll be fit to confront the ultimate danger: going to parties and places where alcohol is served. (Of course you'll need to take sensible precautions—see Chapter 9).

Vacations, too, can still be fun. If you arrange yours around AA-sponsored retreats and conventions, you'll find compatible people and plenty of diversion in safe surroundings. (See the *AA Grapevine* and recovery newspapers for listings of upcoming events.) Resorts and travel agencies, too, have discovered recovery and are creating special packages—everything from Club Med–type vacations† and alcohol-free cruises to rafting and camping trips. Later in recovery, you can expand your vacation vistas further—traveling abroad, going to "civilian" resorts, anywhere your passport will take you. You'll be warmly welcomed and provided with as-needed support by AA groups just about anywhere in the world—people who speak different languages but whose problem is the same. (Usually, someone wants to practice their English, so the language barrier can be minimal.)

"If I didn't like myself, or was feeling down, or maybe had done something I didn't like, I'd call up a girl and she would say come on over and spend the weekend with me. So I would go, and she would tell me I looked good, smelled good, tasted good, did good. I felt good and all was fine. Then I would go home and feel empty again."

Still, you will find it's always safest to travel with your spouse, an AA friend, or someone else familiar with your problem and recovery needs. And pack some AA tapes and reading materials to keep you honest.

Incidentally, you don't have to travel the seven seas or free-fall from an airplane to have fun sober. You'll find

*Such as "Feeling Bingo" and "Recovery," available from Judy Martin, Recovery Games, 675 14th Avenue, San Francisco, CA 94118; (415) 221-6264.

**It's not a good idea to attempt such high-exhilaration activities early in recovery, since they can cause an adrenaline rush that could lead to a compulsion to drink or use. See page 461.

†Package vacations are available through: Sober Vacations International, 2365 Westwood Blvd., Suite 21, Los Angeles, CA 90064 (213/470-0606); Rebos Travel, 58 Green St., Milford, CT 06460 (203/373-3360); Idaho Afloat, P.O. Box 542, Grangeville, ID 83530 (208/983-2414).

enjoyment in the most mundane activities—in taking a course, having coffee with a friend, spending time with your family, going to work, watching newcomers to AA turn the corner, earning your first-year chip. Just watching the flowers grow or the snow fall—things that passed you by when you were drinking or using—can now give you a high.

Sobriety may be an essential lifesaving medicine, but it clearly doesn't have to be a bitter one. There is life after sobriety.

"Since becoming sober, my social life has ceased to exist. In our town, all the gay socializing is in bars—and I know I can't set foot in one without getting myself into trouble."

This is a serious issue for many gay men and women, and one that can't be easily solved. Going to a bar is not just dangerous immediately (you could order a club soda with a twist and hope for the best) but long-term, too. The people you meet at a bar are probably going to be drinkers, and going home with a drinker or starting up a relationship with one could lead you right back to drinking yourself.

So if you belong to a gay AA group, discuss this issue with your fellow members. They probably are all concerned about it. One solution is to establish a social group with friends from AA—in a restaurant or club room somewhere. It could have music, dancing, everything that a gay bar usually has except the booze.

"I used to trust that alcohol and drugs were my friends when I was in trouble. Now I need to trust a better friend—AA."

Of course, going to a bar can lead to more than drinking—it can often quickly lead to sex. And during the first year of recovery new emotional relationships are not recommended. At a time when your life is in shambles, you may be tempted to use the sexual element of it to control others and to escape from your own feelings. This isn't very healthy. It can interfere with recovery and be damaging to partners.

THE BUDDY SYSTEM

Just as swimmers shouldn't swim in deep water without a buddy, it's best for alcoholics/addicts in early recovery not to circulate alone. Whether it's an AA meeting, a sister's wedding, a grandmother's birthday party, or just a walk that will take you past your old happy hunting grounds (bar, liquor store, drug corner), you should try to avoid doing it solo.

A supportive spouse can be a buddy. So can an AA sponsor or AA friend. Try to find people at AA who have similar lifestyles or interests, whose families are compatible with yours, so that you can do social things together. Spending a lot of your time with other recoverees means less time for you to spend off on possibly dangerous tangents by yourself and provides the chance to build strong friendships. (Of course, as recovery progresses, you should add friends with different interests and backgrounds, to expand your horizons.)

Ideally it's best to refrain from all sexual encounters, but becoming involved sexually with anyone raises the very serious issue of the transmission of HIV. *Be sure to take the precautions recommended on page 309 to avoid such transmission.*

BEING ALONE AND LONELY

"I'm fine when I'm at an AA meeting or having coffee with my friends. I'm even okay at work. It's just when I go home and have to be with myself that I feel like I want to climb the walls—or get high."

Many people never learn to enjoy their own company. From the time they're babies, someone's been there to entertain them. When they find themselves alone as adults, they are jumpy and anxious—especially if they haven't learned to like themselves. Alcoholics/addicts use chemicals in the attempt to transform themselves into more acceptable company. Once the chemicals are removed, they're back to feeling uncomfortably lonesome. (Or in desperation, they become couch potatoes and make Oprah, Donahue, Sally Jesse, and the cast of *General Hospital* their constant companions.)

But why feel alone? Turn yourself into good company.

❖ Get loose. Learn relaxation techniques, such as the ones described on page 320, to make it easier to enjoy your solitude. Prayer and meditation have a similar effect, and they help you get in touch with yourself, which is necessary if you are to become a good companion.

❖ Get busy. Take up a serenely solo hobby, such as collecting stamps, knitting, woodworking—anything that will occupy you when you are alone. The time you spend alone passes more quickly and pleasantly, and a constructive hobby gives you a sense of achievement that makes you feel better about yourself.

❖ Get physical. Set up a regular exercise program—in the house (using videotapes or in-home exercise equipment), at the gym, or in the park. Not only will physical activity keep you happily occupied, it will pump endorphins in your brain and lift your mood.

❖ Get educated. Reading the Big Book and other AA materials, and listening to or watching tapes on recovery, will increase your self-awareness. At first this may make you a little less comfortable with yourself, but in the long run, as you realize how much you've got going for you, it will become a recovery plus.

❖ Get serious. Take an inventory or work on your journal (see page 108); this is solitary but important work.

❖ Get connected. Before the loneliness gets to be too much, simply pick up the phone and call your sponsor or another AA friend. As they say in the ads, "reach out and touch someone."

❖ Get out. Limit your time alone to what is absolutely necessary until more progress in recovery kicks in.

11 YOUR LOVE LIFE IN RECOVERY

You've probably been hearing a lot about how normal it is for your sex life to be a total mess in early recovery. Alas, it's true. But it's not true that you have no choice but to grimace and bear it. This chapter aims at helping you (and your partner) understand why you feel as though you're failing Sex 101. It explains which sexual problems are inescapable, at least early on, and how to live with them. More important, it offers practical advice on which problems can be overcome, and how.

SEXUAL INTIMACY IN RECOVERY

An AA joke tells of the wife explaining why she's still a virgin after ten years of marriage to an alcoholic: "All he ever did was sit on the bed and tell me how good it was going to be." But the problems that recoverees—both men and women—have with sex are no joke. Though many believe that by becoming clean and sober they will remove all the barriers to a satisfying sex life, they quickly discover that this is just wishful thinking. Just about every sexual dysfunction Freud and Kinsey ever wrote about—impotence, premature ejaculation, no ejaculation, painful intercourse, frigidity—is common (though not necessarily universal) during the early weeks and months of recovery.

Guide Lines

❖ Your love life in recovery will probably get worse before it gets better. But it *will* get better.

❖ Sexual intercourse and true intimacy are not the same thing. Don't confuse them.

❖ You can enjoy intimacy even if intercourse is a fiasco.

❖ If you aren't in an ongoing relationship, celibacy may be your best bet for the time being.

WHY PHASE ONE RECOVERY IS A ROCKY TIME FOR ROMANCE

There are many reasons why lovemaking is almost always unsatisfactory in early recovery. Some are related to the recoveree, some to his or her partner.

The Recoveree

Any number of factors contribute to making men and women in early recovery less than ideal partners in lovemaking:

Hormone havoc. Some 400 years ago, Shakespeare noted in *Macbeth* that alcohol, "provokes, and unprovokes; it provokes the desire, but it takes away the performance; . . . it sets him on, and it takes him off; it persuades him, and disheartens him; makes him stand to, and not stand to." As usual, the bard was right. In chronic alcoholics, alcohol reduces levels of testosterone (the hormone involved in sexual desire) while at the same time liver damage increases levels of estrogen (the feminizing hormone). As a result, men who drink heavily lose interest in sex. It's also why they sometimes develop female characteristics, such as breast enlargement and loss of body hair. Marijuana, because of its similarity to estrogen, can also wreak havoc causing feminization—breast development (gynecomastia), loss of body hair, voice changes—in males who use it heavily.

In early recovery these symptoms tend to persist because the reproductive hormones have not yet returned to normal. But as hormone levels begin to come back into balance (which usually takes somewhere between a few weeks and several months time), these changes cease and sexual desire returns.

Women don't escape unscathed. As their testosterone levels slide, so does their interest in sex. For both male and female abusers, it's almost as though the chosen chemical becomes the lover. Unfortunately, what starts out as a short-term physical problem for recovering people may end up as a long-term psychological one, when they begin to fear there is something permanently wrong with their sexuality. Awareness that patience is the best cure—while the body heals itself—should make costly sex therapy unnecessary.

A battered nervous system. Alcohol damages the nervous system, including the nerves leading to and from the penis and the clitoris. With these nerves impaired, males may have trouble getting or holding an erection and females may have difficulty achieving orgasm. In better than 95 percent of cases, the nerve endings regenerate during the first six months to a year of sobriety, and erection and orgasm again become possible.*

Medication. Certain medications, such as some of those used for treating hypertension, can interfere with sexual performance.

Low self-esteem. Recoverees temporarily lack confidence and feel insecure and less in control of their lives, all of which can add up to impotence, frigidity, or generally unsatisfactory sex.

Lack of practice. A good many alcoholics/addicts have had no sexual intercourse for long periods before becoming sober. Hard-core junkies, particularly, may have lost all interest in sex while their ecstasy came in capsules or packets. Many alcoholics simply couldn't perform and so abstained. Or their spouses found them repugnant and refused them when they were high or "stinking" drunk.

The removal of the chemical security blanket. During active addiction, many recoverees became accustomed to having sex in a chemically induced haze. Some have never had sex any other way. Now they have to learn, or relearn, how to make love sober.

Unpleasant memories. Sex under the influence was frequently unsatisfactory, unsavory, abusive, dull, even disastrous. It often takes a while for the act of lovemaking to be rehabilitated in the mind of the person in recovery.

Fear of failure. Recoverees who had trouble with sex for years may fear that sober, the problems will continue. This can become a self-fulfilling prophecy.

Guilt. Remorse over how they treated their partner before they became sober, or about one or more acts of infidelity, makes it difficult to perform sexually. The poor performance doubles the guilt, further worsening performance, and the downward spiral continues.

Sex-drug associations. In some addicts, coke and sex become entangled. They use cocaine to get sex, and sex to get cocaine. Just thinking about sex during recovery ignites fantasies in their minds. Since they are trying to avoid the drug, they also, usually subconsciously, try to avoid sex.

Self-centeredness. Some recoverees are still not ready for the kind of unselfish giving of oneself required to achieve genuine sexual intimacy. It's often difficult in early recovery for alcoholics/addicts to recognize, understand, and be sympathetic toward the feelings and desires of their partners.

Stunted sexual development. If they started using or drinking in their teens, the sexual development of alcoholics/addicts (like other facets of their personality) may be stalled in adolescence. They will have to put some effort into maturing before they can achieve satisfactory sexual relationships.

A madonna complex. A male may view his long-suffering wife as saintly—unapproachable, at least by someone as "unworthy" as he. Unable to satisfy sexual desires with his spouse, such a man may search for sexual fulfillment elsewhere, compounding his marital difficulties.

Menstrual irregularities. In females, irregular periods (they can be shorter one month, longer the next) during early recovery can confuse those trying to use the rhythm method, and make even those who don't uneasy: "Why am I late? Could I be pregnant?" This brings unwanted anxiety to the marital bed.

Painful intercourse. A woman for whom pain during intercourse (because of vaginal dryness, spasm, or endometriosis, for example) had previously been numbed by alcohol or drugs may suddenly become painfully

*The cases where impotence may become permanent are almost always among elderly males who have been drinking heavily for decades, and who might have a potency problem related to age anyway.

aware of the discomfort when she becomes clean and sober.

Change-of-life changes. In postmenopausal women, there may be unresolved problems that arose while menopause was masked by substance abuse. Sexual difficulties can be particularly severe if there was little or no intercourse around the time of menopause.

Change-of-age changes. If they are older and have been married and chemically dependent for many years, the last satisfactory sex a couple had may have been when they were barely out of their teens. If they are in their forties or fifties now, sex will not be the same, even when it's good. It almost certainly will be less frequent (it takes a man longer to recover between ejaculations as he ages), the male partner's erection may be softer (but it will probably last longer), and the female's vagina, if she is postmenopausal, may be uncomfortably dry (lubrication will help).

Fear of passing on an STD. Many recoverees are concerned that they might have contracted a sexually transmitted disease, particularly AIDS (see page 306), during under-the-influence sex, and worry about passing it on. Most of these infections can be easily detected and treated. With new tests and treatment evolving rapidly, the prognosis even for HIV is no longer as hopeless as it once was. So it makes sense to seek medical attention quickly, rather than let the specter of a perhaps nonexistent disease ruin your pleasure.

Sexual inhibitions. Even in an age of sex-saturated media, many people still don't know that sex is a problem they can talk about. Even if they do, they may be ashamed to admit failure between the sheets, or feel they don't have the right forum in which to bring up the subject. Doctors and counselors may be uneasy about the subject themselves and fail to give patients an opening. Because many of these problems are embarrassingly unsuitable for discussion in a mixed group, they often aren't raised at AA meetings. The result: many recoverees suffer in silence.

The Spouse or Lover

Often the problems lie partly or entirely with the nonaddicted partner. Returning to a sexual relationship with a newly sober spouse or lover may be difficult for many reasons:

Unsavory memories. Making love with somebody who reeks of alcohol, is high on drugs, is sloppy and unkempt, or is abusive and uncaring rarely leaves moonlight-and-roses recollections. The memories such experi-

TESTING FOR IMPOTENCE

The person who has a nocturnal erection isn't likely to be truly impotent. So for the recovering male who hasn't yet been able to perform adequately, waking up with an erection can be reassuring. If that never seems to happen to you and you're beginning to worry that your sexual prowess is gone for good, try this test.

Take a strip of penny postage stamps (long enough to fit around your nonerect penis with one stamp overlapping) and wrap it around your member. Moisten one end stamp and glue it to the other end stamp. If the stamps pop open during the night, your worries are over. You had an erection.

If they don't, you may want to consider seeing a doctor.

ences do leave aren't likely to stimulate desire.

A mountain of resentment. While the alcoholic was anesthetized by alcohol, the spouse suffered, fully aware, through everything that happened in their troubled marriage. Unless and until it's bulldozed away, resentment about that suffering can be a rocky obstacle to a fulfilling sexual relationship.

"I'd become almost dysfunctional sexually in the last year and a half. When I got clean and sober, I began wondering, 'Hey, am I ever gonna get back to the level I was on before cocaine?' Trying to find out, I wanted to chase every woman I met."

Lack of trust. Sex without trust is not a truly satisfying experience, and a good many spouses are not yet ready to trust their recovering partners.

Lack of forgiveness. There may be bitterness over one or more affairs during the period of alcohol/drug abuse. The husband of a recovering alcoholic/addict, especially, may find it difficult not to brood about her past behavior. Even when the partner has consciously forgiven, the body, controlled by the subconscious, still registers anger.

Fear of disease. If the partner is known or suspected to have been unfaithful, this is a major concern (see page 310).

Fear of inadequacy. Many spouses of alcoholics or addicts who have had affairs freeze up because they worry that they won't be able to perform up to the level of that sexy "other woman" or "other man."

Misunderstanding and confusion. Lack of sex drive and interest on the part of their newly sober partner often is misinterpreted as a sign of rejection, rather than as a piece of the normal pattern of recovery behavior.

IMPROVING LOVEMAKING IN RECOVERY

You could just ignore any sexual problems you're experiencing in recovery in the hope that they will go away. But taking this tack could increase anxiety, damage an otherwise good marriage or other loving relationship, and even lead right back to drinking or drugging. If you don't want that to happen, you need to take some concrete steps to improve your sex life.

Sexual intercourse is the culmination of an intimate relationship. As the personal relationship wilts during active addiction, its sexual component withers in turn. Depending on the problems you've been experiencing, you may find some or all of the following tips helpful in gradually coaxing your relationship back into full flower. Remember, as with other aspects of your life, you can't expect to approach anything like normalcy until the end of the first year.

Lower your sights for now. Don't expect great, or even good, sex right away. Although it's within the realm of possibility, the odds are against it. It's even possible you may not be able to have sex at all. Most people—not just you, lots of people—are unsuccessful at least six weeks into recovery, many for much longer. With so many other important things on your mind and so many challenges to meet in your early months of recovery, for heaven's sake don't feel obligated to make love or to

EXTENDING ERECTION

If premature ejaculation doesn't clear up after numerous unsuccessful attempts at intercourse, you may want to try the Semen Squeeze. Just before ejaculation, squeeze the penis firmly. Then remain fairly still and get your mind off sex for a minute or so (try doing difficult addition or multiplication problems in your head, or speculate on who the next presidential candidates will be). Usually this will prolong the erection and postpone ejaculation. This method of drawing out the act of love isn't ideal, but it's a tried-and-true interim solution until your coupling is satisfactorily back on track.

set performance standards. The *Guinness Book of World Records* can wait. And don't judge the rest of your relationship by the quality or quantity of sexual intercourse. As it is on a honeymoon, patience on both sides will mean more than setting "personal bests."

Set your sights realistically for the long run. The average couple has average sex. A few couples have the fantastic sex idealized and glorified by Madison Avenue and Hollywood. A few find they are totally disinterested in sex. All these variations are normal and none prevents a couple from having a strong, loving relationship. March to your own drummer. What's right for you is what you are comfortable with and not disappointed by.

Concentrate on communicating. Not with vitriolic or aiming-the-blame messages, but with the nonthreatening kind where each permits the other the freedom to express feelings without fear of being attacked for stating them. Share your feelings about lovemaking —when, where, how, and how often— openly and honestly. Talk about pain, fears, what feels good and what doesn't. While feelings are ideal grist for your communications mill, opinions or arguments on who's right and who's wrong should not be.

Remember that there are no norms where sex is concerned; how often the average couple makes love has nothing to do with you. If you and your partner seem to have different sexual appetites, learn to compromise, just as you do about anything else in a good marriage. (But keep any discussions about sex or anything else that threatens to be uncomfortable out of the bedroom.)

Do a little self-examination. Are you really interested in your partner's sexual pleasure, or only in your own? Sex is a way of sharing with the one you love, so share the pleasure. Self-centered sex is not only likely to be unsuccessful, it could be a warning that you aren't working hard enough at your recovery.

Get romantic. Focus on the nonsexual part of your relationship. Work on rebuilding trust and showing you care through deeds, not words (see page 184). Put the emphasis on love, intimacy, and romance rather than on the physical sex act. Renew your courtship—get to know each other all over again. After all, you are not the same two people you were during active addiction. Hold hands, touch, kiss, hug, cuddle, enjoy massage, pleasure each other. The rest can follow when you both feel the time is right.

Understand your partner. Recognize that he or she may need as much help as you do during this recovery period. While you have probably gone for in-

or outpatient therapy, and/or have attended many AA meetings, your spouse is probably still bewildered about what is going on. He or she may feel and act as though you're still an active addict and be torn between feelings of wanting to go and wanting to stay. Al-Anon, reinforced by individual counseling if necessary, can help your partner deal with these feelings.

Help your partner. When it's the wife who's disinterested in sex, it's often because she finds her energy for lovemaking sapped by trying to live the "superwoman" lifestyle: job, kids, housework, homework, cooking, laundry, and so on—often not because she wants to, but because she has to. Every study that's been done shows that most men are not sharing the work load, and addiction magnifies this unfairness. If you hold up your end of it, or even go beyond the call of duty, then you may find she has a lot more energy when bedtime rolls around.

Evaluate failure. If a particular lovemaking episode dies aborning, do a little postmortem to figure out what went wrong. Discussing the problem openly and honestly (but again, not in bed) is often half the journey to a solution. If you identify a clear-cut problem (he loses his erection when he sees her in curlers, she gets turned off when the football game is blaring on the bedroom TV), remedy it before the next try. If the problem is that one or both of you developed poor lovemaking habits during active addiction ("Wham, bam, thank you ma'am," for example), make an effort to slow down and improve your technique. Of course, in many cases the problem may be deep-seated: a hurt that will simply take a long time to heal.

Accept abstinence. If neither of you feels like making love for weeks, or even months, on end and your relationship is otherwise improving, don't worry about it. That's normal for some couples, especially in early recovery. And contrary to the school-yard rumors you may have heard as a youngster, there are no ill effects—either physical or emotional—related to sexual abstinence.

Get ready, get set. When you do feel ready to make love, set the scene carefully. Be sure you are both relaxed (try relaxation exercises or meditation if it helps; see page 320). Eliminate distractions such as the TV or telephone (take it off the hook or turn on the answering machine). If your bedroom is a warehouse for so many bad memories that one or both of you feels inhibited there, try another part of the house, a vacationing friend's apartment, or if you can afford it, a night at a hotel. If there is music you both find romantic, play it. If particular clothing—or no clothing at all—is an igniter, then dress or undress accordingly. Indulge in fantasy, watch a stimulating movie, or read an erotic book together, if any of these activities helps arouse your libido. If intercourse is painful for the female partner because of a dry vagina, apply a lubricant (in gel, cream, or suppository form) before getting started. Postmenopause or during lactation, an estrogen cream may be recommended by your physician.

Have fun up front. Don't forget the foreplay. Kissing, caressing, touching each other's erogenous zones (explore and experiment patiently to find out where they are), will help both of you become physically and emotionally ready for intercourse. Sometimes foreplay alone is enough to send you to sleep with a smile on your lips. The other good stuff can come at a later date.

Concentrate on giving. The odds of successful sex increase when each partner focuses on giving pleasure, rather than just receiving it.

Play safe. Worry erodes sexual enjoyment, so try to banish it from your bed. If there is any concern about the possibility of a sexually transmitted disease, use condoms until all doubts are erased. (See page 309 on how to proceed with the erasure.) Unless one of you is sterile, use some form of contraception until you are ready for a baby, which should probably not be for a while. Many surprise pregnancies occur during recovery, particularly when the woman was unable to conceive previously because of alcohol or drug use and fertility returns suddenly and unexpectedly. Expect it.

Take care of yourself. Work on your recovery. A good recovery, by increasing feelings of confidence, security, and control over your life, will improve your prospects for good sex. Pay attention to your health, too. Sticking to a nutritious diet, getting adequate exercise, setting aside time to relax and meditate, and giving up smoking can boost energy levels and thereby improve sexual performance.

If all else fails. Sometimes couples need outside help to achieve a satisfying sexual relationship or to reconcile differences in what they are looking for. A minor sexual problem in an otherwise satisfactory relationship may not require professional help until a year or more has gone by. In most cases, time will resolve it. A more serious one, such as impotence, may require such help if it hasn't disappeared six months into recovery.

Get help even earlier if the problem is seriously jeopardizing your relationship, if either of you is considering going outside the marriage to meet sexual needs, if feeling like a failure at sex is leaving either one of you feeling like a failure generally, or if there is destructive or violent behavior associated with sex.

Before you seek help from a sex therapist or clinic, have your physician rule out a physical cause of your difficulties. Both illness and medication can cause such problems as impotence in males and frigidity in women. Treating the illness or changing the medication can often result in rapid improvement in bed.

If there seems to be no physical cause, then look for a sensitive therapist familiar with the problems of both sexual dysfunction and addiction, rather than a self-help group. If there is any kind of group therapy associated with the treatment, it should take place among those of the same sex to encourage open and honest discussion. Avoid a therapist who uses drugs as part of the treatment or who is too quick to jump to a diagnosis of "depression." Choose one who is willing to work with the problems that affect your relationship and who sees your sexual problems as secondary to the addiction problems.

Look forward to the future. Remember that with time—and given patience, love, and care—sexual relations frequently become more satisfying with sobriety than they ever were before.

OUT-OF-SYNC SEX DRIVES

You're eager for sex and your spouse isn't interested. Or your spouse is longing for love and you'd just as soon read the telephone directory. She wants to make love every day, and for you once a week is pushing it. Or you're aroused all the time, and she'd rather do laundry.

The marriage in which both partners always want sex with the same intensity at the same time is rare. Such differences are normal and natural; human beings exhibit different levels of sexual desire at different times. In recovery, additional factors can throw a couple even further out of sync. In some cases, the recovering partner is still feeling residual effects of the chemicals he or she abused and the

FLASHBACK INTERRUPTUS

It's conceivable for a flashback (see page 576) to occur during intercourse, and a flashback can turn a passionate Romeo or Juliet into a polar iceberg in a flash. Rather than trying to fight the feeling or deny it, apologize to your partner as lovingly as possible. Explain that you're experiencing some old feelings that make lovemaking impossible for you right now. Your partner should, in turn, be understanding and say, "I'm sorry, too." Comfort yourselves with the thought that better times lie ahead. Then exchange a kiss and abort the mission.

other partner is much more interested in sex. In other cases, it's the reverse: The abuser's hormones have recovered from alcohol's assault during drinking but the spouse isn't quite ready to trust, forgive the past, love and let love. Following some of the suggestions in this chapter may help. So will switching tactics. If you're the one who is more interested in lovemaking, instead of sex on demand try a little wooing. Let your partner know from the first kiss in the morning to the last hug at night, by what you say and do, that you care. Flowers, love notes, phone calls—you know what your loved one likes best. (If you don't, it's not too late to inquire.)

If it turns out that your natural inclinations are out of sync, don't despair. No two partners think exactly alike. But people who make a success of their partnerships know just what to do: give a little here, take a little there. If you both work on the relationship, things will get better. Compromise doesn't make all of the people happy all of the time, but it sure beats feeling unhappy most of the time.

SEX AND SOLO SINGLES

If you are a recovering single person not in a stable relationship, you'll need to approach sex the way an air force jet does mid-air refueling. Very carefully. You'll not only have to face the sexual adjustment problems of married or living-together recoverees, you'll also have to deal with the complexities of "The Chase." In addition, love and libido (the polite word for sex drive) stimulate cravings that are similar in many ways to chemical addiction. Allowed to run rampant, they can lead to self-destructive behavior. The emotional overlap of these cravings could jeopardize your sobriety. For these reasons, it's usually recommended—just as it's recommended that you avoid trying to establish new romantic entanglements—that those not already in a monogamous relationship abstain from sex entirely in early recovery. For establishing a new relationship when you're ready, see page 385. For now:

❖ Keep out of "chase" situations. In fact, run the other way. Hunting and being hunted may be fun, but it's sometimes stressful and always time-consuming. Allow it to take over your life, or even just your free time, and it could drive sobriety down on your priority list. Keep first things (Twelve-Step meetings) first. Get involved with recovery, not with every Tom, Dick, or Harriet.

❖ Strive to be totally up front in all your relationships. There's no policy better than honesty in forming new (or rebuilding old) ones. Create no illusions. Most people in early recovery don't know reality from let's-pretend,

WARNING NOTES

What you don't know about sex can hurt you. Don't forget that:

❖ Both very good and very poor sexual relationships can lead you to using—the good sex because you associate the satisfying feelings with a drug high, the poor sex because you want to get rid of the bad feeling that follows it. If you feel the urge to drink or use following intercourse, speak to your sponsor, take a cold shower, or follow the suggestions on page 162.

❖ If you are going to have a relationship, sexual or otherwise, it should not be with someone who is using—even if you suffer from the delusion that you may be the only one who can help this person get sober. That's like accepting an invitation for a cruise on the *Titanic*.

❖ When you're with a date who is drinking, you may have difficulty differentiating between being thirsty and being horny. Make sure you know the difference. Though neither is a good idea right now, taking a drink is definitely more hazardous.

❖ Guilt-creating behaviors (such as cheating on a partner) can lead to relapse. Avoid such situations; stay honest.

❖ Even if you frequently had unprotected sex without conceiving while drinking or drugging, as fertility returns you can now become pregnant (or make someone else pregnant) inadvertently. Use contraceptives.

but as soon as you know who you are, *be* who you are. When you meet someone who interests you, don't postpone acknowledging your addiction and your recovery-in-progress. Get things straight from the start by emphasizing your top priority: your need to live the AA way of life now and for the foreseeable future. That way, there won't be any misunderstanding as things develop. If "the prospect" cheerfully accepts playing second fiddle to your recovery, you're off to a good start.

❖ Remember that your emotional development, and that includes your sexuality, stopped at about the time you began to drink or use. To have a strong, mature relationship with another person, you are going to have to do a lot of maturing during your first year of recovery. Wait at least until that year is over before acting on impulses that could lead to intimacy or sex. That may sound harsh, but you're not being asked to take a permanent vow of celibacy, and you'll discover that delayed gratification—whether with a high-risk relationship or a high-calorie dessert—is the most satisfying kind.

❖ Use condoms if you do have sex. Now is not the time to add more worries (about sexually transmitted disease or pregnancy) to your list.

❖ Be aware that if you have been sexually active and are not now, it is normal to have sexual dreams, and if you are a male, to have "wet dreams." This doesn't mean you are sex-starved and need to get into bed with the first person you meet, any more than it did when you had your first nocturnal emission at age thirteen or fourteen.

❖ Don't feel guilty if you find you need to substitute masturbation for sexual intercourse for a while. Contrary to any locker-room tales you may have heard, the practice isn't harmful—unless, of course, it becomes an obsession itself.

12

WORK AND MONEY ISSUES IN PHASE ONE

When you get clean and sober, you may look at your work through totally different eyes. You may find you like your job better than you thought you did—or less. Or that you covered up your "problem" less effectively than you thought you had. You may discover that your employer doesn't want you to return because you've worn out your welcome. Or you may recognize that a boss whose ultimatums forced you to go into treatment was really a good guy after all. Though work isn't the most important thing in life in early recovery, few people can afford to neglect it entirely. For some it provides important structure and support.

This chapter will help you learn how to juggle work and recovery in Phase One without dropping either ball. It will also help you to start getting your financial house in order.

WHAT'S ON YOUR MIND?

BOTCHING IT AT WORK

"I've been through treatment, and now I'm ready to go back to work. Things were very sticky before I left. I was pushed into treatment... or else. If I mess up now, I'm history."

You're lucky to have an employer who cared enough about you, as a person and as an employee, to push you into treatment—and on top of that, to welcome you back. Now it's your turn to show those you work for (and with) that they're lucky too, to have someone as reliable and productive as you on the payroll. That won't

Guide Lines

❖ Concentrating on recovery now will make you better at your work later.

❖ Given the choice, Phase One is not the time to make any drastic changes in jobs or careers.

❖ Honesty will be your most important weapon in the battle to straighten out your financial affairs.

be easy. A lot will depend on your keeping your priorities straight and on anticipating (and avoiding) possible pitfalls. If you're uneasy about getting back into harness, you may want to request an "exit interview" with your counselor or physician to discuss your concerns. If feasible, invite your employer or supervisor to sit in.

Once you're back on the job, your responsibilities will be clear:

❖ Prove you're serious about sobriety by staying sober. At this point, working hard at recovery will be even more important than working hard at your job. But give both the best that's in you.

❖ Be sensitive to your coworkers. In all likelihood they've been covering up and compensating for your poor work habits for months, even years. Steamrolling in, in an effort to make up for all those lost days and weekends, is admirable—but not if you crush a lot of people's toes in the process. Think how *you* would like a returning recovering coworker to behave. Then, go thou and do likewise.

If one or two colleagues—a partner, secretary, assistant—have been, in effect, "enablers," doing your work and making excuses for you, and thus enabling you to continue with your drinking, they may now be a little put out to find that this part of their job description has been wiped out. They may not even realize why themselves, but it's often because they resent the loss of either the boost to their self-esteem gained by helping you out or of the kicks they got from knowing you couldn't make it without them. Such feelings are normal initially, but if they can't shake them, reading about enabling on page 501 or even attending a couple of Al-Anon meetings might be helpful.

❖ Apply what you are learning about human relations in your recovery program to your job. Above all, be honest in all your dealings at work. Though you may fear that this will only earn you a swim in hot water, that's unlikely to happen. Your frankness in your reaction to a proposal or your honesty about being unable to complete a job on schedule will surprise people (they aren't used to your admitting you chopped down the cherry tree), but most of the time your telling the truth and nothing but the truth will please them and set all of you free.

❖ Don't try to run the show. Most alcoholics/addicts in recovery still have a need for control, which originated in their inability to control their addiction and which they sublimate by trying to overcontrol every other aspect of their lives. In most cases, your coworkers won't be any more willing to put you in charge than your family is.

❖ Toe the mark. Chances are you have a work history that includes frequent absences, late arrivals, missed deadlines, forgotten appointments. Most employees can get away with dropping the ball once in a while, but you probably won't have that luxury. Just oversleep and come in late once, and everyone will be sure you were out on a binge the night before. Don't fret unduly about that. Maybe everybody *is* watching you. But you earned their distrust. Now quietly go about earning their trust.

❖ Consider entering into a formal Continuing-Care Plan agreement with your employer (see page 236). If there is an Employee Assistance Program (EAP), turning to its staff for advice could be helpful.

Your Twelve-Step or other mutual-help group is the keel helping to restore stability to your life. Your job can be the rudder that helps to restore direction. Don't neglect it.

WHAT TO TELL COWORKERS

"I've been away from my office for nearly six months. I'm very nervous about going back, especially because I haven't seen any of the people I work with for the entire time, and I don't know what they've heard or been told, or at this point how much I should tell them."

Ideally, it's best to take one or two respected coworkers into your confidence before you leave for treatment or begin going to AA. With them you can discuss how and when others at work will be told what is happening in your life. They will feel like partners in your decision, and can support you while you're away by fielding wild rumors before they start to fly.

If that wasn't possible, or just didn't happen, the first thing you need to do is to set the record straight. It's very likely, as you fear, that rumors have circulated in your absence. You can discuss what might be the best step to take with a qualified counselor in your company's Employee Assistance Program, if one exists. If not, arrange to have lunch with a coworker whom you like and whom others respect. Explain exactly what has been going on—treatment, AA, and so on—and how long you've been sober. Make it clear that you'll be staying sober from now on, one day at a time. Point out that you'll work hard to prove you're for real, but that, much as you'd like to, for a while you won't be able to focus on your work with laser-beam intensity. Explain that you sure won't malinger, but your most important job will be the work of solidifying your recovery—as it would be, you might add, if you were recovering from a coronary. Admit honestly that you realize you've let them down in the past, if this is the case, and explain that their support and patience now can make a big difference. You're determined to prove (to yourself as well as to them) that it was alcohol (or drugs, or both) lying down on the job, and not you.

Ask this friend to get the word around to others at the office, so that you won't have to explain one-on-one to everyone. Of course, if someone asks, feel free to talk about your recovery. You'll find that sometimes those who ask the most questions have unresolved drinking or drug problems of their own. But that's okay. Your success (and here's another reason for you to work your program faithfully) could guide them to the help they need. And that will feel pretty good.

"I've heard conflicting advice on whether or not to tell the folks you work with that you've been out because of an addiction problem."

As with so many other issues, there is more than one point of view. Some counselors suggest that you keep your own counsel, telling only your supervisor and those you work with intimately. That may work for some people, but there are several problems with such an approach:

"The first time I applied for a medical internship I opted for honesty and noted on my application that I had been through treatment for alcoholism and was in recovery. I was turned down flat, without a chance for an interview. I still felt that telling the truth was important, but I decided to tell rather than write it. On the next application I made no mention of this disease, got an interview, made a good impression, and then told them. This time I got accepted."

❖ White-lying about where you've been (or about anything else) could be detrimental to your recovery. Never forget that honesty in all things is the concrete on which a healthy sobriety is built.

❖ Keeping people in the dark about what's been going on—offering such ambiguous explanations as "Oh, I've had a problem, but things are better now"—will lead people to imagine scenarios considerably messier than the truth.

❖ Avoiding the truth is a way of leaving a dangerous escape hatch for the future (see page 165). It also leaves you much more open to temptation. If your coworkers aren't aware of your problem, they won't hesitate to push a drink on you at the holiday party or to try to cajole you into joining them at the local pub after hours.

❖ Lying has a way of catching up with people. What if you say you were out with a bad back or some vague complaint, and then later on the truth comes out? How do you look to others then?

This doesn't mean that you have to announce your condition over the company's PA system, or that you should "confess" to every client or business associate. But should the question "Where've you been?" come up, an honest answer is better than a dishonest or evasive one.

OVERDOING IT

"I've been back at work now for three months. Things are really going well. I've been working night and day to prove that I'm not the drunk that I used to be, that I can do as good a job as anyone. But my sponsor says that I'm doing too much, that I should slow down. I don't see why."

You've almost answered your own question. If you weren't so busy at work, you'd quickly recognize the wisdom of what your sponsor is saying. You would have time to look at your life and realize that spending so much of your day buried in your job has to take time away from your recovery work. It is also—as you transform yourself from alcoholic to workaholic—building up more stress than you may be able to handle at this stage.

So let a more experienced head prevail. Do slow down for a while longer. Let yourself at least reach Phase Two recovery before picking up the pace.

If you're having trouble deciding where to cut back, start keeping a record of your daily activities; it can be part of your recovery journal, if you're keeping one. (If you haven't kept one, now could be the time to start. See page 108). Look at the schedule at the end of each day and decide which things could have been eliminated.

Then ax those items the following week. At the same time, be sure there's adequate time penciled in for AA meetings and talks with your sponsor, as well as time with your loved ones.

HARASSMENT

"A friend of mine went into treatment about when I did. He did it voluntarily, and it seems nobody at work bothers him. My supervisor reported me to the company EAP and I was railroaded into treatment. Now they never take their eyes off me. Doesn't seem right."

It's not. Paradoxically, the guy who did it on his own is much more likely to relapse than you are. If someone had taken more notice of his substance abuse (and his slipping job performance) and reported it, he would have had a better chance of a successful recovery. It's possible, of course, that he will make it. It's also possible, because of your negative attitude (remember, that "railroad" can take you out of slavery into freedom), that you won't. That won't be because of unequal treatment at work, but because of how each of you responds to your recovery responsibilities.

In general, alcoholics/addicts whose jobs are on the line if they fail to remain sober enjoy a much better rate of recovery than those who volunteer for treatment. That's because they're painfully aware of what they will lose if they fail, and also because they are more closely supervised by the EAP. The self-referrer may dictate his own treatment terms, fail to follow recommendations, and end up relapsing.

That's not to say that alcoholics/addicts should wait until someone else forces them to get sober. But those who initiate action on their own need to keep firing up their own motivation to maintain momentum.

UNFAIR EXPECTATIONS

"I feel as though I'm constantly being tested. If someone else screws up, people just shrug and send them back to the drawing board. If I make the least little error, everyone puts on that knowing look, and the boss calls me in and and puts me on warning. I'm expected to be better than everyone else. It's not fair."

Life isn't fair. It wasn't fair to your coworkers or your boss when you didn't show up and they had to do the work you were paid to do but didn't. It wasn't fair when you let down your friends and wheedled money out of your family.

Whether your present situation is fair or not is a matter of debate, but not one you are likely to win at the moment. Put yourself behind your supervisor's desk: You abused the trust of those you work with. Now you have to earn it back—the hard way. Expect at least several months to go by before your occasional bloopers are taken in stride the way those of "civilian" coworkers are.

Nor should you be surprised and resentful if your employer demands that you take periodic drug testing or sign an employment contract (page 236), even if it's not required of other employees. This protects your employer in case you should break your word and relapse. But it also protects you, giving you another powerful incentive to keep your recovery on line.

"While my sponsor is not as 'tough' as some, her spirituality is so gentle and real that I want what she has."

MINI-GUIDE

Drug Testing

Drug testing is becoming more and more accepted in the sports arena, government agencies, and corporations—particularly in areas where risk to the public is involved, such as utilities, nuclear power, and transportation industries. Testing is supported not just by management and by federal and most state courts, but by unions and employees in general. No one wants to work in a safety-sensitive job alongside someone who is high or drunk.

The most common type of testing is pre-employment, which is meant to weed out abusers from among job applicants. But the purpose of testing among current employees, drug experts believe, should not be to get them dismissed but to get them into treatment (unless of course their drinking or drug use leads to some kind of catastrophe—a train crash, a fire, an explosion—in which case they may be fired on the spot).

In some companies, employees are screened across the board, usually randomly. In others, testing is limited to those whose behavior at work (absenteeism, lethargy, accidents, mood swings, possession of drug paraphernalia) makes their supervisor suspect current drug or alcohol abuse and to those in recovery, who may have to submit to frequent testing. Though testing procedures vary from company to company, many follow a procedure similar to this one:

❖ Testing is done randomly. The computer simply kicks out a name and that employee is tested. The odds of being chosen are the same each day. You could win the lottery today and then hit the jackpot again tomorrow. Employees may also be tested after an accident or when being considered for transfer to a safety-sensitive job. Tests are performed regularly, on a random basis, on those who have previously come up positive.

❖ The person to be tested is notified, usually by a supervisor, about an hour before the test.

❖ At testing time, an on-site nurse provides the employee with a collection container in which to urinate. To be certain the sample is unadulterated, it is produced in a lavatory with no running water except for the blue-tinted water in the toilet. To ensure that it is fresh (testers know all the tricks), the temperature of the sample has to match the body temperature of the testee. If the person has tested positive before, or if there is a suspicion that tampering may be taking place (odd noises are heard coming from the lav, or the testee seems to be taking an inordinately long time), a person of the same sex may be assigned to witness the procedure. At the very least, any irregularities will be noted and passed on with the sample. If the employee seems to be having trouble producing a specimen, he or she will be given water to drink.

❖ The sample is transferred to a bottle, capped, sealed, and carefully labeled as the employee watches. The employee then supplies his or her employee ID card and social security number to the nurse, and verifies the specimen's source by initialing the sealed container.

❖ A legal "chain of custody" is begun as the nurse passes the sample on to a messenger, who signs for it and takes it to the lab, where it is again signed for.

❖ The sample is subjected to a two-tier procedure. First comes an immunoassay screening test. If negative, the sample is discarded. If positive, it is retested via gas chromatography/mass spectrometry (GC/MS), which is regarded as the gold standard for drug tests, scientifically and forensically. This second test weeds out any false positives on the earlier screening test. Samples that remain positive on GC/MS are then pronounced positive and are required by law to be kept frozen for at least one year for possible retest.

❖ The Medical Review Officer (MRO) evaluates all positive test results. If the chain of custody was unbroken and other possible reasons for an inaccurate result (see below) are ruled out, the test results are confirmed.

❖ The employee will be informed of the test results, usually within a week of submitting the sample. If he or she wants to challenge a positive result, a retest can be requested. The retest is done on the frozen portion of the sample, perhaps at another lab. If the retest is positive, the employee foots the bill (about $80) and the company's procedures for dealing with a drug-use incident are set in motion. If the retest is negative, an investigation is opened to determine what went wrong.

❖ Human Resources (still called Personnel in many small companies) will be informed of positive results. They will immediately remove the employee from safety-sensitive work, as required by law. At the discretion of the employer, there may also be a disciplinary suspension (loss of two weeks pay, for example).

❖ In corporations enlightened enough to provide treatment for employees who test positive, the employee will meet with a clinician (such as the EAP or the MRO), who will take a complete medical, psychiatric, and drug/alcohol history, as well as a social and family history, and decide what the appropriate treatment should be. The prescription will include the faithful completion of a year or more of outpatient treatment, preceded when clinically necessary by a stint at an inpatient facility. Faced with summary loss of their job, most employees accept treatment and make it work.

❖ When the employee initially returns to the job after a positive drug test, he or she must work in a non-safety-sensitive position for at least eight weeks. Then, if a urine test proves negative, the employee may return to safety-sensitive work. Follow-up urine tests are likely to be very frequent, and by law may be witnessed. If there is any sign of tampering with a test, or if any subsequent test is positive, the employee is discharged immediately. (Some employers allow more leeway, but many have discovered that if allowed only one chance, addicts will make good in one. Given two, they'll take two; and so on.)

Be aware that occasionally tests can come back positive even if you haven't come within arm's length of an illegal substance in years. Something as innocent as poppy seeds on your bagel (which give a positive test for opiates) can throw the test out of whack. But because the MRO has to confirm a finding of opiates in the urine by physical evidence (such as intoxication, withdrawal symptoms, or needle

(continued on next page)

MINI-GUIDE

(continued from previous page)
tracks), these little seeds should not cause a major problem.

Many medications can give false positives for certain drugs (ibuprofen, indocin, and other nonsteroidal anti-inflammatory drugs, for example, can make a test positive for marijuana) but only on the screening test. A followup GC/MS will turn out appropriately negative (if Advil or indocin is all you've been taking), which points out how important it is that your job doesn't hang on a less sophisticated test.* Using a Vicks inhaler prior to a drug screen can produce a false positive even on a GC/MS, so if you are subject to testing, avoid the inhaler entirely.

Decongestants, diet pills, codeine cough preparations, anesthesia (even a local given for an injury in the emergency room), and a wide range of drugs used to treat emotional ills, too, can produce positive drug screens. But this isn't a *false* positive, since these are mood-altering and you shouldn't be taking them (at least not without a good medical reason; see page 246).

*You could also come out with a positive for marijuana if you simply breathe in someone else's, so be careful about the company you keep. This kind of exposure could not only screw up your drug screen but your recovery as well.

If you are taking a prescription medication that affects your thinking or level of alertness, don't wait until you're randomly tested. Let your supervisor know. Such use could be a safety risk, affecting your judgment or slowing your reflexes, and could require a temporary transfer from a safety-sensitive job. Because such medication could put your recovery at risk as much as your job, be sure that you take it only under controlled conditions (see page 246).

If you should be involved in an incident at work (a fight or an accident, for example), put drug testing in your corner. If there's any chance that because of your history the episode will be colored by suspicion of drug or alcohol use, request a drug screen immediately to establish your sobriety.

Some industries are beginning to test for alcohol as well as other drugs, and more can be expected to do so in the near future. The most accurate testing is done with a breathalyzer (which measures alcohol in exhaled air) or blood samples (which measure the level of alcohol in the blood). Urine tests are more complicated; employees have the right to demand a blood test instead. Saliva dipsticks may be used for screening, but they are not considered wholly reliable and are not accepted as legal proof of alcohol intoxication or the absence thereof.

FEAR OF BEING FIRED

"I've been out on sick leave, getting treatment for my alcoholism. But I didn't tell my boss. It's a high-pressure business, and I'm afraid if I tell him I'll get the sack. Can't I just keep this whole thing a secret?"

A good recovery is based on honesty, so don't start yours with a lie. It's more important to save your life than to save your job. Besides, you aren't likely to get away with it. Unless your boss or supervisors are off in space somewhere, they probably are aware that you had some kind of substance abuse problem. So call and explain the situation. Or make an appointment to talk in person if you're more comfortable doing that. If your employer wants to know more about your treatment, your present condition, and the prognosis for your staying sober, put him in touch with your counselor, doctor, or therapist.

If you *are* fired—even in a tough job market—consider it, if not a blessing, then at least a long-run plus. You'd be unwise to work in an atmosphere in which a recovering person didn't receive some support. If you really follow your recovery program faithfully, not only will you eventually be able to find employment elsewhere, you'll be a better employee than you ever were before. See page 239 for tips on finding another job, if that becomes necessary.

Often an employer terminates a recovering employee because of misinformation on the subject of drug and alcohol abuse. Education can sometimes lead to a reversal of such a dismissal. If you think your employer is educable and you want to keep your job, ask your counselor or physician to call and explain away the mythology that many people erroneously accept, while pointing out—with lots of examples—the heightened potential of employees who are in recovery. If you're a good producer, a wavering employer may be swayed into an about-face when a strict "second chance" Continuing-Care Plan is mutually agreed upon (see page 236). Your employer can get more information about drugs in the workplace by reading pages 580 to 581 of this book and by contacting Business for a Drug-Free America (204 Monroe St., Rockville, MD 20850; 301/294-0600).

Employers need to understand that the big risks—of lost productivity, accident, poor morale, increased medical costs, and so on—come from employees who have not done anything about their drug or alcohol problems, not those who have. The bottom line: your successful recovery helps your company.

And, in fact, if you are in recovery and *remain abstinent,* you cannot legally be fired because of alcoholism/addiction. You are protected under the Americans for Disabilities Act, which went into effect in 1992.

"Scotch is my boss's middle name. I've started going to AA and have been sober for thirty days. Whenever I go into his office for a meeting, he opens the bar and presses me to join him in a nip. I've been managing to make excuses, but I don't know how long I can keep this charade up."

Assuming you agree that your life is more important than your job, end the charade right now and level with your boss. Don't lecture him; he's not likely to take kindly to the sermons of a reformed sinner. But do tell him that you didn't like what alcohol was doing to you and you've stopped drinking. Explain that he would make it easier for you if he didn't offer you a drink when he broke out the scotch. If he's at all rational, he will respect your request. Of course, if he's boozing all day, he's more likely to be irrational—in which case, you may want to start looking elsewhere for a job.

TEMPTATIONS ON THE JOB

"Now that I'm back at work, I'm scared to death of that first business lunch I have to face. These guys I do business with drink like fish—like I used to."

So far so good. You're scared, just as you should be. The next step is to put off such aquarium lunches—or any other situations exposing you to temptation—as long as you can. In the meantime, set up a meeting over barbells at the health club. Or suggest dining at a particularly nice place where booze isn't served. Or order an elegant, but dry, lunch to be served in your office. When the time comes that you have no choice but to face a two-martini lunch or a party, prepare yourself by reading Chapter 9, "Thwarting Temptation." The tips there should help keep you honest.

A JOB YOU DISLIKE

"I just got out of treatment and have been declared ready to go back to work. I haven't ever really been happy at my job, and it seems to me it's time for a change."

Significant changes of any kind—a career change, a relationship change, a location change—can put your recovery at risk. If your employer welcomes you back to the old job, consider yourself lucky. Looking for a new one now would entail a great deal of stress and anxiety, either of which could make staying sober more difficult. And learning the ropes at a new job would almost certainly divert your energy and concentration away from recovery, where it needs to be.

Toward the end of the year, when your recovery is more solid, you can consider a change. By then you may decide you don't want one. Feelings you remember now as job dissatisfaction may really have been job scapegoating. Think about it: You didn't want to be there—you wanted to be out drinking or drugging. Very possibly some of your coworkers didn't want you to be there either, because of frictions your chemical dependency created on the job. You're a very different person now. You may find the job is different, too.

Since you are probably returning to an environment in which you were frequently drunk or high, it will help if you think ahead about ways of responding to jokes, embarrassment, and discomfort (your own as well as that of others). Your sponsor, EAP, or other recovering employees or friends should be able to help you rehearse your back-on-the-job behavior.

If you still want to change later, you'll be in a much better position to get what you want with a year of solid-citizen sobriety under your belt.

Of course, if you return to the job and find that you're still unhappy with it and the resultant stress is putting your recovery in jeopardy, then you will have to consider looking elsewhere. Discuss this possibility with your counselor or sponsor, and be sure you don't put the blame for your misery on sobriety.

WORKING WITHOUT CHEMICAL HELP

"I've always needed something to get me to work in the morning, then something more at noon to get me through the rest of the afternoon. I'm about to go back to work, and I don't know how I'll get through the day."

You're much more qualified to handle the tensions and stress of your job now than you were when you jump-started your motor with chemicals. That doesn't mean, however, that it will be easy. In many ways, you'll be starting all over as an employee. These tips may help:

❖ Don't wear a Superman cape to work. Remember your new recovery philosophy: "Nobody's perfect—not even me." Don't try to make up for lost years at work in a day or a week. And don't take on more than is practical while you're in early recovery. Rebuild your work life slowly, one day at a time. Tackle a single task, complete it, then move on. That will transmit an important message to those you work with and for: that you can be relied on.

Setting your expectations (and everybody else's) too high will make it impossible for you to live up to them. Your approach to work, as to everything else, should be based on moderation.

❖ Try exercising in the morning to give yourself that ready-to-take-on-the-world feeling. Substitute an exercise high for the kind of chemically induced highs you used to depend on.

❖ Fortify yourself with food rather than chemicals. A breakfast with plenty of complex carbohydrates (whole-grain cereals or whole-grain bread) and a small amount of protein (low- or nonfat cottage cheese, milk, or yogurt; smoked fish, beans, or occasionally eggs or breakfast meats) will keep your blood sugar high and avoid that midmorning crash. A good lunch (again with complex carbohydrates and protein, plus vegetables and fruit) will keep you going all afternoon. Be sure to have a beverage in the morning (but one without caffeine, which is dehydrating), another at midmorning, at lunch, and midafternoon—with some additional fluids in between. Add a light snack of fruit, whole-grain crackers, fruit-sweetened whole-grain cookies at coffee-break times if you feel yourself sagging. See page 304 for more tips on eating for recovery.

❖ If yours is a very-high-pressure position, you might want to consider reducing the pressure during early recovery so that you can channel the major part of your energies into getting better. You can do this by cutting back on your work load, hours, or responsibilities (this may entail a cut in pay, but the payoff will be in survival); by moving from the nightshift to day work (this not only reduces stress, but allows a regular pattern of sleep and meals, more time to get assistance from the company EAP if there is one, and more opportunity to participate in evening meetings and counseling sessions); by switching for the time being to a different, less responsible position at your present firm; by taking a temporary leave of absence and earning your bread with simpler work; or by leaving your present job permanently for one that is less demanding. What is stressful for one person may be relaxing for another. For a deskbound white-collar worker, an outdoor job like landscaping may be appealing. For others, clerical or stock work that doesn't require a lot of interaction with people is a good choice; for still others, "people work," such as retail selling offers a refreshing change of pace. Being successful at something—anything—will help rebuild (or build for the first time) your self-esteem and confidence.

❖ When you start to feel tense or uneasy at work, take a few moments to meditate. If that isn't enough, pick up the phone and call your sponsor or another AA friend. Or stop in to see the Employee Assistance Program person, if there is one at your company. Find an AA meeting to go to at lunchtime or after work—you'll find this kind of support much more uplifting than anything that comes in a bottle or a bag.

❖ Don't fear that drugs have pickled your brains if some things that used to be second nature escape you now. If you learned to use complex machinery or computer equipment while under the influence, you may have to relearn their use now (see page 237). But you should be able to do so easily.

❖ If you're in a highly skilled profession, find out if there is a local AA group made up of compatriots—doctors, lawyers, pilots, engineers, or nurses, for example. Participating in such a group can offer support not just for recovery, but for reorganizing your work life as well. It will give you a chance to discuss issues that are relevant to your job (handling drugs, for example, if you're a physician, or flying sober if you're a pilot). If you work for a large company, seek out others with similar jobs who are also recovering. The Employee Assistance Program person can often be of help. Some large corporations or government organizations are supportive enough to have on-site meetings.

FINDING A NEW JOB

"My boss fired me. I don't blame him. But now that I've finished a treatment program, I need to find a new job. Do I tell a prospective employer about my past?"

This may sound like jobicide, but the answer is yes. Honesty—with yourself and with others—is such a key element in recovery that you really have no choice but to tell all. Most people will be impressed with your frankness, especially in an era when so many resumes are liberally salted with half-truths and untruths. In addition, employers are coming to recognize that those who have gone through the discipline of treatment may actually be better candidates than the typical applicant.

Recoverees often have developed superior coping skills, are more honest and responsible, and relate better to others. Group therapy has made good listeners out of them, and delivering talks at AA meetings has done as much as a Dale Carnegie course to improve their ability to express themselves and to be comfortable speaking in public. That doesn't mean that every employer is going to be delighted to hear that the six-month gap in your employment record is the result of alcohol or drug usage or treatment. But anyone who turns you down on that account alone is probably not the right employer for you anyway.

Not leveling with an employer can not only put your recovery in jeopardy, it can put your job on the line. If the employer finds out about your history from other sources, your integrity is immediately suspect. What if you have a relapse? How do you explain it to your new boss then? So on every level, honesty is the best policy.

Being honest, however, doesn't mean you can't employ a win-win strategy (good for you, good for the employer) in your job hunting. One way to do this is to withhold the information about your alcohol/drug history from your original application and resume. Then when the prospective employer invites you for an interview, put your best face forward, make the best possible impression, and get the job offer. Finally, before accepting it, explain your history. Don't make too big a deal of it. The more emphasis you put on your problem, the larger it will loom in the eyes of others.

In some cases, it may be helpful to have a professional involved in your treatment (your counselor or physician) act as your advocate before a prospective employer, via either a letter or a phone call. If you work in a safety- or security-sensitive or high-risk field—medicine or transportation, for example—it may be necessary for you to go through a probationary period during which you have to continue in after-care treatment or therapy and/or remain active in AA. If there is an Employee Assistance Program where you work, its staff will probably be involved in overseeing your recovery.

There are at least three ways you can assure an employer that you are fulfilling these requirements. One is to have your counselor, doctor, or therapist send regular reports to your employer or to the medical board or whoever is following your recovery. The second is a mutually agreed-upon employment contract (see page 236). The third—a tightrope walk that pins the responsibility directly on your lapel—requires you to compose an undated letter to your employer or other interested parties saying that you have not met your recovery responsibilities and therefore

INSURANCE ASSURANCE

This is how the scenario used to be played out when recovering alcoholics/addicts applied for life insurance from an industry that viewed alcoholism as both a moral issue and a pre-existing condition—as, for the most part, it still does:

When applicants truthfully admitted their past, they were automatically declined, unless they had five or more years of provable sobriety and were willing to pay four or five times the standard premium. The act of signing an application authorizes a company representative to request medical records, talk to neighbors, and search state DUI reports. So if the eager applicant white lied, he or she would be exposed by an insurance investigator, or by a routine printout from the industry's Medical Information Board data bank. Or after the insured's death, further investigation would uncover the deception and the insurer would refuse to pay the beneficiaries.

That scenario is no longer the only one thanks to the Renaissance Group, a New Jersey insurance brokerage founded by two recovering alcoholics with links to 350 other agents around the U.S. If you're a regular member of a support group like AA or of a strong church fellowship and have a minimum of two years sobriety (one year in many cases and as little as six months for impaired physicians being actively monitored by their peers) Renaissance will offer you insurance at the same rates paid by nonalcoholics. The insurance is underwritten by a major company, whose CEO is himself a recovering alcoholic.

Renaissance has a disability insurance program in the works with Lloyds of London and is working on a group health program as well. If you've been turned down for life insurance but meet their sobriety and support group criteria, contact the company at (800) 348-9149 for more information—and, very likely, a standard-rate insurance policy.

are probably back on drugs or booze. The letter is held by your counselor, doctor, therapist, or sponsor and is mailed by prearrangement the moment you miss one or more appointments without good cause, stop going to meetings, or fail to meet other recovery requirements.

"I haven't worked in nearly a year, and I'm nervous about going back to work now that I'm sober."

And so you should be, laden down as you are with the responsibilities of recovery. It may not be best for you to rush right back into full-time employment unless you're driven to it by financial or other demands. A period in which you do nothing but concentrate on recovery can be extremely beneficial. You may be able to do this if you have some savings, can stay with family or friends, or have some other source of temporary support. If that's out of the question, for the time being you should probably consider either a part-time job or one that is less taxing and stressful than your usual work. Once you find that you can handle a lower-stress job competently, you'll feel more confident about tackling a more demanding one.

FEAR OF ADMITTING IMPERFECTION

"We're starting a new project at work and I really am having trouble grasping the details. But I hate to ask for further explanations. I'm afraid they'll start thinking, 'Boy, is she brain-damaged!'"

You don't have to be in recovery to be uncomfortable admitting you don't understand something. A lot of people have felt that way since they were knee-high to a multiplication table. But people in recovery feel particularly vulnerable, fearing that everyone distrusts and thinks poorly of them. So they don't ask questions, leaving themselves open to really bungling the job. Even if the first impression you give is one of ignorance, asking questions shows that you really care about doing the job right. In the long run, that won't be lost on the boss.

In early recovery, part of the problem is physiological. The fog has not yet lifted (see page 311), so grasping information may be tougher for you than for others. But there's no need to relate your queries to your recovery; anyone can ask questions. Just listen attentively, take notes when appropriate, and ask questions when something comes up that you don't understand. Rest assured that when your mind is clearer—and it will be—things will come easier.

HIGH-RISK WORK

"I was a floor nurse in a big city hospital before my treatment for drug abuse. My supervisor is hesitant to take me back. And to tell you the truth, I'm a little nervous myself about being face to face with the drug closet with a key in my pocket."

You are both wise to be wary of the day-in-and-day-out temptation of drugs. For those in recovery, the lid to the cookie jar is generally considered too hot to handle. For that reason it's recommended that recovering doctors, nurses, pharmacists, and

A CONTINUING-CARE PLAN AGREEMENT

Your employers may respect your talents and recognize your past contributions to their business but be understandably reluctant to risk keeping you on because of your erratic history. To protect them and yourself, suggest a tough no-loophole employment contract for a specific period (usually one or two years) that spells out a comprehensive Continuing-Care Plan. Such a plan should, at minimum, require the following:

❖ Your regular attendance at AA or a similar mutual-help group, with full participation including enlisting a sponsor.

❖ Random urine drug screens on request from your employer (at least monthly).

❖ Quarterly reports from your physician or counselor verifying your sobriety and recovery.

❖ Immediate termination of your employment if you fail to uphold your end of the contract.

This type of agreement creates a win-win situation. It gives you a carrot and your employer a stick.

others in a position to handle scheduled drugs (and who abused any drug but alcohol) change positions temporarily, at least for the first year. If that's not possible, then very close supervision of that aspect of the job is necessary—preferably with someone else holding the key. Sometimes an employment contract (see page 236) is useful in such a situation.

WORK DIFFICULTIES

"I've been back at work for a week now, and I can't seem to concentrate at all. Today I tried to use a computer program I should know as well, and my mind went blank. I'm really afraid I'm suffering some kind of permanent brain damage."

Alcohol and other drugs do damage the brain. But in most instances the brain eventually recovers (see page 311), and it's more than likely that yours will too. Still, the fogginess and lack of concentration can be alarming if you aren't aware that they are normal at this stage. Many people report being unable to concentrate long enough to do even a little reading. But the fog gradually clears, and the ability to sit still and apply oneself to a task gradually returns.

Not remembering how to operate a computer program, however, may be related to what is known as "state-dependent learning." If you learned to do something (operate a machine, work a program, do a dance step) while you were in a particular state (such as high on a drug), you may have to learn it all over again when you become clean and sober. The problem is most common with alcohol and benzodiazepine abusers, but it can appear in those who used speed or other drugs, too. Fortunately, the second time around it won't take as long to learn what you seem to have forgotten. The knowledge is there; it just needs to be unlocked. So pull out your program manual and give yourself a fast refresher course.

A NONPRESSURED JOB

"I started drinking in college and barely managed to graduate. But even with a degree I couldn't settle into something, and I still can't seem to. I'm working as a dishwasher, and this has my parents in a tizzy. 'How can a girl with a college degree scrub pots?' is what they keep asking. But for the moment, I'm happy with this low-pressure work."

Mom and Dad don't always know best. Sometimes a child must lead them. In this case, you're absolutely right to stick for a while to work where the heaviest decision you have to make all day is whether to use a sponge or a steel-wool pad. This will allow you to put your focus where it belongs: on your recovery. When you've been sober for a year or so, you can start thinking about career moves. If your folks have trouble understanding this, ask them to read Chapters 27 and 28 and start attending Al-Anon meetings.

LEGAL TROUBLES

"I've got a jail sentence for assault hanging over my head—I punched a guy when I was drunk. Now that I'm sober, is there anyway to get out of serving the time?"

Possibly. Although in some cases a judge will not bend and the time will have to be served, many magistrates will suspend a sentence in a

JOB-HUNTING TIPS

Setting out to find a new job is always daunting. It's particularly unnerving when you are in recovery—still unsure of yourself, still uneasy about the kind of reaction your disease will provoke in prospective employers. But many recoverees have successfully landed good jobs, and you can too. The following pointers should help.

❖ *Do your homework.* Many alcoholics/addicts set inappropriate career goals, often because they are unable to do an accurate self-assessment. If your career goals aren't crystal clear, then you probably should seek some vocational counseling from someone who understands the needs of the recovering alcoholic/addict. Programs for getting recovering people back on their feet vocationally may be sponsored by individual localities, in- or outpatient treatment centers, major employers, the local chapter of the National Council on Alcoholism, or your state department of employment. The best of these programs may include evaluation and assessment, a part-time transitional work program, job-preparedness training, stress management and assertiveness training, job and job-hunting skills seminars, and placement. Some provide only placement. Whether you do it alone or with help, however, you need to explore your goals and aptitudes (a test may help), and gather occupational information before you decide on your direction.

❖ *Network.* If you seem to be having trouble finding an employer who doesn't freeze up at the mention of alcoholism or addiction, ask around at AA meetings for suggestions and recommendations. The AA grapevine can usually point out the "friendly" employers, those who've had good experiences with other recoverees and recognize them as ideal employees. (Some of these employers are so supportive that they give AA workers time off for meetings.)

❖ *Do some role-playing.* Before you face any prospective employers, run through some simulated interviews (with an employment counselor, your sponsor, or a friend). Be sure you are hit with some tough questions during this rehearsal.

❖ *Do it right.* Neatness counts. A sloppy, skimpy resume or a poorly filled-out application will lead a prospective employer to question your ability, whether you mention your alcoholism/addiction problem or not. Your resume should be well-written, neat, grammatically correct, and professional looking. Get help from your sponsor, friends, even a resume service.

❖ *Dress for the role.* Wear to the interview whatever is appropriate attire for the job you are applying for. Avoid flashy, trendy, or radical styles.

❖ *Arrive on time.* Turning up late for an interview could close down a job opportunity before you even open your mouth.

❖ *Recognize that you may not get the job.* There are probably many applicants for a single position, and all but one will be disappointed. This is not a personal judgment against those who don't succeed. Still, because rejection right now may be difficult to handle, be prepared to turn to your support structure if you are turned down. Go to a meeting, call your sponsor, have lunch with an AA friend—and start getting the next batch of applications ready. One thing's for sure: Nobody's going to hire you crouched in the fetal position with the bedclothes pulled over your head.

case like yours, if it's clear that you're serious about your recovery work. Persuading him may require supervision from a physician, counselor, or outpatient program, as well as a probation officer. Talk to whoever is treating you about helping you with your legal problems. Most people in the alcohol field have run into situations like yours before, know the ropes and can direct you to a lawyer (possibly an empathetic recovering lawyer) who knows them even better. If he or she (and your positive attitude) can persuade the judge that you're a new man, there's no reason to put the old man behind bars, and you could (though it's by no means guaranteed) get off with probation.

LICENSE AND INSURANCE DIFFICULTIES

"I got out of treatment a few weeks ago, and I'm ready to go back to work. My problem is that my driver's license was suspended for six months and my insurance was canceled because of some DUI's—and I need a car to go to work."

Ideally you should try to find another way to get to work—a car pool, car service, or public transportation—until your sponsor and/or counselor has confidence enough in your recovery to give you the go-ahead to drive. You may only have one more chance, and you don't want to blow it.

How easy it will be to get your license reinstated at that point depends on where you live and how serious your offenses were. The national furor sparked by Mothers Against Drunk Driving (MADD) and other groups has, justifiably, hardened law-enforcement attitudes. But you may be able to appeal to the motor vehicle bureau for a conditional "hardship" license, which would restrict you to driving to and from work and meetings—with no detours—during your six-month suspension. Letters from a rehab facility physician or counselor attesting to your successful completion of treatment and your strict follow-up in a structured continuing-care program should help. So should a penitent letter from you, explaining that you are now sober and fully intend to stay that way. In any case, you may have to take a special driving class before you can get behind the wheel.

Of course, even with your license reinstated you won't be able to drive without insurance. Theoretically an insurance company cannot refuse to insure a driver with a valid license, but it can "rate" you—that is, charge you considerably more than the careful driver. The overwhelming statistical evidence of accidents and fatalities caused by drinkers and druggers amply justifies the caution of insurance companies in underwriting drivers with DUI's on their records. (Incidentally, they don't wait for you or the courts to warn them. Auto insurance companies subscribe to services like Press Clips, which send them lists or DUI violations reported on local police blotters. The company's computers cross-check their files, and when your name comes up in a match, presto, out goes a notice that your policy has been rated or canceled.)

In most states, the driver who gets his license reinstated can purchase insurance through a state-run indemnity company in an assigned-risk pool of drivers with major violations—people convicted of DUI's, leaving the scene of a motor vehicle accident, drag racing, driving without insurance, or vehicular manslaughter. These are not exactly prize customers, and they pay dearly for their insurance—30 to 50 percent more for liability, for example, or double for collision insurance. Major private insurers often create second-tier companies offering insurance at premiums slightly lower than the state pools.

So the sad news is that it's going to cost you. The good news is that, if you behave, you won't have to surrender your wheels permanently. And the best news is that after five years with a Good Conduct medal, your rates may revert to those of your next-door neighbor, Sam Sober, who never drinks anything stronger than Colombian coffee.

One final note: When you do start driving, you'll need to be extra careful. It could be months before your reflexes return to normal.

FINANCIAL WOES

"I came out of treatment owing everybody in town: the butcher, the grocer, the department store. (Everybody but the liquor store—I always paid my liquor bills.) I'm behind on my mortgage and my car payments. And I don't have two cents in the bank. How can our family survive?"

Alcohol and drugs can destroy not just the human fabric of your life, but the financial fabric as well. Most people find that the walls start tumbling down around them at about three months into recovery, when creditors stop threatening and start phoning collection agencies. So your situation, though desperate, is hardly unique.

Pulling yourself out of your financial hole is possible, but it won't be easy. Certainly, your family is going to have to pull long and hard with you. In 99 out of 100 cases, people in your position can manage to save themselves without having to declare bankruptcy, which should be considered in only the most dire situations.* You can turn to a non-profit debt counseling service to draw up a stopgap financial plan, or try to do it yourself. Such a plan usually includes:

❖ *Calling creditors to let them know what's happening.* Explain calmly and reasonably that you've been through a lengthy illness, that you're finally on the road to recovery, but that you need some time to regroup your resources. If they're willing to work out an extension, you'll repay them slowly but surely. If they're not, you'll be forced to declare bankruptcy and they'll get little or nothing. Assure them that in the meantime you'll refrain from taking on fresh debt.

❖ *Cutting up your credit cards.* Don't just tuck them into a drawer, thinking you may need them in an emergency. Cut them up and dump them in the trash.

❖ *Cutting back on expenses.* Burgers instead of steaks, pasta instead of wild rice. Movies or videos instead of theater tickets. A day at the beach instead of weekends in the country. You know where your spending may be excessive, and where you can best cut it down to size. If you're not sure, keep a diary for a month, writing down where every penny is spent. Then figure out where you can pare.

❖ *Keeping to a budget.* At least until you're back on your feet, you'll need to avoid deficit financing. Decide in advance where every incoming dollar will go, and then stick to your budget like epoxy. Write into your calendar the days on which payments or bills are due, and check that calendar daily. Promptness avoids late payments and

*Get competent legal advice from more than one source. Some bankruptcy lawyers tend to paint a rosy, but false, picture of post-bankruptcy life. You risk losing home, furniture, car, everything. If you do consider bankruptcy, consider a Chapter 13 or wage earner's plan, whereby your creditors are paid a prorated amount of the outstanding debt. An all-out bankruptcy proceeding should almost never be necessary.

establishes a track record that improves your credit rating. When the check has been sent, cross off the item.

❖ *Starting a savings account.* This may seem an impossible goal with all the creditors at the door, but plan to pay yourself before you pay them. Even if you put away just $5 a week, you've begun to construct an umbrella for a rainy day.

❖ *Accepting help—with a caveat.* If you have family or close friends who are willing to lend you cash or to cosign a note to pay off some of your creditors and give you some breathing space, don't be too proud to accept their assistance. But plan to pay it back. It's important for your recovery that you accept ultimate responsibility for your life. That means no more bailouts from those who love you in spite of yourself, and *you* paying the bills *you* owe.

Facing up to your financial responsibility also helps you to see the financial havoc wrought by addiction and increases your motivation for recovery.

"I was sober for sixty days and feeling pretty good—until I got this nasty little note from the IRS. With all the debts I'm behind on, there's no way I can pay what I owe now."

Remember what you used to have to bring to school when you were out sick? A doctor's note. If the amount in question is small, that may do the trick with the IRS too. Get a note from your counselor, therapist, physician, or treatment center explaining that you are in early recovery and that it will be a while before you are financially on your feet again. Take the note, in person if possible, to the nearest IRS office and explain that you do want to pay, but that it will be a while before it will be possible. More than likely you will be able to work out a mutually acceptable payment plan. Or they may work out a loan for you with your credit union or bank to pay off your indebtedness to them. If you run into resistance, ask to speak to a supervisor.

If that still doesn't work, or if you are talking about several thousand dollars or more of indebtedness, you will need professional help to cut a deal with the IRS. Consult a tax lawyer or a tax-savvy certified public accountant (CPA), preferably one who used to work for the IRS or who appears in tax court frequently. Recovery publications often run ads for such professionals, some recovering themselves. But discuss their fees in advance to be sure they're not going to sink you even deeper into your hole. If that seems likely, tap the grapevine at your AA group. You're far from the first recoveree up to the earlobes in debt to the IRS, and someone's sure to have the name of an expert who can help you.

"I've made a shambles of my financial affairs while I was using cocaine, but somehow I managed to end up with a fair amount of money still tucked away in various accounts. I need to use some to pay my outstanding bills, some to live on while I pull myself together, and some should be invested—but I can't think clearly enough to know how to manage things."

Don't try. You've got to focus what thinking ability you can muster on your recovery. Get professional help to deal with the financial mess you've made. Choose someone who understands that this isn't a time for you to be speculating wildly and recognizes that the best investments for you right now are the safest ones.

13

Taking Care of Your Body in Phase One

You will probably notice so many physical symptoms and ailments during the early weeks and months of your recovery that you'll wonder wryly if you were healthier when you were drinking and drugging. No way. What's happening is simple: You're just much more aware of what your body is saying when you're sober. Twitches, aches, pains, and indefinable sensations went unnoticed before, blacked out by your bombed-out brain. Now they are magnified. This is partly because your body's own natural pain-easing chemicals, kayoed by foreign chemicals, are not yet back in full production. But in addition, you're still suffering from the effects of the substances you've been abusing and—double whammy—from the effects of their withdrawal.

While drinking or using you probably ignored colds, fevers, and toothaches, or treated them with the same friendly chemicals you used to treat your emotional ills. Now you'll be more aware of illnesses, and have to treat them very differently. Taking mood-altering medications could lead to a relapse, so you need to be familiar with nondrug methods of treating common illnesses, as well as with which drugs are safe and when. You'll also need to practice catch-up—taking care of any medical and dental problems ignored under the influence (new contacts or glasses, dental work, a prescribed contraceptive). Equally important, you'll need a doctor who knows how to treat people in recovery.

Gradually, if you take good care of yourself from now on, your body will heal and the message it starts sending will be: "I feel great!"

Guide Lines

❖ Your body may feel worse before it feels better.

❖ You can expect to experience a variety of symptoms; some are the leftover effects of the chemicals you took, others are the result of withdrawing them. It's likely that most of these symptoms will disappear gradually over the next six months. A few may linger longer.

❖ The longer you delayed getting treatment, the more symptoms you will probably develop and the longer they will hang on.

❖ Your medical care should come from a physician who is either thoroughly familiar with addiction or willing to learn.

❖ Any medication, by providing a "quick fix," can drag you back into the cycle of addiction; but the most dangerous medications for the alcoholic/addict are those that alter mood.

A GUIDE TO RECOVERY MEDICAL CARE

Health care in early recovery is critical to a successful return to the sober life. But you can't do it alone. You've got to have the right physician, the right dentist, and the right support from your sponsor and others in AA. You also need to know how to distinguish between recovery-enhancing and recovery-imperiling medical care, and how to steer clear of menacing medications, possibly safe for others, but definitely dangerous for you.

FINDING THE RIGHT DOCTOR

Not every internist or family physician understands or can (or wants to) cope with alcohol- and drug-related problems. But it's critical that you find one who's willing, able, and experienced. Here's how to compile a short list of candidates:

❖ Ask your treatment center or counselor to recommend a doctor in your community.

❖ Ask AA friends or acquaintances for a recommendation.

❖ Call your local medical society for the names of area doctors certified by the American Society on Addiction Medicine (ASAM); or contact ASAM directly (12 West 21st St., New York, NY 10010; 212/206-6770). Certification means that a physician has passed a written exam on and has some experience with addictive diseases. Like any other certification, it doesn't automatically guarantee a great doctor. But it does give you an excellent start.

If you can't find an experienced addiction specialist, all is not lost. Give your own doctor or another family physician or internist a short quiz to determine if he or she would be right for you. First, explain that you are an alcoholic (and/or addict) and that you are in recovery. Then ask:

Can you be comfortable having a "sober drunk" (or a "clean addict") as a patient? A negative answer should tell you to look elsewhere. Even an uneasy affirmative response should raise doubts in your mind.

What do you view as the cause of alcoholism and addiction? The doctor who believes it's all a matter of moral weakness or lack of willpower is not for you. You want a doctor who understands that this is a disease, a primary disease that isn't usually caused by emotional or social problems, but more often is their cause. A physician who doesn't understand this could prescribe medications to cure the "emotional" problems, and set you back to where you were before you became sober. The doctor should also recognize (as almost all scientific authorities now agree) that alcoholism/addiction is a treatable, but incurable, disease and that like other chronic conditions, it requires lifelong vigilance to keep it under control.

What is your attitude about prescribing medications for people with alcoholism or addictive disease? The doctor who replies only "Well, I wouldn't give him morphine or barbiturates" is not well informed enough to protect your recovery. You want a doctor up-to-date enough to know that any mood-altering drug, even an antihistamine, has the potential to trigger a relapse and who sees his or her role as primarily supportive—helping the body heal itself.

Have you ever been to an AA meeting? A doctor who has cared enough to attend, either as participant or visitor, will have a big advantage in treating patients with addictive disease.

Correct answers to these questions may not be enough. Correct actions will have to follow. The doctor who says "I believe alcoholism is a disease" and then hands you a prescription for Tylenol 3 (which contains codeine), needs either to be educated or to be dropped.

The ideal doctor for you will do more than provide routine health care. He or she will:

❖ Be familiar with and know how to treat the residual problems of addiction (such as liver disease, neuropathy, HIV infection, herpes).

❖ Help you deal with pain without getting hooked again—treat minor illnesses without using mood-altering drugs, and weigh risk versus benefit in the use of anesthesia or other drugs for serious illnesses or surgery.

❖ Be willing to be your advocate if you have problems at work or at home.

❖ Be well enough acquainted with what's available in and around your community to recommend a counselor or treatment center, if either is needed.

❖ Be knowledgeable enough to be able to help you over the rough spots in your recovery program.

You may have a wonderful family physician or internist who has no experience in the treatment of alcoholism/addiction, yet whom you hate to desert. Ask him or her to read the message to physicians on page 578, and then sit down and discuss whether you can work together to help you get well.

HOW TO HELP YOUR DOCTOR HELP YOU

These days, good health care requires a partnership between doctor and patient, with each contributing what he or she does best. You won't get optimum care from even the best doctor unless you do your fair share.

❖ If your doctor doesn't already know you well, schedule a get-acquainted session so he or she can learn what it was like for you during your active addiction, what happened to make you well, and what it's like now in recovery. If you've switched doctors, transfer all your medical records from other physicians, and from hospitals or treatment centers, to your new provider. (You will have to do this either in person or by sending a signed letter that gives permission for this confidential material to be forwarded to your new caregiver.)

❖ Don't see any other physician without your primary doctor's knowledge. Check any treatment, particularly if it involves medication, with your primary doctor.

❖ Tell the whole truth to your doctor—about your past history, present behavior, symptoms, possible causes, and so on. If you provide only partial or incorrect information, what you'll get back will be partial or incorrect medical advice and treatment.

❖ Don't allow any doctor you suspect of being under the influence to treat you. If such a doctor provides negligent care, you will then share the responsibility for any poor outcomes.

❖ If you have any concerns and questions about the care you're getting, let your doctor know. Be frank, but never belligerent.

❖ Offer to take your doctor to an AA meeting from time to time. It's excellent continuing education for any medical professional.

❖ When a medication is prescribed, politely remind your doctor—who has a lot of other patients on his mind—that you're in recovery. Always ask if the medication is absolutely necessary and if there are acceptable medication-free alternatives. Keep in mind that physicians are under constant pressure (through saturation marketing in journal advertising, at medical convention exhibits, and via in-office visits by sales reps) from pharmaceutical companies to find you a better life through chemistry. And since there's no money to be made by pushing non-drug treatments (nobody makes a dime when you jog or meditate), there is little propaganda to counter this corporate promotion.

Also recognize that for all of us, time is money, and that for busy doctors, a scribbled prescription provides a shortcut to dealing with complicated issues; one-on-one counseling is much more time consuming. If you conclude that a medication is not advisable, let your doctor know rather than meekly accepting the prescription and then tossing it in the first wastebasket you pass. (See page 246 for more on medications; copy page 578 of this book for your physician to read.)

❖ When emotional problems arise, remind your doctor that you'd rather try to handle them through your AA group and recovery program or talk therapy than with a drug. (Of course, serious mental illness may require medication; see page 249.)

❖ Promote your own wellness. Living a healthy lifestyle—no smoking, good nutrition, proper exercise, stress reduction—will lessen your chances of getting sick and of needing any kind of treatment, including medication.

❖ Report symptoms promptly. Don't wait until the blues turn into serious depression or bronchitis becomes pneumonia before calling the doctor.

❖ Follow doctor's orders. If you have reason to question those orders, do so—but don't ignore them.

❖ If you repeatedly find yourself disagreeing with your doctor, and especially if you don't feel you're getting adequate support for your recovery, consider switching physicians.

GETTING REGULAR CHECKUPS

You probably steered away from all doctors while you were using chemicals. Either you were feeling no pain, or you didn't want to hear any bad news. In recovery, you should get into the habit of seeing your doctor regularly, even if you're feeling fine. Periodic medical checkups should be a regular part of your recovery plan. Now that you're no longer living life so close to the edge, you can expect to be around a long time. Preventive health habits, screening for serious diseases, and implementation of health-promotion strategies under your doctor's guidance are just a few of the practices that can help you meet that expectation.

See your physician as early in recovery as possible, and get a thorough physical. When the doctor asks for a drug history, be sure you give a complete one, since the substances you used, how you used them, and for how long will dictate what the examination should emphasize: If it was alcohol, the liver and nervous system will be checked more closely; if cocaine, the heart and nose. If you smoked your drugs, a chest x-ray will probably be in order. If you did them intravenously, tests for hepatitis and AIDS will generally be considered. A history of sexual promiscuity increases the likelihood of AIDS and other sexually transmitted diseases, which special lab tests and cultures can either confirm or rule out. If confirmed, they alert your doctor to the need for treatment.

The doctor will also want to know if you've tried unsuccessfully to get sober before, if you've been through in- or outpatient treatment for your addiction (and where), and if you are presently in a continuing-care program.

THE MEDICATION TRAP

There are two kinds of medications: mood-altering and non-mood-altering. It's the mood-altering variety (everything from antihistamines to tranquilizers) that present the greatest risk and that can set you up for a slip. The very first dose, like flipping a switch, can transform a positive attitude into a negative one. It can also bring on mood swings and anger, as well as a compulsion to drink or use more drugs.

"About five weeks into treatment, I broke my arm. I thought, damn, how am I going to get it set without taking something? Well, a counselor went to the emergency room with me, and the doctor set it while we talked. I still can't believe that I was able to tolerate all that pain. I used to have to take something for the least little twitch."

But there are also two kinds of people: alcoholics/addicts and non-alcoholics/addicts. Alcoholics/addicts can get hooked on an empty capsule if they're convinced it will make them feel better. It's not just their vivid imaginations; their expectation triggers the brain to produce the substances that create a high. It's almost the identical sleight-of-hand that the brain pulls off when it produces the exhilaration experienced when you see your baby born or ride a roller coaster. So, since any medication can feed addictive behavior, alcoholics/addicts must consider any that they swallow, inhale, or take at needle-point hazardous to their sobriety. Of course, most dangerous of all are the drugs on which they were accustomed to getting high.

Treat the decision to take any medication seriously, and any use as a mini-slip. Report the use to those involved in your recovery: your doctor, counselor, and/or sponsor. If you follow these precautions, you are less likely to innocently open the door to a relapse. Your doctor may think there's no need to make a big deal out of taking an aspirin, but long experience demonstrates that sobriety is strengthened by the realization that dependency on *any* medication is risky.

Fortunately, you'll need medication less and less as you progress in recovery. The reason is chemical: Ordinarily, the brain prescribes and promptly administers its own chemicals (endorphins and enkephalins) to combat pain as needed. Alcohol and drugs impair these natural defenses by instructing the brain to stop making its internal painkillers because the body is already overdosing on them from an external source. When you sober up, pain of various kinds may initially be a problem because it takes a couple of weeks for the still fuzzy brain to get the message that it needs to kick in with painkiller production again. But once it does, you will find that a single aspirin relieves pain more effectively than a strong painkiller used to do.

SAFE MEDICATING

In spite of the risks, it's sometimes not possible to avoid mood-changing drugs when serious accident or illness strikes, or when surgery is necessary. If you and your physician or dentist, after weighing risk against benefit, decide that non-drug pain relief (see page 288) won't be sufficient and that a prescription or other risky drug is absolutely needed, there are ways of making certain that it is administered safely. These tips should help prevent a slip:

❖ If the physician handling your case has no experience with addiction, get a second opinion from one who has as to what is the safest medication route for you to follow.

❖ If you're having surgery, regional anesthesia (which numbs the area to be worked on) is preferable to general anesthesia (which puts the patient to sleep) when feasible. Ask your surgeon to request the anesthesiologist to omit the pre-op medications (usually a tranquilizer) if possible. A chat with the anesthesiologist, meditation, soothing music (or music videos), or repeating the AA Serenity Prayer may do just as much for you. Also explore the possible use of hypnotism and acupuncture for drug-free or drug-reduced surgery.

❖ When medication is absolutely necessary, it should, if at all possible, be in a different class from your old drug of choice. For example, if you abused a particular drug (Demerol, for example) taking it or a related one (any other narcotic, in this case), except under the most rigidly controlled conditions, could be fatal to your recovery.

❖ If possible, any needed medication should be administered only in a hospital, where it can be closely controlled.

❖ Whenever feasible, have an advocate at your bedside. This can be a family member who is knowledgeable about safe medication procedures, or your sponsor or another AA friend.

❖ Also have at your bedside the Big Book and other inspirational recovery reading material. If you have a tape player (with headphones if you are sharing a room), a selection of favorite AA tapes will provide further support. Arrange for frequent AA visitors, and if it can be orchestrated, have a mini AA meeting in your room. If visitors are banned, keep in phone contact with your sponsor.

"In my drinking and drugging days, I could take a bottleful of aspirin and not get any pain relief. Now, if I hurt real bad and take one aspirin, it works like a charm."

❖ Following surgery, a strong narcotic for a few days in the hospital will be safer than a tranquilizer for a few weeks at home. The longer you take the drug, the greater the risk—especially if you are in charge of administering it.

❖ In the hospital, arrange for your doctor to leave standing orders with the nursing staff that exempt you from routine sedation or sleeping pills. This kind of medicating is often more for the convenience of the staff than the benefit of the patients, and it definitely is not safe for you. Have your doctor explain your situation to the nurses so you won't have medication you don't need forced down your throat. Because nursing shifts change frequently and nurses on a new shift may not be aware of your doctor's orders, it would be wise to ask each nurse to read your chart before giving you any medications. The biggest risk will probably be when you're fresh out of surgery and groggy. (If an advocate is with you, he or she can do the talking.)

If, in spite of your best efforts, routine medication is handed to you, dump it down the toilet (or have your advocate or a visitor do the deed). Don't leave the pills lying temptingly on your nightstand.*

❖ Avoid medication "as needed by patient." Many hospitals now have technology that allows doctors to prescribe pain medication via an intravenous pump—on demand, as the patient feels the need. With your history, that would be about as safe as giving Al Capone the keys to Ft. Knox. It's better for the nurse to administer your medication, but only on a regular schedule as the physician feels you need it after consulting daily with you and your advocate. This procedure makes life a bit more difficult for the busy, often harried nurses, who can't hand out your medication with everyone else's. But nurses are there to help and will usually cooperate.

❖ Don't accept any medication, unless you're given a very convincing reason why you should take it. If possible, consult an ASAM physician or medical personnel at a chemical dependency treatment program if you're uncertain.

❖ If at any point you don't understand what's happening to you or can't get your point across to the nursing staff, or to a weary resident who's been on duty for twenty-four hours straight, appeal to the attending doctor on call (one is always available). Sometimes it may be easier to reach the doctor on your room phone rather than through the staff. That may not win you any popularity contests, but it won't lose you your sobriety either.

"The first time I saw it, I was amazed. This nurse had been sober for ten years when she went in for surgery. They gave her medication, and she was a different person. It was like she'd never heard of AA or recovery. She was yelling to get out of there because they didn't treat her right, she didn't want to go to detox, and she didn't want to go to AA or to do anything she'd been doing in recovery. It was like she didn't have a problem—which she sure did have!"

*If you manage to avoid medications during your hospital stay, you may get an argument from your medical insurer: Why did you have to be in the hospital if you took no medications? Let your doctor field that question for you. If you need more support, send the claim clerk a copy of these pages.

EXCEPTIONS TO EVERY RULE

Mood-altering drugs *can* be dangerous for anyone in recovery. However, there is a small percentage of people who can not really move into recovery until they are lifted out of deep depression or until they are capable of organizing their thoughts sufficiently to allow them to utilize the tools of recovery. Such life-threatening situations demand drastic action, which may mean the use of psychotropic drugs (usually antidepressants, antipsychotics, or lithium, but not sedative hypnotics or benzodiazepines).

Ideally, these are given during inpatient treatment or are doled out in the doctor's office or by a reliable third party. Once brain function is normalized, such individuals can be gradually weaned from the medication on a trial basis. If he or she continues to function normally, the medication can usually be discontinued permanently. If not, it is continued for a while longer, at which time another weaning is attempted.

A risk of prescribing psychotropic medication is that once the patient escapes the depression, he or she may assume the addiction problem is a thing of the past: "Why go to AA? I only drank because I was depressed." To guard against this, many physicians follow a "no meetings, no meds" policy: If the patient does not faithfully follow an agreed-upon recovery program, the medication is no longer prescribed.

❖ As a general rule, you should be drug-free for forty-eight hours before release from the hospital. In other words, you should be detoxed before discharge. If the surgical or medical problem was severe or complicated and heavy use of medication was necessary, detox alone may be inadequate for relapse prevention. Sometimes it may be necessary to convalesce in a substance-abuse treatment facility for a short time.

When that's not practical, make plans with your sponsor to smother you in AA friends, literature, and meetings until the pharmaceutical fog lifts completely. This could take weeks in some cases. In any case, the first few nights should not be spent alone, but with someone in solid recovery or with a spouse or friend active in AA or Al-Anon.

❖ If medication must be continued after release from the hospital or after leaving the dentist's office, you're not the right person to be placed in charge of administering it. A nonaddicted spouse or friend familiar with the use of drugs in recovery should stay with you (or you with them).* Besides helping in other ways, their judgment about medications will be more objective than yours. Among other things, they should dole out one dose at a time and make sure that you swallow each dose on the spot. A written record of all medications taken at home should be kept, and all remaining medications (when the treatment is ended) should be disposed of with one quick flush.

❖ In the case of a serious mental illness, the decision to use medication (such as lithium or antidepressants) should be made with the guidance of a physician who is well versed in addiction and who will carefully supervise its use. Do not rely on the opinions, no matter how well-meaning, of your sponsor or others in AA who may warn you to "stay away from the stuff." The

*Have whoever is staying with you read this section of the book.

fact is that sometimes such drugs must be used. Of course, precautions similar to those described above should be employed. In addition, the medication and the dose should be regularly reevaluated. As soon as it ceases to be absolutely necessary, it should be discontinued.

❖ For pain relief, always ask if a non-mood-altering drug (such as Tylenol) can be substituted for a mood-altering one (such as Demerol). Also consider non-drug treatments for pain (page 288).

SAFE DENTISTRY

The last thing most alcoholics or addicts think about when they are drinking or using is taking care of their teeth. Many a night they fall into bed drunk or high without taking their shoes off, much less taking time to floss and brush. Sugar-loaded junk-food diets and traces of vomit compound the damage to teeth and gums. So does the failure to schedule regular visits to the dentist, who is about as popular with practicing alcoholics and addicts as an AA meeting. Their mouths are often slowly self-destructing. But thanks to their blessed state of permanent chemical anesthesia, they don't even notice.

Then sobriety brings painful reality. Rotting teeth begin to ache. Swollen, reddened gums feel sore. That overdue visit to the dentist becomes a necessity—and a risk.

By all means go to the dentist. But be sure your dentist understands what is and isn't safe for a patient in recovery. The following points are crucial for both you and your dentist if you're to keep your teeth without losing your sobriety.

❖ Ask what type of mouthwash is used in the office; if it contains alcohol, bring your own or arrange to rinse with plain old-fashioned water. (Of course you should shun mouthwash with alcohol at home, too. And beware of those complimentary little bottles you find in hotel bathrooms; pour the contents down the drain before you start to think about draining them.)

❖ Discuss in advance the kind of anesthetic that will be used if repair work needs to be done. Never agree to nitrous oxide (laughing gas) or any other general anesthetic for routine dental work. A local anesthetic, such as Novocain, Lidocaine, or Marcaine, which numbs the gums but not the brain, is okay. They resemble cocaine chemically but do not appear to be hazardous in recovery. If you get heart palpitations or a racing pulse following the use of Lidocaine, ask if you can get it without the epinephrine component. Also safe for dental work are hypnosis and acupuncture (though not many dentists are familiar with their use) and Transcutaneous Electrical Nerve Stimulation (TENS; see page 292), which stimulates nerve pathways to the gums so you feel no other sensory input (such as the dentist's drill), but is helpful in only one case out of four.

❖ Dentists are licensed to prescribe the same medications as physicians—to sedate, tranquilize, and anesthetize. But they may be even less aware of the risks of medicating a patient in recovery. If you don't forewarn your dentist, he or she may never know. And what your dentist doesn't know can hurt you.

Do not take Demerol, Valium, Tylenol 3, Versed (a new benzodiazepine, which is being extravagantly touted as nonaddictive, as were so many of its predecessors), or any other narcotic (page 288) or tranquilizer (page 278) either before or after a dental procedure. Also avoid any other drug about which you have any doubts. That doesn't mean that suffering has to be synonymous with dentist. Recent studies show ibuprofen (Advil, Nuprin) is even more effective than narcotics when two to three are taken before a

MENACING MEDICATIONS

Some of these gateway drugs are not in themselves hazardous. But because they can open the gate back to addiction for those in recovery, they should be avoided except in life and death situations.

In general people in recovery should avoid:

❖ All sedatives (sleeping pills), including all barbiturates and all synthetics (page 293).

❖ All narcotics (pain killers), including opioids and synthetics (page 288).

❖ All tranquilizers (anti-anxiety agents) including benzodiazepines (page 278).

❖ All stimulants, including amphetamines and antidepressants (page 282).

❖ All antihistamines (except Seldane and Hismanal; see page 276).

❖ All combination medications, prescription or over-the-counter, containing narcotics (usually codeine), stimulants (including caffeine), alcohol, or antihistamines.

dental procedure and the dose is repeated six hours later. If you can't take ibuprofen, acetaminophen (Tylenol) or aspirin will relieve pain effectively enough. If these pain relievers fail to wipe out the pain completely, just remind yourself that a little pain is better than a big slip.*

❖ Use non-drug treatment (such as cold therapy, page 290) when possible for pain after a dental procedure. Also try elevating your head on a couple of pillows when you sleep.

❖ If oral surgery is necessary and a local anesthetic won't suffice, check with your own doctor or one certified by ASAM to see if the planned anesthesia is appropriate, or if there might be a better way. If general anesthesia is indeed called for, it's best to perform the procedure in the hospital, following the guidelines suggested on page 247. If that's not possible, you should have your sponsor or another support person with you at the dental surgeon's office and plan to be surrounded by AA friends from the moment you arrive home until all aftereffects of the medication (including any cravings) have faded away. If you or your sponsor notices a return of cravings or risky thinking, a contingency plan—admission to a treatment center for a short stay, for example—should be implemented.

❖ Follow the Clean-and-Sober Recovery Diet (see Chapter 23), avoid sweets between meals, and brush and floss twice a day to help minimize the need for dental work in the future. Chewing sugarless gum, or nibbling a piece of cheese or a few peanuts, after snacks or meals away from home and toothbrush should also help reduce dental decay.

*It's okay to take prescribed antibiotics either before dental surgery or following it.

SAFE HANDLING OF A MEDICAL EMERGENCY

If you twist your ankle sliding on an ice patch on a winter morning, grill your hand on the barbecue, or slice your finger instead of the bagel, an emergency room visit is probably warranted. But such a visit could be hazardous to your sobriety.

ER staffers are not likely to be well informed on the treatment of people in recovery. If you encounter them on a busy weekend, they *are* likely to be harried, tense, and moving at full throttle. So it's possible they will curtly dismiss any polite explanation you try to give about medications you can and cannot have.

To prevent one emergency leading to another, always be prepared by carrying in your wallet your sponsor's phone number and the numbers of several AA friends, your doctor's number, and a photocopy of the list of Menacing Medications described on page 251.

If possible, call your physician to discuss your problem before you go to the emergency room. If your doctor is out or unavailable, you may be able to buy time with temporary measures—ice packs, for example—until he or she can come to your rescue. You may be lucky enough to have a physician who is willing to meet you at the ER, or at least to call and tell the doctor in charge a little of your history and its risks.

If you can't reach your doctor, try to get your sponsor or another AA friend to meet you in the ER. If you are in no condition to pick up a phone, ask someone else to call for you. When you get to the ER, hand the treating physician or nurse your "Menacing Medications" list. If they seem to be ignoring it and your request not to be given one of these drugs, ask to have your doctor called. If the drug is for pain relief and you can grit it out, tell them you don't need it. Or ask for an aspirin or acetaminophen instead.

When your sponsor or another AA person gets there, he or she can act as your advocate. Between you, you should be able to persuade the ER staff, but you may have to be vigorously assertive. Maybe even obnoxious. Just don't take the word of an ER doctor, no matter how wise he seems to be, that if you've been sober for a while, it's okay to take the drugs. It isn't.

One way to get the attention of a busy or disinterested staff, wherever you are being treated, is to tell them you are "allergic" to alcohol and other drugs with a mood-altering effect. The medicolegal risk of prescribing medications to someone who has volunteered information about an allergy will generally prevent a physician from giving you a drug, unless there is relative certainty that withholding it would be a greater threat to your life.

There are, of course, times when a forbidden medication may have to be used—in life-or-death situations, when the pain is unbearable and nothing milder helps, or when serious mental illness is present. In any of these situations, the special protocol on page 247 should be used.

When the emergency is over and you're left with lingering pain, discomfort, or other symptoms, see the treatment recommendations beginning on page 275 for tips on how to cope without dope.

SAFE CHILDBIRTH

Nurturing a healthy baby requires a healthy body. Few women are ready for this task in Phase One of recovery. Ideally, you should wait until you've had a good solid year of sobriety before attempting to conceive. So it's a good

WOMEN AT RISK

Women in recovery who are experiencing anxiety, insomnia, depression, pain, or other emotional symptoms are more likely to be offered a quick pharmaceutical fix than are recovering men. Be wary of the offer of such medication; be sure you and your doctor are completely familiar with the guidelines for safe use of medication in recovery.

DRUGS IN TERMINAL ILLNESS

Quality of life is paramount when there's not much of it left. For the terminal patient, there's a normal tendency to seek escape from the pain through the use of narcotics. The natural thing for an addictive patient to do is to shrug, "What a way to go!" and choose the drug solution. But narcotics, which may be very effective for other patients, often lose their effectiveness for addicted people after just a few doses. That's because tolerance is reached very quickly. Then you're right back where you started—in pain, but now in relapse too. Sliding back into addiction will not only fail to enhance the quality of the last days of life, it will diminish it and your dignity as well.

Even if you know your condition is terminal, work hard with your doctor to find relief for your symptoms without mood-changing drugs, using all the applicable approaches listed on page 288 along with plenty of emotional support. Then, if narcotics become an essential last resort, at least that option has been preserved.

idea—because fertility usually improves rapidly as recovery progresses—to talk to your doctor about the best type of birth control in the interim, and to use it faithfully. (If, however, you do conceive during this year, see Chapter 14 for tips on improving the odds of having a safe pregnancy and a healthy baby.)

Waiting will also give you and your husband a chance to get into tip-top condition. Improve your diets. Give up smoking. Cut out, or down on, caffeine. Get into a good exercise routine. Make appointments for complete preconception physicals, and if any chronic conditions (such as diabetes or high blood pressure) are diagnosed, get them under control. If you're over- or underweight, make an effort to get as close to normal weight as possible. About three months before you start trying to conceive, stop any strenuous dieting and begin taking a vitamin-mineral formula designed for pregnancy. If you're taking birth control pills, have an IUD in place, or are using a spermicide, switch to condoms before you start trying to conceive (in the case of the Pill, switch three months before). Once you start trying to conceive, avoid x-rays, unnecessary medication, and exposure to possibly toxic chemicals at home or at work. And, of course, work hard at your recovery. A clean and sober mom is the best gift you can give your future baby.

Of course dad should also be clean and sober before attempting conception, since drugs could damage not only his fertility but the baby's future health as well.

A GUIDE TO UNDERSTANDING YOUR RECOVERING BODY

Becoming clean and sober is not going to leave you feeling fit as a Stradivarius. As a matter of fact, an odd assortment of physical symptoms may make you feel as though your strings are popping and your bow has snapped. Some of these symptoms are thanks to the damage done to your body by drugs and/or alcohol (alcohol alone is believed responsible for up to 350 disease processes in humans*), while others are a result of your body's brave efforts to rebound from chemical abuse. Still others are a way of expressing emotional distress through physical symptoms and fall into the category of psychosomatic ills.

Some symptoms will disappear within hours after your last drink or fix; others will take weeks, months, or even a year or more to fade away. Some will require medical attention, some home remedies, others just plenty of patience. Depending on how long you drank or used your drug of choice, and the damage it's done, you may note several of these symptoms, only a few, or, if you're uncommonly lucky, none at all.

Many of the symptoms alcoholics and addicts notice with sudden alarm in recovery were there while they were drinking or using. But, numbed by chemicals, they barely noticed them. And if they did notice, they just tossed off another drink or drug as a chaser. Why not? They were so miserable, the little things in life didn't seem worth caring about. Once sober, they suddenly care very much. Even the smallest symptom sets off a loud alarm, and for the first time in a long time, the signals the body is sending are reliable.

If you belong to certain population groups, you may need to be particularly alert for specific health problems. If you're an American of African descent, for example, you may be more susceptible than other alcoholics to liver disease, heart disease, and certain cancers. If you're a Native American, you are also at greater risk of developing alcohol-related problems more quickly than whites. The illness and injury rate among Native Americans is three times higher than for the rest of the population. Native American women are especially susceptible. Their death rate from alcoholic cirrhosis is thirty-seven times that of other U.S. women and their offspring are three to ten times more likely to suffer from fetal alcohol syndrome. If you're female, no matter what your ethnic heritage, you are at greater risk of developing more serious alcohol- or drug-related medical problems earlier in your drinking career.

Of course, not every symptom experienced in recovery is related to recovery. Like anyone else, recoverees are subject to any and all the ills of humankind, and then some—including any of those mentioned in the Guide on page 275. While many of the symptoms described here are normal in early recovery, most of them should disappear sometime during the first year (see page 404). If they don't, or if you notice any other questionable symptoms, check with your physician.

*Most of these are caused by the irritating effect of alcohol on all body tissues and organs.

THE MOST COMMON SYMPTOMS IN EARLY RECOVERY

Abdominal pain. There are many reasons why your stomach may hurt—a number of them related, at least in part, to the damage inflicted on it by rivers of alcohol. The stomach lining ordinarily protects the muscular wall of the stomach from the acidity of digestive juices. But alcohol can damage the lining, leaving the stomach open to a variety of problems, including bleeding. Damage that alcohol doesn't cause directly, it may exacerbate.

Abdominal pain in recovery—mild, middling, or severe—may be due to gastritis (stomach inflammation), a consequence of your favorite rotgut "rotting" the stomach lining. Or it may be caused by other stomach problems (page 259). Mild pain that is clearly related to the use of alcohol or other drugs will probably gradually disappear on its own, sometimes within a few days of initial sobriety. Antacids and a light or liquid diet may help rest the stomach until healing takes place. More severe pain or soreness, especially if there is any indication of internal bleeding (bloody or black, tarry stools would be one such sign), requires a careful medical workup to be sure that no serious or life-threatening condition lurks beneath the surface.

Cocaine addicts experience abdominal discomfort in the form of bloating, cramping, and gas. This usually lasts only a few days after their last fix. Recovering narcotics addicts—abusers of heroin and similar drugs—can expect cramping and gas to last a bit longer, but these symptoms usually clear up in the first few weeks.

Abdominal soreness. Soreness or tenderness below the right rib cage, often with a feeling of deep pressure, usually is related to liver damage (page 270) or pancreatitis (page 274). In most cases, continued abstinence reverses the condition over time.

Aches and pains. The theory that alcohol numbs pain is true but deceptive. It's like a shopping spree on your credit card—sooner or later, you have to pay it back with interest. That's because alcohol interferes with the body's own ability to handle pain; so when the alcohol wears off—as it does in sobriety—your body isn't ready to deal with it. Consequently, for a while you'll be noticing aches and pains more than ever before. But as your body gets back to normal, so will your reaction to pain. In most cases this will take two or three months, but if you used the slower-acting sedative drugs, tranquilizers, or narcotics, the discomfort will be slower in fading away. See page 288 for ways to deal with pain without falling back into the pain-drug-pain-drug cycle. Also see Nerve damage; Muscle pain.

Acne. Though dermatologists don't recognize a link between alcohol and acne, some alcoholics, particularly young ones, report outbreaks. This may stem in part from poor personal hygiene during active addiction that continues into early recovery. Often the problem seems worse than it is to the young recoveree whose self-image is already in tatters—so discussing the problem with a physician, your sponsor, or someone else you trust may help to put it in perspective. It's rarely a lifetime sentence since the culprit hormones level off after the teen years. See page 293 for ways to deal with acne safely.

Anemia. Alcoholics often suffer from anemia, a shortage of the important red blood cells that carry oxygen. There are several reasons. For one, alcohol damages the bone marrow, which produces red blood cells. For another, there may be internal bleeding because alcohol interferes with clotting, because of intestinal inflammation or hemorrhoids, or because of injury in a fight or a fall during a drinking or drugging binge. Since normal blood clotting depends on healthy liver function, damage to the liver by alcohol makes it tougher for the body to plug the leak, making the bleeding more severe and anemia more likely. Dietary factors also play a role in anemia (most alcoholics/addicts eat poorly), and to compound the problem, alcohol depletes the body of important nutrients or interferes with their absorption. Iron and the B vitamins, particularly B_6, B_{12}, and folic acid, are the most affected by alcohol, and inadequate stores of any of these can contribute to anemia. Many drug abusers, too, suffer from anemia—usually because of poor diet or the secondary use of alcohol.

There may be no symptoms with mild anemia, but extreme fatigue, weakness, palpitations, breathlessness, and even fainting are possible with a more severe case. Check with your doctor if you experience such symptoms. You may need a blood test to confirm or rule out anemia, and nutritional supplements if you do have the problem. The doctor should also make certain that the anemia is the result of past alcohol use and not the symptom of a serious but unrelated disease. Since a red blood cell's life expectancy is about 120 days, it may take several months of sobriety for the cells you now have to be replaced and for alcohol-related anemia to be corrected.

Anxiety attacks. These are extremely common in recovery, and there is much you can do about them. See page 326.

Arthritis. See Joint pain; also see page 261.

Black phlegm (or sputum). See Cough.

Bowel problems. See Constipation; Diarrhea. These may alternate in recovery, which can sometimes be confusing both to doctor and to patient. In some instances, the cause of this seesaw bowel activity is psychological; it's also a common problem in children who grew up in families with alcoholism/addiction.

Narcotics users often pass small frequent bowel movements for one to three weeks in early recovery. This may be a sign of withdrawal for those who suffered from constipation during active addiction, and will pass.

Breathlessness or shortness of breath. This is common in those who smoked cocaine or marijuana, and it can hang on for three to six months, and occasionally as long as a year. Sometimes it is severe enough to seem like an asthma attack. Until this worrisome symptom abates, limit any activity (for example, strenuous exercise) that brings it on.

Shortness of breath may also be a problem for alcoholics who have done damage to their hearts, as well as for former narcotics users. Again, this is a symptom that requires medical evaluation, especially if it gets much worse with exercise or when you lie flat.

Bronchitis. Bronchitis—an inflammation of bronchial-tube air passages leading to the lungs that triggers coughing—can be acute (lasting a short period of time, usually no more than a few weeks) or chronic (lasting more than a few weeks). It may be associated with the smoking of tobacco or other drugs, or it can be caused by a germ, such as a virus or bacterium. When there is a bacterial infection, coughing generally produces phlegm (often thick, yellow or greenish, and possibly foul-smelling), and antibiotic treatment is usually required. Those with chronic bronchitis from smoking are more susceptible to acute infections of the bronchial tree. See also Cough; and page 281.

Chest pain. The stress on the heart caused by cocaine use can trigger chest pain. This pain usually clears up within a few days to a couple of weeks of withdrawal. If it doesn't, major heart damage may have occurred and you should check with your physician immediately. (Do the same with any acute chest pain which lasts for more than 30 minutes and radiates to other body parts—the arm or jaw, for example. You could be having a heart attack, and quick treatment minimizes heart muscle damage.)

Constipation. Constipation (infrequent, difficult-to-pass bowel movements with hard stools) is not unusual in recovery. It may alternate exasperatingly with diarrhea. Constipation is not only uncomfortable in itself, it can also bring on hemorrhoids (page 260), so it's not wise to ignore it. For ways to prevent and treat the condition, see page 285.

Coordination problems. The nerve connections between your muscles and your brain may not be functioning at optimum levels in early recovery, so the muscles may not always do just what the brain commands. Give your body time to heal. In most cases it will within six months, unfortunately some neuromuscular conditions caused by alcohol are permanent.

Cough. Marijuana and crack-cocaine users often develop a chronic cough as a result of using the respiratory tract to deliver their drug. When the drugs are stopped, instead of getting better, the cough gets worse, and dark gray mucus is coughed up. That's because the tiny hairs that sweep the respiratory tract clean, known as cilia, until recently paralyzed by the drugs, suddenly emerge from their coma. Now they fight back, triggering coughing to expel the junk inhaled during drug use. This mopping-up action may go on for weeks, and it may feel at times like terminal TB, but it's just the normal reaction to the withdrawal of foreign substances.

For ways to treat a cough, see page 281. A cough that continues for more than a few weeks, or is associated with temperatures over 101°, needs medical evaluation. That's true even if you've had a smoker's cough for as long as you can remember. If you cough up any blood or experience localized chest pain, you have even more reason to make an appointment with your doctor.

Coughing is, of course, a perpetual problem for smokers. In recovery they often find they are coughing more and are more sensitive to cigarette smoke. This is probably the reaction of an exasperated body saying, "Enough is enough. When are you gonna stop beating up on me?" But that isn't all bad. Even if you aren't quite ready to give up yet, this exacerbation of symptoms is likely to tilt you in the direction of quitting (see Chapter 24).

Diarrhea. Alcohol, which burns like the devil's pitchfork when poured on an open wound, sorely irritates the delicate lining of the digestive tract and often causes diarrhea, nausea, and vomiting. These symptoms may continue for as long as a couple of weeks after withdrawal, but then they should disappear. If they don't, or if you see blood in your stool (it may look red, black, or tarry) or in your vomit, check with the doctor. There could be internal bleeding.

Narcotic addicts may experience diarrhea, or diarrhea alternating with constipation, in recovery. See page 280 for treatment tips.

Dry mouth. See Mouth dryness.

Ear symptoms. Ringing, buzzing, and roaring in the ears are most common among benzodiazepine users in recovery. There may also be a heightened awareness of sound in general, or a reduced ability to hear and discriminate sounds. Most of these symptoms begin to diminish in the early months of recovery.

Changes in immunity, chemical irritation, and poor hygiene while using a drug may all be reasons why alcoholics and drug addicts sometimes suffer from itching or pain in the ear canal or outer ear due to inflammation. If symptoms do not clear up within three weeks of withdrawal, check with your doctor. If fever, redness, or other signs of infection occur, however, call your doctor immediately.

Eye symptoms. "Dry" eyes may be a problem for alcoholics. As alcohol is excreted from the body in tears and other body fluids, it can cause chronic irritation. This in turn decreases the ability of the eyes to self-lubricate, leaving them dry and itchy. Time will remedy this. In the meantime, a soothing eye-drop preparation may help. See also Visual disturbances.

Fatigue. Some of the "I'm-tired-all-the-time" feeling often experienced in recovery is the result of your body machinery working overtime to get back to normal. It may also be the result of vitamin deficiency (particularly of folic acid), which could be causing anemia (page 255), so be sure to take a supplement containing the vitamin.

But some of your extreme tiredness could be caused by your doing too much too soon—in your eagerness to make up for lost time, setting a pace that is unrealistic for anyone, especially someone recovering from a severe health problem. This is not the time to play Superman or Superwoman. Do only the things necessary for your recovery at this point (see page 146). You not only do not have to do everything, you *can't* do everything and survive. And be sure to build relaxation and stress reduction, exercise, adequate sleep, and good nutrition into your daily schedule. They will all help reduce fatigue.

To wake yourself up when you're feeling zonked, get up and walk around (outside, if possible), do some stretching exercises, take a few deep breaths, drink a glass of ice cold water, talk to someone (on the phone or in person). Make sure the room you're in is well-ventilated.

Feminization. Many men would never start using if their dealers were required to put a warning on the drugs they peddle: "Use of this drug is hazardous to your masculinity." But indeed, some drugs are, notably alcohol and marijuana. Alcohol decreases levels of the male hormone, testosterone, and by damaging the liver increases levels of the female hormone, estrogen. As a result, men who drink or use heavily tend to develop feminine characteristics. Breasts may enlarge, body and facial hair lessen, fat becomes redistributed in a more female pattern (heavier around the hips). In most cases, the hormone levels return to normal in four to six months, but in some men the process is slower. In a small percentage of men—usually those who have been drinking heavily for many years—there is enough damage to the liver and the testes to interfere permanently with the return of hormone production to normal levels.

Flaking of the face. During the first week of recovery some people, particularly African-Americans, have what looks like and itches like dandruff of the face. The reason is unclear, but it may be related to the fact that alcohol leaches oils and proteins out of the skin, leaving it dry. The condition may have existed during alcohol use, unnoticed by the sedated drinker. See page 293.

Flashback sensations. Flashback—the sensation of having used a drug when none has been used—occurs during abstinence with many different kinds of drugs, including alcohol. Some former cocaine users experience a cocaine taste in the back of the mouth, often with a numbing feeling, even late in recovery. This appears to be a conditioned response of some kind, often to some stimulus in their environment (a dish of powdery sugar, perhaps). Narcotic users may be suddenly overcome with nausea, as though they had just shot up with Demerol. And former users of hallucinogens (such as PCP, LSD, or marijuana) may suddenly feel high, though they haven't been near the drug in weeks or months.

It's not always absolutely clear whether a particular episode is a flashback or not. But it really doesn't matter what you call it as long as you realize that it isn't harmful—unless it leads to a craving. When a flashback strikes, let being reminded of your drug remind you that you're still vulnerable.

Fungal infections. Male alcoholics are very susceptible to jock itch and athlete's foot. But again, they may be impervious to bodily complaints and so don't realize they are infected until they become sober. Then suddenly the itching and discomfort become unbearable. Simple over-the-counter medication (such as Tinactin) usually quickly eliminates the fungus and its discomforts. If the problem persists, see your doctor. Women alcoholics are also susceptible to fungal infection; see Vaginal infections.

Gastritis (or inflamed stomach). Early in their drinking careers, alcoholics often conclude that drinking actually makes their heartburn quiet down. But that wishful thinking doesn't last long, and soon the discomfort is worse than ever. They may have a burning sensation in the area of the stomach (just above the belt), a sour taste in the mouth, and even vomit frequently. These symptoms are caused by the severe irritation of the inside of the stomach by alcohol and are often mistaken for a stomach ulcer, especially if a doctor isn't aware of your drinking history. This gastritis may become chronic, which is why so many alcoholics also pop antacids or over-the-counter pain relievers, many of which have the adverse effect of producing more stomach irritation.*

Fortunately, with sobriety, the stomach lining heals quickly and within days of the last drink there is usually relief from the symptoms. Of course, if they persist or if there is bleeding or black stool, check with the doctor. An x-ray of the upper gastrointestinal (GI) tract or examination of it with an instrument (a gastroscope) may be necessary. When it will give the information needed, the x-ray is the better choice since a gastroscopy (the scope is inserted down the throat) usually requires a tranquilizer, narcotic, or other medication to make the patient more comfortable and the procedure more effective. If a gastroscopy is required, be sure that any medication is administered under the guidelines detailed on page 247.

Gout. Alcohol's metabolic damage inhibits the breakdown of uric acid. As levels of this substance build up in the body fluid, it sometimes crystallizes in joint cavities, causing the inflammation and exquisite pain of gout. The joint most often affected is in the big toe, but gout can also affect knees, hands, spine, feet, elbows (joints and long bones), and hips. Symptoms may worsen during withdrawal, but then usually begin to improve. With abstinence, the number of gout attacks diminishes, often even if there were other causes of the condition. If alcohol was the prime cause, the attacks usually stop entirely within the year, sometimes almost miraculously. Treatment of symptoms with muscle relaxants and narcotics should be avoided if possible, since it usually boomerangs. Tolerance develops and eventually the medication becomes useless—and for those in recovery there is the added risk of relapse. So the pain of gout should be treated with aspirin, ibuprofen, creams with salicylates in them, or with special prescription medicine for gout, rather than with mood-altering drugs.

Gums, bleeding. Cocaine damages mucous membranes, not only of the nose but of the mouth as well. Bleeding and soreness may continue briefly when cocaine use ceases but should clear up rapidly after that. Alcoholics, too, may suffer from bleeding gums for

*In some people, it is suspected that a tolerance to alcohol develops and the gastritis becomes less of a problem as the alcoholism progresses.

a short while after withdrawal, because of damage to the mucous membranes of the mouth, and to blood clotting machinery, poor nutrition, frequent vomiting of the irritating contents of the stomach, and neglect of basic dental hygiene. Again, this should clear up with abstinence and a change for the better in hygiene and lifestyle. See page 288 for tips on keeping your teeth and gums healthy.

Headache. Where the hangovers of abuse end, the headaches of early recovery sometimes begin. Some, usually centered in the forehead or the back of the head, are caused by tension. Others are probably vascular-type headaches that resemble but are not identical to migraines. In alcoholics, who ruefully wonder why their newfound virtue earns this kind of reward, headaches can continue for as long as a month or more after the last drink. In cocaine users, they may continue to recur on and off for months. Some people who never experienced (or at least never noticed) headaches while drinking or using are bothered by them in recovery for the first time. Fortunately, they are much better equipped to handle them now.

If you suffer from persistent headaches that are also accompanied by nausea and/or vomiting, disturbed vision (double vision, for example), or poor coordination, see your doctor immediately. For tips on treating headaches, see page 283.

Heart palpitations. A rapid or irregular heartbeat may occur during withdrawal—or at any time—because of the use of caffeine, chocolate, or other stimulants. Sometimes they occur for no apparent reason. If such symptoms aren't speedily resolved following withdrawal, and if cutting back on or giving up caffeine (see page 435) doesn't help, it's time to check with your doctor. An EKG (electrocardiogram) to evaluate heart function, a blood-pressure reading, and possibly other tests may be in order. Heartbeat irregularities (particularly what feels like a skipped beat) are fairly common, and though sometimes disconcerting, they are usually harmless. Don't worry about them, but do mention them to your doctor. If a heartbeat problem is associated with loss of consciousness or is set off by exercise, have your doctor check it out immediately.

Heartburn. The alcoholic who lives on beer and antacids, or on scotch with an aspirin chaser, often suffers constant heartburn. If this pain or burning sensation in the center of the chest doesn't disappear after several days of sobriety, check with your doctor. You may be suffering from gastritis (see page 259). Heartburn could also be related to hiatal hernia (see page 270).

Indigestion, gassiness, and heartburn are all common in recovery, no matter what the substance of abuse was. This may be because of the accumulation of drugs in the gastrointestinal tract, or it could be the result of a rebound effect. For example, cocaine stimulates the GI tract; with withdrawal, the system becomes sluggish and starts closing down.

Garden-variety heartburn, experienced even by paragons of sobriety, occurs when the ring of muscle separating the esophagus (which carries food from the throat) and the stomach relaxes or is otherwise pressured. This allows food and harsh digestive juices to back up from the stomach into the esophagus. The symptoms can often be avoided or at least minimized (see page 285).

Hemorrhoids. Many people in early recovery suffer from hemorrhoids, or piles—varicose veins of the rectum that can bleed, itch, burn, or ache. It isn't clear why these swollen veins, which resemble a bunch of small grapes, suddenly become a problem at this point. It may be that they result from constipation or diarrhea associated with withdrawal. Or they could be related to liver disease. Or they may have been there all along (a result of the abusers' irregular eating habits, low-fiber nutrition, and desperate straining during bowel movements); they just weren't noticed or were carelessly disregarded because of the anesthetic effects of alcohol or drugs. Whatever the cause, they can usually be prevented or alleviated (see page 285).

Any rectal bleeding should be evaluated by the doctor before it is assumed that hemorrhoids were the source.

Impotence. This condition is extremely common during early recovery. But take heart, it's not likely to last. See Chapter 11.

Indigestion. See Heartburn; also see page 285 for the treatment of indigestion.

Infection. Alcohol is no friend of the white blood cells we need to fight invading microorganisms. By reducing their numbers and effectiveness, it makes drinkers more susceptible to everything from boils, athlete's foot, and the common cold to bronchitis and pneumonia. With sobriety, the white count goes back up and susceptibility down, though how quickly varies from person to person. To help improve your resistance more rapidly, follow the Clean-and-Sober Recovery Diet (Chapter 23), get adequate exercise, work your program, and deal with tension and anxiety promptly (page 326). If you do get sick, beware of Menacing Medications, such as cough syrups (see page 281) or antihistamines (see page 276).

Infertility. Alcohol and marijuana, by killing sperm cells in the male, interfering with ovulation in the female, and decreasing sex drive in both, can impede fertility. Fertility gradually returns over the early months of recovery. Just when isn't certain, so birth control is a must if you're contemplating making love.

Intellectual problems. Fogginess, short attention span, and other thinking problems are routine in early recovery. See page 311.

Itching. Because signals may get muddled by your damaged nervous system, you may experience some rather odd symptoms, including itching. Though you can try anti-itch ointments and colloidal oatmeal baths, they aren't likely to help very much because the problem isn't your skin, but your nervous system. Meditation may help more than calamine lotion. With time in sobriety nerve endings will heal and itching will ease.

Joint pain. Like virtually every other part of your body, your joints are affected by drug abuse. Achiness should diminish during the first few months of recovery. If it doesn't, it's possible you have arthritis, which may improve but won't disappear with sobriety. See your doctor for diagnosis and treatment. See page 279 for treatment tips.

Leg cramps. Leg cramps, because of flabby muscles, are not uncommon. Be sure you're getting enough calcium (as in dairy products or supplements) and potassium (as in bananas). Stretching and moderate exercise may also help.

Memory problems. A variety of these commonly occur and are virtually always temporary. See page 311.

Menstrual irregularities. The menstrual irregularities that occur with heavy drinking or drug abuse do not suddenly vanish with sobriety. In recovery, a woman's menstrual periods can be longer or shorter than normal, more frequent or less, heavier or lighter. Or they may be totally absent.* This doesn't mean you can't get pregnant—which presents a problem, since an unplanned pregnancy in early recovery is the last thing most women need to cope with. To be safe rather than surprised and sorry, it's a good idea to use some sort of family planning or birth control.

Menstrual regularity usually returns after several months of sobriety, though emotional or physical stress may throw it temporarily out of kilter at any time. If menstrual abnormalities continue beyond the first six months of recovery, they should be discussed with your physician. (Also see Premenstrual tension.)

Minor annoyances. Throughout the day we all experience sensations that we have learned to disregard—a twitch here, a flutter there, an itch, an ache, a pain. But alcoholics and addicts don't learn to disregard these minor annoyances; instead they blot them out with chemicals. Now that your romance with chemicals is over, you have probably become newly and unduly sensitive to these normal body sensations. You may find them annoying, even worrisome, at first. Eventually you may learn to appreciate them.

Some may have an obvious cause (your feet hurt because your new shoes are too tight, or you have a stiff neck from tucking the phone between your neck and shoulder at the office), and eliminating the cause will usually eliminate the associated discomfort. Others (accelerated heartbeat during exercise or in stressful situations) may just be normal signs of a busy body at work and can't be eliminated. They can, however, be ignored, which you will gradually come to do. Still others (frequent unexplained headaches or ringing in the ears, for example) are signs that something may be wrong. You will need to learn to listen to and evaluate what your body is trying to say, to sort out the friendly everyday messages from the dire warnings.

*Of course, if you stop menstruating, it's conceivable that you've conceived. Even if you don't remember any sexual encounter during which you could have become pregnant, consider that if you had blackouts, conception could have occurred during one of them. Take a home pregnancy test or see your doctor to rule out this possibility. Other explanations for absent periods: menopause or eating disorders (page 301).

Mood swings. Almost no one escapes these in early recovery. See page 320.

Mouth dryness. Dry mucous membranes are common during the first few days of recovery. As traces of alcohol quit the body through the mouth, the evaporation promotes a drying effect. When all of the alcohol has been eliminated the dryness generally disappears, too. Drinking plenty of water may help keep the membranes moist and you more comfortable.

Mouth irritation and sores. Poor nutrition and dental hygiene, frequent vomiting, and chemical abuse during active addiction all contribute to making the mouth an uncomfortable place during early recovery. Bleeding gums, canker sores, cold sores, and other infections are all common, but they should clear up as your lifestyle improves with abstinence. Cold sores on the facial skin near the mouth can be prevented in many cases by the application of sun screen before you go into the sun; lesions on the lips may be avoided by applying a sun-screen lip product.

Muscle pain (myalgia) and weakness. Muscle tissue rarely escapes the ravages of substance abuse. It may be destroyed directly by the chemical used, or indirectly by a diminished blood supply resulting from infection, scarring, and narrowing of blood vessels caused by the use of needles. This damage is known as *myopathy.* There may be both pain and weakness, particularly in the arms and legs, sometimes accompanied by trembling and twitching.* Often even the slightest exertion (walking up several flights of stairs, carrying a suitcase, or working with the arms held overhead) causes extreme fatigue and pain. With continued abstinence, your muscles will begin to regenerate and the symptoms will begin to lessen. If the damage is severe, physical therapy may be useful or even necessary. It's best to consult your physician.

The symptoms of a disease called *fibromyalgia* are similar to the muscle problems associated with substance abuse and withdrawal, but the conditions should not be confused. Fibromyositis is treated with medication, but this is not appropriate for the treatment of those in recovery.

Sometimes, just plain old-fashioned lack of use causes muscular weakness and flabbiness. Many alcoholics and addicts get little exercise, allowing muscles to atrophy. A sudden heavy exercise program isn't the cure. Rather, exercise should be reintroduced very gradually (see page 300), to allow muscle tissue to rebuild before being subjected to stress and to avoid injury to joints and ligaments.

Muscle spasms or twitches. Your arm suddenly swings out. Your foot jerks back. Your body seems to be operating independently, out of your control. These random movements are the result of damage to the communications system between brain and muscles, and are usually most troublesome at night when you are sleeping or trying to fall asleep. They will eventually improve, but some muscle jerks are normal in early sleep and may continue. In the meantime, relaxation exercises or meditation (see page 320) may minimize the problem and help you get some shut-eye.

*Sometimes the pain is emotionally caused, though it is nonetheless real.

Myopathy. See Muscle pain and weakness.

Nerve pain (neuralgia). Like muscle tissue, nerve tissue is also subject to injury by alcohol and many drugs, particularly benzodiazepines and narcotics, such as Darvon and Darvocet. A low level of damage can cause pain along the course of one or more nerves. Although the pain usually lessens with time, it can take weeks or even years for it to cease entirely. Though such pain is probably related to years of substance abuse, it is best to double check. Therefore, report it to the doctor so other unrelated causes can be ruled out.

Neuropathy. See Numbness.

Night sweats. These are most common during the early months of sobriety, with the first few days being the most uncomfortable. Anxiety may be partially responsible, but the major cause is probably physical withdrawal itself. When the sweats occur, change to fresh clothes to keep yourself comfortable, use a fan or air conditioner to cool off when possible, and try meditation or relaxation techniques. If sweating begins suddenly later in recovery, consider the possibility of an infection (take your temperature). If you are a woman in the middle years, you may be experiencing the hot flashes of menopause. If sweating continues unabated for more than two or three weeks, gets worse instead of improving, is associated with pain, coughing, stomachaches, back pain, or diarrhea, or if it is so heavy that you have to get up and change your damp sheets in the middle of the night, check with your doctor.

Sweating during exercise, whether the cause is hot weather or that you are under stress, is normal. It's just the body's way of turning down its thermostat (just as shivering is the way the body turns the thermostat up).

Nightmares. Dreams about drinking and using are very common, particularly early in recovery. But not to worry. If you consider waking up in a sweat believing you've just blown your sobriety to be a nightmare, that's good. It means you value your recovery. Start to worry if you find such dreams enjoyable. (See page 164 for more on "drunk dreams" and how to deal with them.) Many recoverees also experience dreams that are difficult to distinguish from hallucinations.

The sudden explosion of vivid, disturbing dreams in recovery is partly psychological, the combined result of anxiety about recovery and fear of insomnia (you know you can't take anything to help you go to sleep). But it's partly physiological, too. While on alcohol or other drugs, REM sleep, the sleep during which dreams occur, was drastically cut back. In recovery there is a rebound, as though the mind is trying to catch up with all that missed dreaming. (A similar rebound effect occurs following certain types of mental illness.)

Even fairly harmless dreams may be unsettling when you have gone so long with almost no dreaming at all. This unwelcome overstock of nightly dreams can last a year or even two, but dreaming will eventually diminish to normal levels. Think of them as free entertainment, be pleased with your vivid imagination, and they may not seem so bad. Meditation should help to calm you after a particularly disturbing episode.

Nose, runny. See Runny nose.

Nosebleeds and nasal damage. As every addict knows, but may be too far gone to care, snorting cocaine can seriously damage the tissues of the nose. It can inflame and damage (ulcerate) and then actually break through (perforate) the wall between the nostrils (the nasal septum). The body responds to the damage by creating extra blood vessels—larger, more superficial, and less protected from bleeding than ordinary vessels. Breathing, especially of dry air, can irritate them and cause frequent, sometimes almost constant, nosebleeds. In recovery, the bleeds eventually diminish and finally stop. But uncomfortable crusting and annoying whistling sounds are two additional reasons why most recovering coke addicts rush to the nearest ear-nose-and-throat specialist or plastic surgeon for nasal repair. Until surgery becomes practical (often not for a year or more because even the unperforated nasal tissues are in such poor condition that the necessary graft may not take), saline nasal sprays (Nasal, Ayr, Ocean),* coating areas inside the nose that are within reach of a cotton swab with Vaseline, or moisturizing the air (see page 281) may help.

For small perforations, sometimes no other treatment is necessary, and the results of surgery, if undertaken, are generally good. But if the loss of septal cartilage has been massive, the nose may collapse, and major reconstructive surgery, mostly cosmetic and often with only limited success, must be attempted. Performing this challenging and difficult procedure on a continuing abuser would be the height of folly, and no reputable surgeon would do it on anyone who has been clean for less than a year, since the longer off the stuff, the longer the damaged tissues have a chance to recover and the better the patient's overall health. Though costly (as much as $5,000 for surgeon and anesthesiologist alone), it is not a particularly painful procedure, and the patient should be back at work in a week or less.

Numbness and tingling. Numbness, tingling, and tenderness, with or with-

*You can make your own salt solution by dissolving ¼ teaspoon salt in 1 cup of warm water. Use a clean atomizer or dropper to administer this, with your head back.

out pain, are common in alcoholics and some drug abusers. In alcoholics the feet are most likely to be affected, though sometimes the symptoms extend to the legs, hands, and arms as well. The cause is usually peripheral neuropathy, a condition in which nerve cells, particularly in the extremities, are damaged. The damage usually persists into recovery (see page 274). It can affect balance and walking, and may continue to be a problem for months and sometimes years. The course of the condition should be followed by your physician. A burning sensation in the feet is a good sign—it means that the nerves are beginning to come back to life.

Benzodiazepine users also experience distorted sensation for many months. But because these drugs don't discriminate among body parts, the sensations are just as likely to affect the trunk as the extremities.

Some patients have found that the B-complex vitamins, particularly B_6 and niacin, are helpful in reducing symptoms of neuropathy. But because they can be dangerous in high doses, you should take them only under medical supervision.

Osteoporosis. Alcohol robs the bones of calcium, making women who drink heavily (even those who are not technically alcoholics) more susceptible to fracture because of brittle bones, sometimes at a relatively early age. Men, too, particularly those who are small in stature, may suffer from osteoporosis, and excessive alcohol intake is the major cause of osteoporosis in men. During recovery, a diet rich in calcium and low in caffeine, combined with weight-bearing exercise such as walking, bicycling, or jogging, may help to improve bone density. For women in menopause, hormone replacement therapy may also be useful.

Since vitamin D is necessary for the metabolism of calcium, and since adequate exposure to sunshine is necessary to produce the vitamin, most of us in temperate climates have lower levels of it in winter—and consequently more bone loss. So for both men and women in recovery, vitamin D supplementation (but no more than the recommended daily allowance, or RDA) is probably a good idea during the short dark days of winter or if one is confined indoors most of the time and doesn't drink vitamin-D-fortified milk.

Pain. Aches and pains you never noticed before—or that you routinely medicated with your drug of choice—may surface during recovery. Now you need to deal with them in non-drug ways (see page 288).

Pneumonia. A cough associated with shortness of breath, rapid breathing, and/or chest pain is usually a sign of an infection of the lungs, or pneumonia. The invading organisms could be bacteria, viruses, or other microorganisms. This is more serious than bronchitis because it threatens the capacity of the lungs to extract oxygen for use by the body. Alcoholics/addicts are particularly susceptible to pneumonia during periods of intoxication, but the risk extends into early recovery, and any such symptoms should be reported to your doctor immediately.

The infection will be confirmed by x-ray, white blood count, and sputum examination. Treatment with injected antibiotics is often sufficient for mild cases. But if breathing becomes difficult, hospitalization, with intravenous antibiotics and possibly oxygen, will be necessary. If an abscess of the lung develops (a fairly rare occurrence), surgical drainage may be required.

Premenstrual tension and other symptoms. Most women who begin experiencing PMS as adolescents learn to deal with the discomforts—more or less. The woman who uses alcohol or other drugs deals with them too, by blocking them out with chemicals. Often PMS becomes a non-issue in active addiction because menstruation ceases entirely. When menstruation resumes in recovery, the accompanying backache, cramps, headache, tension, irritability, and depression may come as a shock. Since alcohol is a major contributor to PMS, the symptoms are often at their worst in early recovery, before the body gets back into the business of manufacturing its own painkillers again. See page 287 for tips on making the best—and the least—of PMS.

Psychosomatic ills. Symptoms of illness in humans can be caused in a variety of ways: by germs, by the reaction of the body's immune system to foreign invaders, by injury, by genetic mistake, by failure of some body system, or by the mind and the emotions. The illnesses triggered by the last two are as real as any of the others and are called *psychosomatic,* meaning that physical symptoms are caused by emotional distress. Psychomatic ills are particularly common in alcoholics/addicts, who have not been world-class champs at knowing, and clearly and honestly communicating, their feelings. Emotional distress expresses itself differently in different people. When things begin to "hurt" emotionally, Tom may get a headache, Dick a stomachache, and Harriet a skin rash. Try to interpret the way your body speaks to you when you're not treating it right. If you're honest with yourself, you'll be better than your physician at figuring out its language.

Of course, neither your doctor nor you should automatically dismiss symptoms because they seem to be psychosomatic. "Psychosomatic" illness often results in real physical damage, so it should be evaluated and treated like any other physical illness.

Runny nose. Sniffling and a runny nose can result from the use and withdrawal of several drugs, particularly opiates. When drugs are taken nasally, membranes in the nose become irritated. They can also be irritated by cigarette smoke. The cooking of drugs also irritates nasal passages. The body fights back with its inflammatory response, increasing secretions. This symptom disappears as the irritation clears up. In the meantime, treat the condition as you would an allergy (see page 276).

Sexually transmitted diseases (STD's). Active alcoholics/addicts are subject to the full gamut of STD's—gonorrhea, syphilis, chlamydia, genital warts, trichomonas (trich), candida (yeast), genital herpes, and gardnerella.* But they are often blissfully unaware of their infections, either because there are no symptoms or because their chemically-deadened brains are out to lunch. This allows the infections to do their dirty work, which can sometimes result in infertility or even serious illness. Recovery is the ideal time to check for such diseases and to stop them in their tracks if they are found. At your first medical checkup in recovery, ask to be tested for STD's. If at any time you notice suggestive symptoms (vaginal or penile discharge or oozing that may be yellowish, green and frothy, and/or foul-smelling; genital warts, blisters, sores, or other lesions; vaginal redness; vaginal odor; genital pain or itching), see your doctor. If you're a woman and the symptoms are accompanied by lower abdominal pain, see your doctor immediately.

Shakiness. Long after withdrawal is complete, some people find they are occasionally shaky and lightheaded, particularly around the time of day they usually drank or took their drugs. It feels much like an attack of hypoglycemia (low blood sugar). Liver damage, weakened muscles, and nervous sys-

*AIDS, of course, is sexually transmitted. It is discussed separately on page 309.

tem impairment may all be contributors in those who drank.

Some alcoholics treat the hereditary tendency to shakiness with alcohol. If you're one of them, hair of the dog is clearly not the ideal prescription for you. The risks of such treatment are obvious. The condition itself though anxiety-provoking is harmless. A high-protein snack may help.

Skin rashes. Possibly because of lowered resistance to infection, as well as a weakening of the skin's protective qualities because of alcohol abuse, some people have repeated skin rashes, and sometimes recurrent boils, for months, even a year or more, into recovery. For tips on skin care in recovery, see page 293.

Sleep problems. Whether you are sleepy or sleepless following withdrawal (and for how long) will depend on the drug you abused and on your personal sleep needs and patterns. From infancy, human beings need widely differing amounts of sleep and take that sleep in different ways (often to their parents' dismay). Most adults can readily describe their normal sleep patterns. But in alcoholics and addicts, the sleep pattern has been chemically disrupted for so long that they usually have no idea at all what is "normal" for them.

In early recovery, they aren't likely to find out. Their bodies are still rebounding wildly from the effects of their drugs of choice. Those who had been using alcohol or other depressant drugs usually find it difficult to fall asleep, and staying asleep just as hard. Those withdrawing from benzodiazepines often can't sleep at all. Those who had been using stimulant drugs, on the other hand, may feel like sleeping around the clock. In a sense they're catching up, and even ten hours a night often seems like a mere catnap.

It takes time for a brain to rehabilitate itself after being under siege during years of chemical warfare. Disordered sleep patterns in recovery may clear up in as little as five or six days, take weeks or months, or hang on for a year or more. In the meantime, you'll lose less sleep worrying about your sleep problems if you keep three points in mind:

❖ There is no such thing as a "normal" sleep pattern. Don't obsess, complain, or even think about being unable to sleep (or sleeping too much). Even among people who've never abused alcohol or other drugs, that legendary eight hours of sleep touted in junior high school health classes is a myth. Sleep patterns vary from person to person, and in the same person at different ages. Some people get along fine on five hours of sleep a night; for others nine or ten never seems enough.

❖ The sleeping pattern you settle into in the months ahead may be entirely different from the one you had before you began drinking or using. You've been sedated or high for so many years that your internal body clock may have been thrown totally out of balance. If you started to use in your teens, you never had a chance to develop an adult sleeping pattern.

❖ Drugs of any kind are not an effective long-term treatment for sleeping problems. If you're not sleeping, or are sleeping too much, see page 293 for non-drug ways of dealing with these problems.

Slowed reflexes. Most drinkers assume that once they're on the wagon, their reflexes will quickly return to normal. Not so. You'll probably discover that not only are your reflexes still slower than normal, your overall motor performance isn't up to par either. (Just where your deficits are may depend on your sex. In general, studies show that women appear to have slower reflexes in recovery, while men seem to make more errors on simple tasks; both make errors on very difficult tasks.) That means you have to be particularly cautious when driving or operating machinery and, at least for a while, should lower your expectations when participating in sports or activities like video games that depend on rapid responses. Over the next few months, your coordination will gradually improve and, if (a vital *if*) you remain clean and sober, eventually it will return to normal. In the meantime, go slow, especially where risk to yourself or others is involved.

Sore throat. Many alcoholics find their throats are raw and red in early recovery. Possible contributing factors include long-term irritation from both downing alcohol and bringing it back up, smoking, and a weakened immune system. Abstention from both alcohol and tobacco will allow the throat to heal in time. For dealing with the discomfort, see page 296.

Tiredness. See Fatigue.

Tremors. See Shakiness.

Vaginal bleeding. Some women experience excessive vaginal bleeding (this is not necessarily menstrual blood) during alcohol detox. This is probably related to the hormonal changes accompanying the withdrawal of the drug, but it's best to check with the doctor to be sure there's nothing else going on.

Vaginal infections. During the early months of recovery many women notice symptoms of vaginal infection. If it's a yeast infection, there will be itching and irritation, and possibly redness and swelling of the vulva (the inner folds of the area around the vagina), along with a thick cheesy discharge. With other types of infection there may be a greenish yellow foul-smelling discharge. These infections require medical diagnosis and treatment, so call your doctor if you experience them. If you have a discharge along with lower abdominal pain, call your doctor immediately or go to the emergency room. You may have a pelvic infection, which could put your fertility at risk. See page 297 for information about prevention and treatment of vaginal infections; see also Sexually Transmitted Diseases.

Visual disturbances. Just when your mind begins to see the world more clearly, your vision may become alarmingly blurred. You may also experience difficulty focusing and find it hard to concentrate on reading. Don't run to get checked for new glasses. Some of these changes relate to normal aging of the eyeballs, but alcohol and other drugs apparently alter the sensitive metabolic balance necessary to maintain stable visual sharpness and acuity. In any case, your eyes are in a state of temporary flux. If they are not extremely disabling or inconvenient, wait at least three to four months for these symptoms to disappear. Then get your eye checkup and new prescription. Obviously, if your safety or someone else's depends on your visual acuity, you may need to get a transitional prescription immediately and may have to go through several more before stabilization occurs.

Night blindness from alcohol use may also persist into recovery. This is apparently the result of an ailing liver's inability to metabolize vitamin A, the vitamin which, as you no doubt learned in public school, helps turn you into an owl at night. Until the doctor says your liver is back to normal, you won't be able to take any vitamin A supplements, but you should be able to safely eat plenty of carrots, sweet potatoes, and green leafy vegetables rich in beta-carotene in the meantime. See also Eye symptoms.

Wheezing. Though addicts can, of course, have asthma apart from their drug use, some develop wheezing (noisy, difficult breathing, especially on breathing out) and other symptoms of asthma because of an allergic reaction to inhaled or intravenous drugs or because of damage done to the respiratory tract by drug use (see page 279).

As you can see, there's many a pothole and not a few flat tires on the road to recovery, and many a puzzling, unexpected, and disquieting physical symptom. Most—maybe even all of them—will be healed by that master physician, Dr. Time. Odds are your symptoms are just recovery-related. But because some of them (particularly sleep problems, gastric discomfort, and pain) could mask disease unrelated to your addiction, it makes sense to have your doctor evaluate them—especially if they continue or worsen past the withdrawal phase of your recovery. That's true, too, of any other unusual symptoms you experience that are not listed here. Now that you've stopped abusing it, your body is on speaking terms with you again, and it could be trying to tell you something.

If no unrelated medical problem is found, it's very possible that your symptoms are somewhat different or just slower in making their exit than most. But it is also possible that these symptoms are alarm bells warning you that your recovery is shakier than you think. Some people, instead of craving a drink or a drug, display an increase in unexplained physical ills (aches and pains, minor infections) or emotional symptoms (mood swings, depression) as a sign of impending relapse. It's a kind of nonspecific cry for help from a body in denial preparing for the worst. Heed the cry. Talk to your sponsor, counselor, or physician about your concern, and together decide what you can do about it. Increasing attendance at AA meetings may be one solution. Another may be some outpatient treatment, or possibly even a short relapse-prevention booster as an inpatient to improve your recovery skills and odds.

HOLDOVER MEDICAL PROBLEMS

Alcoholism and addiction leave their scars, not only on your psyche, but on your body. Some of their effects are long-lasting, even permanent. It's important to stay on the alert for serious medical problems that may result from past drinking or drug use, either immediately or in the future.

Cancer. Alcoholics have an increased risk of certain cancers—most commonly malignancies of the head and neck, esophagus, liver, lung (associated with wine and whiskey), rectum (beer), and breast. Combining smoking (tobacco, and probably marijuana) and drinking increases the risk of esophageal cancer. Smoking alone increases the risks of mouth and tongue cancers, cancers of the larynx, bladder, and kidneys, and of the lung. Abstinence will reduce the risks gradually over the next ten years, but it's wise for those in recovery (as well as everyone else) to be aware of the symptoms that could signal cancer and that require immediate consultation with a physician (page 272).

Gastritis and other stomach problems. The damage done to the stomach and the rest of the digestive tract usually heals quickly in recovery. If symptoms continue well into recovery and simple remedies (see page 285) don't avail, then a medical workup is in order.

Heart muscle damage. That moderate drinking (about two drinks a day) may help reduce the risk of a heart attack, as some studies suggest, is debatable. Not open to question, however, is the fact that heavy drinking and drug use can damage the heart and the blood vessels that serve it and can raise levels of low-density lipoproteins (LDL), the "bad" cholesterol. That puts heavy drinkers at an increased risk of having a heart attack. The risk will diminish as sobriety grows. But in the meantime, be on the alert for possible signs of a heart problem: extreme shortness of breath and/or chest pain on exertion; swelling (edema) of ankles, hands, face; a racing heartbeat; a "fluttering" in the chest; the inability to breathe comfortably when you are lying down. If you experience any of these symptoms, don't panic—there may be a perfectly innocent explanation. But do check with your doctor at once.

Hiatal hernia. It was once believed that peptic ulcers were caused by alcohol consumption. But things change, even in medicine. Now the thinking is that what appears to be a peptic ulcer in alcoholics is usually a hiatal hernia (or sometimes gastritis; see page 259). A hiatal hernia occurs when a portion of the stomach pushes up through the opening in the diaphragm through which the esophagus passes as it carries food to the stomach. Often there are no symptoms. But sometimes, particularly in alcoholics, there are symptoms of heartburn, or gastric reflux (see page 260). This may be because the alcohol dissolves the mucus that protects the lining of the stomach and esophagus, directly irritates the unprotected tissues, and boosts acid production. Dealing with the condition is important because the irritation of the esophagus can cause bleeding and increase the risk of esophageal cancer.

You can minimize symptoms by following the tips for dealing with heartburn on page 285. See your doctor if they fail to help; prescribed medication, or even surgery, may be needed.

Infectious hepatitis. In this type of hepatitis the liver damage is caused by an infectious organism (usually hepatitis B virus, but sometimes hepatitis C), rather than by an overdose of alcohol (as in alcoholic hepatitis; facing page). Since hepatitis B and C are transmitted via the blood or other body fluids, IV drug users usually contract this disease through the sharing of contaminated hypodermic needles.* Symptoms include yellowing of the whites of the eyes and possibly a yellowish tinge to the skin; fatigue and a general feeling of being unwell; bleeding problems, because the damaged liver can't fulfill its role in the clotting of blood; pain, usually in the upper right abdomen; nausea and vomiting; loss of appetite; and loss of the taste for tobacco. Prompt treatment is important.

Liver damage. Though alcohol affects virtually every cell in every body system, the liver takes the most punishment. That's because it's the liver that processes toxic (poisonous) substances, including alcohol and drugs, in our bloodstream, in a gallant attempt to render them harmless. Excesses of alcohol (as little as three drinks a day) and of some drugs taken by mouth can overtax the liver's purifying machinery, eventually causing it to malfunction.

If you have not already had a medical exam during treatment, have one to check liver function, among other things. Doctors keep track of liver health by measuring the blood levels of the "enzymes" (SGOT, SGPT, GGT), which are released into the blood when a liver cell dies. The higher the levels, the greater the liver damage.

Three kinds of liver damage commonly occur in alcoholics:

---

*Hepatitis B, and probably C, can also be passed via sexual intercourse or through accidental contact with infected blood in a hospital setting. Hepatitis A is transmitted through stool contamination and oral ingestion, and so different precautions are necessary. If you're infected, ask your doctor how you can avoid spreading the disease to others.

Fatty liver (steatosis). This condition is almost universal among those who imbibe excessively. The liver, located in the upper right abdomen, is enlarged and tender to pressure, but the alcoholic may notice no symptoms.

The best way to treat your fatty liver is to work your recovery program. With abstinence and a healthier lifestyle, the liver almost always returns to normal. How quickly this happens depends on how much alcohol has been ingested and for how long, and can vary anywhere from two weeks to many months or more. Good nutrition—and taking a supplement containing thiamine and the other B-complex vitamins during detox and after—can help speed the return of normal liver function. It's also suspected, but hasn't been proved, that a low-fat diet may hasten the healing process. Excesses of vitamin A (but not beta-carotene) on the other hand can slow it down, or even damage the liver independently. *Do not* take any supplements containing vitamin A if your liver is still not back to normal.

Alcoholic hepatitis. This condition is more severe than fatty liver. Its cause isn't known for certain, but it is believed to be related to the immune system's response to the toxic effects of alcohol on living cells. Again, there may be no symptoms, but observant friends may spot the telltale jaundice (a yellowing of the skin and the whites of the eyes), resulting from a buildup of bilirubin in the blood. Often, however, there is nausea, vomiting, and loss of appetite; fatigue and malaise; pain in the upper right quarter of the abdomen; and intermittent fever. There may also be weight loss. Perhaps most dangerous and disarming is the fact that as the liver deteriorates, pain and tenderness may tend to lessen or disappear.

If alcohol consumption is continued, the condition gets worse, often progressing to cirrhosis—though sometimes cirrhosis occurs without hepatitis developing. With abstinence from alcohol, about 70 percent of livers eventually return to normal. (Occasionally, the condition gets worse before it gets better.) In an unfortunate 30 percent, the condition persists or even progresses.

Though jaundice is not, as was once believed, a result of poor nutrition in alcoholics, good nutrition can hasten healing. Treatment usually includes a low-protein, high-calorie diet, with an emphasis on thiamine and the other B vitamins, and sometimes salt restriction, depending on complications.

Cirrhosis. The longer an alcoholic continues to drink, the greater the chance of developing cirrhosis, the end stage of the progression that begins with fatty liver. One study showed that one pint of whiskey a day for thirty years gave a drinker a 50 percent chance of developing the condition. Women, because of their smaller size and the way their bodies handle alcohol, can develop cirrhosis on less alcohol in less time. The specific mechanism that leads to the cirrhosis is unclear, though it is speculated that in addition to the direct toxicity of alcohol, malnutrition, the immune system, and/or genetics, may possibly play a role. For reasons that aren't clear, intravenous drug use along with alcohol consumption multiplies the chances of developing cirrhosis. Hepatitis B infection, too, may lead to cirrhosis.

Cirrhosis mugs one in ten victims without a warning symptom of any kind. The other nine may experience nausea, vomiting, and fatigue; abdominal pain; fever; or jaundice. Medical examination may show signs of increased blood pressure in the veins that carry blood containing the products of digestion to the liver. Because the liver is involved in the cycle of reproductive hormone production, there may also be menstrual irregularities or even a complete absence of menstruation in women. Even the most macho of men may suffer embar-

CANCER WARNING SIGNS

Though your first reaction to the heading "Cancer Warning Signs" may be to quickly turn to the next page, not only reading but memorizing these signs could save your life. For almost all cancers, the difference between survival and non-survival is early detection. So if at any point you notice any of these signs, check with your doctor on the very first day you can reach him or her.

But don't panic. While these symptoms are sometimes signs of cancer, they can also be signs of minor illness, of no illness at all, or, occasionally, residual effects of your alcohol or drug abuse. But only a careful examination and review of your history by a physician can tell you for sure what these symptoms really mean. The most favorable verdict, of course, will be a reassuring "No malignancy." But even if a cancer is found, early treatment will tremendously improve your chances of beating the rap.

❖❖ A sore, lump, thickening, or raised warty area in the mouth (with or without pain) that does not heal or disappear within two weeks; white patches in the mouth.

❖ A sore, unrelated to injury, anywhere on the body, that does not heal within two weeks.

❖ Obvious changes in a wart or mole. This includes sudden or continuous growth, itching, bleeding, crusting, erosion, oozing, scaling, softening, hardening, tenderness, or pain. Also suspect are redness, swelling, or the eruption of new blemishes around an existing lesion, and other skin lesions (such as a dry scaly patch; an inflamed red area with a crusting center; a pale, waxy, pearly nodule; or an ulcerated area or sore) that persist for two weeks or more. Requiring immediate medical examination are "ABC" growths: A for Asymmetry (one side is unlike the other); B for Border unevenness (the perimeter is notched or blurred); and C for Color variations (a mixture of shades and colors, including black, blue, brown, red, tan, and white).

❖❖ A persistent cough or hoarseness, unexplained by cold, flu, or smoking, with or without difficulty in swallowing; soreness in the neck; a lump-in-the-throat feeling; or bloody sputum. (Even when a cough is explained by smoking, malignancy can

rassing breast enlargement and demoralizing shrinking of the testicles. The most serious complication of cirrhosis is the occasional development of hepatoma (liver cancer) down the road.

Only a liver biopsy (examining a sample of the liver in the laboratory) positively establishes a diagnosis of cirrhosis.

The core of treatment is maintaining a healthy distance between yourself and the nearest bottle. In less severe cases, those who are completely abstinent have a 90 percent chance of survival for five years; those who are not, only a 65 percent chance. In more severe cases, the five-year survival rate is poorer: 55 percent in abstainers, 33 percent in those who continue their drinking. The odds are best for abstainers who have no liver complications in the first year; their survival rate is 85 percent.

Treatment also includes a nutritious diet, with extra calories if necessary. Depending upon associated problems, sodium and/or protein may be restricted, medication given, or other medical procedures employed. Cases of liver failure may respond to the use be present. All smokers should have chest x-rays as part of their physical.)

❖ Unusual bleeding. Report rectal or vaginal bleeding; recurrent bleeding under the skin (as in unexplained black-and-blue marks or bruises); bleeding from the gums or nose.

❖❖ Blood in urine or stool (bowel movement may be bright red, dark red, or black and tarry); blood in phlegm or sputum (coughed or spit up); blood in vomitus, or vomit that looks as though it has coffee grinds in it.

❖❖ Indigestion that doesn't appear related to something you ate, particularly if it is a new symptom or if it recurs regularly. Other persistent or recurrent intestinal symptoms, such as mild bloating, pain, or fullness; slight nausea; heartburn; loss of appetite. Belching and vomiting, particularly when accompanied by blood in stools or vomitus—also require prompt investigation.

❖❖ An unexplained change in bowel or bladder habits, such as a sudden stretch of diarrhea or constipation, not connected with an illness or your recovery; or a weak or interrupted flow of urine along with lower back, thigh, or pelvic pain, and/or burning or painful urination. Also suspect: pencil-like stools (with narrow diameter).

❖❖ Difficulty swallowing, even food you have chewed thoroughly, with or without soreness in the neck and/or a "lump-in-the-throat" feeling.

❖ A painless thickening or lump in the breast (if you're a woman, do monthly self breast exams*), the testicles (men should also do regular self exams), or elsewhere, particularly the lymph node areas (armpit, groin, neck, and jaw). If you don't know how to do a self exam or need a refresher course, don't be embarrassed to ask your doctor for help. It could save your life.

❖ A generalized feeling of being unwell that just doesn't go away, with fatigue, loss of appetite, weight loss, persistent unexplained fever, and sometimes unexplained pain.

*And, of course, have an annual mammogram. The American Cancer Society recommends that women 40 to 49 have one every one to two years, and those over 50 have them annually. Some experts believe a mammogram isn't necessary until a woman turns 50.

❖❖Be particularly alert for this sign if you have abused alcohol, smoked cigars, pipes, or cigarettes, or chewed tobacco.

of Cephulac (a nonabsorbable sugar known generically as lactulose), which in a massive laxative sweep clears out the gastrointestinal tract, eliminating all toxic substances (including ammonia and bacteria) in its path—substances a sick liver has been unable to process. The major side effect, diarrhea, is a small price to pay for the tremendous improvement that often occurs.

Of course, with all types of liver damage, abstinence from alcohol is essential. If you relapse, irreversible damage could occur, and liver transplants (if they are available for alcoholics at all) are not a dime a dozen. And, in fact, there is some question as to whether alcoholics should be eligible for them. Though it's important to get treatment when recommended for your liver problem, spending all your time worrying about it could distract you from your main task: building a sober lifestyle. Without that, all the treatment in the world won't help.

Optic neuropathy. The eyes do not escape the damage inflicted by alcohol. You won't find it in whiskey ads, but chronic alcoholism leads to reduced vision, blurred vision, vision distortions, spots, and diminished color vision. Smoking compounds the problem. Abstention from both alcohol and tobacco, plus a good diet and vitamin supplements, halts the progression of the condition, but sometimes residual vision loss remains.

Pancreatitis. Inflammation of the pancreas occurs in many heavy drinkers. Though it happens most often to those who have been drinking for ten or fifteen years, the really serious drinker can do a number on the pancreas in as little as two years. Since the pancreas supplies the intestinal digestive juices that normally dissolve the food we eat, it is easy to imagine how disruption of its normal function presents a problem. When these juices are unable to get to the intestines to do their job, they begin to digest the pancreas itself. The end result: pain and digestive problems. The pain, in the upper abdomen, right or left side, is severe and stubbornly steady. It usually radiates to the back between the shoulder blades. Some relief can be obtained by sitting with the knees drawn up, forearms folded across the abdomen. Because the digestive juices aren't operating effectively, nausea and vomiting are usually present, and at times constipation. The patient generally feels sick and is anxious, restless, distressed. The skin may be mottled, and the hands and feet cold and sweaty. The heartbeat may be rapid, and there may be fever. Sometimes there are black-and-blue (or blue-green) marks on the flanks or around the navel, indicating internal bleeding.

Most people begin to feel better after a week of sobriety, but complications can extend the course of the disease. Treatment may include, in addition to abstinence, suctioning of the gastrointestinal tract through a tube in the nose; antibiotics (usually if there is fever); and IV fluids for the first few days, followed by a liquid diet and then a gradual return to a regular diet. If the pain is very severe, narcotics may be necessary—taken under carefully controlled conditions, of course (see page 247). A single alcohol binge can bring a rapid return of pancreatitis.

Pancreatitis sometimes becomes chronic, particularly in people with an abnormal pancreas. Both malnutrition (too little protein and fat) and overnutrition (too much protein and fat) have been suggested as factors in chronic pancreatitis, but there is no consensus in support of either theory. Symptoms of chronic pancreatitis include recurrent episodes of abdominal pain of varying intensity over weeks or months; occasional jaundice; and fatty stools that are difficult to flush. The patient often looks thin and malnourished, and appears older than his or her actual age. The condition can be fatal sometimes. Unfortunately, abstinence does not always prevent recurrence in the last stages of the disease. Pancreatic enzymes are given along with vitamins to reverse malnutrition, narcotic analgesia for pain (but under close supervision), and drugs (and sometimes insulin) to lower blood sugar levels.

Peripheral neuropathy. This condition, which appears to be the result of the direct toxic effect of alcohol on the peripheral nervous system and of vitamin deficiency, usually begins in active alcoholics as a tingling, numbness, and tenderness in the feet, which then creeps up the legs and may later progress into fingers, hands, and arms. Weakness and difficulty balancing become apparent and can make walking awkward, even impossible. The condition can also cause impotence.

Abstention from alcohol doesn't bring miraculous relief. It generally takes months, sometimes years, of sobriety along with a good diet, plenty of foods rich in B vitamins, vitamin supplements, and sometimes medication to eliminate these symptoms. Sometimes residual problems persist. If they do, a medical workup is in order to be sure there is not some underlying disease, such as diabetes.

THE GOOD NEWS: CHRONIC CONDITIONS THAT TEND TO IMPROVE IN RECOVERY

The early recovery health news isn't all depressing. The good news is that some health problems clear up or improve rather quickly following withdrawal.

Diabetes. Alcohol damage to the pancreas and liver tends to worsen diabetes. When they quit drinking, many people who began taking oral medication for diabetes as adults find they no longer need it. Even insulin-dependent diabetics may improve enough so that they are able to give up their insulin shots. If you're a diabetic, your disease should be reevaluated very early in recovery so that changes can be made in your treatment.

Hypertension. Heavy alcohol consumption can raise your blood pressure (as well as that of the people around you). With abstention, blood pressure often returns to normal. Many people who have been on medication while drinking suddenly find they can do without it when they quit. Don't stop taking medication without checking with your doctor, of course, but do have your hypertension evaluated once you are into recovery. You may be pleasantly surprised.

As a precaution, have your blood pressure checked frequently during recovery to be sure it hasn't sneaked up again. To help keep it down, don't smoke, maintain a diet low in sodium (see page 436), watch your weight, and get regular exercise (see Chapter 25).

NON-DRUG APPROACHES TO MEDICAL PROBLEMS

Turn on your TV, open a magazine, switch on the radio, and you will hear that there's a pill to cure what hurts you. Whether it's sinus pain, a cold, a backache, a toothache, or a tension headache, America's fabulous pharmaceutical marketeers can sell you a pill for it. It's no wonder then that from earliest childhood we learn to rely on the quick fix for solving our problems. Well, if you're in recovery, the quick fix is no longer the best fix—if indeed it ever was.

You don't have to be in recovery to look at drugs and medications as a last resort in treating minor medical problems at home. Cultivating such an attitude can not only help prevent a relapse, it can help avoid the mind-set that popping a pill is the answer to virtually every problem in life. It's particularly useful in teaching children to live drug-free lives.

Just as it's important for your general health to learn to read labels in the supermarket, it's important for your recovery health to learn to read labels in the drugstore. Avoid all suspicious ingredients (including alcohol, antihistamines, codeine or other narcotics, sedatives, and stimulants, such as are found in "diet" pills) and any product that warns of "drowsiness."

Of course, sometimes medication is necessary to health and safety. So don't reject it when the benefits outweigh the risks. And there are many medications that do not put recovery at risk, and which may be necessary in certain situations. Antibiotics, for example, insulin, diuretics, anticoagulants, most blood-pressure medications (though reserpine—Serpasil Hydromox, Hydropres, Salutensin, etc.—could be hazardous to some), digitalis, and vitamin preparations. Alcohol-free children's medications that do not contain any other risky ingredients, taken in doses recommended for age twelve and over, may also be okay.*

Knowing what to avoid, what is safe, and what to do as a last resort to treat the most common illnesses will help safeguard your recovery. Remember, you are always better off if you can eliminate the cause rather than simply treating the symptoms.

ALLERGIES

Treatment to avoid: Popping a pill. Particularly dangerous to depend on are most antihistamines, which, though they do counteract the allergic response, are mood-altering. Avoid all allergy medicines containing antihistamines, such as brompheniramine, chlorpheniramine, tripolidine (Actifed, Alka-Seltzer Plus, Allerest, Chlor-trimeton, Congespirin, Contac, Coricidin, Dimetane, Dristan, Novahistine, NyQuil, Sinarest, Sinutab, Sominex, Sudafed, Triaminic and Triaminicin). Also avoid any allergy medication containing alcohol, or ephedrine or pseudoephedrine.

Treatment to substitute: First of all, before you treat, be sure you have allergies. Some symptoms of alcoholism mimic allergy. Alcohol perniciously washes oils and proteins out of skin and mucous membranes, causing runny, sniffly noses, watering eyes, peeling skin. Other drugs can cause nasal symptoms, skin rashes, and assorted allergy-like symptoms. If you are sure allergy is the problem, try a non-drug approach first. There are two ways of dealing with allergy; one is by doing something about the allergen that is triggering the symptoms, and the other is by treating the person having the allergic response. It's best to do both.

The Allergen

Try to identify what it is that's driving your immune system crazy. Sometimes it's obvious (every time a cat pads by, you sneeze and your eyes swell up; or your skin breaks out in hives whenever you eat strawberries). Sometimes a little detective work is necessary. If you think it's a food causing the problem, eliminate one or more suspects from your diet and see if the symptoms subside. If they do, and they then return when you eat the food again, you have your culprit. If it's pollen, note if symptoms worsen when pollen counts are high (local weather reports usually include pollen counts in season). If you always have a reaction in one room of the house and not others, try to figure out what's different in that room. In other words, play allergen detective. If you fail to uncover the tormenting allergen, have an allergist do some skin testing.

Once you know, or even suspect, the offender (or offenders), try to eliminate it (or them) from your life. At home you might try to create one allergy-free room—ideally your bedroom. Consider the following:

❖ *Foods.* Avoid eating anything that triggers a reaction. Always ask before you take the first bite.

❖ *Animal dander.* Stay away from dogs and cats. If you have a pet, you may have to find another home for it (unless you can be desensitized; see page 278). Since the old gray mare may

*Don't rely on any list, this one included. Learn to read labels and look for risky ingredients. Formulas can and do change. For the latest on non-drug ways of dealing with physical ailments, order the "Self-Care Catalog" by calling 1-800-345-3371.

also cause a problem, don't sleep on a horsehair mattress, or at least cover it with a plastic mattress cover.

❖ *Household dust.* Keep your home as dust-free as possible. Dust daily with a damp cloth or furniture spray; vacuum upholstery and carpeting, damp-mop floors, and wash curtains and similar items frequently; avoid chenille bedspreads, velour upholstery, any kind of carpeting, draperies, and other dust-catchers where you sleep; install an air cleaner, and place filters over forced-air vents; avoid fans (which can stir up allergens).

❖ *Carpets.* Rugs and carpets are often hideouts for sinister allergens. Dust, microscopic mites, animal debris, mold, and chemical residues collect in carpet pile and may be almost impossible to get out and keep out. Hardwood, tile, and vinyl flooring are sensible substitutes when carpets are suspect. If you have carpeting that can't be easily replaced, a sturdy plastic covering, though less than elegant, should minimize allergic reactions.

❖ *Molds.* These most often grow outdoors in the summer and fall, but they can be a problem anywhere, any time of year, especially in damp climates. When humidity is high, control the moisture level in your home by using a well-maintained dehumidifier, providing adequate ventilation, and exhausting steam in kitchen, laundry, and bathrooms. Areas where molds are likely to grow (garbage cans, refrigerators, shower curtains, bathroom tiles, damp corners) should be cleaned meticulously with an antimold agent. Limit the number of houseplants in the rooms where you spend a lot of time, and store firewood away from the house.

Out-of-doors, avoid damp wooded areas, particularly where fallen leaves and tree stumps have been left to decay. Be sure drainage is adequate around your house. Rake leaves frequently so they don't have time to begin to grow mold, or have someone else rake them; dispose of leaves and other garden debris promptly. Cover your child's sandbox when it rains. And allow plenty of sun to reach your property (mold thrives in the shade).

❖ *Bee venom.* If you've ever had a bad reaction to a bee sting, see your doctor about the possibility that you are allergic to the venom. If you are, your doctor may recommend that you carry a bee sting kit or may suggest a series of desensitizing injections. In the meantime, avoid airspace that bees or wasps think of as theirs alone.

❖ *Miscellaneous allergens.* There are many other potential allergens that can be removed from your environment as necessary: wool blankets (cover them, or use cotton or synthetic blankets); down or feather pillows (use foam or hypoallergenic polyester-filled ones); tobacco smoke (keep your house

THE BEST MEDICINE

No matter what ails you, keeping your recovery program strong is your best medicine. At least 350 separate diseases have been linked to the use of alcohol; avoiding the chemical for the rest of your life reduces your risk of all of them. A study of men shows that alcoholics who relapse die at nearly five times the rate of other men of the same age and race. Those who stay sober eventually live as long as nonalcoholic men. Experts speculate that the figures are equally grim for women alcoholics and for those who abuse other drugs.

smoke-free; avoid smoke in other locations); perfumes (use unscented cleaning items, laundry detergents, sprays, deodorants, facial tissues, toilet paper, etc.); soaps and cosmetics (use the hypoallergenic types).

Avoiding allergens away from home may be more difficult. Sometimes you can simply steer clear of places that offend (if you're allergic to fragrances, stay out of stores where the air is perfumed; if tobacco smoke is your nemesis stick to no-smoking destinations). Of course, if the allergens are lurking in your workplace, the problem is more difficult. If there is an EAP or a medical staff, consult with them about your problem. If not, speak directly to your employer or supervisor. Possible changes include: limiting smoking to specific well-ventilated areas, moving your work station away from whatever it is that's bothering you, putting in an air-filter system, taking down drapes or picking up carpeting in your office, transferring you to a job with less exposure to allergens, or whatever will help you breathe easier and, not incidental to them, work better.

The Person

It isn't possible to eliminate all allergens from your life. Instead you may be able to change the way you respond to them by undergoing desensitization through gradually increasing injected doses of the offending allergen. Desensitization is particularly effective in allergies to pollen, dust, and animal dander. See your doctor about this.

You can also try treating the symptoms. For example, hot showers and humidifiers (see page 283) for respiratory problems.

Last-resort treatment: Two new antihistamines, Seldane (terfenadine) and Hismanal (astemizole), reportedly do not cross the blood-brain barrier (they don't travel from the bloodstream into the brain) and therefore don't exert a mood-altering effect. In theory these appear safe for recovering people, but only time and experience can guarantee that. The perceived safety of these drugs in recovery may be less as we learn more. Some physiological risks have already surfaced. Seldane when combined with certain medications or when there is liver damage and Hismanal when taken in excessive doses may have serious side effects. Still, if an antihistamine is required, these are preferred. Check with your addiction specialist or a knowledgeable family physician for the latest data.

In certain cases, your doctor may suggest that topical steroids or a short course of oral steroids may be useful.

ANXIETY

Treatment to avoid: Tranquilizers seem like an easy way to rid yourself of anxiety. But the easy way, as you have undoubtedly learned by now, usually isn't the best way. To protect your recovery, avoid all tranquilizers (benzodiazepine) and other mood-altering drugs, including those containing alprazolam (Xanax), buspirone hydrochloride (BuSpar), chlordiazepoxide (Librium, Limbitrol*), clorazepam (Klonopin), clorazepate (Tranxene), diazepam (Valium), flurazepam (Dalmane), halazepam (Paxipam), haloperidol (Haldol), lorazepam (Ativan), midazolam (Versed), oxazepam (Serax), prazepam (Centrax), temazepam (Restoril), thioridazine (Mellaril), thiothixine (Navane), or triazolam (Halcion).

Treatment to substitute: Anxiety can best be eliminated by eliminating its cause. When this isn't possible, coping with the cause effectively reduces the anxiety. Meditation, exercise, relaxation techniques, yoga, going to an AA meeting, and talking to your sponsor or counselor all help. For more tips on dealing with anxiety safely, see page 326.

---

*Limbitrol also contains an antidepressant.

Last-resort treatment: If your anxiety is long-lasting (more than a few weeks), debilitating (interfering with your work or with other parts of your life), or has you thinking self-destructive thoughts, get help from a professional experienced in working with recovering alcoholics/addicts. Talk therapy may be sufficient.

ARTHRITIS

Treatment to avoid: Do not use mood-altering painkillers (see page 288).

Treatment to substitute: Apply creams containing salicylates to the painful joints. Heat (via hot baths, whirlpools, heating pads, or even an electric blanket), special exercises and weight loss (if you're overweight) may also be helpful. One recent study suggests that a vegetarian diet can substantially reduce symptoms—possibly because of the switch from fatty acids of animal origin to those from plants. More studies need to be done, but cutting down on animal fat can't hurt.

Last-resort treatment: Use aspirin, ibuprofen (Advil, Medipren, Motrin, Nuprin), or acetaminophen (Anacin III, Datril, Tylenol), as directed by your doctor; studies show they are generally as effective as stronger drugs. When an anti-inflammatory action is needed, aspirin, ibuprofen, or other nonsteroidal anti-inflammatory drugs (NSAIDs) are best.

ASTHMA

Treatment to avoid: If possible, avoid treatment with antiasthma medicines, such as AsthmaHaler Mist; Benadryl; Benylin; Brethine; Bronkosol; Elixophyllin; Metaprel; Primatene;* Proventil; Slo-Phyllin; Vanceril; Ventolin; or others containing epinephrine, theophylline, isoetharine, terbutaline, albuterol, or other bronchodilators. These drugs produce a stimulant side effect, usually making the user jittery. Fortunately it isn't a pleasant feeling, but then how many addicts do you know who care whether the high they get is pleasant or not?

Treatment to substitute: Preventing an asthma attack is the best way to go, since treatment always has a risk because the usually prescribed medications do affect mood to some degree. If allergies trigger an attack, eliminate as many triggers as possible (see Allergy). If you have exercise-induced asthma, discuss with your doctor how you can get some exercise without experiencing a flare-up. Take good care of yourself and try to avoid colds and other upper respiratory infections, as well as excessive stress, all of which can also bring on an attack.

Last-resort treatment: Treatment with adrenaline or substances that stimulate the airway muscles to open up passages is usually necessary for all but the mildest attacks. So, if you're an asthmatic, there are almost certainly going to be occasions when asthma medicine will be necessary. In general, the use of an inhaled steroid (such as beclomethasone) is relatively safe because, when inhaled, steroids have a primarily local effect. Bronchodilators may also be needed early in an attack to open the airways rapidly. Because asthma treatment carries some risk of relapse, be sure that your care is supervised by a physician who understands this, and that the precautions described on page 247 are observed. For those with bronchial asthma who require continuous medication or medication just before exposure to exercise or environmental triggers, inhaled cromolyn (Intal) may be prescribed. It is not used for acute attacks.

*Primatene tablets are available over-the-counter and can be hazardous during recovery because they contain phenobarbital.

BACKACHE*

Treatment to avoid: All narcotic and other risky painkillers (see Pain, page 288). Muscle relaxants are often prescribed for back pain, but when their effect wears off the back goes into spasm—so in the long run they are not very effective and are best avoided.

Treatment to substitute: Bed rest during an acute episode. Then: exercise, particularly that aimed at strengthening the abdominal muscles that support the back; good posture (with pelvis thrust forward and spine as little curved as possible); care in bending (bend at the knees, not at the waist) and lifting (use your legs, not your back); a firm mattress (sleep with knees bent); chairs that support the spine. Try the pain-relief tips described on page 289. A physical therapist sometimes helps.

Last-resort treatment: The safer pain relievers (aspirin, acetaminophen, ibuprofen). Check with your doctor if all else fails. If you are referred to an orthopedic specialist, make sure that your own physician is involved in approving any prescriptions. If surgery proves necessary, be sure the recommendations on page 247 are followed.

COLDS AND FLU

Treatment to avoid: Medications containing antihistamines (see page 276), and all nasal sprays and drops or mouthwashes containing alcohol or antihistamines. Also avoid decongestants, such as phenylephrine, phenylpropanolamine, phenyltoloxamine, and pseudoephedrine.

Treatment to substitute: Adding humidity to indoor air (see page 282); safe saline nose drops or sprays, such as Ayr, Ocean, and Nasal, or mix your own;** menthol/eucalyptus lozenges; extra-hot fluids (1 cup per hour during the day); Vicks Vaporub; and, of course, chicken soup. Large doses of vitamin C (2,000 to 4,000 milligrams a day) are controversial, but some studies find this reduces symptoms.

Last-resort treatment: Seldane or Hismanal may be helpful (see page 278). Decongestant nasal sprays may provide brief relief, but when their use is stopped, there is a rebound effect: symptoms become worse than before. It may be helpful to use such a spray two or three times to clear the sinuses and then switch over to a saline solution (see above). For fever and aches and pains, take the safer painkillers (see page 292).

CONSTIPATION

Treatment to avoid: Chemical laxatives (such as Correctol, Ex-Lax, Feen-A-Mint, Senokot) are not recommended for anyone because they can damage the bowel. Because they can be habit-forming, they are particularly unwise for recoverees. Stool softeners such as mineral oil are also risky because they sweep out fat-soluble vitamins (A, D, E) along with stool and, if inhaled, can damage the lungs. Old standards, such as Epsom salts and milk of magnesia, which are known as "osmotic agents," are a bit safer, but dependence on them can also develop. Least risky are bulking agents, such as bran, psyllium (Metamucil), and methyl cellulose (Citrucel), but including fiber in your diet naturally is a better alternative. If you're on a laxative, you may have to be weaned from it gradually.

*If sudden back pain is accompanied by fever and/or pain on urination, check with your doctor. You may have a urinary tract infection.

**You can make your own salt solution by dissolving ¼ teaspoon salt in 1 cup of warm water. Use a clean atomizer or dropper to administer this, with your head back.

Treatment to substitute: About one in three people who think they are constipated, aren't. They equate infrequent bowel movements with constipation. But it's as normal to have a movement every three days as it is to have one three times a day. Only when the movement has to be forced, when there is gassiness and bloating, and when the stool itself is dry and hard is constipation present. If you're not constipated, and want to stay that way or if you are and would rather not be, the following will all help:

❖ *Prompt action.* If you don't respond to the urge to go, your body withdraws it. If you deny your body often enough the result is constipation. If you've got to go, go.

❖ *Medication monitoring.* Something as innocent as an iron or calcium supplement or an aluminum or calcium-based antacid can cause constipation in some people. So can a variety of prescribed medications. If you associate constipation with a new medication, let your doctor know. Usually you can switch to a less constipating formula.

❖ *A diet high in* non*soluble fiber.* That means wheat bran (not oat or barley, which, though possibly helpful in reducing cholesterol, are soluble), fruits, vegetables, legumes (dried beans and peas), whole-grain cereals and breads. Also helpful are apples, figs, pears, prunes, prune juice, or prune juice followed by hot coffee. Any hot drink is, in fact, stimulating to the colon. Many people find that hot water flavored with lemon juice first thing in the morning works like a charm.

❖ *Moderate exercise.* A good brisk walk a couple of times a day or a half-dozen sit-ups is often enough to stimulate bowel activity.

❖ *Adequate fluid.* Well-moistened food will make its trip through your digestive tract more quickly and smoothly. Always drink at least a full cup of liquid when you have a high-fiber meal. At least six to eight glasses of water a day (we're not talking soda here) should help not only your constipation problem but keep your skin moist as well.

Last-resort treatment: If these measures fail, check with your doctor. You need a medical exam to be sure there is no underlying disorder. If the diagnosis is just garden-variety constipation, a bulking agent, stool softener, or enema may be recommended for *temporary* use.

COUGHING

Treatment to avoid: Most prescribed cough medicines are in the risky category. So are a number of over-the-counter cough preparations. Many contain alcohol, codeine, ephedrine, pseudoephedrine, hydrocodone, and/or risky antihistamines (page 276) or decongestants (page 280). Risky cough medications include Delsym (dextromethorphan), Dimetane-DX, Fedahist Expectorant Syrup, Triaminicol Multi-Symptom, Vicks Formula 44, and all multisymptom cold preparations.

Treatment to substitute: Humidification of air (see box, page 282); bathroom steam, created by running the shower at maximum heat (but not with you in it); hot liquids (1 cup per hour of chicken soup, other clear soups, tea, fruitade made with hot water and fruit juice); Vicks Vaporub; menthol eucalyptus cough drops, hard candies, or simple throat lozenges (Cepastat, Chloraseptic); Hold cough lozenges; honey and lemon; hot shower (let water beat on your back); ice pack on the neck. If you're a smoker, giving up tobacco will help, although initially the cough will get worse (see Chapter 24).

Last-resort treatment: Call the doctor if you are running a fever with the cough, if the cough is interfering with

HOW HUMID?

A little moisture in the air is a good thing. Too much can cause problems. Ideal moisture levels are between 30 and 50 percent humidity. More dampness than that will encourage the growth of airborne fungi, bacteria, molds, and other allergens, and possibly even some viruses. Check home humidity levels with a hygrometer, or moisture meter, available at hardware stores or via mail order.

your sleep, if it persists without improvement for more than a week, or if you are coughing up sputum that is darkish yellow, greenish, blood-tinged, or has a foul odor. You may have developed a bacterial or other nonviral infection of the bronchial tubes or lungs, or another medical problem that needs attention. The right antibiotic will usually knock an infection right out and will be safe to take in recovery.

Keep in mind that a cough related to a past cocaine or marijuana habit can last weeks into recovery, and needs only symptomatic treatment.

DEPRESSION

Treatment to avoid: All stimulants, antidepressants, and other psychoactive drugs including cocaine, crack, amitriptyline (Elavil, Endep, Limbitrol*), amphetamine and/or dextroamphetamine (Biphetamine, Dexedrine, Obetrol), bupropion hydrochloride (Wellbutrin), doxepin (Sinequan), fluoxetine hydrochloride (Prozac), imipramine (Tofranil), methamphetamine (Desoxyn), methylphenidate (Ritalin), perphenazine-amitriptyline (Triavil), phenmetrazine (Preludin); and others, including Adipex, Cylert, Didrex, Ionamin, Melfiat, Plegine, Prelu-2, Sanorex, Tenuate, Tepanil.

Treatment to substitute: The first lines of defense against depression are activity, people, and, for recoverees, meetings. Get busy. See page 326 for tips on banishing the blues.

Last-resort treatment: When depression doesn't lift within a couple of weeks, interferes with your sleeping, eating, or working, or is triggering self-destructive thoughts, get professional help from a therapist or psychiatrist accustomed to working with recoverees. Often, talk therapy will suffice to pull you out of depression. If it doesn't, electroconvulsive therapy (ECT) may do the trick. If all else fails, medication may be needed; see page 249 for tips on its safe use.

*Limbitrol also contains a tranquilizer.

DIARRHEA

Treatment to avoid: Antidiarrheals containing narcotics, phenobarbital, opium, or other risky drugs (such as Donnagel PG; Imodium A-D; Lomotil; Parepectolin).

Treatment to substitute: Bed rest and fluids (water, weak tea, Gatorade, or orange juice diluted half and half with water). Fluids are important to prevent dehydration, but avoid sugar-sweetened beverages, which can prolong the diarrhea. The doctor may recommend a special oral rehydration preparation to replenish the fluids and other chemicals your body has lost. If you are hungry, eat plain white rice or pasta, or white toast with a fruit spread. It's not necessary to starve yourself, but avoid high-fiber foods (including fruits, vegetables other than potato without the skin, and whole grains), undiluted juices, and milk until bowel movements have been normal for a day or two. Restore milk to your diet last.

Last-resort treatment: To allow nature to sweep the offending virus out of your body, do not take medication for the first six to eight hours. Then take Kaopectate or another kaolin product, or Pepto-Bismol, if needed. Call the doctor if the diarrhea persists for more than two days, or if it is severe (more than two or three times an hour, or eight times a day), bloody, black, or contains worms. Also call if the diarrhea is accompanied by fever over 101° for more than a day or by persistent pain in the abdomen or rectum.

EARACHES

Treatment to avoid: Risky painkillers (see page 288).

Treatment to substitute: Heat applied with heating pad set on low, a hot-water bag filled with warm water, or warm compresses, while waiting to speak to your doctor. Ear infections usually require medical attention. Call your physician; antibiotics will probably be prescribed.

Last-resort treatment: The safer pain medications (aspirin, acetaminophen, ibuprofen).

GASTROINTESTINAL DISCOMFORT

See Constipation; Diarrhea; Indigestion; Nausea.

HEADACHES

Treatment to avoid: All prohibited painkillers (see page 288).

Treatment to substitute: "Take two aspirin" is the classic prescription for headache in our society, but that shouldn't be your first choice. Initially, try prevention. To minimize the likelihood of headache, try the following:

Eat regularly. Many headaches are hunger-related.

Exercise regularly. This may reduce tension, and with it, any headaches related to stress.

Relax regularly. Several very powerful muscles connect to the sides and base of the skull. If you have difficulty

WHICH HUMIDIFIER?

It's not clear whether moisturizing overheated dry indoor air in winter is effective in cutting down on the number of colds in a household, but it does make many people feel more comfortable, reduces dry skin, and may slow the spread of infection. However, the wrong humidifier can backfire. Cold-mist humidifiers encourage the spread of germs and molds in the air, and ultrasonic types, unless scrupulously maintained and used only with mineral-free water, spew out dangerous mineral impurities and possibly other pollutants.

Use instead a vaporizer (which makes hot steam), a warm-mist humidifier (an updated version of the vaporizer), or the newer "wicking" humidifier, all of which appear to be safer than the cold-mist type. Wicking humidifiers are less likely to spread mineral particles (there is a filter to trap them) or bacteria and molds (the water must be treated with an antibacterial). All humidifiers should be maintained according to manufacturer's directions.

relaxing, these muscles tense up and pull constantly. The result: a headache. Learning and practicing relaxation techniques (see page 320) will help not just with headaches, but with many other aspects of your recovery as well. Using your leisure time for pleasurable activities will also help you relax and reduce the chances of tension-caused headaches. Pursuing active hobbies that allow you to interact with others in a healthy fashion (tennis, golf, volunteer work) or produce results (a mess of fish, a bevy of beautiful photos, a patchwork quilt, heavenly homemade bread) are better in the long run than spending time passively watching sitcoms or televised sports events. But it's certainly okay to collapse in front of the tube once in a while after a particularly difficult day.

Get adequate rest and sleep. Lack of sleep and insufficient rest can make your head pound.

Attend AA meetings regularly. Headaches are less likely to be a problem if you unload the feelings that may be causing them.

Cope with problems promptly. The stress of accumulated worries can lead to tension headaches (see page 167).

Avoid tumult. Noisy stores, loud music, raucous parties (which often present other dangers as well), can all induce headache.

Avoid stuffy quarters. Working, sleeping, or living in a warm, smoky, poorly ventilated space can lead to headache. Keep windows open and air circulating at home and at work.

Avoid allergens. If you have a history of allergies, you may get sinus headaches from exposure to a variety of substances, including tobacco smoke, dust, dog dander, perfume, and incense. See page 276 for ways of dealing safely with allergy.

Avoid entirely, or at least reduce, caffeine intake and cigarette or cigar smoking. Both caffeine and nicotine can cause rebound headaches within hours of the last dose as the body cries out for another.

Avoid refined sugar. In some people, sugar in any of its many guises (see page 427) can lead to lightheadedness or headache, possibly caused by a seesaw effect: a rapid rise in blood glucose levels shortly after ingestion of the substance followed by a sudden drop a while later.

If headache does occur, try the following before resorting to the pill solution:

❖ Lie down in a quiet, dark room with your eyes closed.

❖ Do meditations or relaxation exercises.

❖ Eat, if you think you have a hunger headache. But don't *over*eat. That could give you a guilt headache.

❖ If you suspect anxiety or tension is the culprit, deal with the problem that's plaguing you (see page 326).

❖ If stuffy indoor air is making your head spin, get outside into the fresh air for a few minutes.

❖ If your sinuses are pounding, try either hot compresses or alternating thirty-second hot and cold compresses to the affected area for ten mintues four times a day.

❖ For a pain in the head that starts in the neck, apply an ice pack or "ice-pillow" to the nape of your neck. Or apply heat (see page 291), and then get your spouse, a friend, or a masseuse to follow with a good rubdown.

Last-resort treatment: If nothing else helps, you can now take your two aspirin, or one of the other safer pain relievers (acetaminophen or ibuprofen; see page 292) as directed. If your headaches are severe enough to warrant a trip to the doctor, ask about ergot (Cafergot, Ergostat) as a possible medication. If you suffer from persistent headaches, or headaches that are also accompanied by nausea and/or vomiting, disturbed vision (double vision, for example), or poor coordination (unrelated to your addiction), see your doctor immediately.

HEARTBURN

See Indigestion.

HEMORRHOIDS

Treatment to avoid: Any painkillers listed as dangerous on page 288.

Treatment to substitute: To avoid hemorrhoids or minimize symptoms when they occur, try the following:

❖ Avoid the straining that comes with constipation by keeping "regular" (see page 280).

❖ Eat a diet rich in vitamin C (which keeps blood vessels healthy).

❖ Avoid any food that seems to make your hemorrhoids worse (sometimes tomato sauce or other acid foods do).

❖ Keep the rectal area scrupulously clean (use moistened, unscented white toilet tissue, or a bidet if available).

❖ Avoid long periods of standing or sitting; break them up by walking around. Rest or sleep on your side, rather than on your back, and sit on a doughnut-shaped rubber tube, if necessary, to keep pressure off your rectal veins.

❖ Apply heat or cold, whichever is more comfortable (an ice pack, a warm sitz bath), or alternating heat and cold, when hemorrhoids flare.

❖ For relief, use Tucks (individual cleansing pads that are available over-the-counter), or medicated suppositories or topical anesthetics if recommended by your physician.* If your hemorrhoids protrude, swallow your embarrassment and ask your doctor to show you how to tuck them back in.

Last-resort treatment: When you can't cope with the pain, take a safer pain reliever (see page 292). Sudden and heavy rectal bleeding requires emergency medical attention—it could be from twisted and dilated veins or arteries (called varices), which are common in people with liver disease. But if you spot any rectal bleeding at all, consult your doctor. It's probably just from the hemorrhoids, or from the fissures (tiny cuts) that often accompany them; but, particularly in people over age forty-five, the cause could be a more serious problem. In some cases it may be necessary to directly view the interior of the colon via a sigmoidoscopy or colonoscopy, or to administer a barium enema and then x-ray the gastrointestinal tract, in order to rule out malignancy as being a cause of the bleeding.

INDIGESTION, HEARTBURN, FLATULENCE (GAS)

Treatment to avoid: Risky pain medication (see page 288); most antispasm drugs used to treat irritable bowel syndrome and similar conditions (Bellergal-S, Belladenal, Donnatal); other gastrointestinal medications containing risky ingredients (Phazyme PB). Also avoid aspirin and ibuprofen, which could upset your stomach even further.

Treatment to substitute:

For occasional indigestion or heartburn: Exercise patience or try a safe antacid (see below). You could also try

*Hemorrhoid products sold after August 5, 1991 are required to contain only ingredients labeled as both safe and effective by the FDA. Any such items in your medicine chest purchased before that date should be discarded unless you know for sure that they meet FDA guidelines.

a banana, which a recent study shows can often relieve simple GI discomfort. Or a diet 7-Up or Sprite, which some people find work as well as Alka Seltzer and are certainly tastier.

For frequent indigestion or heartburn: Avoid any food or beverage that you've noticed causes discomfort. Possible offenders include: alcohol, of course; hot, spicy, highly seasoned, fried, or fatty foods (including nuts); processed meats, such as hot dogs, bologna, sausage, bacon; chocolate, coffee, or carbonated beverages; citrus fruits and juices; and spearmint and peppermint (even in gum). Also avoid smoking, which encourages the production of stomach acids; pressure on the stomach, from tight belts and garments or from bending at the waist (bend at the knees instead); and stress, particularly at mealtimes. Eat several smaller meals rather than three big ones (but be careful not to eat more total food). Relax, if possible, for half an hour after each meal, and lose weight if you are overweight (see page 299). Sleep with your head elevated four to six inches (use a large pillow or wedge or even some books under the head of your mattress). And avoid belching. Though this may make you feel better initially, in the long run it will make the problem worse.

Last-resort treatment: Try an antacid, such as Maalox, Mylanta, Gaviscon, or Phazyme (but *not* Phazyme PB). Best are those that are low in sodium. Magnesium or aluminum-based antacids are more effective than calcium antacids, which cause a rebound in stomach acidity. If these measures don't help, see your doctor. Persistent indigestion, vomiting, or a change in your bowel habits requires medical evaluation.

INJURY, MINOR

Treatment to avoid: All risky pain relievers (see page 288). Theoretically, some first-aid creams and sprays containing alcohol could be a problem. Practically (unless you're spraying your throat), they are probably okay. When in doubt, do without. For example, use an iodine-based product like betadine for disinfecting rather than alcohol-based witch hazel.

Treatment to substitute: Try RICE (rest, ice, compression, and elevation; see page 290) and other non-drug methods of pain relief see page 288).

Last-resort treatment: The safer pain relievers (see page 292). Check with the doctor if symptoms don't improve or actually worsen in the hours after injury. If a "sprain" still hurts after three or four days, get it checked out. It could be a fracture.

IRRITABLE BOWEL SYNDROME

Treatment to avoid: Most drugs used to treat irritable bowel syndrome and similar conditions (Belladenal, Donnatal).

Treatment to substitute: Stress reduction (see page 320), relaxation, a diet high in insoluble fiber (see page 281), and the elimination of tobacco, caffeine, and other stimulants (which

---

"I knew I couldn't take any kind of mood-altering drug without threatening my sobriety. When the doctor assured me I could take a tranquilizer because I'd been clean and sober for two years, I knew I couldn't take that doctor either. I switched."

---

should be off your list anyway), and possibly of sorbitol should all help. Some people also get relief by eliminating milk products, using only those with added lactase (the enzyme that helps digest milk sugar), or taking lactase tablets before consuming dairy products.

Last-resort treatment: For severe pain, acetaminophen (Tylenol, etc.) will help. If the symptoms don't go away, a full GI checkup by your physician will probably be necessary.

MENSTRUAL/PREMENSTRUAL DISCOMFORT

Treatment to avoid: Medications containing pyrilamine maleate (Midol, Premsyn PMS, Pamprin).

Treatment to substitute: Alcohol and drugs make premenstrual syndrome (PMS) worse, so sobriety should improve the situation. If PMS and menstrual discomfort continue to be a problem, however, there are some steps you can take: Reduce or eliminate caffeine (see page 302) and chocolate* intake as well as sugar; increase your calcium intake; drink plenty of fluids (twelve to sixteen cups daily during the week before you expect your period); work some exercise into your daily schedule. Some women find that vitamin E supplements (200 to 400 I.U. daily) or raspberry leaf tea (from the health-food store) help too.** When tension strikes, try meditation and other anti-anxiety weapons (see page 320). Reduce your schedule when you expect symptoms to be most debilitating. For pain, try a hot-water bottle across your abdomen or other appropriate pain-relief techniques (see page 288).

*Chocolate contains theobromine, a caffeine-related compound, which can also act as a stimulant.

***Don't* take raspberry leaf tea if there's any chance you might be pregnant.

Last-resort treatment: If pain and cramping are interfering with your life, take Motrin or another ibuprofen-only preparation (Advil, Nuprin). If the symptoms are predictable, a pre-emptive strike with one of these might be helpful.

MOTION SICKNESS

Treatment to avoid: Most motion-sickness preparations, including those containing cyclizine lactate (Marezine), dimenhydrinate (Dramamine), meclizine hydrochloride (Bonine), or promethazine (Phenergan). Medicated skin patches, because they exert their effect systemically through the bloodstream, should also be avoided.

Treatment to substitute: To reduce the likelihood of motion sickness, don't read or do close work while in motion; in a car do the driving yourself, or sit in the middle front seat; don't ride on a full stomach; keep your eyes on the horizon; nap for most of the trip, when possible. If you are aboard ship, stay on deck in the fresh air and nibble on dry crackers to suppress nausea. Long popular with sailors, elastic bands worn on the wrists apply a kind of acupressure and often help avoid motion sickness. These "Sea Bands" are available in many drug and health-food stores and shops that cater to boaters.

Last-resort treatment: If nausea and vomiting when traveling are a serious problem, you can use Emetrol liquid, which acts locally and works well for many people. Check with your physician if nothing else banishes queasiness.

NAUSEA AND VOMITING

Treatment to avoid: Most antinausea drugs, including Atarax, Benadryl, Compazine, Dramamine, Marezine,

Phenergan, Thorazine, Trilafon, Vistaril.

Treatment to substitute: Sea Bands (elastic bands that fit around the wrists) reduce or eliminate nausea in many people (see Motion Sickness for where available). Modify your diet: To keep body fluid levels normal, drink water if it stays down (small sips every fifteen minutes may be retained better than large gulps); otherwise, suck on ice chips (fluid is important to prevent dehydration). Gradually add light, nonfatty foods (plain gelatin dessert, clear soup, toast, fruit) as vomiting ceases. Stay as inactive as possible until symptoms improve; rest in bed if you can.

Last-resort treatment: If the vomiting continues for more than twenty-four hours, is bloody, or has a foul odor, or is accompanied by severe pain, call the doctor.

OBESITY OR OVERWEIGHT

See Weight Control.

ORAL HYGIENE

Treatment to avoid: Stay away from products containing alcohol; most popular brands of mouthwash and a few toothpastes (including Aim, Pepsodent, and Close-Up) do. Not only are alcohol-based mouthwashes a relapse risk, they are also suspected of causing mouth cancers. Read labels.

Treatment to substitute: Rinse your mouth regularly with a homemade solution of salt water or baking soda and water (½ teaspoon salt or baking soda to 1 cup water) or use Oxyfresh, Tom's of Maine, or another alcohol-free brand of mouthwash. A nutritious, low-sugar diet, regular flossing, and twice-daily brushing (of teeth and tongue) will also help to keep your mouth fresh, and gums and teeth healthy. Chew sugarless gum when you can't brush or rinse after eating.

Last-resort treatment: See your doctor if you can't rid yourself of mouth odor. Intractable odor probably does not originate in the mouth, but elsewhere in the digestive tract. Finding the cause may help to get rid of the problem.

PAIN

Treatment to avoid: Even such innocent-sounding pain relievers as aspirin and Tylenol can be dangerous in recovery, particularly when they are laced with other ingredients, such as codeine or caffeine. Avoid aspirin or acetaminophen or any other pain medication with added caffeine; prescription analgesics containing codeine (such as Empirin with Codeine, Fiorinal with Codeine, Phenaphen, Robitussin A-C, Tylenol 3); diprenorphine hydrochloride; hydrocodone; meperidine hydrochloride; methadone hydrochloride; morphine or hydromorphone; oxycodone; propoxyphene (Darvon); and pentazocine.

Also avoid all narcotics, including the natural ones: opium (Donnagel, Dover's Powder, Paregoric, Parepectolin) and opium derivatives, such as codeine, morphine (MS-Contin, Roxanol, Roxanol-SR), and hydromorphone (Dilaudid). And the synthetics: butorphanol (Stadol); fentanyl and methadone (Dolophine, Methadose); hydrocodone and phenyltoloxamine (Tussionex); meperidine (Demerol, Mepergan); oxychodone or oxycodone hydrochloride (Percodan, Percocet, Tylox); oxymorphone hydrochloride (Numorphan); pentazocine/naloxone (Talwin); propoxyphene hydrochloride (Darvon, Darvon Compound); and propoxyphene napsylate (Darvocet).

Treatment to substitute: Pain experts are beginning to come to the realization that drugs, though useful in the short run in some cases, are not the best way to deal with pain. Narcotics, for example, don't zap the sources of pain, they just eliminate its perception. But because they make you less aware of the pain, your body is fooled into cutting down on the natural painkillers it produces. As a result, when you stop taking the narcotics, the pain is more severe because your body isn't turning out enough chemicals to relieve it. So you take more narcotics, and a dangerous cycle begins.

This cycle tends to occur with any kind of medication used to treat chronic pain. At first it helps; then gradually, as tolerance develops, more and more medication is needed to achieve relief. This increasing tolerance and dependence is equivalent to relapse for someone in recovery, and it can bring other addictive behavior on its coattails. So if your pain is going to stay with you, learn to handle it without medication.

There are a great many drug-free ways of dealing with pain, some simple, others rather complicated, all worth trying before resorting to medication:

Acupuncture and acupressure. Some kinds of pain, especially those in which there is a localized area of tenderness within the region of a muscle spasm, respond dramatically to these ancient Chinese arts. While acupuncture is done with needles and requires an expert, acupressure can sometimes be performed by kneading or massaging the pressure points—which anyone taught to locate them can do.

Aloe vera. For the pain of simple burns (and to speed healing), applying the juice from a broken leaf of the aloe plant seems to be very effective. Keep a plant handy in the kitchen or purchase a first-aid cream or spray containing aloe.

Biofeedback. If you like playing with gadgets, this technique may work for certain types of pain, especially pain related to tension. Through a system of sensors attached to the skin and a machine that registers body response you can actually learn to control certain involuntary functions and ward off certain types of headache. Biofeedback therapists are usually listed in the phonebook, or you can contact the Biofeedback Certification Institute of America, 10200 West 44th Avenue, Suite 304, Wheat Ridge, CO 80033; (303) 420-2902.

Chiropractic manipulation. Though chiropractors have been known to overstep their area of expertise, treating a variety of medical ills with little success, they can often help with back-related pain. Objective studies have shown that chiropractic treatment may be more successful and faster in relieving lower-back pain than traditional medical approaches—so much so that some orthopedic specialists are learning spinal manipulation themselves. But be sure you have an accurate diagnosis of your problem before accepting chiropractic treatment, and ideally, ask

BEWARE OF AN OVERDOSE

Aspirin, ibuprofen, and acetaminophen are "safer" painkillers. That doesn't mean you can pop them like candy. All can have serious side effects when taken in large quantities, especially on an empty stomach.

Aspirin and ibuprofen both irritate the digestive tract and cause internal bleeding. Acetaminophen can cause liver damage. In more sensitive people, even normal doses can be hazardous.

your physician for a recommendation so that you can feel confident about the chiropractor you consult. Exercise caution and common sense. At least one study suggests that the number of treatments usually has no relationship to the success of the therapy, so don't pawn the family jewels so you can afford a year's worth of chiropractic visits. A few visits may do as well.

Cold therapy. Cold therapy not only dulls the pain of an injury, it can also, by reducing blood flow, decrease swelling and bruising. It's most effective during the first 36 to 48 hours after an injury, or until swelling subsides. Treat bruises promptly with ice cubes (placed in a heavy plastic bag and wrapped in a terrycloth towel to absorb dripping, or placed in a hot-water bottle) or an ice pack.* Apply ice for 10 to 20 minutes every hour or two while you're awake, until the pain and swelling are gone. Alternatively, an injured foot or hand can be soaked in ice water for up to fifteen minutes at a time. Repeat every hour or two.

Minor burns can be treated with cold therapy. Soak in *cool*, not icy, water or apply cool compresses until the pain diminishes (usually about half an hour, though sometimes pain can persist for hours).

Do not apply cold therapy if you are hypersensitive to cold or have poor circulation (if you have Raynaud's disease, for example) or if the wound is open or blistered.

Compression. Compression is a good first-aid technique. It will stop bleeding (apply pressure directly to the wound) as well as reduce the swelling of a sprained ankle or injury (use an elastic bandage or tie a towel around the affected body part).

Elevation. In infection, surgery, or trauma, swelling of the affected area often stretches the pain receptors, which transmit messages of dismay to the brain that are interpreted as pain. Elevating the injured part of the body allows the circulatory system to absorb more tissue fluid and reduce the swelling, lessening the nerve stimulation. This means less pain for you.

RICE FOR INJURIES

As every athlete knows, The best treatment for bumps, bruises, and sprains is RICE. Not the kind that you get in a Chinese restaurant, but *R*est, *I*ce, *C*ompression, and *E*levation. These four steps will more effectively treat a sprained ankle or a bruised wrist than any pill you can pop.

Elimination. Try to eliminate the cause of the pain. If it's a hunger headache, eat. If it's back trouble, get a new mattress, a better office chair, more comfortable walking shoes; and improve your posture and your abdominal muscle strength (by doing safe sit-ups with your knees drawn up, for example). If it's a tension-triggered pain in the neck, do relaxation exercises (see page 320).

Exercise. Keeping your body in good shape with exercise can help prevent painful injury. It can also reduce the likelihood of pain (such as backache) that comes from poor muscle tone. For muscle pain, exercise is often a very successful treatment. Low-impact exercise, such as swimming, may be helpful for arthritis pain. See page 300 for a good recovery exercise program that avoids the mistake of doing too much too soon (another contributor to pain).

---

*Commercial ice packs, though probably less satisfactory than ice from your freezer, are sometimes convenient. Two types are available: one is kept in the freezer ready to use, refreeze and reuse; the other needs no freezing, but is discarded after only one use. You can also use an unopened package of frozen food in a pinch.

Heat therapy. Heat—in the form of a heating pad, hot water bottle, warm compress, hot bath, or a combination of these—can speed healing, relax tense muscles, and reduce stiffness, as well as help reduce pain. Heat is best for treating back or muscle pain, inflammatory-related problems, such as arthritis, and injuries once swelling has subsided (usually after 36 to 48 hours). Moist heat (from a warm compress, moist heating pad, shower, or bath) often works better than dry. Check with your doctor to learn which form of heat (or cold) works best in which situations.

Always wrap heating pads and hot water bottles in a towel to prevent burns, and limit applications to 20 to 30 minutes. Avoid heat therapy if you have a fever, internal or external bleeding, or an infection. If you have a heart condition, check with your doctor before using a hot tub or whirlpool. If you are pregnant, avoid heat therapy to your torso.

Hydrotherapy. Whirlpool baths are best, but any hot bath can help relieve muscle pain, as well as tension and insomnia. A heating pad applied following the bath provides additional comfort—but never use the heating pad during the bath.

Hypnosis. If chronic pain is the problem, hypnotism can sometimes make it bearable. See a doctor familiar with hypnosis, or a reputable hypnotist your doctor recommends.

Ice. See Cold therapy.

Immobilization. Keeping an injured arm, ankle, finger, or leg immobilized will often reduce the pain and encourage healing. This may be as simple as putting your arm in a sling or your finger in a splint, or as complicated as getting a pair of crutches or having the doctor put your leg in a cast.

Massage. A good massage can often reduce tension and pain. If you can't afford a professional, ask your spouse, partner, or a friend to learn the tricks of the trade (from a book, videotape, or practice). The basic techniques are very simple: While you lie on your stomach, the masseur or masseuse uses both hands to knead and stretch muscle groups on the back, arms, legs, hands, feet, and neck. Hot towels, heating pads, and scented or unscented oils will augment the feeling of well-being. And there's a plus: The physical contact can greatly enhance the effort to restore communication and intimacy in a troubled relationship.

Meditation. Meditation isn't a cure-all, but it can be helpful in a wide range of situations, including the battle against pain. The pain doesn't have to be in your head for your head to help you to deal with it. For ways to use meditation, see page 320.

Physical therapy. A licensed physical therapist can often help reduce pain. In many states PT's practice under the supervision of a physician; in others they practice independently. Either way, be sure you get a good recommendation from your doctor before putting yourself in the hands of a physical therapist. If the pain seems to get worse rather than better under such care, don't be afraid to ask questions and to check with your doctor.

Relaxation. Relaxation comes in many packages—a game of tennis, a movie, a concert, a good book, a leisurely walk, a weekend at the beach, quiet meditation, playing catch with the kids. And what relaxes one person may make another person anxious—losing that game of tennis, for example, or playing with young children. Learn what it is that truly relaxes you, and try it even before pain begins to nag.

Rest. While not a panacea, rest seems to be good for most things that ail us, pain included. Whether you're dealing with a jogging injury or a headache, time out for rest usually helps reduce the discomfort. Going forward with exercise or other activities in spite of the pain may seem gutsy, but it's usually foolhardy. The concept "no pain, no gain" may be helpful in emotional therapy or in recovery, but it has no place in physical activity.

Ventilation. If the pain is caused by fear or worry (a tension headache, neck pain, or upset stomach, for example), talking about the problem often helps. In such cases the pain is only the symptom; your body is saying, "Hey, something is wrong!" and it's the underlying cause that needs treating.

TENS (transcutaneous electric nerve stimulation). This method of pain relief relies on low-level electrical stimulation delivered to the skin by a special device. It's believed that this stimulation either blocks the transfer of pain impulses (because the nerves can carry only one message at a time) or that it promotes the release of pain-relieving endorphins. It has been used with varying degrees of success for various kinds of chronic pain, as well as for dental work, childbirth, and back pain. Ask your physician or physical therapist, if you're interested.

Ultrasound. Deep, penetrating sound waves can often unknot muscle spasms and relieve the pain that accompanies them. This, of course, must be handled by a professional. Ask your physician or physical therapist for a recommendation.

Water therapy. See Hydrotherapy.

Last-resort treatment: If you do decide you need medication for acute or short-term pain, you may be pleasantly surprised at how effective an aspirin can be. While you were drinking or using, you probably found little relief from such over-the-counter painkillers because the alcohol or other drugs were suppressing the brain chemicals that deal with pain (as well as those that deal with anxiety and depression). Now these analgesics can bring dramatic relief. Take (as directed) aspirin (Bayer, Bufferin, Ascriptin, Ecotrin, Empirin, and generics); acetaminophen (Tylenol, Panadol, Tylophen, Datril, and generics); ibuprofen (Advil, Nuprin, Motrin, Genpril, Medipren, and generics); or magnesium salicylate (Doan's Pills). Take these medications after eating, not on an empty stomach, and follow with a full glass of water.

Though these drugs are not normally addictive, addicts can become dependent on them, so take them *only* when absolutely necessary. Do not take these painkillers in anticipation of pain (though a doctor or dentist may suggest you do this after an in-office surgical procedure), because this can encourage a return to addictive behavior by self-destructively using pharmaceuticals to solve problems (which in this case may not even exist).

Even extremely severe pain can now be treated without a narcotic. Although studies show that Toradol, an oral or injectable nonsteroidal anti-inflammatory drug (much like ibuprofen), is highly effective in treating pain and doesn't seem to carry with it the danger of relapse, there are serious questions as to its safety.

Any other pain medication should only be taken as described on page 247.

SKIN PROBLEMS

Treatment to avoid: Creams, lotions, ointments, or sunblocks containing alcohol;* hydrocortisone cream. Retin A is an effective treatment for acne, but because it can cause birth defects, and because unplanned pregnancy is a risk in early recovery, it's not the treatment of choice right now.

*Since alcohol can be absorbed through the skin, applying these could make a person on Antabuse sick. They are probably not a problem for others.

Treatment to substitute: If you are on Antabuse, look for alcohol-free skin products. Moisturize dry skin daily, avoid very hot showers or baths, use a mild soap or cleanser only as needed, and try to reduce indoor dryness in the winter (see "Which Humidifier?," page 283).

To minimize acne, keep your skin clean with a mild cleanser or soap (such as Dove). Don't pick at or squeeze pimples. Self-treat breakouts with benzoyl peroxide preparations, available over-the-counter at your local pharmacy. If that doesn't seem effective, your doctor may prescribe a topical antibiotic, such as erythromycin, to spread on the affected areas of skin. Dietary changes aren't necessary unless you note a link between a particular food and an eruption.

You can speed the departure of skin rashes by using very mild hypoallergenic soap, such as Basic or Neutrogena, and using it only where your body is really dirty or smelly. Baking soda or Aveeno (colloidal oatmeal) in your bath water may also help. If the rash is allergic in nature, an over-the-counter cortisone cream may alleviate it. If it is caused by a fungus (as are athlete's foot and jock itch), an over-the-counter antifungal preparation, such as Tinactin or Micatin, may spell relief. Don't stop applying such a medication as soon as the rash is gone; continuing it for an extra week or two will diminish chances of a recurrence. Sometimes a minor rash can become infected with the bacteria normally in residence on the surface of the skin. In many cases, warm compresses or soaks can nip such an infection early. Intense redness, pain, or pus, however, usually indicates problems that cry out for medical attention.

The development of cold sores or fever blisters caused by herpes simplex virus I can sometimes be blocked by taking lactobacillus tablets or capsules at the first twinge. Over-the-counter ointments may also be helpful.

Last-resort treatment: When all else fails in eliminating acne, a fungal infection, or recurrent herpes outbreaks, an antibiotic, antifungal, or antiviral medication taken by mouth may be prescribed by your doctor.

SLEEP PROBLEMS: TOO LITTLE

Treatment to avoid: All sedatives or sleeping pills, including butabarbital (Butisol); butalbital (Fiorinal, Esgic, Phrenilin, Repan); chloral hydrate (Noctec); ethchlorvynol (Placidyl); ethinamate (Valmid); flurazepam (Dalmane); glutethimide (Doriden); meprobamate (Equanil, Miltown); methaqualone (Quaalude); methyprylon (Noludar); phenobarbital, pentobarbital (Nembutal); secobarbital/amobarbital; secobarbital (Seconal); talbutal (Lotusate); temazepam (Restoril); and triazolam (Halcion). All nonprescription sleeping preparations, including those containing diphenhydramine (Nervine, Nytol, Sominex 2) and doxylamine succinate (Unisom).

Treatment to substitute: The most effective ways of improving sleep in the long run, you may be surprised (and should be pleased) to learn, do not come in a bottle. Keep in mind that worrying about not sleeping tends to compound the problem. Lying in bed and thinking "I won't be able to fall asleep" often converts anxiety into reality. The following tips should help you overcome sleepless nights:

❖ Have a regular going-to-bed routine. Go to bed at the same time each night—at least as often as you can. Use standard sleep-inducing tricks at bedtime: a warm bath or leisurely shower, reading, soothing music, a back rub, cuddling with someone you love, making love, meditation and relaxation techniques (see page 320), prayer, warm milk (if it seems to help), or counting backward from one hundred.

If sleeplessness has become a habit, you might try to break the habit by *changing* your going-to-bed routine as much as possible; change the location of your bed or replace the bed itself, if that's feasible.

❖ Have an active day. Get up at the same time every morning (even if you tossed and turned all night); make a point of getting out and spending time with friends or family (isolation may contribute to sleeplessness). Get in some moderate exercise (see Chapter 25) daily; it will make it easier for your body to sleep at night. But don't nap during the day or exercise just before bedtime.

❖ Try to eliminate the stress and anxiety that may be keeping you awake (see the tips for dealing with stress on page 326). Get rid of underlying problems when you can. And if you can't, make a monumental effort not to take them to bed with you. Distract your mind with an engrossing TV show or book, with meditation, or with recovery readings on tapes.

❖ Be sure your sleeping quarters are conducive to sleep. That means the room should be dark, neither too hot nor too cold, and quiet (though not necessarily silent; "white noise" from a fan, for example, may help you sleep). If light streaming through a window is interfering with your sleep, try a heavier window shade or wear eye covers (available at your pharmacy). If noise from outside is the culprit, block it out with ear plugs.

The mattress should be comfortable and not lumpy, the linens neat and smooth. If you are happier with your blanket tucked in tightly, be sure it is; if you prefer looser bedding, arrange yours that way. But don't cover your head with the blankets, since this can reduce oxygen and increase carbon dioxide intake, leading to headache and sometimes abnormal heartbeat, both of which can keep you awake.

❖ Find your natural sleep rhythm. You'll sleep best when your temperature drops; take it hourly for a few days to determine when this happens during the day. Try to time your bedtime accordingly. If your biological clock is set inconveniently—for sleep from 2 A.M. to 10 A.M., for example—it might make sense to try to reprogram it via chronotherapy, a method that attempts to manipulate your internal clock. See your doctor or a sleep clinic accredited by the Association of Professional Sleep Societies.*

❖ Try a different bed. Restless twist-and-turn sleep can be created by pressure points on a mattress. If you suspect this is the source of your problem, turn the mattress over or add a sculptured foam pad called an "egg-crate mattress"; or buy a new mattress or switch to a waterbed or a large air mattress.

❖ Late in the day, avoid eating foods that tend to give you indigestion (which can interfere with sleep). Also avoid a heavy meal just before you turn in. And of course keep away from caffeine, at least from early afternoon on; its effects may not strike until eight hours or more after it enters your system, just when you're slipping under the covers.

❖ Before bedtime, avoid things that tend to stimulate: loud music or entertainment, TV thrillers, animated or angry discussions, and strenuous physical exercise. If you've been to an exciting movie, meeting, or sports event, take some time to unwind (with a bath, book, music; see above) before even attempting to get ready for bed.

❖ Comfort yourself with the thought that if you're in bed with your eyes closed, even if you're awake, you're getting rest.

❖ Don't just lie there. If you are very

*For more information, write to the APSS at 604 Second St. SW, Rochester, MN 55902.

restless and sleep doesn't come in 15 to 30 minutes, get up and do something else. Watch TV, read some AA literature or a relaxing novel, do last night's dishes or sort the laundry. If you just lie in bed and stew, you may be a vegetable in the morning.

❖ Reconsider your sleep needs—they vary significantly from person to person. It's possible you're sleeping more than you think. People who complain of "tossing and turning all night" are observed getting plenty of sleep when they are subjects in sleep labs. You can judge how much sleep you need by monitoring how your day goes. If you aren't sleepy during the day, you're getting enough sleep. You may be trying to stay in bed for too many hours; try cutting back.

❖ Remember that no matter how disruptive this temporary sleeplessness is, it can't compare to the problems that chemical dependence caused in your life. Nobody has ever died from lack of sleep, but people die every day from resorting to pills or alcohol to put themselves to sleep.

Last-resort treatment: If these suggestions don't alleviate your sleeping problem, a medical workup is probably in order. If your symptoms are not directly traceable to withdrawal, ask your physician about evaluation in a sleep laboratory.

SLEEP PROBLEMS: TOO MUCH

Treatment to avoid: All stimulants and antidepressants (see page 282), including caffeine. If you're gulping coffee to stay awake, you're using it as a drug. Beware.

Treatment to substitute: Maintaining a healthy schedule and sleep pattern demands a certain amount of self-discipline—something few active alcoholics/addicts have ever developed. But it's never to late to start. To assist you, get a pocket calendar on which to list your daily schedule and a good clock with a snooze alarm (which will wake you a second time if you don't get up at the first signal). Schedule early morning activities (fishing, hunting, shopping, museum-hopping, berry-picking, hiking) that will lure you out of bed. If you usually just shut off the alarm clock and turn over, have a friend or neighbor telephone or stop by to be sure you get up and get dressed. If you aren't working, fill your days with meaningful pursuits: meetings, visiting friends, classes, good works. Try exercising during the day to increase your energy level. Also try to avoid heavy meals, which can make you drowsy; have six small meals instead of three large ones. Try to keep your activities consecutive, so you won't be tempted to go

THE WILLINGWAY DRUG RULE

"There are two types of drugs: Old drugs and new drugs. Old drugs are addictive. New drugs are nonaddictive. When the new drugs become old drugs, they become addictive and are replaced by new nonaddictive drugs."

What does this riddle mean? Virtually every time a pharmaceutical company introduces a new drug, it is at first hailed as "nonaddictive." Once it's been around for a while it becomes clear that ("Oops!") it is indeed addictive, little comfort for those who have already inadvertently become hooked. So take any claims about a new drug being safe for recoverees with a grain of salt and a ton of caution.

home and crash between them. For example, plan to meet a couple of acquaintances after work for supper and then go right on to an AA meeting, followed by a snack with your sponsor.

Last-resort treatment: If these suggestions don't alleviate your sleeping problem, a medical workup is probably in order. Ask your physician about having an evaluation done in a sleep laboratory.

SORE THROAT

Treatment to avoid: Gargles or mouthwashes containing alcohol; risky pain relievers (see page 288).

Treatment to substitute: Gargling with warm saltwater (1 teaspoon salt to 1 glass water) or hydrogen peroxide diluted according to package directions; sucking on lozenges, such as Chloraseptic, Cepastat or Sucrets; ice pack to the neck.

KIDNEY STONES

The pain of kidney, or renal, stones usually begins in the back just below the ribs on one side or the other. As the stone begins to move down the ureter to the bladder, the pain (the stabbing type that tends to come in waves) travels with it around to the groin and down one side of the abdomen. It's reputed to be the most excruciating that humans experience, except for childbirth. The pain may continue over a period of hours or days, which is why it presents a special problem for the person in recovery. Strong pain relief is usually indicated, and sometimes nothing but a narcotic will help.

If narcotics are needed, you have to assume that the judgment necessary for maintaining your sobriety will be lost. To reduce the possibility that your sobriety will be lost with it, stay in close contact with your AA group, your sponsor, and your addiction physician or counselor during treatment. And take the precautions specified on page 247. Pay extra attention to your program, possibly going to a meeting every day if you're not hospitalized.

If you have such an episode, drink a lot of water (at least 8 to 10 glasses a day) and call a urologist for expert help. The stones usually pass by themselves. If not, you will need help getting rid of them. The longer you are in pain, the more likely you will need heavy-duty pain relief. In some cases, a new technique known as ultrasonic lithotripsy, which pulverizes the stones into small particles that pass in the urine, can be used to eliminate the need for surgery and lessen the quantity of narcotics needed. Sometimes, however, there's no choice but to surgically remove the stone or stones.

As important as dealing quickly with the present episode is finding out what type of stone it was and how the problem can be prevented in the future. Each recurrence puts your recovery in jeopardy. To capture a stone, urinate through a fine strainer until after the stone is passed. Any solid material in the urine will end up in the strainer. Carefully put the stone or stones in a bottle and bring it to your doctor. The type of stone will dictate how you can avoid a recurrence. For example, if it is primarily calcium, then you may have to cut down on your intake of this mineral. Speak to your doctor about this possible preventive measure. Drinking plenty of fluids, especially in hot weather, may also help reduce the chance of more kidney stones developing.

Last-resort treatment: Most sore throats are caused by viruses and require no drug treatment, but if a "strep" throat is diagnosed, antibiotics are recommended. Report to your doctor any sore throat that is accompanied by a fever or swollen glands, or that interferes with your swallowing.

STRESS

See Anxiety.

VAGINAL INFECTION

Treatment to avoid: Any kind of risky painkillers (see page 288). Pain accompanying vaginal symptoms could indicate a serious condition and requires immediate medical evaluation.

Treatment to substitute: The best treatment for vaginal infections is prevention. To avoid this problem, and to hasten its departure if it strikes, observe the following:

❖ Keep the vaginal area clean and dry. Always wipe from front to back after using the toilet, to avoid spreading germs. Rinse thoroughly after showering or bathing, and avoid deodorant soaps, bubble baths, perfumes, or other possible irritants.

❖ Wear cotton—or at least, cotton-crotch—underwear.

❖ Avoid tight pants or jeans, leotards, and spandex exercise outfits.

❖ Follow the Best-Odds Recovery Diet. Be particularly sure to keep your sugar intake low—sugar may provide a breeding ground for yeast (candida) infections. A daily cup of yogurt with live cultures (check the label) may also help to ward off this condition.

Last-resort treatment: See your doctor if symptoms (see page 268) appear. Proper diagnosis and treatment with the appropriate safe medication should have you back to normal in no time.

WEIGHT CONTROL

Treatment to avoid: Prescription appetite suppressants including amphetamines and/or dextroamphetamines (Biphetamine, Desoxyn, Dexedrine, Didrex, Obetrol) and methamphetamine (Desoxyn); Adipex, Bontril, Efed II, Fastin, Ionamin, Mazanor, Melfiat, Plegine, Pondimin, Prelu-2, Preludin, Sanorex, Tenuate, Tepanil; and nonprescription appetite suppressants, including Dexatrim and Acutrim. Also avoid fasting and liquid diet plans, which have not proved to be very helpful. Fasting could lead to drug craving, and the quick-fix weight loss is usually gained back just as quickly.

Treatment to substitute: Reducing caloric intake (by reducing food intake, especially of high-fat foods) and upping caloric outgo (through increasing exercise). See page 437 for dieting details. For many people Overeaters Anonymous is extremely helpful.

Last-resort treatment: If you are extremely obese or are having a difficult time taking weight off, your weight-loss program should be medically supervised by a physician who specializes in the treatment of obesity without drugs.

14

LIFESTYLE AND HEALTH IN PHASE ONE

Health and lifestyle are inextricably intertwined. What you eat, drink, and smoke, how you spend your leisure time, how you conduct your love life—all affect your health and longevity. Eventually you will want to overhaul your lifestyle so that you can be healthier and live longer. Right now you should be concentrating on recovery to the exclusion of everything else. But that doesn't mean you can't start to think about possible lifestyle changes and begin to make subtle adjustments that will head you in the right direction.

WHAT'S ON YOUR MIND?

SUDDEN LIFESTYLE CHANGES

"I'm ready to turn over a new leaf and go on a health kick."

Forget about trying to do an instant turnaround. That's the old you, the alcoholic/addict, thinking. The new you is going to go slowly, consolidating your recovery first and then moving on.

You can, of course, start to move in the right direction by gradually adopting some of the changes recommended in this chapter, but don't try to change too much too soon.

DIET AND NUTRITION

"About the only 'nutritionist' in my life is the kid behind the counter who hands me my fries and double cheeseburger. Should I be concerned about diet during recovery?"

Everyone should always be concerned about diet. But with recovery now your number one pri-

Guide Lines

❖ Remaining abstinent is the number one priority.

❖ Attempting radical changes in your lifestyle now could interfere with abstinence. Changes in diet, exercise habits, and use of tobacco, while clearly desirable, can be distracting and should be made only as you are ready.

❖ Some basic changes begun early can help enhance recovery.

❖ Caring for body and mind, and treating them with respect, are important elements in a healthy recovery.

ority, the nutritional areas for you to focus on at this point are just those that touch on becoming and staying sober.

The suggested dietary changes for Phase One of the Clean-and-Sober Diet are those that research has shown can enhance sobriety. The first five of our Basic Six recommendations on page 304 are simple to carry out, take very little expertise, and can have a big payoff. The sixth, which involves dropping sugar from your diet, is more difficult for some people. For that reason, we suggest that if the prospect of eliminating sugary foods is even more depressing than the "sugar blues" might be, you should wait until your recovery is a little more solid before giving it a whirl. In Phase Two you can move further into dietary changes that enhance your life, and in Phase Three into others that will prolong it (see Chapter 23).

Of course, if you're introduced to a healthful diet in treatment and have someone at home who can take charge of discarding the junk food, oversee the restocking of cupboards with healthful foodstuffs, and put into practice the Clean-and-Sober Diet, then there's no reason why you can't zip through its three phases any time you're ready.

Improving your diet right from the start appears to yield important benefits. Recent research has shown that good nutrition (combined with the Twelve-Step program of AA) results in recoverees having fewer episodes of low blood sugar, less alcohol craving, and a better chance of staying sober.

WEIGHT TO LOSE

"I need to lose fifty pounds—mostly from my beer belly."

Sure, that beer belly's got to go. But dieting isn't a good idea right now. If you've been a drug user, quick weight loss could be almost as dangerous as pouring yourself a double vodka. That's because most mind-altering drugs are stored in fat deposits. If you burn that excess fat too quickly, chemicals deposited in it could be released into your bloodstream in large doses. In this way, it's possible for drugs to act as time bombs, exerting a negative influence on your thinking long after you've stopped using them.

Instead of worrying about losing weight now, just try to eat regular meals that are low in fat, limit snacks to fruits and vegetables, and start a simple exercise program.* That way you won't gain any more weight, you may

*Of course, if you have to lose weight immediately for medical reasons, follow your doctor's recommendations.

even surprise yourself by starting to lose some. If you have trouble controlling what you eat and keep gaining weight, don't worry. Concentrate on your recovery now. Mess that up by trying to diet, and you could end up skinny and dead.

When your recovery is secure and you've begun enjoying life again, it will be time enough to start thinking thin (see page 437).

STARTING AN EXERCISE OR RECREATION PROGRAM

"I'm really eager to get into a good exercise program. Is there anything special I should know because I'm in recovery?"

Absolutely. While every sedentary person who gets into an exercise program should proceed slowly—building up from just minutes a day—those in recovery should move even more slowly. The reason is that your muscles, joints, reflexes, and possibly even your bones are probably far from normal. Depending on how long you've had a problem, your muscles may be weak and even shrunken from disuse and chemical damage. Your joints may be inflamed because of mistreatment or gout. Your reflexes are slow because the connections between muscles and brain are shaky. And your bones may be brittle because of alcohol-related calcium loss.

Jumping into a full-fledged exercise program could lead to your dropping out of it just as quickly because of injury. So while mild exercise, such as brisk walking or swimming, is a good idea, don't do anything more strenuous until your doctor has made certain that your body is ready for it. Then embark on the program described in Chapter 25, which will lead you gradually into a more active lifestyle without unnecessary risk.

"My counselor said I ought to start thinking about some recreational activities. That raised a big question mark in my head. To me, recreation has always meant watching TV. Besides, shouldn't I be concentrating on more serious stuff?"

Recreation—which can include music, dance, indoor games (Ping-Pong, Monopoly, Jeopardy), outdoor games (tennis, golf, fishing, shuffleboard, croquet), hobbies (coin collecting, knitting, model building, gardening), arts and crafts (woodworking, painting, photography, pottery-making), exercise (walking, hiking, rollerblading, bicycling), or just about anything else you enjoy—*is* serious stuff. It's a vital part of a healthy lifestyle—an absolutely safe relaxant and temporary escape from problems—as well as a vital part of recovery. But like you, most alcoholics/addicts have trouble even contemplating recreation. The reasons are many, but each can be overcome.

Limited experience. For most, recreation has for years meant recreational drugs; other activities were usually limited to those that didn't take much effort, like watching TV, movies, or sports events. *Solution:* Remember there's always a first time. That goes for riding a two-wheeler or a roller coaster, or for that matter, the first uncertain steps you took as a toddler. You've broken new ground before and there never was a better time to do it again.

Limited skills. To participate in most recreational activities, you need to have some basic skills, to know the rules and techniques of the game, and to be able to get along with others. Most alcoholics/addicts lack this expertise. *Solution:* It can be learned. Pick a recreational activity that sounds interesting but isn't inordinately complicated. Learn the rules and techniques one step at a time. If you can, take lessons or get some pointers from a skillful friend. Practice in private, before going public. Master it before moving on to another activity.

Limited playmates. Most of your pre-sobriety playmates are probably no more adept at healthy recreation than you are. *Solution:* Share your recreational time with AA friends or sober family members.

Limited time. Certified workaholics can't find time for fun—and believe they shouldn't have any. *Solution:* Remember that recreation is as important to body, soul, and recovery as food. Make time for it.

Unlimited guilt. Most alcoholics/addicts have an I-don't-deserve-to-have-fun or a just-relaxing-like-that-must-be-bad attitude. *Solution:* Improve your self-esteem (see page 316). Everybody deserves to have fun—you included.

Unlimited fear. You may be afraid of:

❖ Interacting socially without a chemical crutch. *Solution:* Recognize that not only can you socialize without chemicals, you can socialize better. Look at your AA experience.

❖ Being embarrassed if you don't perform well. *Solution:* Keep in mind that recreation is not a test of performance; it's meant to make you feel good.

❖ Looking "silly." *Solution:* Stop worrying about how you look to others. Compared to the way you looked high, anything you do looks good.

❖ Having free time at all (because you might fall into your old free-time ways). *Solution:* Filling your free time with constructive activities is much safer than just letting free time happen. (First you have time on your hands, then you have a pill or a shot glass in your hand.)

Don't forget that recreation should be fun. Don't approach it with the same grim determination or compulsiveness you brought to your earlier activities. Every tennis serve doesn't have to be an ace, every swing of your golf club a hole in one. Relax and enjoy.

DANGEROUS EATING HABITS

"I haven't even craved a drink in months. But my sponsor says my eating habits are a problem. I don't see it."

Most people with an eating disorder *don't* see it. Denial is often an integral part of this disease, which makes it very difficult to treat. And untreated it can be fatal. That is probably why your sponsor is concerned.

Eating disorders are rather common in women alcoholics/addicts. One reason is that a life dependent on alcohol or drugs usually seems totally out of control. Sometimes the only area of personal control that remains is food consumption. So some individuals learn to manipulate their food intake—often in very unhealthy ways. The most common eating disorders are:

Bulimia. People with bulimia periodically gorge themselves—eating what to a normal person would be an unbelievable amount of food: a gallon of ice-cream for example, or two whole apple pies, or an entire fried chicken with four servings of fries. But then black clouds of guilt settle in, and they desperately want to erase the evidence of the crime. Bulimics then purge their bodies by either vomiting and/or using laxatives. The forced purging allows the bulimic individual to eat excessively without becoming obese.

Anorexia nervosa. The anorectic individual never pigs out. In fact, she hardly consumes any calories at all, taking tiny portions, picking at what she takes, dumping the remainder into the garbage can. She is obsessed not with eating, but with controlling her eating. She quickly becomes grossly underweight. When friends and family look at her, they see near emaciation. When she looks in the mirror, however, the image she sees is still overweight. So she continues the desperate struggle to get rid of that image. Without help, the anorexic can literally starve herself to death.

"I was at the gym, doing aerobics, and I looked in the mirror and thought for a moment, 'She's pretty.' It was the first time in my life I liked what I saw."

Compulsive eating. The compulsive eater is not very different from the alcoholic or drug addict. Food isn't consumed for survival and good health. It is consumed in order to cover up feelings and make the eater feel better. And it usually leads to obesity.

Eating disorders can carry over from the period of active addiction or they may begin during recovery as a substitute addiction. Many women who suffer from them have a history, often long submerged, of sexual abuse as children.

If you fit any of the above descriptions, then you should get help immediately. If you are either bulimic or anorectic, speak to your doctor about referral to a physician who specializes in treating eating disorders; untreated, they can be fatal. If compulsive eating is your problem, Overeaters Anonymous (OA) may be able to help you. Many people find that AA is not enough to help them with the weight-control component of their problem, but that OA does the trick.

CAFFEINE

"I never have a compulsion to drink alcohol anymore, but I'm very, very big on cola. I know this is really another addiction, and it concerns me."

Caffeine is a drug—a stimulant. Many active alcoholics ingest a lot of caffeine—in coffee, tea, or colas—to counteract the depressant effects of the alcohol. Many continue to depend on caffeine during recovery, as witness the cauldrons of coffee consumed at AA meetings. Whether this is wise or not isn't clear. Research has not yet associated caffeine intake with an increased risk of relapse, but it's possible that there may be some subtle effect. Certainly large doses of caffeine can be hazardous to anyone's health. The equivalent of five or more cups of regular coffee a day can lead to chronic poisoning, with restlessness, headaches, disturbed sleep, heart rate and rhythm irregularities, digestive tract irritation, and diarrhea. The equivalent of seven cups can trigger a mild delirium in some people. It's hard to imagine anyone committing suicide this way, but the equivalent of seventy cups could be fatal.

Recognizing the minor to major hazards of continued caffeine consumption and the fact that many people become jittery (not a desirable state in recovery) after just one cup of coffee, more AA groups and treatment programs are starting to offer a decaffeinated option. Some offer only decaf.

Joining the "decaffeinated generation" at some point is probably a good idea. But if the idea of going through yet another withdrawal right now isn't appealing, getting off caffeine can wait until Phase Three. On the other hand, if you're ready to go for it now, page 435 will tell you how.

SMOKING

"I've been getting conflicting information. Do I or do I not have to quit smoking when I get sober?"

While less than 30 percent of the general population smoke, about 80 percent of alcoholics and addicts use tobacco. That's not really surprising, since tobacco contains nicotine, which is an addictive drug. Some treatment centers now include this drug in their abstention programs. If you haven't gone through such a program, you have to make a decision whether to stop now or to wait until your recovery is more solidly established.

Reasons for quitting now include:

❖ *A no-smoking home group.* Though AA meeting rooms used to be thick with tobacco haze and were often affectionately called "the Smoke House," there is a change for the better in the wind, and some groups now prohibit lighting up. If yours does, you can consider whether you want to quit or switch.

❖ *Protecting your recovery.* Whether or not using tobacco, like using any other drug, can lead to a relapse is unclear. It certainly doesn't do this overtly, or most alcoholics/addicts would never stay sober. But some suspect that there may be a more subtle effect—more like using an antihistamine than using morphine. So it's a factor to consider.

❖ *Protecting your health.* Giving up tobacco could immediately start increasing your life expectancy. If you have a hacking smoker's cough or are at high risk for heart disease because of other risk factors (diabetes or high cholesterol levels, for example) quitting now would be especially prudent.

Reasons you might want to wait include:

❖ *A home group where everyone else smokes.* Quitting right now and attending these meetings might put excessive stress on your recovery. Again, the alternative is to switch home groups.

❖ *Protecting your recovery.* For some people, abstaining from tobacco appears to be so stressful that it takes the focus off their recovery. (Some successful recoverees claim that quitting heroin was easier for them than quitting nicotine.)

Whenever you're ready to toss away your last pack, turn to Chapter 24 for tips that will help you.

"I haven't smoked in years, but friends have been telling me that having a cigarette in my hand will make it easier to stay sober."

Many recoverees have fallen victim to that theory. First of all, there's no evidence that this is true. And in fact, it may be the reverse. Getting hooked on a new substance could be a subtle road back to other addictions. And second, substituting one drug for another doesn't make much sense, especially when both can kill.

Any of the satisfactions you can get from smoking you can get in other ways. If you want to calm your nerves, work out, meditate, do relaxation exercises. Want to keep your hands busy? Take up knitting or pick up a string of worry beads. Crave oral gratification? Keep a supply of sugarless gum, raw vegetables, or air-popped popcorn at hand. See Chapter 24 for more on the dangers of smoking and on cigarette substitutes.

THE CLEAN-AND-SOBER DIET—FOR STARTERS

While you are struggling to establish sobriety, it would be unwise to allow yourself to be distracted by ambitious strategies for instantly changing your dietary lifestyle. But ignoring the effect that good diet can have on your recovery would be equally foolhardy. So, as soon as you can, begin observing the following Clean-and-Sober Basics:

1. TAKE A SUPPLEMENT. It's risky for a person in recovery to depend on a pill for anything. Still, the health and rehabilitation benefits of taking a good daily vitamin-mineral supplement probably outweigh the risk in most recoverees—as long as they realize that the risk exists. If your drug of choice came in pill form, however, you may be better off with a liquid preparation. If you can't find an adult formula, take an infant one—but don't increase the dosage or you could seriously overdose on vitamins A and D.

Keep in mind, too, that a supplement is just that. It's intended to supplement a good diet, not replace it. If you say, "Well, I can have a couple of chocolate doughnuts for breakfast as long as I take my vitamin pill with them," then you're thinking like an addict: illogically. And that's troubling. But if you take that daily pill as insurance, because you know that your body hasn't yet recovered completely from the ravages of alcohol and/or drugs, that's common sense.

The formula you take should include folic acid (or folates), B_6, B_{12}, zinc, and calcium in amounts at or near the Recommended Daily Allowances (RDA) you'll find on the label. If you are anemic, your physician may also prescribe iron. Avoid megadoses of vitamins—particularly the fat soluble ones, such as A and D, which can be toxic at levels not much beyond the RDA—unless prescribed by your physician.

2. EAT THREE SQUARES—PLUS. It may not be easy to get into the habit of eating three meals a day if you've been living primarily on junk foods at irregular times and getting most of your calories from alcohol. But it's a habit worth cultivating. It's particularly important in recovery because skipping meals or living on junk food can lead to episodes of low blood sugar, and low blood sugar can make you jittery, depressed, confused, anxious—all feelings that can bring on a compulsion to drink or use.

To get into a three-squares mode, start with breakfast. If you have little time in the morning, fill your bowl with dry (preferably whole-grain) cereal and fruit the night before; all you have to do in the morning is pour the milk and eat. If you're a coffee drinker, prepare the ingredients (preferably a decaffeinated brew; see page 435) at night, too. Then just boil the water or turn on the coffee maker while you're dressing.

If your work schedule is so busy that you can't find time for lunch, you're working too hard. *Make* time for lunch. Bring a sandwich from home, order in a slice of pizza, pick up a salad on the way to work. Even a quick lunch is better than none.

Most people manage to have a

meal in the evening, so you shouldn't have too much difficulty with that one. If you've already had two solid meals, you'll find less need to pig out at supper.

Many people can't get from meal to meal without experiencing a drop in blood sugar. To avoid such a drop and its possible consequences, have light between-meal snacks—fruit, raw vegetables, whole-grain crackers or bread sticks along with a beverage.

3. GET YOUR FILL OF FLUIDS. Alcoholics, though they drink constantly, can suffer from dehydration. (Depending on one's drinking pattern, alcohol can make the body either retain or eliminate fluid.) Now it's important to keep your body hydrated. So though it may seem like a monumental task, drink eight to ten glasses of water and other fluids (juice, soup, milk) spread out over the day, every day. Do not count coffee (caffeinated or not), regular or decaf teas, or other caffeinated beverages. All of these are diuretic and rob the body of fluid.

4. FOCUS ON THE B VITAMINS. These nutrients are vital for the repair of the nervous system, so try to increase their intake. That means having more whole-grain cereals and breads (become a label reader) as well as some meat and/or dairy products daily.

5. CATCH UP ON CALCIUM. Alcohol depletes the body of calcium, robbing the bones of this vital mineral and often weakening them. The problem can occur in males as well as females. The sooner you start replacing the calcium you've lost the better. Try to drink at least three glasses of milk daily, or eat the equivalent in other foods (see page 430).* To avoid increasing the risk of heart attack while reducing the risk of bone-weakening osteoporosis, stick primarily to low-fat or nonfat dairy products. (They are a gradually acquired taste.)

6. SHUN SUGAR. For some, eliminating sugar is akin to trying to kick one more addiction. So use your judgment. If you aren't suffering from severe mood swings, if attacks of low blood sugar do not seem to be a problem, then you can wait a while before moving on to this step. On the other hand, if you find you are often shaky, irritable, depressed, tired, or have trouble concentrating a few hours after having a sugar-loaded snack, it makes sense to adopt this Clean-and-Sober Basic.

When early humans first developed a sweet tooth, it was a lifesaver. It made them reach for the grapes on the vine, the oranges on the tree, the berries on the bush. This ensured that they got the essential vitamins and minerals found in fruit. Today a sweet tooth is much more likely to lead us astray: to Twinkies, Chunkies, cream pies, and hundreds of other "goodies" that aren't very good for us.

For many people, including those in recovery, there is an additional problem with sugar: it affects their moods. That's why eliminating sugar from your diet as early as possible is recommended. See page 427 of the Clean-and-Sober Diet for a complete explanation of how sugar acts in the body and for ways to make your diet sugar-free without making it pleasure-free.

*If you're under thirty or pregnant, you need the equivalent of four cups of milk.

PREGNANCY PLANNING

"I've got a very spotty past where drugs and alcohol are concerned. How is this going to affect my getting pregnant and having healthy babies?"

Once the drugs and alcohol are out of your system, you're well into a solid recovery program, and your physical condition passes muster with the doctor, you should be able to conceive and carry a healthy baby.* Assuming, of course, that you stay sober. If you have any doubts about remaining sober, *do not try to conceive.* The risk of the devastating effects of alcohol and other drugs on a fetus is too great.

Ideally, conception should be postponed until Phase Two of recovery. The reasons make sense. First of all, by then all the effects of the chemicals you have been abusing should be out of your body. Although some, such as alcohol, clear out much sooner, others, such as benzodiazepines and marijuana, can hang on for six months or even a year. And second, pregnancy puts a strain on your body both physically and emotionally. That strain may be too much for your fragile early recovery to handle safely. For some women pregnancy is a powerful motivator for sobriety, but for others it can be a distraction from the work of recovery. Even if a woman manages to stay sober through delivery during a Phase One pregnancy, there is the danger that if adequate attention hasn't been paid to developing the tools to continue to stay sober, she could relapse under the stress of parenting once the baby arrives.

If you really do want to become pregnant, or if you become pregnant accidentally and want to carry the baby, that's certainly not an impossible task assuming of course that you're clean and sober. (If you're not, see Chapter 3.) But you will have to work particularly hard at your program, because you have only nine months in which to establish a really solid foundation that will give your child the gift of a sober mother.

*Factors other than your drug abuse could interfere, such as being HIV positive or having a blocked fallopian tube due to a previous pelvic infection.

CONCERN ABOUT AIDS

"I can't tell you how many times I went home from a bar with a guy I didn't know. I've never been tested for HIV. Am I better off not knowing?"

Probably not. As treatments multiply, it is clear that knowing—and taking appropriate measures—is best. First of all, not getting tested won't eliminate your worry. And the worry can lead you down the road to relapse. Second, you may not be infected. If it's at least six months since your last such encounter and you test HIV negative, the odds are good that you will stay that way. If you do test positive, that does not mean you have the disease, only that you're infected with the virus. See the following pages for what that means and what treatments are available to slow the development of AIDS or AIDS-related illness.

It is very important, however, to get counseling before testing so that you will be prepared in case of a positive result. You should also be certain that you will have plenty of support to help you adjust if the news is bad. Otherwise you could have an additional threat to your life: relapse.

"I was an IV drug user and I'm terrified that I have AIDS. So terrified that I don't want to know."

AIDS AND AA

AA meetings are usually warm and welcoming. Yet sometimes, for those known to have AIDS or to have tested HIV positive, there are subtle and not-so-subtle signs of rejection. People smile hello, but don't put out a hand to shake. They sit a seat or two away. They avoid holding the hands of a PWA (person with AIDS) at the meeting's closing ceremony. And they fail to invite him or her to join them for coffee after the meeting or for a meal at home. If you find yourself reacting this way to a PWA, it's time to rethink your feelings.

AIDS researchers assure us that you absolutely cannot catch AIDS through casual contact—shaking hands, breathing the same air (in a room or a car), being coughed or sneezed on, hugging, touching. So trying to avoid casual contact is definitely not necessary to protect yourself. It is also definitely hurtful to those who are infected.

Remember that there but for the grace of God, or just plain luck, go you. Reach out your hand (literally and emotionally) to those who need you. It will do you both good.

You're not alone. Most people in your spot feel the same way. Fortunately, the picture is not as bleak as it once was, and there are good reasons for finding out whether or not you are infected. That's true for everyone in recovery.

Intravenous drug users are at high risk of contracting Acquired Immune Deficiency Disease (AIDS) because of their widespread use of contaminated needles. Their sexual partners (male or female) are too. But they aren't the only ones at risk. *All* drug and alcohol users are, because of weakened immune systems and increased promiscuity (heterosexual or homosexual). The risky sexual behavior* may be a result of alcoholic blackouts, the blocking of inhibitions and the wiping out of judgment by alcohol or drugs, or the temporary increase in sex drive triggered by such drugs as crack. Even those with only one partner may be at risk if there is any chance—even a remote one—that the partner may have had risky sex elsewhere or done IV drugs. This is most likely when the partner is a substance abuser, and especially if he or she has been in prison. Of course, anyone who has had a blood transfusion (particularly before 1985) is also at risk.

Even if you have only used IV drugs once since 1977, with your own private works and what you believed to be clean needles, and even if you have absolutely no symptoms of AIDS, getting tested would be a good idea. It's still more important if you shot up frequently. And don't assume that you are in the clear if you've had a recent medical checkup or have been recently hospitalized. A test for HIV (human immunodeficiency virus**) can only be done with your informed consent. If you haven't consented, you haven't been tested.

Testing is a must if you've noticed any symptoms that might be early

---

*Risks, of course, vary. If you shook hands with or hugged someone with AIDS, the risk is nil; you can't catch AIDS with a hug or a handshake. If you tongue-kissed an infected person or had sex with a condom, you have a small risk. If you had unprotected sex, the risk is much greater. Because of blackouts, however, you may not be fully aware of what you did with whom—and it only takes one ill-advised contact to become infected.

**The virus that causes AIDS may also be called HTLV-III, LAV, and ARV.

DON'T DIE OF EMBARRASSMENT

Many people who suspect they might be HIV positive hesitate to be tested because they fear that even getting tested labels them as somehow unsavory. But medical personnel know that seeking a test or being HIV positive isn't a reflection of the kind of person you are (except to show you are wise enough to get tested). They recognize that this is a disease caused by a virus that doesn't know or care whether a victim is an IV drug user or a hemophiliac, gay or straight, a streetwalker or a church-going mother. Seek help—you will find understanding and caring. And if you turn out to be HIV positive, you'll have a much better chance of survival.

Be assured that your confidentiality is protected when you are tested (no one can be told you are positive without your permission) and that the law protects people who are HIV positive against discrimination (in housing, jobs, and so on). From your own point of view, you needn't tell anyone you know except sexual and drug-use partners and those close family or friends upon whom you will have to rely for social and emotional support. You needn't notify your employer, unless your work could involve blood-to-blood contact—for example, if you are a health care worker who handles sharp instruments.

signs of AIDS: fatigue, fever, loss of appetite and weight, diarrhea, night sweats, and swollen glands (lymph nodes), usually in the neck, armpits, or groin. Of course, you can have all of these symptoms and not have AIDS. Nevertheless, if you do have such symptoms for more than two weeks (and can't link them to a "bug" that's going around or to some other cause), check with your doctor. (If you already know you are HIV positive and you develop these symptoms or an unexplained cough, skin rash, fungus infection, or sudden confusion or loss of memory, call immediately.)

Some people in recovery are so worried about the possibility of AIDS that they develop the symptoms even when they aren't infected. If you suspect you have AIDS, don't just crawl into a hole and give up in despair. Get tested. The AIDS may be in your mind, not in your body. If that's the case, get some extra emotional help—from your doctor, your counselor or therapist, or your sponsor.

A negative test, which is most likely, will clear your mind. If you test positive for HIV, ask for a retest (one which uses a different method to detect the antibodies to the virus) to be sure the results are accurate. Though better than ninety-nine out of a hundred tests are accurate, there are occasional false positives—tests that look positive but aren't. If you have your HIV test within six months or less of risky behavior, you should probably be retested after that period, since the antibodies often don't show up for months.

Be sure counseling is offered along with the test, so that if it is positive you will understand the significance of the results. Testing positive for HIV does not mean you have AIDS or that you will develop it in the near future, just that you are infected with the virus. Fewer than one in three people who are HIV positive show symptoms of AIDS or AIDS-related illness within five years of infection, and only about 50 percent at ten years. With the treatments now available, it's possible to improve those odds. Though it's presently believed that everyone who is positive will eventually become sick, treatment can delay the process, prolong life and improve its quality, and in the future may even prevent illness entirely.

But while a positive HIV today isn't necessarily a death sentence, it *is* a warning: to get the best possible treatment, to take the best possible care of yourself, to be alert for symptoms of disease, and, of course, to stay clean and sober.

If you turn out to be HIV positive, you should be scrupulous about not engaging in activities (such as risky sex) through which you can pass the virus on to others. You should also notify anyone you shared drugs or had sex with during the past three years (at least) so that they can get tested. In most states there are programs to assist with contact notification.

Those who test HIV positive or have AIDS need more than treatment. They need emotional and social support (some of this should come from a professional source), good nutrition (which helps strengthen the immune system), and a positive attitude, which might include using relaxation techniques such as meditation and prayer. Concentrating on living well while getting optimum medical care has had a very beneficial effect on many who are HIV positive, keeping them feeling well longer.

For those in recovery, careful attention to their program and abstinence from alcohol and drugs are also crucial, for a variety of reasons. First, without sobriety, attempts to survive are almost sure to fail. People who are drunk or stoned almost invariably forget to take their medications or to keep clinic appointments and in general fail to take good care of themselves. Second, alcohol suppresses the immune system, and could lower the body's resistance to fighting off the virus. Third, sobriety will improve the quality of life (although it may not seem so at first). Fourth, sobriety will reduce the likelihood of risky behaviors that could pass the virus on to others. Finally, because abstention may slow the progression of the disease, it is a way of playing for time—which is important because, with so many medical scientists focusing on it, a cure could come at any time.

SPREADING AIDS

"If I find out that I am HIV positive, how can I continue to live with my wife and kids? But leaving them would be like a double death sentence."

Being HIV positive doesn't have to be viewed as a death sentence any longer; a majority of infected individuals have many good years ahead of them, especially if they get quality medical care. Nor does it mean leaving loved ones. Keep in mind that testing will safeguard rather than threaten your family. And if you should test positive, remember:

❖ You can't transmit the virus merely by living in the same house with someone. AIDS isn't transmitted by using the same glasses or silverware, through hugging and kissing, or in the course of ordinary family life. The only area of concern is when bodily fluids (blood, semen, vaginal secretions, and possibly saliva) are exchanged, as when sharing needles, engaging in sexual intercourse, or tongue kissing.

GETTING HELP

For more information on HIV testing and on AIDS, call your local AIDS hotline (see your telephone directory), your city or state Department of Health AIDS Program, or the National AIDS Hotline at the Centers for Disease Control (800/342-AIDS).

❖ You and your partner do not necessarily have to adopt the monk's way of life, avoiding intercourse entirely. It's often possible to find satisfaction in mutual or individual masturbation. If intercourse is desired, you *must* use a condom. Condoms made of latex do the best job of preventing the passage of the virus and are usually recommended. Put the condom on according to directions before foreplay begins, and keep it on until intercourse is completed. (For a while it was believed that the spermicide nonoxynal-9 could kill the AIDS virus and therefore the spermicide should be used along with the condom. Recent evidence doesn't support this theory.)

❖ Your entire family needs support. Everyone will have questions and concerns, as well as a whole array of feelings (anger, guilt, fear, despair, confusion) that need professional attention and lay support. You can find out about physicians and therapists who do AIDS counseling and about AIDS family support groups in your area by calling your local AIDS hotline or health line (see your telephone directory). Family involvement in Al-Anon will also help everyone weather a crisis.

❖ Your wife should be tested, too. It's possible you passed along the virus before you knew you were infected. This is important information for a female partner to have when thinking about pregnancy. Though not all babies born to HIV-positive mothers become infected, there's no way to assure that a baby won't be, though treatment may help. With research, the outlook for children of infected women could change in the future.

❖ If you work in a job where you might possibly infect others, such as medicine or dentistry, you will also have to be extremely careful to follow the correct protocols for those who are HIV positive.

CONCERN ABOUT OTHER SEXUALLY TRANSMITTED DISEASES

"I've gotten a clean bill of health where AIDS is concerned. Are there any other diseases I could have caught while having sex under the influence?"

AIDS is getting most of the press, but today all sexually transmitted diseases (STDs) are on the rise. Even syphilis, once believed to be almost wiped out, is showing up more frequently than in the recent past. What this probably means is that people are not taking precautions against STDs.

These diseases are passed along through sexual intercourse or through other sexual contact (such as oral sex) that allows the germs from the infected person to pass to his or her partner through a body opening or torn mucous membrane lining. The most common transfer areas are the mouth, the vagina, the penis, and the anus.

The leading villains are gonorrhea, herpes, venereal warts (caused by the human papilloma virus, or HPV), chlamydia, and syphilis. If you think you might have picked up something while engaging in risky behavior under the influence, then you would be wise to ask to be tested for all the possibilities. Many infections are asymptomatic, so you can't rely on symptoms giving you a warning.

If you are infected, you should be treated immediately. Any sexual partners should also be informed and treated as necessary. Until the infection clears, take care to avoid intercourse and other risky sex or to use condoms to block transmission of germs.

Of course, if you notice any symptoms of an STD (see page 266), then you should see a doctor immediately.

15

MIND, EMOTIONS, AND SPIRIT IN PHASE ONE

Although you will wake up to what your body is saying in early recovery, you may feel your mind is not saying anything at all. A reasonable description of the recoveree in this stage is "muddled and befuddled." That's almost certainly how you will feel. But your mind is likely to be so numb and out of focus that you won't even realize how bad your mental state was until you've passed through it. Your emotions, too, may seem frozen at first. Then suddenly the cold haze of winter will lift, your emotions will thaw, and feelings you didn't know you had will burst forth and demand a hearing. Around the same time, you may or may not also experience a "spiritual awakening." Whether or not you do, you will certainly be giving some thought to what spirituality is (there isn't a great deal of agreement on the subject) and the role it plays (or doesn't play) in your life.

WHAT'S ON YOUR MIND?

INTELLECTUAL SYMPTOMS

"I've been sober for nearly two months and my head still feels and acts like a sieve. I can't think straight. Can't concentrate. Can't get anything done. I thought sobriety was supposed to clear my head."

It will . . . eventually. But the haze won't vanish overnight. Your brain is, in fact, probably the slowest part of the body to recover from the ravages of substance abuse. Many brain cells were destroyed during addiction, and new brain cells can't be grown by the body. But fortunately the brain can rewire itself, in a sense, manufacturing new dendrites (nerve fibers) to con-

Guide Lines

❖ Alcohol and all other drugs have an effect on the brain, particularly on its neurotransmitters, the chemicals that transmit information from one brain cell to another. The effects usually continue for some time after withdrawal of the abused substances.

❖ Just which emotional and intellectual symptoms you experience in recovery will depend on the drug or drugs you used, how long and how heavily you used them, and on your brain's reaction to their withdrawal.

❖ Virtually everyone in recovery finds that their emotions are unpredictable and that their moods tend to pendulum from one extreme to the other. Depression, anxiety, euphoria, panic, are all common.

❖ Many people think their minds are clear—until the following week they seem clearer. Indeed, the mind improves progressively. A rule of thumb: one month of fogginess for every year of drinking. This of course can vary, depending on many factors.

❖ Spirituality means different things to different people. You don't have to be a believer to have a spiritual life.

❖ The concept of a Higher Power is open to many interpretations. Your interpretation is as valid as anyone's.

nect the billions of cells that remain unscathed. This takes time. Studies show that though the greatest upgrading in brain function occurs in the first six months of recovery, gradual improvement in emotional and intellectual functioning continues for ten years and more.

A wide range of intellectual and emotional symptoms are likely to trouble you for long or short periods during the first year of recovery. They include fuzzy thinking, difficulty making judgments, mood swings, and an overall feeling of numbness. You may sometimes feel disconnected from your surroundings, like an outsider looking in.

Short-term memory may also be diminished. (You're walking down the hall and suddenly can't remember why or where you're going. You dial a phone number and panic when it starts ringing because you can't remember whom you're calling.) Lack of concentration is also frequently reported. (You sit down to read your favorite author and can't get past the first page. You find yourself rereading the same paragraph over and over before it sinks in.) Problem-solving ability may be hampered. (You can balance your checkbook by following the directions, but can't deduce what to do by logic.) Difficulty grasping spatial relations is also a common complaint. (You're handed a map to help you get to a special AA meeting and can't make head or tail of it.) And some people forget skills learned while under the influence—a condition called "state-dependent learning" (see page 237).

All of these symptoms are common, almost universal, and all gradually disappear. Many people in recovery report that the fog starts to lift after three months, others after six months; the minds of others are still swimming in pea soup at the end of the first year. Good short-term memory sometimes does not return until the end of the second year. Some people are happily oblivious of their shortcomings while they are in the haze. It's not until they come out of it that they're able to look back and realize how limited they were.

Progress varies from person to person and may be particularly slow with abusers of certain drugs (such as the benzodiazepines), but almost everyone can look back at last week, last month, or last year and say, "Hey, I'm doing better!"

SUPERSENSORY PERCEPTION

"Though my brain seems numb, my senses seem extra-sharp. So sharp I think I'm going to go bananas. Every sound, every light, seems magnified a thousand times."

Very perceptive of you to notice. Many recoverees share this augmented sensory perception. A group of schoolchildren can sound like a thundering herd of elephants. A fly buzzing around your head, like a jet fighter. A dripping faucet, like Niagara Falls. The light you usually read by may suddenly seem too bright. The lights in your shop, too glaring. Your vision may be distorted. Even your sense of touch may be affected—a wool sweater that never bothered you before may suddenly feel so itchy you can't keep it on. All thanks to the snarled communications system in the brain.

These symptoms will all gradually disappear over the next few months. But in the meantime, bombarded by these sensory experiences, you may find you want to scream by the end of the day—much like a colicky baby, who has also been getting too much sensory stimulation. Instead of screaming, take time to meditate or do relaxation exercises. These will calm your nerves in the way that a ride in the car calms a crying baby. You could also try ear plugs to drown the excessive sound and tinted glasses to dim the bright light.

PARANOIA

"On my last cocaine binge, I really snapped. I thought everyone was out to get me, including my parents and my best friend. I barricaded myself in my room and was saved only when the police broke in. Most of those feelings are gone, but after six weeks of being clean, I still feel a little uneasy, a little threatened."

That's the cocaine talking. Cocaine, as well as some other drugs, increases the levels of certain neurotransmitters in the brain, and it's not unusual for cocaine users to experience psychotic behavior, including paranoid delusions—the everyone-is-out-to-get-me syndrome. Things start to improve when you stop the drug, but it takes a while before the messed-up neurotransmitter system gets back to normal. That's why many cocaine users in early recovery still feel a bit paranoid.

"When I was in aftercare, the counselor would ask me how I felt and I would say, 'Well, I guess I'm okay.' And she would say, 'There are four feelings: mad, sad, glad, and scared. Which are you?' And I would sit there and say, 'Well, I'm not mad,' and I had to go through each one to think how I felt. Now, if I'm mad, I know it."

If you're feeling that way, try to relax. Things will get better. In the meantime, you may want to stay in safe surroundings for a few weeks or even a couple of months—a treatment center, an extended-care facility or halfway house, or the home of someone you feel you can trust (and who is familiar with the needs of recovery). If the feelings threaten to get out of hand at any point, be sure to seek help immediately from an addiction professional.

"I just got out of treatment and I'm embarrassed to see friends and relatives. I'm sure they all know, and everyone is saying, 'There goes the alcoholic.' I'll bet that's why no one has called or stopped by."

This paranoia is also drug-induced, but in a different way. The alcoholic/addict is accustomed to being the center of his universe, to thinking that everyone else is noticing what he or she is doing. Forget it. Most people have problems of their own to worry about.

If some folks are commenting behind your back, it's better they should say "Here comes the alcoholic" and know you're sober than to whisper "There goes the drunk," which is probably how they referred to you before you went into treatment. Instead of hiding, let them know who you really are: not the person behind the bottle, but the person who's put the bottle behind you.

Unless they have drinking problems of their own, friends aren't staying away because they fear they are stigmatizing themselves by socializing with an alcoholic. Remember, they were your friends when you were stinking drunk. They're probably just uncomfortable, embarrassed, unsure of how to approach you. It's the same problem people have when a friend has a serious disease. The reason they don't call is not because they don't care, but because they are ill at ease.

Put them at ease by making the first move. Invite them to dinner, or to a movie, or whatever you usually do together. Assure them up front that you can understand it if they're uncomfortable, and are wondering what to talk about with you and what to say about your "problem." Let them know that you'll be happy to answer any questions they have, but that you don't intend to bore them with the gory details. (Then be sure you don't. It's so easy to get caught up in the excitement of recovery that you think everyone should be.) You might also invite a close friend or two to go to an open AA meeting with you, so that what you've done and are doing won't seem so strange. Once they've had a chance to see that sober doesn't mean weird or humorless, and that you aren't going to bore or preach to them, they'll loosen up.

Beware, however, of old drinking or using buddies. What's making them

"All the drinking I did was an attempt to suppress the intense self-hatred and incredible feeling of inadequacy in myself generated by a very successful dad. This led to lying and attempted suicide. I wanted to drive off a cliff, but I knew I'd live and be quadriplegic, and I wouldn't get any liquor. So I put a shotgun in my mouth. But I couldn't bear the thought of my brains splattered all over the wall."

uncomfortable is your sobriety—it sends a message they just don't want to hear. Not seeing them now is good for their drinking or drugging, but it's twice as good for your recovery. (This is no time to become a reformer; your recovery isn't strong enough. Wait until you're well into your second phase before trying to sober up your friends.)

GREAT EXPECTATIONS

"So I'm sober. All my expectations still come to nothing. What's the use?"

If you know the Dickens novel, you know that great expectations often come to nought. If we expect the world to go from Hell to Camelot overnight, and all our fantasies to come true the moment we're sober (our families welcoming us with open arms, landing the first job we apply for, winning the lottery), we set ourselves up for a Grand Canyon–size fall. Sure, those things happen, but they're the exception, not the rule. That doesn't mean you should throw all your dreams, hopes, and aspirations out the window—they're what keep the world (and us) moving forward. Work for those dreams with all your might. Just don't *expect* that they will surely come to pass. If they don't, you won't be disappointed and depressed. You'll just turn the page and start writing the next chapter in your life.

BRAIN DISORDERS

"I've been told I have a brain disease called Wernicke-Korsakoff syndrome. What does that mean?"

Once known as two separate entities ("Wernicke's encephalopathy" and "Korsakoff's syndrome"), this disorder of the brain occurs in a small percentage of alcoholics. Wernicke's is considered the first phase of the disease. In it, the patient is confused, seems to be staring a lot, has some form of ataxia (lack of coordination, especially stiffness in walking), and exhibits impaired memory. In the more advanced Korsakoff's stage, the alcoholic seems superficially better. The confusion lifts, though there may still be some disorientation as to time and place. The most obvious symptom that remains is usually impaired short-term memory (a story told five minutes earlier is repeated, for example); sometimes long-term memory is affected as well. The classic way the memory defect shows up is with "confabulation," which sounds like lying but is really the patient filling in the gaps in memory with imaginary happenings as a defense against being found out. It's scary and embarrassing not to be able to remember something that just happened. So you pretend you do.

Injections (oral doses won't work) of large amounts of thiamine (vitamin B_1) can sometimes produce remarkable improvement in some symptoms. Memory takes the longest to return and often does not return completely. The earlier this condition is treated, the better the chances of its being reversed.

Very rarely, so much damage has been done that the brain is unable to process new information. The only information left in the memory bank is what was learned before the damage

> *"The less I expect, the more humility I have, and the more serene and happy I am. And the more I feel that life is on my side, not out to get me."*

occurred. Known commonly as "wet brain," this condition isn't reversible. But don't worry that this is your problem—obviously you managed to assimilate the new information your doctor gave you. Stay sober, and you will be able to do a lot more than that.

"I've been sober for a couple of months. But I've been so confused and am having such memory problems that I wonder if I could be getting Alzheimer's."

An alcoholic has no greater risk of Alzheimer's than anyone else. Since the symptoms you're experiencing are common at this stage of recovery, chances are good that it's your past alcohol abuse and not Alzheimer's that's at the root of them. Speak to an addiction specialist if you're concerned, especially if symptoms worsen instead of improving. He or she should be able to reassure you, and possibly may even be able to give you shots of thiamine to speed your recovery.

LACK OF SELF-ESTEEM

"I'm sober, but when I look around at other people I realize I just can't measure up. I'm not pretty, and I'm not real smart, and I don't have a lot of talents."

It's the nature of the alcoholic/addict to feel inadequate. They feel that way not because they are truly inferior (many are among the most beautiful, talented, successful people in the world), but because they hold themselves up to quixotic expectations, and they believe others expect as much of them too. While they underestimate themselves, they usually overestimate others. Other people are happier, better-looking, smarter, more successful, richer, more talented. You name it, someone else has it better or does it better than they do.

Substance abusers use chemicals to substitute for good feelings about themselves, to cover up what they see as their inadequacies, to paint themselves a personality that they believe can't exist without this help, to turn themselves into someone else. Often they tear down others (spouse, children, associates, friends) in order to elevate themselves on a false pedestal of superiority.

Part of the work of recovery is to rebuild self-esteem, to learn to accept yourself as you are, and to know that what you are is good. The following tips can help:

❖ Stay clean and sober. Involve yourself in AA, one of the best modes of strengthening self-respect. Work the steps.

❖ Understand—with your heart as well as your mind—that alcoholism/addiction is a disease. People who drink or use are sick, not bad. That includes you.

❖ Recognize that there's good in every human being. Look for it in others, and in yourself too. It's there. When you do a life history or inventory or your daily journal, be sure to list the positives, strengths as well as weaknesses. Don't consider things that were well-intentioned but turned out badly, or mistakes that you've tried to correct, to be negatives. If there are shortcomings you can change, make an effort to do so, with the help of your Higher Power. If there are some that you can't change, accept that.

❖ Avoid trying to bolster your self-esteem by feeding your ego. The woman who dresses seductively in an attempt to attract men is doing that. So is the man who bullies women. Though both may briefly feel good about themselves, the real emptiness inside is not filled.

❖ Keep your word—to yourself as well as others. You can't respect yourself if you don't.

❖ Learn the difference between self-respect and selfish self-centeredness. Find a few people you really trust, and ask them to point it out when things you do for your "self" are dishonest or at the expense of others.

❖ Determine what your values are (see page 335), and examine them to see if they are healthy. If they aren't, rebuild them first; if they are, live by them. If you don't, you can't respect yourself.

They say in AA:
"Poor me. Poor me. Pour me a drink."

❖ Surround yourself with people you respect, who care about you and accept you for who and what you are—people who won't be taken in by, or even interested in, the false you.

❖ Make amends when you reach the Ninth Step (see page 112) so you can eliminate unnecessary guilt. Such guilt can demolish your self-esteem.

❖ Keep your goals realistic—which in early recovery means *very* modest—and then work hard to meet them. This is not the time to take risks. Staying sober one day at a time and ninety meetings in ninety days are challenging but realistic goals; getting your life back in order in ninety days is not.

❖ Accept that you are human and, like everyone else, can make mistakes. But don't leave it at that. Put those mistakes to work for you, learning what you can from them so they won't be repeated.

❖ Like yourself—you deserve it, especially now. Show it by the way you care for yourself, in the way you eat, exercise, dress, and treat yourself generally. Don't do this because you want to "look good" to others; do it for you. The more you act as though you like yourself, the more you will.

❖ Before you act, don't ask yourself "What will others think if I do this?" Instead ask "What will I think of myself if I do this? Will I respect myself more? Or less?" That doesn't mean you should ignore the effects of your actions on those around you; you won't feel good about yourself if you are hurting others. Just don't base your actions on their opinions.

❖ Stop comparing yourself to others. Everybody's different. And each of us has the potential to be wonderful in our own way—you included. We just have to find what that way is.

"My whole life is a disaster. I can't help thinking that my alcohol problem is somehow punishment for my being gay. I feel like a total failure."

Your life is a disaster because of alcohol, not because of your sexual orientation. It's common for alcoholics—heterosexual as well as homosexual—to look upon the catastrophies in their lives as punishment for their perceived misdeeds rather than as a result of the substance abuse itself. They have the erroneous belief that bad things happened to them because they were bad people—that such things don't happen to good people. What you've got to make yourself understand is first, that being homosexual isn't "bad," and second, that bad things do happen to good people all the time—whether they are gay or straight.*

The sense of worthlessness that you're experiencing is both a common

*It may be helpful to read, *When Bad Things Happen to Good People,* by Harold Kushner, and *Accepting Ourselves,* by Shep Kominar.

symptom of and an important contributory factor to alcoholism/addiction. The feeling may be directly related to any number of causes (lack of support and encouragement while growing up, child abuse, learning disabilities, and so on) common to both heterosexual and homosexual alcoholics/addicts. But if you're gay, lesbian, or bisexual, there are often additional factors that have damaged your self-esteem over the years:

❖ Hearing from all sides—your family, your religious institution, your friends, your school system, the TV, the movies, deejays on the radio—that you, or at least what you are, is bad.

❖ Staying in the closet, and perhaps grimly participating in the ridicule of gays, telling homosexual jokes, and pretending to be what you are not—feeding your guilt.

❖ Living in fear—fear of being found out if you stay in the closet, fear of being rejected or hurt (even physically) if you come out.

Part of your task in recovery will be not just to give up drinking but to start to rebuild your self-esteem. You may be able to do this just by going to an empathetic AA group (one that is all or partly gay may be best) and working with a supportive sponsor. Or you may also need counseling from a therapist who has experience in helping recovering homosexuals. Don't suffer needlessly. You have every right to feel good about yourself.

PANIC OR ANXIETY ATTACKS

"There have been a couple of times this week when I was in an uncomfortable situation and my heart began to race and I got all sweaty and had trouble breathing."

What you were probably experiencing was a panic or anxiety attack. The symptoms usually include rapid, irregular heartbeat, perspiration, sweaty palms, increased blood pressure, and difficulty catching one's breath. Some people also have hot flashes or chills, dizziness, shaking or trembling, choking, nausea or abdominal discomfort, numbness or tingling sensations, and altered perceptions of sight, sound, and time. Many feel some detachment from their environment and fear they are dying or going crazy. A person experiencing a panic attack can be so frightened that it's difficult for others to calm her. These attacks are common in early recovery when the brain chemistry is still disturbed. The brain is no longer being regularly tranquilized by chemicals, but neither is it making its own tranquilizers yet. So when increased sensory stimulation (like an "uncomfortable situation") triggers anxiety, there's nothing to calm it down. Once you experience such an episode, it can feed on itself. Even the fear of having a panic attack can trigger one.

HYPERVENTILATION

Anxiety or panic attacks sometimes lead to hyperventilation, from breathing in too much oxygen during the rapid breathing. The symptoms are dizziness or lightheadedness, blurred vision, and tingling and numbness of fingers and toes. If you're feeling a lot of anxiety, keep a small paper bag in your pocket or handbag. If you experience the signs of hyperventilation, simply blow into the bag. If you don't have a bag available, blow into your cupped hands. Then inhale the exhaled air. Repeat several times, and you should feel better. If you don't, call your doctor.

There are ways of heading off these early recovery anxiety attacks, and of stopping them once they begin. First of all, avoid caffeine in coffee, tea, colas and other soft drinks, and over-the-counter medications.* Also avoid its cousin theobromine in chocolate and cocoa. (Decaffeinated or caffeine-free beverages are okay, and carob, available in health-food stores, makes a good chocolate substitute.) Second, make a serious effort to learn meditation, deep breathing exercises, and other relaxation techniques (see page 320), which can help break the cycle. These are excellent tools to use in recovery anyway, because they can both head off an impending panic attack and curb one that's begun. Third, try to identify the precipitating factor—a person, a situation, a place, a chemical (such as caffeine)—and try to avoid or defuse it. If every time you see your mother-in-law (or your smart-aleck older brother, or your once-best friend), there's a blowup, avoid meeting for a while. Then gradually try to work out the personal differences and understand the triggers before resuming contact.

If you begin to have panic attacks very often (four times a week or more) or if they begin to interfere with your life, you should seek help. Safest and most effective for those in recovery is probably cognitive-behavioral therapy, developed by David H. Barlow, Ph.D, at the State University of New York at Albany. The therapy focuses on changing the panicky thinking about panic attacks and uses no drugs. Studies show it to be about 80 percent effective long term.**

*In restaurants, when they bring the beverages, don't be shy about reminding waiters that you ordered the decaffeinated brew or a caffeine-free cola.

**For the name of a therapist who treats panic disorder with cognitive therapy write to the Center for Stress and Anxiety Disorders, 1535 Western Avenue, Albany, NY 12203.

"Very early in my recovery I wasn't thinking clearly. But I knew I needed something tangible as my Higher Power. I picked the doorknob, as crazy as it sounds, and it helped."

FEAR

"I've been in recovery for three months, but I still seem to be living in fear. Fear that I'll lose my job or my wife and kids or that I'll have a slip. Am I going crazy?"

No. You're in the process of becoming sane. For most people in addiction, fear becomes a way of life. When they get sober, the fear is still there. It's not surprising. The ability to look at the future with self-confidence can only be built on a track record of successes, and early in recovery about all you have to look back at is a long, sad history of failures. As you pile up small victories—anniversary chips among them—you'll begin to lose your fears and feel confident that things are going to work out after all.

The best way to pile up successes? Doing your personal best on the job. Showing your wife and children that you care. And following your recovery program faithfully. Right now, your fear serves a useful purpose, reminding you day after day how important it is to do what's necessary to stay sober. Self-confidence too early might sabotage that effort.

If at any time your fear becomes disabling—so that you are unable to go to work, unable to relate to your family, unable to go to meetings—get professional help (from your physician, counselor, therapist) immediately.

MEDITATION

The very word *meditation* repels some people. It sounds like something that only people with turbans or shaved heads should do. But meditation is far from far-out. It's just doing some controlled thinking, or mind exercises, to make yourself feel better—physically, mentally, emotionally. It's like turning on a private educational TV in your head and tuning in to yourself. You can do it while you're sitting in your living room, lying in your bed, walking along the beach, or jogging in the park. As you become more adept at it, you'll be able to use meditation to calm yourself in stressful situations.

There are almost as many different approaches to meditation as there are air flights to Atlanta. Three that work successfully in recovery are:

RELAXATION MEDITATION. The purpose of this type of meditation is to relax completely, both body and mind. This may be accomplished by emptying the mind of extraneous thoughts and focusing on breathing, on your movements if you're walking, on a peaceful scene, on a nonsense word, or on a simple, repetitive prayer or thought. For some people, yoga does the trick. For others, reading escapist literature (something that is pure fun and doesn't relate to your life in any way) works as relaxation meditation.

Relaxation meditation is good for getting the kinks out on a regular basis, but it is also valuable for reducing anxiety in a tense situation (before a job interview, when you're about to begin a difficult discussion, when you're mugged by a sudden craving). Just a minute or two of deep breathing can lower your blood pressure and reduce your level of stress.

Good relaxation exercises include: In a comfortable position and with eyes closed, breathe in deeply and say, "I am . . . ," then breathe out and say, "relaxed." Then: "I am . . . calm and serene." You can stop there, or you can follow that by imagining that you're breathing in and out through your feet and then (several times, in turn) your legs, your abdomen, your chest, your back, your arms, your face, your scalp—which indeed your cells are doing. Or just concentrate on relaxing your body, part by part.

CONTEMPLATION MEDITATION. This form of meditation gives you a chance to think about the past day or days, about failures and successes, and about how you can make the next day better. When you have trouble getting started, use one of the standard meditation books (see below) to turn on your meditation machinery.

LIFE-IN-ORDER MEDITATION. When responsibilities pile up faster than the available hours, it's useful to take time out to reorder priorities and

MOOD SWINGS

"One day I feel great, the next just awful. There doesn't seem to be any rhyme or reason for my moods—they just come over me."

Many people in early recovery feel like a punch-drunk boxer in the ring: he's up, he's down, he's up, he's down. But unless the moods are so extreme that they interfere with your functioning (you're so up that you go out and buy a new car you don't need with money you don't have, or so think about the things that need to be accomplished. Having a small pad and pencil handy to jot down key words (but not for extensive note-making) during this type of "meditation" is helpful.

Many recoverees use all three types of meditation as needed. Those who make meditation a part of their daily lives swear by its effectiveness. If you're a novice, the following tips will help you get started.* Try it. You almost certainly will like it.

❖ Meditation takes practice. You may not "get it" at first, but if you keep trying, eventually you will.

❖ Set aside a regular time each day for meditation. Some people find the early bird catches the spirit best; they meditate in the morning, before everyone else wakes up. For others the end of the day, perhaps when they are in bed, is most conducive to communing with themselves. Still others find that walking (or jogging) focuses them best. Experiment to discover what works best for you.

❖ Choose a quiet place until you become skilled at meditation.

❖ Empty your mind of extraneous thoughts before beginning. There are several ways to do this: Breathe in and out several times, focusing on your breathing and nothing else. Or close your eyes and count to one hundred.

❖ A soft musical background (classical, religious) or sounds-of-nature tapes (waves lapping against the sand, a breeze rustling through trees) help some people get into the mood for meditation.

❖ Visualization of a place you associate with serenity (a tranquil mountain stream, a deserted beach at sunset) or imagining yourself floating serenely on a cloud can also help set the mood. You can focus on a painting or photo in the room, or summon up a scene in your mind. Try to do more than just "see" the scene; try to feel it—through sound, touch, smell, even taste. Try to relax your body as well as your mind.

❖ If it will help you tune in to yourself, tune in to someone else first by listening to AA tapes. Choose the talks of people who have similar backgrounds and problems. Or read recovery meditation material, such as *The 24 Hour Book, One Day at a Time, Alateen One Day at a Time.*

❖ Use contemplation meditation as a way of taking your daily inventory. Ask yourself, "Have I been honest in all my words and actions today? Have some of my thoughts, words, or actions benefited me (or my ego) at the expense of others?" See page 108 for more suggestions on taking your recovery pulse through a daily inventory.

*If you want to know more about meditation, one of many useful sources is *The Three-Minute Meditator* by David Harp and Nina Feldman.

down you can't get yourself out of bed or out the door), they are a normal part of recovery.

The reasons for these mood swings are not absolutely clear, but it's suspected that both psychological and physiological factors are responsible. Physiologically, alcohol and drugs seem to sabotage the brain's ability to produce the internal tranquilizers (neurotransmitters) that keep our moods in balance, and that keep us from getting carried away emotionally. It's as though the brain says, "Hey, with all that Valium coming in, I don't need to make any more." When you stop popping the Valium (or whatever drug you're using), the brain doesn't pick right up and start producing. It takes a while for it to realize that its external supply has been cut off. Meanwhile, brain function tends to be less organized and predictable. The result is both emotional instability (which leads to mood swings) and sensory instability (which can lead to itching, ringing in the ears, and other sensory aberrations). Hormone changes may also flip-flop your moods as your body struggles to stabilize them.

Psychological reasons, too, account for roller-coaster moods. Emotional maturation stops when you start drinking or using drugs. You are now attempting to whiz through missed developmental stages in a compressed time period—like a teenager late for a date, and with all the up-and-down emotions of a teen. In addition, like anyone coping with a recently diagnosed illness, you're going through a great deal of stress. Sometimes you feel good because things are going well; sometimes you feel bad because they're not. Or you're afraid the good days can't last. If you work your program faithfully, however, they will definitely outlast the mood swings.

EXTREME EMOTIONAL REACTIONS

"I feel like such a fool. I seem to overreact to everything and everybody. I cry when my boss tells me to retype a letter, get angry when my husband asks if I picked up the clothes from the cleaners, and am ecstatic when I hear from an old friend."

In case you don't recognize them, those are emotions you're feeling. Everybody feels them—everybody, that is, except working alcoholics and addicts. They stuff their feelings, take the edge off their emotions with chemicals. The plan is to get rid of the bad feelings, but of course the good ones get smothered too.

"The first time I came for treatment, I thought I had a spiritual experience. I came in and said, 'I lost my wife, got picked up for DUI. I'm willing to do any damn thing. If you tell me to eat manure, I'll do it.' A few days later, I felt great. My wife forgave me. She paid my DUI fine. I said, 'I'm no alcoholic. I wanna go home.' So much for my spiritual experience."

Emotions don't usually start to surface early in recovery. The first months, and sometimes longer, are spent in a benumbed state. But once they come back, watch out! They spill out all over, like the Johnstown flood. And dealing with them is difficult because they've been dammed up so long that they're strangers.

What can you do? Recognize that overreacting is normal, and that it won't last forever. Usually by the end of the first year, the extremes begin to modify. Episodes where you overreact become fewer and then disappear almost entirely. In the meantime, talk to others who've been through this. This is no time for stiff-upper-lip stoicism. "Sharing yourself" will be more important now than at any other point in your recovery. Trust your comrades in recovery with your until-now secret (sometimes even from you) thoughts, fears, and feelings. Do that and you can expect to achieve a degree of recovery stability that would not be possible if you had to carry the burden of toughing it out alone.

If your emotions threaten to overwhelm you, don't hesitate to get additional help. You may want to see if there is an outpatient program in your area that treats alcoholism/addiction, or to consider individual therapy from a qualified counselor or therapist (see page 47).

LAUGHTER AND TEARS

"I've gone to a couple of AA meetings, and I wasn't surprised that some of the talks moved people to tears. But I was surprised at all the kidding around and the laughing. It seems to me that sobriety is a serious issue and we should treat it soberly."

There's an old saying that "laughter is the best medicine." That's one of those folk remedies that, like garlic, may turn out to be surprisingly valid. Physicians have learned in recent years that people who laugh a lot appear to have a better chance of defeating serious illness than those who somberly ration their grins. Laughter may actually trigger biochemical reactions capable of strengthening the immune system. Consciously putting a smile on your face can apparently make you feel good, even if you didn't feel good to start with.

Humor does more than just help heal. It makes it easier to look at our problems. It's a booster shot for camaraderie. People who laugh at themselves and their lives together enjoy each other and build strong personal friendships. Humor also acts as a safety valve for all that seriousness and fear that people in early recovery face every day.*

So instead of worrying that laughter at AA meetings is inappropriate, let yourself go and join in. That may seem difficult early in recovery, when periods of depression outnumber those of joy, but it will get easier as your recovery gets stronger.

Slip laughter into your private life, too. Funny movies, funny books, funny television shows, can make your life brighter. So can seeing the absurd in difficult situations during the day. Instead of fuming when you pick the wrong line at the supermarket (the one where everyone in front of you is either arguing about a price, cashing a check, or paying with food stamps), laugh at your rotten luck. Jean Cocteau said, "Angels can fly because they take themselves lightly." Try flexing your wings.

But even the best of medicines can have negative side effects. With laughter, it's the risk that it can become a diversion that interferes with the important work of recovery. Some people find that it's easier to crack jokes than to make the serious effort required to move beyond that. So you're wise to be wary of making humor an end in itself. If laughter is used to keep life comfortably superficial, it could lay the foundation for serious problems later.

DEPRESSION

"My boyfriend and I both got sober at the same time. Six months later I still seem to be depressed a lot, but he hardly ever is. How come?"

How depressed you are in recovery depends on several factors. One is the drugs you used. Those who used cocaine or amphetamines are more likely to be severely depressed than those who chose alcohol or other drugs. Another is your sex. In general, women are depressed more often than men (though men, losing some of their macho status in the mod-

*Just be sure your wit is aimed at yourself and your disease and isn't intended to make fun of others.

STRESS: GOOD GUY OR BAD GUY?

Is stress all bad? It all depends on how much we have, how long it lasts, and how we handle it. If we have no stress at all, we don't grow or learn—there's no incentive. If we have too much we may fold under it, and suffer a wide range of physical and psychological ills. A moderate amount of stress in our lives seems just right (the ideal amount varies from person to person). But even mild stress—if we don't know what to do with it or if it goes on and on without relief—can trigger distress.

A moderate amount of stress is already built into recovery: the stress of staying abstinent and learning how to live without chemical support. So it's important not to add more stress on top of this by thinking too much about the past or trying to do too much in the present (at home, at work, at play). Remember, both good events (a wedding, a baby) and bad (a divorce, being fired) can be stressful.

It's also important to know how to:

❖ Minimize stress—using exercise (see Chapter 25), relaxation, and meditation (page 320).

❖ Cope with stressful situations (see page 167).

❖ Deal with the common consequences of stress: depression and anxiety (see page 326).

Your most useful *de*stressor right now is your support group. Increase your meeting attendance whenever stress increases.

ern world, seem to be trying to catch up in the depression department). Still another factor is the kind of expectations you have for yourself. In general, people who get depressed are perfectionists. Sometimes that is the result of parental expectations projected in childhood. Perfectionists expect everything (and everyone, themselves included) to be perfect. When it's not (it rarely is), they're depressed. Often people who tend to become depressed lack the ability to go to others for help. With no outlet for their emotions, they turn the heat inward. The stage is now set for depression.

"I remember talking to God the night I went into treatment. For the first time I didn't bargain with him ('I'll give 10 percent of my income if you . . . '). I didn't promise. I just said, 'Help me or let me die.' And He started right there, at that moment."

A major reason for depression in recovery, of course, is biochemical. It's those mixed-up brain signals again, and an inadequate supply of norepinephrine, the neurotransmitter that controls moods. Still, there are ways of stimulating the brain to produce more of the chemical—without using chemicals (see page 326).

Some of the signs of depression (such as sleep disturbances, difficulty concentrating or thinking clearly) are also a normal part of early recovery. They will pass. Many of the tips on page 326 will help them to pass more quickly.

But if you find that lack of pleasure in the things you used to like to do (at home, at work, at play) persists, if you feel somehow that you don't deserve to be happy, if your low mood is keeping you from functioning at all, or if you're thinking self-destructive thoughts, seek professional help. But be very sure the person you choose understands the problems involved in the use of medication in recovery (see page 247).

FEELINGS OF LONELINESS AND ISOLATION

"Sometimes I feel totally alone in the world, more cut off from my family and my friends than when I was using drugs. I don't understand why."

By anesthetizing the brain, the organ in the body that allows us to live comfortably at peace with others, alcohol and drugs surround the user with a Great Wall of isolation. Many active alcoholics/addicts think they are relating well to others, but this is rarely the case. At best, they make superficial connections.

Theoretically, because sobriety reverses the anesthesia, the wall should come tumbling down in recovery. But there are a couple of reasons why this sometimes doesn't happen.

Some recoverees rationalize that being a loner is "the way I am." This isn't because they don't like people, but because they're afraid people won't like them. Since they fear rejection, they pretend—even to themselves—that they prefer to be alone.

Many failed to develop the skills needed to get along successfully with others before they started using drugs, particularly if they began drinking or using in their teens. Most people in active addiction use chemicals as a way to make friends, and feel lost socially when they go sober.

If you're fearful of rejection or lack social skills, you need to build your confidence along with such skills as listening, sharing, caring, helping. The ideal place to do that is in the secure and welcoming environment of AA. (Also read about relationships in Phase One, Chapter 10.)

Since inevitably there will be times when you'll be alone, you will also need to learn to spend time with yourself without feeling lonely. See page 212 for how to do this.

It's very important to address this feeling of isolation because it's a one-way street to relapse if you don't. Fortunately, if there is any truism in successful recovery, it is that you don't have to be alone any more.

FINDING YOUR FAULTS

"When I first got sober, I thought to myself, 'Hey, I'm pretty terrific.' I didn't notice that I had any character defects. Now I keep finding new ones every day. How come?"

It's that powerful instinct for survival in each of us. If you had recognized all your character flaws when you first became sober, guilt and depression probably would have driven you right back to drink. This sixth survival sense—plus the normal fogginess of early recovery and the inability, out of long habit, to be honest with yourself—kept you from being able to see the real you. And a good thing, too.

As your head became clearer and you began to learn the importance of honest self-evaluation, that quintessential imperfect you emerged. But that's okay. Now you have the tools for dealing with these character flaws, for hammering minuses into pluses. But remember, you aren't expected to be a paragon of perfection. The goal of recovery is to continue to make progress, not to become perfect. Nobody ever is.

TWENTY-THREE WAYS TO DUMP DEPRESSION AND ANXIETY

Every one of these tips has worked for someone. With time and experience, you will know which work best for you. Most of these ideas can help with both depression (D) and anxiety (A), though a few are best for one or the other. Of course, when depression, anxiety, or any other emotion gets out of hand and interferes with your functioning, it's time to seek professional help.

GET OUT. You've heard it before, now hear it again. Go to a meeting—especially if you don't feel like going. You become what you do. It's an act of faith, and it works. (D&A)

GET YOUR FEELINGS OUT. Call your sponsor, an AA friend, your spouse, or someone else you trust, and talk about your feelings or your problems, specifically and honestly. Sharing the load makes it lighter. Can't reach anyone? Try listening to the reassuring taped messages growled by a plushy and cuddly Sponsor Bear (available at recovery bookstores and other outlets) until you can.(D&A)

GET UP AND DO SOMETHING. The urge to crawl into bed and hibernate is typical during depression. Don't give in to it. Do something, anything, preferably with someone you like. Change where you are and whom you are with. (D)

LEARN FROM OTHERS. Read material and books on recovery from AA or other sources; use the index to find topics that apply to your personal situation; read that all-time bestseller, the Bible; get a lift from other people's experiences by listening to or watching recovery tapes that AA friends recommend (hundreds are available; see page 570). (D&A)

BE WITH OTHERS. Company beats misery. Avoid being alone as much as possible. (D)

DO FOR OTHERS. Stop thinking about yourself and do something for someone else. Send your mom some flowers; write a poem for your sister's birthday; take over a household chore your spouse usually handles; volunteer to spend a night staffing a homeless shelter; cheer up an elderly relative or friend with a surprise visit; take your kids to a funny movie. If you're far enough along in recovery (and your sponsor approves), do some Twelfth-Step work helping another alcoholic/addict who's worse off than you. (D&A)

MAKE A CHECKLIST. Are you taking the right dose of recovery medicine: going to meetings, conferring with your sponsor, making a daily inventory, helping (not controlling) others? (D&A)

MAKE A GRATITUDE LIST. Be thankful for what you have rather than wishing for what you could have had. Make a list of people who like you, who love you. Count the miracles that have happened to you, including your sobriety. Draw up a balance sheet—a personal audit—comparing what you are now with what you were when you first became sober. Your progress will probably startle you. (D&A)

MAKE A WORRY LIST. Include all the things that are bothering you, then cross off all those that don't have to be attended to today. You can worry about those tomorrow. Next to the remaining worries, note what steps you can take to deal with them. Then start dealing. (D&A)

TRY DISTRACTION. To get away from your problems for a little while, divert yourself with something you enjoy—a crossword puzzle, a jigsaw puzzle, a video movie, needlepoint, a good book (serious or escapist, whichever relaxes you best), a hobby (if you don't have one, start shopping for one). Or tackle something that needs doing—letter writing, closet cleaning, dog grooming. Some people keep a list of tasks that need doing for just such an occasion, and get pleasure out of crossing something off. (D&A)

TRY INSPIRATION. Listen to soul-stirring music, drive down to the ocean and watch the sun set (or rise), hike in the woods, climb a mountain, visit a house of worship, listen to your favorite AA tapes or read the Big Book or other inspirational recovery literature. (D&A)

TRY EXERTION. Go for a walk, a jog, a bike ride, a swim; shoot some baskets; play a game of tennis; or do whatever you consider both fun and exercise. Or get your exercise accompanied by a sense of achievement by doing physical work that needs to be done—neglected chores such as chopping wood, moving furniture, washing windows, scrubbing floors, mowing the lawn. (D&A)

TRY RELAXATION. Use the relaxation techniques on page 320 or any activity that helps you unwind, such as sports, fishing, gardening, hiking, golf, bird watching, movies, TV, reading for pleasure, music, hobbies, listening to tapes (AA or other), a hot bath, a long drive, a short nap. Get a massage or give one. (A)

TRY MEDITATION. A little mind control can do wonders. See page 320 for how-to. (A&D)

TRY SUPPLICATION. Prayer, especially the Serenity Prayer (page 102), can also work wonders. Try to learn the will of your Higher Power, however you interpret it. (A&D)

TRY ILLUMINATION. Some cases of depression, particularly in women, are related to Seasonal Affective Disorder (SAD). With winter's shorter days and weaker sun providing less light in their lives, some people become deeply depressed. Light therapy, during which they are exposed to bright light for several hours during the day, miraculously brings them out of the doldrums; see page 332. (D)

TRY MANIPULATION. Of your diet, that is. Sugar is sometimes at the root of bouts of depression or anxiety (see page 427). Cutting it out of your diet may lift your mood considerably. (D&A)

TRY INVENTION. Be creative. Build something, paint, sew, sculpt, cook, compose a melody, write a poem or short story (perhaps drawing on your experiences with drugs or alcohol, turning something bad into something useful). (A&D)

TRY A LITTLE TENDERNESS. Be kind to yourself; you deserve it. Share something special with your spouse, partner, or family. (A&D)

GIVE IN. For one day, stop fighting your depression and give in to it. Say, "Okay, today I feel like a frog in a bog, so I'm going to go to sleep early. When I wake up tomorrow, I'm going to feel much better." Don't, however, give in tomorrow. (D)

GIVE OVER. Turn whatever it is you can't handle over to your Higher

(continued on following page)

(continued from previous page)
Power. This is not a cop-out, but a way out. Make a small cardboard "God Box," or order one from a recovery bookstore (see page 572). If God isn't your Higher Power, you can label your box: "Higher Power Box." When you have a problem, write it out on a piece of paper and put it in the box for handling. (A&D)

BUT DON'T GIVE UP. Remember that today you may feel down, but tomorrow is a new day. These feelings have always passed before, they will this time too. And remember, your attitude does not have to be dependent on your feelings. It can be up even when you're feeling down. (D)

CALL FOR HELP. If you're too depressed to do any of the above, call your sponsor, an AA friend, your spouse, a friend, your doctor, or your counselor as your first line of support. (If possible program the numbers into your phone; then all you have to do in an emergency is push one panic button.) If your depression still hangs on stubbornly, speak to your doctor or therapist or consult a treatment center. You may need additional outpatient or inpatient treatment, or psychiatric help from someone who is trained in addiction medicine (see page 46). Also get help if your behavior or feelings indicate that anxiety or depression may be driving you in the direction of a relapse. (A & D)

ASKING FOR HELP

"Maybe it's ridiculous, but I'm very uncomfortable depending on others for getting sober."

Your alcoholic thinking is telling you that if you just try a little bit harder, you can do it yourself. But your alcoholic thinking, as it has so many times before, is leading you astray. Real men may or may not eat quiche, but they certainly are strong enough to ask for help. It's only the weak, afraid of exposing their weakness, who hesitate. So show your strength by leaning on others at this critical juncture in your life. Trying to wield control at this stage in your recovery can be suicidal, because in the addict, control triggers compulsion (see page 151). This doesn't mean that you won't be able to stand on your own two feet ever again. It just means that you have to get strong enough in your recovery before you can attempt it. Once you reach that point, other novice recoverees will turn to *you* for support and guidance.

FEELING YOU'RE GOING CRAZY

"Lately, I've been feeling like I'm going crazy."

If you're together enough to think you may be going crazy, you probably aren't. This feeling is a common complaint in early recovery, partly because of the lingering effects of the chemicals you used on your brain, and partly because of the stress of trying to adjust to a new life that sometimes seems overwhelming (many new parents also feel they are losing their minds). This feeling rears its head only occasionally and soon passes.

Sometimes, however, the feeling pervades your life, indicating more serious problems beneath the surface. Take a look at yourself. Are you taking prescription medicine that may be clouding your thinking? See page 247 if you are. Have you gotten away from your recovery program, missing meetings, forgetting to consult with your sponsor, avoiding Twelve-Step work? Getting back to your program can help you feel better. Are you doing too much, too soon? Keeping up a hectic pace can drive anyone to the edge; slow down (and read page 148).

If you can't pinpoint a problem that is causing your unhappy state of mind, or if you are having hallucinations (seeing or hearing things that no one else sees or hears) or suicidal* or violent thoughts, you should get some professional help immediately. See a therapist who is familiar with alcoholism/addiction (see page 47).

SELF-PITY

"I just got back from an office party. I felt like such a jerk standing there sipping 7-Up while everybody else was guzzling champagne. Why me? Why do I have to be the one who can't drink?"

That's like asking why your six-year-old nephew came down with leukemia or your uncle suffered a heart attack. You have a disease, and in many cases we don't know why some people get sick and others don't. Sometimes it's heredity. Sometimes environment. Sometimes a combination.

In the end why doesn't matter. What matters is what you do about it. Treatment can make a difference for your nephew—most children can survive leukemia. Changing his lifestyle can make a difference for your uncle, greatly reducing the chances he'll have a repeat coronary. As for you, sticking to your recovery program is what will keep your disease under control. Which, of course, you realize.

"In my prayers, I used to beg and plead. But now I just talk to God, turn it over and ask him to take it. It works for me."

But feeling sorry for yourself for having to stick to it could be dangerous. Every time you say, "poor me!" you are looking at what's going wrong with your recovery rather than what's right. It's the pessimist versus the optimist. And studies show that in every situation—whether it's snagging a new client or defeating an illness—the optimist always comes out ahead.

Look at the positives in your life: You feel better, you look better, you aren't having any more blackouts or picking up any more DUI's. Think about all that progress and you'll think "Lucky me!" You'll accept the change in your life as a desirable alternative to death.

Of course, you could make the choice to go backward. Every day you have that option. To join the boozers, knowing what that will mean to your life. Or to keep sipping 7-Up. It's your move.

ANGER AND RESENTMENT

"I find myself angry a lot of the time. I know that's not good, but I don't know what to do with my feelings."

Well, at least you know you have feelings. That's a positive sign. But since anger is one of those emotions that often leads to relapse, being angry much of the time isn't so positive.

Anger in itself is normal. There's no one who doesn't feel angry sometimes, and anger can be a catalyst for good. Anger about seeing people sleeping in

*Call the suicide hotline (1-800/621-4000) if self-destructive feelings are strong.

WHEN DEPRESSION IS NORMAL

A death in the family, a divorce, the loss of a business or a job. To different degrees all such events evoke sadness and depression. These feelings are part of the necessary mourning process. How long they last and how deep they are depends on the kind of loss we've experienced and our own reaction to it. If we don't allow ourselves to express these feelings immediately after the event, the bottled up emotions will eventually spill out in some less appropriate way. So allow yourself to mourn when something bad happens. It's not only okay, it's necessary. Then when the pain begins to dull, gradually use the antidepression suggestions on page 326 to help you start feeling better.

the streets can lead to efforts to get more affordable housing for the poor. Anger about a child being killed by a drunk driver can lead to tough legislation against those who drink and drive. Anger about what alcoholism/addiction is doing can help you save your life and your family.

But anger is also unleashed in unhealthy ways. A parent angry at a crying baby can lash out and harm it. A child, angry at his parents for not letting him go to a weekend party, may try to "get even" by not studying for an important test. Anger can also blind us to possibilities, to truths, to our own shortcomings. And of course, a person in recovery can use his or her anger as an excuse for getting bombed.

Anger deflected—usually from someone to whom you can't show anger to someone more vulnerable—can also be detrimental. Your boss chews you out at work, you snap at your spouse when you get home. Your mother, while babysitting, throws out some important papers, you start screaming at your kids. This kind of anger solves nothing and spreads the misery. Also futile is anger that is a result of exhaustion, lack of sleep, poor planning, guilt, and other feelings that have nothing to do with the final trigger.

Letting anger simmer or covering it up isn't necessarily any better. Some studies suggest this could be detrimental to health, though the scientific juries are still out on that one. And pent-up anger could, like uncontrolled anger, lead to relapse. Still, many people are afraid to express anger, afraid that they will antagonize others. This is especially true of those who grew up in families ruled by alcohol or drugs. Expressing anger when they were young meant being humiliated, being physically abused, or having love withdrawn. Expressing it now is still scary. But necessary.

So what can you do with anger? Recognize that it exists. Accept it. It's okay to be angry. It's what you do with it next that really counts. Keep a pocket log of situations that infuriate you, and try to evaluate why they do. Sometimes we are angriest with others when there is a grain of truth in what they are saying. When that's the case, don't shoot the messenger. Figure out what you can do to rectify the flaw in yourself.

In some cases, you may find you don't have a good reason for your anger. It is all, after all, in your eyes as the beholder. You could resent your boss for not giving you a promotion yet, or your family for not appreciating the miracle of your hard work and discipline in recovery, or the judge for not throwing your DUI case out of court, now that you've been in recovery for six months. On the other hand, you could be more realistic in viewing these events. You could say, "Gosh, I was drunk for twelve years. What can I expect from people in six months?" When you put yourself in the socks of the person you're angry at, you may find that they had no choice and that you would feel the same way. Or that they had problems of their own that led them to hurt you (your boss was under pressure from his boss, the judge was feeling the heat from Mothers Against Drunk Driving, and so on), that they deserve empathy rather than anger. Once again it's a matter of being a pessimist (seeing only the black clouds above you) or an optimist (looking beyond them toward the rainbow that promises a better day ahead). The optimists of this world always do better handling affronts.

Sometimes anger is justified—as when someone has treated you or someone unjustly, or has been dishonest, cruel, or unkind. But even justified anger can be dangerous to your recovery at this point. The emotional energy you spend in expressing it is much better spent on your recovery work. When possible, wait until Phase Two to start venting righteous indignation.

Try to settle down before you express your feelings (if the old "count to ten" doesn't work, count to one hundred—or wait an hour, or twenty-four). Then be calm and assertive rather than angry. Anger just leads to more anger, and it's close to impossible to get your point across clearly when your mood's black and you're seeing red. It's at such moments that we do and say things we later regret.

When you can't get rid of your anger directly, do it indirectly. Tell someone else, someone you can trust and who isn't emotionally involved, how you feel (in person or in writing), tell yourself (on tape or in writing), or, as so many do, unburden yourself at an AA meeting. Or ask your Higher Power to free you from your anger (using prayer and meditation, or just jotting down your feelings and dropping them in your God Box). When anger is directed at a situation, do something positive to eliminate it (if you're angry about your car breaking down every day, get it

CUTTING ANXIETY AND DEPRESSION OFF AT THE PASS

It's good to know what to do if depression or anxiety strike. It's even better to know how to cut the risk of their striking in the first place. Here's how:

❖ Work hard at your recovery program.

❖ Learn coping (page 167), decision-making (page 358), and communication (page 373) skills.

❖ Learn to express feelings and share worries.

❖ Avoid procrastination. (A long to-do list is both depressing and anxiety provoking.)

❖ Keep busy with positive activities, but not so busy that you are exhausted or have no time for recovery work.

❖ Organize your time to reduce stress; writing it down helps to give you an overview.

❖ Get adequate daily doses of exercise, meditation, and relaxation.

❖ Keep your expectations realistic; remember, especially, not to expect perfection (from yourself or others).

❖ Stay honest. (Getting caught in a lie—or fear of getting caught—is one of the major causes of anxiety.)

LIGHT UP YOUR LIFE

If you find that you're depressed when the days grow short, you may be one of the estimated 5 percent of Americans who suffer from Seasonal Affective Disorder (SAD). Recent research has pinpointed the cause of this seasonal problem: not enough light. The answer, logically enough, is more light. You can light up your life this way:

❖ Spend more time outdoors, especially when there's snow on the ground to reflect the light. Don't wear sunglasses, since the light has to enter the eyes to be effective. (Of course, if your eyes are supersensitive to snowglare, you'll have to skip this one.)

❖ Try to bring the outdoors in—outdoor light, that is—by keeping shutters, curtains, and blinds open, and by making sure shrubs aren't blocking the windows. At work, try to work near a window. Use light, bright colors indoors to reflect the light that does come in.

❖ Add adequate artificial lighting. Full-spectrum fluorescents are best; halogens can cause headache or eye strain, and tanning lamps and plant lights (which contain ultraviolet rays) can cause serious eye damage. Therapists often recommend a light box containing eight 40-watt bulbs or the equivalent, with a reflector behind them and a light-diffusing cover.* You work, read, exercise, or watch TV about three feet from the lights for anywhere from thirty minutes to three hours or more a day, depending on how long it takes to brighten your mood. Morning exposure seems to work better than light later.

❖ Take your vacations in the winter, and fly off to a sunny clime.

If you believe you're suffering from SAD, speak to your therapist or physician, or contact the Society for Light Treatment (P.O. Box 478, Wilsonville, OR 97070) or NOSAD, a nationwide support group (P.O. Box 40133, Washington, DC 20016).

*Light boxes are expensive, but they can be rented. Some insurance companies will foot the bill.

fixed, get a new one, switch to mass transit, carpool with someone else).

Sometimes, the best way to get rid of anger is to turn your mind to something else—go to a movie, head for the gym, listen to your favorite music. Or to look for the humor in the situation (there always is some). Or you can apply stress reduction techniques (see page 324). Before you know it, you'll wonder why on earth you were so angry.

However you deal with your anger, your goal is to get rid of it, not to fuel it and keep it simmering. Once you've talked about it or done something about it, it's time to forget it and move on.

If you can't seem to deal with your anger at all—if you don't feel it or can't express it, or are afraid that if you do you will hurt someone or be hurt yourself—then you need to share this feeling with others, starting with your sponsor. If you continue to fume, if your fuse is too short and explosions come too often, that could be a warning sign that your recovery is in trouble. Get professional help.

Finally, turn anger into a positive force in your life. Use your anger at the misery in your past as a motivation to work hard at your recovery. As you move along in recovery, you should be feeling anger less often and be able to handle it better.

When the anger is coming at you rather than out of you, you have to try to see past the angry words and even the nasty epithets. Listen for what is really being said, try to fathom the underlying cause of the anger (a friend is angry because you are late for an appointment, but what's really rankling is that you missed her birthday). Remember, we all say things we regret when we're angry, even to people we love or like or respect. Your responding to anger with anger serves no constructive purpose at all. Instead try to deal calmly with the issues (but not with personalities or old hurts, unless they are at the bottom of the tiff). If you do start burning, use the above suggestions to cool off.

WHAT IS SPIRITUALITY?

"A lot of people at AA are always talking about spirituality. But some of them haven't seen the inside of a church in forty years. What would they know about spirituality?"

Spirituality isn't just something people find in church. It isn't necessarily synonymous with religion. And it doesn't mean the same thing to everybody. Dr. John Mooney used to say that we had three types of existence: the body, the mind, and the soul. The body is pretty easy to understand. The mind is becoming more so. But the soul is the toughest part of ourselves to fathom.

In a practical sense, spirituality can be said to embrace the sweet mysteries of life, those aspects outside the realm of science and intellect: faith, trust, love, truth, compassion. Employing spirituality in recovery and working to strengthen it in ourselves can help carry the benefits of traditional medical care beyond its physical limits.

Achieving real spirituality takes a long time for most people. That's probably why the notion of a spiritual awakening isn't mentioned until the last of the Twelve Steps (see page 110). For many people, a *rude* awakening comes long before a *spiritual* one.

"I'm not a believer. Feeling the way I do, I don't see how I can go through the motions of AA, which rely on belief in a 'Higher Power.'"

Nobody has ever counted heads, but you can be sure that there are many members of AA who are not "believers." Unfortunately, there are many potential members who are put off, as you seem about to be, by having to accept the concept of a Higher Power.

When Alcoholics Anonymous was founded, its members sensed that they needed more than religious tenets alone to keep them sober. They'd been preached at and moralized at and denounced from every pulpit in town, but they were a lot more worried about their next drink than about hellfire and damnation.

At first "Higher Power" was intended as a reference to God. But as AA's membership grew and came to include many agnostics and atheists, along with members of every religion, it became clear that the definition of that personal Higher Power had to be

"When I went into treatment, I felt I'd turned my life over to God. Then I thought I was doing so good I could take over again. And I was right back where I started—only worse. You can't be an Indian-giver with God."

left to the individual member. Of course many people in AA choose to consider God their Higher Power. Some came into AA with that belief; others first came to believe as they struggled with recovery. But a not inconsiderable minority finds a different definition more comfortable.

Unless you actually *planned* to mess up your life with alcohol or drugs, you've already realized that there is a power stronger than you are: the negative power that overwhelmed you. From there it's no big leap to accepting its positive equivalent: a power that can help you overcome addiction.

"I turn to my Higher Power for more than strength. I look to Him for guidance, as a sort of metaphysical Answer Person. When I don't know what to do in a particular situation, I think, 'How does my Higher Power want me to handle this?' Somehow I always get an answer—a good one."

That Higher Power can be God. Or it can be an unnamed power, the power that created the universe. Or it may be the power of acceptance and love in your AA group.

Relief pitcher Tug McGraw wasn't explicit when he urged his fellow New York Mets on to a baseball pennant championship in 1973 with the battle cry, "You gotta believe!" Did he mean in God, in themselves, or what? He never specified, nor did he need to. His teammates successfully filled in the blanks. With time and a lot of reflection, so can you.

"When I was young, my parents taught me that 'God helps those who help themselves.' That's why I have trouble with the idea of surrendering and turning it all over to God."

Your parents were right. God can't do it alone. You can't expect your Higher Power to take over and change your life while you sit back and relax. You've got to do your part: go to meetings, talk to your sponsor, work the steps, examine your behavior. Only then you can ask your partner in recovery, your Higher Power, to remove your defects, keep you sober, make you a better person.

HAVING A SPIRITUAL EXPERIENCE

"I saw the Virgin Mary when I was using. Boy, was I ever spiritual! But I haven't had any spiritual experiences since I'm sober."

Recovery is not one long spiritual experience. Few of us are saints, and those spiritual moments happen only rarely for most people. But when they do, we know it.

The spiritual experience that helps recovery—actually the AA Big Book now calls it a spiritual awakening—doesn't come with a flash of lighting, a thunderclap, and a vision of a white-bearded Charlton Heston on Mount Sinai. It's not external at all. It's something that happens within you. Deep down. It's the moment when you are willing to surrender, to stop fighting, to turn yourself over to that Higher Power, when you realize that this Power is going to do for you what you couldn't do for yourself.

For some people, the road to a spiritual experience comes through meditation and prayer. For others it comes

EVALUATING YOUR VALUES

Values are the ideals that guide (or should guide) our actions, the moral and ethical framework by which we live. When we are unsure which road to take, our values provide a map. An important part of learning who you are in recovery is determining what your values are. The odds are pretty good that you gave little thought to your values while you were under the influence, and that your behavior did not live up to those values that were buried inside you. Now is the time to unearth them and to start living them. The sad truth is that people who don't live up to their value systems in recovery usually don't stay sober.

How do you dig up and identify your values—and learn to live by them?

PRIORITIZE THE POSITIVE. Make a list of the most important things in your life: family, religion, work, play, friends, hobbies, music, art, sports—whatever matters a lot to you. Then rearrange them in order of importance.

EVALUATE. If you started drinking or using drugs at an early age, you may not have had the opportunity to form sound values; if you started later and used for a lengthy period, your values may have become distorted. So see how they stack up against the values of those you respect. Compare what you've decided is important in your life to what is important to your spouse, your parents, your children, your minister, your sponsor, and others you trust. Now go back over your own list and refine it with the newly gained insights.

NULLIFY THE NEGATIVE. Make a list of the things that are not only not important, but that you would like to banish from your life forever. This will probably include alcohol and drugs. It may also include promiscuous sex, extramarital affairs; lying, cheating, and other forms of dishonesty; laziness and procrastination; unkindness; wallowing in guilt or self-pity; and pessimism.

PLAN AHEAD. Think about the ways you can build and enrich those parts of your life that are most important to you, as you move into Phase Two of recovery. Think about ways of ridding your life of the negatives.

KEEP LOOKING IN THE MIRROR. Do a daily inventory. When you look back at each day, notice whether or not you behaved in ways that enhanced those things you value most. Did you avoid those negatives you are trying to eliminate? If family is an important value, did you remember to call your spouse when you realized you would be late for dinner and he or she might be worrying? Did you make a special effort to be able to attend your child's school play? If career advancement is important, did you blow a big deal by watching Monday night football or your favorite sitcom instead of putting the finishing touches on your proposal? (Does this mean that enjoying life and free time is more important than your career—which is fine if that's higher on your values list—or just that you aren't trying to live up to your real values?) Did you refrain from telling that cute, new office assistant that you're married because the subject never came up, or because you're thinking of raising a more interesting subject later?

If you keep asking yourself—and honestly answering—questions like those, you'll not only find your values, you'll begin to live them. In the process, you'll come to love and respect yourself a lot more.

through peace and serenity, and a faith that everything is going to be okay. Through putting hopelessness, guilt, and self-pity behind you. Or through accepting life as it is, recognizing that it's not always going to be the way you want it to be. It might come in doing something for someone else and putting aside selfish wishes. In seeing the beauty in a simple pot of dahlias or in a sunset or a baby's smile, things you never even noticed when you were high. In feeling good—naturally, not artificially—almost for the first time you can remember. When you have the option to choose between doing something right and doing something wrong, and you choose doing right—now that's a powerful spiritual experience.

"I used to lie in bed for hours at night wondering why I couldn't sleep. I finally figured out it was to give me a chance to talk to and listen to my Higher Power, to think about and look at myself. Now once I've finished my prayer and meditation, I fall asleep like a baby."

Some, particularly those with a strong commitment to intellectualism, have trouble from the first with the concept of spirituality. They're likely to refuse to recognize a spiritual experience even when it comes complete with thunderclaps. That's unfortunate, because those people in recovery who expand their spirituality seem to do better than those who don't.

But being spiritually aware is no guarantee of staying sober. The best of us are always just one drink or one fix away from big trouble.

PRAYER

"I've tried praying, but nothing happens. What's the use?"

When you dial a friend on the telephone and get a busy signal or no answer, you try again. If you don't, you won't make contact. It's no different with praying.

Many people seem to get a busy signal or no answer when they call God. Very few achieve the quick response—what they might term a spiritual experience. But if they keep at it, regularly and faithfully, experience shows they will eventually get through.

How do you know you've gotten through? No, not by that bolt of lightning. Not even by having your prayers answered—what you're asking for may not be what your Higher Power has in mind. Success may be so gradual, so slow that you don't even realize at first that something is happening. You may not recognize it until someone you haven't seen for a long time comments on how much more "together" or at peace you seem. Or maybe you just start feeling good.

Persevering is often difficult for alcoholics/addicts. They like quick solutions, immediate gratification—orgasm without love, satisfaction without effort. But if you give up, one thing is sure: You'll never get through.

DAILY MEDITATION

"Meditation sounds like some fringe religion stuff. It makes me feel uncomfortable."

Prayer has been described as talking to God, meditation as listening. For some people that means listening to God, to others just to their inner selves. But in the hectic outer-directed culture we live in, we so rarely take time to listen to our inner voices that some of us have come to think of meditation as flaky. Not only is taking the time to stop and listen not flaky, in recovery it's downright necessary. For ways of making meditation meaningful, see page 320.

THE ROLE OF RELIGION

"I've got a friend who used to be into drugs and alcohol in a big way. Now she seems to have gotten straight just by joining a church. She doesn't go to any self-help group or work the Twelve Steps—but she seems fine."

There is certainly more than one way and one place to find sobriety. Some people do manage to turn their lives around by turning to religion, but only if they've managed to avoid the very real pitfalls of this approach.

Anyone who hopes to walk this way needs to remember:

❖ Withdrawal from some drugs urgently requires medical assistance (see page 78), so even if you don't intend to go for out- or inpatient treatment or to Alcoholics Anonymous, consulting with a qualified physician before attempting detox makes sense.

❖ Recovering from alcohol and drug abuse takes more than giving up the substances that have wrecked your life. It means learning how to live sober—how to work, play, and relate to others without the use of chemicals. This mission can be accomplished (often with the aid of books such as this one) within the context of a religious life, but it can't be ignored.

❖ A major task of recovery is learning to deal with one's emotions without chemical crutches. Again, this can be done without AA, but there certainly should be some sort of support and advice from someone who understands alcoholism/addiction—a cleric or a counselor with addiction training, for example.

❖ It's easy to replace one obsession with another—chemical highs with religious fervor, for example. While this might be all right early in recovery, when you need to focus on getting better—and certainly beats being stoned all the time—a religious conversion that begins to interfere with rather than enhance your work, your friendships, or your family life could drift from being a positive recovery force to becoming a negative one.

"There was this big storm, and I saw a huge tree come falling down. It was then that it came to me, 'Hey, I haven't seen a tree in sixty years!'"

"There doesn't seem to be a unanimity of opinion among AA people I know about the role of religion in recovery."

People have always argued about religion and its role in our lives, and probably always will. Like everything else in life, whether religion is good or bad for your recovery depends on how you use it. If your religious teaching tells you that your alcoholism or drug abuse is a moral problem and all you have to do to get better is pray, that could be detrimental to your recovery. If, on the other hand, your faith allows you to view this addictive disease as you would any illness, and you lean on it to strengthen your sense of values, your family, your orientation toward your Higher Power, it could have an extremely positive effect on your recovery.

16
For Teens Only

You may feel you've already made such a mess of your life that it's too late to do anything about it. But that's like giving up on a baseball game in the second inning because you're a few runs behind. As a teenager you've still got six or seven innings—sixty or seventy years—left to go. And the quicker you change your ways, the more extra innings—and healthy years—you're likely to have ahead.

This chapter will get you started turning the game around. It discusses some of the concerns of teenagers who are trying to become clean and sober. As you move along in recovery you will probably want to read other parts of this book as well. The more you know about the disease of alcoholism/addiction, the better your chances of beating it. With hard work, you *can* come out a winner.

WHAT'S ON YOUR MIND?

WORKING AT IT

"I know my folks are right. I've got to stop drinking and using. But I'm very nervous."

That's normal. Deciding to get help for your drinking or drug problems now is smart. But it is also scary. It's scary for grownups too, but your situation is a little different than theirs. Most of them have had time to develop and mature and, with years of experience, they learned fundamental living skills. Simply because you haven't lived as long, it's less likely that you have. That could be a disadvantage: You have so much to learn. But it's an advantage, too: You are still at a point in your life where learning comes easy. Older alcoholics/addicts have to break old habits and learn new ones. You have as much to learn, but less to unlearn.

That's not to say it will be easy. Most chemically dependent teens haven't had the opportunity to develop a value system, to learn how to organize their time, how to succeed in school, how

Guide Lines

❖ The sooner the use of alcohol and other drugs is abandoned, the easier recovery is.

❖ The use of chemical substances in the teen years slows down growing up. So recovery is a time for catching up.

❖ Learning to deal with friends, parents, and educational choices is a major part of recovery for teens.

to be helpful at home, how to take care of their personal needs, how to communicate skillfully and successfully with friends or family. So not only will you have to get sober and work on staying that way by doing all the things we talk about in this book, you will also have to take on the very important job of "growing up."

It's a big advantage to be starting to deal with your substance abuse problem while you're young. If you get help now, every opportunity in life will still be there for you: You can go to college, have a career, start a family, do anything you want to do. If you learn the lessons of recovery well, you will not only be able to do what your non-addicted friends can do, with your new skills and self-discipline you may be able to do more.

On the other hand, if you continue using drugs, your education and your career training will be disrupted, leaving gaps in your life that may never be adequately filled. Your freedom to live your dreams will become more and more limited. Doors will start closing. Eventually the only door left open will be the one to drug taking.

So get help now. The sooner, the better. Your life and your freedom to live it are on the line.

"I was a zombie for months. My sponsor would call and say, 'Tonight is a meeting at such-and-such time and such-and-such place.' He had to do it every day, or I couldn't remember where I had to go."

WHY BOTHER?

"I'm sixteen and I've been using cocaine for nearly a year. It's been a horrible year and I know I have to stop. But a friend said that you can't get off cocaine once you're hooked—that it's no use trying."

Doctors once believed that cocaine addiction was impossible to control, but we know now that that's not true at all. In fact, in some ways, those addicted to cocaine have an advantage over those who abuse alcohol. The effects of alcohol abuse are slow in showing up, so it may take years before the alcoholic is willing to admit there's a problem. Not so with cocaine—as you apparently know by now.

Cocaine users have no trouble recognizing they have a problem. When you're sixteen and sell your mother's silver for a drug high that is going to last for thirty minutes before you go out to sell her china, denial is difficult.

Because the realization of cocaine addiction comes fast, users don't have years of a deeply entrenched addicted lifestyle behind them that has to be restructured in recovery. So don't let anyone tell you that you can't give up cocaine. You can. If you don't, you risk not only ruining your life but ending it prematurely.

FITTING IN

"I just went through a session with my parents, my older brother, and our family doctor where they convinced me that I had to stop drinking beer and smoking pot. Well, maybe they saved my life. But what kind of life will I have? All my friends drink. I'll be the odd guy out."

Maybe it's your friends who should be out—of your life. There are certainly kids in your school who don't rely on chemical substances to have fun—kids who enjoy sports, who like to dance, appreciate music, go to movies, have parties. If you're afraid you can't be one of them, maybe it's because you've never tried. Or maybe it's because you're unsure of yourself (99 out of 100 teens are) and are afraid to try to be one of the gang without some chemical reinforcement. If that's the case, talk to your doctor or counselor. There are lots of ways a young person can build up his or her confidence.

❖ *Participate in a recovery program.* Recovery programs (for adults as well as teens) help build self-esteem. The longer you stay clean and sober and savor your victory, the better you will feel about yourself.

❖ *Stay away from your old crowd.* The kids you used to drink or do drugs with should be off limits, at least for now. This will probably be easier than you think, because once they know you are sober and intend to stay that way, they are likely to take a walk.

❖ *Build a new life around your recovery program.* There are other kids who've been through the same kinds of turmoil you've been going through and who are now clean and sober. You can learn more from them than from anyone else. But you can also have good times with them. These are the same kinds of kids you used to hang out with, but now you and they no longer need booze or drugs to be the life of the party. For a while, focus on their friendship.

❖ *Take good care of yourself.* This is something you probably weren't too good at before you became sober. Shower regularly; keep your hair well groomed; floss and brush your teeth. Pay attention to what you eat, avoiding junk foods and soda packed with sugar (see Chapter 23 for what a healthy recovery diet should be like, and enlist help from your parents in following it at home).

❖ *Get into a fitness mode.* Exercise is a great way to get a healthy high. So get into sports (anything you enjoy or would like to learn to enjoy, from roller blades to ice skating, from tennis to cross-country skiing). If sports don't excite you, then try walking, jogging, dancing or weight training. They can all make you feel better, occupy your time constructively, and start you on the road to a lifetime of fitness. (See Chapter 25 for more exercise tips.)

❖ *Find new role models.* Look around at the kids in school. It's possible that you will be able to tell who drinks and uses drugs and who doesn't by the way they dress or wear their hair. Think about dressing like the most productive and successful kids in the school. At first it may seem more natural to dress like the losers who are into chemicals, but that will change.

❖ *Modify your musical taste.* You probably recognize how much music of a particular type (maybe rap or

START A REBELLION

Doing something because everyone else is doing it is the way of sheep, not of tough, smart people. If it's the norm to drink and use drugs in your school, start a counter-revolution. Get together with a group of friends and sign a pact, promising you won't drink, smoke, or take drugs. Get as many kids as you can to join your revolution.

country) was a part of your drinking and using drugs. Listening to that kind of music now could be a cue to a relapse (see page 171). That doesn't mean that you have to abandon such music entirely, but play it only occasionally, and then in a setting different from the one you used to listen to it in. If escaping into the familiar beat triggers old user feelings or weakens your enthusiasm for recovery when you hear it, turn it off and keep it off. Try to give your new life a sound track of fresh musical memories. Experiment with other kinds of music—rhythm and blues, or '50s ballads, or classical music, or show tunes—for a while.

❖ *Think about your goals in life.* Who do you want to be? What do you want out of life? What do you want to contribute to society? Sober, you are much more likely to be able to clarify what these goals are, figure out how you can achieve them, and then progress toward them one step at a time.

❖ *Learn some basic truths about life:*

1. *No one is perfect.* No one—not your parents, not your teachers, not your friends, not the president of the United States or the star halfback on your favorite football team—always does the right thing at the right time. We all goof. Start accepting that in yourself, as well as in others.

2. *Life isn't always fair.* Bad things happen sometimes, to good people and to bad people. We can be defeated when bad things happen to us, or find something good in what has happened. Maybe you have to move in the middle of high school, leaving the kids you've known all your life. You can fold up and be miserable in your new school, or you can start making new friends and building a whole new and interesting life. Just keep in mind that it isn't what fate does to you that's important in the end, but what you do with your fate.

3. *Every journey begins with putting your shoes on.* Recovery may seem like an impossible dream and an endless journey, but you don't have to get there in a day. And you won't be traveling alone—the path has been clearly blazed by the hundreds of thousands of successful climbers who've preceded you. The view from the top, and the exhilaration and pride you'll feel once you've reached it, are worth all the sweat it's going to take.

Once your recovery becomes firmly established (this may take six months or even a year), you should begin to expand your horizons. Seek out new friends in school. The best way to do this is to get involved with sports, clubs, or a social service group (maybe one that visits hospitals or an old folks' home). You'll find that the kids who are clean are much more likely to do well in school (you'll also find that better grades are one of the perks of sobriety) and to have outside jobs and be active in school affairs. But while it will be important to broaden your base of friendships, you should not abandon your AA connections. They will remain your lifeline for a long time to come.

Also start thinking about what you want to do in the future; set short- and long-term goals. With a marker in the distance, you will be able to measure your progress more easily.

RESISTING DRUGS

"I just returned to school after six weeks of drug treatment and a long summer vacation. What do I do when my old friends try to get me back on drugs?"

That needs to be figured out before anyone makes an offer you may have trouble refusing. Peer pressure in high school can be tough to fight, but you can resist. All you need are the right tools. You probably got some of them in treatment, and you'll pick up others as you continue in AA meetings. Discuss the question with your counselor, your AA sponsor, and other kids in your school who are in AA. The following may also be helpful:

❖ Think ahead to situations you may come up against and plan exactly what you will do in each one of them. Acting out some of the situations with your sponsor or counselor will make it easier for you to handle them when they occur in real life. Even if you are scared or nervous, try to appear not to be. Stand tall, look directly at the person who's approached you, and speak firmly, confidently, leaving no doubt that you mean what you say.

❖ Don't get into a debate with someone who is trying to get you high. A drug pusher doesn't have to use facts in an argument; fiction works better. Say no and leave the scene as soon as you can.

❖ Stay away from old playmates and old playgrounds as much as possible (see page 171). Let everyone at school know you've been to treatment and are going to AA; hang out with other AA kids or straight kids. Troublemakers among your old friends will keep their distance.

❖ Don't be afraid to ask for advice. If you are upset, confused, or unsure of what to do, asking for help is a sign of strength, not weakness. You might speak to your sponsor, drug counselor, an AA friend, your guidance counselor, your clergy person, or a friendly teacher. If you feel comfortable doing so, speak to one or both of your parents or to another relative. They were all teens once, and peer pressure was every bit as heavy then as it is now.

❖ If you're ever tempted to get involved with drugs or alcohol again (and you will be), think about the consequences and weigh the long-term risks against the short-term benefits. Remember what life was like when you were using—a little heaven, a lot of hell (see page 156). Think about who else you'll hurt (besides yourself) if you relapsed. Think about messing up your schoolwork and your future.

❖ Whatever you do, don't let other kids make decisions that so intimately affect your life and your health. It's your life, and you're in charge of it.

HOMECOMING FEARS

"My father's done nothing but scream and my mother nothing but cry since the school counselor called them in to tell them I got caught with a bag of cocaine. I'm going through treatment now, but I don't know how I can face going home."

Your parents are probably just as worried about your homecoming as you are. You can't blame them for their reactions—they were clearly upset by what you did. Partly because they love you and were afraid of what drugs could do to you—addiction is, you know, a fatal disease. But partly because of their own guilt (Where did we go wrong?) and partly because they see you as an extension of themselves (What will people think?).

During treatment you'll have lots of

time to think about what happened, to learn about your disease, and to evaluate yourself and your life. Your parents need to use this time to think about it too, and to learn about the disease, and to evaluate themselves and the life of the family. Ask that your counselor or doctor urge them to do all of the following:

❖ Attend the family portion of your treatment program, if there is one. If not, ask if your parents can spend some time with your counselor before you go home.

❖ Attend Al-Anon meetings regularly. It's at these meetings that they will find they aren't alone, that there are thousands of other parents in the same situation and that they can help one another.

❖ Read Chemical Dependency: A Family Disease (page 467), which explains alcoholism/addiction to the family and friends of people in recovery and makes suggestions for helping not just the alcoholic/ addict but the entire family.

❖ With you and your counselor, set up a contract for behavior and interaction in the home when you get back. There will probably be very tight limitations on spending money, use of the car (if it's allowed at all), hours, and so on. Your parents will be expected to give you love and the basics (food, clothing, shelter, education), as they are legally bound to do while you are a minor living at home, but not much more.

You will be expected to follow the rules laid down, to do your share of the chores, to do schoolwork faithfully. The more specifically the obligations are spelled out in the contract, the easier it will be for everyone to keep to them. List, for example, the chores you will be responsible for (cleaning your room, doing laundry, cooking, caring for the dog, running errands) and when they will be done.

For your part, you will have to be very understanding when you get home. You hurt your parents a lot, and eventually you will have to think about how you can make amends for that (see page 372). Right now the best way to do that is to work hard on your recovery. You will have to understand that your parents must stop enabling you—that means they will no longer give you the kind of support that allowed you to develop a drug habit and get away with it for so long. It may take some time for them to trust you again. You will have to earn that trust. Maybe the best way for you to understand what your parents are feeling is to put yourself in their shoes: How would you feel if your child did what you did?

Rebuilding relationships will be a very important part of your recovery, but because your family has probably not been functioning well for at least a while, it's likely you will need some outside help. That's why you should continue in some kind of continuing-care program for a considerable period of time. Then, when problems come up, you will have a qualified counselor to discuss them with. It may be helpful for all of the family to tape some conversations at home and then listen to them with the counselor present. Sometimes people don't realize how what they are saying affects other people; playing the conversation back gives them the opportunity to do that. You might also want to keep a journal of feelings and events to discuss with

JUST SAY YES

Everyone tells you to say no to drugs and alcohol, but what do you say yes to? That's a question you may think about often. There are plenty of good answers. You can say yes to life, to a career, to your parents, to God, to your school, to taking care of your body. You can say yes to the future.

your counselor or your sponsor at AA (see page 114).

Some issues may have to be mediated by a counselor or other third party. Partly because feelings in family relations can easily become explosive. Partly because young people and their parents often see things from different angles, and feel that different things are important. You may like to play music at 100 decibels in the house; your parents may hate it. Talking this over with the counselor and reaching a compromise (you play the music for a couple of hours after school until your folks come home*) may help.

Rebuilding relationships with your family is important, not just for sentimental reasons but for your future. Parents are around to provide more than food, clothing, shelter, and education. It's through a working partnership with your parents and the daily trade-offs and interactions of home life that you'll develop the living skills you will need in the adult world. Chores and responsibilities may not be fun, but they are as important to your development from teen to adult as learning to walk and talk were in your graduating from baby to child.

CONFUSED ABOUT SEX

"While I was using drugs, I slept around a lot. I've got a reputation at school now, and all the guys seem to expect it. But at the moment I feel very confused about sex."

You don't have to be a teenager to be confused about sex. These days many people are. But such feelings are particularly common among teens who started using drugs and/or alcohol early. It's easy to understand why. After all, adolescence is when you start learning how to relate to members of the opposite sex, to develop a sexual identity. If you're under the influence of one chemical substance or another all the time, you don't learn how to do that. Your sexual experiences aren't the loving and caring kind that help you grow as a human being. Sex may even become a commodity you trade for drugs or money.

Sexual confusion doesn't disappear with abstinence, and there are many ways it can surface in early recovery. Some people, like you, are simply confused and unsure and wondering "now what?" Others may act out sexually to prove themselves—usually because they feel inadequate. They've come to believe that being a real man means sleeping with any female who comes along or being a real woman means slipping into the sack with any male. Some may become very active with those of the opposite sex because they have homosexual feelings that frighten them. Or they may feel drawn to those of the same sex because they see heterosexual sex as scary or risky. Some jump into bed on a date because they haven't learned how to communicate any other way—it's easier to make out than to make conversation.

But the recommendation for adults to avoid sexual relationships in the first year of recovery (see page 204) holds even more so for teens, whose sexuality, like other parts of their personalities, is still in the developmental stage. The emotional toll of intimacy will interfere with your efforts to build sobriety and rebuild your life. And don't let anyone tell you otherwise.

It's probably obvious to you why it may be dangerous to have intercourse with someone who drinks or uses drugs—do sex together and in no time at all you'll be doing drugs (or booze) together. But it can be equally dangerous to have an intimate relationship with someone who is also in recovery.

*Don't forget, however, that loud music, whether rock or anything else, can damage hearing.

Both of you could sabotage your sobriety by focusing on each other rather than on the task of getting better and staying that way.

There are other risks to having sexual intercourse, risks that could interfere not only with your recovery but with your future as well. You know what they are, but may prefer to push them from your mind when thinking about sex. One, of course, is pregnancy. In some areas of the country, boys no longer count how many girls they've made out with but how many they've made pregnant. You certainly don't want to become such a statistic. Pregnancy could be particularly dangerous to a developing fetus now, before the effects of the chemicals you've been abusing have completely cleared from your body. In addition, the stress of a pregnancy could completely derail your recovery as well as ruin any plans you have for the future.

The other major obvious risk is infection with the AIDS virus or another sexually transmitted disease. Even with the best of protection (that means condoms), there is no 100 percent safe way of avoiding such infection, short of saying no to intercourse completely.

The less obvious risk of teens—in recovery or not—having sexual relationships is that such behavior often interferes with the development of a healthy sexuality and of important interpersonal skills. If you always go to bed on the first date, you never really learn the kinds of give-and-take that should develop on many other levels (conversationally, intellectually, emotionally) for one to grow into a complete and mature person. You can also come to view sex as an obligation, or as a physical act, or as a casual activity (like watching TV or going to a dance). But it should be much more than that. In fact, sex isn't really the right word for what happens between a man and a woman who love each other. Making love is a much better term. And to make love, you have to know what it means to really love another person, to care more about that person than you do about yourself.

So give yourself time. Any guy who doesn't want you to have such time is not the guy for you. A few minutes of pleasure mean more to him than the rest of your life. And he's probably just trying to prove he's a man by "conquering" as many women as he can.

Of course later, when you feel ready for a complete, loving relationship (but not ready for parenting), be sure to use a safe method of birth control (speak to your doctor, the nurse at the school clinic, or someone at Planned Parenthood or a local clinic for advice on what will be best for you). Also be sure that you take proper precautions to prevent becoming contaminated with the AIDS virus (see page 306) or other sexually transmitted diseases (such as gonorrhea, chlamydia, syphilis, herpes, and genital warts). These diseases, although they get less press than AIDS, are more common. For a woman, some infections can lead to cancer in later life or do damage to your fallopian tubes now, which could prevent your having a baby later.

SCHOOLWORK

"I'm a high-school senior, and I've been drinking since I was in the sixth grade. My school records are a mess, and now that I'm sober, I'd like to try to make my last year a good one. How can I do that and still go to AA meetings every night?"

Maybe you can't. You have to get your priorities straight. Sit down with your parents and your school counselor, and if possible your drug counselor, and see if you can get a reduced work schedule. It's conceivable that you can graduate six months or a even a year behind your class.

PEER PRESSURE

When people talk about teens and drugs, they often refer to "peer pressure." That means pressure from friends. You've probably seen or experienced this a lot. Peer pressure can be good: It can get a kid to participate in school activities, take good care of his body, or become a serious environmentalist. Or it can be bad: It can get a kid to use alcohol or drugs, skip classes, have sex before he or she is ready, shoplift, or lie to parents. You have to be a strong person to resist peer pressure to do something you know is wrong. It helps to keep in mind that, no matter what lead or leader you follow, *you* are responsible for—and will pay the price for—what you do.

That way you can focus on recovery without entirely neglecting your school responsibilities. Gradually, as your sobriety becomes stronger, you will be able to shift more of your time and energy to school.

But don't try to do it all now. If a part-time schedule isn't possible, it may be wise to ask for a six-month leave of absence, which will give you time to concentrate fully on recovery. Ideally, you should spend several hours a day in an outpatient or continuing-care program in which you can sharpen your recovery skills. You could also do some volunteer work or take on a non-stressful part-time job.

Once you do go back to school, you should be able to do well. Not only will you not be hampered by chemicals in your body, but you will have learned a lot—about yourself, about dealing with other people, and about the importance of responsibility.

Missing some school time may seem an extreme measure, but if you had fallen ill with another disease or been hurt in an accident and hospitalized for months, you'd have thought nothing of postponing your return to school. Education is important, but your first job is to get your illness under control.

The fact is that going back to school immediately could be difficult. Your work will probably be better than it was while you were drinking or using, but it's unlikely to be first-rate until the fog of early recovery clears. Some people find the fog hangs on as long as a year (see page 311). You may also find that you have to relearn some things that you were sure you knew (like using a computer, for example), because things learned under the influence of drugs or alcohol are often lost when one becomes sober.*

Whenever you do return, it will be important that a professional at your school be acquainted with your situation, help you to get readjusted, and be available to help you if a problem comes up. Ideally this person should be a trained alcohol and drug counselor. If your school doesn't have such a professional on the staff, discuss your condition with the guidance counselor or the school nurse.

Your first instinct might be to try to go back to school and keep your alcoholism a secret. But remember, honesty is an important part of a recovery program, so it would be better to level with at least one person there. It would be even better for you to let everyone

*If your school performance doesn't begin to get better, talk to your guidance or drug counselor about the possibility that you might have a learning disability. This is nothing to be ashamed of—many very successful people have such disabilities and have overcome them. You can too, if it's recognized.

know—not by making an announcement, but simply by mentioning that you are a recovering alcoholic if the subject comes up. That way it will be easier for you to say no when a drink is offered casually at a party, or when drugs are being passed around at a football game.

If the other kids know you are in recovery, you will also be able to be a role model for those who are still chemically dependent. You may even be able to become involved in a peer counseling program, where you can help others. In addition (although this may be something you have mixed feelings about), you are less likely to be welcomed into the group you used to pal around with, a group you would be better off staying away from.

If there are other kids in your school who are recovering (and the odds are very good that there are), there may already be an AA group meeting there, possibly at lunch or after classes. If there isn't, then it may be a good idea to get one going, or at least to set up some sort of weekly or twice-weekly group. Speak to your school counselor about this possibility. It would give all of you a chance to share your concerns about getting back into the swing of things at school and to support each other during this difficult time.

In some schools, you may be asked to agree to a written or verbal contract that spells out what is expected of you now (see page 236). It may include a requirement for drug testing (page 228). If it does, think of that not as "they don't trust me!," but as a way of earning trust.

"I was expelled from college in my freshman year for drug use. Now that I've gone through a treatment program, I'm not sure whether I should return to school for the second semester or wait until the fall."

A lot depends on the campus atmosphere. If drug and alcohol use are a major problem, it may be better to wait until your recovery is better established—which will also allow you more time for "the fog" to lift. Your school should be willing to grant you a leave of absence. College won't do you any good if you relapse, and you certainly won't be a credit to the school. But if you do take a leave, be sure that you fill your time constructively. Discuss this issue with your counselor. If you both believe you can handle going back to classes, first make certain that you have a strong continuing-care plan (see page 236). Then set up a meeting with the dean and try to arrange for a light schedule for next semester. If you receive this special consideration, put it to productive use by keeping your nose in the books and your seat in AA meetings.

Most young people in recovery do very well when they return to school. The motivation and maturity gained in recovery are valuable tools in the education setting. And being clean and sober gives them a competitive edge over students whose minds are still clouded by chemicals. Keep that in mind as you work on your recovery and make your plans.

PART III

MOVING INTO PHASE TWO:

Repairing and Enjoying Your Life

It may happen suddenly. It may happen gradually. The fog begins to lift. The depression, anger, resentment, embarrassment, and pride that were hallmarks of your early recovery slowly diminish, in both intensity and frequency. The self-centered, me-first attitude that was so much a part of your addiction (and that actually helped you through early recovery) is lessening. You're beginning to be concerned about others, about how what you say or do affects them. Reality, which you once did anything to avoid, is easier to face now, even when it hurts. You've candidly evaluated your past actions toward others, your work, and other aspects of your life through a fearless, though hardly painless, moral inventory, and have begun to look at yourself in the mirror long and honestly.

Life may not be fun yet, but you are beginning to want to enjoy yourself. You are entering a time of growth and maturation, a time when all the richness of life (with its ups and downs), which so long eluded you, can be yours. You recognize that living life at the end of a loaded pistol is a risky way to find excitement, and that the best way to enjoy life's rewards is, finally, to lay that pistol down.

17

Maintaining Sobriety in Phase Two

You feel sure you are ready to move on—to start to rebuild relationships, to start having fun. But it's a little intimidating. How do you do this without jeopardizing your recovery?

WHAT'S ON YOUR MIND?

AM I CURED?

"I haven't had a drink for a year, and can't remember the last time I even wanted one. Doesn't that mean I've proven I'm okay now? Can't I give up all this AA stuff—and maybe have an occasional drink at a party or wine at dinner with my husband?"

It seems logical. You feel great, you've been sober for a year, you don't crave alcohol anymore. You must be cured. But it could also seem logical to the diabetic: I haven't had a fudge brownie in a year, I'm feeling great, I must be cured.

The logic in both cases is illusory. The diabetic feels good because she has controlled her diet and taken her insulin. You feel good because you've abstained from alcohol. Your diseases are controlled, but even with today's advanced medical knowledge, they are not yet curable.

Still, for many alcoholics and addicts (as for some diabetics), the idea that their disease is incurable is a hard one to swallow. It's just about this time in recovery, when things are going really well, that a sense of denial rears its treacherous head once more and the recovering person begins to think, "I never really had a problem." (There's an AA saying: "When health returns, the liar revives.")

You may not be able to keep your mind from speculating, but you can

Guide Lines

❖ Reaching Phase Two means you've made a lot of progress, but it does not mean you've "recovered." Alcoholism/addiction is at present an incurable disease, and your best hope is to continue to get better by remaining abstinent.

❖ The boundaries between phases sometimes blur. A sudden setback can set you right back into Phase One. Many people bounce back and forth between phases for a while before they become firmly established in Phase Two.

❖ Phase Two is a time for well-thought-out change, for calculated risks, for becoming the best you can be.

❖ Though recovery work is no longer the sole focus of your life, it shouldn't disappear from your world entirely.

keep your body from acting on wild speculation. Stick to your recovery schedule now, with even more fervor than before. You may find that when you are flying high, you need more support not to drink than when you were somewhere between down-in-the-dumps and rock bottom.

With rare exceptions (and would you want to bet your life on being one?), controlled drinking almost never works for alcoholics/addicts—as many who've tried it could tell you. This is as true after twenty years of sobriety as it is after one. You are never cured of alcoholism/addiction. Even the staunchest of AA stalwarts have been known to slip if they become careless about working their programs—ten, twenty, even thirty years after they first climbed woozily onto the wagon. You can judge from their experiences what an "occasional drink at a party" could do to you.

DEALING WITH TROUBLES

"Things have been going really well for me. So well that I'm worried what I will do if something really bad happens."

You will handle it. If you've learned anything in recovery, you've learned that bad things happen even to the best of people. But you've also learned that human beings can survive almost anything, buttressed by those we love and by friends in our support group.

A lot also depends on how we view "bad" events. It sounds Pollyannaish, but it's true that even the most devastating occurrences can have their positive sides in the long run, if we make an effort to look for them. Say your employer goes belly-up. You could moan and groan about your bad luck. On the other hand, you could say, "Hey, now I have the chance to try something new!" Or say your marriage breaks up. You could berate yourself ("I'm a failure. I couldn't keep my marriage together.") or you could take a more positive stance ("I'm going to learn everything I can from the mistakes I made this time around, and I won't make them next time."). Or say you break your leg the first day of a ski trip and have to spend your vacation propped up in a chair. You could spend six days moping and complaining, or you could use the opportunity to read some good books, meet some new people around the fire in the lodge, write in your journal, do a lot of meditating, send notes to friends you've lost touch with, and go home feeling you salvaged a rotten situation and had a relaxed and restful time.

When you find it tough to see the bright side, working your AA program (meditating, reading, doing step work, calling your sponsor, going to meetings) will usually help. It's always easier to grouse, of course, just as it has always been easier to pour a drink or pop a pill.

But when you're trying to stay clean and sober and make your life better, taking a negative view of life is like fertilizing weeds. In the end all you have is a bunch of tall weeds. A positive view is more like cultivating a vegetable garden, which will yield plenty of body-and-soul food to carry you over the dark cold months. No doubt cultivating a vegetable garden is more difficult than dumping fertilizer on a patch of weeds, but the rewards justify the extra work. So does looking for the silver linings in your life. For starters, here's one silver lining worth celebrating: If you've gotten this far, you've already put in most of the work.

FEELING BETTER, BUT NOT PERFECT

"I have been on the straight and narrow for more than a year now. I'm doing everything I'm supposed to. Gone to meetings, gotten back with my wife. How come my life is still so far from perfect?"

Look around you. You may see a lot of people whose lives you think are perfect, but the fact is that nobody's life always is. Not even Mr. and Mrs. Wonderful's down the block, the ones with the three Wonderful children, wonderful house, two cars, three TVs, four bathrooms, and a wonderful crab-grass-free lawn. There may be days when life seems idyllic for them. But there are days when both cars break down, the cable goes haywire, the four toilets back up, the lawn sprouts dandelions. Days when Mr. W. forgets he's supposed to pick up the kids, and nights when Mrs. W. forgets that Mr. W. is bringing his boss home for dinner. You can imagine how perfect their lives seem then. Yet, basically the Wonderfuls are a happy couple.

Maybe, at this point, your life is a lot less "perfect" than the Wonderfuls'. You may even think of it as still a mess. But that's okay. You can't get back everything you lost or achieve everything you dream of all at once. You are still in the process of recovery, and probably will be for years to come. Your goal isn't perfection, but progress—day to day, month to month, year to year. If you can look back and see that progress, you're doing fine.

But maybe when you compare life now with life six months ago you *don't* feel you're making progress. Recovery is often a case of two steps forward, one step back. For some people the first year is a case of one step forward, one back. They finish the year not noticeably advanced from the day they went dry. Perhaps they were in so dense a fog for so long that now they are incapable of dealing with reality and won't be until months more of recovery have passed. Inevitably, in such a case, the time it takes to build a solid foundation for recovery is prolonged. Many of these people aren't ready for Phase Two after a year, or even two years. That could be your situation. If it is, don't fret. You're building a foundation for that new productive person you will become in Phase Two. Skimp on that foundation, try to finish it in a slap-dash hurry, and you're sure to regret it when the walls cave in on you. Take all the time you need, or you may find yourself redigging your Phase One foundation over and over and over again.

CRISIS MANAGEMENT

You've lost your job, or your love, or are under temporary stress. Suddenly you feel as though you're sliding back and all that progress you've made in recovery seems no more than a memory. Now is the time you need to take shelter in the foxhole of Phase One, with more support group meetings, sponsor conferences, meditations, and readings. Don't let embarrassment, pride, or cockiness keep you from temporarily retreating. Once the shelling stops, you'll be able to emerge once again into the less sheltered Phase Two.

But over the next months you should start to see progress. If you don't, or if you've experienced any of the following, it's possible that your recovery needs some overhauling:

❖ Close calls or even a few periodic relapses.

❖ Delayed withdrawal symptoms.

❖ An inability to deal with reality.

❖ A lack of enthusiasm for enjoying life.

❖ Frequent bouts of depression, anger, resentment, pride, embarrassment.

❖ A continuing focus on self and recovery as the center of your universe rather than a readiness to reach out for new experiences or care about the needs of others.

The problem may be that you are missing one or more of the essential ingredients for successful recovery. If so, there's help out there—you just need to locate it. An addiction specialist can guide you. You may need to go into inpatient or outpatient treatment if you've never been in it, or check in for a booster if you have (see page 551). And you will also need to pay more attention to your recovery program: more meetings, more sponsor contacts, more reading, more meditation, and more basic Phase One work.

Or the problem may be that you've been doing your recovery work so well and enjoying it so much that you've gotten stuck in the comfortable and comforting Phase One survival mode. Some people get so involved in the security and selfishness of early sobriety that they just never get past it into the rewards and the enjoyment of life that comes in the next phase. If your recovery is solid and you meet most of the milestones for the completion of Phase One (see page 350), then you should start taking tentative steps into Phase Two. This section of the book and your support group contacts can help you, but your courage and hard work will be needed in the effort to regain title to your life. The rewards will be well worth that effort.

If some days you feel as though you're making progress and other days you seem stuck, it's possible that you are hovering somewhere on the cusp between Phase One and Phase Two. Many people swing back and forth as the two phases overlap. One day they are stepping bravely out into the world, the next they are back in the womb of their early recovery phase. That's okay, as long as you move in the direction of more days in Phase Two and fewer in Phase One, and as long as you work at it instead of despairing.

For some people, there comes a moment when, suddenly, they realize they've changed, when the recovery way of life becomes their way of life.

That moment may come after one year or five, or even longer. For others, there's a more gradual awareness that things are getting better. Again, this perception can come early in recovery, or not until several years into it. But come it will.

UPS AND DOWNS

"Last week I was convinced that everything was going to be okay, that I'd turned the corner. This week, I feel awful again."

You've just made a very important discovery: Sometimes life is a bowl of cherries; sometimes it's only the pits. Your senses were addiction-dulled for so long that you probably never realized that fact. Or maybe you used chemicals to cover it up. Now you have to look this reality squarely in its not-so-pretty face: In even the best of recoveries, in even the best of lives, there are ups and downs. Paradoxically, it's often during the down periods, the times of stress, that we do most of our growing and maturing—*if* we know how to deal with them.

Your bad days may indicate a need for more work on your recovery. Or maybe they're a figment of your interpretation. More likely they are a normal part of life. Use all the living skills you've developed in recovery (decision making, relaxation, stress management, positive thinking, and so on) to deal with them. And don't forget your AA support system.

"They say half-measures avail us nothing. I thought that half-measures would avail me 50 percent, or nine-tenths measures, 90 percent. But I found out they mean nothing. I have to go all the way. That's why I'm in treatment. I'm not crazy about it, but I am crazy about living."

HANDLING SUCCESS

"Why is it that every time I tell my AA friends that things are going great, that I've never been so successful, they give me a funny look and tell me to 'Watch out'?"

They know from experience that a smooth, straight road tends to make the driver careless, and getting careless can lead to an accident. In your case, a crack-up of a different sort. That doesn't necessarily mean you're in trouble if your life isn't filled with dips, bumps, and treacherous curves. It just means that you can't allow yourself to be lulled into believing there will never be a sudden rockslide ahead; you have to be alert, with your eyes open every minute.

Your friends also know from experience (their own) that alcoholics/addicts, so long used to down experiences, often begin to feel uncomfortable when things continue to go well for a while. They begin to question their good luck and find themselves asking, "After all I've done to others, do I really deserve this great life?" Or they start waiting for the other boot to drop: "Things are going so well, I know it can't last." Both of these attitudes can hinder recovery.

Sometimes things go so well that you begin to believe you *do* deserve it, that there is something special about you. You may even begin to think you are so smart and so unique ("terminal uniqueness" is how that frame of mind is often described) that the rules that apply to others in recovery don't apply to you. You may drop values and people that, for a while, were important to you. This feeling of power coupled with a loss of humility can affect not just your work and your relationships, but your recovery as well. The next logical step is the dangerous thought: "Hey, I bet I could drink now without any problem!"

You don't have to fear success. You just have to learn how to handle it safely. It will help for you to do the following:

Remember your Alamos. You may be headed in the wrong direction if you've forgotten where you've been. Remind yourself by looking periodically at old mementos (videos, photos, letters to yourself, ultimatums from creditors, or anything else that shows what "the good old days" were really like), by working with other human wrecks just beginning their recoveries or coming out of treatment, by sharing your story at AA meetings and listening to the woeful tales of others.

Share your wealth. Your success will mean more to your life and your recovery if you share your hard-earned wealth of experience with others. How you do this will depend on you, your skills, your contacts, your financial resources, and so on. You may be able to help educate youngsters about the risks of alcohol and drugs, make the community more aware of the seriousness of the problem, lobby against the liquor lobbies, work with people in recovery. See Chapter 30 for other ways you can work in the community to improve attitudes.

"When I first got into treatment, I thought I knew everything. The longer I'm sober, the more I realize how much I don't know. It seems like growing in reverse, but actually, I think that's real growth."

WHERE'S THE FUN?

"My first year of recovery was the toughest year of my life. But I made it through. Is it going to stay this tough? Is life ever going to be fun again?"

No and yes. No, it isn't going to stay this tough. And yes, life is going to be fun again—if you let it be. You've reached the point in the recovery process where you should begin to concentrate more on the enjoyment of life in all its facets. This doesn't mean that you will wake up tomorrow morning to find the world is filled with perpetual sunshine and the fruitbowl of your life with sweet ripe cherries. But it does mean that you can begin to think about more than merely surviving without drugs and/or alcohol. Just what direction your thoughts take will depend on what sounds like fun to you. Time with the family. A great social life. Pursuing a fascinating hobby. Exotic travel. Playing or watching sports. Enjoying the arts. Exploring new vistas.

But all your fun shouldn't come from doing "fun" things. You need to learn to get enjoyment out of life itself, to get a buzz from staying sober just as you did from drinking or drugging. This can be tough for alcoholics/addicts, who have so long been in hot pursuit of instant pleasure, focused on cause and effect rather than process. Rushing headlong toward the next high, you've never paused to admire the flowers on the road of life. Now is the time to take the time to enjoy those flowers.

MAKING AND USING LEISURE TIME

"I feel like I'm ready to go to fewer AA meetings. But I'm so used to doing this every night that I'm afraid I won't know what to do with my free time."

When you started going to AA meetings, you probably complained that you had no free time for anything else. Now that free time threatens, you are concerned again. That's because change, even for the better, tends to make us tense and uneasy. Moving and switching jobs both generate high stress levels. But, with the right attitudes, both can light up your life.

Similarly, with the right attitude, your newly found leisure time can go a long way in helping you rebuild your life. Change that transforms you as you grow in recovery is actually essential to your return to health.

So welcome the challenge that more leisure time brings. Filling it fits in perfectly with two major goals of this phase of recovery: rebuilding relationships and learning to enjoy life again. To further the first goal, organize your free time so a great deal of it is spent in mutually enjoyable activities with those people (family, friends, coworkers) with whom you are trying to reestablish a good relationship. Limit solitary activities (like building models or watching TV), but don't abandon them entirely if you really find them fun.

If you have children, many of the activities you choose should include them. They have probably been the prime victims of your substance abuse; let them now be the beneficiaries of your recovery. But in trying to reconnect with your children, don't forget your relationship with your spouse. Some special time should be set aside each week for the two of you alone. (See Chapter 19 and following for more on relationships now.) Again, look for ways to combine your two goals—fun and relationships.

Part of your recovery will be learning how to make decisions in consultation with others. For most alcoholics/addicts, going off on one's own is an established behavior pattern. (You didn't ask your spouse when you decided to stop off at the bar on the way home from work, or check with your kids before you got drunk on the night of the school play.) Changing that leap-before-you-talk piece of your personality now will take a conscious effort. When planning activities with family or friends, don't dictate what the activities should be. Consult the others involved, and occasionally take dictation yourself. A good way to do this within the family—and to show that things are changing for the better—is to hold regular family meetings (see page 193).

Another important aspect of your recovery is service to others. So if you're ready for it, consider spending part of your leisure time in community work

Fill your leisure time wisely by observing the following:

❖ Choose activities that will build an insurmountable wall between you and dangerous playgrounds and playmates.

❖ Be certain your plans are consistent with your financial resources. You may still have the inclination to do things that are unrealistic. Stifle that urge (cut up your credit cards, if you have any left), or you could end up sabotaging your efforts to get your life back on course financially.

❖ Avoid overprogramming. Leave some time for relaxation, some time to "do nothing." You still aren't ready to get back on a nonstop merry-go-round.

❖ Avoid overdoing it physically. If you've been a couch potato for a while, this is not the time to catapult yourself into strenuous physical sports and games. Those should wait for Phase Three. Ease your way into, or back into, a physically active life with milder exercise, such as walking, swimming, or casual biking. And do so only after you've had a medical checkup and have your physician's okay to go half-speed ahead.

If you're having trouble figuring out just what you want to do, try drawing up an interests inventory. Think about all the things that you enjoy, or suspect you would enjoy. The possibilities now are virtually unlimited. Also factor in whether or not you have AA friends, or other sober friends, who enjoy those activities too. Use the inventory as a take-off point for planning activities. You may have to sample a number of possibilities before you settle on the ones you want to concentrate on. But even that should be fun.

FEAR OF SLIPPING UP

"A friend in AA, who's been sober longer than I have, just had a really bad slip. He's dry again, but boy, it makes me worry that it will happen to me."

It can happen to anybody. Alcoholism/addiction is an incurable disease, and a fairly large percentage of those who try to become sober or clean have one or more relapses. It's no disgrace, but it is a warning that the "slipper" was doing something wrong—or omitting something right. A slip can be demoralizing, but it can't take away what was learned in recovery and it can teach a great deal about how to apply that knowledge more successfully the second time around.

If you want to avoid your friend's fate, continue working your program faithfully, going to support meetings regularly, and shunning situations where temptation is great. Also read Chapter 29, which deals in depth with the issue of relapse.

MAKING DECISIONS

"Following the suggestion of my sponsor and other AA friends, I avoided making any major decisions during my first year or so of recovery. Is now the time to start thinking about a change?"

Probably. Until now, your major goal in recovery was, wisely, to stay sober. Now it's time to put new life in your life—and that requires some decision making. To discover whether you are ready for making decisions, take a little inventory:

❖ Has your judgment (as evidenced by your behavior) improved since the days when you were drinking and/or using? To get an accurate and fully objective assessment, you'll have to ask others—your sponsor, family members, friends, coworkers—this question too.

❖ Do you have a better idea of who you are and what your goals are? Comparing past inventories to present will help you decide.

❖ Have you improved your interpersonal skills? Can you relate to others without threatening or feeling threatened? Are you able to "read" other people more accurately?

❖ Are you mostly free of resentment of others and envy of what they have?

❖ Do you think you will be able to handle a decision that ends up with a bad outcome? Even the best decisions sometimes do.

If you can answer yes to all these questions, then, yes, you're ripe for change and ready for decision making. But don't try to change everything in your life at once. Take one issue at a time, preferably starting with a minor one (no harm done if it goes bad), and apply the following basic decision-making principles to it:

Identify the problem or decision to be made. Some people never even get this far—they just let things happen. It could be a relatively minor decision: Do you really need a new car? What model should you buy? Is it time to get your apartment painted? Where should you go on vacation? Or it could be a major, life-shaking decision: Should you move to a new community? Should you quit your job? Should you end your marriage?

"You know, after five years I think, gosh, everything ought to be fine. I ought to be able to live one day at a time and not ever have to worry. Then I realize that I have a lot more growing to do. It's like cleaning out a closet. You clean out the front; then you go in deeper. And just when you think you're finished, someone (maybe you) has dumped some more stuff into it. So you have to keep cleaning."

Gather data on the subject. Some you will have from past experience; some you will have to seek out. Have your old car checked to see how much life it has left; look into prices and styles of new cars. Get several estimates on the cost of painting your apartment. Check on possible vacation destinations, the costs, the time involved, and what you could do when you're there. Look into the cost of a move, the time involved, how it would affect your life, friends, family, work. Look at other work options, what they would mean in terms of career, money, lifestyle, and so on. Go to a marriage counselor with your spouse to see how your marriage looks to an outsider.

Do some field research. How have other people solved similar problems? AA and AA people provide an infinite supply of case histories—on tapes, in talks, in the Big Book, at meetings. Whatever it is you're contemplating, you will probably find others who have been there before you. Study these case histories closely, then factor their successes or failures into your decision making—you may be able to avoid making a guinea pig of yourself.

Know your personal values and your goals. In making any decision, your values and goals come into play. Is having a new car important to you? Maybe it is for safety reasons. Or prestige. Or to help you achieve your goal of getting to work on time. Is a clean, fresh apartment important? It is if one of your goals is to improve the environment in which you live. If recovery is an important goal (and it should be for the rest of your life), would a vacation on that exotic island with no Alcoholics Anonymous group meet or defeat that goal? If strengthening family ties is an important value, would moving to a new community enhance or undermine that objective? What if independence is an important goal? If career advancement is the bull's-eye in your target, would a new job help you hit the mark? If you believe in the sanctity of marriage, would divorce with no attempt at reconciliation be in keeping with your values?

Look at your options. Thoughtfully list all the possible solutions, along with the risks and the benefits of each possible outcome. How will they affect

ONCE MORE WITH FEELING

Many people find that even if they did their Fourth Step (the moral inventory; see page 112) in Phase One, it's helpful to repeat it now. This inventory may look very different from the one you did when your judgment was off, your psyche focused inward, and your head stuffed with cotton wool. You will probably find that now you can remember more, evaluate better, identify behavior patterns that were invisible earlier, and see yourself and others in a very different light. The priorities you must set in this phase of recovery will mean more when they are derived from an updated analysis of where you've been and where you are now.

you (emotionally, physically, financially), your recovery, and other people? Will they be easily reversible, or once done, carved in stone?

If you buy a new car, it may get you to work on time and impress your latest love, but you may not have enough money left to pay your rent. If you don't buy a new car, your finances will be in better shape, but getting to work on time with the old clunker will still be a problem.

Painting the apartment is expensive, but the benefits of increasing its resale value and improving your mood are significant. If you don't paint, the dismal living environment could contribute to the onset of depression, and you know too well where that could lead.

The advantage of that get-away-from-it-all exotic island is its isolation. That's also its disadvantage: lots of tempting, tropical coolers and no AA support group. Some of the other places you've been thinking about may offer AA groups but lack the offbeat appeal.

An advantage of moving would be the opportunity to start fresh, away from dangerous playmates and playgrounds. A disadvantage would be leaving the safety of the familiar and those you love, and possibly wounding them in the process.

Divorce offers a new beginning, but it might mean hurting and leaving children you love or giving up a relationship that still has some meaning.

There may, of course, be a long list of risks and benefits for any one decision. Sometimes, when you look at your list you can see immediately which decisions are good bets (those with a long list of benefits) and which are not (those with a long list of risks). Sometimes, however, the picture looks relatively balanced. Then you have to go on to the next step.

Minimize risks or increase benefits, when possible. This technique can improve the prognosis for any decision.

The financial strain of buying a new car could be reduced by buying a good secondhand car or overhauling your old jalopy. The benefits could be improved by using the car to start a delivery service in your spare time.

Reduce the risk on the paint job with a do-it-yourself compromise that'll save money *and* give you a much-needed sense of accomplishment. Or save by avoiding expensive wallcoverings and sticking to basic cream or white, so that if you do sell, you won't offend any buyers.

Decrease the risk and increase the benefits of visiting Happy Island Paradise by coordinating your trip with two or three friends from AA. You can share the fun and conduct your own backbone-reinforcing meetings.

Reduce the risk of moving by choosing a community where you know someone, or where there is a particularly good continuing-care program. And don't just check out living quarters, shopping, and schools—check out a couple of AA meetings too. Increase the benefit of the move by finding a really good job in the new town.

Reduce the risk of either staying in your marriage or getting a divorce by getting the best possible family therapy and putting your all into it. Improve the outcome either way by strengthening your recovery. That will make your life better, whether you're married or single.

Develop a strategy. Every decision employs a strategy, even if you aren't aware of it. The *chaos strategy* is often an unconscious one: You make a decision without thinking through your options and their possible consequences. Then there's the *delaying strategy:* Sometimes you postpone making a decision pending more information; sometimes you just plain procrastinate. The result is an unplanned decision not to decide. Then there's the *wish strategy,* in which you take the choice you desire most, no matter what the risks—it's betting on the long shot. The *safe strategy,* in which you take the plan most likely to succeed, even if the outcome won't be as rewarding, is betting on the favorite. And the *escape strategy,* in which you select the plan that will avoid the worst outcome even if it will not bring the best result, means you are staying away from the betting window entirely. Finally there's the *combination strategy,* which balances desirability with safety—getting a chance at the big money while hedging your bets. This last strategy offers the most but is the most difficult to apply because it demands careful use of decision-making skills.

Carry out the decision. The best of decisions, or the worst, are meaningless unless they are implemented.

Accept responsibility for the decision. That doesn't just mean that if things go wrong, it's your fault. Or that if things go well, you get a medal. A decision is, in some ways, like a baby. We should put a lot of thought into planning it (though sometimes it just "happens"), and then we need to nurture it. Decisions, like babies, don't start out good or bad. They are what we make them. If you decide to buy the car, paint the apartment, go to that fantasy island, move to another town, or stay in that marriage, your responsibility doesn't end there. Now you have to make your decision work—for yourself and for the others involved. Because this type of commitment can be difficult for people in recovery, it requires heavy duty attention.

If you find you are making decisions without following an organized game plan such as the one above, or if you recognize that a decision is rife with risks but make it anyway, you are acting compulsively—much the way you did when you drank or used drugs. This probably means there are holes in your recovery program big enough to sink you.

18

YOUR SUPPORT GROUP IN PHASE TWO

The biggest mistake people make when they enter Phase Two is to cut back on AA-related activities, and much too soon. It's common to become overly confident once the cornerstone of recovery seems solidly in place. It's easy, especially if one has the wrong attitude, to yawn at meetings that "hash and rehash the same old stuff night after night." And it's tempting to forget about meetings entirely—to let down and spend your free time with family and friends, just catching up and having fun.

WHAT'S ON YOUR MIND?

CUTTING BACK ON MEETINGS

"I've been going to four or five meetings a week for the last year. My wife thinks it's time for me to cut back and spend more time with the family, but I'm scared of going to fewer meetings. How many should I go to?"

With terry robes, one size fits all. Not so with Phase Two recovery programs. Each person needs to find the combination of meetings and other AA activities that fits him best.

Many people are able to cut back on meetings once they've built a solid foundation of recovery. But most, like you, are wary about doing so. Understandably. Meetings have been their lifeline for a year or more, and they wisely hesitate to let go. Indeed, they shouldn't. But they can safely loosen their grip.

Now's the time to start evolving an AA program that fits into your life, instead of fitting your life into your AA program. Your new schedule may in-

Guide Lines

❖ There is no simple formula for deciding how many meetings are appropriate for the recoveree entering Phase Two.

❖ For many people, this is the time to expand AA activity by becoming a sponsor for one or more newcomers to AA.

❖ Even those people who can safely cut back on meetings now may occasionally (at times of stress, for example) need to rev up their attendance.

clude fewer meetings (but perhaps more meditations and reading at home), your own private mini-meeting with an AA friend over lunch a couple of times each week, attending occasional retreats, talking to your sponsor often, becoming an active sponsor yourself. More important than going to a specific number of meetings is living the lifestyle promoted at meetings.

"I always thought that my sponsor wasn't especially fond of me because I bothered her all the time. Then when I started sponsoring, I realized she was probably getting as much out of it as I was. I know I do with the people I'm sponsoring."

Cut back gradually, cautiously, with a lot of support from other AA members and your sponsor to supplement the applause from your spouse. It will slowly become clear just how many meetings are ideal for you. But it's important to remember that cutting back to two meetings a week isn't an irrevocable decision. You have to be flexible. You do have an illness, and if it flares up, or threatens to, you may need some extra treatment. So if you have a bad day, you should feel free to go to an extra meeting. If you're having problems at work, you may feel better if you go to a meeting every night for a couple of weeks. And if you (you should be more in tune with your feelings now) or your sponsor notices that your old attitudes and behavior patterns have begun to reappear (you're resentful, angry, negative, depressed), it will be clear that you've dipped below your "therapeutic dose" of AA; increase your weekly meetings for a while to be sure you don't slip and fall. And don't overlook the inspirational booster-shot value of AA conventions and retreats to get the positive momentum going again. There's nothing quite like their concentrated AA time.

"I haven't been at a meeting in three months. I was feeling so good, I felt I didn't have to go. Things aren't so good now, and I know I need to go, but I'm embarrassed about going back."

Just the fact that you hesitate to go to a meeting is a sign that you sorely need it. You're focusing on yourself and your feelings so much that you think everyone at the meeting is going to point a finger and sneer, "Hey, there's Jane. She hasn't been to a meeting in months. How come she's coming

CONFIDENTIALITY

Though you are not acting in a professional capacity when you sponsor another recovering alcoholic or addict, you must remember to keep whatever you are told in this relationship strictly confidential. No doctor-patient, lawyer-client, or priest-confessor relationship is more of a sacred trust. If sponsors began blabbing about their sponsees, not only would individuals be hurt but the entire system would fall apart. Treat your sponsee's confidence as you would like your sponsor to treat yours.

If a friend or family member of your sponsee asks for confidential information entrusted to you during your tenure as sponsor, the answer has to be no. If, however, you feel that withholding the information would foster dishonesty or could hurt someone, encourage full and appropriate disclosure by the sponsee. Sometimes the sponsee really needs to ventilate something that's been burning a hole in his or her psyche. If he or she is willing to share it, listen. If not, urge sharing it with a close family member or friend, or writing it in a life history that can later be burned.

Being a sponsor does not cloak you in any kind of legal immunity. If anything you believe to be ongoing criminal activity comes up in your relationship with a sponsee, sever your ties immediately. Use your own judgment as to whether or not the information should be passed on to someone else. Unlike a professional, you do not have a legal responsibility to take action if someone gives you information that could harm someone else, but you do have a moral obligation. For example, a threat to

back now?" The fact is the others all have problems of their own. They may not even have noticed that you were away. If they did, they won't be judgmental. No one at AA can afford to be. And you're not the first, and won't be the last, to make that sudden U-turn.

By all means, put your pride in your pocket and get back to going to meetings. You'll be welcomed with open arms. And this time, don't stop going on the first sunny day.

BECOMING A SPONSOR

"A friend asked me to be his sponsor, but I'm not sure I'm ready."

Questioning your readiness is a good sign. You're not willing to assume this major responsibility without being sure you can handle it. Ask yourself these questions:

❖ Have you personally worked all of the Twelve Steps?

❖ Do you have enough sobriety under your belt, and is it the kind of sobriety you think others could benefit from? Some people are ready to become sponsors at the end of a year; others aren't ready until a year and a half or two years have passed.

❖ Do you feel very secure in your recovery?

❖ Do you have enough time to give to being a sponsor without stealing time from your own recovery and from your family and other responsibilities?

❖ Do you feel you have the energy to give to helping another alcoholic or addict?

❖ Do you feel able to emotionally distance yourself from other people's problems?

someone's life should not be ignored.

There are several ways of handling it. You could call in another AA member, but consulting a physician or counselor would probably be better, since as professionals they are more experienced in handling such problems. If danger seems imminent, consult a professional immediately. If there's no one you can contact, you may have to warn the person at risk and possibly call the police. The need to prevent serious harm supersedes the confidentiality of your sponsor-sponsee relationship. These situations arise very rarely, but when they do, your response may be a crucial factor in the outcome.

Some areas are grayer than a direct and immediate threat to someone's life: suspicion of wife abuse, for example, or of child molestation. The course to take in such a situation is not always clear-cut. But if you suspect that your sponsee is either a perpetrator or a victim of such acts, find a family counselor or physician to discuss the problem with. Such a professional can advise you on a course of action and help to get you off the "hot seat."

It's important for your sponsee to understand from the start that it's not the role of the sponsor to pass judgment, but rather to encourage the newcomer to grow, to avoid repeating the mistakes of the past, and, one day at a time, to recover. Any tales told you about past misdeeds will be held in strictest confidence. Equally important is your sponsee's understanding that you will not participate in any illegal activity, and that any ongoing behavior that threatens the well-being of another person will require—and receive—action.

❖ Do you know how AA works from the perspective of an insider—someone who's participated in meetings, not just observed?

If you answer yes to all of these questions, then you are ready. If not, give yourself and your recovery more time. But whether you become a sponsor now or later, do take on that task. Research shows that sponsors have the very best sobriety success.

"I'm a middle-aged man, and my recovery is real good. I'd like to share what I've learned by becoming a sponsor to someone else. How do I find a sponsee?"

Sometimes the sponsee (or "pigeon") finds you first—just walks up to you at a meeting and makes the proposal. Sometimes you have to take the initiative and approach a tentative newcomer. Either way, you want to be sure you have a good match.

You don't have to be as choosy in picking a sponsee as you do in picking a mate, but the fit should be as comfortable as an old boot for both of you. You might get your first clue to a possible sponsee from something he says at a meeting, that makes you think you can help him. In addition, the right sponsee for you should be:

❖ *Of the same sex.* This will, for the most part, eliminate the distracting games people play when opposites attract. (If you're gay, see page 119.)

"I wanted to feel better real bad. Feeling good was as good a spiritual experience as I could get."

❖ *Of similar background.* That will make it easier for him to identify with you, easier for you to understand his needs. But be wary of letting your attention focus too heavily on the things you have in common (if you are both doctors, for example, you may spend too much time discussing how to get a revoked license back, too little on recovery issues). If this is a possibility, enlist a co-sponsor who can deal exclusively with hard-core recovery while you handle more specific items.

❖ *Available when you are.* If you work days and he works nights, you may never have time to talk.

If you're approached to sponsor someone, sit down and talk to him about his needs and how the relationship might work before saying yea or nay. If, after the discussion, you don't feel the chemistry is right, it's okay to say so. Honesty is, after all, the best policy. But do help the person to find the right sponsor and assure him that even if you can't be a sponsor, you can be a good friend and supporter.

"I'm already sponsoring one woman, and another has asked me to sponsor her. How many people is it okay to sponsor?"

There is no simple formula. Some folks—retirees, for example, with plenty of free time and years of accumulated wisdom—manage to successfully sponsor a dozen or more, while others—busy, young, or insecure people—have their hands full with one. How many you can handle will depend on your personality (are you overwhelmed or invigorated when your kid sister and your mother call on the same day to moan and groan about something?) and on the amount of time you can spare (do you need forty-eight hours in a day to take care of the responsibilities you already have, or are you at loose ends wondering how to fill empty hours?). Whatever you do, don't increase your "case load" too quickly, and pull back at any time if you feel you are giving less than your best to all your sponsees. Your goal is to help others and yourself, not to get your name in the "AA Book of World Records."

BEING A GOOD SPONSOR

"Though I've been on the receiving end, I'm not quite sure what to do now that I'm becoming a sponsor myself. The woman I'm sponsoring has a pretty shaky recovery, and I don't want to make it worse."

You're starting off on the right foot by taking your role seriously. Though you won't be responsible for the failure or success of the recoveries of those you sponsor (in the end it's up to them), it is important for you to do the best job you can.

❖ Let the person you are sponsoring know that what you are doing is part of your own recovery, and not taken on as a professional responsibility (even if you are in a helping profession).

❖ Make yourself as available as possible to her. That doesn't mean that if your sponsee has insatiable needs, you must be available every minute of the day and night. Sometimes a really troubled person needs two or three secondary sponsors, so that if the primary sponsor isn't available, fallback people can take over. Suggesting speaker tapes—especially those that may be reminiscent of your sponsee's own life—to be used when you're not available may also be helpful. But if a sponsee continues to need round-the-clock support, she probably needs professional treatment.

❖ Arrange to meet regularly with her on a one-to-one basis.

❖ Monitor her recovery; be sure she is working her program, moving along on her step work. Encourage her to read the Big Book and other appropriate material, meditate daily, and create other structure in her life.

❖ Keep her informed of meetings, conventions, retreats, and other recovery-oriented events that may be beneficial to her. Get her actively involved in AA. Encouraging her to set up chairs before a meeting or fold them afterward, to make coffee, read aloud the Serenity Prayer, the Twelve Steps, or the Twelve Traditions, and to eventually chair a meeting or give a talk will make it clear that recovery is much more than just observing, listening, and taking up a seat at meetings.

❖ Make it easier for her to get to meetings. That doesn't mean donning a chauffeur's cap before each meeting, but when you can, stop by on your way and give her a lift, or arrange for someone else to do it. If she drives, have her pick you up occasionally.

❖ Make an effort to introduce her to others (in AA and elsewhere) who may be helpful to her recovery or who have had to deal with similar problems.

❖ Nudge her in the right direction, based on your own best judgment of what she needs to be doing at any particular time. But keep in mind that change is often gradual rather than pronounced, and as long as she isn't stuck, she's doing okay.

❖ Don't play "Dear Abby." Basically you're not supposed to give advice, but to act as a nonjudgmental sounding board; to guide, not direct. If your sponsee is trying to decide whether or not to continue her marriage, discuss her options with her and tell her you will support her no matter what she does, but be sure to remind her that she is the one who has to live with her decision. You can, however, help her move through the decision-making process (see page 358). Expect that some of the issues she brings up in early recovery will be compulsive echoes of the unmet need to drink or use. Your attentive ear, mature behavior, and thoughtful response will help her move toward healing.

❖ Respect her privacy. Just as anything you hear at AA is confidential, so is anything you hear from the person you are sponsoring. There are exceptions, however, when someone's safety is threatened (see page 364). If you think you will hesitate to take action or be unwilling to make that judgment at a critical juncture, then being a sponsor may not be for you.

❖ Don't try to control. Alcoholics/addicts, active or sober, tend to try to control their world and everyone in it. Don't enable, don't hover, don't do everything for your charge, leaving her nothing to do for herself. Expect that your sponsee will take many wrong turns on the road to recovery. Guide her so that she will learn not to make the same mistake twice.

❖ Don't use your sponsee in the wrong way. A sponsoring relationship is meant to satisfy your recovery needs as well as those of the person you are sponsoring. But it if begins to satisfy a personality need, if you use this person as a substitute for your family, as an excuse for leaving work, or as a reason for not accomplishing things in your own life, you are abusing Twelfth-Step work, not using it positively.

❖ Avoid business and financial relationships with those you sponsor. Lending $10 here, $20 there, or especially larger transactions, will take you out of the objective counselor area, where you must be if you're going to be of any help. What you can provide is more valuable than money. If there are financial needs, help your sponsee find a practical way to meet them.

Remember that sometimes it takes a fairly assertive, even aggressive, ap-

HOW TO HELP YOURSELF BY HELPING OTHERS

At AA they say "You have to give it away to get it." And that's a well-proven truth. It's by helping others with alcohol and drug problems that you are constantly reminded who you are, where you came from, and what you could be again. You will feel better about yourself and the progress you've made when you reach out and help somebody. Studies show that when people help people, the givers benefit even more than the receivers. And long-term surveys have shown that one of the most important factors in recovery is being a giver—sponsoring someone else. Among "graduates" of one rehab program who sponsored another person, better than nine out of ten (91 percent) had complete or stable remissions.

In the community, too, there's great satisfaction in bringing order into lives beset by turmoil. Be wary, however, of overextending yourself; tiptoe into the water rather than dive in headfirst. Don't choose tasks that are impossible to deal with, that are stressful, tedious, or take too much time. At first avoid regular commitments, like volunteering to teach an adult education class or tutoring a child in reading every week. If you have a rough week, feel on the brink of a relapse, or have one, you won't be able to meet such a commitment.

It's not as easy as it once was to do Twelfth-Step work. In the old days, you could always find another drunk who was sobering up and sit with him in his bedroom through the detox. Now many drunks go through formal detox programs, and finding ways to help them may take more effort.

Let your home AA group know that you are now ready to do Twelfth-Step work and to become a sponsor. Offer to sit with someone going through detox; to chair an AA meeting; to talk one-on-one with a person in early treatment, someone who is just considering going sober, or someone who is sick or having problems (or to talk to groups—whatever you feel most comfortable doing). In most cases your offer will be snapped up quickly. To find out where your help may be needed, check with:

❖ Your family doctor.

proach to get an alcoholic/addict's attention. But persistence usually pays off. Also keep in mind that you are not responsible for the sobriety of those you help. You can't take credit for their successful recoveries, and you're not responsible for their relapses. They must be responsible for themselves.

If you find that your relationships with recovering alcoholics/addicts is taking a toll on you, there is help. You now meet the membership requirements for Al-Anon. Go to a meeting now and then, especially when one of your pigeons is dropping a lot of stuff on you.

AA-FOREVER PHOBIA

"I've been dutifully attending AA meetings several times a week. But the thought of having to go to meetings forever is pretty awful."

Maybe it is. But how does it stack up against drinking or taking drugs forever? Most people would say pretty well. Millions in this century have died as a result of their addictions to drugs and alcohol. Have you ever heard of anyone dying from an overdose of AA?

❖ The local hospital—particularly if there is a busy emergency room or a detox or addiction unit.

❖ Detox centers.

❖ Treatment centers, particularly those run by nonprofit groups.

❖ The local police precinct or the Legal Aid Society—through which you can help those in trouble with the law because of their addictions.

❖ Local schools, public or private, elementary or high school, that have, or would be interested in having, drug and alcohol education programs. Colleges, particularly junior or public colleges, may also be interested. Or make your offer directly to a teacher or educator you know.

❖ Your minister, rabbi, or priest. Many clerics are interested in helping parishioners with drug and alcohol problems, but they usually have little training and experience in the area. Most don't know where to start and have trouble not sounding preachy. You can help them do their job better.

❖ Community leaders. Many communities are frantically seeking ways of dealing with the growing drug epidemic. Don't hesitate to use your voice and your energy to influence public policy (see Chapter 30).

❖ Prisons, jails, houses of detention, and other penal institutions. Up to 85 percent of those confined to such institutions have problems associated with alcohol and drugs. They've hit bottom hard, are at least temporarily sober (and very likely miserable), and if ever they had a teachable moment, this is it. A visit from you could change their lives. You may be the only example of recovery they will ever have a chance to learn from. Getting access won't be easy. Penal institutions aren't known for their compassion. You may have more success if you make the approach with other AA members, perhaps offering to run a regular AA meeting on-site. (Such meetings are becoming more common.)

You can also volunteer in community work that is unrelated to addiction and alcoholism. Tutoring adults or youngsters, serving on a committee at your house of worship, being a hospital volunteer, delivering meals to seniors, can give you a feeling of achievement, boost your self-esteem, and enrich the lives of others.

The problem may be that you still haven't accepted the fact that you have an incurable disease, one you have to work hard to keep from killing you. Going to AA meetings is, for most people, the heart of that effort. Those who continue to be active in AA over the years are less likely to relapse than those who drift away.

But you may recoil at "AA forever" even if you accept the incurability of your disease. Most people are frightened of the idea of almost anything labeled "forever"—even a marriage. That's why the one-day-at-a-time concept developed in AA. All you need to do is go to a meeting today. Worry about tomorrow tomorrow. And as for forever—well, it's a long way off, so why waste energy worrying about it now? You can decide to quit going to meetings at any time. You won't have to fill out any forms, make any pronouncements, get permission from anyone, or even reveal your plans to a soul. Stopping is, in fact, easier than starting, or coming back, or continuing. Maybe too easy. This day-at-a-time approach gives you the freedom to elect or reject sobriety. When you were drinking or using drugs you didn't have that choice.

19
YOUR RELATIONSHIPS IN PHASE TWO

For a year or more now, you've been hearing: "Concentrate on your recovery, on your own needs. Healing relationships is important, but all you should do for now is just patch and postpone them." Your family or other loved ones have heard over and over how important it is for you to focus on getting better, even if they feel left out for a while. Everyone has waited—perhaps patiently, perhaps not so patiently—for the moment when you could switch your focus from self-healing to relationship-healing. Now is that time.

WHAT'S ON YOUR MIND?

REGAINING TRUST

"You'd think that after thirteen months of sobriety I'd have won back my family's trust. But my wife and children still act like I'm Jack the Nipper."

Proving to them that you could stay sober was just the first step in regaining the trust of those around you. It was enough in early sobriety, but it isn't enough now. Now you have to prove that you're not just a drunk who no longer drinks, but a thoughtful, caring person. While you were drinking, your behavior was certainly self-centered. It continued to be during early, necessarily selfish, recovery. Now you have to move and grow beyond your old self and begin to show concern for others by giving yourself, your time, and your energies as gifts to those you care about.

You gain trust and respect most easily when you respect and trust others. You learn people's needs only when you begin paying attention to how they feel, and to how what you do

Guide Lines

❖ Even after a long period of sobriety, many recoverees have a distance to go before they can fully regain the love, trust, and respect of those around them.

❖ Most families with alcoholism/addiction problems have to start all over—learning how to communicate, finding out what "normal" in relationships is, discovering what being a family really means. It isn't easy, but it can be done.

❖ This is the time for recoverees to make amends for all the hurtful, thoughtless things done unto others during active addiction. Be careful not to deepen the hurt in the process.

affects those feelings. Now is the time to listen, to pay more than ear service to what they say, to learn to take criticism without exploding in anger, or running off to your sponsor.

In Phase One you built a protective wall around yourself to allow for healing. Now it's necessary for you to raze that wall and become more open and vulnerable to allow for emotional growth. That's difficult, because the tendency of the alcoholic/addict is to be defensive, which builds the wall higher. But by following the recommendations throughout this chapter, you will be able to open up communications channels, both incoming and outgoing. This will cause you pain at times, but you can handle it now. And it's the kind of pain that "hurts good"—the kind that inevitably leads to emotional gain.

FORGIVING OTHERS

"I have a lot of hostility toward many people in my life, and I know this hostility is getting in the way of my recovery."

You're absolutely right. You can't go on with your recovery with a cancer of anger and resentment growing within you. You have to forgive and forget, if not for the sake of those who have wronged you, then for your own.

You can tell yourself you forgive a particular person, but this is a lot less effective than actually forgiving in a more concrete way. The quickest, most direct way is to make a phone call, or speak to the individual in person. In most cases, the person you're addressing will be someone you care about (or you wouldn't really be so angry toward them), so let them know that too. Assure them that now that you've gotten your feelings off your chest, you want to let bygones be bygones. Whatever happened in the past is past. And then live by that statement—don't bring up the issues you've forgiven them for again. Accept gestures of kindness on their part as a kind of penance, even if you know that isn't the way they view it. It may make it easier for you to be totally forgiving.

Maybe you don't feel *ready* to forgive some people for certain things. Try to discuss those feelings with them, in an attempt to understand why they did what they did. This may make forgiveness easier. It could even end up with some very emotional moments of hugging, kissing, and crying.

In some cases, you may find it difficult, even impossible, to pick up the phone or pay a visit. Try writing a letter. If you feel you can't mail it, tuck it into your drawer. Maybe you'll be able to send it later, maybe not. But at least you will have made the gesture of forgiveness in your heart. Now live by it.

In some cases, you shouldn't make direct contact: with old friends who are still drinking and drugging, for example, or with drug dealers. But you can still forgive them. (They may have led you to gin or cocaine, but they didn't make you drink or snort.) Again, try doing it in writing. Mail the letter or burn it, depending on the situation, but use it to ventilate your anger. Then move into a forgive and forget mode, and get on with your life.

MAKING AMENDS

"I hurt so many people when I was taking drugs that I don't know where to begin to make amends."

You can start by going through your "fearless moral inventory." (If you haven't already made such a list, you've either slighted or somehow overlooked the Fourth Step, and now's the time to do or redo it; see page 112.) Look for the names of those individuals you have hurt, and put them on your amends list. Once the list is complete, decide how you are going to make up for the pain you caused each person on it. In most cases, saying you're sorry—in person, in a letter, or over the phone—will be relatively easy. Proving you mean it may be tougher. That is usually best done by taking direct action to remedy the wrong.

You can go to your parents and apologize for all the misery you've brought them. The fact that you've now been clean for a year or more will help to show them you're sincere (something they desperately want to believe) and on the right track. But there will also have to be changes in your behavior. Things like holding a job, keeping regular hours, spending time with them.

If you've hurt someone financially—by taking money from petty cash or the cash register at work, from your wife's cookie jar, from your dad's wallet, from your best friend's vacation savings—then try to make amends by paying them back. Steady token payments of even a few dollars a week —until you can afford more—prove your action as well as talk.

If you've been lying to your spouse (or parents or friends or boss) for years, apologizing will be a lot less effective than being scrupulously honest from now on. If you regret and owe amends to your children for the years when you missed parent-teacher nights, didn't show up for Little League games, were unavailable to help with homework, by all means tell them you're sorry you failed them. But your apology will be meaningless unless accompanied by a new availability, making up for all that lost time and those missed opportunities.

If you physically injured someone while under the influence, perhaps you could help with her physical therapy, if that's appropriate, or read to her if she's laid up, or run errands for her; pay something toward her medical bills, if that's possible. If you ruined a neighbor's garden when you and your friends went on a drug-and-destroy rampage, offer to replant it, or weed it if he has already replanted. If you disappointed a teacher by dropping out of school, let her know when you earn your degree. If you told untruths about friends that may have hurt their reputations, make public acknowledgment among your mutual acquaintances that you were wrong.

Some people put off making amends because of embarrassment. Although that reason for inaction may seem a poor excuse to others, feelings are real no matter what other people may think. And even if you are embarrassed, you still need to make amends. Amends are to be avoided only when they'll hurt someone else, not when they hurt you.

There are ways, however, of easing the discomfort of making amends. Try writing out your apology with no fixed plan for what will happen when it's completed. If writing it turns out to be not so difficult after all, you may end up mailing it. Once you've seen it on paper, you may even feel that you can deliver the message in person. Or you may find you are still uncomfortable, in which case you should take it to your sponsor to discuss. Eventually (for reasons that are hard to explain—they just work), you will *have* to make those amends in order to have a successful recovery.

If trying to apologize directly would embarrass or hurt the other person or reopen old wounds, you aren't absolved. But you can make amends anonymously. Send flowers or a gift or a donation in the person's name to a cause he or she supports. If some of the people you want to make amends to are no longer alive or reachable, then do a kindness for someone connected to each of them, directly or indirectly. Send a donation to a charity they cared about, help out a surviving relative, volunteer your time to help an organization that was important to them.

What if you never learned the names of the people you hurt? Can you still make amends? Maybe not directly, but if you're creative, you can come up with something that seems appropriate. Maybe you lifted some mufflers and gloves from a street peddler who's long since moved on. Find another peddler, buy some mufflers and gloves, and donate them to a homeless family. Or you upchucked all over the coat of a stranger on the subway. You might offer to get some clothes cleaned for someone you know who is down and out. If you can't come up with any amends that fit the crime, do some public service or make a monetary gift which at least *you* know is meant to make up for a specific act.

Sometimes an apology isn't accepted graciously. It may even be rejected outright. That's okay. Though you may feel better after making amends, that's only part of the purpose. The idea also is to make up for the harm you've done to others. If they are not willing to forgive and forget, you will just have to live with that. You tried. Now what you have to do is try to live so that you never inflict wounds like that again.

ESTABLISHING OR REESTABLISHING COMMUNICATION

"After what seems like a lifetime of drinking and a year of meetings every night, I came out of my fog realizing I hardly know my wife and my children. I don't even know how to talk to them."

Though you may feel a burning desire to "fix it," to create one big, happy TV sitcom family overnight, resist it. A recovering family is a lot like an individual trying to become sober. It takes a long time to heal. Relationships change and grow slowly. Suspicion and skepticism die hard. Understanding comes one day, one thoughtful loving act at a time. Since the level of your recovery influences your family's, the family unit will usually trail somewhere behind you. But there are things you can do to help nudge it along:

❖ Be sure you have begun to make amends. With your family, it will take a lot more than a simple "I'm really sorry, guys." Your behavior toward them every day (coming home from work on time, helping out around the house, participating in family events, attending school activities, and most of

(continued on page 376)

VERBAL INTERCOURSE

It's no accident that the word "intercourse" can refer to either verbal or physical communication. The two have much in common. To be successful, each must engage and touch the other person. Sadly, both often fail to touch the other at all. If you want your messages to those you care about and to others in your life to be meaningful, remembering the following will help.

EVEN POOR COMMUNICATIONS MAY BE A GOOD SIGN. In the first phase of recovery, communication is often nonexistent, or almost so. Any communication, even if it is shaky and tentative, is a sign that a relationship is, at least, no longer brain-dead. Recognizing the importance of slowly and gingerly fine-tuning this weak transmission and reception is crucial to improving any relationship.

HONESTY IS THE BEST COMMUNICATIONS POLICY. If family members always level with each other—even when it may be painful—then they can always trust each other. That doesn't mean intentionally saying spiteful or hurtful things ("Wanna know the truth? You have morning breath!"), but giving honest answers and opinions when asked ("I'm worried I may have halitosis." "Well, you do sometimes. But before you start fooling with mouthwashes, maybe just try flossing your teeth at night."). If you can't learn the truth from those you are close to, where else can you learn it?

A LOT IS LOST IN THE TRANSLATION. What you say is often not what other people hear, and a lot that you hear isn't what other people are saying. You may have heard this before, but keep it in mind during actual conversations. ("There's a great movie playing at the Bijou" can mean nothing more than that. But it can also mean "I'd love to see that great movie." If you don't make that clear and the person you're addressing doesn't pick up on it, you may resent spending the evening as a couch tomato.) Particularly when discussing serious matters, don't leave understanding to chance. Be sure you've made your point by repeating it in different ways (not, of course, to the point of tedium or annoyance), and then (not irritably) ask your listener what he or she heard.

If you are the listener, don't try to read more—or less—into what you hear. If you have an interpretation, repeat it to the speaker to see if you have it right. If you don't, ask more questions.

SNAP JUDGMENTS SMOTHER DISCUSSION. Say "That's a stupid idea!" a few times, and the person you've said it to will stop coming up with ideas. At least for you. Say "There you go blowing your stack over nothing again" often enough, and the other person will begin to stuff feelings. Instead of judging, listen, accept what they have to say, and accept their feelings as real (they are, whether you like it or not). Then express your own feelings or opinions ("That's not a bad idea, but maybe we could . . ." or "I'm sorry you feel angry . . ."). By passing judgment on another's attempts to communicate, you create a totem pole with you on top. From that point on, equality in the relationship—and real communication—becomes impossible.

THE BODY SPEAKS. You've heard this before, too: Body language can be powerful. The language of the limbs often expresses what the other person is really thinking or feeling better than words. But it can also be misunderstood. Your wife's clenched fists while talking to you may mean she has a terrible headache, not that she is terribly angry. So you can't jump to conclusions about body language, any more than you can about the verbal kind. If you think the body is saying something that the mouth hasn't, just ask.

ANGER BREEDS ANGER. An angry person is not a communicating person. If your spouse comes home from work late and you start ranting and raving, the response will almost certainly be ranting and raving in self-defense. If, on the other hand, you say, "I am really upset about your being late. I was afraid something had happened to you. I didn't know whether to hold dinner. Please, next time call me so I won't worry," you are likely to get an apology. Remember that of all the feelings bottled up in alcoholic/addict families, anger is the most destructive. Restoring the caring and nurturing lost in active addiction can cut off the anger at its source.

KNOWING VALUES IS VALUABLE. Knowing your own values and those of the person you are talking to makes real communication much easier. You can measure what someone says against the values you know he or she holds. If, for example, you know your spouse really cares about religion, you won't assume that the glumly reported Sunday morning headache is an excuse to avoid going to church. When you sense a conflict between what the other person is saying and the values you believe he or she holds, raise the question and explore it. If values have been vague in your family, start talking about them and defining them now (see page 335).

FRIENDS—EVEN SPOUSES—NEED NOT AGREE ON EVERYTHING. You like burgers and she likes quiche; you love rock and he loves classical; he watches PBS and you love sitcoms. They say opposites attract, and certainly some very happy marriages have been built by people with different interests and tastes. But those who succeed have something very important in common: mutual respect. Not only do they respect each other's opinions, they listen to them without belittling.

PRACTICE HELPS MAKE PERFECT. Rehearsing (in the shower, while getting dressed in the morning, in the car on the way to work) what you are going to say ahead of time can help make it easier to say something you might otherwise find difficult: criticism of some kind, for example. It will also help divorce your statement from the emotions of the moment. In some cases, role-playing with a surrogate can help too. But beware of anticipating a negative reaction from the person you are going to talk to. That can tint your words the wrong color.

(continued from page 373)
all, being there when anyone in the family needs your support) will tell them better than words that not only are you sorry, you don't intend to fall into the same traps again.

❖ Be sure you have forgiven anyone in the family you harbor resentments against. If you are still angry with your wife for throwing you out when you were drunk, or for spending a lot of time away from home, it's time to wipe those slates clean.

❖ Be sure your family understands your illness. Your explanations may fall short. Ideally, those who are old enough will have read about alcoholism/addiction here and in other recovery literature, spent some time with a variety of audio and video tapes, and started attending Al-Anon or Alateen meetings when you first became sober. If they didn't, they should become involved now. An AA family retreat or convention is an ideal way for families to learn from each other in a fun, low-pressure atmosphere. Another good way is socializing (a picnic, fishing, a visit to a museum, a carnival, or whatever your family likes to do) with another family in the same phase of recovery, preferably one that shares interests and values similar to your own. If your spouse and children (or your parents) resist learning about your illness, a talk with your counselor, physician, or someone from your treatment center should do them some good. Or try a reverse intervention (page 200).

❖ Be sure you've grown beyond the egotistical and self-centered stage of recovery. If you're forgetting birthdays, anniversaries, and to call home if you're delayed at work, you still have a way to go.

❖ Find places in your life where you and your spouse, or you and your children, have overlapping interests (bowling, sports, art, camping), and plan activities around them. These should be areas where there are no obvious conflicts or threats to any of you, so that the activities can be relaxing and fun for all.

❖ Learn to respect the individuality and autonomy of each family member. This is often something that alcoholics/addicts and their spouses have trouble with. If you can't accept the fact that your teenaged children can make some decisions on their own, or that your spouse can decide whether or not she wants to work, professional counseling may be needed. Your spouse, too, may need it, if she finds it hard to stop trying to control you—as she probably tried to do for years while you were under the wrong influence.

❖ Be open to change and growth. No one stays the same from year to year—at any age. Accept and applaud this in yourself as well as in your spouse and children.

❖ Improve your communications skills (see page 374).

❖ Once intra-family communication on noncontroversial issues seems solid, you can begin to identify areas of conflict and try to work on them. If you find that every time you try, someone (or everyone) explodes, then you should back off and not try to handle such issues on your own. Get some professional family counseling, or your attempts at building family harmony will end in family discord and disintegration.

LEARNING WHAT NORMAL IS

"I'm the alcoholic daughter of two alcoholic parents. My husband is also from an alcoholic family. We are expecting our first child and want to raise him in a normal atmosphere. But we don't even know what normal is."

Most alcoholics/addicts don't. That's true in many aspects of their lives, and abstaining from alcohol and drugs will not automatically teach them—or you—what is normal. The only way to learn is to try to analyze which parts of your life were dysfunctional. Maybe it was your home life, or your work, or your school. Or maybe all of the above. Then you have to go outside of your own experience to learn what normal is. If it's family living that doesn't work for you, read and discuss together some good books on families and family interaction (see page 570). Then try to alter your ways of relating and behaving within the family.

Take decision-making, for example. You may have grown up with family decisions made in the heat of battle, with the spoils of victory going to whoever shouted the loudest or verbally (or physically) abused the others. Those without the power to win learned to meet their needs by manipulation or by going outside the family completely. These sick behavior patterns persist long after the drinking or drug use stops.

In a normal family, people sit down and discuss decisions that affect everyone. Say they are trying to decide what to do on Sunday. If there's general agreement, they go with it. If not, each member voices his or her wishes. Perhaps dad wants the family to spend the day fishing, mom wants to go to church, and the kids want to see a movie that's playing in town for only one more day. Then they negotiate. They try to see if the decision is more important to one member of the family than the others. The wishes of the person to whom the issue is most vital may get priority, or at least extra weight. Perhaps in this case, since it's the last day for the movie, the kids get the nod. But since they can see the movie in the afternoon, the family can also go to church in the morning. In that case, dad gets left out.

That's where compromise comes in. Next week the family can get up early and get in a full day of fishing. But if mom's religious convictions are so strong that missing church would upset her, then maybe in the future, Saturday can be devoted to movies one week, fishing the next, with Sunday mornings reserved for church.

In a normal family, people aren't heavily invested in the need to control events and one another. In alcoholic/addict families, unrelenting control is usually paramount, with the addict determined to push all the buttons. Other family members are bullied into following the addict's rules, reasonable or not. The kids have to do their homework at a certain time, eat every string bean on the plate, play only with selected friends; the spouse has to have dinner on the table at exactly the right moment (or be home for dinner at that moment), has to go out or stay home, spend money or not spend it, dress, choose friends, all according to the addicted member's whim. The nonaddicted partner, in turn, tries desperately, and unsuccessfully, to control the addict. In fact, the alcohol and drugs are controlling and frustrating them all.

In order to move toward having a normal family, both spouses have to learn to let go, to give each other and their children the freedom to control their own lives—with a little help from a Higher Power.

In normal families, feelings are shared and expressed as a necessary part of family communication. In the addicted family, feelings are buried six feet under. What is going on (or how each family member feels about what is going on) is rarely discussed either within the family or with others on the outside. An artificial sense of well-being is created by a conspiracy of silence that leaves each person experiencing a growing sense of insecurity, inadequacy, and shame. In your quest for normalcy, everyone in the family will have to learn that it is not only okay to open up and talk about what one feels inside, but that it is healthy, even necessary, to do so.

Normal families get angry and have fun, spend and save, work and relax in moderation. Not so the addicted family, where everything is done to excess, where life is lived on the edge. Pursuing normalcy will mean pursuing the middle road in all things.

All families have goals, traditions, rituals. Often they aren't talked about or even thought about, but they are there, and if asked, normal families can usually articulate them. In alcoholic/addict families, the goals, traditions, and rituals are usually crowded out by alcohol and drugs. Children, and even parents, may become confused and uncertain as to what the family really wants, what's good for it, what it believes, what it stands for.

To clear up the confusion, you need to sit down together to think about and discuss what you want your family goals to be, and then think some more about how you can structure your lives to meet those goals. Your goals needn't mirror those of the family next door or across the street; they may be very different. And it isn't enough to know your goals; you need to work together to make them happen.

Begin by establishing traditions, rituals, and ways of doing things in your home that reflect your values and goals (see page 335). If caring about the less fortunate is an important value, for example, make it a family tradition to put loose change in a charity box. If education is an important value, set aside a special time each day for family reading, study, or learning something new—like conversational Spanish for next summer's Mexican holiday.

All illnesses tend to upset family functioning. If mom is in the hospital undergoing gallbladder surgery, everyone has to change or add roles temporarily to compensate. Dad may cut down on his hours at work, sister may have to do the cooking, brother may have to get a paper route to make up for some of mom's lost income. This temporary stress can actually strengthen a family. But if the illness turns out to be chronic or long-term, as alcoholism/addiction is, family functioning can be totally disrupted. Each member (and each member's interactions with every other member) is affected by the illness, and in recovery, each may need patience and help in reconnecting.

In a normal family, each member cares about the others, and about what each needs, wants, feels, and thinks. In the family unhinged by alcohol or drugs, where for so long members had to be on the lookout for number one, it takes time to learn how to care for the others appropriately. But it can be done. The best medicine for the family wounded by alcoholism/addiction is unconditional love, given and accepted. And time.

Sometimes those who come from dysfunctional families, even when they are sober themselves, can't learn to switch over to living in a normal family mode without professional family therapy. At times this dysfunction is so ingrained that it takes a second generation—sometimes even more—before it is effectively lopped off the family tree.

"My fiancée keeps telling me that the way I relate to other people, even now that I'm sober, is very strange. She's so concerned about it that she refuses to set a wedding date."

A perceptive woman. Most alcoholics/addicts display abnormal human-relations patterns outside the family as well as within it. You go to buy a car and don't get the price you want, so you stomp out of the showroom in a fury—as though you think this salesman is out to get you. Or you stifle that response and feel exploited and despondent. A more normal reaction is to grant the reality that you and the dealer have different goals (he's trying to make a living selling cars and you're trying to get the best buy you can). The appropriate response would be: "Well, your price is higher than I want to pay. I'll do some more shopping around and see if I can do better. If I can't, I may come back and see you."

Or your boss tells you that your most recent report just doesn't hack it. You react defensively, accusing others and constructing elaborate alibis for yourself. A more sensible reaction would be to reign in any anger and ask calmly, "Where did I fall short? What can I do to get this report up to speed?" Or to explain clearly why you disagree with your superior's evaluation.

The alcoholic/addict tends to take criticism as a personal attack, disagreement as a personal affront, calamity as a personal assault. But by this stage of your recovery, with your judgment sounder and your ego, hopefully, stronger, it's time to begin to evaluate such situations more rationally. Time to recognize that everybody gets criticized, sometimes unfairly, and to understand that this kind of criticism may have less to do with you than with the person dishing it out. Maybe your boss is worried about his own job, or about root canal work scheduled for that afternoon. Or maybe he still drinks and resents your sobriety. Whatever the reason, your flaring up won't improve matters. Nor will it help when the criticism is justified. That's when you need to remember that nobody is always right, and that being wrong is okay. What isn't okay is trying to defend your position when you know you erred.

If you don't seem to be able to change your patterns of behavior on your own, professional counseling may be needed—before you set that wedding date.

FEAR OF BECOMING VULNERABLE

"My husband claims that I'm afraid to really open up to him, that I'm always afraid to try something new. And I think he's right. Is this part of my disease?"

You don't have to be an alcoholic/addict to be afraid to open yourself up to another human being or to dread trying something new, particularly if it is going to have an uncertain result. Doing these things makes a person vulnerable, and many, many people fear exposing themselves to rejection or failure that way. But you're more likely to harbor this fear if you are an alcoholic/addict. Alcoholics/addicts tend to be defensive, to build walls to hide the weakness of their inner resources. They fear and dam up emotions because emotions put them at risk (if you don't love, you can't lose). But opening yourself up to emotions and new experiences, letting yourself be vulnerable, is essential to a good recovery.

The fear of being vulnerable appears in marriage or other relationships when you hold back, reluctant to give yourself wholeheartedly and completely. Or it could show up in a fear of meeting new people, of taking a new job, of going to a different AA group, of reading anything other than AA literature, of going to an AA convention, or of going out to dinner in a restaurant that serves alcohol. Until you acknowledge the fears and accept the risks, you won't get beyond them. You will continue to live in fear, to live a life that is about as fulfilling as watching diners through a restaurant window. Taking emotional chances opens opportunities for emotional growth. This growth helps melt the icy grip of fear.

Sometimes fear of the unknown keeps the alcoholic/addict from seek-

ACQUIRING ASSERTIVENESS

Assertiveness is not in the behavior lexicon of most alcoholics/addicts. Instead of being assertive, they tend to be totally passive or extremely aggressive. They usually swallow their feelings and reactions until, reaching a critical mass, they explode of their own oppressive weight in a ball-of-fire temper tantrum. That may not get them what they want (though it does guarantee anger and resentment from the other party), but it feels good. On the other hand, if they grit their teeth and contain their feelings, they're the ones who become angry and resentful.

Assertiveness is a way of making a point without being offensive or hurtful. How does it work? Say a husband is always late for dinner. That's been his style for the past fifteen years—not because dinner is set so early that he can't possibly get home in time, but because no matter what time is agreed on, he manages to putter around at odds and ends until the clock strikes "late." Traditionally his wife and children have always waited for him, with resentment mounting by the minute. When he finally arrives, she either rails at him, tosses his meal in his lap, or sits down to dinner simmering in silence. Everyone is out of sorts for the rest of the evening, with one or the other seething like a saucepan about to boil over.

Calm assertiveness is the better way: "Honey, you were late to dinner again tonight. If you're late tomorrow, we'll have to eat without you." She is firm but not angry, then segues neatly into the upcoming school board elections. The next evening, if he's late, she sits down to dinner with the children at the agreed-upon hour. When her husband barges in with "I'm starving. Where's dinner?" her response is neither angry nor punitive, but matter-of-fact: "We've already eaten. Your dinner is in the oven." If he blows up, she leaves the room without attempting to score debating points.

Using this approach, the wife is much more likely to get on-time family dinners than if she is aggressive or passive. But even if she doesn't there is a lot less fighting (it takes two) and family turmoil, and she's no longer a bitter and resentful doormat. She's a person with some control of her life, who can take pride in having changed herself (whether or not it eventually leads to a significant change in her significant other).

ing professional help for a troubled relationship. It's almost as if she's thinking, "Well, things are far from great—in fact they're lousy—but at least I know what I have. Who knows what will happen if counseling changes us?" But this let-sleeping-relationships-lie resignation can seriously hamper growth and progress in recovery.

Some fears, of course, are well-founded. Refusing to dine in a restaurant that serves alcohol could handicap you socially and in business, so it's a risk that you probably need to learn to handle in this stage of recovery. But driving through the part of town in which you used to buy drugs, or stopping off after work at the bar in which you used to get soused every evening, is a risk that won't help you grow and could push you down the slippery slope to big trouble. Clearly, you need to learn to exercise good judgment, to differentiate between a risk worth taking and one that's just plain foolhardy.

Unbuckling your psychic suit of armor to allow yourself to be vulnerable isn't easy. You may have to practice. ("Today, just for today, I'm going to give myself as a gift to my husband. I'm going to be completely open and available." Or, "Okay, I'll go on a trip with you, but only for a weekend. Just let it be a place where drinking isn't the main activity." Or, "Okay, we can go to a restaurant with a liquor license, but let's take a couple of friends from AA along.") Practice may not make you perfect, but it will help you grow.

REBUILDING FAMILY TIES

"Now that it's time for me to start pulling the family—meaning my wife and kids—together again, I don't know how or where to begin."

It all begins after you've said you're sorry. It continues with your spouse and kids waking up to find a cheerful, clean-shaven dad in the living room, getting ready to leave for work, instead of dead drunk on the couch with bottles scattered about him like fallen leaves.

Sobriety alone cannot reverse the damage. Healthy communications is the second priority (see page 374) now that the first one, your recovery, is well underway. But you can't force-feed change down family members' throats. Improvements in family relations are most likely to occur when the whole family participates democratically in change-making (see page 193) and slowly gets the feeling that things—most of all you—have indeed changed for the better.

Relationships must be cultivated gently and patiently. Don't expect problems that were years in the making to be resolved with a few quick hugs and kind words—no matter how sincere—just because daddy's finally come marching home clean and sober. You were stoned or drunk during much of their childhood, when your children were young, immature, and very impressionable. The impact of your behavior as an addict/parent—particularly on teenagers—may be greater than they show or you can imagine. You have your work cut out for you. Chapter 26 can serve as a guide.

A CHANGE FOR THE WORSE

"The first year of recovery, things seemed to be going pretty smoothly between my wife and myself. Then,* bang, *everything seemed to go haywire. I looked at my marriage and I said, 'Why am I living with this person?' "

Your spouse is probably asking herself the same question. During your first year of recovery, while you just concentrated on getting better, your relationship was not your number one priority. Now suddenly, with your sobriety solid, your neglected relationship is back on center stage, and getting bad reviews.

This is very common, but not necessarily an ominous sign. Your marriage may seem terrible. The old sick-sick relationship no longer works, and you haven't yet developed a new one. That's unsettling to many alcoholics/addicts and their spouses. The familiar status quo, bad as it was, was a known quantity. Each of you knew how to relate within it. Now you're two different people who have to get to know and learn to live with each other all over again. The first step is to honestly evaluate your relationship: to see what kinds of problems bedevil it and what can be done to remedy them. Look at all of these areas:

Intimacy. Sex is certainly part of intimacy, and many marriages require at least an adequate sex life to endure. But intimacy is more. It's being able to expose not just one's body, but one's innermost being to the other person. This is tough for someone who has been stuffing feelings for years, but it's necessary (see page 379).

Expectations. Though unrealistic expectations can be a problem for anyone, they seem particularly common among alcoholics/addicts, possibly because they tend to be perfectionists. Inspect your expectations. Do you want too much? Do you expect your spouse to be perfect? To meet 100 percent of your needs? Are you looking for that storybook marriage—the one that doesn't even exist in storybooks anymore? Remember that no marriage, like no life, is without its rough moments and hard times.

Psychological baggage. Key words or phrases ("I'm thirsty," "I can't," "Don't you dare!"), key sounds (the front door slamming, a spouse crying, hard-rock music), key sights (a bottle of gin, powdered sugar, a vial of prescription pills), can all trigger memories and feelings from the past. If the feelings are good ones, that's fine. But for many, particularly alcoholics/addicts and those who lived many a grim moment with them, they can be very negative. Discuss with your mate the memories that each of you would be happy to forget, and how you can avoid triggering them. Each of you should also learn how to deal with them if they do come up. Talking (with a sponsor or a friend or therapist) may help some people; for others writing down their reactions works well. If either of you seems unable to deal with past associations, and is distraught or angered by being reminded of them, professional help should probably be sought.

Physical baggage. Debts, physical handicaps or illness, and poor occupational skills are all forms of physical baggage that can hamper a marital relationship and that won't go away overnight. Each must be tackled individually. Time and patience along with problem-solving skills will all help.

A house, a child, some furnishings, a few dishes—anything that's left from a *previous* relationship can also lead to discord in a present one. Some of those things can be tossed out if finances permit (furniture, dishes, even a house), but others (such as children) can not. So the new spouse may have to learn to live in a house once shared with another, or to accept the fact that another woman's children are very important to her husband.

Resentments should be aired, not smothered. Just saying "I hate living in her house!" or "Her wallpaper drives me up the wall!" may ease the pain. Or discussion may lead to doing some inexpensive redecorating if a full-scale job isn't possible. Or a timetable and a budget for change can be set. (Just knowing that relief is on the way eases pain.) If the thorn is a child (or children), the resolution may be more difficult. It may be helpful to remember that though the child belongs to a stranger, he or she is also part of the spouse you now love. If resentment can't be conquered, then counseling is called for.

Threats. In every relationship there are elements that threaten its stability. Maybe the problem is money: bills mounted while you were abusing substances, and your finances are now very shaky. So when your spouse wants to go out to dinner, there is a row. Or maybe she gets jittery and irritable when you unilaterally accept an invitation to a party where you might be tempted to drink. Or when you turn to your sponsor or an AA meeting for support, rather than to her.

Sometimes just recognizing that the threat exists is enough to exorcise it. More often some discussion is necessary between the partners to instill comfort and reassurance so the threats can be banished forever. If your spouse knows that you're worried about money and are upset about spending freely on dinners out, she may be willing to pull back. Or if you understand how concerned she is that you might relapse, you may be willing to avoid risky invitations for the time being—at least without consulting her first. If she admits she's jealous when you turn to your sponsor rather than to her, you can explain that it's like turning to your doctor; it's part of your treatment.

Unhealthy dependencies. If you are dependent on your spouse (or she on you) for some secondary gain (financial security, prestige, lifestyle), and you feel that without that gain life would be nearly impossible, or unhappy, or unrewarding, you put yourself in a weak position. It enables your spouse to strap a dog collar around your neck, tugging at it when she wishes. If this is true in your relationship, you need to identify your area of weakness and then figure out how to loosen the collar. If money is the matter, maybe you need to get a better job or learn how to live on less. If it's prestige—doubting yourself while basking in your spouse's reflected glory—then you have to work on developing your own sense of worth (see page 316).

Not that *inter*dependence in a relationship is sick. It is, in fact, healthy, as long as it's not heavily one-sided. Perhaps one spouse provides most of the financial support and the other keeps the family going emotionally and physically. This is fine—as long as each appreciates the other's contributions. If you suspect that your dependence may be out of balance, get a second opinion from your sponsor or a professional.

Support-group envy. At this point in the relationship, your spouse should understand the benefits you (and she, indirectly) get from your group and from your other recovery activities. Ideally, she should be involved in them herself. If she knows how AA works but still feels jealous of the time you give to it, there is probably something else going on. Maybe you really aren't giving her enough time and attention; maybe you haven't conveyed your willingness to carry your fair share of family responsibilities. Or maybe she doesn't like the new you—the you who doesn't need her as much. Just as control of the chemical takes high priority in the addict's life, control of the addicted person often becomes important to the spouse. Being at least partially deprived of that role could be at the root of her feelings. In that case, get her to read Chapters 27 and 28, persuade her to go to Al-Anon if she hasn't already, and ask her to consider the possibility that some counseling might help.

Old habits. Almost everyone who lives with another person finds some of that person's habits annoying, even infuriating. (Hey, nobody's perfect.) The problem is exacerbated in homes where alcohol and/or drugs have played a role because the habits are often associated with the addictive behavior, long after the abuse has ceased. A vexing habit can be something as seemingly minor as dropping cigarette butts in the toilet or leaving the cap off the toothpaste. Or as emotionally major as nonchalantly coming home late or forgetting birthdays and anniversaries. It could be yesterday's stockings and underwear littering the indoor landscape, wordlessly declaring that the other spouse is the servant who has to pick them up. Or walking in the door after work and always expecting dinner on the table—even if the other working partner just walked in the door too.

Often the fact that the other person is upset by the behavior isn't mutually or openly acknowledged, despite the head of steam clearly building up. So the first step is to identify which habits irritate each of you. Then you need to negotiate and work out a mutually satisfactory agreement. It may turn out to be as simple as: "I'll pick up my clothes if you remember to cap the toothpaste." All that then remains is for each of you to do your best to live up to the pact. Or it could be more complicated, and the final agreement may require some changes to make getting rid of bad habits easier: "I'll put up some hooks inside the closet door and try to remember to hang my clean clothes there; but could you buy a hamper for me to dump the soiled things in?" Or it may require accepting that nobody, not even the one you love, does everything right: "I'll try to remember to cap the toothpaste, but if it turns out I can't help being a slob, maybe we should just use separate tubes." (There will still be one cap lying around, but it's a step in the right direction.)

Incompatible interests. You like the symphony, he likes stock-car races. That can spell trouble for your marriage. Or enrichment—he escorts you to the symphony, you accompany him to the races. You'll find either that you can actually enjoy each other's interests or that an evening never seemed so long. If the latter is true, you might try exploring some new interests you can enjoy together (baseball or bicycling or fishing for bass). Occasionally you can give each other a gift of self in sharing racing or Rachmaninoff, but mostly you can each follow those interests solo—though perhaps less often than you'd like. Take it one event at a time, and you should be able to work out the differences.

Fears. Everyone has them. Fears of relapse, of unfaithfulness, of desertion, of inadequacy, of crime, of what people are saying, of uncertainties about the future.

When you have a fear, there are two points to examine: the fear and the problem you are afraid of. The fear is certainly real, but the problem may not be. Discuss your fears with your spouse if you can (or with your sponsor if you can't). If you're obsessed with fears, they can take control of your life as thoroughly as drink or drugs. Your mind and emotions are then not free to work on your relationship (see page 319).

If after you've tried to work on these aspects of your marriage, the picture still looks bleak, seek professional help. Don't go to therapy as a last-ditch effort, but with a wholehearted commitment to try to make your marriage work. Without such a commitment, therapy is almost certain to fail. Of course it may fail even if you give it your best shot, but at least you'll be able to look back and say you really tried. And hopefully you will have learned something about yourself. Future relationships will benefit, improving the odds of your converting today's misery into tomorrow's success.

It's possible that you, like so many other people, are afraid to go to couples counseling. Maybe you don't want to hear that you're at fault in any way. Or that it might help to do some things differently. Maybe you fear having to reveal hidden feelings, having to make "public confession," or just being vulnerable (see page 379). Maybe you'd rather dump your marriage than salvage it.

But if you avoid therapy now, you may regret it later, when you go into a new relationship with all the same weaknesses you brought to your present one, with about as much of a future as honey around a bear.

Some people find, even after extensive effort, that their marriage and their sobriety can't coexist. Because sobriety is number one, because they will die without sobriety, they choose divorce. Others choose divorce because they are no longer the same people they were when they married; they are two strangers who cannot live together. If divorce is the way you go, you'll need to start a new life. If there are children, you'll need to build it on the foundation of the old one.

FINDING A NEW RELATIONSHIP

"My longtime live-in girlfriend and I broke up when I became sober. She's still into drugs and booze, and I know that we'll never get back together. At first I was desperate to find another woman. Now I've learned to live alone, but there is still a loneliness, a hole in my life that I'd like to fill. Is this the time? How do I do it without mucking up?"

Now that you're no longer "desperate" to find a new woman, you probably are ready to start looking. Like a drug, a relationship pursued compulsively to satisfy dependency needs will eventually prove self-destructive. So before you build a bedroom relationship, be sure you've solidly finished the work of early recovery. Don't slip into intimacy as you've done almost everything else in your life up to now: impulsively and emotionally. Pay attention to the traffic sign that says "Slow."

To build a relationship and make it fly, you need the right tools or it'll never get off the ground. Brush up on your communications skills (see page 374), and decide what you're looking for. You now have the freedom to make decisions about whom you want to be with and what is important to you—something you couldn't do when drugs or alcohol controlled all your moves, or in early recovery when your program had to be the number one item on your list.

To understand and remember where you're coming from, review your moral inventory. If in leafing through it you find you weren't as honest as you could have been, it's time for a rewrite. (If you missed doing one earlier, do it now—see page 112.) Analyze your words to see what your behavior was toward members of the opposite sex, what was wrong with it, and where you can do better. Understand what you got out of relationships: which parts were good and which bad. Think about the kind of relationship you'd like to have, the kinds of values you'd like to share, and the qualities you want to develop: perhaps the thoughtfulness of flowers, of unabashedly holding hands in public, of complimenting when you admire a new hairstyle, and keeping your opinion to yourself when you don't. Use this evaluation as a basis for your dating behavior now.

Don't start by looking for the mate of your dreams; that paragon of perfection you want to spend the rest of your life with. At this point, the last thing you need is the pursuit of a new obsession. Try mingling in groups for a while—with married couples and singles interested in a common activity or outing. That should help brush the rust off your socializing skills without the pressures of discovering one-on-one encounters. Then date people you like but don't have any intention of becoming serious with, emotionally or physically, giving yourself the chance to be alone with someone of the opposite sex without stress. Should you be rejected or the evening turn out less than perfect, the pain will be minimal. After relearning how to relate in short-term relationships and developing some basis for comparison, you'll be better prepared when Ms. Right comes along. But don't go out hunting for her, or fantasize Mlle. Ordinaire as Ms. Right, just because you're hungry for a permanent relationship.

If you started thinking about the kind of person you would like to have a permanent relationship with back in Phase One, then you probably have a pretty good idea of what you're looking for. If not, it's time to do a little inventory listing the traits that are most important to you.

You may feel most comfortable with certain kinds of people—AA people, for example, or those who are sports-minded or intellectual. You may want to spend all your time that way, trying to meet someone with a similar comfort level. Or you may want to explore venues you're less comfortable in, meeting people who are different from those you've always known. Though initially more difficult, you may find this to be more stimulating. Also, it could give you fresh perspectives on life and yourself, plus the chance to grow in new ways. For many people who are trying to resume an active social life, a combination of the two works best.

Once you've tested the dating waters casually, you can think about going out with someone you're really interested in. Even then, don't rush the relationship. Let it mellow sufficiently so that you're good friends before you're great lovers. If the relationship starts to get serious, take the time to examine it objectively (love that's blind oft goes astray).

What are possible problem areas? Friends, interests, background, religion, rungs on the socioeconomic ladder, education, attitudes (toward money, morals, children, family, work, alcohol, drugs), and goals are all possible areas of disagreement. Is either of you in the relationship to fill needs that really should be met by recovery? (If you can't think of any problem areas, you aren't being honest or looking hard enough.) Map these territories, and see if you can come to an accommodation. If areas of conflict persist and you're considering marriage, get some professional premarital counseling. Many more options exist before you march down the aisle than after the minister says, "I now pronounce you . . . ."

"A very nice man at my office just asked me out. I would like to date him, but what if he finds out about my history of drug use?"

He should find out about it—from you. Let him know that you do not intend to relive your past, but that you don't feel it's fair to him to lock the skeleton in the closet and throw away the key. Explain that you don't enjoy rattling bones, but it's impossible to build a healthy relationship on deception. You needn't go into great detail on a first date. Just mention that you are recovering, and for that reason you can't drink or use drugs. Should the relationship bloom, you may want to take him to an open AA meeting, give him some reading material, introduce him to some of your AA friends. If any of this turns him off, it's better to know it now than later.

FINDING TIME FOR FAMILY FUN

"I know that I need to spend more quality time with my family. But I am so involved in AA that I don't quite know how to do this."

Your problem is shared by millions of others in Twelve-Step programs, and most eventually solve the problem to their family's satisfaction. Some of the ways this can be done:

❖ Examine your schedule and see where you can plug in more family time. Can you steal it from work, leisure time, volunteer activities, or must you encroach on your AA time? In fact, you may be far enough along in recovery that it's safe to modestly downsize your AA involvement (see page 362).

❖ Fit AA in at noon, at breakfast, or on the way home from work if such meetings are available in your community. That way, you can keep up your AA involvement and expand family time too.

❖ Reduce other outside activities (church, school, community work) to a minimum. Make family and recovery activities number one and two.

❖ Invite your spouse and children to some open meetings. They'll learn a lot, and it will give you more time (and empathy-building shared experiences) together.

❖ Get your family involved in Al-Anon, Alateen, or Alatot as appropriate and available. Although this is not time spent with you, their involvement will deepen their understanding of your problem and bring the family closer together.

❖ Plan weekend trips and longer vacations around regional AA conventions or other events. This, too, will add to family togetherness and will broaden knowledge and understanding of the disease that afflicts you.

Remember, too, that the idea of "quality time" is often misunderstood. Any time you spend with your children in a loving and caring atmosphere is quality time. You could be preparing dinner while your toddler plays a little concert with the pots and pans on the floor. Or balancing the checkbook as you periodically answer (or try to) questions from your teenager who is deep in geometry. Or picking out the clothes you'll be wearing to work in the morning and explaining to your ten-year-old how to coordinate colors and fabrics.

There are endless ways of being part of your children's lives, even when time is limited: walking to school together, saying prayers together before bedtime, watching and discussing the TV news together, going to the supermarket and reading labels together. And it's all quality time, as long as you reach out and make contact with them. On the other hand, you could spend every minute of every day with your children and make no contact at all. For more tips on child-rearing in the recovering home, see Chapter 26.

MAKING AMENDS WITH YOUR ESTRANGED FAMILY

"My wife and I have been separated for nearly four years. I haven't spoken to her since I became sober. Should I call just to let her know how I am?"

It's too late to rewrite history, but it may be possible to shape the future. Sometimes relationships in active addiction still hold the ingredients for healthy renewal in recovery. If contact has been severed completely, do an inventory of the relationship before attempting to reestablish communication. Was it loving, caring, and generally healthy, aside from the chemical dependence? Do unexorcisable ghosts—violence, incest, or child abuse, for example—still haunt the past? Would the relationship be supportive of your newfound way of life or jeopardize it? Would harsh rejection sour your recovery at this point?

If the answers to these questions are favorable, or at least not totally negative, and you still have fond memories of your ex (and, so far as you know, she's not remarried), it can't hurt to make contact. Usually a letter is least threatening and allows you to explain the reason for your contact without the phone suddenly going "click" in your ear. Regrets, amends, and optimism about the future may all be part of your correspondence. But bad habits die hard, and it will be difficult to avoid manipulation, so it might be a good idea to solicit review and editorial input from your sponsor before you lick the envelope. What happens next will depend on how your addressee responds to this first exploratory epistle.

You may have the door slammed in your face. If so, at least you can go on with your life knowing you tried. Or there may be a cautious opening. In that case, the same kinds of exploration of the relationship described on page 382 will be necessary before deciding whether or not there's a future for the two of you the second time around.

GOING IT ALONE

"I've just broken up with a man I lived with for five years. I haven't ever lived alone. I'm not sure I can adjust to it."

If you can adjust to sobriety and make it to Phase Two, you can adjust to anything, including living alone. It will be different, but not necessarily bad. It will give you a chance to look at yourself, your likes and your dislikes, without always having to measure them against someone else's. So take this breakup as an opportunity for growth.

If you find you are lonely at first, some of the tips on page 325 should be helpful. Increase your support-group meetings for a while to protect both against loneliness and depression. Keep up your AA friendships. See your sponsor as often as you can. And start enjoying yourself. You can get up and go to bed according to your own schedule without worrying about someone else's biological clock. You can watch your favorite TV shows, order in your favorite ethnic food, pick a color for your bedroom wallpaper without consulting anyone else.

Those are the pluses. And for some people they may outweigh the minuses. If they don't for you, consider a roommate for the time being. We're all different. Some people revel in being alone. Others crave human companionship. Follow your instincts and be comfortable with them. If you're having a hard time alone, talk to your sponsor, and if necessary a counselor.

POOR RELATIONSHIP SKILLS

"I think I may have met the perfect guy, but I'm afraid I'll chase him away the way I've chased every other man I've known. Even when I like a guy I seem to do things that push him away—put my cigarette out on his new tweed jacket or slam his hand in the car door."

What do you do to show you *don't* like a guy? Your behavior is probably not at all unusual among those who come from addicted or alcoholic families. There are several possible reasons. For one, you may fear intimacy, and being nice could lead to real intimacy (the kind that brings two soul mates, not just two bodies, together). So you avoid being Miss Congeniality at all cost. For another, you may associate closeness and love with hurting—connecting all the way back to a childhood where those you loved hurt you emotionally or physically. So you always hurt the one you love.

It's more than possible that you have no notion of what a good relationship entails. Maybe you didn't see one at home and were unable, while drinking and/or drugging, to learn. Perhaps you don't like yourself very much (and deep down don't see how anyone could possibly love you), so you really can't like anyone else. Or when you do like someone, you treat him the way you think you should be treated: badly.

Though there may be some perfectly rational reasons for what seems like irrational behavior, the behavior can be changed. But some of it is deeply ingrained and impossible for you to erase alone. Reach an understanding with others so that when they notice you doing these things (it'd be hard not to hear the howls of your wounded date), they'll point them out to you. That should make it easier for you to change. But also read some of the advice for good relationships in this chapter, talk to your sponsor, and if you feel you still need help, get it professionally.

GENETIC TROUBLE AHEAD

"I'm a recovering alcoholic, and I'm marrying a man who is also recovering. Does this mean our kids are doomed to follow in our unsteady footsteps?"

Medical science doesn't know enough at this time to answer your question with any certainty. It does appear that the stronger the family history (and in your case, the history would be powerful), the more likely that the offspring will be susceptible to addiction. Researchers are searching for a possible gene for alcoholism/addiction, and it could be tracked down soon. Meanwhile, we all know families in which the disease is rampant.

What clouds the issue is the fact that alcoholism/addiction expresses itself in many ways. It may be not one disease but several, each with a different origin and a different pattern. Environment and culture, alone and in combination with genetics, also play important roles. So, although any children from your union could be at a higher than normal risk for alcoholism because of genetics, there is a lot you can do to see that the environment in which they are raised reduces that risk. (See Chapter 26 for help in raising drug- and alcohol-free children.)

AN AA ROMANCE?

"I feel that I'm ready for a serious relationship now. There's a young woman at my office who I'm very attracted to, but shouldn't I stick with someone from AA?"

We can't always control where Cupid's arrow lands, but we should attempt to stay out of range when we suspect the wound could be fatal. And that depends less on whether the object of your affection is a member of AA than on whether she has the right qualities for you as an individual and a recovering person.

There are obvious advantages to taking up with another AA member. She understands where you are coming from and where you want to go. She recognizes the importance of AA meetings, respects the close relationship you have with your sponsor, and appreciates the need for absolute abstention. If you both have good recoveries, you will have common values and goals, and the communications skills developed in recovery will make your lives better. Many of the incompatibilities that normally come up in a relationship will have already been weeded out. You will have a social support network that many people lack today—even on-call lay marriage counselors among your friends.

But in some cases, there could be drawbacks. If either or both of your recoveries are shaky, if either of you has neglected portions of your program, or if either of you is en route to a slip, you could be headed for a hand-in-hand dive off the same cliff.

The disadvantages of seeing a person who is not affiliated with AA are equally clear. She may not accept or understand your close ties to AA, may balk at the frequent meetings and be jealous of your sharing confidences with a sponsor and friends. The honesty and openness of healthy interactions may be threatening to an insecure individual. On the other hand, there would be some advantages too, especially if she is willing to learn about chemical dependency and become involved in your recovery. If she comes from a strong, nonalcoholic family background and does not dabble in drugs or alcohol herself, she could bring stability into your life. Children, should there be any, could benefit greatly from the supportive stable family background of a nonaddicted parent.

More important than where you meet the person you want to make a new life with is the kind of relationship you share. If it's built on a solid foundation of healthy interaction, love, mutual understanding, common goals, and honesty, the odds of its succeeding are very good.

LIVING TOGETHER

"My boyfriend who is also in recovery has asked me to move in with him on a sort of trial marriage basis. Is this a good idea?"

No one can give you a clear-cut answer to that question. But there are some things you should think about before you answer it for yourself.

❖ *Your value system.* Alcoholics/addicts often do things abhorrent to their value systems that they wouldn't do if they were sober. Now in recovery you need to start to "do the right thing." If you think living together before marriage is immoral, it won't be a good experience. If you have no problem with it, then you might consider it. But consider some other things as well:

❖ *Your situation as someone in recovery.* Recovery with its risks of relapse is a precarious time. It is more so if both people in a relationship are in recovery. For some such couples, a trial run at living together may avoid a disastrous marriage.

❖ *The level of commitment.* Are you intending to get married in the future? Are you comfortable that there is commitment on both sides? Or if there is none, are you comfortable with that?

As you make up your mind, remember that no carefully considered decision is good or bad. It's only what we make of it.

20

YOUR WORK AND FINANCES IN PHASE TWO

Until this point in your recovery you've been repeatedly warned, "Stay put. Don't make any drastic changes in your working life." At last that advice can be junked. Now, if change is what you want and it makes sense, it's not only okay, it can actually be good for your recovery. It's time to decide, "What next?"

WHAT'S ON YOUR MIND?

A JOB YOU HATE

"I stayed with a job I really disliked during the first year of recovery because I was advised not to make a change until I was on more solid ground. Well, I'm sober fifteen months, and I'm still unhappy at work. Can I look elsewhere now?"

That's a question only you can answer. In order to answer it, you have to ask yourself some other questions:

❖ Are your feelings about your job generating emotions, such as anger and resentment, that could jeopardize your recovery? Are these feelings really related to your job, or do you feel angry and resentful about everything in your life? If the feelings are indeed related to your work, then switching jobs may make a lot of sense. If they aren't, changing jobs won't cure what ails you. Try instead to deal with your negative emotions directly (see page 329) before you type that resignation letter.

❖ Are you expecting too much? No job is perpetually rewarding. There are in the best of jobs, as in the best of lives, bad days and good ones. Take another look at your job in the light of this basic truth, often overlooked by alcoholics/addicts taking a refresher course in Life 101.

Guide Lines

❖ Phase Two is the time to evaluate your career and to see if a change would make sense.

❖ The decision-making and other skills learned in recovery should be used to plan the next move, and to determine whether this is the right time to make it.

❖ Now is also the time for recoverees to get their financial house in order—and keep it that way.

❖ Is it the place where you're working that doesn't seem right, or just the job? Would a promotion give you what you need? If you've been there a while, you probably didn't grow much in the job while you were drinking. Now that you have a year or so of responsible behavior under your belt, talk to your boss about the possibility of promotion, about the education or training that might be needed to achieve this, and the help, if any, that the company could offer. If you can't move up, then maybe you should move out—assuming jobs in the field of your choice are currently available.

❖ Do you have something else in mind that you'd rather do? Sometimes, years of addiction keep a person from acting on his or her dreams. This phase of recovery is a time to think about taking chances, about reaching for the stars. If you've had your eyes on a particular celestial body, go for it now.

If you have nothing else in mind, think about (and actively explore) other options before burning this bridge. Consider career counseling. With what you've learned about yourself in recovery, you'll be in a much better position to figure out just which new direction is right for you. Depending upon your skills and interests, almost any job (don't even *think* about becoming a bartender) should be open to you now.

❖ Is the star you've been yearning for really reachable? People with addictions often dream impossible dreams; be sure that isn't what you're doing. If it is, reassess. If you're uncertain, do some market research. Take some courses or do some volunteer work in the field you're contemplating. If you're a salesman who always wanted to be a fireman, don't quit sales cold turkey and buy a Dalmatian. Join a volunteer fire crew or sign up for a training course first. (If you decide you can't take the heat, you can stay out of the firehouse.)

❖ Does what you want to do require retraining? If it does, is this a possibility right now? Do time and financial constraints make it impossible? If training is needed and feasible, decide how this can best be handled, and if it can be done before you leave your present job (which would be ideal).

❖ Are you reading your feelings correctly? Is it really your job you hate? Or do you want to move on because you suddenly feel you're ready to conquer the world? Or are you bored and antsy in general? If your problem really isn't your job, look at the rest of your life—relationships, for example, and leisure time—and try to see what can be done to enhance it. If you can get everything else on track, it may not be be so terrible to be in a place you're not crazy about 9 to 5.

If you decide that now is the time, your chances of making a successful move are very good. Put as much energy and ingenuity into job hunting as you used to put into hunting chemicals, and you're sure to do well. See page 238 for tips on job scouting.

A JOB YOU LOVE

"I just got a new job, and it's fantastic! I can't believe that it's really mine, that I'm doing just what I want to do after years of going nowhere."

There are two things to say to someone who has landed a great job: congratulations—and be careful. The reasons for the congratulations are obvious: you're recovering from a serious disease and now rebuilding your life. The reasons for the caution may be less obvious.

Though it's wonderful to have a job you like, it's important not to get the notion that a job can make you happy or make your life perfect. A job is, well, a job. It isn't, or shouldn't be, your whole life. It's just one leg of the tripod that supports a stable, well-balanced existence. There's also the family/friends leg and the relaxation/play leg.

Psychiatrist Karl Menninger wisely defined happiness in twelve words: "something to do, someone to love, and something to look forward to." Becoming dependent on your work, leaning too hard on the "something to do" leg of your life (or on any single leg) for all your support and satisfaction, can topple you by regenerating that old familiar self-destructive trait: dependence. When we become so dependent, our self-image begins to dim: "Without this job [or spouse, or country club membership], I wouldn't be a complete person." Then the fear of losing the job becomes so all-encompassing that the joy disappears and is replaced by resentment and depression. The prime source of happiness becomes a source of unhappiness.

To reduce your dependence on your job, be sure you're getting some of your happiness and satisfaction from other parts of your life: take a course; plan a trip; take up a hobby or get involved in sports; become active in your religious community, or in another volunteer organization not related to your work. If you're part of a family, make time for outings with your spouse and/or children; if you're not, make an effort to find friends or someone special to fill the void. Above all, don't neglect the recovery activities that have brought you to this point.

Then feel free to enjoy that fantastic job.

CAREER DIRECTION

"I lost my job (along with my girlfriend) long before I went into treatment. Since I've been out of treatment, I've had a couple of sales jobs, but nothing with a future. I don't know if I should go back to doing what I used to do or try something new."

For the last year or so, while you were in the first phase of recovery, people have probably been telling you, "Don't rock the boat." Now's the time for you to start rocking—to think about making changes, including a major career move if that's what you want. You're not likely to be happy at this point in your recovery, or to continue your emotional growth, if you stick in the mud of jobs that give you a sense of *dis*satisfaction.

It sounds as though you're having trouble convincing yourself that you really have a choice. Many people in active addiction are so used to failure, and to reacting to crises rather than making decisions, that in mid-recovery they still have difficulty comprehending their newly won freedom to make positive choices at times and places of their own choosing.

You may be unhappy because of fear of floundering, but you're actually in an excellent position. You aren't

THE POWER OF POSITIVE THINKING

Nothing that occurs in our lives has a negative or positive value unless we assign it that value. Events are just things that overtake us. Even in what seems to be the worst of events, we can find something positive if we look for it. That's a capital-letter If. A lot of alcoholics/addicts (and other born pessimists) paint everything with tarred brushes, interpreting life as a never-ending series of misfortunes and conspiracies. To have a healthy recovery, you need to start cleaning your brushes.

The positive side may not always be immediately apparent. Say you lose your job. Chances are, even if it was a job you were content with, that there were things about it you didn't like. Or that you have some other things you want to do but had put on the way-back burner because it was hard to say no to health insurance benefits and a weekly paycheck. Or the job tied you to a community you really didn't want to live in. Or kept you from taking six months to do something crazy, like backpacking across the U.S.

You have the power to make losing the job the best thing that ever happened to you. Now you can find a better one, switch careers, move to a new city, take that dream trip. That's not to say that there might not be some pain involved in the job loss, as well as some apprehension—especially if the economy happens to be in recession at the time—but focus your eyes on the bright side and you could turn a valley into a peak.

chained by feelings of loyalty and responsibility to an old job you dislike. You're free to reshape your work life as you've already begun rebuilding other pieces of your life.

If you want to go back to the career you were pursuing when your addiction derailed you, you have a much better chance of success the second time around. That's thanks not only to your sobriety, but also to all you've learned in recovery about yourself and about dealing with others. Success is possible, too, if you harbor an old or new dream about doing something light-years away from your present work: say, becoming a fishing guide in Florida or a dude ranch cowboy.

You may be considering switching to a helping profession (it happens to many people in recovery). Recovery is all about change. A computer programmer decides she wants to be a nurse. A high-school teacher contemplates a career as a writer. And a lot of folks (possibly more than ought to) altruistically decide to devote their lives to drug and alcohol counseling. (See page 397 for the possible pitfalls in such a decision.)

If you're not sure which direction a career choice should take, make a list of all the things you might like to do (see decision-making, page 358). Don't censor yourself; consider nothing out of reach. Then look at each possibility and think about the pros and cons—what's feasible, what's not; which ones your talents are fitted for; which ones appeal only because they're glamorous (TV anchor person, Las Vegas dancer) and aren't realistic. There may be something that you really like but aren't ready for yet. Or something you'd never thought you could master but are ready to go for now.

Professional career counseling may be helpful if you're uncertain about whether your skills and your dreams can live together happily ever after.

"Just about all the people I went to law school with are successful attorneys now. At this point I have to restart from scratch, and it doesn't make me feel too good about myself."

You should feel *very* good about yourself. You're clean, sober, and professionally born again. Envying others you perceive as more successful is dangerous anytime, but especially in recovery. Look at yourself instead—at who you were a year or so ago, and at who you are now. That man (or woman) in your mirror has a great opportunity to realize his (or her) potential, more so than most people ever can.

Just don't expect things to be better two weeks from Tuesday. Recovery from the gradual and complex disease of alcoholism/addiction is gradual and complex. Job satisfaction during that recovery can be slow to improve. For many people, one study shows, it still isn't there after 3½ years of sobriety. By 6½ years, most people begin to feel more power in and satisfaction with their jobs, as well as closer to career goals in relation to their contemporaries. And things keep getting better from there.

Of course, that may all seem a long way off. Right now you should use a different measuring stick. True, you haven't yet caught up with old friends and colleagues in material terms. (Life isn't fair—while you were busy being actively alcoholic, they were being lucratively workaholic.) But some of the assets accumulated in sobriety—an understanding of life earned the hard way, self-awareness, emotional stability, improved social skills, spiritual fulfillment, and even the ability to remain sober one day at a time—can't be bought by even the most materially wealthy person you know. Those assets are in many ways more meaningful

KNOW THYSELF, KNOW THY JOB

You can't make sensible decisions about the right job or career for yourself unless you know who you are. And nobody knows who you are better than the new open and honest you. You are in fact the world's expert on the subject. So sit down with a sheet of paper and do another inventory, with a different objective in mind. List your strong qualities, your weak ones, your likes and dislikes. Do you get along well with people? Are you good with numbers? Are you reliable? Always on time? Do you enjoy physical labor? Do you hate sitting at a desk for eight hours a day? Do you get bored with repetitive tasks? Do you like regular hours? Travel? Do you like to take orders or give them? Does a high noise level disturb you? Is a particular salary level important to you? What about advancement opportunities?

If, expert that you are, you find you can't come up with as many qualities and preferences as you'd like, ask someone who knows you well—your sponsor, a friend, a relative, your cleric—to help you complete your list.

Once you know your likes and dislikes and the personal qualities you can bring to a job, you need to match those to the kind of work you're considering. If you don't know what the noise level will be, or the boredom factor, or the after-hours work, or the travel time, or even if the job involves a lot of partying and two-martini lunches, research the answers carefully before attempting to make a decision.

than the big bucks in their bank accounts. Would you really want to trade?

STARTING A BUSINESS

"My business started to go downhill when my drinking got real bad. I finally had to declare bankruptcy. I recently inherited some money, and I'd like to use it to start another business."

Starting a business, as you already know, is very stressful. Still, at some point in your recovery you should be ready to handle such stress. The question is whether or not this is the right time. The only way to find out is to do a personal/professional inventory.

❖ Is your recovery sound and stable? If it isn't, the stress of starting a new business could wreck it. You should feel good about yourself and be well into Phase Two, with plenty of Twelve-Step work under your belt. If your recovery begins to deteriorate, could you afford to neglect your business to care for yourself? Would someone else be able to take over for you? Consult with your sponsor or sponsors and with your counselor, if you have one, to get their evaluation of your readiness for this kind of heavy-duty entrepreneurial effort.

❖ Is your health back up to speed? Do you have the energy—emotional and physical—for embarking on this venture? Are you doing all that's necessary to keep in good shape? A physical examination by your doctor and a discussion with your counselor or therapist, if you have one, should be part of this assessment.

❖ Can your recovery tolerate the time demands of a business start-up? Will those demands cut into the time needed for AA or other support group meetings? Is there a way you can integrate those activities, people, or meetings into your business routines? It's easier to do this at start-up than to have to reorganize in a crisis later.

❖ Can your relationships tolerate the demands of a business start-up? Phase Two is the time you should be rewiring frayed connections to your family or other significant people in your life. Will business matters distract you from this?

❖ Do you have a sound business plan? Many communities have a small business development authority to assist in preparing a written plan. In any case, someone who understands start-up businesses and can be completely objective should review and critique it for you.

❖ Will the nest egg you inherited cover start-up costs and pay you an adequate salary for the next six months to a year? (Or longer, since most new businesses take two years or more to break even.) Can you cope if there's an economic downturn? If you'll need additional financing, have you talked to a banker to see if it will be forthcoming? If you will need credit from suppliers, have you made sure you'll be able to get it?

❖ Have you carefully evaluated every aspect of your plans, and gone over them with a variety of people with expertise in the field and with no emotional ties to you or your enterprise, to be sure that the project is sound from a business standpoint? Though Phase Two is a time for taking calculated risks, it isn't a time for rash decision-making.

If the answer to any of these questions is no, then the answer to whether you should be starting a business now is also probably no. That doesn't mean you won't be ready in six months or a year. Just be sure to go slow and to evaluate every angle before taking the plunge.

If it seems sensible to go ahead, there is assistance available from local, state, and federal agencies, including the Small Business Administration office in your state. Since those in recovery are covered under the Americans with Disabilities Act, you needn't worry about your history disqualifying you for help—as long as you remain sober. If proof that you're in solid recovery is needed, letters from your doctor or counselor and sponsor should do the trick.

WORK AS THERAPY

"I'm the only daughter of a very well-to-do family and I've never held a job in my life. Though I've been sober for over a year, I still don't feel like I'm very worthy. My sponsor suggested I get a job."

To feel good about themselves, human beings need to feel useful. Being born with a golden spoon in your mouth doesn't eliminate that need, and taking on a job is one of the best ways of satisfying it. The kind of job you should look for depends on your own view of the world and your talents.

If you think that what makes a job important is the work accomplished rather than the money earned, you could consider volunteer work—anything from "candystriper" at a local hospital, to tutoring disadvantaged students, to organizing and running a special drive for food for the homeless through the Junior League. Some volunteer jobs require person-to-person compassion, others organizational skills. Helping alcoholics and addicts requires an expertise you've painfully acquired while going through recovery. You know where your strengths lie. Apply your volunteer efforts accordingly.

If a salary is important for your self-worth, scour the "Help Wanted" section of the Sunday newspaper for a job that will utilize your abilities without requiring past experience. Or talk to people at AA meetings about job possibilities. Don't try to get a job through your family or old friends, because you need to network and feel successful on your own.

If you want to prove you can do hard physical work, look under "waitress" or "sales clerk," or even "landscaper's helper." If you want to prove you can work well with people, look under "receptionist," "sales," or other people-to-people categories. If it's your intellectual abilities you want to demonstrate, scout for an assistant's job at a newspaper, a publishing house, a university, or if you like crunching numbers, an accounting firm. You may need to take a typing course or learn to use a computer for some of these jobs, but that's all to the good. Mastering this kind of equipment will give your self-esteem a boost.

BECOMING AN ALCOHOL AND DRUG COUNSELOR

"I used to be in sales, but I never liked the work. From my experience with Twelve-Step work, I think I would make a very good drug counselor."

Sit down with half a dozen patients in a treatment facility, and five of them will tell you they want to switch careers and become substance-abuse counselors—maybe even start their own centers—when they get out. By the time they finish treatment, only one or two still picture themselves in this role. For most people, the desire to help others is not a new career direction, just a natural part of recovery. In some, the interest in counseling is a form of denial of their own treatment. ("I'm not really the person with the problem. These other folks are.") In a psychological sense, it's easier to project your faults and impose your personal needs on others than to attend to them yourself.

A year later, few recoverees are still interested in actively pursuing a career in counseling. But even for those who are, it's still too early to make this decision. When you've been sober for at least two years, have done a good deal of Twelfth-Step work, and have a solid Phase Two recovery, you can certainly consider this kind of career change. But you have to really examine your motives. In a sense, Twelfth-Step work is selfish work. It's a way of aiding your own recovery as much as (or more than) someone else's. But the drive to do this is not a good foundation on which to base a career. And trying to help others professionally before your own needs are met can do more harm than good.

Think carefully: What attracts you to this kind of work? If it's an unselfish desire to help others, that's certainly a noble goal and one that should not be discouraged. But counselors aren't the only people who help others. Any job in our society that isn't criminal in nature contributes to the good of all—the police officer and the sanitation worker, the file clerk and the forester, the farmer and the teacher, the waitress and the social worker. Doing what you do best and doing it well is the way you can best contribute.

Do you really understand the nature of substance-abuse counseling? It's an often frustrating job because you can't "cure" your client. In a sense, your client has to cure himself. You may be able to keep this in mind when you do Twelfth-Step work and not feel responsible every time someone fails. But when you begin to do this kind of work professionally, you're more likely to forget it, to feel guiltily responsible, or to start playing God. It can lead to your becoming personally involved with a client or to depersonalizing and distancing yourself, either of which can create problems for both of you.

There's a high burnout rate in substance-abuse counseling, and it's especially high when the career is chosen for the wrong reasons. Warning flags abound: increased cynicism and negativism, emotional fatigue, increased irritability, feelings of anger directed at yourself or others, loss of caring, and feelings of helplessness and lack of control. There may also be signs of physical stress and psychosomatic symptoms, exhaustion and illness, marital and family conflicts, and in fact, disruption in all areas of the counselor's life. The risk of burnout can be minimized if counselors who work together are alert to each other's needs. Time should be scheduled regularly for colleagues to discuss and address recognized and unnoticed problems.

Finally, substance-abuse counseling is not the highest paid of professions, and with third-party payers eager to cut back on payments for treatment, there may be fewer jobs available.

If on thoughtful consideration, you're still convinced that the most important thing you can do with your life is to help others learn to "just say no," that's certainly all to the good. But professional training is then in order. Your own treatment and your affiliation with AA familiarized you with the tools for helping others, but they didn't anoint you "counselor." Most states have associations of addiction counselors that offer an educational route to certifications. At least two national associations offer reciprocity between states for certified counselors. Some states license counselors, but requirements vary widely. Most require education plus experience. Some allow partial experience as credit for what was learned in personal recovery.

Counseling can be a wonderful and rewarding profession but sometimes it's not the best career route even for those who want to work in the substance-abuse field. Before you make your final decision, consider some of the other areas in which you could help: nursing, government service, the ministry, medicine, social work, law enforcement, teaching. If you have a family and switching careers might be difficult, you can satisfy your need to help others by doing volunteer work or by sponsoring several people in your AA group. (For more ways in which you can help others while helping yourself, see page 368.)

HIGH-RISK WORK

"I was a pilot before I got fired for getting to the airport drunk. I've been absolutely sober for the last two years and completely out of touch with the industry. Is there any chance I can get a flying job now?"

Federal regulators have justifiably put everyone in the transportation industry under the microscope—and the Breathalyzer. All people employed in this field are monitored closely for alcohol and/or drug problems. Pilots have one of the oldest and most successful recovery programs to turn to when there are such problems. If you adhere to a solid program of recovery, and can prove it, you will almost certainly be able to return to flight status if you want to and are otherwise qualified. For obvious reasons, you can expect to be monitored closely and drug-tested frequently. This is good for you—as well as for the rest of us.

CREDIT-MENDING NOW

"I lost all my credit cards—along with everything else—while I was using drugs. I'd like to start to reestablish my credit. How can I do that?"

Very cautiously. Even if you could get all the credit you wanted, it's probably a little early to deal with the temptations it would raise. But gradually reestablishing your credit is a good idea.

During Phase One you lived within your means, began repaying past-due obligations, and avoided further financial entanglements. That's a great start. Now you need to figure out a way to demonstrate your new financial stability to the lenders we all need at one time or another. The best way is usually to borrow a small amount of money—even if you don't need it—then pay it back on time (or ahead of time).

Here's a simple six-month, six-step plan for mending your credit:

1. Establish a savings account. Assuming you've been putting some money away weekly as recommended in Phase One, you may already have one with several hundred dollars in it. A minimum of $500 is probably what you need. If you have less, or none at all, borrow some from your family or a friend, or start scrimping now and build an account.

2. The personal loan. Once you reach your $500 goal, wait two or three weeks (you don't want to look too obvious) and then try to borrow against it. Go to a bank officer (dressed for success) and tell him or her that you want to clear up some obligations and don't want to empty your savings account. Fill out an application for a six-month loan, explaining you're reestablishing credit after a long illness (there is absolutely no need to say what it was unless you choose to). If they offer you more than your collateral, refuse it (both for safety and to show you are prudent).

3. The checking account. Take the proceeds of the check in cash (or cash the check you are handed), then go directly to a competing bank, open a checking account, and deposit the $500 in it. Ask to start the numbers in your new checkbook at 500 or 1000 (which will give them the look of coming from an established account).

4. The timely repayment. Now you have a savings account and a checking account, each with $500. It looks good on your credit record. As soon as the numbered checks with your name printed on them arrive in the mail, start paying back the loan—twice a month instead of monthly so that your debt is repaid three months early. Don't do it any faster than that. If you do, it won't show up on the credit bureau's records. You can stretch payments out to six months, but three will earn you an even more positive credit rating. Don't, however, empty your checking account in the process of repaying the loan. Make several deposits into it during this time, so that it shows positive monthly activity, and so a little nest egg begins to grow.

5. The credit purchase. Once you've paid back the first loan, go to a store that extends credit for purchases and buy something small (a TV, a kitchen table). Agree to pay for it in six months. Again, repay twice monthly and be paid up in three. You may need to tighten your budget to keep your cash flow positive.

6. A looking-good credit rating. By the end of six months you will have built up good credit at two banks and a store. If you borrowed the original $500 from friends or family, now's the time to repay them (regaining their trust) and start putting your own bucks into your savings account. Continue to handle your credit carefully. Avoid borrowing anything you can't pay back easily. If you do get a credit card, be sure to repay it in full every month. Avoid creating new debt that would be difficult to handle if you had a slip. Be realistic about what you can do, and what could do you in.

Once you've begun painting a new credit picture, make every effort to white-out the old. Get a copy of the guidelines in the Fair Credit Reporting Act (available at any local credit reporting bureau and most banks) and follow them to wipe the slate clean. Remember you do not have to mention the specifics of your illness, and be sure to point out your new improved reliability (naming banks, stores, and so on where you now have good credit).

"I messed up my finances while I was drinking. In the year-plus that I've been sober, I've really tried to live within my means. I want to buy a car, but will I be able to get credit? Do I have to tell about my drinking problem?"

When you borrow money, you aren't obliged to sit in the confessional. You are, in fact, protected by law from being required to divulge confidential medical information. If the question of a credit history littered with no-pays or late-pays comes up, you can say you went through a "period of illness" during which you struggled to keep up with bill payments as best you could. If the lender is uneasy about your ability to keep to a payment schedule now, offer to take out "credit disability insurance," which is inexpensive and will make your payments for you if you are out of commission.

Applying for a loan with collateral behind it—the auto loan you're eager to get, for example—is probably ideal. In tough economic times, most car dealers are so delighted to make a sale that credit checking may be less than rigorous, and your willingness to use the dealer's in-house financing (like GMAC) should simplify matters. Once you've shown that you can make on-time payments regularly, it will be eas-

YOUR FINANCIAL STATEMENT

In order to get credit, you may need to present a statement showing your assets (what you own or are owed) and liabilities (what you owe). Even if you aren't trying to get credit, it's probably a good idea to put together such a statement to see where you stand financially.

Draw a line down the center of a sheet of paper. Head one side "Assets," the other "Liabilities." Under assets, list the dollar value of: savings, checking, money market accounts; certificates of deposit; stocks and bonds; real estate you own (use market value); automobiles owned (give make and year); life insurance (use net cash value); any other assets you own (itemize). Under liabilities, list all your regular obligations: rent or mortgage payments (with unpaid balance and months left to pay); outstanding loans, including personal and automobile loans (list the creditors, payments and balance); revolving credit accounts (including store and credit card accounts); alimony and/or child support; stock pledges; and anything else you owe.

If your liabilities exceed your assets, you're in debt.

On another sheet of paper, again make two columns, one headed "Monthly Income," the other "Monthly Expenses." Under income, list your wages, interest, dividends, commissions, and so on. Under expenses, list rent, mortgage and other loan payments, insurance, real estate taxes, mortgage insurance, utilities, tuitions, and other household expenses. This will give you some idea of how much discretionary income you have left for food, transportation, and miscellaneous expenses. If there is very little difference between income and expenses, you are seriously overextended. It's generally recommended that a family's (or individual's) total regular obligations not exceed 40 percent of their net (or take home) pay. Reaching 60 percent certainly doesn't mean you need to panic, but you certainly should be wary about taking on any further debt and should make an effort to reduce what you owe now.

ier to get other loans. But at this point, except for necessary purchases (such as that auto you need for transportation), it would be a good idea to avoid overcommitting yourself. This is rebuilding time. Build up your financial status, put some money in the bank, and continue to live within your means. Once you've shown that you're a solid citizen, it will be safer for you to consider obtaining credit, and safer for the lender too.

"I was forced to declare bankruptcy when I first became sober because I was so deep in debt. I worry that I will never be able to rebuild my credit rating."

Consider yourself lucky. In early Rome, creditors could recoup a debt by selling the debtor's family into slavery. If the sum realized on the auction block failed to square accounts, the creditors could then liquidate the remaining assets in a vengeful let-this-be-a-lesson-to-you dismemberment, awarding each creditor a piece of the debtor, with the largest share going to the principal creditor.

Today, the only thing the creditors divide up are your assets—and your credit rating. It may take as much as ten years to get the bankruptcy expunged from your credit record. You will automatically be rejected by most credit card systems, and probably turned down for credit purchases of cars and appliances. You may, to your surprise, find some credit lenders dangling credit cards and other temptations before you. Ignore them. Not just because they are often fringe lenders who charge exorbitant fees and very high rates and repossess the moment a payment is overdue, but because you're not ready to be lured back into debt. Put your financial house in order one brick at a time. Learn how to handle your own money before you start playing with someone else's.

"I need to refinance my house to get my financial life in order. But I've had such terrible experiences in the past with bankers and credit collectors that I'm starting off angry—and I haven't even been turned down yet."

Before you worry about your finances, you'd better worry about your recovery. Here you are blaming bankers and credit collectors for your financial failures while you were in active addiction. Go into this with a chip on your shoulder and not only won't you get a loan, you're going to build up resentments that could lead to a slip.

Think about the way you used to handle money. If you were like a lot of alcoholics/addicts, you spent your money freely (mostly on the wrong things), neglected bills and other obligations (probably including your mortgage), ignored dunning letters. If you were the banker, how would *you* react to such a customer?

So before you make an appointment at the bank, clean up your attitude. Then go to the bank that holds your present mortgage and level with them. Explain how alcohol got you into deep financial trouble, and that you've been sober now for a year or more, have your disease under control, and are trying to get your financial life in order. Say you're sorry you caused them so much grief in the past. Avoid being arrogant, but don't get on your knees and plead for help either.

You may get a well-intentioned lecture. Listen to it patiently; you may learn something. But in most cases you will get a hearing. The bank, after all, is in the business of making loans. If they hold your old mortgage, they won't increase their risk very much by giving you a new one. They may want to set certain stipulations before discussing refinancing (such as a letter from your counselor, physician, treatment program, or AA sponsor). Bringing such a letter with you to the meeting will help assure them of your sincerity.

21

MIND, BODY, AND SPIRIT IN PHASE TWO

As the eminent baseball philosopher and realist, Yogi Berra, once said, "It's not over 'til it's over." That's true in recovery, too. The time at which all the physical, intellectual, and emotional problems of recovery are finally over varies from person to person. Some recoverees find that all the symptoms that have plagued them from the day they became clean and sober are gone by the time they reach Phase Two. That goes for the residual effects of drug and alcohol use as well as the effects of withdrawal and abstinence. They feel "normal" for perhaps the first time in many years. Others are still experiencing a variety of leftover problems—occasionally physical, but more often emotional or intellectual. For most, these will gradually disappear over the next year, but for a few they may hang on longer. While mind and body heal, for those who are really working at their recovery, so does the spirit.

As symptoms fade, however, attention to health of mind, body, and spirit should not. This is a time to reinforce the safe, healthy habits you introduced in Phase One, and to plan on augmenting them in Phase Three.

WHAT'S ON YOUR MIND?

A PHYSICAL EXAM NOW

"It's been a year since I got sober. I feel really fine. Do I need to see my doctor for any reason?"

Whether you feel fine or not so fine, you should be sure to get an annual physical exam. Just what the exam should include will depend on which chemicals you abused, so be sure that you give your doctor a

Guide Lines

❖ Physical health will certainly have improved by now, but there may still be some lingering symptoms. Taking care of your body, so long treated as something that didn't belong to you, remains a priority still.

❖ Emotional and intellectual symptoms will also have improved, but some of them may have lingered.

❖ Though embarking on full-scale dietary and lifestyle changes is not a priority until Phase Three, there are some health habits you can institute now that will make you feel better sooner.

complete substance-abuse history.

For most people in the second phase of recovery, a medical checkup will differ little from checkups typical for their age group. But because certain cancers are more common among those who've abused alcohol or tobacco and it isn't clear just how long the risk remains, the checkup may also include a chest x-ray, careful examination of mouth and neck, tests for blood in the stool, and for women, a mammogram. Because the circulatory system is also affected by alcohol and drug use, blood pressure should be checked and cholesterol levels assessed.

During this phase, if you experience any old or new symptoms that are unexplained (by a virus going around, for example, or something you ate), be sure to see your doctor about them. They could be remnants of the abuse to your body when you were using or drinking, or they could be psychologically triggered (psychosomatic) physical ailments caused by the stress of restructuring your life. But they could represent a new medical problem, major or minor, that needs prompt attention. Hear-no-evil denial is no stranger to people who are or have been seriously ill. It occurs with many diseases, not just alcoholism/addiction, and not listening to your body's polite warnings is always risky.

MEDICATION CONCERNS

"I need to have some minor surgery and my doctor recommends I take some Demerol for the pain. He said that with two years of sobriety, I shouldn't have to worry anymore."

What you have to worry about most is the state of your doctor's knowledge about alcoholism and addiction. Suggest that he read the material beginning on page 244, as well as A Note to Physicians (see page 578), which is written to help (and to update) family physicians who are not addiction specialists.

Reading this material, your doctor will realize that you are at as much risk from mood-altering drugs now as you were the day you got sober. And you will be at as much risk twenty years from now. Don't let any physician, your friends, or that addict inside of you tell you otherwise. If surgery is necessary, all the precautions suggested on page 247 *must* be observed.

RESIDUAL SYMPTOMS

"I am still bothered by leftover symptoms from my alcohol and drug use. Is this possible?"

Considering that every one of your billions of body cells was susceptible to injury during active addiction, it isn't surprising that your body's repair crews have not yet repaired all the damage even a year or more after you became sober. A few people continue to have memory deficits, but for most that problem will go away. Some extremely serious cases of cirrhosis may be resistant to treatment. And many people find that numbness and tingling in fingers and toes bothers them for years. It may be years, too, before anxiety attacks disappear completely and you feel your moods are well balanced.

Still, most symptoms that were noted in early recovery should be gone by now. If you still experience some of them, see your doctor. There could be a reason other than recovery residuals.

GASTROINTESTINAL PROBLEMS

"It's been fourteen months since my last drink (I'm still counting months), and I am still very gassy. I also sometimes have abdominal pain and nausea. Is this normal?"

It's not unusual. Sometimes an irritable digestive tract takes more than a year to calm down, and intestinal gas, nausea, and abdominal pain continue to linger. But because these symptoms could be caused by some underlying physical or emotional disorder, they should be checked out by your doctor. If you get a clean bill of health, stop worrying. Do try the tips

SYMPTOMS IN PHASE TWO

Happily, some symptoms that were bothersome in early recovery (see Chapter 13) will now have cleared. (If they haven't, it's likely there's another cause, unrelated to recovery; the problem should be checked out by your physician.) The symptoms most likely to have disappeared by now include abdominal soreness; acne; anemia (unless there is severe liver disease); bleeding gums; breathlessness (except in smokers and those still subject to anxiety attacks); chest pain; coughing up black mucus; dry eye; dry mouth; ear inflammation; flaking of the face; fungal infections; gastritis; heartburn; increased susceptibility to infection; inflamed ears; infertility; itching; lack of coordination; leg cramps; menstrual irregularities; mouth sores; night sweats; ringing in the ears (tinnitus); shakiness; skin rashes; sore throat; tremors; and visual disturbances.

Some symptoms, however, continue to plague some recoverees well into mid-recovery: anxiety attacks; fatigue; flashback sensations; hemorrhoids; intellectual problems; memory problems (but memory should continue to improve); sleep problems.

Other symptoms may also be hanging around, but they are less universal: aches and pains; bowel problems; bronchitis (in smokers); feminization traits (in men with severe liver damage); gout and arthritis (which usually improve but don't disappear); headaches; impotence; joint and muscle problems; mild pain from old surgical scars; minor annoying sensations; muscle atrophy (but it should not get progressively worse); muscle pain, weakness, and twitching (not progressive); nightmares; nosebleeds (if nasal drugs were used); numbness (not progressive); pain; peripheral neuropathy (numbness and tingling); runny nose.

on page 285 for avoiding indigestion, but try not to be so distracted by what's going on in your abdomen that you forget the really important "head work" of recovery and life-rebuilding in this phase.

LIVER DAMAGE

"I still seem to have yellowish skin and some abdominal pain. Does that mean my liver is still bad?"

Most alcoholic liver damage is reversible through sobriety. Very rarely, however, the liver will continue to deteriorate. The symptoms of serious liver disease include yellowing of the skin, dark-colored urine, fatigue, enlarged visible blood vessels on the skin (particularly the nose and chest), and flushed (reddish) palms. If you have any of these symptoms, you should see your doctor. The doctor will want to do liver function tests to determine the degree of damage to the organ, and then decide on a treatment plan (see page 271).

It's likely that your problems are the result of alcohol abuse, but it's also possible that you have viral hepatitis. That can be tested for, too—and it's important to uncover such an infection since it can be spread to others.

BRITTLE BONES

"I took a flop recently on an icy sidewalk. It didn't seem all that bad, but I did break my arm in two places. The doctor said my bones are brittle."

Alcohol interferes with the absorption of calcium by the bones. As a result, many heavy drinkers—male and female, though the problem is usually worse in women—end up with brittle bones. There are things you can do to strengthen your bones. One is to be sure that you get plenty of calcium (at least 1,200 milligrams, or the equivalent of four glasses of milk, daily; see page 430). You also need adequate amounts of vitamin D, which helps metabolize the calcium. If you're not a sun-worshipper 365 days a year, and if you're getting your calcium from a source other than vitamin D-fortified milk, you need to be sure there is vitamin D in your daily nutritional supplement. Do not, however, take more than the RDA for vitamin D without your doctor's supervision; too much can be toxic.

Avoid a diet high in protein, which also seems to interfere with calcium absorption; and avoid caffeine, which does likewise. Do a lot of weight-bearing exercise—walking, biking, jogging, but not swimming (see Chapter 25). If you're a woman near menopause, you might discuss with your doctor the wisdom of taking estrogen, which can enhance bone density.

A SAFE PREGNANCY

"I've been sober for eighteen months. I'm feeling fine, and the doctor said it's okay to go ahead and get pregnant. Is there anything special I need to do?"

Your baby prepares for birth for nine months; it's a good idea for you to make some preparations too. These days, most women do. Childbirth classes help them to understand labor and delivery, as well as how to deal with the pain of the contractions in a natural, and if possible drug-free, way. For the woman in recovery this preparation is especially important. To give your baby the best odds of being born healthy, and to be sure you come through pregnancy, labor, and delivery without hazard to your recovery, do the following:

WHY ARE YOU GOING TO THE DOCTOR?

For some people (particularly those who got their drugs one way or another from medical sources), going to the doctor is inexorably tied in with abusing drugs. If you find yourself thinking up excuses for going to the doctor more often than is usually necessary, ask yourself why. Could it be that the addict in you is working its way toward a relapse? (See Chapter 29.)

❖ As soon as you know you are pregnant (and a home pregnancy test can tell you so only one day after your first missed period), visit your obstetrician or family doctor. Even better, if you're planning a pregnancy, get a checkup from your family doctor or obstetrician *before* you conceive.

❖ At your first doctor visit, explain that you are in recovery, so that in case of an emergency, your physician will be aware of the special precautions that need to be taken (see page 244).

❖ Work hard at your recovery, for your baby's sake as well as your own. A relapse could be disastrous for you both. And keep in mind that you aren't the only pregnant woman who is supposed to stay off alcohol and drugs. It's an absolute must for every woman carrying a baby.

❖ Attend a childbirth education class. If you don't have a husband to join you as coach, or maybe even if you do, ask your sponsor or another AA friend to come to classes too. Taking a childbirth class and practicing the breathing exercises faithfully doesn't guarantee that you won't need medication during labor and delivery, but it will improve your chances of having a drug-free birth.

❖ Discuss labor and delivery anesthesia with your practitioner. A local anesthetic, such as a pudendal block (to allow for a painless episiotomy) or an epidural (which numbs your lower body but doesn't affect your mind), can safely be used by women who are recovering. A tranquilizer or Demerol, on the other hand, could be a problem and should be avoided if at all possible. To avoid temptation, ask a professional familiar with your double-bind (such as a doctor certified by ASAM) to make the decision as to whether or not medication is needed. The longer you've been in recovery, the higher your pain threshold will be and the more likely it is you'll be able to tolerate the pain.

❖ When you go into labor, be ready with a collection of stratagems for avoiding the use of medication. Have your sponsor or another AA friend on hand, if possible.* Hold a mini-AA meeting in your room. If that's impractical, take along some AA tapes to play or some books to read (though you may have difficulty concentrating on written material). Meditation, relaxation exercises, counter-pressure (your coach puts pressure on your back—with a rolling pin, a ball, or his hand—to counter the pressure from inside), and possibly TENS, acupuncture, or hypnosis may also help you deal with the pain (see page 288).

If the pain becomes more than you feel you can bear, report this to the practitioner. Based on your behavior, your description of what you are feeling, and how far along you are in labor (if delivery is imminent, you may be able to hang in there), he or she will decide on the wisdom of giving you medication. First choice should be a local anesthetic. If oral medication is needed, it should be administered as described on page 247.

*Studies show that having a female support person in the room during labor greatly reduces the need for both medication and cesarean deliveries.

THE CLEAN-AND-SOBER DIET—PHASE TWO

In early recovery you had to focus on getting better, on saving your life. In this second phase of recovery, you have to concentrate on repairing and learning to enjoy your life. It's not until Phase Three that the focus shifts to extending that life, making it healthier. It's at that stage that you will have to put a major effort into changing your dietary ways. Still, making some changes as you go along will make that final transition easier—and help you feel better along the way.

Continue with the six Clean-and-Sober Diet basics you learned in Phase One: (1) Take a supplement; (2) eat three squares—plus; (3) get your fill-up of fluids; (4) get more than your share of foods rich in B vitamins; (5) catch up on calcium; and (6) shun sugar.

In addition:

❖ *Start becoming aware of what you eat.* Once a month during the next year, for example, on the first day of the month, keep a log of everything that goes into your mouth. Look at it at day's end. Do you seem to be eating as much, less than, or more than you thought? Do most of the items on your list look pretty nutritious? Are there a lot of high-fat foods or junk foods? Are you on target with the Basic Six above? If not, try to do better. Hold on to your logs so you can look them over when you're ready to start the full-fledged Clean-and-Sober Diet.

❖ *Become a label reader.* Start becoming aware of what's in the foods you eat. Get to understand the ground rules: Ingredients are listed according to quantity (the first ingredient is the most abundant, the last, the least); "flour," "wheat flour," and "enriched flour" all mean white flour, in which a majority of the nutrients have been refined out; a fruit "drink" is not a juice; "no cholesterol" does not mean low-fat or even that a product is nutritious, just that the manufacturer is pushing a button he thinks will hype sales.

If you have a nonemergency cesarean section, you will probably have an epidural, which won't affect your recovery and will allow you to view the birth and to feel alert after it. Again, if general anesthesia or other medication is needed, it should be given in a way that avoids triggering a relapse. And don't take medication home with you for postpartum pain—it won't be good for you or, if you're nursing, for your baby.

Do remember that it's important to involve your partner in all of your preparations for childbirth, as well as in the delivery itself. If you do, you will find pregnancy a wonderful opportunity for growth in your relationship as well as in your family.

LINGERING PSYCHOLOGICAL SYMPTOMS

"My first year or so of recovery was a breeze. Now I am suddenly feeling depressed."

The party—that is, sobriety and the exhilarating feelings that go with it—is over. Now there's nothing to do but go home and live in the real world. Many people feel that way as they move from Phase One of recovery to Phase Two. As a result they may experience bouts of depression and/or anxiety. They feel a lack of direction. Now that they have their disease under control, they aren't sure what's next. Allowing yourself to stagnate rather than grow during this period can be risky. Instead, look for new challenges and goals—in your recovery work, in your job, in your relationships.

Still another reason why so many people find Phase Two difficult is that suddenly living a life of moderation can be interpreted as "boring." That's the life that most of the world lives—and for the most part enjoys—but alcoholics/addicts are used to living on the edge. They have some difficulty recognizing the pleasures and joys of life minus the "thrill." If that's the case with you, read how to put some healthy, constructive excitement into your life on page 209.

Fulfillment in recovery is based on what you do with yourself, not on what you put into yourself.

GETTING MORE RELIGION

"I've stayed away from church for the last year and a half because I didn't feel ready to accept the sacraments. Now I do, but I'm a little nervous about that little sip of wine."

Good for you. You should be nervous about it. In fact, you shouldn't have it at all. Before you go back to church, have a talk with your priest. Explain your dilemma and ask if grape juice or another nonalcoholic beverage can be substituted for the wine used sacramentally in some houses of worship. This is an accommodation commonly made in churches and synagogues of all denominations and, therefore, it should not be a problem in yours.

"I have to admit that I haven't been in church in years. Before I got sober it was because I always had a terrible hangover Sunday morning. Once I got into AA, it became my 'church.' Now I'm beginning to feel like I need more 'religion' than I get at AA."

While they are in the process of healing, many recovering people find that AA fulfills their spiritual needs. But, like you, many find that once well along the road to recovery, they want more of a spiritual life and that old-time religion seems appealing. That's a healthy sign, and looking for more than you get at meetings in no way makes you disloyal to AA. In fact, one study of a group of recoverees who went through inpatient treatment showed that 27 percent later attended religious services weekly, and another 36 percent occasionally.

So by all means, think about going to church. You may feel less isolated if you go to a church that is frequented by other AA members, or at least one that has a spiritual leader who recognizes alcoholism/addiction as a disease, not a sin.

Becoming active in your church can enrich your life in many ways—socially as well as spiritually. Like AA, a religious congregation can offer a supportive community in which to grow and thrive. But because it isn't based on a philosophy of abstinence and recovery, such a community is rarely completely adequate for those in recovery. So while joining a church can be a very beneficial part of your recovery, it shouldn't substitute for your Twelve-Step program. Sticking like epoxy to such a program is virtually always a necessity for a solid and sustained recovery.

EXAGGERATED MOOD SWINGS

"My first year of recovery seemed to go pretty well. Now, thirteen months after my last snort and my final shot, here I am experiencing all these emotional jags. Crying one minute, feeling euphoric the next. I've always prided myself on my control of my emotions. It's totally gone now."

Congratulations! The fog's lifted. Your brain has probably been shrouded in the clammy mists of residual chemical damage for the past thirteen months. Prior to that, your shots and snorts neatly anesthetized your feelings. Now the emotions you've been stuffing for years have escaped at last. Because they are unfamiliar, and you don't know yet how to deal with them, they're spilling out like jelly beans.

Not to worry—you'll learn how to handle them. It's something like the sensations when your arm "falls asleep." At first it's numb (like your emotions until now), then it tingles as circulation begins to return (that's what they're doing now), and finally it normalizes (which, presently, your emotions will too).

Actually, that foggy time is a useful period in recovery. If those emotions had come crowding back at the start of recovery, you'd have had an even harder time dealing with them. The fog (which can last from a few months to a couple of years) provides a grace period during which nothing is felt too strongly. Problems and emotions hover in the background. All one has to do is go to meetings and abstain.

Still, the "awakening" can come as a shock. Everything seems to be going so well (as it was for you), and suddenly reality strikes. Fortunately you're now in a stronger position to strike back: Accept the fact that you have feelings, and that feelings are okay. Even crying is healthy—it works some chemical magic in the brain that improves our mood. Use the techniques for banishing depression and anxiety described on page 326, and for dealing with anger on page 329; they will help.

Remember, nobody's perfect—and you're not expected to be. If you were raised with a different notion, get rid of it right now.

LACK OF ENTHUSIASM

"My recovery is going okay. I've been sober for nearly two years. But I don't seem to have any enthusiasm for life. I'm divorced, with grown children, and I just seem to go through the motions every day. Isn't there something more?"

That's just what you should be finding out in this phase of recovery: Life *should* be more than just going through the motions. You need to take some steps to eliminate the blahs.

The way to do that is to find something that excites you. It could be something you've been dreaming of for years, or something brand new and freshly alluring. Maybe you always wanted to sing, but marriage and the need to earn a living interfered with that goal. Now you can start thinking about it again. You can't expect to become an overnight recording star, but you can join a chorus or choir—every town has at least one. Or become involved with a theater group that produces musicals. Or volunteer to teach singing to kids at a school or house of worship. If it's the glamourous life rather than the singing that's appealing, get involved in fund-raising for a local

DEFECTS PICKED UP IN ADDICTION

Human beings have a wonderful way of adjusting to their life situation in order to survive. Think about it: If you don't get enough food, your metabolism resets and burns what food you do get more slowly. In a tight situation, you get a burst of adrenalin to provide the energy needed to fight or flee. If you are drinking or using drugs, you develop a variety of character traits in order to guarantee that you get a supply of the substance you believe you need to survive—you become self-centered, learn to manipulate others, lie, cheat, cover up, and get by one day at a time.

You probably recognize some of that survival behavior. And maybe you've noticed that it hasn't entirely disappeared. You may even be clinging to it as an old friend, possibly believing that you can't live without it or that by now it's an entrenched piece of your personality. But you can, and it's not.

Now is the time to look at each of these traits individually and to decide which ones you want to hang on to and which ones you need to shed. You will probably notice and need to work on others, but these are the most common ones that people develop in addiction:

SELF-CENTEREDNESS. This probably was important to you not only in active addiction but in early recovery. It was what gave you the ability to stick to your program and to focus exclusively on getting better. It did its job; now you have to dump it. If you continue in the self-centered mode, you won't be able to heal relationships, improve your work life, or build a better social life. You could, in fact, U-turn right back into relapse. So stop singing that solo *mi–mi–mi* aria and join the chorus. Start focusing on the needs of others, listening to what they have to say, giving them help when they require it. Start thinking about your family, your neighborhood, your town, your country, the world at large.

DECEPTION AND DISHONESTY. You wouldn't have survived active addiction if you had told the truth to your loved ones, your boss, your coworkers, your dealer. ("Sorry, Charlie, I used the $500 I owe you to buy coke from another dealer" would not have been accepted graciously.) But you won't survive recovery if you don't start telling the truth, the whole truth, and nothing but the truth now. Instead of covering up mistakes (everyone makes them), you have to learn first to acknowledge and then to learn from them. You can't continue to manipulate others, to lie to and deceive them, and still get better. Dishonesty and recovery are strange bedfellows. One of them has to get up, get dressed, and go home.

ONE-DAY-AT-A-TIME LIFESTYLE. Ironically, most alcoholics/addicts learned to live one day and one fix at a time during active addiction. ("I only have enough money for today's fix. I'll worry about tomorrow tomorrow." "I'm too hung over to go to work today. I'll try tomorrow.") That one-day-at-a-time philosophy is one to hang on to. It transfers easily to recovery. The difference is in the emphasis—from staying high one day at a time to staying sober.

Changing or redirecting these traits may not be easy. It will take conscious effort, thinking about each act each day. But do it you can. If you're to make recovery work, do it you must.

theater group or symphony.

Or maybe you have been looking with longing at those who have young children or grandchildren. You long to hold a baby in your arms again. Well, there are thousands of babies in need of arms just like yours—at hospitals, foundling homes, and homeless shelters. Volunteer. It will give you a good feeling, and it will help those babies more than you can know.

Or perhaps you've a newfound hankering to fly a plane or a hang glider, to learn to play tennis or the piano, to write books for children or features for a newspaper. Whatever your dream, you can make it come true in some way. Talk to your sponsor about it, or a friend. Think about the ways you could reach your goal. Try it out tentatively—see if it fits comfortably, if it's really what you want. If it is, go for it.

But there's something you should know. Though getting involved in something new can bring fun and excitement to your life, even banish the humdrums, it won't bring you happiness. Happiness is something that each of us has to find inside ourselves. Depending on anything outside for happiness—be it a chemical, a person, a job, or a new undertaking—is risky. Your happiness lasts only until the chemical wears off, the relationship falls apart, the job becomes routine, or the new becomes old. As Abe Lincoln once said, "Most folks are as happy as they make up their minds to be."

PART IV

ON TO PHASE THREE:

Prolonging Your Life

Consider the world and all the people in it: presidents and princes, rock stars and real estate tycoons, plastic surgeons, attorneys, next-door neighbors. Ask yourself, "Is there anybody I'd like to trade places with?" If your answer is no, there's a good chance that you're ready for Phase Three.

If, on the other hand, you long for something you don't have, long to be someone you're not, or long to be somewhere else, your Phase Two work is incomplete.

Accepting yourself, unconditionally and "as is," combined with having completed the rebuilding and having fun work of Phase Two (the checklist on page 419 will help you determine this), means you're ready to help yourself do three things: continue to strengthen your sobriety, improve your health and your health habits, and live as long as your genes, luck, and better nutrition and preventive health care will allow.

Of course, if you're not doing well, there's the tendency to avoid the work you still have to do and to be over eager to move on to the next phase of recovery. To be sure that isn't the case with you, go over the checklist with your sponsor, who can give you an unbiased appraisal.

22

RECOVERY ISSUES IN PHASE THREE

By now you're considered an old pro in recovery circles. You've struggled through Phase One, literally saving your life. You've toughed out Phase Two, repairing your life and learning to enjoy it in new ways. But that doesn't mean you won't still run into tough times and bad days and that there are no more issues to resolve.

WHAT'S ON YOUR MIND?

NO NEED FOR AA MEETINGS?

"I've got my four-year chip, feel great, never have a craving. I've got a whole new life—married to a guy who never used and didn't mind giving up an occasional beer to marry me. We're expecting a baby. I'd never want to go back to the horror that was my life before. So why can't I just forget about AA and get on with my new life?"

You could, but it would be risky. Even in pre-antibiotic days, not everybody died of bacterial pneumonia. Without treatment, the strong and the fortunate would survive it today too. But since there's no way to judge who would live and who would die, sensible doctors give antibiotics to every patient with bacterial pneumonia. It's very possible, even probable, that some alcoholics/addicts could survive without AA. But since we don't know which ones, it's best for everyone to continue taking their "medicine"—in this case, meetings. Surveys of recovering people show that giving up meetings is the leading indicator of imminent relapse.

It's dangerous thinking to assume that you would be one of the special ones, that you're "different." It would be much safer to continue your affiliation with AA, even if it's at a lower level of activity. If you're determined to cut back drastically, observe the following safeguards.

❖ Keep to a meeting schedule, even if you go no more often than once a week. Circle your meeting time on the calendar, and don't allow anything—

Guide Lines

❖ The temptation to consider oneself cured is great at this point, but very dangerous.

❖ It may make sense to make some changes in your AA life, but abandoning it is risky for most people.

❖ Now is the time to start thinking about taking steps to prolong your life.

outside of a serious emergency—to interfere with your attendance. If an emergency does come up, circle a makeup date and keep it.

❖ Go to extra meetings as soon as you begin to experience negative feelings that are difficult to handle: anger, depression, boredom, worry, anxiety. Or—very important—when your life goes on stress overload.

❖ Continue working your program: take periodic inventories or keep a journal; meditate or read Twelve-Step literature; call your sponsor when you have questions or concerns and meet with him or her periodically. Give your sponsor permission to confront you if you start to stray.

❖ Include AA friends and events (retreats, parties) in your social schedule.

"I sit there and think, That's the worst AA talk I've ever heard. He's so boring. Next time I hear he's going to speak, I'm not coming. Then invariably somebody comes up to me after the meeting and says, 'That was the best AA talk I've ever heard. That man saved my life.'"

❖ Reach out and help someone occasionally, for yourself as well as the recipient. And remember, one of the best predictors of quality long-term recovery is sponsoring others.

BOREDOM WITH AA MEETINGS

"I've been going to AA for six years, and lately I find that I've heard it all before. I'm bored."

You could consider going to meetings in another part of town occasionally, or cutting back on meetings. But the problem may be more your attitude than the quality of the meetings. You can't change the speakers you now find "boring," but you can listen differently. You can dissect their talks and think how each element might apply to your life. (Of course, in the dissecting you may find the talks weren't so bad after all.) If you think meetings at your group tend to be weak, offer to serve as chair and implement your ideas to strengthen them. Your expertise, learned over many long years, can be harnessed now to help newcomers, who may be as disappointed with the meetings as you are—and may walk out and never come back. So instead of just "thinking," help them (and yourself) by speaking up.

Of course, if other people are content with AA sessions that leave you feeling angry, bored, and impatient, it may be you and not the meetings in need of dissecting. When AA is coming out of your ears, it's not getting to your brain. Talk to your sponsor, do an inventory, figure out what's behind your negative thinking. And deal with your feelings before enough resentment builds up to damage your recovery.

STARTING A NEW AA GROUP

"A couple of friends and I have been thinking about starting a new nonsmoking AA group. We recently quit smoking, and going to meetings at the 'smoke house' is getting really uncomfortable."

Starting your own Twelve-Step group is relatively easy. It just takes two people, operating under the Twelve Traditions. You don't have to register at first, or affiliate in any way. Later, when the group is well off the ground, it's a good idea to register with Alcoholics Anonymous General Services office. The information and assistance they provide can help your group to function more effectively.

Virtually any reason for starting a new group is a good reason, and offering a smoke-free atmosphere certainly is one. There are plenty of others: a more convenient meeting time (lunchtime, or 7 A.M., or before dinner); to cater to beginners or professionals, women or families, gays and lesbians, the hearing-impaired, or any specific group; to focus on the Twelve Steps or any other particular aspect of the program; to set up a meeting with coworkers at lunch hour or after work.

You can meet anywhere: in people's homes, in a hospital, church, or synagogue, in the cafeteria or a meeting room at work, in an existing AA clubhouse (you rent the space). Passing the hat at meetings takes care of rent and utilities as well as expenses for refreshments (usually coffee and cookies, which are nice but not absolutely necessary). It's also nice to have packets of AA materials and (in big cities) citywide meeting schedules to hand out to newcomers, along with Big Books to sell at cost.

Will your new group succeed? Bill Wilson believed that any group that did a good job helping drunks would prosper. Any that didn't would just fade away.

AA ADDICTION

"I know that a lot of people start cutting back on AA activities after three or four years. I feel as though doing that would be like cutting off my arm. Could I be addicted to AA?"

Possibly. Some people in recovery do substitute a dependence on AA for their dependence on chemical substances. Obviously it's a safer dependence, but it is a dependence nevertheless.

If you find that AA meetings are still more important than anything else, if AA activities interfere with your work, family life, or social development, if a check of your calendar reveals that the only free-time activities penciled in involve AA, you may be using AA in an unhealthy way. In that case, you're going to meetings but probably not getting very much out of them. You're not growing as you should be, and your recovery is "stuck." Examine this issue with your sponsor or with others at meetings and try to get unstuck. If you can't, then get some professional help. (But be sure that the professional you consult understands the problem is with you and not with AA.)

Of course there are people who make AA the center of their lives, who spend most of their free time with others in the fellowship or at AA functions, and who nevertheless have a very healthy recovery. Their relationships—within the family and outside of it—are flourishing. Their work lives are satisfying and successful. And they find time to exercise, see a movie, enjoy a ballgame or give community service. If that's you, continue to enjoy your "addiction."

LACK OF DIRECTION

"I've been sober for nearly three years. I feel pretty good, but I still haven't gotten my act together as far as work goes. I keep trying this and that, and not finding a comfortable niche anywhere."

You could say that you're wandering. Or you could say that, with all kinds of interesting challenges and opportunities ahead, you're exploring. It's all in how you look at it. But it's best for recovery (and life in general) if you look at it positively.

You're not stuck in a dead-end job you dislike. You have no long-term obligation to an employer. You're free as a bee flying flower to flower to find something that's right for you. The question is, how?

First of all, if you aren't sure what you want, it might be a good idea to go to a career counselor. The perfect job may be waiting for you out there—you just need to find out what it is. And a good career counselor should be able to help.

Second, it may not be the job choice that's the problem, but your own attitude. No job is always wonderful or always perfect. Every job stresses us, bores us, or makes us want to punch the boss (or, at least, a wall) sometimes. Maybe you expect too much. Or maybe you're still nursing a lot of negativism, a quality that can sink your sobriety as well as your working life. Work harder on your recovery, or if you think it might help, see a counselor.

Third, use the decision-making skills you've learned in recovery (see page 358) to decide on your next step. Look at various options, examine their pluses and minuses, and then decide which one is best for you. See page 238 for more on getting a new job.

Look at your recovery, too. Your work is something that should have been attended to in Phase Two. If you are still floundering, you have more work to do in that Phase (see Chapter 20).

DEALING WITH SICKNESS NOW

"I've just found a lump in my breast. If it turns out to be malignant, I just don't know how I'm going to face it."

Don't worry until you know for sure—but don't delay in seeing your doctor. If you do indeed turn out to have cancer, don't despair. You've done a good job of fighting one fatal disease; you can do a good job on this one too.

Recoverees who've been through this ordeal have found that what they learned in fighting addiction helped them fight other serious diseases, including cancer. If it's a false alarm, celebrate. If it's not, let your doctor, and these suggestions, be your guide.

❖ Take your illness one day at a time. God (or your Higher Power) won't give you more than you can handle, and you *can* handle this.

❖ Keep working your program faithfully. Being seriously ill could lead to relapse (which you don't need now) if you get careless.

❖ Use meditation, prayer, the love of family and friends, and sharing your feelings with your group to get you through difficult moments.

ARE YOU READY FOR PHASE THREE?

CHECKLIST

YES	NO	
		RECOVERY PROGRESS:
☐	☐	I have no desire to drink or use drugs
☐	☐	Participation in my recovery program has become second nature
☐	☐	I am more disciplined
		FAMILY/RELATIONSHIPS PROGRESS:
☐	☐	Relationships are functioning well
☐	☐	Communications are restored
☐	☐	Problems are discussed, not swept under the table
☐	☐	Feelings are expressed
☐	☐	Kids (if any) are getting attention
☐	☐	Kids have opportunity for emotional growth
☐	☐	I have a network of supportive friends
☐	☐	I interact with others
☐	☐	I give as well as take
		EDUCATION/CAREER PROGRESS:
☐	☐	I have or am getting the education to do the work I want to do
☐	☐	I enjoy my work and my place of work or my schooling
☐	☐	My job allows me to grow and to meet long-term goals
☐	☐	The stress of work is no more than I can handle
		RECREATION/FUN PROGRESS:
☐	☐	I've learned how to have fun while clean and sober
☐	☐	I am able to relax and have a good time
☐	☐	I have found new forms of recreation and relaxation

❖ Keep a positive attitude. Optimism is one of the best medicines against any illness.

❖ Try to adhere to as normal a schedule as possible. If you can, get up and go to work or to a meeting after a chemotherapy treatment. Avoid long stretches in bed or at home alone, which could lead to self-pity and other negative thinking.

❖ During surgery, be sure that all the precautions described on page 247 are observed.

❖ Try to deal with pain in non-drug ways whenever possible (see page 288).

❖ Remember, we can grow through pain and hardship—though it may be difficult to believe that while you're going through it. It was rough, but you certainly did grow through your addiction and the rocky early days of recovery.

IMPROVING THE ODDS

"I used to be a gambler. I gambled with my money and my life. No more. Now I'm looking for sure things. How can I stay healthy?"

Unfortunately there are no sure things in life. Tomorrow a meteor could land on your house and turn you to dust. But while you can't guarantee yourself a long and healthy life, you can improve the odds considerably.

Regular exercise. Getting a minimum of thirty minutes of continuous exercise at least three times a week (see Chapter 25) will improve your cardiovascular health, reducing your risk of stroke and heart attack. If you begin any exercise program more strenuous than walking, be sure to follow this familiar advice—get your physician's okay first.

Weight control. Maintaining normal body weight (see page 437) will also reduce the risk of premature death.

Smoke-free living. Using tobacco (or exposure to other people's smoke) considerably increases your risk of dying of cancer, heart attack, and stroke. For best results, avoid both active and passive smoke.

The clean-and-sober diet. This diet—low in fat, salt, refined grains, and sugars, and high in fiber—isn't a panacea, but it does improve your odds (see Chapter 23).

Stress control. Stress can have a positive effect on our lives, or a deadly one. It all depends on how you handle it (see page 324).

Good medical care. Regular checkups can ensure that elevated blood pressure and cholesterol levels are controlled, that such illnesses as cancer are detected early, and that medical problems relating to your recovery are dealt with as they arise.

A low-risk lifestyle. Avoiding risky sex, the use of drugs or alcohol, and dangerous playgrounds and playmates can help extend your life expectancy.

Seat belts. And, last but not least—this should be as automatic as looking both ways before crossing the street, but it's often ignored. Wearing seat belts whenever you drive or are a passenger in an automobile greatly improves the odds that you will survive a collision and live to enjoy your recovery. Having air bags in your car's front seat improves them even further.

FILLING IN THE BLANKS

"A lot that happened while I was drinking and using drugs is a total blank. Family and friends sometimes allude to things that I don't remember at all. Is it better to leave it that way?"

This is one Pandora's box worth opening. You couldn't lift the lid earlier in recovery, while you were struggling to save and then rebuild your life, because you weren't ready to deal with what might come swarming out. Now, however, you can start looking back objectively at what happened and at what you did.

Explain the blanks in your memory to family and friends, and ask them to help fill them in. Tell them that you want to know what happened, what you did that might have hurt them, and how they felt, so that you can better make amends. This will not only help you understand their feelings about the past better, but it will also allow everyone to talk freely about it. No more walking on eggs.

Add these incidents to your list of necessary amends, and make those amends. Sometimes amends won't be enough. If you uncover behavior that could be seriously damaging (such as sexual abuse or incest), then both you and anyone else involved will need professional therapy (see page 203).

A LEADERSHIP ROLE IN AA

"I really do appreciate what others have done for me at AA. Now that I've been sober for three years, how can I show that appreciation?"

Alcoholics Anonymous is a voluntary fellowship that depends on members well into recovery to give of themselves and their time to make it work. This may sound like a public service announcement, but you can show your appreciation by becoming more active in service work in AA, and carrying AA's message to others.

Governed by a board of trustees, AA is organized at the group, district, state, national, and international levels. Groups send delegates to represent them at periodic district conferences or assemblies (usually quarterly). Each district sends representatives to the state meetings. Each state sends reps to national meetings, and an international convention, held every five years, is attended by thousands of interested members from around the world, many of them non-delegates.

Getting involved at increasingly higher levels will be of service to others, and will also provide a valuable outlet for your growing talents and skills. Those who've taken this route usually find that they get much more than they give.

A SLIP

"I had a slip after a disagreement with my girlfriend. One of my sponsors said it was partly her fault that I slipped. The other said, 'No way.'"

No way is right. Part of what you need to learn in recovery is that you can't pin your slip on anyone else. Only you are responsible for your behavior. So read Chapter 29 to try to pinpoint what really led up to your slip and to find out what you can do to prevent another one.

Though your girlfriend isn't responsible for your slip, she can support your recovery more effectively and make her life with you more understandable, if she goes to Al-Anon. If she's still talking to you, suggest that she begins going to meetings as soon as possible.

If she drinks or takes drugs, you may need to rethink your relationship. Spending a great deal of time—or even a little time—with someone who isn't abstinent could lead to another relapse.

"I've been sober for four years, and last night I was at a party and feeling pretty low and I gave in and had three drinks. I stopped, which I thought was pretty good."

You might have been better off if you'd gotten stinking drunk. Then you would have remembered what it was like in the "good old days" when you were drunk often. The blackouts. The vomiting. The hangovers. The shakes. Stopping after three drinks may tempt you to think you can do it again, that you are "cured" and can now return to drinking socially. Don't test this thesis. It's a loser. Instead follow the tips in Chapter 29 for steps to take after a slip.

LISTENING TO YOUR BODY

"My stomach's been acting up lately. I don't know whether this is some residual thing from using alcohol for so long or something I should be concerned about."

The damage done to your body by substance abuse should almost certainly be solidly repaired by now. The only exceptions would be severe damage to the liver (see page 270) or to the nervous system (see page 274). Any gastritis or other intestinal symptoms should be gone.

So listen carefully to that signal (and any others) your body sends you. Now that you are sober, they should be more reliable—unclouded by either the chemicals themselves or their many side effects. You may be feeling so well in other respects that you're tempted to ignore your body's warnings, but that is as much a form of denial as refusing to recognize the signs of substance abuse.

Any digestive-tract symptoms that do not clear up in a few days, or that recur frequently, should be reported to your doctor. See Chapter 13 to check out any symptoms that concern you, and to see how they should be handled.

23

Eating Your Way to a Long-Lasting Recovery

The more research that's done on the effects of diet on health, the clearer it becomes that what we eat and don't eat may be a major factor in how well our bodies function, and for how long. Perhaps equally important, research is starting to show that diet may be a significant factor in the treatment of addiction.

What we eat is important, but a good diet is not a guarantee of a long and sober life. It only gives us the best odds of achieving one.

How we eat is important, too. Eating too much or too little, or eating compulsively, is as dangerous to health and recovery as eating the wrong foods.

The Clean-and-Sober Diet described here has the potential to improve both the quality and length of your life and enhance your recovery. It's up to you to decide whether or not to follow it.

A Guide to Eating in Recovery

You're already aware that alcohol, tobacco, and other drugs have the potential to damage virtually every cell in your body. The same is true of poor nutrition. Too little calcium and you can develop osteoporosis (brittle bones). Too little iron: anemia. Not enough vitamin C: scurvy (with weakness, weight loss, bleeding, anemia). Insuffi-

Guide Lines

❖ Every time you eat, you can choose foods that prolong your life and improve your health.

❖ Diet is not a panacea, but it is a major factor in the prevention of numerous health problems.

❖ Diet does appear to affect recovery; a good diet appears to affect it positively.

❖ Compulsive eating and other eating disorders are particularly common among alcoholics/addicts.

❖ Techniques learned in recovery can be used to reach or maintain ideal body weight.

cient thiamine: beriberi (with damage to the nervous system). Too little beta-carotene and/or vitamin A: decreased night vision, blindness, dry skin, poor bone and tooth development and maintenance, possibly even an increased risk of cancer and heart disease. Insufficient vitamin D: weak bones (rickets) in children, osteomalacia (soft bones) in adults, increased risk of certain types of cancer. Too little fiber: increased risk of some types of cancer. And so on, almost ad infinitum.

But poor nutrition isn't only getting too little of necessary nutrients. Getting too much of some nutrients can also sap health. Too many calories and we become obese and are at added risk for heart disease, stroke, diabetes, and other serious diseases. Too much fat and cholesterol and the hazards of heart and blood vessel diseases, and some cancers, increase. Too much vitamin A (but not beta-carotene) can result in fetal damage in pregnancy, headaches, nausea, irritability, peeling skin, hair loss, bone pain, retarded growth in children, menstrual problems, even death. Too much sugar leads to dental decay, obesity, mood swings, possibly a variety of other ills and for the addict, possible relapse. So poor nutrition can be defined as too little of the right things or too much of the wrong things.

The only way to avoid the destructive effects of drugs is to abstain. But happily, there's no need for you to abstain from eating. All that's required is to gradually retrain your taste buds, and to switch from poor-to-mediocre nutrition to good-to-excellent. Which, incidentally, does not mean boring and tasteless meals. Good-for-you food can taste good too.

GOOD DIET, GOOD RECOVERY

It's easy to see that what you eat affects your health and longevity. But does it really make a difference to your recovery? From preliminary research, the answer appears to be yes. Animal research first suggested that diet could have an impact on addiction. When rats fed a diet of refined carbohydrates (similar to the white flour, high sugar diet of most Americans) were offered the opportunity to drink both alcohol and water, they preferred the alcohol. But rats whose diet consisted of high protein and complex carbohydrate foods proved wiser. They spurned the alcohol and chose the water chaser.

Massive studies of recovering alcoholics/addicts have not yet been carried out to see if humans react the way the rats did. But some small studies have shown that eating a particularly nutritious diet—rich in complex carbohydrates (whole grains and legumes) and protein, with no sugar or caffeine, plus a vitamin supplement—can greatly enhance the chances of abstinence in recovery. In one of these studies, 81 percent of those on this diet remained sober compared to 38 percent on a regular diet. The old image of AA members going out after the meeting for coffee, apple pie á la mode, and a smoke is changing as we learn that the time spent together talking after the meeting is the critical part of the formula—and that we can, and probably should, substitute good stuff for the rest.

No diet (or pill or potion or anything else) can offer a money-back guarantee of either a long and healthy life or an abstinent one. But the diet that follows is designed to improve your chances of achieving both.

THE CLEAN-AND-SOBER DIET

Active alcoholics/addicts are usually nutritionally deprived—so much so that drinking to excess leads inexorably to malnutrition. Why? One good reason is that alcohol's empty calories often replace the more useful elements of a normal diet. For example, the alcoholic who puts away 5 ounces of 86-proof gin a day consumes 375 calories (or 15 percent of a young male's average daily requirement) in booze alone. Someone who downs two six-packs per day guzzles 1,800 calories (or 66 percent). That leaves little room for food (no room if the drinker is a small-size female). But if two or three meals a day are consumed as well, it leaves plenty of room for a beer belly. (The alcohol actually encourages the development of body fat.)

The second reason for malnutrition in alcoholics is the damage alcohol inflicts on the body, particularly the digestive tract, interfering with efficient utilization of whatever nutrients are consumed. This results in a variety of problems: an increased risk of osteoporosis because of decreased metabolism of vitamin D; impairment of brain production of proteins; and most commonly, deficiencies of vitamin A, folate, vitamin B_6, and thiamine (B_1). Deficiencies of zinc, iron, magnesium, vitamin E, vitamin K, and phosphate are not unusual.

When alcohol is imbibed, these deficiencies, as part of a truly vicious cycle, slow its metabolism, giving it more time to do corrosive damage to body cells. Less information exists on nutritional damage caused by other drugs, but it's well known that many drugs have a pronounced effect on organ systems and body metabolism that could jeopardize nutritional health.

The Clean-and-Sober Diet is designed to overcome the malnutrition caused by alcohol or drug abuse, to start you on the way to optimum health, and to discourage cravings that can lead to relapse.

THE SEVEN NUTRITIONAL COMMANDMENTS

In Phases One and Two you were introduced to some nutritional basics (see page 304). Now you are ready to expand your knowledge of nutritious eating. Start by absorbing these Clean-and-Sober nutritional commandments.

Variety Is More Than the Spice of Life

It's the key to healthy eating. First, because no single food contains all the nutrients needed to sustain life, so eating a wide range of different foods makes it much more likely that you'll get those necessary nutrients over the course of a day or week. And second, because eating a lot of particular food makes it more likely that when your TV anchorperson announces that one food or another has been contaminated by pesticides or has just been discovered to be unsafe, you'll find yourself thinking, "Omigosh, I've been practically living on the stuff!"

So vary your daily intake among the Essential Eleven choices (see page 429). Do what investors are supposed to do: diversify. Enjoy a wheat cereal one day, oats the next, a seven-grainer the third. Or mix them all in your bowl daily. Vary dinner side dishes: brown rice, couscous, corn, chick-peas, and so on. When you buy fish, try salmon one night, trout another, bluefish a third. Do the same with all your other Clean-and-Sober choices.

Food Should Not Have Emotional Strings Attached

Food and feelings should be separate. Most of us grew up associating food with feelings, good and bad. In childhood, food was a reward and withholding of it was punishment. Certain foods made us feel warm and safe (the favorites mom made to cheer or comfort us); others made us feel angry (the spinach we were forced to eat before we could have dessert); still others brought on guilt feelings (candy bars or ice cream sneaked behind our parents' backs). Separating these foods from our feelings now isn't easy, but it's necessary if we are to avoid eating problems (eating too much or too little). Food is food, and we should eat it for its own sake (for pleasure or sustenance), not in order to feel better emotionally.

Three Squares Are Sensible; Fasting Is Folly

Eating three moderate-size meals a day (one of which should be breakfast) with small snacks in between, or six smaller meals, keeps your blood sugar up and your appetite in check.

Fasting (or even skipping meals) can be dangerous, and offers no health benefits. Periods without food can lead not just to hunger (a common craving trigger), but to a serious drop in blood sugar, which in turn can lead to mood swings, depression, disorientation, irritability. These feelings, of course, can put recovery in jeopardy.

For some people, observing an occasional religious fast day doesn't seem to result in serious difficulties; others become so shaky and disoriented that they risk relapse. If fast days are part of your religious life, try one and see how it goes. Be sure you have support—from your sponsor, and AA friend, or a family member—in case you start to fold. If it goes well, fine. If not, end your fast and next time don't fast at all. No religion requires you to fast if it imperils your life.

Just as the body is distressed by starvation, so are the emotions. Anger and depression with prolonged fasting are not unusual and can also threaten recovery.

If you do fast periodically for religious reasons, keep in mind that you are more vulnerable on such days, and be alert to warning signs that you could slip.

All Calories Are Not Created Equal

The 275 calories in a jelly doughnut and coffee with cream and sugar are not equal to the 275 calories in a heaping bowl of instant oatmeal made with nonfat dry milk and diced dried apricots. It's not hard to guess in which selection the calories offer serious nutrition along with their food energy. And the oatmeal keeps blood sugar levels level a lot longer than the doughnut, which could lead to a blood sugar dive and midmorning apathy. So choose your calories wisely.

To reduce your risk of heart disease and cancer, most of your calories should come from vegetable sources like fruits, vegetables, whole grains, dried beans and peas. A much smaller percentage of your calories should come from animal sources, such as fish, poultry, lean meats, nonfat or low-fat dairy products. Very few of your calories should come from foods high in fat, sugar, or refined grains.

Sugar Highs Can Lead to Sugar Lows

The average American consumes 130 pounds of sugar a year, which translates to 666 sugar calories a day—calories that are totally devoid of nutritive value. For a 125-pound woman, who needs about 2,000 calories a day, that would mean that nearly a third of her daily calorie requirement would provide no nutrition at all. And she would have a hard time getting her Essential Eleven from her remaining caloric allotment. But if the average American takes in 130 pounds of sugar annually, that means there are a lot of Americans consuming more (as well as a lot consuming less). If you're recovering, it's very likely you're heavily on the "more" side of the equation. This is bad news for several reasons.

❖ You can't possibly consume high levels of sugar and be adequately nourished (unless you overeat).

❖ Sugar definitely causes tooth decay, but recent research also fingers it as increasing the risk of diabetes in the later years. That's an added risk you don't need—especially for the new, improving you, who can be reasonably confident of having and enjoying the later years.

❖ You could put yourself in the same nutritional boat you were in when you were using alcohol, with sugar's empty calories standing in for the empty calories of alcohol. Unlike complex carbohydrates, which are packed with vitamins and minerals, sugar can't repair the damage done to your body by alcohol or other drugs.

❖ Your body may be unable to handle sugar normally. There are at least a couple of theories why this may be so. Some researchers believe that alcoholics are victims of either a glucose intolerance or an out-of-whack glucose metabolism caused by alcohol's depletion of glycogen stores in the liver and consequent interference with normal pancreatic function. (Glucose is the form of sugar that circulates in the blood and is used by the body for energy; the pancreas produces the insulin that controls blood-sugar levels.) This leads to crazy swings in blood sugar: soaring sharply when you eat sugar or drink alcohol (giving you a short-lived high), dipping dramatically as the pancreas produces great quantities of insulin in response. Since a steady supply of glucose in the blood is necessary for normal brain function, sudden dives can leave you depressed, irritable, fatigued. Which makes you want more sugar (or alcohol). It's suspected that this see-saw effect when consuming sugar on blood sugar may last for months or even years into recovery.

Other researchers suspect there is a dysfunction (possibly alcohol-induced in some addicts, genetic in others) of tiny structures in the brain that are critical to both the regulation of glucose metabolism (the way the body uses blood sugar) and the production of the brain chemical serotonin (involved in mood regulation). When blood sugar drops in these individuals, the amount of serotonin does too, and they become depressed, irritable, impulsive, even violent. So it's possible you could be courting relapse by consuming even average quantities of sugar.

❖ You could be a sugar addict. Some researchers believe it's possible to become addicted to sugar just as it is to alcohol, and for basically the same reasons. They believe there are withdrawal symptoms (dizziness, lethargy, chills, nausea, shaking, swimming vision, severe headaches, cravings for

SUGAR SLEUTHING

Emptying the sugar bowl and tossing out the Twinkies won't eliminate the sugar in your life. If you really would like to try a sugar-free diet (and for some people in recovery this may be the best way to go), you'll have to start reading labels. Sugar is found in the most unlikely places (breads, salad dressings, hot dogs, barbecue sauces, ketchup, pickles, and a wide variety of processed foods) and under the most unexpected names (honey, maple syrup, sucrose, brown sugar, turbinado, dextrose, invert sugar, raw sugar, corn syrup, fructose, high-fructose corn syrup). Avoid all products containing any of these sugars. That doesn't mean giving up the sweet life entirely. There are dozens of goodies on the market (cookies, candies and candy bars, ice milks, sorbets, frozen yogurts) sweetened with fruit juice or fruit juice concentrates, which do not appear to cause havoc with blood sugar in most people. Many are also fat-free. Try some of these (most often they are found in health-food stores, but they may also turn up in your favorite supermarket) and pick up a "sugar-free" dessert cookbook. Fruit-sweetened goodies will satisfy your sweet tooth without throwing your body chemistry out of whack. Not everything found in health-food stores, however, is healthy. You have to read labels there, too.

more sugar; possibly also palpitations, anxiety, sweating, diarrhea) when the sugar addict abstains from sugar, and that it takes from twelve days to three weeks to lose the physical compulsion or craving for sugar. It's been suggested that this addiction tends to run in families.

There is some evidence that affected individuals have a physical need for carbohydrates—which are, after all, the basic ingredients in alcoholic beverages. Those who've studied this phenomenon describe sugar addiction as a progressive disease with predictable symptoms. Sugar addicts go from eating for pleasure, to problem eating, to an addiction to specific foods and symptoms that mirror alcoholism. These sugar addicts can no longer control what they eat, hide the foods they crave, and use food to relieve tension, boredom, frustration, and uncomfortable feelings. For them, total abstention from sugar is the answer.

Giving up, or at least drastically cutting back on, sugar may not be easy, particularly if alcohol was your drug of choice. The alcoholic is used to sugar rushes (from alcohol, which is absorbed quickly into the bloodstream) and still craves them when sober. Candy bars, cookies, and so on are a quick and easy substitute for alcohol. But they offer only temporary relief. With sugar, as with alcohol, the rush stops suddenly and the blood sugar level plummets quickly, triggering a craving for still more sugar.

Though it is important in recovery to have frequent snacks, in the long run it's a lot better to rely on complex carbohydrates and protein than on sugar for this purpose and for supplying energy needs.*

The Less Tinkering with Foods, the Better

Generally, the closer a food is to its

*Some rehab programs limit sugar immediately; others do not, on the theory that early recovery is enhanced if patients don't feel they are being deprived of anything (other than their drugs).

origins when you eat it, the better it is for you. Not only does fresh food retain more of its original nutrition, it is also less likely to have had a lot of questionable chemicals added to it en route from farm to fork. So favor fresh or fresh-frozen fruits and vegetables, and grains that are "whole" and have not been refined. Avoid heavily processed foods, foods the farmer wouldn't recognize. Read ingredients lists to be sure that you're getting a real food and not a chemical cocktail. There are some who suspect that chemical food additives (those unpronounceable ingredients we see so often on processed foods labels) may play a role in addiction. Basically, the less processing, the less likely it is that a food contains these chemicals—or alcohol, caffeine, sugar, or anything else that might interfere with recovery.

You Can't Do It Alone

If you go on a healthy food kick and the rest of the family munches on doughnuts for breakfast, lets M & M's melt in their mouths at snack time, and enjoys their sandwiches on white bread, you'll have a hard time not joining the party. Enlist the help of those you live with, explaining that a good diet is essential not only for your continued recovery but for the good health of every one of them. Whoever does the grocery shopping should be very familiar with the Clean and Sober Diet—which is, in fact, a healthful diet for everyone.

THE ESSENTIAL ELEVEN

You could set up a chemistry laboratory in your kitchen to be sure that you get all the nutrients you need every day. Or you could just be sure to get your Essential Eleven.

The portion sizes and nutritive values for the Essential Eleven listed below are for fresh fruits and vegetables, raw or cooked, unless otherwise noted. Nutritive value may be a bit lower in frozen produce and considerably lower in canned.

Some foods give you double or triple credit. Broccoli, for example, qualifies as a green leafy vegetable serving, a vitamin C food serving, and a calcium serving. Feel free to combine partial servings to make complete ones: one and a half cups of pinto beans and a half cup of collards equal a complete calcium serving.

Limit your intake of foods labeled,† since they are very high in fat.

1. Whole-grains and legumes—6 to 11 servings daily. These foods are rich in many of the nutrients that alcoholics and addicts lack, including the B vitamins and trace minerals. And, though dieters used to think otherwise, they are not fattening—as long as they aren't slathered in butter or drowned in rich sauces. Consume the larger number of servings if you are male, very tall, trying to gain weight, or otherwise need a lot of food energy.

With occasional exceptions, all breads and cereals should be whole-grain. And don't confuse these concentrated complex carbohydrates with simple carbohydrates like sugars,

DINING DANGER

Danger at the dinner table is an ever-present possibility. It can lurk in the pot roast simmered in red wine, the strawberries soaked in cognac, and the whiskey-flavored pecan pie. Even the best of diets can be a losing proposition if you aren't careful. So know what's in the food you eat—at home or away. And remember that, contrary to accepted folklore, the alcohol doesn't evaporate even after long cooking.

which should be avoided.

One complex carbohydrate serving equals: 1 slice bread; 1 small roll; ½ bagel; 1 small pita; ½ cup cooked brown or wild rice, millet, kasha, unpearled barley; 1 serving ready-to-eat or cooked cereal or grits; 1 tortilla; 2 to 6 crackers; 6 to 8 breadsticks; ½ to ⅔ cup cooked beans (kidney, lima, chickpeas, pinto) or peas (lentils, split peas, black-eyed); 1 ounce pasta; 2 tablespoons wheat germ.

2. Calcium-rich foods—2 to 5 servings daily. How much you need of calcium foods will depend on your age, gender, and other variables. For example, women generally require 3 servings, but this requirement increases to 4 during pregnancy and 5 when nursing. According to the most recent recommendations, both males and females require 4 servings until they reach their mid-twenties. Some experts believe supplementation with calcium during the young adult years will help to avoid osteoporosis later. Anyone with a history of alcoholism probably requires more calcium (possibly the equivalent of 4 servings, no matter what their ages) rather than less, to compensate for the years during which their bones were deprived of the mineral by alcohol.

One calcium serving equals: 1 cup skim (nonfat) or low-fat milk or plain yogurt; ¾ cup calcium-added milk or calcium-fortified orange juice; ¼ cup Parmesan cheese; 1 to 1½ ounces hard cheese, such as Swiss or mozzarella; 4 ounces canned salmon or 3 ounces canned sardines, with the bones; 1 cup cooked collard greens; 1½ cups cooked kale, collards, mustard or turnip greens; 1¾ cups broccoli; 2 corn tortillas; 10 dried figs; 3 cups cooked Great Northern, navy, or pinto beans.

3. Beta-carotene-rich vegetables and fruits—2 to 4 servings daily, or more. Green leafy and yellow vegetables and yellow fruits are the primary dietary source of vital beta-carotene, which is converted by the body to vitamin A. It's believed that beta-carotene may protect against some forms of cancer, so this is a particularly important nutrient for those who have abused alcohol or tobacco and are at an increased risk for cancer. These plant products are also often rich sources of trace minerals, such as zinc and chromium, and of fiber.

One beta-carotene serving equals: 11 asparagus spears; ¾ cup broccoli; ⅓ cup cooked beet greens, turnip greens, kale, collards, or chard; ½ small carrot; 1½ cups deep green lettuce (romaine, Boston, Bibb, escarole); 1 tablespoon canned unsweetened pumpkin; ¼ cup mashed winter squash; ¼ small sweet potato or yam; 1 large tomato, ¾ cup cooked or puréed tomato, or 1½ cups tomato juice; ¾ cup vegetable juice; ½ large red bell pepper; 2 apricots or 4 dried halves; ⅛ small cantaloupe; ¼ large mango; 2 nectarines; 1 large yellow peach; 1 plantain.

4. Vitamin C-rich foods—1 to 3 servings daily, or more. This vitamin is important for everyone's good health. It helps normal tissues stay healthy and promotes healing of damaged tissue. In large doses it may reduce heart attack risk and it is especially important for the smoker, who needs at least 2 servings daily.

One vitamin C serving equals: ½ cup strawberries; 1½ cups fresh blueberries; 1½ cups most other berries; ¼ cantaloupe or ⅛ honeydew melon; ½ grapefruit or ½ cup grapefruit juice; 1 small orange or ½ cup orange juice; 1 large lemon or ½ cup fresh lemon juice; 1 small kiwi; ½ large mango; ½ cup broccoli or Brussels sprouts; ⅔ cup cauliflower or kohlrabi; 1 cup cooked red or Chinese cabbage, or 2 cups cooked green cabbage; 1 to 2 cups cooked greens; 8 okra pods; 2 small tomatoes, ½ cup tomato purée, or 1 cup tomato juice.

5. Other fruits and vegetables—2 servings daily, or more. In ordinary quantities, these fruits and vegetables do not supply the daily requirements of vitamins A and C, but they do provide many important vitamins and essential trace minerals, and (except in juice form) plenty of fiber.

One other fruits and vegetables serving equals: 1 apple, 1 cup apple juice, or ½ cup unsweetened apple sauce; 1 small banana; ⅔ cup sweet cherries; 3 small fresh figs; 1 pear or white peach; ¾ cup diced pineapple, 1 pineapple slice, or 1 cup unsweetened pineapple juice; 2 plums; ⅔ cup most berries; ¾ cup sliced rhubarb; 2 cups diced watermelon; 1 cup dried raisins, apple rings, or currants; 5 dried dates, 3 dried figs, 2 dried pear halves, or 5 large prunes; 5 or 6 asparagus spears; ½ avocado*; ¾ cup green beans; 1 cup beets, eggplant, shredded Savoy cabbage, sliced Jerusalem artichoke; 2 large ribs celery; ¼ head iceberg lettuce; ½ cup sliced mushrooms; 9 okra pods; 1 cup sliced onion or diced turnip; ⅔ cup sliced parsnip, peas, or snow peas; 1 small potato; 2 ounces seaweed or kelp; 4 to 6 radishes; ½ cup water chestnuts; ½ cup zucchini.

6. Protein-rich foods—2 full or 4 half servings daily. This requirement is higher for pregnant women (4 full servings) and for others with special needs. It may be reduced to 1 to 1½ servings temporarily (on doctor's orders) in those with severe liver damage (vegetable protein may be tolerated better than that from animal sources). But patients with milder damage benefit from adequate protein intake, so check with your physician. Protein is particularly important in recovery because it helps to keep blood sugar level and repairs damaged tissue. Having some protein with each meal will help keep your blood sugar from dropping between meals, triggering a craving for sweets (or worse). Remember, partial servings can be combined to meet the full requirement. For example, 1½ ounces mozzarella and 2 ounces high-protein pasta equal 1 full protein serving. See Heart-Healthy Hints for tips on choosing protein foods.

One full protein serving equals: 3 to 3½ ounces fish (fresh or canned); 4 ounces lobster or scallops; 5 ounces crab or clam meat; 3½ ounces shrimp; 3 ounces lean or 4 ounces fatty veal, beef, lamb, or pork (the more fat, the less protein); 2½ ounces white chicken or turkey meat, or 3½ ounces dark meat; 5 to 6 ounces tofu; ¾ cup low-fat cottage cheese.

One half protein serving equals: 1¾ ounces mozzarella, Swiss, or other lower-fat cheese; 1¼ ounces nonfat Cheddar or other nonfat cheese; 2 ounces high-protein pasta or 4 ounces regular pasta; 3 egg whites or 1 large egg plus 1 white; 1½ glasses (12 ounces) skim (nonfat) or low-fat milk; 1 cup plain low-fat yogurt; ¼ cup grated Parmesan cheese; 2½ to 3 tablespoons peanut butter.

7. Iron-rich foods—some daily. Small amounts of iron are found in many of the fruits, vegetables, grains, and meats you consume every day. Being sure to eat some of the foods that are particularly rich in iron will help ensure that you don't suffer from iron deficiency anemia (women in their childbearing years are most subject to this condition because of monthly blood loss, but alcoholics for a variety of reasons are also susceptible; see page 255).

Iron-rich foods include: beef; blackstrap molasses; carob flour or powder and baked goods made with them; chick-peas (garbanzos) and other dried peas and beans; dried fruits; Jerusalem artichokes; liver and other organ meats (but these are high in cholesterol and

*This food is too high in fat to be used to meet the Essential Eleven requirements on a regular basis.

may also be contaminated with chemicals, so have them rarely if at all); oysters; pumpkin seeds; sardines; soy beans, soy products (tofu, miso), and baked goods made with soy flour; spinach.

8. Water and other fluids—eight 8-ounce glasses daily, or more. No matter what your favorite fluid was in the past, your choice now should be water, and plenty of it. No problem—you're used to imbibing fluids, and this one is calorie- and caffeine-free and the very best thirst quencher. If the water in your area is suspect, consider buying bottled water that comes from a pure water source or installing a water filter on your own system. If water is at or near the bottom of your list of favorite beverages, drink it icy cold, perhaps with a twist of lemon or lime. Or choose seltzer or sparkling water. Round out your fluid requirement with soups, fruit and vegetable juices, decaffeinated teas and coffees, sugar- and caffeine-free sodas, milk (which, however, is only two-thirds fluid), and juicy fruits and vegetables.

9. High-fat foods—in very limited quantities. A totally fat-free diet is nutritionally unwise (unless it is medically indicated and adequate supplementation is given) because we all require what are known as "essential fatty acids." But too much fat is definitely a health hazard (linked to both cancer and heart disease), and federal guidelines recommend that the average American consume no more than 30 percent of his or her daily calorie intake in the form of fat. That means that if you need about 2,100 calories a day, no more than 630 of them should come from fat.* Since it takes only 70 grams of fat (5 Clean-and-Sober fat servings or about as much as you would find in a single hefty slice of quiche) to reach 630 calories, this requirement is easily filled—and almost as easily overkilled.

Some experts consider 30 percent high, and suggest that 20 percent would be a better ceiling (or 420 out of a 2,100-calorie diet). Still other experts recommend a 10 percent limit (or 210 out of 2,100-calorie diet). So monitor your fat intake carefully, and err on the side of too little rather than too much. Don't forget that fat used in cooking and preparing foods counts, too. If you've fried your eggs in ½ tablespoon margarine (½ serving) and mashed your tuna with 1 tablespoon mayonnaise (1 serving), include those amounts in your daily tally.

One half serving of fat equals: 1 ounce cheese (Swiss, Cheddar, provolone, mozzarella, blue, Camembert); 1½ ounces skim-milk mozzarella; 2 tablespoons Parmesan cheese; 1½ tablespoons light cream; 1 tablespoon heavy (whipping) cream; 2 tablespoons whipped cream; 2 rounded tablespoons sour cream; 1 tablespoon cream cheese; 1 cup whole milk; 1½ cups 2 percent milk; ⅔ cup whole evaporated milk; ½ cup regular ice cream; 1 cup whole-milk yogurt; 1 tablespoon light margarine; 1 whole egg or 1 yolk; 1 tablespoon peanut butter; 2 small biscuits**; ¼ to ½ cup commercial granola (varies with brand)**; 1 slice cake, 3 cookies, 1 brownie (varies with recipe)**; 1 typical muffin**; 9 French fries**; ½ cup white sauce**; ⅓ cup hollandaise sauce**; 1 tablespoon light mayonnaise; 1 egg or 1 egg yolk; ¼ small avocado; 6 ounces tofu; 7 ounces light-meat turkey or chicken, no skin; 3½ ounces dark-meat turkey or chicken, no skin; 4 ounces fresh or canned salmon; 3 ounces canned tuna in oil.

*You can determine your approximate calorie needs this way: Multiply your ideal weight by 12 if you're sedentary, by 15 if you're moderately active, and by 22 if you're extremely active. In general, men need more calories than women, larger people more calories than smaller ones. See the table on page 434 for the appropriate number of fat servings for your weight and level of activity.

MINI-GUIDE

Heart-Healthy Hints

❖ Reduce your overall consumption of fats. When you cook with fat, make olive or canola oil your first choice; corn, safflower, and sunflower oils should be second choices. Avoid palm kernel and coconut oils, as well as all hydrogenated shortenings (shortening that stays solid at room temperature). Spreading a pat of butter on bread once a day won't sabotage your diet; eating more than that might.

❖ Reduce your intake of foods that are high in cholesterol, including eggs (limit yourself to three or four yolks per week), poultry skin, red meat, organ meats (eat rarely), and full-fat dairy products.

❖ Cook and bake with egg whites, discarding the yolks. Two whites will usually substitute nicely for one whole egg in most of your favorite recipes.

❖ Use low- or nonfat milk, yogurt, cottage cheese, sour cream, ice milk, and frozen yogurt. Use hard cheeses only in small quantities (as seasoning), and always choose those that are lower in fat and sodium; or use nonfat cheese.

❖ Chill soups and gravies and remove the fat; then reheat to serve.

❖ Beware of commercial baked goods and prepared foods; they are generally very high in fat and sodium and low in fiber.

❖ When cooking at home, sauté onions, mushrooms, vegetables, fish, and so on in a nonstick pan sprayed with vegetable cooking spray. If more oil is needed, add a couple of teaspoons of olive or canola oil. Avoid fried foods.

❖ Buy low-fat ground meat. Sauté ground meat slowly, and drain off all fat before proceeding with any recipe using loose ground meat, such as chili, spaghetti sauce, and so on.

❖ Increase your intake of high-fiber foods, such as whole grains, fresh fruits, vegetables, and legumes (dried peas and beans).

❖ Increase calcium intake and reduce sodium intake (see page 436).

One full serving equals: 1 tablespoon vegetable oil; 1 tablespoon regular margarine or butter; 1 tablespoon regular mayonnaise; ¼ cup premium ice cream (16 percent fat)**; 2 tablespoons regular salad dressing†; 1 croissant or doughnut**; 1 piece Danish or other pastry**; 1 serving apple or other fruit pie**; ½ serving pecan pie**; 1 large waffle (regular recipe); 3 to 6 ounces lean meat (varies with cut); 1 to 1½ ounces fatty meat; ¼ roasted duck, meat only; ½ fast-food burger; 1 small chicken drumstick, fried; ⅓ chicken breast, fried; ¾ cup tuna salad.

**These foods are too high in fat and too lacking in nutritive value to be a regular part of your diet.

†Since the fat content of salad dressings varies, read the label; each 14 grams of fat is 1 fat serving. In homemade dressings, each tablespoon of oil is equal to 1 fat serving.

10. Calories—enough to keep your weight where you want it or to get it there, but no more. Though calories do count, you don't have to count

YOUR DAILY FAT LIMIT

The following table provides fat intake maximums (at both 20 and 30 percent of calorie requirements) for typical weights. If you fall somewhere in between, average the two closest servings to figure your own maximum. Unless you are underweight, it is probably wise to try to stick closer to the 20 percent maximum rather than the 30 percent. The number of servings suggested takes into account the fact that the average person consumes at least one 14-gram full fat serving during the course of day in dribs and drabs from "low-fat" foods, such as breads and cereals; low-fat milk, yogurt, and cottage cheese; legumes (dried beans and peas); and many fruits and vegetables. If you would like to stick to a 10 percent maximum, just halve the 20 percent figures.

Your ideal weight (pounds)	Your activity level	Your daily calorie needs	Your maximum fat intake in grams (30%/20%)	Your maximum full fat servings (30%/20%)
100	1	1,200	40/27	3/2
100	2	1,500	50/33	3½/2½
100	3	2,200	73/50	5½/3½
125	1	1,500	50/33	3½/2½
125	2	1,875	62/42	4½/3
125	3	2,750	92/62	6½/4½
150	1	1,800	60/40	4½/3
150	2	2,250	73/50	5/3½
150	3	3,300	110/72	7½/5
175	1	2,100	70/47	5/3½
175	2	2,625	88/59	6/4
175	3	3,850	128/85	9/6

them. Just weigh yourself every day at the same time of the day, with the same type of clothing (or lack of it), preferably on an empty stomach, to see if what you're eating is moving your weight in the direction you want it to go. If it's not, read the material on weight control on page 437.

11. Vitamin supplement—one a day or as prescribed by your physician. Alcoholics/addicts enter recovery with a year to dozens of years of below-par nutrition—because they have usually paid little attention to eating and because the substances they have used have robbed their bodies of much of the little they did manage to take in. So a vitamin pill (or several) may be prescribed for you. If such supplementation isn't prescribed, you may want to take a daily vitamin-mineral supplement as insurance—although if you adhere faithfully to the rest of the Clean-and-Sober Diet, it may not be necessary after the first months of recovery.

Keep in mind that this pill should *supplement* good eating habits, not replace them. Because the danger lies in the person and not the chemical, you should also recognize that there is a risk in your depending on a pill for anything. (It can be as psychologically addicting to pop vitamin pills as any other pills.) Think of this as a food supplement, which it is, not as a drug or medication to solve your nutritional problems.

Don't think that if taking one vitamin supplement may be useful in recovery, taking a lot of them will be even better. Some vitamins are toxic in large doses, and doses higher than the RDA should be taken only on the advice of your physician.

HERBAL TEASE

Herbal teas sound safe and natural. But herbs are drugs, and some of them do have a mood-altering effect. Although many of the national-brand herbal teas may be okay, avoid any that stimulate or change your mood or give your heart "skips" or palpitations. And stay away from exotic herbals, especially sassafras and comfrey, which can damage your liver—the last thing you need in recovery.

CAFFEINE AND YOUR RECOVERY

Caffeine (found in coffee, tea, many soft drinks and medications) is a drug. It has some definite mood-changing effects (it peps some people up, paradoxically calms others down), and heavy users experience both side effects and withdrawal symptoms. But as yet no research has linked this very common drug directly to relapse. Still there are a good many reasons to eliminate caffeine from your recovery life: If you have panic attacks, agoraphobia (fear of crowded places), mood swings, or similar problems, they may be related to the consumption of caffeine. Since a panic attack could lead to relapse, the caffeine could be an indirect trigger. Some people get the same kind of rush from caffeine that they get from alcohol and sugar—and the same kind of letdown later. Another reason caffeine may be risky in recovery.

If you are hyper, restless, agitated, or experience sleep problems or palpitations, caffeine may be the culprit. Caffeine may also aggravate premenstrual syndrome (PMS) or irritate an ulcer (even decaf coffee may be irritating). In very large doses (more than 8 cups of coffee a day), caffeine can cause a variety of serious symptoms, including restlessness, headache, disturbed sleep, heart irregularities, digestive tract irritation, diarrhea, and delirium in some people. That may sound like a lot of coffee, but not a few AA members drink as much at one meeting.

Many of the charges hurled at caffeine remain unsubstantiated. Caffeine doesn't seem to be related to cancer, high blood pressure, or high blood cholesterol levels (though, oddly enough, it's possible that coffee—decaf or regular—may raise cholesterol if prepared by boiling rather than the drip method). On the other hand, the claim that it can improve athletic performance has gone unconfirmed. It may slightly increase endurance, but this possible benefit is far outweighed by the fact that it increases fluid loss,

TO SALT OR NOT TO SALT

That is a question that can't be answered unequivocally. We do know that all human beings need some sodium to survive. Nature in her wisdom lightly salted many common foods (milk, carrots, and celery, for example) with this mineral. Humankind originally salted foods to preserve them, but we didn't stop when refrigeration became available, and we continued to add massive quantities of sodium to our food products. We know now that we don't need large amounts of this mineral in our diet. Whether or not excess sodium is involved in the development of high blood pressure (hypertension) and stroke in some people, isn't clear, however. Some recent studies have raised questions about what had been medical gospel. Still, until all the answers are in, the U.S. government recommends limiting intake of salty (high-sodium) foods.

If sodium is linked to hypertension, salt limitation is particularly important for alcoholics, since alcohol, like sodium, is linked to high blood pressure. Aim for no more than 2,500 to 3,500 milligrams of sodium a day (unless you are put on a salt-restricted diet by your doctor and are limited to less). Limiting sodium intake is becoming ever easier as more and more foods are labeled for sodium content. Processed foods (frozen, canned, bottled, dehydrated)—other than those that are intended to be low-sodium—usually are high in sodium and should be generally avoided.

Add salt at the table rather than during cooking (most people use less this way), and use spices, herbs, lemon juice, vinegar, and other seasonings generously to reduce the need for salt. Avoid salted nuts, pretzels, pickles, herring, olives, prepared salad dressings, and other highly salted foods, as well as any processed main course with more than 450 milligrams of sodium, or side dish or dessert with more than 200 milligrams. Packaged baked goods can be particularly high in sodium, so watch breads, cakes, muffins, and their cousins, and stay away from those containing more than 200 milligrams a serving.

heart rate, and jitters, all of which can interfere with performance.

Cutting down on caffeine may be particularly important if you give up smoking. While you smoked, nicotine helped metabolize the caffeine more quickly; without the nicotine, more caffeine will remain in your bloodstream longer (see page 455), and you could suffer from a suddenly concentrated jolt of symptoms from the drug.

Reducing or eliminating your caffeine intake takes planning:

Avoid "cold turkey." Giving up caffeine suddenly can result in a wide range of unpleasant withdrawal symptoms: headache, irritability, fatigue, lethargy. So it's probably a better idea to taper off by reducing your intake a quarter of a cup at a time. You can do this by gradually drinking less coffee, tea, or cola. Or you could replace the caffeinated beverages with decaffeinated a little at a time. (Some folks like to start by blending decaf and caffeinated coffee, each day reducing the proportion of caffeinated until their cup is caffeine-free.)

Keep your energy up. Replace your caffeine kick with better nutrition, regular meals and snacks that are high in protein and complex carbohydrates and low in sugar (which will keep your blood sugar levels from falling, thus forestalling that tired "Boy, do I need a cup of coffee!" feeling). Plus regular exercise (in the morning it can get you going as well as caffeine; in the mid-afternoon, it can give you a lift).

Switch beverages. An icy glass of water, juice, or lemonade can be a terrific warm-weather pick-me-up, and decaffeinated coffee or tea is a good cold-weather substitute for your usual caffeine fix. Even better, try hot juice tea: a spoonful or two of your favorite fruit juice or frozen juice concentrate mixed with boiling water and, if you like, some cinnamon or nutmeg.

YOUR WEIGHT IN RECOVERY

Most people in recovery have a weight problem. Some are grossly underweight after years of lots of drinking and very little eating. Others bulge disconcertingly as they swap a craving for alcohol and drugs for a craving for food. Still others have eating disorders.

For each individual, there's a best way of controlling weight. For those who choose to lose (or not to gain), the following points are fundamental:

❖ Apply to weight control the same principles you use in controlling your addiction to alcohol and/or drugs.

❖ Keep a food diary for at least a week. Write down every item that goes into your mouth, when, and why. Evaluating this record will help you understand where you're going wrong and indicate how to straighten up and eat right. For example, if you find you always nibble and nosh while cooking, chew gum instead, or dramatize your good intentions by binding a kerchief over your mouth, or take a vow of abstinence while cooking. If you eat whenever you're tense, learn to do re-

GETTING STARTED WITH THE CLEAN-AND-SOBER DIET

You want to improve your diet, but where do you start? Start by looking at what you're eating now. If you're like most Americans, you may be unpleasantly surprised, even shocked. If you started keeping a food diary back in Phase Two, look at it now. If you didn't, keep a daily diet diary for a week. Compare what you've been eating to the Clean-and-Sober Diet. This will give you some idea of how far you have to go and point out your most glaring faults.

Next, sweep the cupboards clean—and the refrigerator and freezer, too. Get rid of foods with refined carbohydrates (white flour, white crackers, breads, refined cereals), sugar in any form (cookies, cakes, candy, ice cream), hydrogenated shortenings (those like Crisco that are solid at room temperature).

Restock the shelves with whole-grain breads, cereals, and flours; peas and beans (dried or canned); frozen vegetables; fruit-juice-sweetened cookies and muffins; frozen fruit juice concentrates for cooking and baking; nonstick vegetable spray; canola and olive oils. Replenish fresh fruits and vegetables regularly. Continue developing your label-reading expertise so you won't be misled by food package hype.

If you want to "cheat" with an ice-cream cone or a hoagie occasionally, do it outside the house. Or bring one serving home and eat it. But don't store any nutrition-poor foods in the house.

laxation exercises instead (see page 320).

❖ Follow the Clean-and-Sober Diet faithfully, with the alterations noted below. Plan meals in advance so you won't be tempted by last-moment compulsions to eat the wrong things—like that plump bag of French fries still lurking in the back of your freezer.

❖ Don't diet or fast. Your goal should be not so much losing or not gaining weight as changing your eating style; this way, any weight loss will be permanent and not just a passing success.

Our bodies are designed for survival. Internal feedback systems trigger fierce self-protective instincts when our physiology senses danger. Fasting, or cutting back drastically on food intake, sends the message that the world in which you live has become hostile and is threatening to starve you. You respond with intense feelings of hunger for anything filling and a lot of it, nature's way of stocking up in hard times. Unless your idea of a "Perfect 10" is the Goodyear blimp, it's critical to avoid this survival urge to eat more.

Fasting or greatly reducing food intake over longer periods also sparks survival activity and is self-defeating for those trying to shed pounds. The body resets its metabolism—the way food is burned—so that it can get by on fewer calories. The more you starve yourself, the less food you need to survive. With your metabolism lowered, you may fail to lose weight even on a low-calorie diet; and as soon as you start eating "normally" you begin to gain.

❖ Avoid liquid diets (unless medically indicated); they can be as addicting as alcohol, and sometimes as dangerous. Those who manage to stay on their liquid diet do lose weight, but they become fearful of eating. Once they return to real food, they usually fly out of control. Will the L.A. Dodgers manager Tommy LaSorda keep off those 30 well-advertised pounds he lost? Well, the big bucks he earns each time the commercial runs are a strong incentive, but some studies have shown that 98 percent of liquid dieters regain what they've lost.

❖ Don't try to lose more than ½ to 1 pound per week. Weight lost slowly is much more likely to stay lost.

❖ Cut the fat. Combined with exercise, this is the single dietary change that can make it possible to drop pounds and keep them dropped. Reduce your fat intake to 10 percent of your calorie intake (one-third the usually recommended 30 percent). Be on the alert for hidden fat (ask for salad dressings and sauces on the side in restaurants and use only a sprinkling; better still, use plain lemon juice or piquant balsamic vinegar on salads); avoid all fried foods and luncheon meats (even the "low-fat" variety) entirely; before cooking, remove skin from poultry and carefully trim fat off meats; avoid high-fat or whole-fat dairy products as well as butter and margarine (they are equally fattening), except in tiny quantities. If you must have a spread on bread, use a "light" one. Since most commercial baked goods are extremely high in fat, buy those that are fat-free or fat-reduced.

❖ Drink plenty of fluids, particularly water, during the day. (Some researchers suggests that ice water chills the body, causing the metabolism rate to increase and thus burn food more rapidly, but that isn't clear.)

❖ Avoid completely any foods that trigger further eating (the I-can't-stop-at-just-one foods). That means keeping them out of your home and turning your back on them at parties. These include (alas!) peanuts, chips, and almost anything containing sugar.

❖ Concentrate on foods that are high in bulk and nutrition and low in fat and calories, that will fill you up not out, such as: air-popped popcorn (use an imitation butter spray if you crave the

WILL SUGAR SUBSTITUTES HELP CONTROL YOUR WEIGHT?

Maybe. A recent study showed that subjects consumed less sugar and fewer total calories when they drank aspartame-sweetened soft drinks, and they actually lost weight. But other studies have shown no weight loss with the use of sugar substitutes. The reason: the would-be dieters, proud of putting sweetener rather than sugar in their tea, blithely rewarded themselves for their virtue with a Danish (or doughnut or cheesecake). So it seems that *if* you substitute a lower-calorie sweetener* for sugar (in soft drinks, coffee, ice cream and the like) *and* consume a diet that is otherwise low in fat, sugar, and calories, you can lose weight. But that's a major "if."

*Aspartame (Equal, Nutrasweet) and saccharin (Sweet 'n Low) are low-calorie sweeteners. Saccharin, because of possible cancer risks, is sold with a warning label. Sorbitol and mannitol (found in ice creams, candies, gum) don't cause the same kinds of shifts in blood sugar that sugar does, and they don't cause cavities, but they yield as many calories as ordinary table sugar. They can also cause diarrhea in some people.

butter flavor), raw vegetables, fresh fruit, green salads with low-fat dressings. If you hate preparing raw vegetables, buy them ready-cut at the supermarket or a local salad bar.

❖ Eat frequent small meals or snacks to avoid hunger. Waiting to eat until you're very hungry may lower your blood sugar and your resolve.

❖ Start a meal with a salad (topped with low-fat dressing or just some lemon juice or balsamic vinegar), raw vegetables, a clear soup (made without fat or cream), or a glass of water, to take the edge off your appetite before getting to the more caloric part of the meal. Take small portions, eat slowly, avoid seconds, and make it your policy to leave a little something on your plate. As soon as you have finished your meal, get up from the table and, ideally, leave the kitchen-dining area. Or chew sugarless gum while you clean up.

❖ Never eat on the run or without thinking. Savor your meals in a leisurely fashion, enjoying the food with the senses of smell and sight as well as taste. Never eat standing up, while watching TV, or at your desk. Limiting where you eat will limit how much you eat. Requiring yourself to set the table and sit down, even for a snack, may sometimes make that snack seem like more effort than it's worth. Between meals, keep the kitchen door closed to remind you to think before you eat. Have healthy snacks readily available and visible in the fridge (keep ready-to-munch vegetables in a covered glass bowl) and store the high-calorie stuff in the back behind the milk.

❖ To avoid eating out of boredom, stress, or depression, learn alternative ways of dealing with these states of mind (see pages 322 and 326), all of which can also interfere with your general recovery. Eat for the right reason—because you are hungry.

❖ Change your playgrounds, playmates, and routines, at least for a while. That means avoiding the places where you ordinarily eat the wrong kinds of foods (fast-food haunts, ice-cream parlors, and so on), the people you tend to overdo with (those who can't finish a meal without a rich dessert), and the events in your daily life that are related to eating too much (watching TV in the living room, for example; watch in the bedroom instead, and institute a no-eating-in-bed rule).

❖ Don't reward your abstinence from alcohol, cigarettes, or other drugs with food at this stage of recovery. Choose a movie, a book, a ballgame, a concert, a video, a tennis racket, or anything else you've been hankering for.

❖ Use cues to keep your goal in mind: a picture of you thin—or much fatter than you want to be—taped to the refrigerator door. A scale in the middle of the kitchen. A new slimmer-size dress or suit hung conspicuously in the bedroom.

❖ Eat something before going to a party where you might be tempted to eat too much. Then stay away from the food and beverage tables, keep a diet soft drink or seltzer in your hand, and use your mouth to talk a lot. Plan on having something to eat near the end of the party, and then just take small portions of the things you really relish.

❖ Never waste calories on empty-calorie foods that you don't absolutely love. If you're going to binge, make it a good one.

❖ If you have a compulsion to eat a food you know you shouldn't, try substituting another activity (take a shower, begin a crossword or jigsaw puzzle, go for a walk, play the piano, phone your sponsor) or try stuffing yourself with safe foods like air-popped popcorn, broccoli, carrots, celery, red peppers, apples, pears, and so on. In general, deal with food cravings as you would any other cravings—with distraction, postponement, relaxation exercises, and so on. Remember, this craving too shall pass.

❖ Don't completely deprive yourself of treats—that will lead to self-pity and uncontrolled eating. But enjoy them out of the house and in small quantities (one scoop of your favorite ice cream, for example, or half a slice of creamy cheesecake or a sliver of pecan pie) in controlled settings (where you can't have more than you plan on having). Walk half a mile (or more) for your longed-for delicacy, enjoy it, then walk half a mile back. This will erase calories as well as guilt.

❖ Get some exercise every day. Your options are many: brisk walking, jogging, bicycling (stationary or moving), cross-country skiing (again, stationary or out in the snow), aerobics, folk dancing. Swimming, though a good aerobic exercise in many ways, isn't much for burning calories. The heavier you are and the faster you exercise, the more calories you will burn. In general, covering 1 mile (walking or running) will burn 100 calories. If you begin any exercise program more strenuous than walking, be sure to get your physician's okay first.

❖ When you slip up, forgive yourself. Don't wallow in guilt and self-pity. Just get right back to your good dietary habits.

GAINING WEIGHT

To the overweight of the world, difficulty in gaining weight sounds like a wonderful dream. But to those who can't seem to gain an ounce, it's a frustrating nightmare. If it's *your* nightmare, there are ways of awakening from it.

Before making an attempt to put on pounds, however, you should get a thorough checkup to be certain that there is no medical reason behind your inability to put on weight. Once you get a clean bill of health, try the following tips:

❖ Keep a food diary for a week. Are you getting at least three substantial meals daily, with snacks in between? What kinds of foods are you eating? Compare your intake with the Clean-and-Sober Diet. Are you getting your Essential Eleven? If not, start working on making them a part of your life.

❖ Eat efficiently. Avoid filling up on salads and high-bulk low-calorie foods. Get your Essential Eleven of fruits and vegetables, but emphasize foods that go down easily and pack a big nutritional wallop: meats, fish, cheese, beans, breads, cereals, and in small amounts, avocados and nuts. Be sure you're getting 30 percent of your calories from fat (choose vegetable sources over animal, and olive and canola oil over others). Given the choice, take the higher-calorie food rather than the lower—a banana over an apple, salmon over sole, and a baked potato over a side of green beans.

❖ Examine your eating environment. You should be sitting down to meals and not eating on the run. Mealtimes should be relaxing and unhurried. Try to allot at least twenty minutes to a meal (thirty would be even better).

❖ Exercise only moderately. The compulsive jogger who does ten miles every morning burns so many calories that it's almost impossible to compensate for them with food. So try to limit yourself to no more than thirty or forty minutes a day, preferably every other day. If you have trouble cutting back, you may need professional help to deal with your obsession.

YOUR IDEAL WEIGHT

Just what constitutes ideal weight is still very much a matter of debate. Federal guidelines were recently changed to allow more leeway to those in middle and old age. Those guidelines are shown here, but keep in mind that some experts think they are too generous, and that most of us would be better off weighing somewhat less than the recommended weight. The higher weights generally apply to men and the lower to women.

Height	Ages 19 to 34	Age 35 and Over
	Weight in Pounds	
5′0″	97–128	108–138
5′3″	107–141	119–152
5′6″	118–155	130–167
5′9″	129–169	142–183
6′0″	140–184	155–199
6′3″	152–200	168–216

WHEN EATING—OR NOT EATING—BECOMES THE PROBLEM

Alcoholics/addicts are particularly susceptible to eating disorders in recovery. This may be because of their general tendency to carry things to extremes, or it may be rooted in an abnormality in the brain's reward system which stimulates addictive behavior in the first place. For many recoverees, compulsive eating replaces compulsive drinking or drug use. Anorexia nervosa and bulimia are also particularly common, especially in women. So be on the alert for the signs of either or both of these conditions as you progress through recovery. They may be difficult for you to self diagnose, however, since denial is often a prominent element in eating disorders.

Anorexia Nervosa

This disease is characterized by a morbid fear of being fat and a distorted view of one's own body. People with this condition (85 to 90 percent are women) look in the mirror and see themselves as fat, even when they are so thin that their bones are becoming prominent. It may all start with an ordinary weight-loss diet. The anorexic reaches his or her first goal, and is so delighted that another lower goal is set. Losing weight becomes so gratifying, confers such a sense of power and control, that as each target is met, a new one is set. The downward spiral continues until weight dips dangerously low. Losing weight becomes the most important thing in life—more important than family, work, health. Sound familiar? It's an addiction.

Anorexia nervosa most often develops in the teen years, but it can occur at any age, especially during recovery. Anorexics tend to be achievement-oriented perfectionists who nevertheless lack self-esteem. Many come from families genetically loaded for addiction and have subconsciously chosen what they see as a safer option. Warning signs of anorexia include significant weight loss of 15 to 25 percent below desirable weight, frequent trips to the scale during the day, and such eating rituals as measuring and weighing everything that is to be eaten, cutting food into tiny pieces, pushing food around the plate without eating it, discarding food surreptitiously, eating on the sly. Eventually menstrual periods in women become irregular or cease entirely, and excess body hair may begin to sprout. Anorexics are usually fatigued, depressed, and weak, with a below-normal body temperature and a re-

TREATMENT FOR FOOD ADDICTION

Food addiction is a serious problem in our society. Many people use food in ways similar to the way they use drugs. They begin by eating certain foods for the "lift" they get from them and end by becoming compulsive eaters, unable to control their eating.

There are now programs available in various parts of the country to help those addicted to food. Many are hospital-based. Such treatment may begin with detoxification, followed by abstention from binge foods, then individual and group therapy leading to Overeaters Anonymous. There is usually a vital family component. Check with your physician or addiction professional.

SOURCES OF HELP FOR EATING DISORDERS

National Association of Anorexia Nervosa and Associated Disorders (ANAD)
Box 7, Highland Park, IL 60035
(708) 831-3438

Anorexia Nervosa and Related Eating Disorders (ANRED)
P.O. Box 5102, Eugene, OR 97405
(503) 344-1144

National Anorexic Aid Society (NAAS)
5796 Karl Road
Columbus, OH 43229
(614) 436-1112

American Anorexia/Bulimia Association (AA/BA)
418 E. 76th St., New York, NY 10021
(212) 734-1114

National Institute of Mental Health
Eating Disorders Program
Building 10, Room 3S231
Bethesda, MD 20892
(301) 496-1891

Overeaters Anonymous,
World Service Office,
P.O. Box 92879
Los Angeles, CA 90009
(213) 542-8363

duced interest in sex. In spite of muscle weakness, they often become addicted to exercise as part of their fanatic weight-control program.

Bulimia

Bulimia can develop after anorexia takes hold, or it can start without previous anorectic behavior. This condition is characterized by binge eating followed by forced purging (usually through self-induced vomiting and/or the use of laxatives, diuretics, and emetics, such as syrup of ipecac, but sometimes through strenuous exercise, fasting, or the use of diet pills). The binge may involve an immense amount of food (eating a gallon of ice cream along with a couple of boxes of chocolates, for example; an intake of 3,000 to 50,000 calories in a two-hour period is not unusual) or an ordinary meal with the family. After either, bulimics feel remorseful and guilty over their lack of control and secretly purge themselves.

Like anorexia, bulimia is most likely to begin in the teen years but can start at any time. It is more common than anorexia, and some believe that one in five women try purging themselves at one time or another. At least 1 million Americans are estimated to be seriously affected, roughly 5 to 10 percent of them males.

Bulimia is less obvious to others than anorexia, since bulimics can maintain their normal weight or even be overweight. (The weight range is from 15 percent below to 15 percent above normal.) Bulimics binge in private, so others rarely know how much they are eating. While the anorexic revels in a sense of control, the bulimic feels guilty and out of control, and is therefore more likely to be depressed. The anorexic's addiction is to thinness, the bulimic's to excessive eating. Some bulimics actually steal to support their eating habit (again, a familiar addictive behavior).

There are, however, some physical signs of bulimia: puffiness in the cheeks or under the chin caused by swollen salivary glands, abnormal menstrual periods, excessive tooth decay and gum disease (a result of the acidity of the vomit that is frequently induced), and scars on the back of the hands (from forcing fingers down the throat to trigger the gag reflex). Depression and self-injury (such as cigarette burns) are also common.

The Health Consequences

Both anorexia and bulimia require professional treatment. Without it, they can lead to serious medical problems, including thinning of the bones (osteoporosis), irregular heart rhythm, rupture of the stomach, deterioration of other vital organs, inflammation of the pancreas, and infertility. If a woman with an eating disorder does become pregnant and continues her behavior, she could put both herself and her baby at risk. Eating disorders can be fatal. Six to 10 percent of people with eating disorders die as a result of starvation, cardiac arrest, or suicide.

Some of the side effects of these illnesses are less serious but nevertheless disturbing: dry skin; brittle, splitting nails; dry, thin hair; cold, blue hands and feet; broken blood vessels in the eyes or face; tooth decay and gum disease.

Those who become fat as a result of binging can overwork their hearts, suffer from diabetes, impaired lung function, or kidney problems.

Getting Help

Don't be embarrassed about an eating disorder. Like other addictions, it is a medical problem and requires prompt medical help from experienced professionals. Be open and honest (as you've learned to be in recovery) in describing your eating problem to your physician. Treatment should be individualized, and may be given on an outpatient or hospital basis, through psychotherapy, nutritional reeducation, and group or family counseling. Participation in a special Twelve-Step group for bulimics (part of an Overeaters Anonymous program) may also be recommended.

Not all psychiatrists or addiction professionals are sufficiently savvy to help patients with eating disorders. The experience of the professionals you see will be more important than their specialty background.

A NUTTY PARADOX

Nuts are high in fat and too much fat in the diet increases the risk of heart attack. True. But a recent study of Seventh Day Adventists, whose members eat a lot of nuts, greatly *reduced* their risk of heart attack. More studies are being done to confirm these results. In the meantime, don't go nutty eating nuts. But do feel free to include a few in your diet daily.

24

TOBACCO: WHEN LIFE GOES UP IN SMOKE

You've already given up at least one old friend—alcohol or a kindred substance. Why should you have to give up this last dependency, one you may be clinging to for dear life? For just that reason: dear life. In this country, tobacco use is the major cause of people dying before their time. If you want to live to enjoy your sobriety, it's time to give up smoking.

A GUIDE TO QUITTING

SMOKING AND RECOVERY

Smoking has not yet been positively linked to relapse, but as it is increasingly recognized as an addictive drug, it's likely that future research will show that it is. Many public health experts already say that since tobacco use is so costly to society and increasingly seen as "antisocial," it should be lumped together with the other drug addictions. A growing number of rehab centers and addiction specialists now feel that treatment has not been successful until the patient grinds that last cigarette into the dust.

Smoking certainly has been a major cause of death, even among those who stay in recovery. Bill Wilson, cofounder of Alcoholics Anonymous, Marty Mann, founder of the National Council on Alcoholism, and Dr. John Mooney, who founded Willingway, all died as a result of their heavy smoking. We know too much about the hazards of tobacco addiction to allow this needless loss of life to continue.

WHY QUIT?

Smoking is linked directly or indirectly to about 400,000 deaths annually

Guide Lines

❖ Smoking reduces your life expectancy. Quitting starts to erase the damage almost immediately. Smoking also reduces the life expectancy of those with whom you live, work, and play.

❖ Nicotine, a major component of tobacco, is an addictive drug. Smoking may be a relapse risk.

❖ Though giving up smoking is sometimes even more difficult than giving up other drugs, it is possible to quit permanently—if you are well motivated and use what you've learned in recovery about dealing with addictions.

❖ The techniques for quitting outlined in this chapter can be used whether you quit when you first become sober, now in Phase Three, or any time in between.

(each year wiping out a city the size of Columbus, Ohio) and causes 11 million cases of chronic illness. Like drinking, it can turn so many parts of the body into disaster areas that it's not absurd to speculate that hard-pressed life insurance companies may someday decline to pay death benefits on the grounds that voluntarily stuffing a cigarette in your mouth twenty to sixty times a day could be considered the equivalent of committing premeditated suicide.

Cigarettes encourage the development of heart disease and stroke; cancers of the lung, esophagus, mouth, pancreas, bladder, and throat; disabling chronic lung diseases such as emphysema and chronic bronchitis; duodenal ulcers; and osteoporosis—all potential killers. They are also linked to cervical cancer in women (a danger compounded if a woman is exposed both to her own smoke and smoke from others around her).

Dropped carelessly into a wastebasket or limply onto a bed or between sofa cushions by a sleeper, the cigarette is a major igniter of fatal fires. Then there are the nonfatal effects, which, if they stopped to think about it, would-be-sophisticate teenaged smokers might consider a fate worse than death: prematurely wrinkled skin, yellowed teeth and fingertips, tobacco breath and stale-smelling clothing, enfeebled taste buds and sense of smell. For females, there is the increased risk of not being able to have a baby. For males, an increased risk of impotence.

Cigarette smoke doesn't stop there. It seems to interfere with the way the body deals with certain nutrients (vitamin C, for example), drugs (caffeine, for one), and some medications. The painkilling effect of analgesics, for example, is weaker in smokers, so they require larger dosages. If you smoke and have to take medication for surgery or some other reason, the fact that you may require more than normal doses could unexpectedly wreck a previously successful recovery from alcoholism/addiction.

As almost everyone but see-no-evil smokers knows by now, the clouds of smoke they exhale are a keen and present danger to nonsmokers with whom they live or work. (Greater love hath no spouse than one willing to live with a mate who's slowly killing her—or him.) Exposure to secondhand smoke transforms the nonsmoker in the home or workplace into a passive smoker at increased risk for both cancer and heart disease. It even makes the family pet more susceptible to lung cancer.

For children, neither a smoke-filled womb nor a smoke-filled room is healthy. During pregnancy, maternal (and to a lesser extent paternal) smoking, increases the risks (in part because of carbon monoxide poisoning) of a baby being born too early and too small, dying around the time of its birth, having long-term physical and intellectual deficits, and being hyperactive in childhood.

If one or both parents continues to smoke after the baby is born, they expose their child to an increased risk of illness (particularly respiratory ills, such as asthma and bronchitis) in infancy and childhood, and possibly to a greater chance of developing lung cancer later in life. Knowing that, what parent wouldn't quit? Many don't know, don't want to know, or feel shame and guilt but keep saying, "No way I can break this habit."

As with the damage to smokers themselves, damage to offspring is dose-related: the more cigarettes smoked around your children, the greater the risk. Your smoking also doubles the risk of your children turning out to be smokers and, since smoking is a gateway drug, of turning them on to other drugs as well. Of course, if you smoke, you may never need to worry about your children. Smoking doesn't do it to everyone but it can interfere with fertility by lowering a man's sperm count and often his sexual desire.

If better health for yourself and your loved ones, a longer life span, and possibly less risk of relapse aren't incentives enough to persuade you to quit, consider the money that goes up in smoke every time you light a cigarette. With cigarettes selling for well over a dollar a pack, the two-pack-a-day smoker ends the year $1,000 poorer. And that doesn't include the added costs of medical care, work time lost because of smoking-related illness, and replacement of cigarette-burned clothing and household goods.

Though the bad news about tobacco sounds really bad, the good news is pretty good. If you quit—no matter how long you've been smoking or how old you are—you reduce your risks of many of these negative outcomes and increase your potential life span.

Some people in recovery have already given up smoking by the time they reach Phase Three, either because the treatment program they participated in attended to cigarettes along with other drugs right from the start or because health or other personal considerations motivated them to quit on their own. If you aren't one of these, now is the time to concentrate on smoking cessation.

Laws against smoking in airplanes, restaurants, and other public spaces have certainly made it harder to smoke, but only one person can totally legislate cigarettes out of your life. That move—disarming those little white time bombs in your purse or pocket by dropping them into the nearest garbage can—is up to you.

SMOKING ADDICTION: HOW TO KICK IT

For those in recovery, giving up smoking may be both harder and easier than for other people. Harder because for many recoverees smoking becomes the new crutch, and they lean so hard on it that some claim giving up cigarettes is more difficult than giving up alcohol or drugs. Easier because the very same principles used to break alcohol/drug addiction can be applied to a smoking addiction.

Dismayed and disgruntled smokers find they can no longer indulge at work (at least in many places) and that in private living rooms, public meeting places, classrooms, restaurants, airports, planes, and trains, they are treated like lepers in their most contagious stage. With so many places where they can't light up ("Sure you can smoke—just bundle up well and exhale out there in that snowstorm"), more and more smokers are throwing up their hands and their cigarettes. You may feel like doing that, too.

Since 1964, when the surgeon general first announced that smoking was hazardous to health, more than 41 million people have quit smoking. Another 1.5 million quit each year. Are they any smarter or tougher than you?

A smorgasbord of approaches has been developed over the years and is constantly being refined and improved. The box on page 456 can help you decide which approach may be best for you.

You have an edge. You know that it won't be enough just to stop smoking, that you will have to reorganize your life to be tobacco-free, that you will have to change your playgrounds and playmates and maybe even your daily schedule (at least for a while), and that you won't be able to have a smoke "now and then" because the match that lights that casual cigarette will reignite your addiction. But perhaps what makes you strongest in your winning battle with nicotine is that you've developed coping skills (in place of a "coping cigarette") to turn to when you're tense or nervous.

In some ways, quitting is easier in this country than ever before because smoking has become an "Ugh!" habit, less and less socially acceptable. In spite of the tobacco industry's smoke ring press releases, only a modern Rip Van Winkle could fail to know that tobacco can put you to sleep permanently.

Many teens, unfortunately, are not yet tuned in, but in other age groups it's no longer considered "sophisticated" or "smart" to smoke. With nearly three out of four Americans nonsmokers, smokers can't help but notice that every time they pull out a pack of cigarettes, there's someone conspicuously fleeing across the room or holding their ground and saying firmly something that would have been considered rude barely ten years ago: "Yes, I mind very much if you smoke."

In general, the following can help anyone who wants to quit. Some tips will work better for some than for others; try those that you think will work best for you.*

To Begin Your Campaign

❖ Reject tobacco as a "friend." Most smokers have an emotional attachment to their little packs of cigarettes that parallels a friendship. They think of tobacco as loyal in difficult times, available for support when times are bad, and nonjudgmental when other friends are gone. The first step to success in laying down the weed is changing your relationship with it. See it as your enemy, the killer-out-to-get-you it truly is. Some of this readjustment is a mind game you must play with yourself, but some simple techniques, such as those below, may also help.

❖ Brainwash yourself. Read all the material you can find about the hazards of smoking. Reinforce the notion that smoking is a dirty habit by not emptying your ashtrays (in the office, your car, at home), flicking ashes on the floor, and keeping windows closed and any air-cleaning equipment inactive. Remind yourself that you share the hazards of every cigarette (or even more so, every pipe and cigar) with those you love and like around you—spouse, children, unborn children, friends, coworkers. Use positive reinforcement to enhance your idea of yourself as a nonsmoker. Imagine yourself enjoying *not* smoking, breathing clean, fresh-smelling air, enjoying the taste of food as your taste buds revive, feeling new bursts of energy as the carbon monoxide leaves your lungs.

---

*If you are chronically depressed, you should get treatment for this problem at the same time as you try to quit smoking (see page 328).

❖ Evaluate your habit. Are you truly addicted to tobacco? Do you smoke every day? Do you have to have a cigarette when you get up in the morning? Do you find yourself lighting up almost every hour during your waking day? If the answer to these questions is no, you may not be addicted and chances are good that you can give up smoking easily. Of course, unless you've been smoking for only a short time, this isn't likely. Most recovering alcoholics/addicts are every bit as addicted to their tobacco as to their other drugs of choice.

❖ Decide on your "stop date." You can pick a particular date in advance (a family birthday, a holiday, the first day of the next month or the new year, a day you'll be somewhere that smoking is prohibited, or the next Great American Smokeout). Or on a day when you feel awful, just say to yourself, "Today I feel lousy. Smoking is the main reason, and I'm not going to smoke anymore."

❖ Announce your stop date publicly. Tell friends, family, and coworkers that you are planning to quit and when. Bet a friend or relative $5, $10, or more that you'll quit as scheduled.

❖ If a spouse, other family member, close friend, or colleague at work smokes, try to enlist them in an all-out joint campaign to quit. Working together will make quitting easier.

❖ Keep track of your habit for a week. Up until your designated quitting day, keep a diary of each cigarette you smoke and when, where, with whom, and why you smoked it. This will help you find substitutes for cigarettes once you do quit, and to know which playgrounds and playmates need changing. Also note how badly you needed each cigarette, on a scale of 1 to 3 (with 1 indicating the greatest need), so you will have some idea of which smokes will be easy to give up and which difficult. Keeping a diary will also show you just how much you are smoking—all those cigarettes smoked without your even realizing it will now become real.

❖ Remind yourself how awful smoking is by taking a day to overdo it: smoke at least double your usual quota of cigarettes, smoke until your eyes and throat are irritated, until the very thought of another cigarette alarms you. If the feeling stays with you the next day, try to go cold turkey (continuing on page 452). If it doesn't, or if you return to your regular smoking ways, continue with the steps below.

❖ Using your diary, try to figure out what motivates you to smoke: oral gratification, to keep your hands busy, to steady your nerves, to ease anxiety or depression, to look mature or confident, or simply for pleasure. Then think about appropriate substitutes and start using them occasionally now (see page 452 for examples). If you smoke in the belief that it keeps your weight down, as do many young women, also read page 454.

❖ Again, using your diary, analyze what triggers a desire to smoke. Do you always have a cigarette with coffee? Okay, then switch to tea—at least until your abstinence from cigarettes is comfortable. Do you always have a cigarette when you talk on the phone? Then try to make your calls from a smoke-free zone. Is the coffee break always a time to light up at work? Then move to a nonsmoking zone the moment you hear the coffee wagon bell. Is the end of a meal the signal to pull out a pack? Then get up from the table as soon as you've had your last bite, and busy yourself with dishes or something else. Do coffee and dessert say "light up?" Then skip them for a while, or have them away from the table—in front of the TV in the living room, for example.

❖ Based on the notations in your diary, evaluate which cigarettes during the day you are least dependent on. Try eliminating them now by asking yourself before striking a match, "Do I really need this cigarette?"

❖ Write down the reasons you want to quit on a pocket-size card and carry it with you. Attach the card to your cigarette pack with a rubber band. Whenever you reach for a cigarette, read the card first. Postponing lighting up may allow the craving to pass without your yielding to it. This will also help you reduce the number of cigarettes you smoke, and thus taper your intake of nicotine, before you quit.

❖ When your ashtrays overflow, empty them all into a large glass jar. Dampen it down with a little water, and keep the jar where you can see its nasty contents. Before you light up a cigarette, open the jar and sniff.

❖ Make smoking a chore. Put cigarettes in an inconvenient place; keep matches and cigarettes in different rooms; if you're right-handed, smoke with your left hand. Buy cigarettes only by the pack, and don't buy a new pack until you've completely finished the old. Or better still, don't buy cigarettes at all. Depend on cadging from friends and neighbors. Create nonsmoking zones, or times, or positions. Tell yourself you won't smoke in the car, won't smoke within fifteen minutes of eating a meal, won't smoke standing up, and so on. Adopt these rules one at a time; don't move on to the next until you are successful at the previous one.

❖ Postpone gratification. When you feel a compulsion to smoke, wait ten minutes before lighting up. After a few days, try to extend that to fifteen minutes, then half an hour, and so on. Fill the waiting time with appropriate distractions (see page 452). Have your first cigarette of the day later and later in the morning. When you do light up, smoke only half of the cigarette.

❖ Switch to low-tar filtered cigarettes, preferably to a brand you don't like, as you get closer to your stop date.

❖ If you're worried about gaining weight once you've quit, start exercising (by now, you should be breathing easier) and take other measures to prevent that from happening (see page 455).

❖ Frequent places where smoking is prohibited (movie theaters, museums, houses of worship, buses or subways, shops, the nonsmoking sections of restaurants, and so on), and avoid locales you associate with smoking. If the AA meeting you usually attend is not nonsmoking, find a meeting that is. If there isn't one, gather a group of nonsmoking recoverees and start one (see page 417). If you must be somewhere where smoking is permitted, stick with the nonsmokers. If smoking is permitted where you work, set your own limits and make your own rules—decide, for example, that you can smoke only in the lounge or on breaks.

❖ Ask friends not to smoke around you, and stay away from friends who just can't oblige.

❖ Get rid of all your smoking paraphernalia—lighters, matches, ashtrays, cigarette boxes, pipes, and so on. Give them away (if there's anyone you dislike enough) or just throw them away. If you have costly cut-glass ashtrays, convert them to nut dishes (but keep them filled). If you have a silver cigarette box or case, use it for something else or sell it for the silver. Don't pick up matchbooks on your way out of a restaurant—reach for the toothpicks instead.

❖ If you have more than two cups of coffee a day or the equivalent in other caffeinated beverages (colas, teas, and so on), begin to cut back on your caffeine intake over a period of several weeks to prevent caffeine rebound as your nicotine intake drops (see page 455).

NICOTINE GUM, NICOTINE PATCHES

People smoke for two reasons. One is behavioral—oral gratification, something to do with their hands, a way of dealing with stress. The other is nicotine addiction. Recent research tells us it may be useful to deal with these factors one at a time, behavioral first and addiction second. This allows the smoker to give up the most dangerous part of the habit (the smoke-filled lungs), while temporarily continuing to get nicotine from nicotine gum or the newer nicotine-dispensing skin patch. This approach hasn't been linked to drug or alcohol relapse, so it appears safe to use in recovery. It must, however, be used under medical supervision.

If you use the gum, you have to follow directions carefully (it's not like chewing Chiclets) or you could end up with unwanted side effects, such as nausea. Since food and drink—particularly coffee and colas, but also milk and fruit juice and many kinds of solids—can interfere with its absorption, the gum should not be used immediately after, or with, anything but water. A waiting period of at least 15 minutes after food or drink is a good idea.

Most people find that starting with twelve pieces a day (each chewed when a cigarette is craved) works to replace the nicotine they've been getting from tobacco. The frequency is gradually whittled down to zero. As use is tapered off, it may be necessary to cut the gum into smaller pieces. The gum should not be used for more than six months.

While the gum works only for smokers, not for those who chew tobacco, the nicotine patch, which is taped to the skin, can work for smokeless tobacco users too. The patch is easier to use than the gum, and appears to have fewer side effects. The first patch releases nicotine approximately equivalent to one cigarette per hour into the wearer's bloodstream. Patches are gradually reduced in size and potency as the nicotine habit wanes, and then are eliminated entirely. The patch should not be used for more than three months.

The patch is newer but early results of use indicate a fairly high success rate with it. Both patch and gum are more effective when tied to a formal smoking-cessation program. This route to a smoke-free life isn't for everybody. Those who have certain heart conditions and pregnant women and nursing mothers should not use it. It may also be risky to smoke while wearing the patch, though this isn't clear.

❖ As the day for quitting approaches, get your teeth cleaned by a dental hygienist and resolve to keep them that way. (Brushing after each meal will reinforce the idea of keeping your mouth fresh, and you'll be less likely to want to foul it with vile-smelling tobacco.) Air out your car, your house, and your clothing (even better: get everything washed or dry-cleaned) so that as you become a nonsmoker, you'll smell like one. Ask your employer if you can be moved to a nonsmoking area, or if one can be created for nonsmokers if it doesn't already exist. If you're the boss or are self-employed, make your own workspace a smoke-free zone. Post no-smoking signs in your home as well.

❖ Shift your addiction frame of reference. Think of nicotine as your drug of choice, of smoking as your active addiction, and of yourself as an addict with a desire to stop smoking. To meet the challenge, increase your attendance at Twelve-Step meetings.

❖ If you think it might help, plan to quit while you're on vacation. A totally different environment, a locale where you've never smoked, where your daily routine is completely different, may make quitting easier.

❖ Find an informal smoking cessation sponsor—someone who's successfully quit and is willing to talk you through your own ordeal.

Once the Big Day Arrives and You've Puffed on Your Last Cigarette

❖ Continue the preparatory behaviors outlined above (changing playgrounds and playmates, making smoking difficult, thinking of the negatives of smoking and the rewards of not smoking, substituting other forms of gratification, and so on).

❖ Be sure your home, your office, and your clothing are free of tobacco and all its accoutrements (a long-lost or just-in-case pack in the back of your desk drawer is as certain an invitation to failure as a stash of coke or a fifth of vodka under the mattress).

❖ Change your self-image, as well as the image others have of you, to "nonsmoker." When the subject comes up, instead of saying "I'm trying to quit," say "I don't smoke."

❖ Speak to your smoking-cessation sponsor regularly, for support and advice.

❖ Improve your diet to improve your chances of being a successful quitter. See the the Clean-and-Sober Diet, Chapter 23, and the special tips for those who smoke or smoked.

❖ Exercise regularly. This will help keep your weight from soaring and your mood from plunging.

❖ Drown yourself in drink—water, that is. Be sure to have at least eight 8-ounce glasses of water every day. Water helps to flush the nicotine out of your system. A tall, cold drink of water may even banish a craving for a cigarette. Some ex-smokers find tomato or orange juice helpful, too (but you pay a modest calorie premium).

❖ Apply what you've learned during your recovery from drug or alcohol abuse to giving up tobacco. This is just another addiction and should be treated as such. For extra help, you may want to locate and attend meetings of Smokers Anonymous in your area. But keep in mind that though you may be able to take your other addictions one day at a time, you may have to stay away from cigarettes just minutes at a time. One study showed that smokers trying to quit encounter a craving about every five minutes. Though most begin to lose their cravings before the end of the first year, a few experience at least occasional compulsions to smoke for years.

❖ If you have a craving, tell yourself you can wait for that smoke. Do something else instead. The craving will pass whether you smoke or not. Select the substitute activity that most fulfills the need you think you smoked for. Substitutes include:

Relaxers. If you believe you smoke to calm your nerves, try relaxation exercises and other routes to calm (see page 320). When cigarette craving strikes, sit down and relax your body. Slowly inhale deeply, then exhale. Repeat several times until the urge fades.

Mouth fillers. If you think you smoke for oral gratification, find some satisfying substitutes. Use, for example, an empty cigarette holder, raw vegetable sticks, sugar-free chewing gum or mints, or a plastic straw.*

Hand busiers. If you think that you smoke because you like to have something in your hands, occupy them with knitting, needlework, drawing, painting, sculpturing. Or do jigsaw puzzles; play solitaire or video or computer games; take up a musical instrument; try simple carpentry; make a phone call (unless you always smoked when talking on the phone); finger worry beads, roll a couple of marbles, Silly Putty, or children's clay around in your hand; make paper airplanes, or do origami.

Mind occupiers. Keeping your mind off smoking and on other things may help. Try reading (a challenging book or a light and entertaining one), learning a new computer program, studying a foreign language, doing volunteer work, taking a course in something related to your work or totally unrelated—anything that will require you to concentrate hard and keep your mind focused anywhere but on the smoke you're craving.

Short-term distractors. When the craving stirs, depending on the time or place, you could try turning on the tape deck or MTV and dancing; turning down the lights and making love (substitute a snack for the after-sex cigarette); getting up and going for a short walk; taking a leisurely bath; going for a bus ride or going anywhere else that smoking is prohibited.

❖ Don't despair if you slip and have a cigarette; just remember that you don't have to have two. Call your sponsor, a co-quitter, or the local American Cancer Society and talk about it. Learn from your slip. Remind yourself why you quit smoking.

❖ If you smoke to calm your nerves or relax, to keep going, to give yourself a lift, to distract yourself from worries, to choke off negative feelings or for "good" feelings, see Chapter 15 for healthy ways of meeting these needs. If you're tempted to use cigarettes to help you cope, ask yourself, "Will smoking this cigarette solve my problem?"

❖ Get help if you need it. If you have difficulty abstaining, sign up for a formal program (see page 456). You can also try hypnosis or acupuncture, which helps some people, or nicotine gum or skin patches.

❖ Reward yourself for your abstention. This will also improve the odds of success. Use tangible rewards (a movie or show, new clothes, a concert or ball game, a ski weekend, but not food) or psychic ones (tell yourself how terrific you are, how proud you are of yourself and how proud others are of you; how you and your house smell and look better—no more stained teeth and fingers, holes in your clothes, upholstery, rugs). When eating, notice how good food tastes and smells. Day in and day out, remind yourself how much money you're saving. Put what you would have spent on tobacco in a piggy bank, and use the savings for something special. Of course, your real reward is something money can't buy.

❖ Be persistent. Like an infant taking its first step, if at first you don't succeed, try, try again. You *can* do it.

DEALING WITH NICOTINE WITHDRAWAL

It's only in the past twenty years that scientists have definitively agreed that tobacco is addictive, but it's been no secret to smokers—fingers trembling as they greedily sucked in that first long drag in the morning—for a lot longer than that. As with any addiction, giving up the substance you're

*Some studies show that people who use such cigarette substitutes rather than finding other things to do, such as house or yard work, tend to be more successful at quitting. It wasn't clear from the study if the subjects happened to be people who smoked for oral gratification, or whether this technique would be valuable for any and all would-be smoke enders.

hooked on invites a bombardment of withdrawal symptoms, with individual variations. Not everyone experiences every symptom. Some lucky people go through withdrawal feeling nothing but regret at losing a friend they've relied on. Symptoms are mild in some, intense in others.

Nicotine is a psychoactive substance that works at specific sites in the brain as a relaxant, while paradoxically acting elsewhere in the body as a stimulant—accelerating heartbeat, elevating blood pressure, and giving a generalized lift. The body responds to the withdrawal of the drug in many ways, some of which are uncomfortable but none of which are life-threatening. The most common:

❖ A decrease in heart rate and blood pressure.

❖ Tingling or numbness in the extremities as circulation improves.

❖ Difficulty sleeping; vivid smoking dreams.

❖ Restlessness.

❖ Increased coughing as the respiratory system function improves and enthusiastically takes on the job of clearing out accumulated mucus and other junk.

❖ Dry mouth, because less mucus is produced.

❖ Slight sore throat, and possibly sore gums and tongue.

❖ Fluid retention, with some slight swelling of hands and ankles.

❖ Psychological distress, including intense cravings, nervousness and tension, depression (with bouts of crying), fatigue, irritability, light-headedness, aggressiveness.

❖ Impairment of both physical and mental performance, with lack of concentration and temporary loss of creativity.

Less common symptoms include:

❖ Headaches.

❖ Constipation and other intestinal ills.

❖ Muscle aches.

You may experience all or only a few of these unsettling phenomena. As with any withdrawal symptoms, there are ways of minimizing the discomfort. To reduce nervousness (by slowing the release of stored nicotine into your bloodstream), increase your intake of fruit, fruit juice, milk, and mixed greens and temporarily cut back on meat, poultry, fish, and cheese. Avoid caffeine, which can only add to the jitters. Get plenty of rest (to counter fatigue) and exercise (to replace the kick you used to get from nicotine). Let your mind go fallow for a few days, if necessary, doing mindless tasks or going to the movies or other places where smoking is prohibited.

The worst of withdrawal lasts only a few days to a few weeks. The benefits last a lifetime—a lifetime in which the odds of it being longer and healthier shift significantly in your favor.

SMOKING AND YOUR WEIGHT

Women seem to have more trouble giving up smoking than men. One possible reason: young wives' tales that smoking keeps weight in check. Giving up cigarettes, many women believe, will turn them into hopeless humpty dumptys. Senior citizens and the very overweight also buy into this fiction.

It's true that nicotine, a stimulant, does speed up metabolism. And on average, smokers do weigh less than nonsmokers, but the difference is only seven pounds. (And given a choice, how many women would willingly shorten their lives by twenty years just to be 110 pounds instead of 117?) Though marginally lighter, smokers

THE CAFFEINE CONNECTION

Because nicotine moves caffeine out of the bloodstream very quickly, smokers tend to drink copiously of beverages high in caffeine. When quitting smoking, overdoing caffeine is the wrong way to go. Continue to go heavy on coffee and colas after giving up nicotine, and the caffeine buildup in your bloodstream could exacerbate many of the nicotine withdrawal symptoms you may experience—among them irritability, nervousness, anxiety, inability to concentrate, and sleeplessness.

All that caffeine could also increase the risks of coronary heart disease and, if a woman is pregnant, of a low-birthweight baby. So it is very important to gradually cut down on caffeine *before* giving up cigarettes. Otherwise "cold turkey" nicotine withdrawal could lead to excessive blood levels of caffeine, even to caffeine toxicity. How do you get off caffeine? See page 435.

wear more fat around their middles, the kind of fat associated with an increased risk of heart disease, diabetes, and early death.

In spite of smokers' worst fears (and best excuse), studies show that only one in three people gains weight upon giving up smoking. The other two stay the same or lose weight, and even the gainers usually put on no more than ten pounds. So it's usually recommended that when giving up smoking, you stop worrying about being body fat-free and concentrate on becoming smoke-free. Work at taking off any added pounds later. Of course, if scale-ophobia deters you from taking the cure at all, you'll want to employ some of the hold-that-waistline strategies outlined below from the moment you crush that last cigarette.

There are a variety of reasons why an ex-smoker may gain weight. And there are a variety of ways of circumventing them:

❖ Because food tastes and smells better, the reformed ex-smoker tends to eat more of it. Overcome that urge by learning to savor those smells and flavors. Eat slowly (and *con mucho gusto*) rather than hurriedly shoveling it in.

❖ Food becomes a substitute for smoking as a way of coping with boredom or stress. Learning to deal constructively with boredom (page 209) and stress (page 324) will help to reduce this problem.

❖ A craving for foods high in fat and sugar, some authorities suspect, may be triggered by nicotine withdrawal. Overcome this by adhering faithfully to the Clean-and-Sober Diet. And always think before you eat.

❖ Particularly during activity, nicotine seems to increase the metabolic rate, as it does other body processes. Without it, food is burned more slowly. Push your metabolic rate right back up there by getting more, and more frequent, exercise. With medical approval, exercise for thirty to forty-five minutes, five to seven times a week. Start slowly, but be consistent.

You can also keep weight gain to a minimum by:

❖ Eating six small meals a day rather than three large ones. This will keep your blood sugar from falling and leaving you ravenous, weak, or otherwise uncomfortable. Favor low-fat, low-sugar foods and those that offer oral gratification, such as popcorn, raw vegetables and fruit, and crunchy whole-grain breadsticks. Satisfy any craving for sweets with fruit or low-fat

WHICH WAY TO GO?

The best way to quit smoking depends on you. Some people do better alone, others in group programs, still others with individual counseling. Here are the most common options.

SELF-HELP HELP. About 15 to 20 percent of Americans seem able to quit on their own, using self-help materials provided by a variety of organizations, such as:

The American Cancer Society's pamphlet *How to Quit Cigarettes*; call (800) ACS-2345 or your local ACS affiliate.

The American Lung Association's brochure *Freedom from Smoking*; call (212) 315-8700 for the number of your local affiliate.

The National Cancer Institute's *Clearing the Air* or other smoking cessation materials; call (800) 4-CANCER or write to the Office of Cancer Communications, BLDG. 31, Room 10A18, Bethesda, MD 20892.

The Seventh Day Adventists' *Tobacco Magazine* and booklet *Stop Smoking*; call (800) 253-3000.

The American Academy of Family Physicians' *AAFP Stop Smoking Kit,* available through your family doctor.

You can enhance your chances of doing it yourself by finding friends willing to quit with you. Talk to each other several times a week, meeting for lunch in person or on the phone, for mutual support.

GROUP THERAPY PROGRAMS. Success rates are much higher when the smoker attends a clinic or group program—ranging from 16 to 55 percent success after one year, with a median of 28 percent. For-profit programs don't appear to be any more successful than free groups. Such groups are available through:

The American Cancer Society (Fresh Start support groups); call (800) ACS-2345 for the number of your local affiliate.

The American Lung Association (Freedom from Smoking clinics); check with your local office.

Many local hospital and medical centers.

INDIVIDUAL THERAPY. A wide range of psychotherapeutic and behavior modification approaches are available through individual therapy, and success rates average about 21 percent. Therapy is most successful when the client is motivated and the therapist is experienced. With those smokers who are susceptible to suggestion, hypnosis (especially self-hypnosis) often works, but it should be administered only by a licensed physician or therapist. Acupuncture also works for some people.

INPATIENT TREATMENT. When all else fails, inpatient treatment may work. Provided by some treatment centers, it is modeled on drug and alcohol treatment but usually lasts no more than a week. Aftercare at Smokers Anonymous or other group programs is usually recommended. You can expect to pay out of your own pocket, since few if any health insurance companies will cover the cost of smoking cessation programs (though because of potential long run savings, perhaps they should).

fruit-sweetened cookies or other treats. Or eat something sour, which may banish a craving for sweets.

❖ Eating regularly. Never wait for hunger to take over. A preemptive attack on your refrigerator puts your intellect instead of your appetite in control of what goes into your mouth.

❖ Drinking lots of ice water, which will fill you up without filling you out, and may hike your metabolic rate as your body burns more energy to warm the icy fluid.

❖ Getting up from the table immediately after you've eaten your fill. Don't linger and nibble. Do anything—wash the dishes, phone a friend, walk the dog, walk yourself—to fill time and keep from overfilling body.

❖ Telling yourself you will not gain weight. This is the kind of prophecy only you can make self-fulfilling.

❖ Following the tips for dealing with cravings on page 162 and the additional tips on weight control in recovery on page 437.

If you find your weight going up when you stop lighting up, ask yourself if you could be subconsciously eating up a storm to justify going back to "weight-control smoking." If your weight threatens your smoking abstinence, try Overeaters Anonymous (OA). Based on the same Twelve-Step principles and traditions as AA, and on abstinence from certain foods (you choose which ones), these groups have helped thousands to control their weight problems. There's no law against being a member of more than one Twelve-Step recovery program. Lots of people are.

YOUR SMOKING HABIT: DEALING WITH THE DAMAGE

Most of the detrimental effects of smoking disappear in the years that follow cessation. But sometimes damage to the lungs lingers on in the form of chronic obstructive pulmonary disease (COPD), which may also be called chronic obstructive lung disease (COLD) or chronic lung disease (CLD).

This disease is quite common in substance abusers, not so much because of the substance abused (unless it was smoked) but because so many substance abusers of every stripe also abuse tobacco. If you're one of these and haven't already quit, now is the time to get the job done.

"I just take one day at a time. I will not smoke. It doesn't matter how miserable or how upset I get, I won't take one right now. Maybe later. Maybe tomorrow. But not now."

CLD develops over a long period of time, with the first damage (to smaller airways) occurring after the first few years of smoking. If smoking stops early enough, this damage is reversible. That the smaller airways function less well is usually not obvious to the smoker, but coughing and excess phlegm usually are. In general, the more cigarettes smoked, the more hacking and spitting. Smokers may also notice that as the years go by, it becomes harder and harder to blow out those candles on the birthday cake—or to do anything else that requires a lot of expiratory breath, such as blowing up a balloon. Lung disease takes different forms in different smokers. Various combinations of emphysema, asthma, and chronic bronchitis are common.

If you smoke, and especially if you experience a lot of coughing, excessive phlegm, increasing breathlessness, or other respiratory problems, you should be checked for lung disease. The examination may include a chest x-ray, stethoscopic examination and percussion (or finger-tapping) of your chest and back, and testing of your breathing capacity as you blow into a peak-flow meter.

Some medications used to open up respiratory passages when there's an asthmatic component (theophylline, for example) can make the patient hyperactive and anxious, which can contribute to a destabilization of recovery and a risk of alcohol or drug relapse. Cough medicines also usually contain risky ingredients. So it's wise to avoid such medication unless absolutely necessary, and to use it with the guidelines on page 247 when it is necessary.

Infection is a frequent complication of CLD. These infections of the bronchial tubes (bronchitis) or lungs (pneumonia) can be treated with antibiotics. Such use of antibiotics for documented infection is not generally hazardous to recovery, but the antibiotics should not be used with tranquilizers or pain medications.

Whenever possible, non-drug treatments are the way to go. Any or all of the following may be helpful in treating CLD: physical therapy to improve breathing, postural drainage,* and sometimes inhalation of steam or humidified air. Those medications that are inhaled and have minimal systemic effects (such as steroids and bronchodilators) can also be beneficial and may reduce the necessity for higher doses of systemic medication.

Eventually we may have cures even for those severely crippled by tobacco use. Meanwhile, for most smokers in recovery there's a better way: Stop now, before it comes to that.

*The purpose of postural drainage is to allow bronchial secretions to drain out of bronchial tubes so that they can be coughed up. Ask your doctor to demonstrate the proper technique.

25

EXERCISE IN RECOVERY

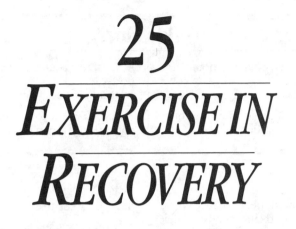

You've heard it before: Exercise is good for you. It can lower your weight, your blood pressure, and your cholesterol levels, reduce your risk of heart disease, stroke, and osteoporosis, possibly boost your immune system, and (not unimportantly) prolong your life. What you may not know is that it can enhance the odds that your life will remain a clean and sober one.

A GUIDE TO EXERCISE IN RECOVERY

It's a little more work than bending your elbow, but exercise is the perfect replacement for the couple of drinks that helped you unwind after work. It improves self-image, chases sleep problems, and often alleviates symptoms of mild to moderate depression and anxiety. Exercise helps control weight by burning calories and speeding up metabolism, makes stress easier to handle and reduces its effects on the body, and enhances social skills and thinking.

Possibly most important, it helps reconstruct lifestyles. A health-oriented life that builds in regular exercise usually has no room in it for the use of drugs or the abuse of alcohol. Indeed, the few studies that have been done show improved abstinence rates for those in exercise programs compared to those who remain inactive.

Exercise is not just for the young and healthy. In some form, it can benefit almost anyone at any age.

BEFORE YOU START

It's likely that after years of being under the influence and a period of inactivity during early recovery (to allow damaged muscles and joints to heal) you are not a candidate for the Olympics team. Before setting out on any exercise program more strenuous than walking, you should undergo a complete physical and get your physician's blessing. Depending on your age and condition, it may be recommended that you take an exercise stress test, in which your cardiorespiratory (heart/lung) fitness is evaluated as you first walk then run on a treadmill or other exercise machine.

Guide Lines

❖ An exercise program should not be embarked upon without your doctor's okay.

❖ For the sedentary, exercise must be introduced gradually.

❖ Listening attentively to your body when you exercise can prevent injury and illness.

❖ Exercise is a good thing. Like any good thing, it can be overdone.

The test should be preceded by a careful screening exam to ensure that you can undergo it safely. The stress test isn't infallible, and it's usually recommended only when there is some suspicion that heart disease may exist or when an individual is at high risk for such disease (as some people in recovery are). A pre-exercise physical exam may also check your flexibility and muscular strength.

DECIDING ON A PROGRAM

The best exercise program for you will depend on a mixed bag of factors—your health, your age, your personality and interests, your physical limitations or disabilities, your daily schedule, and the facilities available to you. One thing's sure: There's a program that's right for you. The ideal program for the healthy individual includes the "big three": aerobic exercises, strengthening exercises, and flexibility exercises. Choose activities you enjoy and can look forward to. Do them with a buddy if you enjoy company, by yourself if you're basically a loner. If you need structure to strengthen your commitment to regular exercise, join a health club or exercise class. If you can afford it, get a trainer.

Exercising with other recoverees affords a bonus, making the time spent exercising beneficial to recovery as well as to body and soul.

Aerobic Exercise

Aerobic exercise is rhythmic, repetitive activity strenuous enough to demand increased oxygen to the muscles, but not so strenuous that demand exceeds supply. The most popular aerobic exercises include walking, jogging, bicycling (stationary or moving), tennis singles, cross-country skiing (stationary machine or the real thing), jumping rope, aerobic dancing, and swimming.* Exercise that is too strenuous to be sustained for the twenty or thirty minutes necessary to reach a "training effect" or that makes you gasp for breath (sprinting, for example) or that is not strenuous enough to get your pulse rate up (such as tennis doubles) is not considered aerobic.

Jogging, the wave of the future in the 1970s, is still around but comparatively at ebb tide. As more research was done, it became clear that some types of aerobic exercise were safer than others. Walking and cross-country skiing, for example, are less likely to lead to injury than jogging or high-impact aerobic classes. (The latter have been linked to inner-ear damage, with dizziness and hearing loss. It isn't clear whether the damage is permanent, and whether its cause is vigorous jumping or just plain loud music.) Aerobic dancing offers the benefits of

*Swimming, while it is aerobic, is not weight-bearing and does not appear to strengthen bones against osteoporosis or to help in paring off pounds.

dancing in a healthful atmosphere, but be sure it's the low-impact variety to avoid risks that could outweigh that benefit.

Weight Training, or Muscle-Strengthening Exercises

Weight training involves putting a muscle group under a heavy load, then contracting and finally relaxing it. This can be done with simple barbells or with one of many contraptions (Nautilus, Soloflex) designed for the purpose. But you don't have to be that high-tech. Results soon begin to show even with old-fashioned push-ups or chin lifts, where the weight is you. When the importance of exercise was first recognized in the 1970s, weight training was considered not only unnecessary but possibly harmful. Today its

FITNESS FOLLY

Wouldn't you know it? Exercise, for all its benefits, has its downside for alcoholics/addicts (and for others as well). Since exercise stimulates endorphins, the body's natural feel-good chemicals, there is a definite link between exercise and addiction. In addiction, the feel-good chemicals are poisons supplied from sources outside the body, but the final action pathway in the brain is probably the same. Runners describe a "high" with intense exercise, and there are cases where people chasing that feeling neglect family, work, and other healthy activities.

Exercise is great, so long as it doesn't become a replacement for other things in your life. If you have to exercise rather than go to meetings, have dinner with your family, finish a paper for school or a report for work, if you go out in spite of foul weather or serious injury, exercise is a problem, not a solution. Studies have shown that exercise addicts are very similar to people with eating disorders. Both have unhealthy preoccupations with weight and body fat, and both push their bodies beyond healthy limits—exercising through pain, for example.

Even if you don't feel that exercise has become an unhealthy addiction, there's potential danger if you spend too much time at it. Too much time spent exercising could keep you from working on your recovery or relearning interpersonal skills. Or if you push yourself too hard and too far, it can result in injury, the disruption of sex hormones (throwing the menstrual cycle out of whack in women and lowering sperm count and sex drive in males), an impaired immune system, and even an increased risk of osteoporosis.

But the greatest danger, ironically, is of exercise making you feel too good. So good that you think, "Hey, now that I'm healthy again, I don't have to work my program. Now that I'm healthy, I can control my life. Maybe I can even drink again."

Of course, you can't. The fact that you can control your life enough to exercise doesn't mean you can be a "controlled drinker." One central fact must not be allowed to slip your mind: Alcoholism/addiction is a disease, and diseases can't be controlled through willpower.

Like everything else in your life now, moderation should be the goal. And just to be on the safe side, your exercise program should be monitored by your sponsor, counselor, or addiction specialist.

If you seem to be having trouble controlling your exercise activity, you may need to try to apply the Twelve Steps to this part of your life. Try beginning with "I admit I am powerless over exercise."

LET YOUR HEART BE YOUR GUIDE

Many physicians recommend that you keep track of your heart rate (or pulse) while you exercise to be sure that your exercise is neither too strenuous (your pulse races too fast) nor not strenuous enough (your pulse goes up only slightly). The formula for determining your target pulse rate (what your pulse should be during the most strenuous part of your exercise) is simple, though individual variations make it a less than perfect procedure.

To figure your maximum heart rate, subtract your age from 220. Your target heart rate is anywhere from 65 to 85 percent of that, but 75 percent is probably a good average to strive for. So if you're thirty-five, your maximum heart rate is 185 and your target heart rate is about 140 (220–35 = 185 × .75 = 139). If you're very fit, it may be difficult to get your heart rate up to 140 no matter how hard you work out. So don't worry if you're stuck at 120 after a twenty-minute run.

On the other hand, if you're out of shape, your heart may soar to 140 beats a minute before you've gone more than a block or two, in which case you will have to take it more slowly until your conditioning improves. Some physicians don't feel it's necessary to bother with pulse taking; they believe that most people know they are overdoing when they feel fatigued or can't catch their breath or talk while exercising.

role in a complete exercise program is well documented. Properly supervised weight training can increase your ability to engage in an aerobic program by strengthening your muscles and endurance and reducing your risk of injury. It will also make you more fit for other chores—gardening, moving furniture, carrying children. It may even raise blood levels of the good cholesterol (HDL), lower total cholesterol and blood pressure somewhat, and possibly reduce the risk of heart attack from unaccustomed exertion. For the recovering alcoholic/addict, it's a way to rebuild muscle mass and restore muscle tone weakened by years of abuse and disuse.

Flexibility Exercise

Well designed and properly performed stretching exercises (including some forms of yoga) enhance flexibility, maintain and extend freedom of movement, and help you dodge the stiffness that ordinarily comes with age. (The flexible person doesn't have to retire from tying his shoelaces at 65.) To be effective, they should be smooth and rhythmic rather than bouncy or jerky. Like weight training, flexing can improve your aerobic performance, but it's not clear that doing stretching exercises before and after your aerobic workout will prevent injury. Some studies show that done regularly, such exercise does reduce injury frequency. But doing it only sporadically is worse than not doing it at all.

EXERCISING SAFELY

Exercise is a lifestyle-enhancer, but like every endeavor it involves some minor risks. Keep in mind all of the following in planning your program.

Start Slowly

If you're like a lot of alcoholics/addicts, you tend to plunge into things headlong—new drugs, new kicks, new activities. The physical and mood changes you're looking for with exercise come slowly from consistent, ever-increasing efforts. If a fierce compulsion to "get into shape" rules your exercise plan, you're sure to do too much too soon, damage unprepared muscles and joints, and cause needless aches and pains and possibly serious side effects. Discouragement could make you an early dropout, in itself a serious side effect.

So, if you've been sadly sedentary, limit yourself to no more than five minutes of strenuous exercise the first few times out. Your body seems to be adjusting well to your chosen activity? Great. Extend that exercise period by a couple of minutes each day until you reach twenty to thirty minutes. If walking—than which nothing is safer—is your exercise of choice, start off with ten minutes and work up to an hour.

If you have a new pair of running shoes that you're itching to use, cover half a mile by walking two blocks or their equivalent and then jogging one. In later sessions (which because of stress to legs and back should be on alternate days), work up to two jogging and one walking, then drop the walking and, if you're having no trouble with breathlessness, keep adding blocks until you've reached your target of a couple of miles or more.

If you want to do weight training as well, don't worry about looking like a wimp. Start with the very lightest weights (even if they seem too easy) and work with them for several days, increasing the number of lifts gradually over a week or more, before moving to the next size weights. When you do move up, start with just a few lifts of the heavier metal, and then work your way up again.

With stretching exercises or calisthenics, do just a few repetitions of each for a few days, then add a couple more for a few more days, working your way up to ten or twelve repetitions or more. It may be less of a chore and more effective to do two or three short sets of stretching exercises during the day, rather than forcing yourself to do one long session.

Start each workout slowly in order to give your cold muscles a chance to warm up. Walk a few blocks at a leisurely pace, pedal your stationary bike or walk on your ski machine slowly at loose tension. Then do your stretching exercises, if you elect to do them at this point, and finally get into the heart of your workout. It's especially important to warm muscles gradually in cold weather.

Learn to Breathe Properly

Breathing incorrectly can sabotage the benefits of exercise, and occasionally

TAKE A WALK

A business contact suggests meeting for drinks. A colleague at the office wants an hour of your time to discuss a new project. You spouse is upset that you haven't had time to talk about summer vacation plans. What do you do? Suggest going for a walk. Whether it's an important business deal, complicated office politics, or choosing between the beach and the mountains that's on the agenda, there is no more relaxing or private way to talk—without interruptions, temptations, or environmental stress.

Choose a park if one's available, an indoor mall if the weather's inclement, or just the downtown streets if that's all that's available. Not only will you get more accomplished in less time, you'll get some top-notch exercise in as a bonus.

SUPER SENIORS

A frail ninety-five-year-old woman pumping iron sounds more like a TV sitcom than a scientific study. But scientific study it was, and with startling results. The old folks in this study not only didn't suffer any injuries from weight training, their muscle mass and strength increased dramatically, giving them the edge over those twenty years younger. In many cases, canes and walkers were thrown away, weakness disappeared, and a whole new lifestyle became available to the active senior.

So this exercise section is not aimed just at the young people in recovery, but at everyone who gets a green light from his or her physician. Those with high blood pressure will have to be closely supervised by knowledgeable medical personnel, at least at first. But most men and women over sixty-five, with no serious medical problems, should be able to participate in such a program.

may be dangerous. So make sure that you know or are instructed in the proper breathing techniques for the exercise you choose. This is particularly important with weight training, in which you should take a breath as you begin a movement, then let it out at the peak of exertion. If you hold your breath instead, your blood pressure could rise to unhealthy levels.

Set Realistic Goals

Alcoholics/addicts tend to think big and go to extremes: "I'm going to start running today, and by two weeks from Tuesday I'll be ready for the Boston Marathon." That kind of thinking will doom your program to failure. So set attainable goals and aim to meet them gradually. Moderation should be your byword in exercise, as in everything else in your recovery. The ultimate goal is to achieve a healthy and sustainable exercise program. Don't go out to set world's records. Go out to enjoy each day's physical activity and the good feelings it brings.

Be Consistent

Exercising one week, then skipping the next will avail you nothing. By the time your sedentary week is over, many of the benefits of your active one will have disappeared. Exercising like crazy for a month, then skipping two months, will do you no good physically and could actually increase the risk of injury. So could playing tennis for hours every day during the summer, then hibernating during the winter. To have a beneficial effect, exercise has to be as regular as the six o'clock news, at least three times a week. Devise a plan you can follow.

Tune In to Your Body

Remember that you're not into abusing your body these days. So listen when it speaks to you through fatigue (slow down or quit for the day); pain (take the stress off the injured body part, or rest up completely until the injury is healed); dizziness or light-headedness, headache or nausea (stop, and check with the doctor if these symptoms appear again when you're working out). Those macho athletes who insist "no pain, no gain" are neither physicians nor physiologists, and a lot of them end up in splints and wheelchairs.

If you're so winded that you can't carry on a conversation while exercising, you're overdoing—slow down or stop. But in general, relax, enjoy, and stay loose. Don't allow a fear of injury to interfere with your concentration;

because it increases muscle tension, fear will actually make you more injury-prone.

Chest pain during exertion that subsides after a few minutes of rest may be "angina," a serious sign of heart disease. This pain is usually in the midline of the chest, but it can be felt in other places, such as the jaw or arm (usually the left). In this condition, fatty deposits partially block one or more arteries supplying blood to the heart. With heavy exercise, an inadequate blood flow results in pain. Many therapeutic options are available, so you should see your doctor within a day or two of experiencing angina. If the pain is severe and doesn't go away in fifteen or twenty minutes, you should call an ambulance or have someone drive you directly to a hospital emergency room. (If, as recommended earlier, you've had a complete medical checkup before starting your exercise program, this isn't likely to occur.)

Adapt to Your Schedule

If you plan an exercise program that's impossible to carry out, it will be just that. So plan one that will work for you. New research shows that you can break your exercise up into smaller segments throughout the day with no reduction in benefit. So if you don't have time for more than a five-minute warm-up, a ten-minute run, and a quick cool-down and shower in the morning, don't throw in the towel. Instead, add a brisk twenty-minute walk at lunchtime and another short run before dinner, and you've got three exercise periods that add up to a good program. If you can barely drag yourself out of bed in the morning, much less drag yourself to the jogging trails, do all your exercise before dinner. But do it.

If you find that your exercise program is cutting into your recovery program, consider combining the two. If you can do it in a park or somewhere else where traffic poses no danger, listen to recovery tapes while you jog or walk. Watch recovery videos while doing a stint on a stationary bike. Get your exercise walking, instead of driving, to AA meetings.

Mix It Up

Unless there is one activity that you love above all others, you may find that varying your exercise will be less boring and will give different muscle groups more attention. It may also be beneficial, research shows, to intersperse a more concentrated exercise with a lighter one. So if you usually walk, jogging a block now and then may give you more fitness in less time. (This won't help you lose weight, however, unless you spend more time exercising.) In weight training, you should avoid stressing the same muscles two days in a row. Alternate muscle groups, so that each has a day to recover before being put to the test again.

Don't Run on Empty

Avoid running or other strenuous exercise on either a full or an empty stomach. If you exercise first thing in the morning, have a light high-protein snack before starting out. Carry a flask of water or diluted fruit juice with you to replenish fluids lost en route; this is particularly important in hot weather. At the end of your workout, drink some more and enjoy a hearty breakfast. Salt replenishment is not necessary; lots of water is.

Dress for the Part

Your exercise clothes should be appropriate to the exercise, comfortable, breathable, and not restrictive. Ideally, footwear should be designed for the particular activity; it should fit comfortably and be well cushioned. The best socks are, surprisingly, not cotton, but orlon or acrylic because they absorb the moisture from sweaty feet and whisk it away. They are also less likely to cause blisters.

PART V

CHEMICAL DEPENDENCY: A FAMILY DISEASE

What Every Family Member Should Know

Most active alcoholics/addicts want to believe that their drinking or drug use hurts no one but themselves. When they become sober, they begin to recognize the misery their behavior has caused those that they love. But they may be less in tune with the more subtle effects their chemical dependency has on the family.

Children are often the most innocent of bystanders and the most damaged. No matter what their ages, they show the scars of parental chemical dependency. They are also at risk of becoming dependent themselves—unless parents take steps to make their children dependency resistant.

Other adults in the family of the alcoholic/addict may also be innocent and damaged bystanders. But they can do a great deal to protect themselves in such a relationship (whether the alcoholic/addict is spouse, parent, child, or sibling) and to avoid being codependent. They must also learn how to stop "enabling" the chemically dependent family member.

26

THE CHEMICAL CHILD

If you're a parent, your chemical dependency has affected your children. If you closed your eyes to that fact when you were actively drinking or using drugs, that was just another form of denial. Now you've got to scrutinize your children as you do every other aspect of your life, and assess the damage. You will not only have to rebuild your relationship with your children, you may also have to help rebuild each child's sense of self. You will need to understand the risks your child faces, what you can do to reduce them, and how to recognize and deal with a child's suspected substance abuse.

PARENTING IN THE CHEMICALLY DEPENDENT FAMILY

Generally, the children of active substance abusers experience a wide range of emotions—confusion, anger, shame, fear, guilt, anxiety, loneliness, helplessness. If their home is one in which feelings are swallowed rather than shared, they tend not to express them. Parents may recognize that something is wrong, but it's often not clear just what.

ALCOHOLISM/ADDICTION AND THE YOUNG

If ever the sins of the fathers (and mothers) were visited on the sons (and daughters), it's in the chemically dependent family. Some children in substance-abusing households continue to do fairly well; others have a hard time with just about everything they do. How and to what degree a child is affected by parental alcoholism or drug abuse also varies, depending on many factors.

❖ Are both parents addicted, or just one? If one, which one? The emotional scarring is more severe when it's the mother (traditionally the primary caretaker) or when both parents are addicted.

❖ How severe were the symptoms of addiction? Generally the more severe, the greater the impact on the child.

❖ Was there a strong caretaker other than the addicted parent or parents—a loving aunt or grandparent, for example? Such a caretaker often helps to ease the child's sense of hopelessness and improve coping skills.

Guide Lines

❖ All children are affected by a parent's addiction, although sometimes the damage isn't visible to the unpracticed eye. The most composed and serene-looking child may actually be the most hurt.

❖ Individual children, even in the same family, can be affected in different ways. Some may be as good as they can be, others as bad; some may withdraw, others try to clown their way through their misery.

❖ Children of alcoholics/addicts are at high risk for developing the disease themselves. The only sure way they can beat the odds is by not drinking or using drugs at all.

❖ You can't drug-proof your children, but there are steps you can take, starting now, to greatly reduce the chance that they will turn to alcohol or drugs.

❖ All parents, but especially those who have alcohol or drug problems themselves, need to be alert to the signs of substance abuse in their children.

❖ Did the mother and/or the father drink or abuse drugs around the time of conception? Did the mother drink or abuse drugs during pregnancy? Either can affect not only the physical health and intelligence of children, but their ability to learn from experience—someone else's as well as their own.

❖ How old was the child when the addiction first became a problem? When did the parent became sober? Was the child born pre- or post-sobriety? How a child reacts to physical and emotional abuse by the addictive parent depends upon the interplay of these factors. The longer the parent's involvement with alcohol and/or drugs, the greater the child's emotional difficulties.

❖ What was the child's place in the family? In general, firstborns react differently than last-borns, and middle children differently from both (see facing page).

❖ Was there family cohesiveness in spite of the addiction? If the family was somehow glued together (usually by the nonaddicted parent, an older sibling, or another adult in the household), problems may be less severe.

❖ Did the family manage to stick to its general direction and goals in spite of the addiction? The more the addiction derailed these goals, the more difficult it is to get the children back on track.

❖ How did the nonaddicted parent respond to the situation? Those unable to cope with not having their personal needs met find it difficult to meet their children's needs, and an emotional domino effect occurs. On the other hand, strong spouses, particularly those attending Al-Anon, may be able to give strong support to their children through their own emotional recovery, lessening the impact of the other parent's addiction.

❖ How much did the child understand? Was he or she a terrified and confused bystander who saw all and was told nothing? Or was he or she given some insight into what was going on in the family, information about the disease of alcoholism/addiction and its effects, and emotional support during the time of the addiction (from the nonaddicted parent, from family or friends, from a group such as Alateen, from a physician or therapist, or from a helpful teacher or school counselor)? This kind of support reduces emotional scarring in children.

❖ Were family members allowed, even encouraged, to express feelings? In families where feelings are regularly stifled, the emotional development of children is stunted. Later, these youngsters find chemical use an effective way of dealing with pent-up emotions—at least at first.

❖ Was the child's independence fostered? Youngsters who learn to stand on their own two legs do fairly well, even in a family suffering from chemical dependency.

❖ Did physical or sexual abuse compound the emotional abuse in the home? This always puts a child at higher risk for developing problems and requires professional assistance to help with recovery. It may take some effort to uncover such abuse, since it usually occurred under intoxication and parental blackouts may have obliterated it from memory.

❖ What is the level of education of the parents and the economic stability of the family? Lower education levels and lack of economic security tend to compound the negative consequences of a life lived with a chemically dependent parent.

"My mom would say to me, 'Look, you're obviously an alcoholic. It runs in the family.' When the cops brought me home one time, she didn't scold, she just said, 'Look what you got yourself into—what you're doing to yourself.' Her not yelling at me made me realize sooner that I had a problem."

❖ How resilient is the child? Each human being responds to life stresses differently, and some bounce back from adversity more easily than others.

HOW THE YOUNG RESPOND

In general, children handle stress differently than adults or teens. When living in a hostile or frightening environment, they are unable to ventilate their feelings, seek outside help, or pick up and leave. They are, in effect, trapped. To survive, most children develop chameleon-like defensive personalities and behavior patterns as the family slides into dysfunction. And although no two families are exactly alike—not even drug-abusing families—certain motifs seem to repeat again and again. You may see one or more of your children in this typical family constellation:

The Hero or Martyr

One child in the addicted family—it can be a girl or a boy and is most often the oldest child*—generally becomes the family caretaker: looking after the younger children, making excuses for the parents, taking responsibility for chores ordinarily handled by adults. This child, who is less likely to fall into addiction at an early age, tries, often fruitlessly, to reestablish normal family functioning. The "hero" often goes into one of the helping professions, becoming a doctor, teacher, counselor, or nurse, for example.

Just because these youngsters seem so "together"—seldom displaying anger, depression, or antisocial

*Although the birth order often determines which role children in an addicted family will take, they may take other roles depending upon how many siblings there are and on individual family situations.

behavior—it shouldn't be assumed that they are unscarred by parental addiction. They may be in as much emotional turmoil as the acting-out child—and sometimes more.

The Troublemaker

This child—frequently a second-born—is the one who gets into mischief a lot and ends up being the family scapegoat. Instead of focusing on the real causes of the family's dysfunction, everybody points at the troublemaker. This behavior also serves to take the limelight away from the "hero" sibling. Parents and others often project their own guilt or inadequacy onto this poor kid, who may be the only one who is showing obvious pain.

The Lost Child

This child—often a third or middle child—is less angry and more lonely. He or she doesn't expect anything, and doesn't get it. Because of the absence of a family role model and meaningful loving interactions, this lost, or invisible, child hasn't learned how to connect emotionally with anyone, is shy and afraid to speak up, usually avoids confrontation and stress, will leave the room (mentally or physically) when there's a fight, has school problems, and has few friends. Although the family is relieved at this passivity after coping with the "troublemaker," this child may be worse off than the older sibling. These children usually show their misery by their inability to share (they treasure possessions, perhaps because that's all they have) and through a variety of psychosomatic health problems (bed-wetting, allergies, tics). If they don't get help by the time they get to junior high school, they may begin to use sex to make up for the lack of emotional intimacy at home. Although these youngsters seem the most pathetic, they aren't lost for good. If identified and helped, they do recover.

The Family Mascot

Often the baby of the family, this child is usually more protected than the others. But though this leaves them in the dark about what's going on, last-born children nevertheless experience tension, anxiety, and fear. They have all of the feelings but none of the facts. With their confusion and fear bottled up inside, they tend to develop phobias (about the dark, school, babysitters). They often have trouble concentrating and may be hyperactive, discharging all the family feelings through their humor, teasing and clowning around. They draw attention away from (but of course don't solve) family problems with humor and entertainment. Nobody takes them seriously, and so they become slow learners and underachievers. But they may also appear quite well adjusted in social situations. When they get older, they are at particularly high risk for tranquilizer abuse.

Adult personalities are in part imprinted during childhood, and the roles that children take on in order to cope in a family buffeted by addiction usually continue into adulthood unless appropriate treatment helps them to straighten out their feelings about themselves and others.

FEELINGS IN COMMON

Whether they withdraw or act out, most children in substance-abusing families suffer from severe embarrassment and shame because of parental behavior. They see the knowing looks and hear the whispered comments ("Jane's mother didn't make it to the conference. She must be, er, you-know-what again") and the derisive ones ("Hey, Tommy, your old man smells like a brewery! Did you see him fall over the garbage can coming up the walk?"). And they cringe. Even the silence of friends trying to look the other way can be painful. To compound their misery, they usually feel guilty about being ashamed. They feel they are betraying the family when they fail to defend mom or dad to friends or strangers. Once they are old enough, children take sides, cutting themselves off from either their friends or their family.

But perhaps these youngsters are most upset and confused by the uncertainties and inconsistencies of their seesaw existence. The role reversals, for instance, when the nonaddicted parent has to jump in and take over the responsibilities of the addicted one. "Who's going to pick me up at school today?" Maybe no one. Or "Who's going to give me my bath today?"

Then there are the dramatic mood swings: Mommy is kind and loving when sober, withdrawn when drunk; Daddy is friendly and fair when sober, violent and unjust when high. And, the dramatic swings in atmospheric pressure: The home is sometimes morosely silent and at other times an angry and tumultous parental battlefield. Occasionally (but rarely), it may even be normal.

Perhaps most damaging of all, there are the swings from bright hope (when the sick parent promises to stay sober or clean) to darkest despair (when that promise is broken). This behavior damages the child's self-image ("If Mommy really loved me, or if I were really good, she would stop drinking forever"), builds a basic distrust (which unless reversed can color all future relationships) and increases guilt (because they hate and fear when he's drunk the very same father they love when he's sober).

Because their emotional resources can't fix their problems, children in substance-abusing families may also experience physical symptoms—sleeplessness, unexplained aches and pains, upset stomachs, and so on—related to the family's dysfunction. Though these symptoms should always be checked out with a physician, if no physical cause is found (as is usually the case), the symptoms can be expected to abate gradually as the emotional pain lessens—either because the parent and family are in recovery or because the child is getting therapy.

PUT IT IN WRITING

Even before they can read, simple lists spelling out their responsibilities are appealing to young children (use colorful pictures cut from magazines). It makes them feel grown up, makes clear what's expected of them, and lets the parents shed the role of "nag." Start with something as simple as, "Hang up coat" (be sure there's a hook that's easy for your child to reach); "Put soiled clothing into the hamper"; "Wash hands before meals"; "Brush teeth after meals"; "Carry your plate to the sink after eating." As your child grows, more responsibilities can be added, but always be sure they are realistic.

HELPING YOUR CHILD

While you're going through recovery, your child will need to do some recovering too. Don't naively assume that once you become sober, everyone in the family will feel better and all the problems related to your drinking or drug use will miraculously disappear. They won't.

If your children are old enough, don't let them indulge in such wishful thinking either. Let them know it's going to be a long haul for everyone (see page 197), but that at least now you'll all be pulling together. It will help for them to become educated about alcoholism/addiction. If they are

"There's always the temptation to ask questions, to challenge, to lecture, to sermonize, when someone in your family is drinking or using—especially when it's a teenager. I learned in Al-Anon that this doesn't accomplish anything."

young, read to them or have them read some good children's books on the subject. A selection of the best appears on page 573. If they are teenagers, they can read Chapters 27 and 28, and should also become involved in Alateen.

These measures should be helpful, but they may not be enough. Some children need one-on-one professional help to make them feel better when their parent becomes sober. Seek help from a counselor or therapist trained in treating children of addicted families if your children seem extremely withdrawn, are getting into trouble at school or with the police, refuse to discuss your alcoholism or addiction, or repeatedly talk about hurting themselves or wanting to die.* Professional help is also an absolute necessity if they've been subjected to any sexual or physical abuse at home.

Because your children will be at high risk of marching to the same drummer you did, you should take positive steps to make them as drug-resistant as parentally possible.

*Children trying to appease their troubled family often accept much more guilt than they could ever deserve, and often talk about how everyone would be better off without them. A prolonged desire to "be dead" often precedes suicide attempts by teens.

ENDANGERED SPECIES: CHILDREN AT RISK

All children today, particularly in the teen years (because of adolescent insecurity, lack of family cohesiveness, and pressure from peers and the surrounding culture), are susceptible to the lure of mind-altering chemicals and the dependency that often follows. But children in drinking and drugging families face an increased risk because of genetic or environmental factors, or more likely both. Once they start to experiment, they have a higher tolerance than other youngsters.

It may seem logical to you that having witnessed and suffered the swath of misery bulldozed through the family by your addiction, your children will steer clear of alcohol and drugs. But that rarely happens. Children are often not yet ready to learn from the mistakes of others, particularly if "other" is spelled "mother" or "father." In fact, the influence of environment begins very early. Kids in substance-abusing families often start using sooner than other youngsters. They frequently feel, "I can't beat 'em, so I may as well join 'em. If this stuff my folks are using is so great that it means more than even their own children, I guess I ought to try it too." In addition, familiarity breeds comfort. These youngsters are much more comfortable in the familiar world of alcohol and drug use—no matter how unhappy it is—than in an unfamiliar abstinent one.

When one parent has a drug or alcohol problem, the children are four times more likely to develop one of their own than are kids in families with no substance abuse. If both parents have a problem, the kids are eight times more likely to succumb. There's no absolute way to know which children in which families are susceptible, but a handful of traits—some possibly inherited—appear to be good predic-

GRANDCHILDREN AT RISK

Sometimes the children of an alcoholic/addict recognize, loathe, and want no part of the parent's disease. Resisting peer pressure, they stubbornly abstain. But unaware of the genetic factors in the development of chemical dependency, they don't take any special precautions with their own offspring. A big mistake. As every parent should remember, kids often inherit some of their traits from grandparents. This means that they are as likely to inherit grandpa's alcoholism as they are his musical talent or red hair.

These children should be forewarned: abstain as their parents have done, and they can avoid the disease. Some try limiting themselves to an occasional drink in a social setting, but only time will tell if this is liquid Russian Roulette.

Parents of these genetically "marked" grandchildren should take the preventive steps listed on page 476, steps that can help to "immunize" any child against chemical dependency.

tors of substance abuse.

One study found that novelty or thrill-seekers and those youngsters who have no fear of harming themselves have an almost twenty-fold risk of becoming alcoholics. Another found that those who are fearless, assertive, and easily bored (again, the thrill-seekers) are three times more likely to fall victim to the disease. Yet another suggested that youngsters who've experienced one or more serious bouts of depression or anxiety disorder are at increased risk. And still another concluded that behavior problems before age fifteen (damaging property, playing hooky, school suspensions, running away from home) are predictors of alcohol/drug abuse/dependence. But more study needs to be done to confirm these findings.

Some fascinating experimental work underway may lead to blood tests to confirm genetic risk potential, but those tests are not widely available and their validity is not yet satisfactorily established. Even should these tests become routine, they won't be able to predict every child at risk because it's likely that there are several types of addictive disease, and that not all are inherited. Environment certainly plays a role.

The problems that result from raising children in a home affected by substance abuse don't end with this generation. Unless there is some sort of intervention, these children grow up, marry, and tend to have families that function just as poorly as the one they grew up in.

But that doesn't mean that you have to sit by and let your kids fall victim to the disease that has ravaged your life. Recognizing the risks, you can take steps—starting with your own recovery—that can help your endangered children avoid your wasted years.

CAN YOU ADDICTION-PROOF YOUR CHILD?

The magazine headline "You can addiction-proof your children!" probably sold a lot of newsstand copies. And it would be great if parents—especially those who've had their own addiction problems—could addiction-proof their offspring. Unfortunately, we can't—no more than we can control the substance abuse of a spouse, parent, or friend. Each individual, including your child, is in the end responsible for his or her own behavior. No matter how smart, kind, or sober you are, you can't guarantee that your child will not get into trouble with drugs and/or alcohol.

Remember that in spite of the damage that alcohol and drugs have done to their lives, teenagers, sensing the allure these substances have had for their parents, will often be seduced themselves. Subconsciously, some may even yearn to imitate dad or mom (even though mom and dad nearly died) and become active in and enjoy the camaraderie of AA—which they tend to believe means they've got to develop a drinking or drugging problem first.

Although you can't prevent your child from going your way, you can try to reduce the risk by the way you live your life from now on and by the values you pass on. Creating a drug-free atmosphere at home, practicing good parenting skills, and supplying your children with the facts about addictive disease and the tools to resist peer pressure, will increase the chances that they will be able to do a lot more than "just say no." If, in spite of all your efforts, a child does choose to experiment, use, or abuse, you are not responsible. And, though you may feel terrible, you're not a failure as a parent.

"My folks broke up three years ago when I was fourteen, because of my mom's drinking. She's real bad off. I'll never be like that. I like to get drunk. It feels good. But I only drink on weekends."

MAKE YOUR HOME A DRUG-FREE ZONE

❖ Stay sober and work hard at your recovery. The example you've set in the past has been abominable. By now you are beginning to see that you've got to do (and can do) better for your family as well as yourself.

❖ Keep your home free of alcohol and drugs (except for those prescribed or recommended by a physician, following the guidelines on page 247). Don't allow a sip of beer or other alcoholic beverage to be offered to a child of any age, no matter how adorable relatives think this is. The body provides a natural barrier to alcohol: taste. For most people it is an acquired taste (new drinkers often start with ginger ale and a dash of whiskey, and keep reducing the former and augmenting the latter as their tastes adapt). Giving sips of alcohol to kids breaks down that barrier dangerously early. Since we don't know how much alcohol or drug use "primes the pump" of addictive behavior (some claim it was the first sip or first snort that hooked them), abstinence is the most effective early prevention strategy.

❖ Include tobacco as an off-limits drug. If you keep your home tobacco-free, you greatly reduce the risk that your children will take up the habit. That's important because tobacco is a gateway drug for other drugs; kids who don't smoke rarely become drug users or abusers. And another good reason: Tobacco is the single most dangerous killer drug in the U.S., in the sheer numbers of people it buries each year.

❖ Let your children know by the way you act, as well as by what you say, that drunkenness is neither funny nor acceptable, and that alcohol is neither the only nor the best way to celebrate or have fun. Tell them how embarrassing it is to get drunk, to pick fights with your friends and throw up at a party, and to generally make a fool of yourself. It's definitely not "cool." Adhere rigorously to a policy of discouraging drinking and driving as well as drinking and any other potentially risky activity (such as swimming or biking). Don't close your eyes to the fact that Uncle Jack has had three martinis at a restaurant dinner and then intends to drive home. Don't countenance cousin Sarah's plans for a dip when she arrives at your beach house blotto. Make a point of reminding your children that everybody has to be extra-cautious both when driving and when crossing the road because of the danger from drunk drivers.

❖ Instruct children never to drive with someone who has been drinking. Make it clear that it's *not* embarrassing to turn down such a ride, and that it's downright dumb to accept it. Make sure they always have an alternative way to get home in such a situation. This should include phone or cab money, and someone they can call if you're not at home to pick them up.

❖ Counter—both by words and by action—the old "better living through chemistry" attitude that surrounds us all. Comment on the absurdity of TV commercials, billboards, and magazine ads that make it sound as though a pill can cure any problem. Make the use of pills (even an innocent Tylenol) a last-resort treatment in your home. Use non-drug treatments whenever possible. And of course, avoid using alcohol as a treatment. (Some alcoholics report becoming hooked as children when parents gave them such drinks as milk laced with blueberry cordial to help them sleep or to calm a tantrum.)

❖ Don't try to live up to the Joneses next door or the Smiths down the block. Let your family know that you don't have to have an automatic garage door opener just because everyone else does, or a vacation in the Bahamas at Easter because your partner does, or to serve alcohol at a christening because it's traditional. Consistently do what you believe is right for your family, even if others look amused or askance. Teach your children to respect individual differences, at home as well as elsewhere.

❖ But do try to influence the Joneses. Most families would like to keep their children from abusing drugs and alcohol but don't know how. If parents establish a common front, they can go a long way toward creating a community atmosphere that discourages such abuse. This includes being sure that all activities for youngsters and teens are properly supervised and are substance-free (see page 488), providing good parental role models (which means adult parties don't focus on alcohol and are drug-free, medicine chests are not filled with mood-altering drugs, parents don't use alcohol or drugs to sleep, calm down, cheer up, or wake up), and making a combined effort to influence school and community policy in this area.

❖ Explain to your children why your home is drug- and alcohol-free: "Our family is not like most other families. We have this illness called alcoholism (or addiction)." Explain that they are likely to have the problem too, unless they are really careful and learn all they can about how to enjoy living without using drugs and drinking. Admit to them that it won't be easy: "It's going to take all of us working and talking it out together. You'll have a lot of pressure from friends, TV, wherever you go. If you see any drugs at school or you're offered any, you need to let us know. We want to try to help you, to suggest ways you can handle those situations."

BE AN EFFECTIVE PARENT

❖ Create a caring environment. Human beings require nurturing, love, and praise in order to thrive and survive. If children don't get these at home, they either become withdrawn and depressed or turn elsewhere to find them. Most often they turn to a peer group, where in order to earn their strokes they may have to do things that conflict with the values they learned at home: drink, use drugs, have sex, steal, bully, and so on.

In your home's nurturing environment, children should know that come what may, they will always get love and moral support and that these won't be withdrawn as punishment or as the consequence of undesirable behavior. Building a strong relationship with your children now will mean that in times of crisis your love, support, wisdom, and experience won't be shut out of your child's decision-making.

❖ Be honest. Dishonesty is the soil in which the seeds of addiction germinate (see page 202), and being honest in all your dealings with your children as well as with others is the single most important preventive strategy any parent can have. That means being honest about feelings, about what you've done in the past, about missteps in the present.

Show your kids by your actions that you can be trusted to keep your word. That's the only way you can expect them to keep theirs. Parents who break their promises have children who do likewise. Trust your children as long as they earn that trust. Increase privileges when they adhere to rules, reduce them when they don't. In effect, that gives them a choice.

Also be open about other family problems—financial or job-related, for example. You need not go into great detail, but it's important for them to know that problems are a part of life and that you don't run away from them, that you discuss and reach decisions about them without a "Shh! The children are listening."

❖ Try to be consistent. Nobody can be perfectly consistent (or consistently perfect). Nor will it always be possible for you and your spouse to agree on parenting issues. You are, after all, individuals who may have been attracted to each other by your differences. But even if you disagree on some points, try to develop a common ground—possibly one that uses a little from your column A, a little from his column B—for dealing with the children.

Presenting a unified parental front may be more important than whether the decision is right or wrong (it's probably not completely one or the other). And showing the children how you handle your differences amicably will be a lesson for them in human relations, compromise, and diversity. If your differences start to lead to the children playing one of you against the other or to the children being caught in the middle of your fractured parental coalition or to other family friction, seek help from a qualified counselor.

❖ Admit to making mistakes, and be willing to change course if you seem headed for disaster. This may be difficult at first, since, like many alcoholics/addicts you're probably accustomed to sticking to an obviously erroneous position in spite of logic and common sense. But it's important to try. Kids who don't learn that everyone makes mistakes, and that it's all right to admit it, may either try too hard to succeed or not try at all—and eventually attempt to cover up their normal imperfections with chemicals.

❖ Don't stifle thought and opinion in your home. Listen to your children without criticizing or carping. You don't have to agree with them, but they should not feel intimidated about voicing their views. If you won't listen to their opinions, how can they possibly feel free to stand up for them in front of others—friends, teachers, and, later, spouses and employers? Children who are regularly bullied by parents don't develop self-confidence and will either become bullies themselves or let everyone else bully them.

Set aside some time during each day (after school with milk and a snack, at the family dinner table, before bed) when distractions (such as TV, radio, record players, phone calls, and so on) are banned and family members have a chance to talk to each other. Regular family meetings ("every Monday night over pizza") will also help ensure that there is time in your busy schedule to discuss family problems. Be willing to listen to constructive criticism from your children. Invite comments on changes for the better in your own attitude and behavior, and solicit suggestions for further improvement.

❖ Don't stifle feelings and emotions in your home. Be sure there is plenty of hugging and laying on of hands—the warm and loving, not punitive, kind. Also be sure that it's clear that it's okay to show anger, disappointment, fear, frustration, or other negative feelings. Don't belittle, laugh at, or be angry about your child's feelings. Accept them as real and make it clear that you are glad that your child feels free to express them. If your child seems reluctant to express feelings or to talk about something that is a problem, try to create an opening that will make it easier: "Gee, you seem upset about something. You may feel better if you talk about it. And I'm ready to listen whenever you're ready to talk."

Also make it clear that feelings, no matter how strong, should not in any way interfere with love among family members. Emphasize that regardless of how angry or disappointed you may be about some event or behavior, you'll always love your child and you believe that your child (even when screaming, "I hate you!") feels the same way—or will when the anger subsides. There are no strings attached to family love. (Okay, let's be sentimental—only heartstrings.)

Talk about and evaluate feelings—the feelings of friends and family members, of characters in books, on TV, in movies. Discuss the feelings your child may have after failing a test in school, getting a good report card, winning a tennis match, forgetting a homework assignment. Describe your feelings when your child tells you an untruth, when you break a favorite china platter, when your spouse is late for dinner, when the car gets a flat tire in the middle of a busy street.

"I was mad when my parents learned about letting go. I lost my keepers. But in the end I got my self-respect back. Now we have a great relationship."

Talk about acceptable ways of expressing feelings: through words ("I am very angry"), actions ("I am so angry that I am not going to allow you to watch TV tonight"), or lack of action ("I am so angry that I need some time to cool off and don't want to talk about this right now"). And talk about unacceptable ways: physical violence, throwing things, hurting someone in other ways (by getting them in trouble, lying about them, making them feel bad about themselves). For more on dealing with anger, see page 329.*

It's also important to discuss ways to deal with feelings and "feel better." That means figuring out why we feel the way we do and determining what actions or behaviors can alter that feeling for the better. Problem-solving and decision-making (page 358) skills can all be useful at this point.

You may find it difficult to express feelings yourself (most addicted people do), but it's important that you learn

*For pamphlets on "rethinking" anger, for parents and teens, write the Institute for Mental Health Initiatives, 4545 42nd St., N.W., Suite 311, Washington DC 20016, or call (202) 364-7111.

how, for your own sobriety as well as for your child's.

❖ Make your home a place for family members to bring their concerns. If your child brings a problem home and is scolded or ridiculed, you can be sure that next time the problem simply won't come home. Your child may take it elsewhere or may not deal with it at all. If, on the other hand, you handle the small ones (about schoolwork or a playmate) with sensitivity, your child is more likely to bring you the bigger problems later on.

If during your years of substance abuse your child lost faith in you as a confidant, be sure that there is someone else he or she can talk to until you reestablish rapport. It can be someone at Alateen, a grandparent, an older sibling or other relative, a minister, priest, or rabbi, a teacher, guidance counselor, or doctor. It should be someone your child likes and trusts. Make it clear that this person will not report to you or consult with you without your child's okay.

❖ Give your children your time and attention. When work, social activities, sports and television are perceived as taking priority over family (as drugs or alcohol once did), kids often build up resentments that later show up in rebellious behavior, including drug use. Be sure that there is plenty of time for family dinners and/or other family events every week, and schedule outings and trips together regularly.

Attention, like love, should never be used as a bartering tool—it's a child's due. Children who get too little attention often find negative ways of getting it. Flunking a course, being called to the principal's office to be reprimanded for playing hooky, and coming home after curfew drunk tend to attract more attention from busy parents than getting straight A's, being called to the principal's office to be thanked for tutoring younger students, or coming home on time. Be sure to make as much fuss—or maybe more—when you catch your kids being good as when you catch them being not so good.

❖ Set limits and house rules. A country without laws is ungovernable. So is a family. Some rules can be set by adult fiat, others by family discussion. Rules should always be spelled out clearly—in writing if everyone likes that idea. Everyone should be expected to adhere to the rules, and the consequences when rules are broken should also be clear, specified in advance, and always carried out promptly—except when all agree there were extenuating circumstances (see page 484). What the consequences should be can be discussed in advance with your children. Youngsters can often be very tough on themselves and may come up with more severe penalties than you might, so temper them if necessary.

Your offspring can always be expected to test the limits you set, so leave a little leeway. That way it won't be disastrous if they overstep them a bit. When kids do overstep or otherwise misbehave, don't label them "bad." It's the behavior that you should object to, not the children.

❖ Know when to say no—and mean it. If parents (perhaps wanting to be loved) never say no, then why should their children (perhaps wanting to be liked) say no when offered drugs? But pick your arenas carefully and don't say no to everything. When it's rational and safe, let the younger generation win a round now and then. Whether you say yes or no, don't just flatly announce your verdict. Let your children in on the decision-making process, so that they realize how one comes to a wise decision (see page 358).

❖ Provide supervision. If neither parent can be at home when your children are, be sure that someone reliable is. Or look into after-school programs sponsored by schools, houses of worship, or community centers. When kids aren't supervised, they may assume that it's okay to do anything at all, since apparently nobody cares. You don't have to be a genius to guess (and you'd be right) that latchkey children are at twice the risk of abusing alcohol, tobacco, and marijuana as are children who have someone to look after them when they get home from school.

❖ Avoid corporal punishment. Be alert for signs of abuse—physical, emotional, or sexual—from the other parent or other adults in or out of your home who have contact with your child. If there has been any child abuse in the past or if there is any occurring now, *seek professional help for the family.*

GIVE YOUR CHILD THE TOOLS TO RESIST TEMPTATION

Self-Esteem and Self-Respect

Youngsters who like themselves are less likely to try to become someone else through the use of chemical substances. Kids who respect themselves are less likely to allow others to push them into unwise behaviors. Of course, building self-esteem isn't easy, but there are some techniques that work.

❖ Respect your child. Unless parents show they esteem a child, it is difficult for that child to value him- or herself.

❖ Be realistic about your child's abilities. Don't expect a child to behave or perform like an adult, and don't expect more than your child can give. When kids feel they can't live up to exaggerated expectations, they often lose respect for themselves.

❖ Applaud work well done. Catch your child being good, and reinforce this behavior with a pat on the back, a hug, a high five, or simply words of praise. But don't applaud poor performance or your child will learn to distrust your evaluations.

❖ Encourage more effort when work doesn't match ability, but *never* belittle. "You stupid kid—why can't you ever do anything right?" is hurtful and ineffective. Much better when the performance is mediocre is "That's not bad, but I bet you can do even better." When it's downright poor, try "You must be very upset about this. Let's try to figure out what went wrong so this won't happen again." Then take steps together to help your child do better: agreeing on a regular study time; teaching research, study, or other needed skills; and arranging for a tutor if necessary. But always keep those expectations realistic—check with a teacher or other professional to be sure you're on target.

❖ Nurture both innate talents (art, sports, music, writing, mechanical skills, sociability) and areas where your child tends to have less ability. Where there is natural ability, there should be striving for excellence; in the other areas, for competency. Becoming a proficient and successful human being builds self-esteem.

❖ Encourage good work skills. From a very early age children can learn to participate in the work of the family—picking up toys, setting or clearing the table, helping put soiled clothing in the washing machine, drying the dishes, and so on. What is expected of each family member should be clear, and there should be penalties for nonperformance (see page 484). Helping out with chores will help boost the self-esteem of children as well as make them feel more a part of the family.

❖ Place a premium on completion of activities. Addicted people are accustomed to putting their substances of abuse first, and are used to abandoning projects uncompleted. Learning the importance of finishing what they start not only helps children build their feelings of self-worth but also gives them a frame of reference for comparison, should addiction become a problem later in life ("Hmmm . . . Something must be wrong; I'm not getting anything finished these days.").

Self-Reliance and Independence

You can only make your children independent by loosening your controls (within reason and taking safety into account, of course). You start letting go when you first leave a baby with a sitter, when you allow a toddler (perhaps with your heart in your mouth) to climb the monkey bars at the playground, when you send a preschooler off on a playdate. Then there's the first sleep-over, the first trip to the store alone, the first afterschool job. Later you foster self-reliance in your children when you let them make some of their own decisions and suffer the consequences of their behavior.

Good Health Habits

Children who have learned to respect and take care of their bodies—through good nutrition, regular exercise, brushing and flossing, getting regular checkups, observing safety precautions (always wearing seat belts, for example), and avoiding exposure to hazardous chemicals in the environment (pesticides, radon, etc.)—are less likely to fall victim to substance abuse. Who, after all, would want to mess up a body they've worked so hard to take care of?

Self-Comforting Skills

Don't encourage the use of outside resources (food, drink, pacifiers, gifts) to make an upset child feel better. Instead offer love and support, but not so smothering that it doesn't allow the child a chance to work out of the misery alone. Suggest a trip to the playground, recite a favorite poem, sing a song or listen to music, play catch, draw or paint a picture, do a puzzle. Older children can go for a walk or a jog, turn to music or books, even learn to meditate. They can also learn to think through a situation, and learn how to use both problem-solving and decision-making skills to deal with their feelings.

Ability to Delay Gratification

Children who are overindulged (they get what they want when they want it) and who find their parents oversubmissive (they give them what they want when they want it) find it hard to delay gratification in the teen years. For instant happiness, they often turn to chemical substances. Kids need to learn that some things are worth waiting for—a hard concept to get across in this fax and microwave world, but a vital one.

With toddlers, the delays to gratification are brief: "Mommy will get that book for you in just a few minutes; I'm fixing lunch." With school-age children, they grow longer: "I know all the kids have Smasheroo, but if you've already spent your allowance, you'll just have to wait until next week to buy one." Teens should be able to wait longer still: "Having a car of your own would be great, but you just got your license and I think we need to see how responsible you are at driving the family car before we think about that. We also need to work out a plan for sharing the costs. Let's discuss this again in six months."

Impulse Control

Children who get their hearts' desires by screaming or pouting find loss of control a very useful bargaining chip. Let your children know that you won't even listen to their requests unless they calm down first. As they get older, they also need to learn to control negative impulses. The toddler may swing

"Sure I don't do well in school. How can you think about Shakespeare or biology when you have to worry about whether you're going to get beat up when you get home?"

at a friend who appropriates his wagon; the older child should learn how to negotiate the return of a toy. But keep in mind that children don't learn to control their impulses if they live in an environment where adults don't control theirs (to yell, spank, or take what they want). Self-control is learned best in a home that is neither overly permissive nor overly strict, and where fairness and rational behavior are the golden rule.

Mood-Maintenance Skills

A teenager doesn't need drugs to experience mercurial mood changes, but many of them turn to drugs to alter moods they are uncomfortable with. To avoid this happening in your family, talk about moods, mood changes, and ways of dealing with them. Let children know that it's normal to feel great some days, not so great on other days. Transmit to your child all the techniques recommended in this book for avoiding and coping with extreme mood swings (good diet, exercise, meditation and relaxation exercises, good sleep habits, anti-depression activities). Never recommend the use of alcohol or another drug (or food, for that matter) as a way of dealing with depression, anxiety, or any other unwanted mood.

Problem-Solving Expertise

Children who learn to face problems head on, and to cope with them will not have to turn to chemicals as a coping tool. Even rather young children can understand that acting on feelings alone can be a mistake. A baby (who likes the sensation of rolling and rolls right off the bed) may feel and then act, but older children and adults should add thinking to the equation.

Decision-Making Skills

Too many children are led into drugs because they are unused to making decisions. Teens are less likely to use drugs if they make their own decision rather than have their parents decide for them. From earliest childhood, give your child the opportunity to make choices: "Do you want to go on the slide or the swings first?" "Which dress do you want to wear to the party?" "Would you rather go to a baseball game or a movie?"

As your child gets older, allow more leeway in decision-making (as long as health and safety are not at stake). Teenagers should be encouraged to make most basic decisions in their lives (what courses to take, which clothes to buy, which music to listen to, which friends to see, what to spend their allowance on). But they will need plenty of input from an understanding adult. Guide them in the decision-making, using the tips on page 358. Help them consider the possible consequences, both positive and negative, of any decision, how they and you would feel about such a decision, and how the decision would affect them and others in the long run. However, once the child's mind is made up, he or she should be allowed to act on the decision—even if you consider it a poor one—without adult interference or second-guessing. Let them learn through experience that they have to live with the consequences of their decisions. A child watched TV instead of doing homework? Don't write an excuse note in the morning; instead let him or her face the music at school.

LET THE CONSEQUENCES FIT THE CRIME

When we punish, we are making a show of power. We are telling our children that the only way we can control them is by brute force, or its psychic equivalent. But a show of power is an indication of weakness, not strength. Kids recognize this and try to take advantage of it. A show of force, whether in the international arena or in a family, inevitably generates a show of counterforce. The result: a battle royal. So on many levels, punishment is ineffective and counterproductive.

Because it's good for children to learn that every act has a consequence, it's better to think in terms of natural consequences than of punishment. If they don't hang up their clothes, put away their games, books, and records, or make their beds, their rooms begin to resemble the city dump. You could yell and scream and maybe force them to pick up. You could revoke their TV privileges and pick up yourself. Or you could just allow the chaos to mount, letting your children see what happens when one doesn't clean one's room.

Let them face the embarrassment when friends come to visit, the difficulty of finding a clean pair of socks in the morning or of locating the project they were working on for school, lost somewhere in the debris. This approach does more than teach youngsters that their acts have consequences and that they can take responsibility for their own lives. It also reduces friction and increases mutual respect. There are no lectures, no shouting matches, no tears and recriminations. Of course, you will need to help them develop the skills required to meet their responsibilities (make their beds, put away toys, etc.).

Letting the consequences fit the crime can also work in other situations. The youngster who is late for dinner has to fix her own or go hungry. The one who blows his entire allowance on video games doesn't have any funds left for a Saturday night movie and isn't given a handout. And the one who carelessly drags mud on the living room carpet on a rainy day has to vacuum it up before going on to any other activity.

Of course, sometimes the consequences of a youngster's acts are so severe that parents must prevent them. You can't let a teenager who doesn't swim well go out in a boat without a life jacket, or one who has had a drink drive your car. You can't permit a youngster to stay out every night until 2 A.M., or live on doughnuts and burgers. Sometimes the parent just has to be the boss.

Children, as well as adults, need to understand that there are two kinds of decisions: critical decisions and toss-up decisions. With critical decisions, the right choice is just that: critical. Critical decisions usually involve health (to smoke or not to smoke), safety (whether to call your parents or to drive with someone who's been drinking), or the future (whether or not to use birth control, if having sexual intercourse). If they make an unwise decision on any of these, the damage may be done before they have a chance to recognize their mistake and change their mind.

With toss-up decisions (for a child that can mean which friends to invite to a birthday party, selecting a prom outfit, even picking a summer job) however, it's how they live with the choice and how they make it work that really counts. If your child invited a favorite classmate, who tends to be wild to his party, he should be willing to agree to send him home if he acts up). The prom outfit doesn't look quite right? Accessorize it to make it more attractive. Becoming a summer camp counselor turns out to be boring? Arrange some fun activities during times off. You're not stuck with toss-up decisions forever. They can be changed—incrementally or entirely.

Good Judgment

Good decisions require good judgment. In addicted families, many judgments are based on faulty premises. Some of those most likely to be noted—and copied by children include:

❖ I'm the center of the universe.

❖ The world should be fair—in other words, I should have everything I want.

❖ Power and dominance are necessary weapons of self-preservation.

❖ Good things happen. Bad things happen. There's not a thing we can do to change them.

❖ The world, my country, my state, my family, my school, my boss (or someone else) "owes me."

❖ Pain and emotional discomfort are bad and should be avoided at all cost.

Learning early how false these "truisms" are will enhance your child's ability to make sound judgments. So will your good example.

Hobbies and a Healthy Social Life

Youngsters who are busy—with school clubs and other afterschool activities, lessons, sports, scouts, karate, youth groups, or hobbies (music, computers, collecting, and so on)—are less likely to turn to drugs as an escape from boredom than are kids who hang out at the local mall or video arcade. Encourage activities that provide healthy ways to have fun and keep busy. And since the expectations of a peer group play a major role in a child's development and behavior, encourage friendships—at least while you still have some control over this—that are unlikely to lead your child into temptation.

A Set of Values

Values are taught primarily through example, but in a world where values outside the home often clash with those inside, it's also necessary for parents to reinforce living room lessons by talking to their children about things they think are important: honesty, charity, tolerance, respect for authority, concern for the environment, or whatever. But don't preach what you don't prac-

SPELL IT OUT

Children are born knowing how to cry and suck (and they're often better at the former than at the latter). Everything else must be learned—usually from the parents. In an alcoholic home, this kind of teaching is often neglected, and many children don't know how to accomplish the simplest chores. Now's the time to make up for this in your family. When you want toys put away, or dishes dried, or the bed made, don't just bark the order out. Instead, explain the objective or purpose of the task. With a young child, break the chore into its components (putting the toy back in the box, fitting the cover on, making room on the shelf for it, and so on). Demonstrate the first time, then help the next. Finally, let the child do it under your watchful eye, and offer constructive (not sarcastic) comments. From then, they're on their own.

tice; it won't work. In the end, children tend to do what their parents do, not what they say. Parents are often angered when they see their own behavior in their children. This anger confuses children—"What's wrong with doing what my parents do?"

A Healthy Skepticism

Children need to learn to see past the glitz and under the surface in a variety of situations. Start by watching TV with your child and analyzing commercials as well as the behavior of various characters. Point out the con artists (the health hucksters, for example, who purport to be providing objective information in a commercial, but whose goal is to remove money from viewers' pockets and put it in advertisers'), the wise guys trying to persuade others to do something that may not be right or good for them, and the weaklings, who are led around by the nose, even though that nose may get cut off.

A Spiritual Life

Strong religious faith, of any kind, can help deter drug use. If that is something you are comfortable with, pass it on to your child with love, inspiration, explanation, and information. But be aware that a belief system that stifles growth and thinking; has the potential to provoke rebellion.

Realistic Expectations

Children need to know what you've been trying to learn in recovery yourself: that nobody's Ms. or Mr. Perfect. Not parents. Not teachers. Not friends. And not themselves. We should all try to do our best, but shouldn't beat up on ourselves when we do less. To feel good about themselves, kids need to not only recognize their strengths but accept their weaknesses and mistakes. The idea that if you're not perfect you're nothing is as destructive to children as to adults.

Information

Education (but not scare tactics) is one of the best weapons against drug and alcohol abuse. Ideally, education about the effects of drugs and alcohol on body and soul should begin in early childhood, but it's never too late to start. Be sure you make it clear that beer, wine, and hard liquor pack the same wallop—kids often don't know this and think, for example, that beer is "a safe drink." Avoid preaching (there's nothing like a reformed sinner for preaching), but do talk about your own experiences. Urge your child to go to Alateen (see page 490) or other family-oriented AA meetings in order to learn from others. If it seems necessary, get your child some private tutoring from a smart drug counselor. Giving information certainly isn't a guarantee, but it helps ensure that even if a child does dabble in drugs or drinking, he or she knows that there is a way out, an alternative to that kind of lifestyle. Such prepping may lead children to seek help sooner if they do get in trouble.

Emotional Strength

Children become strong through a combination of support (love and attention, plus assistance when necessary) and freedom (plenty of opportunities for making choices, taking calculated risks, and so on). They also benefit from adult guidance. Standing up and being different isn't easy. Discuss this with your child:

"How are they going to treat you if you don't drink or accept drugs?"

"They're gonna laugh at me or drop me."

"Which do you think will take more courage and character—accepting or saying no?"

Talk about peer pressure, about the risks of doing what others do, not because you want to but because you feel you have to. Tell them about the little Scandinavian lemmings—the ultimate symbolic example of peer pressure—who follow each other into the sea and drown.

When your child does say no in such a situation, he or she may not feel happy about the decision at first. Your congratulations could lift fallen spirits. Such attention now, shown in support of a wise decision made in a difficult situation, reinforces the concept that making the right choice usually leads to positive results. Down deep we all feel better when we adhere to our own value systems, and at some point your child will too.

Situational Skills

Some children have an easy time with new situations; others need to be taught how to handle them. How do you deal with a classmate—especially one you really like—who offers you a beer at a party? Or a smoke at a football game? How do you respond when an older kid you're a little afraid of offers you a joint? It's not easy to just say no. Discuss how they can handle such situations. Given the opportunity to think about it, they may have some good ideas of their own. If not, you can offer some approaches—but be ready to have some of them shot down as totally unrealistic.

The goal is to help children be assertive ("No, thanks, I really don't want a drink"), rather than aggressive ("No way—do you think I'm as stupid as you guys?") or passive ("Er, well, I don't know. Maybe if everybody else is . . ."). Rehearsing a wide range of possible scenarios in advance—even if you all feel silly playacting at first—will make it easier for your youngsters to deal with them confidently and without hesitation when they come up.

Goal Tending Skills

Goals are what keep us going and doing our best in life. We need short-term goals (getting homework done on time), medium-term goals (learning to play the piano), and long-term ones (becoming a concert pianist). Striving for unreachable goals, however, is frustrating and self-defeating (for example, finishing homework in the first hour after school, when pent-up energy levels are highest and the playground beckons). Goals, particularly short-term ones, should be realistic (finishing homework immediately after dinner, before the TV is turned on). Encourage your children to meet their goals (help them set a time and place for doing homework, prohibit distractions like TV or phone calls) so they won't hate themselves in the morning.

WHAT DOESN'T WORK

Some parents have tried to head off problems with alcohol or even drugs by telling their children, "If you want to drink or use drugs, do it at home." This almost invariably backfires, and the kids end up with serious problems. Trying to give a child a "bad" experience with tobacco, alcohol, or drugs (making them use the substance until they feel

SURVIVING PARENTHOOD

Being a parent is never easy. It's even tougher if you've lost some rapport with your child because of your own drug or alcohol abuse. But many of the same tools you rely on for surviving in recovery can be useful in surviving as a parent. On days when you feel like locking the kids in their rooms and throwing away the key, think of some of the basic mottoes: "One day at a time." "This too shall pass." And say the Serenity Prayer.

sick) also usually fails. If the first use is bad, a kid with an inclination toward addiction (like your own) will usually just keep trying until it gets better, and it will, as tolerance develops.

Limiting drug education to "just say no" usually flops too, because it tends to maintain the romanticism of drugs and it doesn't deal with the major drug problem in this country: alcohol. The slogan has contributed enormously to awareness of the drug problem, but it's just a starting point. And it's worthless if youngsters aren't helped to develop qualities and attitudes that make drugs unnecessary in their lives.

Force and coercion are not effective in preventing drug or alcohol abuse, either. Children who are abused, either physically or emotionally, may cower and submit to parental power at home. But in the long run, they are more likely to rebel and seek escape through drugs than are those who are treated with fairness and firmness.

RECOGNIZING A TEENAGER'S DRINKING OR DRUG PROBLEM

Parents who spend a lot of time listening to, talking with, and observing their children are more likely to be tuned into what's normal behavior and what isn't. Still, even actively involved parents may overlook—or subconsciously deny—the earliest signs of a substance-abuse problem.

Some of the clues youngsters exhibit when using drugs or alcohol are fairly subtle, but others are rather obvious:

❖ Many hours spent alone, especially in their room; persistent isolation from the rest of the family. This is particularly suspicious in a youngster who hasn't been a loner up until now.

❖ Resistance to talking with or confiding in parents; secretiveness, especially in a child who had previously been open. But be sure your child isn't being secretive because every time he tries to confide in you, you jump on him or break his confidence.

❖ A definite change for the worse in performance and attendance at school and/or job or other responsibilities as well as in dress, hygiene, grooming. Frequent memory lapses, lack of concentration, and unusual sleepiness.

❖ A change in friends from acceptable to unacceptable. Your child may switch to a totally different group of friends, or the crowd that he has always hung out with may change in character and behavior—becoming wilder, rowdier, less interested in school and other responsibilities.

❖ Pronounced mood swings with increased irritability, hostile outbursts, and rebelliousness. Your child may sound like a con artist and seem untrustworthy, insincere, even paranoid.

❖ Lying, usually in order to cover up drinking or drug-using behavior as well as sources of money and possessions; stealing, shoplifting, or encounters with the police. Cash, prescription drugs, liquor, valuables may vanish from home: that twenty-dollar bill you left on your dresser, mysteriously disappears.

❖ Abandonment of wholesome activities, such as sports, chorus, social service and other clubs, religious services, teen programs, hobbies, and even involvement in family life.

❖ Unusual physical symptoms, such as dilated or pinpoint pupils, bloodshot eyes, frequent nosebleeds, appetite changes, digestive problems, excessive yawning, the shakes.

❖ Curfew breaking. Coming home late and then having trouble getting up and getting it together in the morning.

Don't jump to the conclusion that your child is using when you see such behavior. Evaluate the situation. Such

PARTY GUIDE LINES

Get together with the parents of your teenager's friends and draw up a list of rules for teen parties in the community. Agree that you won't allow your children to go to parties that don't meet these standards. The following guidelines can serve as a foundation. If some parents refuse to agree to standards, make their homes off limits.

❖ Before the party, make it clear that no alcohol or drugs will be allowed.

❖ Make clear what the consequences will be if this rule is broken.

❖ Give your child the responsibility to tell all the invited guests about the no-alcohol/no-drug rule.

❖ Know the guest list in advance, and make it clear that no crashers will be allowed.

❖ Be sure the party is continuously supervised by a reliable adult who is always visible. No guest should be admitted who has been drinking or using drugs.

❖ Set a time limit for the party, and stick to it.

signs may be due to illness or family disruption, such as divorce, illness, or death. Sometimes substance abuse may coexist with one or more of these other causes. Some behaviors, however, leave little room for doubt:

❖ Alcohol on the youngster's breath.

❖ Drug paraphernalia stashed in pockets, drawers, school bags, or other hideaways: seeds or leaves, cigarette papers, roach clip (little metal holder for marijuana so it can be smoked right down to the butt), hand-rolled "cigarettes," empty cans bent in the middle and covered with soot and multiple pinholes (a homemade crack pipe), small plastic bags of a white powder,* glass pipes with tubes (for crack/cocaine), plumbing fixture joints (for cooking up vapor to inhale), empty capsules. Most parents have never seen drug paraphernalia, and may accept such lines as "Oh, that pipe? It's for a chemistry project." If a display of such items is available in your city (ask the school, the police, or a drug-abuse hotline), go and see it—even if you don't suspect your child. It pays to be knowledgeable.

❖ Obvious hangovers, blackouts, drunken or high behavior, slurred speech, poor coordination. Also frequent vomiting (although this could be associated with an eating disorder).

Of course for parents, seeing is not always believing; they may be as much in denial as the kids.

Parents may also cop out by saying, "I couldn't breach my child's trust by searching his room." Well, the Supreme Court has never declared parental search to be illegal. You are still the adult and you are still responsible for what your children do—including their possession of an illegal substance. New drug laws are more punitive than ever before, and often the judicial discretion allowed in the past, which frequently got both parents and kids off the hook, has been eliminated. If your child has cocaine or hash concealed in a bureau drawer, you could lose your house or car, even go to jail.

*To confirm that your find is actually cocaine, call your local health department, medical society, or a drug treatment center for information on where to have such materials tested. Do not call the police at this time, because your child needs professional help not punishment.

ALATEEN

Alateen is a division of Al-Anon for twelve to twenty-year-old children of alcoholics.* A group is usually sponsored by a member of Al-Anon and sometimes co-sponsored by a member of AA. The sponsor is present at meetings but does not ordinarily speak unless spoken to. The purpose of the meetings is to give youngsters the chance to discuss their experiences, encourage and help each other understand the disease of addiction, the phases of recovery, and the principles of Alateen, and share effective ways of coping with their problems in substance-abusing families. Like AA and Al-Anon, Alateen's group therapy is based on the Twelve Steps. Ideally, regular attendance at Alateen should help youngsters put their parents' condition in perspective and achieve some order in their own chaotic lives.

Alateen is an important forum for youngsters in alcoholic families, giving them a chance to voice their thoughts in a safe, nonjudgmental atmosphere, frequently for the first time in their lives. These youngsters have often not been able to express their feelings at home and have avoided discussing their problems with friends at school. At Alateen they find soulmates—kids just like themselves with the same feelings and fears. The mutual support found at Alateen can diminish the loneliness in the lives of these youngsters, and can increase their feelings of self-worth by helping them understand that they aren't responsible for their parents' behavior, that they aren't stupid or worthless.

Bringing high-risk teens together doesn't automatically provide a magic cure. A poorly run Alateen group can, in fact, act as an enabler to support teen drinking instead of helping the youngsters deal with the problems of living in a substance-abusing family. Youngsters in Alateen may drink because they are angry and want to get back at their parents, or because they are young and think, "That's my father's problem. It won't happen to me."

Denial can become infectious at meetings with even a few rebellious teens. So try to pick a group that discourages such thinking. Discussions should focus on the experience of living in a substance-abusing family and on examining the damage that alcoholism and addiction have

*Children of alcoholics who have substance-abuse problems of their own also need to attend AA or another Twelve-Step program.

Youngsters (like parents) deserve trust only as long as they earn it. It's a good idea to set up a family policy early on that says that "Because we love you and care about what happens to you, we reserve the right to search your room and your belongings for evidence, if at some point we think you might have a drug or alcohol problem." (Ideally, this should be a two-way street. Children should have the right to search parental possessions, or even demand a drug screen, if they have reason to suspect a relapse.)

If you have any suspicion that your child is involved in the use of drugs or alcohol, don't hesitate to bring the subject up. The sooner the problem is identified and treated, the better the chances that your child's future will be safeguarded. Raising the subject will be easier if you already have good communications in the family. It will also be easier if you raise the issue at a time when no one is in a hurry to go somewhere else. Avoid selecting a time done to these families. Groups where the focus of discussion is getting high on Saturday night, or where drinking and drug use are romanticized, could seduce a youngster who hasn't yet dabbled in alcohol or drugs.

If you have a choice (often you don't), try to pick a group with a strong, involved sponsor who is filling the needs of the youngsters, not his or her own needs. The sponsor should not talk down to group members, and the kids should feel comfortable confiding in him or her. You should also feel comfortable with this individual as role model and chaperone. If possible, select a group with a majority of youngsters in your child's age group and with similar social interests.

But even a less than perfect Alateen group can be beneficial. It may not prevent youngsters from experimenting, but it will alert them to the warning signs that the experiment is about to fail, deteriorating into abuse. It will also teach them where and how to get help and prepare them for moving into an AA group, if that becomes necessary.

If your teenagers balk at going to Alateen, you might let them test the concept out at a weekend recovery retreat in a fun location. These retreats give teens a chance to meet others in a similar situation on neutral territory, which they may find less intimidating or embarrassing. They may then go home ready to try an Alateen group in the neighborhood. Attending open or family AA meetings with you may also be helpful as a learning experience and as a way to interest a teenager in going to Alateen.

If your child is a preteen or younger, there aren't a lot of Twelve-Step resources. Some communities have what are known as "Al-Atot" or "Pre-Alateen" groups (this is not a formal designation). Most often these are little more than baby-sitting services. But even getting kids involved in such simple adult-led activities as talking or drawing pictures about experiences in an alcoholic home can be enlightening for others in the family and therapeutic for the child.

Children with significant emotional problems, no matter what their age, need more than Alateen. They should see a professional therapist who is experienced and qualified to deal with the children of substance abusers. These children rarely require hospitalization, so any suggestion that the child be referred to an institution should be followed up with a second opinion. And remember, a child's treatment is not likely to be successful unless the rest of the family gets help too.

when everybody is tired and out of sorts.

Raise the issue calmly and give your child plenty of opportunity to respond. He or she may feel out of control and be grateful for the chance to unburden, and for your offer of support. Discuss the ways in which you can seek help together. AA meetings may be an important starting point if your child has only been experimenting with alcohol and/or drugs. But evaluation by a professional is also important. This can be your pediatrician or family doctor, a minister, rabbi, or priest active in Twelve-Step programs, or a school counselor.* Teen drug counseling is best provided by someone trained in both child/adolescent therapy and drug rehabilitation.

*Unfortunately school drug counselors, where they exist at all, are often overburdened and unable to give individual attention to youngsters. If this is the case at your child's school, seek help from a mental health clinic or a private therapist.

No matter what their backgrounds, parents should not try to play the professional in such a situation. We are too emotionally tied to our children, too often see them as an extension of ourselves and their behavior as a reflection on us. These are not good criteria on which to base decisions. Since our kids are dependent on us financially (as well as emotionally), we have an unfair advantage over them; we may be able to force our own judgments on them, whether those judgments are right or wrong. So leave the counseling of a child with a substance-abuse problem to someone else.

"You can't drink unless you have someone to take care of you, covering up for you. The hardest thing my parents ever did was to tell me not to call them anymore."

STEPS TO TAKE WHEN YOU SUSPECT DEPENDENCY

If it's clear that your child has gone beyond experimenting with alcohol and/or drugs, then you must move quickly to get a professional evaluation and to decide on the best course of treatment. You might consult your own counselor, teenagers you know from AA or their parents, a nearby rehab facility or drug therapist, as well as your child's doctor or school counselor for advice. If an intervention seems in order, see page 508 for how to arrange one. And see Chapter 16 for more on the subject of teens and addiction.

It's possible that your child will be grateful that you care enough to want to help. On the other hand, your child may not only be ungrateful, he or she may be furious with you. "Look who's lecturing!" may be the tone of the response. You may get an outright denial (which doesn't ring true) or an admission-but-no-problem defense, in which case you're at a standoff.

Don't drop the issue, institute curbs, or start a shouting match. Instead, get an objective professional (such as an adolescent pediatrician or a drug counselor) to referee. Explain to your child, "I don't think you're a bad person. But I do think you're a person who needs help. I'm worried about this because the chances of your having a problem like mine are very great. I know you think there's no problem now, and maybe there isn't. But let's get an impartial opinion from someone who knows more about these things than either of us."

Make it clear that you're not going to see a counselor because your child has a drug problem, but because you aren't able to agree on the subject. This eliminates your being antagonists and allows you to slip into a supportive role—which is the one you should be playing. If your child still refuses to own up to the behavior and your suspicions are shared by the counselor, suggest a drug screen to settle the matter. If your child refuses, you can assume it would be positive. If your child balks at seeing a counselor, you can also assume a problem exists. As the parent, you then must take steps to see that your child is treated—ideally in an inpatient setting away from the distractions that have already helped lead him or her astray.

No matter what your child's response, you should begin adopting the preventive measures in this chapter if you haven't already. These will help you develop a family environment that will discourage future drug or alcohol use, and will make recovery easier for everyone. Stress honesty and openness, encourage the free expression of

THE STAGES OF TEEN ABUSE

According to the American Academy of Pediatrics, there are three stages of drug use among teens:

EXPERIMENTING WITH DRUGS. There is strong peer pressure to dabble recreationally in drugs. This use is usually limited to weekends, and in most cases, there is no lasting change in behavior.

ACTIVELY SEEKING DRUGS. A threshold toward dependence is crossed when drugs are used to produce good feelings or to relieve stress. Use usually spreads to midweek, and there may be marked changes in behavior and school performance. Immediate help is needed.

DESPERATELY SEEKING DRUGS. Now there is a complete loss of control over drug use. Attempts to limit use can cause withdrawal symptoms, including depression, moodiness, and irritability. Other signs of drug use may be noticed, including the sudden disappearance of money or household goods to pay for drugs. Immediate professional help is needed.

ideas and feelings, and discuss safe ways of coping with emotions.

There should also be a strict rule of no alcohol or drugs in the house for anyone (both parents included, even if one is not alcoholic). To protect everyone against the possibility of violence (self-inflicted or against others), get rid of all guns or other potential weapons. Jewelry or other valuables that could be stolen to sell for drug money should be put in a bank vault, just in case.

"I knew I had to stop picking up my daughter's messes, stop enabling her. I realized that she could die from her disease. I had to accept that. But I wasn't going to contribute to her dying. I was able to tell her she couldn't continue to drink and live at home. Throwing her out was the hardest thing I ever did, but it saved her life."

Though you shouldn't dwell on past misbehavior right now, you will have to set up specific ground rules governing present behavior—in effect a contract between you and your child. This is probably best done with the guidance of your child's therapist or drug counselor. The contract (in writing, with every detail spelled out) should specify the responsibilities of all parties. For example, that parents will continue to provide food, clothing, shelter, education, and medical care. The child's half of the bargain will be abstention from alcohol and drugs and adherence to household rules. Hours, household responsibilities, car-use privileges (these probably shouldn't be reinstated without a lengthy period of sobriety and good behavior) should all be delineated, along with the consequences if your child does not live up to the contract. The consequences can range from loss of privileges for returning home past curfew to commitment for treatment (page 497) to—harsh as it may sound—being turned over to juvenile authorities for using prohibited substances. This should only be a last resort, since this kind of situation puts

WHO'S RESPONSIBLE?

When a child gets in trouble—it hardly matters whether that "child" is twelve or twenty—parents feel that damage control is up to them. Pride ("If my kid doesn't look good, I don't look good"), embarrassment ("What will friends, relatives, teachers, the community think?"), and obligation ("What kind of parent abandons a child in trouble?") are behind the rush to help. When substance abuse is the problem, desperate parents usually end up taking full responsibility for trying to deal (no matter how hopelessly) with the situation and all the youngster has to do is shrug and drug. He or she has gotten the message: "You can't stay clean and sober by yourself." So there's no use trying.

Well *we* aren't capable of keeping them sober, either. Though we hate to admit it, we are truly powerless when our children are abusing drugs. And the more we fight it, the worse the addiction becomes. Letting go is the answer. But, as every parent knows, letting go is one of the most difficult things in the world, especially if the process wasn't started early. To put your hands in your pocket and say, "Now, son, it's up to you to make your own way" is tough for any parent and in direct contradiction to the nurturing instinct.

But instincts sometimes mislead us. When our children are young, certainly nurturing is necessary. Even when they are grown, there are times when they need our help, and we should always be ready to give it. But our children also have to learn to take on the world by themselves. If the lioness keeps feeding her cubs, they will never learn to hunt. You can't provide all your children's needs, solve all their problems, get them out of all their predicaments without leaving them helpless.

Nor can you cure their alcoholism/addiction; they've got to take on that problem by themselves. The more you allow them to suffer the consequences of their behavior, the less you will feel the guilt—and the responsibility for making them well. Lay down the oars or your children will never learn to row. They may just drift listlessly for a while. But you have to believe that eventually each child will realize that no one is coming to the rescue, and will pick up the oars and start rowing. At that point, it's okay to throw him or her a rope, to "help those who help themselves." Until then, it's time for the Serenity Prayer. And a lot of support from Al-Anon.

troubled kids together with other troubled kids and results in double trouble.*

The contract should specify the ways in which the youngster can gradually gain additional privileges—by sobriety, regular school attendance and improved grades, having clean drug screens, attending AA meetings faithfully. From this arrangement your child should learn that trust has to be earned back slowly, but that like little deposits in the bank, brownie points add up.

Drug and alcohol use in teenagers is often accompanied by specific behaviors (bizarre clothing, hairstyles, music, language, eating habits, entertainment) that can create a risk-laden atmosphere if continued into recovery. These behaviors should be discouraged and may be included in the contract. The

*You can't evict a minor (although in some states a child becomes emancipated simply by using drugs) without professional recommendation, and in most cases a child would have to go into a youth home of some sort. Try treatment first (see page 496).

family as a unit should do all it can to promote change in these areas, with everybody paying more attention to good health habits, careful grooming, and so on.

Infractions should be met with a quick response. Children don't benefit when their parents let them get away with breaking their word. It isn't easy to throw your own child out on the street or to turn her over to juvenile authorities; it will probably hurt you but help your child. Like the parents who loathe letting a young baby cry it out because it seems so cruel, parents of drug-abusing teens loathe being so harsh with them. But it is really the kindest thing you can do—for the baby, who learns to fall asleep on its own, and for the teenager, who has to learn that in the end, no one can pull him out of addiction but himself.

Grown children who live at home, or who return home in trouble, should also be required to agree to a contract that includes abstinence. And they too should be evicted if they fail to live up to their part of the bargain. Don't back down on this part of the pact, even when your child pleads, "If you'll just give me my own apartment, a car, college tuition (or fill in the blanks), my

CAN YOU AFFORD IT?

The cost of treatment for substance abuse can seem astronomical to the average family. And an employer or insurer willing to cover the cost for an employee may not be willing to foot the bill for the employee's adolescent child. But the cost of not getting treatment will be higher. It can cost a child's future. Or a child's life.

Even in the short term, the costs of waiting until things get worse before putting a youngster into treatment can be great. Thousands of dollars can drain away in lawyer's fees (the teenager has been picked up for driving while intoxicated); auto repair (he ran the car into a tree); increased insurance premiums (they usually go up when there's a claim); tuition spent in vain (when a youngster is expelled during the school year); money and goods stolen from the home or family business (to support a drug habit).

There are nonfinancial risks, too: youngsters hurting themselves or others, flunking out of school, falling behind their classmates, losing a chance to get into a good college, getting pregnant (or getting someone else pregnant), becoming infected with HIV or another disease transmitted sexually or via IV needles. Can you afford treatment for your teenager? The question should really be: Can you afford *not* to get treatment?

If your medical policy won't cover treatment and you don't have the financial resources to pay for it yourself, there may be other options. Check with:

❖ Your local department of youth services.

❖ The counselor at your child's school.

❖ The EAP at work, if there is one.

❖ Your doctor, clergyperson, or therapist.

❖ One or more local drug hotlines.

❖ Local treatment programs (some may have grants or public funds for treating young people).

❖ The National Council on Alcoholism and Drug Dependence, Inc. (800/NCA-CALL), which offers information and referral services for children and teens (as well as adults) seeking help with alcoholism and other drug dependencies.

TREATMENT FOR TEENS

The quality of the treatment program you choose for your teenager can make the difference between success and failure. The program should do more than get youngsters off alcohol and other drugs. It should teach them the skills they need to live a drug-free life.

All of the standards for judging a treatment program in Chapter 3 also apply to choosing one for your teenager. But there are some additional concerns. The attitude toward teenage alcoholics/addicts is often much more punitive than toward chemically dependent adults. Frustrated parents, teachers, counselors, law enforcement people just want to send them away "to be fixed." So these youngsters often wind up at programs that are rigid and harsh, where punishment is the prime teaching tool and children are deprived of their rights. Instead of learning responsibility and accountability in such an atmosphere, the youngsters often learn a jail house mentality from other "inmates."

For most teens, a more relaxed program that allows youngsters some responsibilities and demands accountability should be the choice. Of course, even in such a program, if a youngster abuses the freedom, then more control will have to be imposed. Some therapeutic communities (see page 58) have excellent programs for teens, others are too harsh and throw the youngsters in with hardened felons.

In most cases, a mixed age patient population is most beneficial, but there are also some very fine programs designed especially for teens. Examine any program carefully before having your child admitted. Discuss the possible choices with your physician or the therapist who is advising you.

Speaking to former patients and their parents also will give you a better view of the program than

problems will be over." Continue to be available for constructive help when needed (like driving your child to a treatment center or paying for medical or dental care or groceries), but don't let yourself or your financial resources be used to enable drinking or drug use. If you settle any necessary expenses, make the payments directly; *never* hand money over to a child who is using.

Parents who turn to eviction as an act of last resort may feel both a sense of relief and a sense of guilt. It's okay to feel relief—you've gone through a very terrible time. Having this child out of your life for the time being will remove an immediate burden, from your shoulders if not your heart. But while relief is warranted, guilt is not. You did the best you could; no one can do more than that. If you allowed yourselves to burn out now, you would not be available when your child needed and wanted your help later on.

What is happening must be explained in understandable terms to any other children in the family—who may otherwise think you cruel and side with their sibling. They should be invited to attend Alateen, Al-Anon, or open AA meetings and be given counseling as needed. Also expect them to meet the same standards set for the sick child: no alcohol, no drugs, clear-cut hours, and so on. Don't neglect them now, or they may be your next problem.

Through all this, you will have to work hard at your own recovery. Nothing will be more beneficial to your child in the long run than this. If the speaking only to staff.

Some relatively new programs are wilderness-based, challenging youngsters to survive without the amenities of civilization. While these may have appeal in certain cases, they are ordinarily better saved for later in recovery, when the youngster no longer thinks he or she can conquer the world.

There are some important factors to insist on when choosing program:

❖ Leaders should be certified or accredited for outdoor activities as well as in addiction counseling.

❖ The program should have a good safety record; qualified medical personnel should be at hand at all times; and instant communication with a rescue group should be available in case of sickness or injury.

❖ Adequate equipment, food, and drink should be provided (at least one teen has died because of lack of water in such a program).

❖ Though physical exertion can be required, it should not be beyond the capacity of the youngsters involved, since many have not yet regained their normal coordination and strength. Risks to life and limb should be avoided.

❖ The atmosphere should be supportive and loving like an AA meeting, not punitive like a chain gang.

❖ How long has the program been in existence? What is its track record in giving teens a good start on recovery? Ask for a list of participants in several outings, along with phone numbers. Call each name on the list for a reference.

❖ Check to see if there is state or other licensing; check with the Better Business Bureau in the area where the program is headquartered.

❖ Be sure the program is Twelve-Step based and that the leaders recognize alcoholism/addiction as a disease.

stress of your child's substance abuse seems to be threatening your sobriety, increase the number of AA meetings you attend, start going to Al-Anon meetings, and/or seek additional group or individual counseling.

27

Living with Someone in Recovery: Your Role

"Never send to know for whom the bell tolls," John Donne wrote hundreds of years ago; "it tolls for thee." Donne was writing about death, but his thought applies equally well when catastrophic illness strikes a family.* A diagnosis of terminal cancer pronounced on one member affects every member. When the potentially terminal illness is chemical dependency, every family member is also affected.

A GUIDE FOR SIGNIFICANT OTHERS

If you live with—or care deeply about—someone who is chemically dependent, recovery is a crucial time for you. With recovery comes the opportunity to rebuild and reinvigorate relationships, but this will be successful only if everyone works hard at overcoming the insidious effects of the disease. To participate in this effort you need to understand the phases of recovery as outlined here. For a more thorough understanding of what the alcoholic/addict is going through also read the parts of the book aimed at the recoveree.

Nobody needs to tell you that the chemical dependence of your spouse, child, parent, friend, or lover has sent shock waves through every part of your life. You feel them every day. But

*We use the term "family" to apply to both traditional and nontraditional relationships.

Guide Lines

❖ Everyone in the family of an alcoholic/addict is affected by the disease.

❖ The significant others who play important roles in the disease process (by enabling, for example) play equally important roles in the recovery process.

❖ You can hate the disease (alcoholism/addiction) but love the person who has it.

❖ Each individual is responsible only for his or her own recovery, not for that of other family members (except young children). No matter what you do for yourself, some members of your family may remain sick.

❖ Once individual family members recover, they can work together toward the recovery of the family unit.

❖ Al-Anon offers a way out—from controlling others, being controlled by them, and having to lie or otherwise compromise your values for them.

what you may not recognize is that this disease has powerfully affected your own behavior.

HOW ALCOHOLISM AND ADDICTION AFFECT THE FAMILY

When serious illness strikes one member of a family, the others experience denial, anger, anxiety, depression. They do all they can to help the patient, or they retreat in confusion and distress. It's the same when the disease is chemical dependency, but the impact is felt while the disease is developing, long before anyone suspects anything is wrong and long before a diagnosis is made.

Gradually, as the drinking or drug use takes over, the family—instinctively committed to self-preservation—begins to change. Members alternately exhibit super-responsibility and powerlessness, self-blame and blaming the alcoholic, anger and forgiveness, hurt and fear. They try to manipulate, reason, beg, and browbeat the addict into cleaning up his or her act, almost always unsuccessfully. As the disease progresses, the chemically dependent person loses more and more control over his or her own life while, ironically, often taking control of the increasingly tangled and distorted lives of other family members. The term often used to describe those involved in the troubled and troubling life of the alcoholic/addict is "co-dependent." But their dependency is on the substance abuser, not on the substance.

Here are some of the ways in which family members alter their conduct in order to cope with the stress and unpredictability of life with a chemically dependent person:

Covering up. The alcoholic/addict makes liars of us all. When a chemically-created problem occurs, family members usually step in—as much to cover their own embarrassment as to cover up for the addict.

If the sick family member doesn't get home in time for a dinner party or is too hung over to go to work, the spouse delivers an alibi to the host or the boss. If mother is too drunk to bake a cake for the school bake sale, daughter may bake one herself. If father forgets Little League practice, his son tells the coach that his dad is out of town. If the car gets smashed up, it's quietly repaired. If the driver is jailed for DUI, bail is paid. If money is spent wildly, cuts are made elsewhere. In rare cases, a parent or spouse even takes the rap for the alcoholic/addict's passing bum checks or abusing a child.

In effect, well-meaning family members or significant others enable the alcoholic/addict to sail merrily (though erratically) along despite severely worsening disease. And this makes it difficult for anyone, particularly the foggy-thinking alcoholic/addict, to recognize the important fact that a major problem exists.

The substance abuse and its damaging consequences are covered up. The painful feelings they produce are suppressed. The distress is there, but it's kept under wraps.

Rationalizing. Rather than acknowledge the increasing disability from substance abuse as a disease wildly out of control, family members often explain it away with rationalizations: "After all, he's under pressure." "Everybody lets loose once in a while." "It's those awful friends she hangs out with."

Withdrawing. If a husband fears his wife will take two cocktails too many and make a scene when they go out with friends, they stop going out. If a youngster can't be sure her dad won't be blotto when she gets home from school, she doesn't come home until late and doesn't bring friends with her. If a wife can't rely on her husband to discuss and settle family issues, she simply carries the load alone, never consulting him. If a young child finds mom doesn't respond to his needs, he stops asking.

"I did such stupid things when Charlie was drinking—always trying to control him. I would pack the kids in the car and go to the bar to bring him home. I threatened the liquor store owner with prosecution if he continued taking his checks. I got the older kids to spy on him to see where he hid his liquor. I let him take the baby in the car when he went for a haircut—hoping he wouldn't drink with her there. But deep down I knew he would."

Blaming. Family members may blame themselves for the catastrophe that has overtaken their home: "Maybe I haven't been helpful enough, (or loving enough, or made enough money, or been obedient enough)." Some come to think there's nothing wrong with the substance abuser; their own behavior becomes so distorted and the addict's rationalizing so convincing that they begin to believe they themselves are the problem. Of course they may—simultaneously or alternately—blame the substance abuser: "You've ruined our lives. You've messed up our kids."

Haranguing and controlling. As it becomes more and more apparent that something is wrong (though exactly what is often not clear until much later), there is a lot of shouting, begging, recriminating. One or more family members may try to control and redirect the erratic alcoholic/addict—sometimes to the point of obsession, but always unsuccessfully.

Checking out. When they fail to help their sick loved ones with kindness or to change them with sound and fury, some family members simply give up. They check out, either physically (by staying away from home a lot or moving out) or emotionally (by withdrawing into themselves). They go about their own lives as best they can. If they're smart, they may improve them by attending Al-Anon meetings.

Unfortunately, these approaches, except for the last, are doomed to failure. They actually enable the substance abuser to continue to stagger toward his inevitable fall while increasing the stress on everyone else.

When an individual limps because of an injury, weight is taken off the damaged limb and extra stress placed on other parts of the body, disrupting the mechanics of walking and causing pain or injury elsewhere. It's the same in a family. As stress and responsibility are shifted away from the "sick" member to others, an imbalance results. That imbalance in family dynamics doesn't disappear the moment sobriety begins. Just as extensive therapy may be needed to help the lame person walk normally, so extensive emotional therapy may be needed to help the lopsided family straighten out. This takes time and effort. It's a major task of the recovery period.

GETTING READY FOR RECOVERY

Before recovery can begin, three important steps must be taken. You can play a much needed supporting role in all of them—but remember, you can't control the situation.

1. Recognition. First of all, the chemically dependent family member must recognize that there is a problem. The

ENABLING

You can hardly be involved with an alcoholic/addict these days without hearing the term "enabling." What does it mean? Simply that those who live and/or work with addicted people tend to adapt in such a way that they make it easier for them—indeed *enable* them—to continue their substance abuse. Spouses take over the responsibilities of the sick partner, make allowances, forgive unforgivable behavior, and continue trying to be loving and caring in the face of abuse. Parents close their eyes to suspicious behavior, hand out generous allowances, write absence notes for questionable illnesses.

Why do people enable? Not, oddly enough, for the benefit of the sick person—enabling harms the alcoholic/addict. They enable in order to meet their own needs. It's an attempt to restabilize the relationship, to counter growing alienation, to lure the alcoholic/addict back into the relationship by providing a counterforce to the alcohol and drugs that seem to be tugging the other away. Although this tactic may work very effectively to draw an alienated but non-addicted family member back into the fold, it's ineffective and actually counterproductive when used with victims of alcoholism/addiction. Enabling is a poor-quality glue. It not only doesn't succeed at keeping the marriage, family, or friendship together, it allows the disease to progress to a more serious stage and worsens the prognosis for a good recovery.

THE SILENT CRY FOR HELP

The teenager who's using "accidentally" leaves a crack pipe in the family car. The young mother who's drinking too much keeps complaining about vague symptoms. The alcoholic who already has a glove compartment full of DUI's nevertheless weaves into the car to drive to the liquor store for another bottle of vodka—knowing, maybe hoping, he'll get caught. All are trying to call attention to their misery in the only way they know how.

Friends and family need to be alert to such cries for help, and ready to answer them. Your help may not seem appreciated at first, but it certainly will be further down Recovery Road.

light may dawn first when an employer or a school counselor orders the alcoholic/addict to shape up or ship out. A close and caring friend may urge the alcoholic/addict to seek help. Or maybe you finally took on that thankless task yourself. Because denial is a part of the disease, your significant other may be the last to know there's a problem—or at least to admit it. In some cases, you may both be in denial. Read Chapter 2 to identify the clues that suggest a problem.

2. Acceptance. Recovery will go absolutely nowhere until the chemically dependent person is willing and able to accept the diagnosis. Some have reached the point where they are ready to throw in the towel and say "I am an alcoholic (or drug addict)." Others are more tentative and are only willing to say, "If you (or my boss, or all my friends) think I am an alcoholic (or drug addict), then I will stop drinking (or using drugs)." This is still a form of denial, but it allows an opening through which the sunlight of truth may eventually shine. If denial continues to be strong ("You're crazy—I don't have a problem at all"), an intervention may be needed (see page 508). Even if that doesn't work immediately, you've planted a seed for future salvation.

3. A decision to get help. It's not enough for the chemically dependent person to say "Okay, I'll stop." That's only the beginning of a new beginning. There must be a decision as to how a new drug- and alcohol-free life can be achieved. There are a variety of approaches to treatment, all outlined in Chapter 3. Your understanding of the addicted person and the severity of his or her problem, as well as your knowledge of family finances, medical coverage, child care needs, and so on, make you a key person in helping to direct and decide which of the treatment methods makes the most sense. Ideally, that decision should be made in consultation with a trained professional (physician, psychologist, cleric, or counselor), other interested family members, any employer or school officials who may be involved, and of course the alcoholic/addict.

"I felt guilty when my mom was nearly killed driving drunk. Like it was my fault. I tried real hard to be good, but I could never figure out what she wanted from me."

DETOXIFICATION

Recovery can't actually begin until all use of alcohol and drugs ends. For some people detox—the withdrawal from alcohol or drugs—is extremely difficult; for others it is fairly easy. Much depends on the substance involved, the degree of dependence on it, and the individual's reaction to being deprived of it. Before your family member undergoes this process, read up on what it's like (see Chapter 5) so that you'll be better able to be supportive.

UNDERSTANDING THE PHASES OF RECOVERY

Alcoholism and addiction develop over a period of time in fairly clear-cut stages, and so does recovery. Understanding the stages of recovery gives families and significant others an idea of what to expect during this far-from-easy time.

Phase One Recovery

During this period—which usually lasts a year or more—recoverees focus almost entirely on getting well. It's a question of survival. If they don't succeed at staying clean and sober, eventually their addiction will kill them. It's important for you to respect their need to pursue sobriety (even though that means a lot of nights out at AA meetings) as faithfully as they once pursued their drugs of choice. It's okay to be an enabler of sobriety.

The recoveree in Phase One: You will probably find that sober, your mate, parent, or child is a "new" person. Not necessarily better, at least at first, but certainly different. You knew what to expect when drugs or alcohol were in control and you learned to adapt. Now you have to start learning what to expect from this new sober person.

For a while it may be like living intimately with a stranger. That won't be easy. This stranger may appear unstable at times, even act drunk or high (a dry drunk; page 161). In early recovery the body is in a recuperating mode (sleeping a lot is common), the mind is cloudy, behavior is unpredictable, and emotions are explosive. The person accustomed to using chemicals to smother or deal with feelings will suddenly not know what to do with them. Don't be thrown by the fact that your spouse is chipper and smiling one day and depressed the next, or that your teenager comes home from school day after day and crashes on the couch in front of the TV instead of socializing. For most people it takes a good year, sometimes much longer, for the mind to clear and emotions to level off.

What may seem like floundering or a lack of direction—in school, at work, in his or her social life—may make you feel that the recoveree is well on the way toward becoming a sober failure. But that's normal behavior in early recovery. At this point the recoveree is still focusing on getting better. Everything else has to wait. The self-

> **CAPTURE THE MOMENT**
>
> If a family member or close friend is not yet clean and sober, capture them on film. Whether with a video or a still camera, get them looking their worst: coming in from his all-night drunk, vomiting her guts out, standing next to a smashed-up car or an injured passenger. These films will be valuable tools to use later, when a craving threatens to sabotage recovery.

centeredness you probably came to hate is still there, but now it's directed toward renewal instead of destruction. It will continue through Phase One.

Family response in Phase One: Individual family members and friends may react differently to recovery. Many will be genuinely pleased. Parents who were embarrassed, guilty, disappointed, and disturbed about their children's drinking or drug use usually feel cautiously optimistic because abandoned hopes may yet be fulfilled. Spouses whose marriages were clearly doomed by substance abuse are often cheered by the possibility of recovery.

But though virtually everyone claims to be pleased about sobriety, many really aren't. Some of those close to the recoveree harbor subconscious resentments, particularly where the active addiction satisfied a personal need. The wife who took over handling the family finances because her husband was irresponsible when drinking is annoyed at having to relinquish the power of the purse. The mother whose nest refilled while her drug-using daughter was unable to pay her apartment rent fears loneliness when the girl sobers up and regains her independence.

The physician, disappointed that his son wants to be a musician instead of a doctor, is no longer able to blame that choice of career on drugs and bad company. A sibling who was subconsciously delighted that her brighter, more attractive, but chemically dependent, sister was no longer looked upon as the family's pride and joy now resents the way everyone is cheering her on. And adult children grimly watch the possibility of an eagerly anticipated early inheritance slip away when an alcoholic parent they said was better off dead sobers up.

Sometimes recovery is subconsciously resented and resisted by the family member whose life revolved around Al-Anon while the addiction was active: "If the addict becomes sober, what will I have to do? Everything I worked so hard to adjust to will change, and I'll have to start all over again."

If anyone in the family is consciously or subconsciously fighting recovery, professional counseling should be sought. This type of attitude can sabotage a fragile recovery—and most, early on, are very fragile.

Your relationship in Phase One: Expectation (that with sobriety comes a perfect family) and reality (there is no such thing as a perfect family) are on a collision course in early recovery. Sometimes there is a brief honeymoon, with everyone on his or her best behavior to avoid triggering a slip, and everything seems perfect. But it isn't real and it rarely lasts. There are too many unresolved issues—resentments, guilt, money or job troubles—that will have to be dealt with in Phase Two. If your life remains problem-free well into that phase, you are probably wishfully glossing over and unwisely failing to address them.

"When I first got sober, I expected my wife would be thrilled that I wasn't drinking and that I came home from work on time every day. I thought she'd welcome me with open arms, feed me like a king, let me crash in front of the TV after my AA meeting, and not blink when I slept till noon on the weekends. Instead she acted like I was the one who should be doing things for her."

Finding that sobriety doesn't mean a suddenly perfect relationship often comes as both a surprise and a disappointment. Significant others often feel like *insignificant* others in early recovery, when for a time relationships seem to become worse rather than better. If you find your spouse, partner, parent, or child distant at first, don't be surprised. Those in early recovery have to put their best efforts into staying sober, which means that when you want to talk or go out or entertain, they may not have the time or the physical or psychic energy to participate. Nor are they ready to deal with past problems and issues—this kind of discussion will usually have to wait until later in recovery.

That doesn't mean that there should be no time at all for your relationship. It's a good idea to plan some time every week for spouses to spend quietly together—talking, engaging in a common hobby, listening to music, or whatever they enjoy doing jointly. They should also take every opportunity to go to meetings together, visit with friends from AA or Al-Anon, view AA videos or read meditations, or spend time with others whom they enjoy sober. Parents and children, too, should set up special times to spend as a family.

In a sense you will need to get to know one another all over again. Without the alcohol and/or drugs in your lives, you are truly different people. If it's your mate who's recovering, it's like the early stages of courting, where you go slowly and try to learn what you can about the other person. If it's a child or parent, it's as though you're starting fresh with a new family and have to get acquainted. It's difficult, but starting from neutral territory has some real benefits. You can toss away old feelings and animosities and try to be the person you always wanted, but couldn't quite manage, to be. Work gradually toward real communication, which probably won't be achieved until sometime after the first clean and sober year.

But don't expect that your relationship will eventually become old-fashioned Hollywood-happy-ending perfect. No one and nothing in the real world meets that romantic ideal.

"I spent the last ten years covering up for my husband's drinking, picking up the pieces every time he messed up, doing his job and my job in the family. Now that he's sober, nothing's changed. I'm still the workhorse. It's not fair."

Your role in Phase One: Read all the chapters on Phase One so that you know what to expect and what goes on in early recovery. If honesty fell victim to addiction (as is usually the case), start resurrecting it, not just with the recoveree but with everyone else in and outside of the family. Cooperate in making the house an alcohol- and drug-free zone (see page 507). If you do the cooking, be sure you know about the relapse traps in some foods (see page 182). You could also help strengthen recovery by steering your recoveree into the Clean-and-Sober Diet (see Chapter 23). Most important, get involved in Al-Anon or Alateen.

But don't expect to choreograph your loved one's recovery. That's his or her job. It's not up to other family members—not even parents—to get the recoveree to meetings or to counseling sessions (unless a non-driver asks for a ride). Nor are you expected to check for alcohol on the breath or to examine belongings for signs of drug abuse—though in some cases this may be part of a parent-child or spouse-spouse agreement when trust has not yet returned. Work, instead, on improving yourself through Al-Anon's Twelve-Step program.

Phase Two Recovery

While Phase One was dedicated to sobriety in an effort to survive, Phase Two, which also usually lasts a year or more, should be devoted to learning how to enjoy life: rebuilding relationships, reevaluating career goals, getting back into recreational activities. If serious problems beset family relationships and professional therapy was not sought earlier, now is the time for it.

Your role in Phase Two: So that you know about the kinds of problems and feelings that crop up in Phase Two, read Chapters 17 through 21. This is a very important time for you, and for your relationship with the chemical-dependent person in your life. The spotlight is on that relationship, and its future is on the line. It takes two people to make it work, but only one to wreck it. You'll both have to give it your all. You'll both have to be open, sharing, caring, thoughtful, forgiving, and most of all, not controlling. You will have to learn how to communicate (page 373), how to express your feelings without rancor (page 329), how to have fun together. If underlying issues have been swept under the family rug until now, this is the time to start addressing them. Avoiding the task now can lead to a serious explosion in the future, and a relationship in which important issues are never discussed is a poor example for your children. The pattern will be passed on to future generations if it isn't broken now.

If the recoveree seems to be struggling in Phase Two, talk to him or her about the possibility of extending Phase One work (see page 353).

Your relationship in Phase Two. The real work of rebuilding your relationship takes place now. The suggestions in Chapter 19—on learning to communicate, to share, to reassign responsibilities—are for both of you. While you go about these tasks, remember to keep your sense of humor. Laughter is a dividend of sobriety.

"My mother started working the Al-Anon steps when she was eighty-five. She started talking to some members of the family for the first time in years. Going to Al-Anon helped her forgive my alcoholic father for abandoning her. I think she died happier because she learned to live and forgive."

Phase Three Recovery

At this point, the focus shifts to extending the life that was saved in Phase One and revitalized in Phase Two. Now is the time for the recoveree to think about instituting good health habits—the Clean-and-Sober Diet, freedom from tobacco, and an exercise program—if they aren't already in place. Phase Three is also a time in which many recoverees, having developed a solid recovery lifestyle, think about cutting back on AA. This should be done *very* cautiously (see page 415). Phase Three—the equivalent of normalcy—continues for the rest of the alcoholic/addict's life.

Your role in Phase Three: Significant others in the life of the recoveree are every bit as important to the success of Phase Three as they were to the earlier phases—maybe more so. It's virtually impossible for one person in a household to change his or her eating habits if no one else cooperates. The Clean-and-Sober Diet is a family affair that will benefit everyone.

It's also difficult to stop smoking if those you live with are still puffing away. So again, quitting should be a family project. Exercise can often be carried out independently, but for many people having an exercise buddy makes it much easier to stick to a program. And an early morning or evening walk is a great time either to "catch up" or to discuss (and often solve) family problems. Even if you don't join with the recoveree in getting active, you should avoid grousing about the time spent jogging, walking, or pumping iron (assuming it isn't a case of Fitness Folly; see page 461).

Your continued support of the recoveree's AA activities is also important. Most people maintain their sobriety better when they don't detach themselves completely from AA. If the recoveree finds that every chip he collects puts a chip on your shoulder, if she hears a litany of complaints about AA stealing too much time from you and the family, he or she could drop out. In the long run, that could be as bad for you as for the recoveree.

YOUR ROLE IF THERE'S A SLIP

Many alcoholics/addicts have a slip or a relapse at some point, most often early in recovery, and you could be living with one of the unlucky ones. Family members need to be alert for the most obvious warning signs: the recoveree starts feeling sorry for him- or herself, muses about missing the action at the bar, talks about the good times, and starts wondering "Am I really an alcoholic?"

Reading Chapter 29 will help you understand what can trigger a relapse, what the warning signs of trouble are, how to head off a relapse, and what the recoveree needs to do if one occurs.

"When my husband got into treatment, he was a junkie S.O.B.; when he left treatment, he was just an S.O.B. He had to work on this. He finally realized he couldn't construct another way of life unless he reconstructed himself."

KEEPING ALCOHOL AT HOME

The best show of support you can give a family member who has a drug or alcohol problem is to remove all mind-altering drugs and alcohol from the house. Parents (and spouses) sometimes refuse to give up their drinking "just because Val has a problem," and they lock up the liquor instead. This doesn't usually work. It sends your recoveree the message that he or she is expected to do something you are unwilling or unable to do yourself: abstain.

That's the kind of action that can be judged unjust and can breed resentment. If you're unwilling to clear out the liquor, you have to consider why. Are you trying to spite, tease, or challenge your child, spouse, or parent? (This would be a very unhealthy and unproductive way of dealing with the issue.) Or are you unable to quit drinking? (If that's the case, it may be time to consider seeking help yourself.)

Whether or not you want to continue social drinking when the recoveree in your family is not around is an issue you have to think about, too. The answer will depend partly on whether an occasional social drink leads to another and could lead to your getting home soused or wanting to continue your drinking at home.

MINI-GUIDE

STAGING AN INTERVENTION

What can you do when someone you love has a drug or alcohol problem and continues to deny it? Or when someone close to you has a relapse and refuses to acknowledge it? You can arrange an intervention.

WHAT IS AN INTERVENTION? An intervention is a group meeting at which family, close friends, and possibly a professional facilitator try to persuade an alcoholic/addict that he or she has a problem and should seek treatment. The intervention should stress the importance of the family's needs, allowing family members to ventilate their feelings and frustrations to the alcoholic/addict, with a supportive group present to help them make their case. But it is not a time to beat up on the alcoholic/addict, to punish or get even. Its purpose is to help, out of love and concern.

An estimated nine out of ten interventions succeed in getting the alcoholic/addict into treatment. But even those that don't succeed give family members the feeling that, no matter what happens, at least they tried.

A really successful intervention helps not only the alcoholic/addict but those around him or her. It stresses the importance of their needs and persuades them that, whether or not the goal of getting their loved one into treatment is met, they need to change their own lives. It can also be therapeutic, since it affords a forum in which they can finally tell the alcoholic/addict how they've been hurt by the disease, allowing them to ventilate their feelings and frustrations with a supportive group present to help make their case.

WHEN IS AN INTERVENTION A GOOD IDEA? When an alcoholic/addict has rejected other unmistakable attempts or suggestions to get treatment, is practicing denial and self-deception, and there are no other strong factors (such as job, medical, or legal problems) to motivate seeking treatment.

WHEN IS AN INTERVENTION NOT A GOOD IDEA? When there is little ammunition with which to approach the alcoholic/addict. Until you have your preliminary planning meeting, you may not know whether the ammo is there or not.

IS PROFESSIONAL HELP NECESSARY? When family relationships are fairly strong and when the person you are trying to reach does not have a history of mental problems, violence, or self-destructive behavior, family and friends may be able to handle the intervention alone—after being carefully coached by a professional. It's preferable, however (especially if you suspect that the alcoholic/addict might blow up or otherwise react badly) to recruit the services of an experienced professional both to set up the intervention and to take part in it.

WHO SHOULD PARTICIPATE? Pick those people who are closest to the chemically dependent person and the most influential. This could include close family members, close friends, a clergyperson, doctor, business associates. Bringing in those outside the family helps by making it clear that knowledge of the problem and concern about it have spread. The group should be large enough (a minimum of two individuals) to have an impact and to show there is some interest and power behind the effort, but small enough to still be personal and manageable and not overwhelm your target (no more than eight or nine).

Avoid asking anyone whom you know, or even suspect, has a drinking or drug problem of his or her own. Such an individual could, by subtly (perhaps unconsciously) defending substance use, sabotage all your efforts. Also exclude those who always immediately trigger anger in the alcoholic/addict, which could blow up the intervention before it gets going. Nor should very young children or grandchildren attend. Until they are eight or nine, youngsters can neither understand nor contribute to an intervention. Young children could distract from the issues at hand, giving grandpa the excuse to dandle junior on his lap and ignore the goings-on. Or their presence could be irritating ("How could you shame me before my granddaughter?") and cause an alcoholic/addict to bolt. But older children and adolescents are generally very effective participants at an intervention.

HOW IS AN INTERVENTION CONDUCTED? There are usually nine basic steps.

1. *Decide whether an intervention is necessary.* If you feel that a child, spouse, family member, or close friend is in need of help and he or she refuses to seek it voluntarily, or if a recoveree has a relapse and is not seeking help, discuss the situation with one or two other key players. If you agree that an intervention is called for, continue with the next step.

2. *Make a list of all potential participants.*

3. *Contact a professional* who is experienced at conducting interventions. To find one, ask for a referral from AA or Al-Anon friends, an addiction specialist, a local treatment program (but not one you intend to use, since this could represent a conflict of interest), the American Society of Addiction Medicine (ASAM—see page 46), or a local alcohol awareness council. Before agreeing to hire the professional, ask about the costs and manner of payment, and check his or her credentials and approach.* Talk to the professional in person and try to gauge if he or she comes across in a loving, compassionate way and will be able to direct family energy constructively. Avoid someone with a punitive, militant approach. Ask for a couple of references, and check them out.

4. *Arrange a preliminary planning and education meeting.* It will be helpful to have the professional there to explain how the intervention will work, to show films, to provide some alcohol and drug education, and to explain the workings of AA and Al-Anon. Family members should be advised to attend one or more Al-Anon meetings before the intervention, so that they will better understand their own feelings, the alcoholic/addict,

(continued on following page)

*The fee, which usually covers two or three planning sessions and arranging such logistics as the location of the intervention, may vary from $500 to $1,500, although some community groups may offer this service for less or even at no cost. Some individuals may stage interventions as part of their Twelfth-Step work.

MINI-GUIDE

(continued from previous page)

and the disease they are dealing with. Reading this chapter, as well as Chapters 2 and 3, will also be helpful.

Have everyone who will attend the intervention make a list of situations where they were hurt by the drinking or drug-related behavior. Each incident should be a firsthand experience and accompanied by the following information: when it took place; where it took place; what the behavior was; how it related to alcohol or drug use; what was wrong with it (it was embarrassing, dangerous, hurtful, financially damaging, detrimental to business, and so on); and how it made the person recounting the story feel. When possible, be specific about amounts of alcohol consumed or pills swallowed. Use recent incidents rather than those that can be dismissed as "ancient history."

Warn all participants to avoid bringing up issues (such as an affair) that are not common knowledge and could stun the subject or other participants. Letting such a cat out of the bag could wind up with everyone getting scratched.

5. *Get the facts on treatment.* You can't just surround the drinker in your family and say, "You've got to get treatment." Someone who has been blind to the need for treatment is in no condition to research the options and decide how to go sober. Deciding *to* go sober will be hard enough. So read the material in Chapter 3 carefully, and then explore, or ask someone else in the group to explore, the various options, including inpatient treatment, outpatient treatment, individual therapy, and Alcoholics Anonymous or another Twelve-Step program alone.

Speak directly and at length to potential therapists, treatment center personnel, and so on. Don't sign up with the first center you interview. (Talking to one is helpful. By the time you've talked to people and inspected facilities at three or four, you've spotted strengths and flaws you wouldn't have noticed earlier, and you're almost an expert.) Also get information on how treatment can be paid for (citing the cost of treatment is a popular way for an alcoholic to squirm out of getting help; see page 50), the possibility of time off from work, and availability of space at an inpatient center if that's the choice. Be sure to block all potential escape routes. For example, review both business and family responsibilities and see how they can all be met or postponed while the patient is getting sober (the fact that a big deal is pending or a family vacation has been promised is another way to get out of treatment).

6. *Hold a rehearsal meeting.* A rehearsal should lower the temperature at the actual intervention, helping the participants feel calmer, better prepared, and more confident. It also allows the family to confront in advance the emotions stirred up by the intervention process. If these were to surface at the actual intervention, the whole operation could be endangered. Everyone who is going to be at the actual intervention should be at the rehearsal. Someone unacquainted with the process could wreck it. One of the participants should play the role of patient, so the players will not be talking to air.

Bring out every piece of information that you might want to bring up at the intervention. Each person should now present the items on their lists, calmly and in a non-judgmental way, just as they would present information suggesting that a family member has another disease. Each should talk of the ways in which the drinking or drugging has affected them personally, how they have been hurt, upset, angered, embarrassed, or frightened by it, how it is running or ruining their lives. Each should close with a plea for the subject of the intervention to get help.

Decide on what the consequences should be if the subject refuses to stop drinking or using drugs. These should not be a cluster of idle threats, but actions that each of you is willing to take. Depending on the situation, they may include separation, divorce, loss of children, loss of employment, loss of financial support, eviction from the home, and so on.

If during this rehearsal some participants seem dubious about the process, are afraid of angering or alienating the alcoholic/addict, or unexpectedly play defender, ask them not to attend the real thing. By general agreement, edit out weak or unconvincing episodes. If information comes up that could be too upsetting to the subject, that should not be used early in the intervention. This may be more effective later—especially if the subject is reluctant to get help. If facts upsetting to those at the rehearsal come up, they will need to be dealt with too—by the professional present or by another counselor.

7. *Make final preparations.* As needed, reserve space at a residential treatment center, make an appointment with a therapist or at an outpatient clinic, pack bags, and arrange such major and minor details as transportation, pet care, childcare, or time off from work. Do whatever is necessary to make it easy to get the alcoholic/addict into treatment immediately should the intervention prove successful.

8. *Set up the intervention.* Choose a locale the subject can get to easily. Ideally, it should be neutral territory—a doctor's office, a motel room, a church meeting room. If you think it will be impossible to get him or her there, settle on doing it at home as a last resort. The room should be chosen and arranged so that there is no easy escape and, if violence is a possibility, no ready access to weapons.

Be sure to pick a time when all essential players can be present. Getting the star there, of course, will be a challenge. One approach is to say that you've been seeing a counselor (the intervention counselor) as a family "to deal with the problems that you've created in our lives," and that you will be expecting him or her to join you for a one-time-only meeting. Then, with the time and place set, extend the invitation to that meeting. Try to be upfront, but do whatever is necessary to get him or her to the intervention.

If you get absolutely no cooperation, beard your lion in the den. Pick a time you're sure the subject will be at home and is likely to be most lucid. Then have all the participants converge on the house together. If the subject retreats to the bedroom, follow. If he or she tries to escape through the front door, block it with the sofa.

(continued on following page)

MINI-GUIDE

(continued from previous page)

9. Do your lifesaving work. Calmly (or as calmly as possible) have each participant list and describe the events that have been damaging to work, family, health, safety, and so on. Reading from prepared texts or index card notes will reduce anxiety and make certain that nothing important is omitted. The attitude should not be vindictive, but rather sorrowful. Love and concern should constantly be emphasized. When everyone is finished, ask, "Is this the way you want to live your life?" and urge the subject to "please get help."

Clearly spell out the consequences to follow if help isn't sought—but only if you are really ready to follow through on them.

WHAT ARE THE POSSIBLE OUTCOMES OF AN INTERVENTION? In the vast majority of cases, when an intervention is carefully planned and well executed, the person being addressed agrees to get help. Sometimes, however, the response is "I promise, I'll stop drinking this time—but on my own." How do you respond? You can remind him or her about the number of times this promise has been made and broken. If the answer is adamant, you can say okay, "One more try." But extract a promise that if there is any further drinking or drug taking, the next step will be professional treatment. You can suggest that in the meantime, attendance at AA meetings will be beneficial.

Even if you don't succeed in persuading the subject to get clean and sober, the intervention has not been a failure. First of all, you've planted some important seeds. Even if they don't sprout immediately, it's possible that they will in the near future. Second, you've done your very best to help, so you needn't feel guilty if your family member continues this self-destructive behavior. And third, the rest of you have recognized the problem for what it is and can—and should—take steps to help yourselves (see Chapter 28).

28

LIVING WITH SOMEONE IN RECOVERY: YOUR CONCERNS

Sober members of the family often have more questions about recovery than the alcoholic/addict, whose mind is still in a chemical haze. Though sobriety is something family members desire, it's also something for which most are totally unprepared. It's like getting married or having a baby: Even if you're eager to leave the single life or to have a child, the prospect can be daunting. What will it be like? Can you handle it? What should you know to make it easier? The same questions arise about recovery.

WHAT'S ON YOUR MIND?

RESENTMENT

"I resent being told that I should go to Al-Anon. After all, my husband is the sick one."

Your feeling is a natural one and not uncommon. But the more that is known about the disease of addiction, the more it's seen to affect everyone in the family. The concept that family members are "co-dependent" has become such an important one that some doctors are trying to get it classified as a bona fide medical diagnosis.

Whether they succeed or not, the fact is that even if your husband refused help, you'd benefit from getting it yourself. And your getting it would help him. When family mem-

Guide Lines

❖ Both you and your recovering family member will behave differently in sobriety than during active addiction. But (at least at first) that doesn't guarantee a better relationship.

❖ Your concerns and the trials and tribulations you're enduring are not unique, although you may feel they are. Millions of others have experienced them, as you'll discover at Al-Anon.

❖ Faithful adherence to a recovery program—including Al-Anon and Alcoholics Anonymous—usually starts to heal relationships before the end of a year. If yours doesn't start improving by then, seek professional help. If issues of sexual or physical abuse are involved, or serious disagreements fester, seek such help much earlier.

bers learn to stop enabling and turn their own lives around, the alcoholic/addict often finds himself without the supports that have kept the roof from caving in on him. And that gives him a choice: either clean up the wreckage of his life or, eventually, die pinned beneath it.

There's another plus in your going to Al-Anon. You're the one whose mind isn't impaired by chemicals, so you can learn more quickly than your spouse and help him as well as yourself, without, of course, taking over and running his show.

If he becomes involved in his recovery and in AA and you don't go to Al-Anon, he'll grow and mature and you'll stay just where you are. That isn't good for a relationship, and many a marriage has floundered in recovery because one of the partners refused to work at getting better.

"Till he got treatment I only saw what drugs were doing to him. When he couldn't go on, I always had to keep going. I didn't realize the wear and tear on my own life. When I really looked at myself, I didn't like what I had become."

YOUR ROLE DURING DETOX

"I'm very nervous about my husband going through alcohol withdrawal at home. But his doctor seems to think this is okay."

It's sensible to be nervous. Detoxifying the body from alcohol or other drugs is a serious procedure and requires serious attention from everyone involved.

In some cases it is possible to safely withdraw at home; see page 78 for the kinds of situations in which this can be accomplished safely and successfully. If your husband fits this description, then home detox is a viable option—*if* it is very carefully planned and carried out.

The first step is to have every adult in the household read the pertinent sections of Chapter 5 (including the Mini-Guide to Home Detox) so that they are familiar with detoxification procedures. The process should also be explained to the children at a level they can comprehend.

This will be a difficult experience. The atmosphere will be tense. You'll see an alarming exaggeration of symptoms you've observed before when your husband ran out of booze or drugs for even a short time. Your husband will necessarily be the center of attention, but don't neglect your own needs, or those of your children or other family members during the detox. It may be a good idea for very young children to stay with grandparents or a friend during the withdrawal because what goes on could be frightening to them.

CONCERN

"My wife is about to enter a residential treatment program, and I'm concerned about what I can do to help her in her fight against an addiction to pills."

This is going to be a tough time for your family—for a while, maybe even tougher than what you went through while your wife was addicted to drugs. Though your wife will have to fight her own battle, there are several things you can do to support her.

Stand tall behind her. When she goes off to treatment, she needs to feel that you fully support her struggles to get the monkey off her back. Don't disparage her (she didn't plan on getting hooked on pills) or her efforts (the battle will be tough enough even with support). Put the energy you used trying to control her and her habit into supporting—but not controlling—her recovery.

Keep the home fires blazing. Your wife will have enough to worry about without worrying that things will fall apart while she's away. So assure her that home and hearth will be secure. If you have children, make plans for their care that will remove any doubts she may have that they'll be okay. Cut back on your work hours if possible, so that you'll be home with the children during evenings and weekends at least. If your children are preschoolers, call on grandparents, other relatives, close friends, or paid sitters to oversee their care during the daytime. Arrange for school-age youngsters to attend an afterschool program or to visit friends (supervised by parents) until you get home.

If you have to cut corners while trying to play both mother and father, let the dust build up under the bed, use paper plates and frozen foods, and let the children wear the same jeans until they stand at attention beside their beds. But try to get the house in order and the laundry and dishes done before your wife's return, even if it takes paid help. Coming home to a messy house could put a damper on her recovery as well as her homecoming.

Clean house. It won't be enough for your home to pass the white-glove test. It will also have to pass the clean-and-dry test. Carefully search the house for alcohol, pills, other drugs, or drug par-

AL-ANON

Al-Anon is to you what Alcoholics Anonymous is to the alcoholic/addict in your life. Like any support group, it reminds you that you're not alone and offers structured advice from those who have been through it before you. Like AA, Al-Anon is a Twelve-Step program, again more a fellowship than an organization, run entirely by volunteers. You get the most out of Al-Anon if you attend meetings regularly, work the steps, and enlist a sponsor.

aphernalia that may be stashed in odd places (the top shelf in the closet, under the mattress, in the laundry hamper), and get rid of everything you find.* If there are tapes or magazines or other paraphernalia that were part of your spouse's pill-taking lifestyle, get rid of them, too. If you're not sure just which items need to be disposed of, speak to the counselor.

Keep in touch. But write to your wife, rather than telephoning. In early recovery, memories are short, feelings are volatile. Things may be said on the telephone in haste or anger that you (or she) would be unlikely to put in writing. In addition, telephone calls can be distracting to someone in treatment, and a phone conversation can be played back mentally and misconstrued by the participants.** A letter, in black and white, is much harder to misinterpret. It remains exactly as it was written, can be read over and over again, and a counselor or friend can help interpret it if there is any doubt.

Letters can be referred back to at a later date, dramatizing how much progress has been made. Unlike a phone call, they can be tucked into a drawer and saved forever. The letters you write should be honest and newsy. Express your feelings and concerns, but before you raise issues that could be distracting or embittering, check with your spouse's counselor.

Do use the phone to keep in touch with the counselor. The better your rapport, the greater the free exchange of information. The counselor (who in a way will be counseling both of you) will let you know just how much you should be involved in treatment. Since each situation is different, follow this advice as closely as you can.

"Recovery seems to be contagious. My brother just picked up his three-month chip. I could do cartwheels across the room!"

The counselor can let you know how your wife is doing (at some centers you may get this information from the nursing staff), and in turn you can provide insights that may be helpful to those treating her. If at any time during treatment you discover something about her substance abuse or behavior that you think could be useful in her care, phone it in. And call immediately if you get the idea from sarcastic remarks in her letters that she's going through the motions of complying with the program without "getting it."

If her letters are filled with resentment and anger toward you, or seem designed to make you feel guilty, recognize that they are coming from someone who is going through an extremely difficult time. Speak to the counselor about them. This will not only offer her fresh insights into your spouse's feelings but will also help you deal with the letters yourself.

But keep away. Many treatment centers do not permit any visiting until the family session at the end of treatment. Even if the unit your wife is in allows it, you should consider staying away—especially early in treatment, when visits tend to trigger addictive behavior and arguments.

There are other advantages to avoiding personal visits during your spouse's treatment. You will both be doing some changing in this period

*During treatment, your wife's counselor may be able to discover where the stuff is stashed. Your wife may not remember, however, if it was hidden during a blackout, when much of the most deceptive behavior occurs.

**Many treatment programs recognize this, and limit or prohibit telephone calls while encouraging letter writing.

and will appreciate the differences more fully if you don't see each other as the changes are occurring. Some of the really bad feelings may dissipate during the separation. And then, of course, absence makes hearts grow fonder. If you haven't seen each other for several weeks, the reunion may even feel like a honeymoon.

Help yourself. You're likely to feel left out at this point, even distant. Until now you've been heavily involved in trying to help your spouse one way or another. Now someone else has taken over. You may actually find yourself feeling jealous of the counselors working with her, and thinking that someone else may succeed where you failed. But getting your spouse well wasn't your responsibility. It isn't even the responsibility of the counselor, who will only be guiding her. The addicted person has to get herself well.

You may feel a whole host of other emotions—anxiety, denial, anger, guilt, fear. Though these emotions are par for the course, they won't make you too pleasant to come home to, and learning to deal with them will help you both recover. Now is an ideal time to do this, and there's no better place to begin than at Al-Anon meetings (see page 515).

If after several meetings your anxieties are not relieved, or if you're feeling as if all the worries are on your shoulders while your spouse is being waited on and catered to in a fantasyland treatment center, consider seeking therapy for yourself beyond Al-Anon. Your spouse's counselor or treatment center can probably recommend the best way to go about this.

Helping yourself while your spouse is in therapy doesn't mean shifting your dependency elsewhere in your search for solace and support. Some partners end up having affairs or painting the town technicolor, and getting into trouble themselves. You should be making lifestyle changes to foster family recovery, not family disintegration.

Help each other. Participate in the family segment of your spouse's treatment program. The content of this series of sessions depends upon the resources and philosophy of the particular program and the needs of the patient. But most treatment centers involve significant others in some way, usually during the last week or several days of treatment (see page 518).

"When my son picked up his three-year token, he wanted me to be the one to present it. I didn't know what I could say. I'd never done that before. I got up and said, 'By birth you're my son. By choice, you're my friend.' Then he got up and said, 'I thought my mother was going to cry, but I'm the one that's crying.'"

Help others in the family. You may not be the only one suffering the effects of your spouse's alcoholism. If there are children, they're certainly not unscathed. If they've been involved in her life recently, that may also be true of your wife's parents and siblings. Play St. Bernard. Guide everyone toward the appropriate help: Al-Anon for adults, Alateen for teenagers, individual or group therapy for those who need extra assistance.

Inform yourself. Learn all you can about alcoholism and addiction. Read this book and others; listen to tapes; view videos on the subject (see page 570 for a list of helpful materials). Go to open AA meetings to learn what your chemically dependent family member is going through and what the

WHERE YOU FIT INTO TREATMENT

You may feel a bit nervous as the time nears for you to participate in the family segment of the treatment program, though probably not as nervous as your spouse, child, parent, or friend felt on entering treatment. But chances are you will quickly settle into the routine and enjoy the experience. Along with the relatives and friends of other patients, you'll discuss and learn a lot about your needs, the needs of the patient, and those of other family members—and (if it could be a problem) your own alcohol and drug use.

Before you zero in on the flaws in your relationship, you and the patient will be encouraged to grow separately—through counseling, group discussions, education, and support from staff, other family members, and other patients in treatment. Now's the time to ask about the things you might do unwittingly to sabotage recovery, and about how you can avoid being an enabler. Talk to staff people who are members of Al-Anon, and if there's an Al-Anon meeting nearby or on the premises, ask to attend with one of them.

Even the best of family sessions won't solve all your problems. A lot of unfinished business will remain for you both to keep working on when you get home. A weak family program—and there are bound to be some—may leave you feeling frustrated, uneasy, and unsure how to proceed when you leave. If you feel that your concerns weren't sufficiently addressed during family treatment, seek additional help elsewhere. Al-Anon members in your local community should be able to recommend a resource.

AA experience will be like for her. That's as important as going to Al-Anon to learn what you'll be going through yourself.

CONTINUED DRINKING

"My husband has gone to AA a few times to please me, but he hasn't stopped drinking. His drinking doesn't seem to bother him, but it's driving me crazy. Still, I know he has an illness and I have to stand by him."

It's true your husband's alcoholism is a disease, but that doesn't mean he has the right to make you sick, which is clearly what is happening. To keep your own sanity yet live up to your obligations as his wife, you can do the following:

❖ Discuss your feelings with your spouse. Drinking behavior usually puts feelings on the back burner. If you're being hurt by his drinking or drug use, talk about it calmly and rationally, avoiding anger, accusations, ultimatums, and nagging. Communicating the pain you feel because of your love for him will make further steps in addressing the problem less difficult.

❖ Arrange an intervention. On page 508 you can learn how to go about using this technique to try to get your spouse to recognize his need for treatment. You can't, however, force him to get help. His recovery, like his drinking, is his responsibility.

❖ If the intervention fails, make it clear to your spouse that his drinking is unacceptable. If he wishes to continue drinking, if his need for alcohol is stronger than his need for family, you should prepare yourself to live without him at some time in the near future. And as calmly as possible, warn him to prepare to live without you.

❖ Develop some autonomy for yourself, starting with your own checking account, savings account, or amassing of other assets. A nest egg will give you the security to make good your threat. Examine your earning power. You may need to return to school or get some vocational training. Financial dependence on the addict is a chain that binds you to a sinking ship. That kind of dependence also erodes your feelings of self-worth, making effective actions and decisions on your part more difficult.

❖ Go to Al-Anon. You aren't responsible for your spouse's recovery, but you are responsible for your own. At Al-Anon you will meet others who are facing, or have faced, the same problems you are struggling with. Their love and support will guide and strengthen you, whether your spouse gives up drinking or not and whether you leave him or not.

❖ Be grateful for the AA meetings your spouse did attend. Once an alcoholic/addict goes to AA or to treatment, even under duress, he's never the same. The experience may not keep him sober, but it can sure ruin his drinking or drugging. That's because some of the foundation for substance abuse has been undermined permanently. Going to AA or treatment and just looking around at all those ex-alcoholics/addicts grinning and hugging, tells him that when he's ready for it, there is a way out, that addiction is not the only way to live.

❖ If all else fails, a separation may be necessary. But make that a last resort. It almost always leads to divorce. However, a brief, amicably agreed-upon period apart—a breather, in effect—may give each of you some time to think, gain perspective, and rebuild energy.

"My husband, who's now retired, seems to think treatment is a revolving door. He goes in to dry out every few months. I don't know what to do. If it weren't for the great support I get in Al-Anon, I don't think I would survive."

There are several possible reasons for your husband's failure to stay sober. All of them are remediable.

❖ The treatment he's been getting is either not adequate or not appropriate for him. Different people require different types of treatment. Consult Chapter 3 for tips on picking a treatment program. Get additional advice, if necessary, from AA or Al-Anon friends, a qualified physician, or a certified addiction counselor.

❖ Your husband needs more than treatment. Most people do. In fact, the continuing-care program (see page 71) is usually more important in achieving long-term sobriety than the treatment itself. So be sure that the treatment facility he attends sets up a very intensive continuing-care schedule. For your husband it should probably include some sort of outpatient program.

❖ He is suffering from one or more

"When I got out of treatment, there was no band playing for me. My family and old friends weren't glad to see me. Thank God. I couldn't have handled that then. I would surely have used them to resume my addiction. Instead they stayed cool and I stayed sober."

underlying psychological problems that are interfering with his ability to assimilate treatment. Check with a qualified therapist to determine if treatment for such problems should be carried out in conjunction with the treatment for substance abuse.

❖ He is bored with his life and no longer feels valuable. Many retired people suddenly feel at loose ends, and drinking often becomes a problem at this point even if it wasn't before. If this seems to be the case, encourage him to become active in some community or church work, paid or voluntary, that seems relevant to him.

❖ You are too involved in his recovery to allow him to remain sober. Examine your own attitudes. Do you feel, deep down, that if he becomes permanently sober you will lose your reason for being? Or that you will have to become less involved in Al-Anon? Do you have enough to do in your own life without being your husband's caretaker? If not, you should probably look into getting a job, doing some volunteer work, or taking up a productive hobby. Your husband will do better when he has to look after himself.

DENIAL

"I've been going to AA for six months. I admit I'm an alcoholic. But my wife still drinks herself sick every night. And takes prescription pills to boot. Why can't she see what's happening?"

Your wife isn't ready to admit that she's sick. The term that's commonly used to describe this very common symptom of the disease of alcoholism/addiction (as well as of some other diseases) is "denial." This kind of denial isn't lying to others, it's lying to oneself. That may not be the perfect description of this kind of behavior because it makes it sound as though the individual is stubbornly refusing to see reality. That isn't so.

"At Al-Anon I learned more than how to cope with the drunk in my family. I learned a healthy way of living that is relevant to every part of my life."

More likely, the refusal stems partly from the effects of alcohol and/or drugs on the brain, and partly from the inability to come to grips with reality. It's the same attitude that people have when they hear they or a loved one has any incurable disease. They just don't want to believe it because it's too painful to face. Eventually, however, as they begin to come to terms with the dreadful news, they begin to be able to look at and even live with it.

An intervention that includes her physician (see page 508) may help your wife face up to her disease. If that doesn't work, you have to take steps to protect the rest of the family. First and foremost don't let your own recovery program slip, even if it means a separation. Start going to Al-Anon to increase your understanding of your role as the spouse of an alcoholic/addict. Be sure that your spouse is not in a position where she can do harm to any children in the family or to the family finances. And let her know that you won't be an accomplice to her self-destruction. Don't make excuses for her. Suffering the consequences of one's addictive behavior in many cases is the catalyst that converts self-destructive abuse into self-preserving recovery.

"My husband thinks my son may be using cocaine. I can't believe this. He comes from a good Jewish home and never saw anyone use drugs."

Children from good Jewish homes, as well as good Christian homes and good atheist homes, have been known to use drugs. It happens. The problem of substance abuse is so pervasive in our society that no one is immune. So seek help from your rabbi if he is familiar with substance abuse and its treatment. If not, call your local JACS office, if there is one (see page 133), or your local Federation of Jewish Philanthropies. Many Federations support recovery programs.

Because getting drunk or using drugs seems so foreign to Jewish life, many Jews feel too guilty and ashamed to admit their problem or the problem of a loved one. But the fact is that there are suburban Jewish housewives popping pills, Chassidic businessmen getting drunk, and Orthodox students experimenting with cocaine. In fact, experts estimate that the rate of chemical dependency is the same in the Jewish community as in other ethnic groups.

Read page 488 to see if your son may indeed have a problem, then get help for him. It would be un-Jewish not to.

KLEAN AND KOSHER

For information on treatment programs that are sensitive to the needs of traditional Jews (kosher diets, religious observance, and so on), call the Addiction Assistance Line (718/968-8154) or your local JACS office.

"My brother has decided he has a drinking problem. That's ridiculous. We're Jewish and I've never heard of a Jewish alcoholic."

A lot of people haven't heard of Jewish alcoholics. But there are plenty of them. Tradition has it that Jewish people don't get drunk. The distaste for drunkenness in Jewish life probably goes all the way back to the bible, where both Noah and Lot got themselves into trouble by getting drunk. And indeed, up to a generation or two ago drunkenness was frowned upon and relatively rare. The only occasions on which drinking was encouraged were two holidays: Purim, when it was customary to drink "until one couldn't distinguish between Haman, the villain of the Book of Esther, and Mordechai, the hero," and Simchat Torah, when enthusiastic celebratory drinking to commemorate the giving of the Torah, or first five books of the Bible, to Moses was encouraged. So, although occasional drinking problems did exist, they were less common than in the general community.

Many adult Jews can look back on childhoods where the only wine ever seen in the home was the thick, sweet type used for religious purposes, and where hard liquor was reserved for special occasions such as weddings or bar mitzvahs. Few of today's Jewish children, however, will look back on such childhoods. With the assimilation into the American social scene in the last decades has come the assimilation of such customs as social drinking, drinking unrelated to religious ritual. And with this shift has come an increase in alcoholism in the Jewish community.

Still, this increase has been kept mostly under wraps, leading to a community-wide denial. Most Jews, like you, continue to be unaware that alcoholism is becoming more widespread in their community or that drugs, both licit and illicit, have also become a problem.

Fortunately there is a growing recognition among Jewish leaders that Jews are no longer immune to alcoholism/addiction. More rabbis are learning about the disease and opening their synagogues to Twelve-Step programs.

Now is the time for you to become enlightened too. Learn about alcoholism/addiction and about the role of family members. What your brother needs now is your support, not your denial.

DISGUST

"My husband has been an alcoholic for years. I finally threw him out of the house about six months ago, and I thought, 'Good riddance.' Now he calls me and says he's been in treatment for alcoholism and he's sober and wants to see me and the children. I still say, 'Good riddance.' "

Who can blame you? This man was a malignancy destroying your family and you're not willing to risk his coming back and doing further damage. On the other hand, he may no longer be the same ugly person you've known in recent years. Treatment often changes people completely, not only bringing them back to their predrinking selves, but usually making them better human beings than they ever were before.

Still, if you don't want to see your husband, no one can force you. Of course the courts may force you to allow him to see his children. But do you want it to come to that? Do you want this kind of contention between you? A better course may be to agree to a meeting with him, perhaps in the presence of a counselor or therapist. Talk about the issues between you, the problems you see as insurmountable. If the first meeting goes well, perhaps you'll agree to further counseling. Keeping an open mind could eventually lead to opening your heart. If it doesn't, it could at least lead to a more amicable separation (which could save you both a bundle in legal fees).

Your spouse's illness (alcoholism *is* an illness) affected you and affected your children. Whether you decide to see him again or not, you should do something about undoing some of the damage. Reading this part of the book will help. So will going to Al-Anon. If his recovery and remorse are genuine but you continue to act as though he is still drinking, you and your children could be the big losers as your spouse gets well.

"I used to think, 'How can he love me and love this drug, too?' He would say, 'It kills me to do this to you.' And I would think, 'I'm the one who needs to kill you.' It was only when I learned about his disease that I finally understood."

HESITANCY ABOUT AL-ANON

"My daughter's drug counselor said I should go to Al-Anon. Isn't that group really for wives of alcoholics?"

The largest single segment in Al-Anon is probably made up of wives of alcoholics, but there are also parents, children, husbands, live-in lovers, and friends of alcoholics and drug addicts. Don't hesitate to go because you're embarrassed or are worried that people will point and whisper, "Poor thing. She's the mother of a drug addict. What did she do wrong?" In fact, instead of taunts, you can expect support from other Al-Anon members. They are there to get help and to give help, not to judge. Many have had experiences similar to your own and would be the last people to pass judgment on someone else.

Many of those you will meet at Al-

Anon have already learned a lot at meetings. You'll realize that as soon as you hear them talk. You may fear, of course, that even though Al-Anon worked for them, it won't work for you, that if you change yourself or the way things are done in your family, everything will fall apart. Talk to them about your fears. They probably felt the same way when they put a first tentative foot inside the door of a meeting. But they found out that the program could work for them—and it can work for you.

"I've heard that Al-Anon meetings are primarily for wives. I'm a husband, and I feel like I'll be out of place."

It's true that traditionally, Al-Anon has been mostly for wives of alcoholics. But times are a-changing. Although statistically there are more male alcoholics than female, and there probably will always be an imbalance of females over males in Al-Anon, more and more women are seeking treatment for alcoholism/addiction and more are going to AA. A sensible result: more of their husbands are turning to Al-Anon for help and there are now all-male groups in many communities.

Some Al-Anon meetings may still be primarily aimed at wives. If you find that's true of the first meeting you go to, try another one. You're almost certain to find one where you'll feel at home. If you don't, ask your wife where the husbands of some of her AA friends go. If they don't go anywhere, you might consider starting your own Al-Anon group (see page 417). Whatever you do, don't let the absence of a perfectly compatible meeting keep you from getting the sanity-saving benefits of a support group like Al-Anon.

COUNSELOR VS. FAMILY

"Our nineteen-year-old daughter just finished a drug treatment program and says she doesn't want to come home. She says we don't know what's best for her, and her counselor does. I just don't understand."

It always hurts more when your child cuts the umbilical cord than when the obstetrician does it. It's particularly difficult when you think

PARENTS IN AL-ANON

Some parents of teenagers who have abused alcohol or drugs find that although Al-Anon is helpful, it would be even more so if it were geared more directly to their special interests and concerns. If there are several Al-Anon groups in your community, look for one whose members feel the way you do and set up parents-in-Al-Anon meetings. Focus on issues like: how to balance detachment and control with a fourteen-year-old; what should be expected of teens in school; how much and what kind of contact is best with teachers and school counselors; when is individual therapy needed; dealing with other children in the family; what to do about undesirable friends.

Rather than replacing regular Al-Anon meetings, these meetings should supplement them. Even if you don't seem to be getting help from these meetings at first, keep going back. One day the light may suddenly switch on and you will find the help you need. If not, consider professional therapy.

it's premature, that she isn't ready to survive on her own. But it has to happen sometime, and this is probably a very good time for your daughter. Her recovery from addiction requires that she learn to walk without crutches of any kind—chemical or parental—guided by those most knowledgeable about her disease. This is an unsettling but necessary scenario. So relax and give the treatment a chance to work.

Letting go doesn't mean that you're a failure. At some point every parent has to let go. And it doesn't mean you have no role to play in the recovery process. There is much you can do to support your child's recovery, including learning all you can about her illness.

If you find that you can't keep your hands off your child's life, you need to take another look at your own. Do you have enough (between work and play) to occupy you? Do you feel lost now that your child is no longer sick, no longer a child, no longer in need of your care? Many parents, particularly mothers, feel this way. But hanging on isn't good for them or their children.

The best way to deal with these feelings is to start going to Al-Anon meetings faithfully. There you'll find kindred spirits who've had or are still having trouble letting go. If you still feel lost and empty, see a therapist for individual or group therapy.

"I thought mothers didn't go to Al-Anon. Mothers are supposed to know what to do. I cried the whole time at the first meeting. After the meeting, two mothers came up to me up and said, 'We know how you feel.' It was the first time I'd found anyone else who really understood."

GUILT

"My son just called up from the drug treatment center we sent him to, one that was very highly recommended. He said he hates it there and we should come and take him home. The counselor says he's not ready to come home. I'm so torn."

That may be just what your son wants you to feel. Remember, he's still an addict and (even in recovery) will always be an addict. Part of the disease of addiction is the need to manipulate others—which could be what he's trying to do with you.

Whether it's a child or another family member who is grumbling, the action you should take is the same. Tell him not to make an impulsive decision, to stay where is for a few days. Make it clear to him that this is a medical decision and that you aren't qualified to decide what's best for him. Say you will consult the doctor, counselor, or team that referred him, and have those professionals evaluate the situation.

What the referring professionals have to decide is: is your son trying to manipulate his way out of treatment? Is he just having difficulty adjusting to the rigors of a treatment program? Or is there really a problem with the program? It sometimes happens that an alcoholic/addict ends up at a treatment facility that, even if it is a good one, isn't quite right for him. If that's the case, then switching is called for. But the new program should be at least as intensive as the present one (in other words, if he's in an inpatient program don't switch him to an outpatient one) and also as highly regarded.

If, on the other hand, the professionals decide your son should stay put, continue to support the efforts of the treatment center and the counselor who's handling his case. This will give your son the best chance of getting well. If necessary, refuse his phone calls—but continue to write to him frequently to show that you care. Ask the counselor to act as a buffer between the two of you right now.

Whatever you do, don't let your son walk away from his commitment to get treatment. And don't feel guilty. He may not agree now, but he will appreciate your efforts later. You're doing what's best for your child. (And that includes showing him that his days of manipulating you are over.)

AN EMPTY NEST

"Our daughter just went through treatment at a good rehab hospital. Now they seem to think she ought to stay at an extended-care facility for six months. I don't understand why when she has a good home to come home to."

She probably has too good a home to come home to. Fledglings pampered in their nests may never learn to fly. Your love and concern for your daughter are important to her, but right now she needs to try her wings. Give her that chance, even if it's difficult for you (it almost always is).

An empty nest can be a lonely place. The best way to banish that feeling is to find other interests. There are a lot of other people out there—young and old—who can benefit from your love and concern. Share it with them. And at Al-Anon share your worries about your child and about your own life with other empty-nesters.

They say in AA . . .
"Pain is necessary—misery is optional."

SUSPICIONS

"My mother and I keep arguing about the martini she has before dinner every day. I've measured the gin it it, and it's more like a triple martini. As soon as she takes it, her memory goes completely. You tell her something, and the next minute she's forgotten it. It also seems to be affecting her memory in general. How can I get her to stop drinking?"

Tell your mother that alcohol causes premature aging of the brain, and that it is almost certainly the cause of her memory problems. Even small amounts of alcohol can masquerade as senile dementia. If concern about memory loss isn't enough to scare her into sobriety, then she has an alcohol problem. Talk to her physician. He or she may be able to prescribe sobriety for health reasons. If that doesn't work, try to persuade your mother to try abstention for a couple of months. During that time, keep track of her memory lapses. Have things improved? If so, then you should be able to persuade her to continue abstention in order to keep her brain as healthy as possible.

"My mother has been suffering from memory loss, blackouts, and dizzy spells, and has had several minor falls. I don't think she's a secret drinker. I believe her symptoms come from taking too many prescriptions and other pills."

You may be right. It's generally recognized that many older people are being overmedicated. Sometimes it's the physician or physicians who are overprescribing or miscalculating the dosages. Sometimes it's the older person herself who is misusing the medication—taking too much too often, mixing prescription and over-the-counter (OTC) drugs, or taking pills prescribed by several different doctors. The more she takes, the less aware she is of what she's doing, and the more the misuse escalates into abuse. The symptoms you describe could of course be related to aging, but it is very possible they point to just such abuse.

Get your mother some professional help quickly. Unless certain of her medications are necessary for survival, the best route may be a drug-free test period, possibly in the secure environment of a hospital. During this test the doctors can assess which medications are really needed and which are excess—and dangerous—baggage. Once your mother is stabilized, all medication, including OTC preparations, should be supervised by one physician. The doses should be carefully calculated to be age-appropriate (most drugs are tested on younger people and recommended dosages are too large for older people). To be sure that Mom doesn't mess up again, it would be a good idea for the medication to be doled out by a friend, relative, visiting nurse, or other responsible person.

THINGS GETTING WORSE

"My husband hasn't had a drink in three months. This is his longest period of sobriety in fifteen years, and the kids and I thought our lives would finally be good again. But things seem just as bad as they were before—maybe even worse."

Giving up alcohol is only the first step on a long road. And though it's the most important step, if the others aren't taken, the journey is certain to lead to a dead end.

So don't expect a healed spouse or a healed family overnight. Expect that things may even get worse before they get better. What you can do to take care of yourself and your children during this difficult time is to start going to Al-Anon meetings. (Check your local telephone directory for a phone number and call for the meeting nearest your home.) There you'll learn how you can make it through from others who have experienced the same struggles. There are some basic principles that you will have to absorb and make part of your life:

"My father is sober; my mother is drug-free now. But there's no joy in their lives. Something is missing. Sometimes you need to talk about painful things to get some closure. My mother always refused to talk about anything. She left me feeling outside. But Al-Anon has helped me."

Each of us is responsible for our own behavior. You will have to learn that you were not responsible for your spouse's drinking (or the drinking or drug use of anyone else in your family) and that you aren't responsible for his sobriety now. He's the one who lifted the glass to his lips, and he's the one who has to be sure that he never does it again. You are responsible only for what *you* do.

Your behavior is the only yardstick by which you should judge yourself. If your spouse (or your child or your parent) behaves badly, you may feel sad about it. But since it isn't your responsibility, you shouldn't feel guilty. Just keep tabs on yourself. If you're doing what you should be doing, you're doing all that can be expected.

We can't control or change others. It always seems so easy when we are young and still believe in fairy tales. We fall in love with the guy who drinks too much or the girl who behaves like a spoiled child and we are sure we can, through our love, change them. Of course we can't. But we keep trying, and usually make things worse. In recovery you have to accept that if your spouse is to stay sober, he will have to do it on his own. You can be supportive, but you can't be responsible. You will have to let go of the puppet strings, which have probably been so tangled for so long that you haven't been able to wield control anyway.

We shouldn't rely on others for our happiness. Until now you have probably been miserable when your husband was drinking and happy when he was sober, your own moods dictated by his behavior. From now on, try to get your happiness from what you do. Remember, the alcoholic/addict in your family didn't become sick to make you miserable and he isn't trying to get well (or shouldn't be) to make you happy. He should be doing it for himself. And you should also do what you must to make your life better.

If he doesn't show up in time for a party or some other event (because he's drunk or just plain thoughtless), go yourself. If you enjoy music and he doesn't, it's okay for you to go to a concert on your own or with friends. Be as nice to yourself as you've been to other people—even spoil yourself occasionally. You deserve it, and this will help build your own self-esteem. Without feeling good about yourself, you won't be able to feel truly good about anyone else. It will also make "detachment with love" possible.

You have to separate the disease from the person. If a family member has Alzheimer's, you hate the disease but you don't stop loving the person.

Recovery is a slow process. As it would if he'd just gone through major surgery, it will take time for your partner to heal. So be patient.

TRUST

"My husband lied so much in the past that I don't trust him to tell me the truth. I see him go down the street in the direction of the liquor store and I panic, even though that's the only way he can get anywhere from our house."

Like a mistreated dog who cringes every time he sees a rolled-up newspaper, you're conditioned to expect the worst when your spouse walks out the door. It takes a lot of time and loving attention for that dog to become "reconditioned." It will take the same to change your reaction to your husband's behavior. Like the puppy, you will have to see for yourself that time after time the old response, the one you fear, doesn't occur.

The first step in breaking the pattern? Talk about your feelings at Al-Anon and with your sponsor. You'll find that lack of trust is common. It takes a long time to regain, but one day you realize that you're no longer living "a life of quiet desperation," no longer waiting for the next bomb to drop. You don't automatically break into a sweat when your spouse heads in a dangerous direction, or comes home late, or forgets an appointment.

You will also need to learn that even if the alcoholic/addict does slip, you can be okay. You, as a free and independent human being, needn't depend on anyone for your strokes. That's easier for us to say than for you to make a part of your philosophy, but you've got to start taking responsibility for your own happiness, start finding contentment within yourself. Many Al-Anon members who've made the effort have been pleasantly surprised to learn it's possible.

WHAT ABOUT A CURE?

"Our daughter is in treatment for alcohol and drug abuse. Can we expect that she will come out cured?"

At present no one is "cured" of alcoholism/addiction. It's a treatable, but incurable, disease. If you expect your child to come out of treatment not only clean but with all her problems scrubbed away, you may be in for a major disappointment. Treatment is only the beginning of the road back for an alcoholic/addict. It will give her the tools for turning her life around, the information she needs to know about the disease that has ravaged her life (and yours), an introduction to Alcoholics Anonymous, and some insight into the problems that her substance abuse has caused. Most of all it will give her the freedom of choice to stay sober or go back to drinking and using. But that choice won't be made by a committee. It will be up to her.

You can support her when she returns from treatment (or still better, before she returns) by going to Al-Anon yourself and taking a crash course in learning all you can about her disease. When one person in the family has it, everyone has to work at getting well.

You can also support her decision to remain sober. But you have to learn how to avoid enabling should she choose not to be sober (see page 501).

"I thought once the chemical wasn't there, it would be the end of all the craziness and our family would return to normal. But I found that this is a lifelong process."

If you make it very clear that she gets no help from you at all if she resumes her chemical abuse, abuse will be a lot less attractive. Combined with what she learned in treatment, this may make it possible for her to become clean and sober again—hopefully permanently.

RESENTING A NEW INDEPENDENCE

"My wife came back from treatment for alcohol addiction a different person. She seems stronger than she used to be. She doesn't seem to need me or even want my help. And (it's hard to admit this) that makes me uneasy."

Most ordinary folks would stand up and cheer when a spouse who's been having problems is suddenly stronger and more independent. But people who have been living for any length of time with an alcoholic or addict are far from ordinary. They're more likely to sit down and cry (or an emotional equivalent). They have become dependent (in fact "co-dependent") on their familiar role in a sick relationship.

The fact that your wife appeared weak and in need of your help when she was drinking made you feel, at least subconsciously, strong and useful. By getting back on her own size 7-C's, she's robbed you of the chance to play the hero, and (again, perhaps subconsciously) you don't like it. You may even feel that if she is well and doesn't need you any more, she might up and leave. You've become obsessed with, and dependent on, taking care of her (Where is she? What is she doing? Is she sober?).

You may also fear that those responsibilities that you took over when she was unable to meet them (doing the income tax returns, arranging play-

"I used to get annoyed when my wife went to AA meetings. I would say, 'I think you should stay home with the children.' And she would say, 'If I don't go to meetings, I'll drink.' Then I finally realized going to AA was the difference between life and death for her, and I stopped resenting it."

dates for the children, shopping for the groceries, or whatever) will gradually move back into her court. It's goodbye martyr. For some people this is distressing—consciously or unconsciously.

There may also be the worry that she will resume those responsibilities, have a relapse, and throw everything into chaos again.

Here are some ways of dealing with those concerns:

❖ Get a really good recovery program going yourself, with a strong emphasis on Al-Anon.

❖ Find a new identity for yourself that doesn't depend on taking care of your spouse. It can be coaching a Little League team, volunteering to tutor disadvantaged youngsters, or taking up a hobby. As you get busier, you'll find family chores naturally reassigning themselves as you have less time to give to them. (And who wants to have to figure out all those "simplified" IRS forms anyway?)

❖ Recognize that you have to let go. It won't be easy, but hovering over your spouse, playing private eye at her every move, will not give her a chance to grow as she must in recovery.

❖ Slowly begin relinquishing responsibilities in bits and pieces (preferably wait until Phase Two to begin). This will be more comfortable for both of you (she may be as worried as you are about resuming everything at once).

❖ As communications begin to improve later in recovery, talk more about responsibilities and how you can share them. Every couple (whether they have an addiction problem or not) needs to work this out on their own timetable, in their own way.

ADDICTION TO AA?

"Now that my husband is sober, I think he has a new addiction: Alcoholics Anonymous. It doesn't matter what else is going on in our lives, he's got to go to AA. AA is obviously more important than me or our children—and I've become resentful."

Would you be resentful if your husband had a stroke and was required to go for physiotherapy every day? Probably not. Well, this isn't any different. Your husband has a potentially fatal disease and AA is an important part of his treatment.

Knowing that your husband had to go for physical therapy every day (and, perhaps, that you'd have to be the one to drive him) would not be fun. And knowing that there are AA meetings day after day after day isn't either. But treatment for any disease isn't meant to be fun—it's meant to make the sick person better.

There are ways of making this early phase of recovery easier on everyone in the family. Go to some of those AA meetings with him—and take the children along if they are old enough to sit quietly and understand some of what is going on (usually about age seven). Go to Al-Anon meetings yourself to unload some of that resentment and to get the support you need. Build some time into your schedule for the two of you to spend alone—it could be dinner out once a week; or a late dinner at home after the kids are in bed and he's returned from an early AA meeting; or a quiet half-hour before bedtime (switch off the TV, turn on the answering machine) talking over the events of the day, reactions to them, and feelings about them, and possibly reading some simple meditations or prayers together. Also set up some special family times for something everyone enjoys doing together, at least once during the week. It could be bowling, skating, swimming, a movie, a visit to a museum or zoo, a picnic, or whatever makes all of you feel like one happy recovering family.

Evaluate your feelings honestly. Could you be resentful of AA because it has done for your husband what you couldn't do? Many spouses and family members feel that way about treatment, AA, sponsors, and counselors. It's understandable, but it's not productive. Because of your close relationship to the alcoholic/addict, you can't possibly do what an objective professional or a fellow AA member can do. Accepting that fact will make you feel better about your spouse's AA experience, as well as about yourself.

DISCOMFORT WITH AL-ANON

"I really am very uneasy about going to Al-Anon. From what I've heard, it sounds like a lot of simplistic and mindless spiritual hocus-pocus."

Forget hearsay: Rely on the evidence of your own ears and eyes. They'll tell you there's no hocus-pocus at Al-Anon but rather, if you give it a fair chance and a lot of effort, a good bit of magic. Yes, you may be uncomfortable at the first few meetings. That's natural enough. But you'll find a lot more peace of mind there than mindlessness and more down-to-earth practicality than spirituality. You will hear stories just like your own from people feeling the same pain you've felt, and the same frustrations and confusion. The difference between you and those participating in Al-Anon for more than a brief time is that they've learned how to deal with the problems of chemical dependency in their families in a healthy way, something that can be as good for you as it's been for them.

"I had a lot of anger when my husband was drinking. I wanted to kill him. I actually handed him a loaded gun and invited him to shoot himself. I threw kitchen knives at him. At family meetings they taught me ways to work on my anger, to channel it constructively—by saying the Serenity Prayer, going to an Al-Anon meeting, calling my sponsor, going for a walk, mopping the floor, whatever."

So don't allow the possibility of discomfort with "spirituality" deprive you of the benefits of Al-Anon. If the first group you go to seems too focused on the spiritual for your comfort, try another. If there isn't another, just determinedly filter out those aspects of meetings that put you off. Reading the material on spirituality for the alcoholic/addict throughout this book may help you understand that the subject can be interpreted in many ways and that even those who consider themselves "unspiritual" can live with AA and Al-Anon if they try.

Look upon Al-Anon as sanity-saving medicine. A spoonful of the good humor, common sense, and open-arms friendship you'll find at meetings will help the medicine go down.

LIQUOR IN THE HOUSE

"My husband is now gung-ho for sobriety, and he wants me to get rid of all the liquor in the house. Just because he has a problem, I don't see why our friends can't enjoy a drink when they visit. Or why I can't."

If your husband had a violent allergic reaction to tobacco smoke, would you object to banning smoking in your home? You need to examine your reasons for resisting banning liquor. Your motivations may be obvious or deeply buried, but they are probably very much like those of other family members in your situation.

A conscious or subconscious wish to sabotage your spouse's recovery—not out of malice but out of fear. Fear that if your spouse becomes sober, your life will change. It's a realistic concern. But if you both work at it, the change should be for the better.

A desire to make your spouse suffer as you've suffered. Fired by normal resentments, you ask: "Why should I make it easy for him by making our home an alcohol-free zone? Why shouldn't I make his recovery as tough as he's made my life all these years?" The answers, if you think about it, are obvious. If he suffers, and especially if he fails in his attempt to keep sober, you will suffer too.

An inability to face giving up liquor yourself. If you feel you can't live in an alcohol-free house, you may have an alcohol problem too. Many of those who live with a chemically dependent person are so obsessed with their mate's behavior that they fail to recognize their own. A person who is truly a social drinker can take booze or leave it. If you can't leave it, or have trouble leaving it, start attending some AA meetings along with those of your Al-Anon group.

Whether you want to give up having an occasional drink out of the house is a personal decision. Just as many husbands decide to give up alcohol for nine months in support of pregnant wives who can't drink, many spouses decide to do likewise to support a husband or wife in recovery. You have to decide if giving up alcohol entirely is worth it for you—thinking about what the benefits are, and how important the losses might be.

WHO'S IN CHARGE?

"Our nineteen-year-old son is in an outpatient treatment program and living at home. I tried to sit down with him and make a schedule to be sure he gets to meetings and therapy sessions. My husband says I should let him handle it by himself."

In this case, father knows best. Your son has to be the one to get himself to meetings—that isn't your role. In fact, the less involved you are in your son's recovery program, the better. If you try to chauffeur him through life, he'll never learn to drive on his own.

You can provide food, shelter, medi-

"The most loving thing I can do for my family is stop trying to control and intervene in their lives."

A CONTINGENCY PLAN

The best way to deal with a slip is to prevent it (see Chapter 29). The next best way is to agree on a contingency plan in case one does occur. So at some point in early recovery, the family (or other significant others) should sit down and discuss what will happen if there's a slip. This plan needs to be tailored to the individual and the situation and should, if possible, have input from an addiction professional.

For example, you could let your husband know that if he starts using again, you will call his boss at the public utility and say, "Joe is operating nuclear power plant controls under the influence again." Or your wife could agree that if she has a slip she will enter the inpatient treatment program she's been trying to avoid by going to AA. Or you could make it clear to a child who's just gone through treatment that if he slips, he's out of the house. Whatever the plan, it should be put into effect immediately if a relapse occurs.

cal care, and schooling, if that's the deal, but otherwise it's time to let go.*

A HOLIDAY SLIP

"My father was doing really well once he started to go to AA, and then he went to an office Christmas party and came home smashed. My mom and I are crushed and don't know what to do. Should we have stopped him from going to the party?"

That certainly wasn't the Christmas present you wanted, but we don't always get what we want. Your distress is understandable but not constructive. If you've been going to Al-Anon or Alateen, you know that you can't control the alcoholic/addict in your home (and certainly not at his office party) and that you're not responsible for his actions.

Your attitude, however, will make a difference. Don't cry, harangue, or threaten over this slip, or allow it to break your heart or spirit. A slip or two along the road to sobriety is not unusual. It's helpful to have a contingency plan ready for such occasions (see below). If you don't, set one up at the first opportunity. For now, let your father know that you aren't shocked or disappointed (though you may indeed be very upset), and that you're still there to support his recovery. You could also explain that you're nervous when he doesn't go to meetings, distressed when he drinks, and worried about the impact of his behavior on the family. Make clear that whatever his reason or excuse for drinking, it's not good enough.

Hopefully this was just a momentary slip and your father will get right back on the wagon. But if he heads for the corner bar tomorrow, bite your tongue, even if it hurts. Don't tell him to call his sponsor or to go to a meeting. That's his responsibility. And it could backfire—he might go out to drink to spite you.

Instead of trying to control your dad (which you know has never worked), let him know that you've decided to

*The exception to the rule: When the alcoholic/addict is suffering from organic brain damage and memory is poor, it's okay to remind him about a meeting or to call his sponsor when it seems necessary.

MATTERS OF LIFE AND DEATH

Does it ever make sense to step in to prevent your loved one from self-destructing? Sometimes. If your spouse, parent, child, or friend is high on drugs or alcohol and about to drive a car, taking away the keys could save a life, or several. Likewise, if he or she intends to operate machinery or work at any safety-sensitive job while under the influence, you can prevent a catastrophe by notifying a supervisor. Ideally, it's best to discuss this type of situation in a moment of relative sobriety, but even if you haven't, you have a moral responsibility to take action. If suicide or violence is threatened, step in and call the police.

get help for yourselves. You and your mother should go to an Al-Anon (or Alateen) meeting for the support you need. Call your sponsor, an Al-Anon friend, your clergyperson (if he or she is familiar with alcohol problems), or a doctor, counselor, or therapist you or your dad has worked with before. Try meditation, prayer, exercise, or any of the tips recommended for alcoholics who are upset (see page 326) but which work just as well for "civilians."

It's tough, but you need to detach yourselves from this situation, to look at it from the point of view of "innocent bystanders." That's healthier for you than taking your father's drinking as somehow your responsibility.

If you had tried to stop him from going to the party, that wouldn't have worked. You can't put him in mothballs. In a sense, it's what your parents have had to do with you as you got older—allowing you to be your own person, and make your own mistakes.

This situation isn't easy for you. But if we want the dignity to live our own lives as we see fit, we have to give the same opportunity to those we love.

RELAPSE

"My husband just relapsed for the second time—just when things were going well. I'm so angry I could scream!"

Go to an Al-Anon meeting instead. If you absolutely have to scream, lock yourself in the bathroom to do it. Fight the urge to scream at your spouse. That kind of behavior may give you a momentary sense of satisfaction, but in the long run it won't help either of you. Anger and screaming beget screaming and anger. Certainly you should express your feelings, but calm down and think before you speak or act. An alcoholic/addict is much more likely to criticize himself if others don't beat up on him first.

But remember, if he wants to kill himself with chemicals, you can't stop him. If he hasn't been in treatment, you might try an intervention aimed at getting him into an inpatient program. If he's already been to one, a different inpatient facility or a long-term outpatient program might be called for. If he refuses to take the necessary steps, then you may have to take some, such as asking him to move out. Or moving out yourself.

"The guy I live with went through a treatment program because his employer insisted. Now he's drinking again, as if he didn't learn anything."

It's doubtful that he didn't learn anything, no matter how scornful he may be of the experience. There's one thing that treatment is guaranteed to do: destroy one's innocence about alcoholism. Your friend will never again drink as casually and obliviously as he did before. He's been told what he's doing to himself, and the nature of his disease. When he drinks, he can no longer say (at least not with any conviction) "I drink because of my girlfriend (or my parents or my job, or because I'm crazy)." When he sits at a bar, there will be a sense of paranoia (any moment someone will flash a badge and say, "I'm from AA—you're coming with me"). Best of all, a door will have opened. He will know where to turn for help when he's ready for it. That doesn't guarantee that he will at some point seek help voluntarily, but it improves the odds.

You can help by not enabling his drinking or allowing him to trap you in his web. Going to Al-Anon to learn how you can detach yourself will help both of you.

"When I first started to go to Al-Anon meetings, I thought that everyone else's family was pretty much like mine—lots of screaming and crying, a lot of unhappiness and fear. I was amazed to find that families could really be happy."

AN ABUSIVE SPOUSE

"For twelve years my husband drank himself blind every weekend, and for twelve years he physically abused me every weekend. He's been sober for three months and wants to move back in. I don't know if I should let him."

If in the past you were seriously injured (broken bones, bruises, cuts), if you had to seek medical aid at your doctor's office or the emergency room, or if you had to call the police because of his violence, the answer is certainly no—not yet. Assuming you still have feelings for him and would like to make another try at your marriage, he should not come home until the situation is evaluated by a professional accustomed to dealing with family abuse.

You should also talk to your spouse about his abusive behavior when he was drunk—with a professional on hand to referee. Before you share the same living quarters, contingency plans should be in place for the possibility of a resumption of violence or drinking. For example, if he drinks or attempts to hurt you again, you will pick up and leave for an unspecified safe haven immediately, one to which he can't possibly gain access. He will then have twenty-four hours to vacate the premises permanently. If you think he might not keep his word, work out a legal contract to that effect in advance.

Whether or not you decide to give him another chance, you should get counseling for yourself so that you will have another chance, too. You need to learn your rights and how to protect them.

MISSTEPS

"I'm a nervous wreck because I'm afraid everything I do is going to upset my wife and that she'll start drinking again."

Family members often go from walking on eggs with an alcoholic/addict to walking on eggs with a recovering alcoholic/addict. By sweating your every move, you're inadvertently continuing that old pattern of thinking you control your mate's destiny. You don't. You shouldn't. She has to learn to stay sober no matter what you do to annoy, offend, or even enrage her.

Stop worrying about saying or doing the wrong thing, and begin to express yourself honestly and effectively. (Most of us think we're getting our message across when we really aren't.) If you're upset about something, say so—not vindictively, but calmly and openly. By sharing your experiences and strengths, you can help each other find answers. But you have to accept that your answers and hers may not always be the same. For help in improving communication, see page 373.

SOBRIETY AND SEX

"Since my wife has stopped drinking, she hasn't shown any interest in sex."

Don't take this disinterest personally. Very few people in early recovery are interested in making love. There are a great many reasons, some related to hormonal changes, some to psychological and emotional unreadiness, and some to relationship factors. You can speed your spouse's return to a normal sex life in several ways:

❖ Read Chapter 11 so that you understand completely what is going on—for her and for you. Also try the tips suggested in that chapter.

❖ Don't put the pressure on. That tends to turn the romance off.

❖ Woo your spouse instead. Remember how it was when you first met? Remember how your romance was kindled? Rekindle it.

❖ If you think she may be worried about having contracted AIDS or another sexually transmitted disease (or if you are worried that she may have), ask her doctor to suggest testing (see page 306).

❖ Give it time. Like everything else in recovery, rebuilding your sex life often is a slow and steady process that takes patience.

❖ Work on the relationship (see Chapters 10 and 19). Satisfying sex may be impossible until you two feel comfortable with each other again. Work on communication, trust, and enjoying each other in other ways. If infidelity was a symptom of addiction, you will need to talk about it, possibly with a professional marriage counselor.

❖ If the lack of a sex life is interfering with your relationship or with recovery, or if it persists into the second half of the year, get professional help.

HELPING YOUR CHILD

"Our son is in an outpatient drug recovery program and seems to be doing well. He's gotten a job, but he needs a car to get to and from the job. Of course he doesn't have a penny and could never get credit. We can afford to get him a secondhand car—but should we?"

Parents with kids in recovery have to walk a very narrow line between helping and enabling. Sure your child may need help, especially if his life has been a mess for a couple of years or more. But you've got to avoid giving the kind of help that will enable him to go back to using drugs.

First of all, offer only no-frills assistance. Limit it to the necessities of modern life: food, basic clothing, shelter, and transportation. Second, if he's living at home, have him contribute toward his room and board. Also expect him to be a participating family member, helping with the marketing, cooking, dishes, laundry, cleaning, or wherever his participation is needed most.

Finally, tie all assistance to adherence to his treatment plan. If he stops going to counseling sessions or meetings, or starts seeing old friends and going to old playgrounds, cut it off immediately. (Of course, let him know in advance that there are strings attached.) Not only will this set the ground rules for your help, it will also teach him the important lesson that even a free lunch has its price and every action its consequences. Smart people try to foresee them.

If you do buy him a car, keep it in your name and register him as one of the drivers (you may have to pay a premium for insurance). Build in a goal for him to strive for. Let him know that at a certain point in his recovery, perhaps after two years of sobriety, you will sign the vehicle over to him.

HAVING HAD ENOUGH

"My father has been an alcoholic for as long as I can remember. Now because his employer finally told him that he had to quit drinking or lose his job, he has gone for treatment. Well, that's great for him. But Mom and I feel that we've had enough and don't want him back in the house."

Think about what you're saying. For years while this guy was drinking, you let him live with you. Now that he's hoping to turn his life around and behave himself, you want him out. Does that make sense?

Even if it doesn't, your sentiments echo angrily in thousands of other homes every day, probably for several reasons: resentment and anger—rejection is a way to get even. Fear—is he really going to go straight? And role changes—now that he's promising to behave, the delicate balance of relationships in the family is likely to change. And change, even if there's a chance it might be for the better, is always unsettling.

But your father has a disease. Now, when he's trying to do something about it, is not the time to bar the door against his return. Now is the time to give him your support. Try to stick together as a family, or at the very least, keep your options open until you've given his sobriety a chance and can better judge whether or not all the hurts can be mended. In the meantime, learn all you can about his disease. Go to Al-Anon. If you need it, get professional help. But don't throw in the towel until you've had a chance to clean up the mess. Good stuff could be underneath.

SELF-DESTRUCTIVE THOUGHTS

"My wife has been sober for six months, but she still seems depressed a lot of the time. Several times she's alluded to feelings of not wanting to live. How seriously should I take such comments?"

Very seriously. Many people who talk about suicide actually attempt it, and suicide is especially common among alcoholics/addicts,

"I didn't want my husband to begin to take back any responsibilities unless I decided to give them back. I didn't want to let him have his name in the phone book. I didn't want him to drive a car. I didn't want him to pick up the children at school. He had lost his rights in my eyes by reason of what he had done."

even those in recovery. So get professional help for your wife immediately. If you don't know where to turn, look up "Suicide Hotline" in your local telephone directory—most communities have one. If you can't find one, call your local mental health center or hospital emergency room. Don't delay. And don't assume you can put it off if your spouse suddenly feels better. Many suicides are attempted at "I feel much better" moments. They often feel better because they've decided to go ahead and end it all.

"The most powerless I ever felt was when my daughter was using drugs. It was only when she got real bad and I accepted that she could die that I was able to detach. I knew there was nothing I could do to help her. But I knew I wasn't going to contribute to her dying, either. What a burden that lifted!"

BREAKING THE NEWS TO GRANDPARENTS

"Our son has a serious drug problem and is beginning inpatient treatment. I don't know whether or not to tell my parents, who dote on him."

Grandparents and their grandchildren have a very special relationship. If your parents live nearby and see your son often, they probably are aware that something is wrong. If you withhold information from them, they will feel hurt and left out. They also may think that something even worse is going on. And finally, you will miss the support you can get from them.

How to best broach the subject will depend on your relationship. If your parents are easy to talk to, tolerant, and understanding, then just come out with it. If you think they will be crushed, you may have to hold off letting them know the extent of the problem immediately, or you'll have an extra problem on your hands—comforting them. In that case, wait a week or two. Then when treatment is going well, sit down and talk with them. At the same time, have your son write a letter to them, with the help of his counselor. It will reassure them that although there is a problem, the process of bringing it under control is underway. The same kind of letter should go to grandparents who have been told all.

If your parents live far away, there's no rush to tell them until you see them, since hearing the news from you in person will be easier than getting it via a letter or the telephone. But don't wait too long, or they will begin to wonder what the tension they feel, even at a distance, is all about.

Grandparents, like others in the family, need to be educated about the disease of alcoholism/addiction. Get them some written material, perhaps have them read this chapter, even invite them to an Al-Anon meeting. Keep them posted on their grandchild's progress. Grandparents can also be a source of information. They may know about other alcoholism/addiction problems in the family: "Oh, yes, Uncle Joe drank like a fish. It killed him." Or "Sarah's daughter Mary swallowed pills like candy. They kept it quiet, but she was hospitalized for a while."

Of course, if either or both of your parents have an unacknowledged drinking problem of their own, they may be more difficult to confront. They will probably deny your son's problem as they deny their own. On the other hand, they may also become aware of the family nature of the disease and be willing to take steps to help themselves. If they don't, when your son is home and doing well, he might want to be involved in an intervention with them. He would be strong medicine.

THE SAFETY OF A GRANDCHILD

"We have a daughter who was sober for a year and then started drinking again. We're heartsick. She's divorced and has a three-year-old child, and we think he isn't getting the care he needs."

You can't do anything about your daughter, other than arranging an intervention (see page 508) and getting her into treatment. As painful as it is, she is the only one who can make decisions about her life. About all you can do is pray—and go to Al-Anon yourself.

But your grandchild is a different matter. If you suspect he is being abused or neglected, it's your responsibility to do something about it. If a carefully staged intervention doesn't work, if your daughter persists in her abuse of alcohol, you should talk to her about her child's welfare. Offer to care for him until she decides to get sober. If she refuses, retain a lawyer and seek temporary custody of the child. Difficult as it may be, avoid anger and recriminations toward your daughter. That won't be constructive. Keep in touch with her, let her know you love her, allow her to see the child if you gain custody, but don't do anything that will help her to continue drinking (see Enabling, page 501).

PART VI

THE REST OF YOUR LIFE IN RECOVERY

Making the Most of Your Chemical-Free Life

As you progress from phase to phase in recovery, most of your early fears and concerns will drop away and be forgotten. One will, however, stay with you for the rest of your life: the fear of relapse. Whether you swore off your once-favorite chemical yesterday or ten years ago, or even twenty years in the past, your disease can become active again if you lower your guard.

Another major recovery concern that should stay with you forever is "payback"—what you can do in a concrete way to help others find the joys of sobriety as a way of saying "thank you" for your own second chance at a new life.

29

RELAPSE ALERT

Most accidents are programmed to happen. A distracted parent allows a toddler to play near an open stairway. A harried cook neglects to wipe up a spill on the kitchen floor. A sports fan polishes off a six-pack at a game and then heads home behind the wheel of his car. The tragedies that follow are almost inevitable.

It's the same with relapse. It usually begins long before the recovering addict yields to the prodding of a companion or of a treacherous inner voice with "Oh, what the hell! Why not?" So it's important to become familiar with attitudes and behaviors that can undermine recovery, to be alert to situations that can trigger relapse, and to recognize warning signs that your recovery is about to take a turn for the worse.

A GUIDE TO PREVENTING AND SURVIVING RELAPSE

It's no secret that the risk of relapse is greatest in the first few months of being clean or sober. That risk diminishes with time, but it never completely fades away. Many life events—for example, ill health—can send the risks soaring once more.

Those with the incurable disease known as alcoholism/addiction are always walking the edge of a cliff. Just one false move, one misstep, and they can tumble deep into the abyss of drinking and drugging. After the fall it's not impossible to haul oneself up again. But you can spare yourself a lot of bruises if you build a good strong fence between you and the cliff. Whether you just picked up a thirty-day chip or took a bow at a meeting for thirty years, continued vigilance is the price of sobriety.

WHAT IS RELAPSE?

Relapse is a medical term describing the return of signs and symptoms of a disease after an apparent recovery. You can have a relapse with the flu—and you can have one with the disease of alcoholism/addiction. In neither case is the prognosis grave. It's likely you will recover from both, but while the flu will probably be self-limiting and go away on its own, you'll have to take a very positive steps to recover from relapse into alcoholism/addiction.

A person in recovery is considered to be in relapse when he or she starts drinking or using again. The behavior can be out of control or there may be an attempt to control it. A slip, on the

Guide Lines

❖ It's possible to recognize a relapse before it happens, and to take steps to prevent it.

❖ Although many people in recovery relapse once (or more often), relapse certainly isn't necessary to a solid recovery.

❖ One drink or one drug doesn't have to lead to an irreversible relapse.

❖ A relapse isn't the end of the world—not if you learn from it how to avoid a repetition.

other hand, as we use the term here, is taking that first drink (or drug) or two and getting help before going further.

Anywhere from 10 to 60 percent of those in recovery will have at least one relapse. (The percentage depends on whose statistics you use. No two programs have the same success rates.) Most relapses occur early in recovery, and the prognosis for those who relapse early is better than for those who relapse later. Of those who relapse after a solid foundation in treatment, most will eventually have a successful recovery. These people come to understand relapse not as a failure but as a lesson in how to succeed, not as a sign that they should resign themselves to a life of substance abuse, but as a sign that they need to work harder at escaping that life.

MYTHS RELATED TO RELAPSE

Because relapse is shrouded in shame and embarrassment, many myths have grown up around it—myths that may endanger recovery if they aren't recognized as such. You may have heard these recited as gospel:

"Relapse is inevitable." Sometimes people in recovery hear so much about relapse that they begin to believe it's part of getting better. "I might as well have my slip now and get it over with" is not an uncommon attitude. But in fact, most successfully sober individuals have never relapsed, and the chances of staying sober in the long run are better if you don't relapse.

"I've been close to a slip only once in all the years I've been sober. I got on my knees, said the Serenity Prayer, and sweated. The compulsion passed."

"Relapse inevitably means failure." For some people, relapse *is* an important part of recovery. They aren't truly committed to sobriety the first time around; they haven't experienced enough pain to persuade them that they can't safely drink or use drugs. But they learn something each go-round, and by the time they're truly motivated to remain clean and sober permanently, they've acquired the tools to get the job done. Of course, those who don't learn from their relapses are doomed to more of the same.

"Relapse can't be prevented." Not only is it possible to prevent a relapse, it is possible for the great majority of people in recovery to do so successfully. Avoiding relapse is much less a matter of willpower than of being knowledgeable about what causes a relapse, how to minimize the risk in unsafe situations, what the signs of impending relapse are, and what to do if a slip is about to occur.

"Relapse after a period of sobriety and it will take months or years to hit bottom again." Alcoholism/addiction is a progressive disease. It continues to get worse in a kind of shadow progression during recovery. Those who relapse usually find that when they wake up "the morning after," they are in worse trouble than when they swore off. In fact it generally takes only a few hours to a few days to reach bottom in a relapse.

LAPSES THAT CAN TRIGGER A RELAPSE

If you've been in recovery for a while and have really been paying attention, you can probably come up with a long personal list of behaviors and attitudes that could put you at risk for relapse. Your list may include the following:

Dishonesty. Shakespeare said it first, but it's a reminder that can't be repeated too often: "To thine own self be true." Self-deception denies your disease, dodges your responsibilities, neglects the fundamentals of your recovery program, rationalizes unwise actions, and fails to evaluate you (or your good and bad traits) honestly.

You live outside your own value system—cheating on your spouse, defrauding your employer, breaking the hearts of your parents. A sociopath, whose mental illness makes him hostile toward society and its moral code, might not have a problem with this, but most of us are uncomfortable living a lie. And this discomfort can jeopardize recovery. Even if you aren't ready to admit that what you are doing is wrong, if you know someone is being hurt by it, you are still endangering your recovery by creating uneasy feelings of guilt. Such feelings are hard to live with, and it's natural to want to smother them with drugs or drown them in gin.

It's just as necessary to be truthful with others—at home, at work, at play. Failing to confide the truth, nothing but the truth, to those trying to help you—physicians, counselors, sponsors, others in AA—is another way dishonesty can sabotage recovery. Sometimes we lie as a way of protecting ourselves, hoping to avoid the consequences of the truth. But in the long run, the consequences of lying are always worse. We lose the respect of others. Perhaps worse, we lose self-respect.

Those with successful recoveries will testify that absolute honesty is the single most important factor in preventing relapse. See page 202 for more about dishonesty and recovery.

HALT. Hunger, Anger, Loneliness, or Tiredness can make you vulnerable to relapse, so be sure to guard against each of these. Eat three square meals a day, with regular snacks in between to keep up your blood sugar level and ward off hunger. Talk about your anger and examine it honestly. Take charge of it before it begins to take charge of you (it is believed to act as a mood-changing drug, making people do things they wouldn't do otherwise). Remain active in a recovery community such as AA, and attend meetings often enough to keep loneliness at bay. Regular social activities with recovering friends are also helpful. When loneliness troubles you, immediately call a sponsor or AA buddy. Avoid overdoing at both work and play to avoid fatigue; don't take on more than you can handle. Exercise regularly, since moderate amounts of exercise increase energy levels.

Unrequited thirst. Finding yourself thirsty (especially hot and thirsty) with nothing to drink but a frosty beer can be extremely risky. So avoid such situations by being sure that, whether you are sailing a boat, cheering your favorite team at a ball game, or playing a sweaty set of singles on a tennis court, you're well-supplied with frosty sodas, juice, or ice water. If necessary, bring your own thermos.

Negative feelings. Resentment, ingratitude, self-pity (telling yourself you're the victim of bad luck rather than someone who's made poor choices), pessimism (your thermos is always half-empty rather than half-full), impatience (you crave instant gratification—one day at a time isn't good enough), frustration ("Why can't everything go just the way I want it to?"), are all attitudes that can undermine recovery. If you don't acknowledge these feelings and deal with them quickly and constructively (see Chapter 15), they will inevitably lead you over the edge of Relapse Cliff.

"On a flight to Hawaii, free miniature drinks were passed out and I got off the plane with a pocketful for my 'friends back home.' It suddenly dawned on me that I was an alcoholic, and I got rid of them as soon as I could."

Unrealistic expectations. Expecting too much too soon (a trait typical of alcoholics/addicts) can lead to disappointment and resentment, which in turn can lead to the nearest bar or dealer. In early recovery, it should be enough that at the end of each day you can say, "I've stayed clean and sober today." See page 315 for dealing with expectations realistically.

Unattended-to Phase One issues. If you haven't worked Steps One, Two, or Three, if you never got a sponsor (or don't really confide in the one you have), if you haven't dealt with other basic issues of early recovery (Chapters 6 through 15), then your recovery has a weak foundation. This will make it difficult for you to be strong when faced (as you will be daily) with temptation.

Unresolved Phase Two issues. If problems in your relationships, your work, or other aspects of your life still have not been adequately faced and resolved, they will make negative feelings simmer and eventually come to a boil. If this is the case, return and finish your Phase Two work now, before its unresolved issues finish you. Most winners in recovery agree that they can't afford the luxury of "emotional litter" in their lives. Dealing with emotions rather than ignoring them keeps that litter from piling up. See Chapters 17 through 21.

Renewing old friendships. Once recovery seems well established, it may seem silly or over-cautious not to see an old friend you used to drink or use with. "She called and sounded so friendly—why shouldn't I see her? Am I supposed to live the rest of my life like an orchid in a hothouse?" But unless and until that person is in recovery too, you're in permanent danger of picking up where your relationship left off. (See page 173.)

Getting back on the old merry-go-round. As recovery progresses, feelings of invulnerability are likely to recur: "I'm doing great. Seeing some of my old playmates, visiting some of my old playgrounds, won't bother me a bit." But that's like skydiving without a parachute: the odds are definitely not in your favor. If you find yourself in-

"My house was wiped out by a tornado. I lost $20,000. I just sat on the ground and cried. If I'd had a bottle, I would have drained it. But my friend said, 'Hey, man, you can get another house. You still got you. *God made sure you were somewhere else when that twister came.'"*

vited to a party or other event that is important to attend but that you suspect could be risky, take an AA ally along if at all possible. Study the partying tips on page 180 and use them to plan your every move ahead of time: What will I do if offered a drink? A joint? A snort? When you're on the spot, stick to your plan like the tortoise to his shell.

Remembering the old days—otherwise known as "romancing the drink [or the drug]." Putting a shine on the bad old days ("Hey, remember that time when we all got loaded and . . . ?") can make them suddenly seem like good old days. Don't dwell on the past or you'll dwell in it. If someone else tries to romanticize your drinking or drugging days, put on the brakes with your own memories: "Yeah, and you vomited all over yourself and your date." If you're the one who starts romanticizing, bring yourself up short.

Indulging in doubtful habits. Nicotine (in tobacco) and sugar (in most processed foods and almost all desserts) have been associated with relapse in some recoverees. Although studies haven't shown this scientifically, a number of observers nevertheless believe it's a fact. Other compulsive behaviors—gambling, sex, eating—may also weaken defenses against relapse. So follow the life-extending, sobriety-sustaining health habits recommended in Phase Three.

Shifting the blame. If you can always find someone or something else to blame for your problems, past or present, you aren't putting the responsibility for your life where it belongs: in your own lap. By relinquishing your responsibility to deal with your life, you return to the irresponsible behavior of addiction. The next step is to return to addiction itself.

SITUATIONS THAT INVITE RELAPSE

Sometimes those in recovery don't do anything specific to set themselves up for a relapse, but life itself sets them up. Certain situations, while not inevitably leading to relapse, do weaken one's defenses. The only protection: eternal vigilance. If you find yourself in one of the following situations, stay constantly aware of the risk of relapse. As necessary, take the steps on page 547 to be sure that the moment passes you safely by.

Bad times. Not surprisingly, many people relapse when something goes awry in their lives. Almost any major problem can trigger a slip, including the death of a spouse, child, or other loved one; the loss of a job; natural catastrophe (a home destroyed by fire or flood, for example); or an illness—anything from a cold to cancer.

Good times. While you might be alert to a possible slip when things go wrong, you're much less likely to be wary when everything's coming up daffodils—you inherit a substantial sum of money, you patch up your marriage, you get a great new job or a promotion. In fact, most people tend to let their guard down completely when everything is going right. They toast themselves mentally: "I'm doing great. Staying sober is easy. I don't have the problems others have. I'm in control." Gradually, counseling sessions are canceled, "better" ways are found to spend evenings than going to AA meetings, and before you know it, you've slipped on a banana daiquiri.

Milestones. Being sober for thirty days, six months, one year, or five years is certainly something to celebrate. But it should also be a reminder: *Keep working your program.* A clean and sober anniversary can be a time of confidence and elation ("Everything's going so well!"), of anxiety and depression ("Things are going *too* well; it can't last." or "They aren't going well enough"), or of complacency ("This sobriety is a breeze; now what?"). Unless it's also a time of caution and reflection, a recovery milestone can put recovery at risk. Don't be the runner who, having crossed the finish line and achieved his goal of running a marathon, bronzes his running shoes and takes to his rocking chair.

Few people pick up their chip and then celebrate with a binge, but many think, "Okay, I've proved I can do it. Now I can relax a little." They take to that rocking chair, skip the next meeting or neglect to check in with a sponsor, and their sobriety becomes vulnerable. The riskiest clean and sober anniversaries, experience shows, seem to be three months, six months, and one year.

Vacations. Getting away from it all can be a tonic for anyone, recovering or not. But because that often takes vacationers far away from their usual support systems, it can also be a great opportunity for a gin-and-tonic relapse. So pick and choose vacation destinations thoughtfully. Choose recovery-related retreats and conventions in early recovery, and later on stick to resorts and destinations that stress sobriety. When possible, share vacations with support group friends. For tips on sober getaways, see page 210.

"I was on a cruise with booze offered all over the ship, night and day. I suddenly felt a desire to drink. I prayed real hard, and the desire never became a compulsion."

Change. Starting a new relationship or breaking up an old one, switching jobs, and moving all seem to increase the risk of relapse. It's not surprising—all rank high on any psychologist's list of super-stressors. They all involve ventures into the unknown, and the attendant high anxiety creates an uneasy thirst. So if you can avoid or postpone them, make no major changes until you are solidly in Phase Two, and even then be alert to the potential risk.

Boredom. Once the early work of recovery is completed and work and relationships are on an even keel, the addict may long wistfully for excitement—often for the wrong kind. If you crave the rush that excitement brings, get it the safe way (see page 209).

Illness or physical ailments. Aches and pains—headaches, backaches, surgery, dental problems, injuries, or other physical complaints—all have been linked to the start of drinking and drugging. Not surprisingly, they've been linked to relapse too. Sometimes that's because of the anxiety and depression the illness triggers. Sometimes it's because of the medications prescribed to chase the pain.

Some people in recovery feel safe taking a prescribed medication (sometimes, even a sleeping preparation), as though the doctor's imprimatur somehow magically prevents a drug from acting like a drug. Not so. The patient believes he can control such usage, but more often than not finds out too late that he was wrong. Result: relapse. And the fact that the drug was prescribed and used with the best of intentions, and that relapse was accidental, doesn't help its victim one bit.

So if you experience frequent headaches, intestinal disturbances, muscular spasms, or any other symptoms, be alert for signposts warning that you're speeding toward what might be called a medically prescribed relapse. If you become seriously ill and require medication for either treatment or surgery, or if you're about to have a baby and think you might need pain relief in labor, be sure that you and your physician follow the guidelines discussed on page 247.

Unexpected exposure. You're a nurse, and you find yourself with the key to the narcotics cabinet. You're doing the spring cleaning, and you turn up a cache of vodka you'd forgotten about. On the commuter train en route home every evening, you start running into a guy you used to get high with. If you don't have a workable plan for such eventualities, relapse is only a misstep away. So be sure you plan ahead (see page 549).

Triggers: something you see (powdered sugar spilled on the table, a photogenic frosty mug of beer in a TV commercial, the outfit you used to wear to wild parties); something you hear (rock music you associate with shooting up, soul music that takes you back to your drinking days, the music you were listening to the first time you smoked a joint); something you smell (bourbon or stale beer, the perfume worn by the girl you used to do cocaine with, vanilla extract when you're baking a cake, an acrid whiff of marijuana from the joint of a passer-by); something you taste (nonalcoholic beer or wine, ice cream artificially flavored with rum, a bowl of pretzels or salted peanuts like the ones canny bartenders use to double your thirst); something you touch (grains of sugar, a leather jacket, a flat mirrored surface or a highly polished oak countertop). Any of these flashback stimuli (see Chapter 9 for more of them) could trigger a craving for alcohol or drugs. Again, vigilance—being prepared for psychological ambushes—lessens the danger.

"This guy I knew was sober for eighteen years. He made a million dollars. He got so cocky, he was sure he could handle anything, including just one drink. He took it, never got sober again, and six months later he was dead."

RED FLAGS

Relapse doesn't just happen. There's an early warning system built into recovery. If you're always on the alert for its red flags—behaviors that quietly (or noisily) signal that a relapse may be imminent—you can head off a slip before it happens. If any of the following are suddenly part of your life (or if they've been part of your life in recovery all along), then take the preventive action on page 549 immediately. There's no time to lose.

Elaborate excuse-making. When you find yourself going to great creative lengths to rationalize or explain away your behavior—why you missed a couple of meetings, why you've been late to dinner every night for a week,

SMOKING: A RELAPSE FACTOR?

For years, recovering addicts and alcoholics deprived of their drugs of choice puffed desperately at cigarettes, getting what lift they could from nicotine. While the rest of the population was abandoning the smoking habit by the tens and hundreds of thousands, those in recovery smoked passionately on. It was easy to mistake an AA meeting for a political convention.

Then a few things happened. First, recoverees (and those treating them) began to realize it wasn't enough just to save their lives through sobriety and to enjoy them through fulfilling relationships, work, and play. It was also important to extend their lives through improving health habits—which clearly meant that smoking had to be reconsidered.

Second, the world in which recoverees were living became more and more smoke-free. Workplaces. Restaurants. Movie theaters. Public transit. Finally, reports began emerging suggesting that nicotine, as a mood alterer, might trigger relapse by having a depressing effect on the recovering addict. It was already known to open the gates to teen involvement in other drugs.

This led to a sudden flowering of "No Smoking" signs at AA meetings—first for isolated seating sections, then for entire groups. And some treatment programs asked sensibly, why not withdraw patients from nicotine at the same time they withdraw from other troublesome substances? And so they did.

Suspicion is rampant, but it's still unclear whether or not nicotine is a relapse factor. What is clear is that this is a drug every recoveree (and everyone else) is better off without.

or why a report at work is long overdue—you are probably tottering on the brink.

Panic in the streets. Or anywhere else. Anxiety or panic attacks (page 318), thoughts of suicide, compulsive behaviors (gambling, promiscuous sex, page 154), and eating peculiarities (page 442), are sure signs that your life is getting out of hand. They require immediate attention. If seeing to your Phase One priorities doesn't get you better fast, seek help from a professional.

Irresponsibility. You start avoiding your commitments, failing to do what must be done. You do things that you know are not in your own best interests, or that are in the worst interests of those you care about.

Breaking the rules. The rules laid out for aftercare no longer seem to apply to you. You've "forgotten" to refill the prescription for Antabuse. You make a beeline for your old haunts and hangouts instead of detouring around them. You don't see the need to promptly make amends when you make a mistake. You stop taking inventory.

Lying low. You used to check in with your sponsor a couple of times a week. Suddenly you realize it's been more than two weeks.

Sick thinking. How can you tell your thinking is running a fever? You start missing the action at the bar and wonder if it really was the alcohol that caused your problems. While sipping a soda, you ponder the possibility of an innocent little "scientific experiment" in social drinking. You feel sorry for yourself. You start to dial your sponsor when temptation invades your mind; you abruptly hang up. You act on impulse rather than with forethought.

Strapping on spare parachutes. You discover that you've kept the numbers of pushers or liquor stores in your phone file, but you reason that they're important reminders of the error of your old ways. You decide to leave them there as historic markers. You turn down a ride to a meeting with an AA friend because you know you can't stop for a drink with him "just in case" you need one. When an old drugging buddy calls to ask "What's happening?", you reply vaguely rather than with a clear, firm "I'm finished with drinking and drugging. I've joined AA." (See page 165 for more on escape hatches.)

Treading water. You've hit a plateau. You follow your program faithfully, but things are not getting better day to day, month to month. If this lack of progress continues for six months to a year, it's time to think about seeking professional help, even if you had treatment (in- or outpatient) earlier. Some people are so sick initially, their ability to think so dampened by drugs, that treatment is less effective than it could have been. For these people recovery often stagnates, and some form of booster treatment *without waiting for relapse* is often the way to go.

Going to hell with yourself. You find yourself forgetting to take a bath, roll on the deodorant, brush your teeth before you slip into bed, get your hair cut, wash your clothes, see the doctor when you are ill. The next thing you're likely to forget is your sobriety. Keep an eye open for deteriorating personal hygiene. A deteriorating recovery program often lies behind it.

Switching poisons. Alcohol is your nemesis, so what could be wrong with smoking a joint or two? You're a cocaine addict who never had trouble with alcohol, so why not just switch to harmless social drinking? Or tranquilizers were your downfall, so why should a short snort be a problem? The answers will swiftly become evident (page 160).

"I was stressed and strung-out and could feel negative feelings building up, but I didn't tell anyone. I could have talked to my principal or the counselor at my school, or to my sponsor. But even before I took that first drink, pride and my alcoholic thinking took over. I said, 'I'm going to handle it myself.' I did. I went out and got drunk."

Denial. If any of the above describes your behavior, yet you insist you aren't at risk for relapse, you've just followed Alice down a rabbit hole into Wonderland. Your denial could be taking the form of refusing to believe that, now that you're sober, you have an alcoholism/addiction problem at all. Or you may be denying other problems—health problems, financial problems, relationship problems, work problems. Continued denial of reality could lead to giving up on recovery and trying to escape your problems in an old familiar way: through the brief Nirvana of substance use. The only way to "escape" problems is to face them head-on and just plain wrestle them into submission.

HEADING OFF A RELAPSE

If you notice any of the mentioned red flags (or any like them) waving in front of your face, try any or all of the following suggestions to avoid falling off the wagon and under its wheels. Remember, the compulsion to drink or drug will pass, *if you do something else.*

❖ Call your sponsor (or counselor or addiction specialist) immediately. Here's where that list of emergency numbers in your purse or wallet comes in. If you fail to contact the first person you call, work your way down the list until you do reach someone.

❖ Go to a meeting. If your usual meeting isn't on, go to one that is—across town or, if necessary, in another town. Make no excuses. Spare no expense. Do whatever it takes to get you there.

❖ Increase the number of meetings you've been going to. You may have to do a meeting a day—or more—for several days or weeks to get back on track.

❖ Put mileage between yourself and temptation. If you're a health professional, ask a trusted colleague to take charge of your key to the narcotics cabinet. Walk out of a party or other event the moment you begin to sense "that old feeling" coming on. Say sayonara to the "friend" urging you to have "just one."

❖ Try relaxation techniques, meditation, prayer, reading (the Big Book or other inspirational materials), pick-me-ups (munchies, exercise), or other methods of smothering a compulsion to use or drink (see page 162).

❖ Sign up immediately for a recovery weekend or retreat. Total immersion in a convivial, sharing, understanding atmosphere for forty-eight hours can be a very sobering experience.

❖ Remember what pre-sobriety life was really like. Now is the time to pull out that cache of rub-your-nose-in-it materials you prepared in early recovery (the history, letters, photos, videos, etc.) so that you don't forget to remember all the gory details. Ask yourself what it is you want to get out of the drink or drug that's tempting you, and whether there might be a better way to reach that goal. Also think about the long-term effects of that drink or drug on you and on those you love most.

Our surveys of successful recoveries indicate that perhaps the most powerful force restraining people who feel a compulsion is pure old-fashioned fear—of sliding back into hell, of pain and degradation, of dying.

❖ Always be prepared. Know what you would do in a whole list of perilous "if" situations: if you suddenly discover a bottle of liquor you buried long ago under a pile of sweaters in the cedar closet. If you're offered a joint by a new friend who doesn't know your history. If an emergency room doctor prescribes a mood-altering drug for the blinding pain of an ankle sprained on the ski slopes. If you run into an old drinking or drugging buddy.

Know not just roughly what you would do, but precisely, including the very words you would use. Anticipate the kind of response you might get in return, and decide how you would handle it. Role-play with AA friends to prepare for the real thing. Rehearsing sticky situations beforehand opens up a prepared escape route. And knowing

"Though I went to meetings regularly and worked my program faithfully, I never called my sponsor when I had a bad time. I didn't want to bother him with my burdens—he had enough of his own. Besides, I didn't need someone to tell me if I was right or wrong; I had to run my life my way. I didn't realize I was setting myself up for a slip."

"I went to a bar to drink. I had just seen a TV report on a drunk who had killed some kids. I had been a drunk driver, too, and I just couldn't order the drink. I got up and left."

what to expect from yourself helps you live up to your expectations.

❖ If you feel a slip is close and fear you'll fail the challenge, consider giving yourself a "booster" at a weekend retreat, a refresher program, or an in- or outpatient treatment facility.* Signing-in before you actually have a slip, you skip the detox portion of the treatment and move directly to dealing with your mental state—which is where the problem is, anyway.

❖ If you spot a pattern of regular slips, or a cycle of periodic sobriety followed by slips, try to head them off. If, for example, you seem to relapse every six months or so, check in for a booster after four or five months. This tinkering with your body's clock could block that relapse.

❖ Strengthen your recovery. Thoughtfully and honestly evaluate your recovery program to expose the weaknesses that keep you tottering on the brink of relapse. Then return to Phase One (Chapters 6 through 15) to find the best ways to overcome them. Also study Chapter 5 of the Big Book (How It [AA] Works), and suggest discussion topics at meetings that you think will be helpful. Dropping back to square one (in this case, Phase One) now, *before* a slip, will be a lot easier, and more productive in the long run. It's like a talented rookie shortstop in a batting slump being sent down to the minors for a few weeks to work on hitting the curve ball. If he looks upon it as a learning opportunity, not a disgrace, he'll be back. And so will you.

*Some treatment centers do not accept sober people, and most insurance carriers will not cover treatment for someone who hasn't relapsed. You may be able to arrange an admission for mental health reasons or for an impending relapse, and be covered that way.

IF YOU DO SLIP

First of all, remember that one slip (taking that first drink or fix) does not an irreversible relapse make. A close call or an actual slip doesn't mean you're a failure, just that your recovery program needs immediate first aid. For some people, one or more slips, or even a full-blown relapse, may become a meaningful part of their recovery process. The following steps can turn a slip into a learning experience—one that, instead of damaging your recovery, will strengthen it.

❖ Recognize that you made a mistake, but that you don't have to compound it. One drink doesn't deserve another.

❖ Don't surrender to the "Now that I've had one, what difference will a few more make?" despair. The difference could be considerable—between being sober this time next year and being dead.

❖ Leave the scene of the crime without a moment's hesitation. If you're at home, dump the drug or alcohol down the toilet before you go, or it will be awaiting you on your return. Your destination should be an AA meeting, your sponsor's home, the home of another AA friend, your counselor's or doctor's office, or some other safe haven.

❖ Get immediate help—from your counselor, your doctor, your treatment program, your sponsor, or whoever you feel would be most useful in directing you back to the road to recovery. Pick up the nearest telephone and start calling your list (page 162); keep trying until you reach someone. Don't be embarrassed to ask for help. You are not the first person in recovery to slip, and you won't be the last.

❖ No relapse "just happens." Once the immediate crisis is over, do an inventory to try to determine why you slipped. Look over the risky attitudes, behaviors, and situations described in the preceding pages, and see which may have been responsible for your fall. Were there physical cues—sights, smells, sounds, tastes—that triggered your actions? Figure out how to evade or alter them in the future, and take measures to be certain that you do.

❖ Reinforce your recovery program as though you were starting from scratch in Phase One: go to more meetings, rework the Twelve Steps, read the Big Book and other literature, do more meditations, and so on.

❖ Consider a treatment booster shot—in- or outpatient.

❖ Assure yourself that you can succeed. You can.

IF YOU RELAPSE

If at any time in recovery you return to your drinking or drug-using behavior, even only sporadically, you are in relapse. Taking the appropriate action is critical to your survival:

Get short-term help. Don't think about it—do it. As soon as you can pull yourself together to make a phone call, call your counselor, sponsor, doctor, treatment program, or another strong, reliable AA person. If you wait until you hit bottom again (even if it's just a few days), it's no melodramatic exaggeration to say that you may not live to make another stab at recovery. Leave a message if you can't reach someone, then call the next name on your list. Don't stop calling until you've reached a sympathetic and sober person who is able to come immediately. Alternatively, call a cab to take you to an AA meeting. When you get in the taxi, ask the driver to take you directly to your destination "even if I change my mind on the way."

Detoxify. If you experienced withdrawal the first time you quit, you are likely to again, even after just a small dose of alcohol or another drug. Since withdrawal symptoms are generally more severe the second time (or subsequent times) around, you may require medical detox.* A few days of hospitalization by your family doctor may be all you need. If you—and someone you trust, who has considerable experience in these matters—decide that you don't need hospitalization, fully and carefully follow the procedures on page 80 for safe home detox, even if you didn't the first time. Attempt this only if you have an AA member or another steadfast, knowledgeable, and thoroughly reliable friend keeping the vigil with you. If your AA clubhouse has cots, you may be able to withdraw there.

AN INFORMAL RELAPSE SURVEY

Of 91 sober Willingway alumni surveyed informally, 22 reported a relapse at some point in their recovery, another 38 recalled a close call, and 31 had neither a relapse nor a close call.

*Most people who had the DT's the first time will have them again, usually in a worse form, but a lucky few escape them the second time around. Some people who didn't have the DT's the first time do the next.

Get long-term help. If you didn't go the formal treatment route the first time around, now is a good time to try it. If you did but lacked motivation the first time, professional treatment may be particularly valuable now. If you really open up your mind, all the words you listened to but didn't make a part of your life then should now finally make sense.

If you have a history of periodic sobriety and relapse, professional treatment may be not only valuable but absolutely necessary for your survival. Impaired judgment from drinking could set you up for self-destructive behavior, even suicide. Typically, relapse is a time when many people alternately seethe with anger and wallow in self-pity: "I'm never going to climb out of this hell. Nobody gives a damn about me. My family'd be better off without me. I might as well end it all."

There are a variety of professional treatment options (see Chapter 3). Which you choose will depend on your health, your addiction, your wallet (or your employer's), and personal factors.

Down the line, you may be able to further protect your recovery by agreeing to drug testing at work or school, or by having your sponsor or counselor agree to report you to your boss or dean at the first sign of a slip (see page 236).

"The first time I went to treatment, I wasn't honest. I didn't think the counselor would want to hear or would understand what I'd done. It was something I was ashamed of: adultery. I really didn't put much significance on telling. I thought, 'I can handle this on my own. Let me handle the other stuff first.' But that attitude led to my downfall."

Spotlight your shortcomings. You didn't relapse accidentally, unless a friend with a distorted sense of humor sneaked some booze or hash into your beef goulash. (What were you doing associating with anyone who could think that was funny, anyway?) The newly sober recognize that they have a lot to learn about recovery. But relapsers sometimes feel that they are experts on recovery, that the relapse was "just a fluke." If told "What you need is ninety meetings in ninety days," their smart-aleck response is likely to be "I know what I need, and that ain't it!" But someone who lacks the humility necessary to crawl back on the recovery wagon is likely to see it roll away without him.

If you want to get sober again—this time for good—the first thing you're going to have to admit is that what you know about recovery couldn't fill a shot glass. Then start your program over from scratch, soul-searching for the chinks in your recovery armor that made it possible for drugs or alcohol to seep through. You can go to your old AA group, or if you find it more comfortable, make a fresh start at a new group, one where you aren't recognized as an old-timer.

Re-focus on recovery. Eventually, what you learn from your relapse will allow you to carry a powerful message to others. Right now you have to forget about being a sponsor or helping other people, and instead look after number one. Even if you've been sober for years, a relapse means you have to drop everything and concentrate on the work of recovery—on Phase One work. You'll probably complete it in less time than you did the first time around, but you need to "get it" better than you did then.

Making meetings mandatory. Don't ever let going to Twelve-Step meetings become a random activity; structure your life so that meetings are a routine part of it. Going to the same meeting at the same time and in the same place each day (or later in recovery, once or twice each week) will strengthen the habit—though the Twelve-Step meeting on Monday night, for example, may not be with the same group as the one on Friday afternoon.

Link your meeting attendance to your regular routine. Go to a meeting on your way home from work, while you're out for your exercise, or en route to an evening class. That way you know where you're going in advance and don't have to make a fresh decision each time. You can say to friends, "See you next week," or arrange to meet someone for a meal before the next meeting or to drive there together. If you find yourself trying to choose between going to a Rotary meeting (or a movie, or a basketball game) and going to your regular AA meeting, there could be trouble ahead. If you reach the point where you find yourself choosing the movie or a game over the meetings, or chronically missing meetings for other reasons, take action. There's very likely a relapse in your future.

Unmask the villains. Carefully examine your current involvement in AA (do you have and regularly confer with a sponsor? have you gotten careless and cavalier about attending meetings? do you read the Big Book and other literature often?) and your life (are your relationships healthy, is your job interesting and on track, is there too much stress, too little fun in your life, too few friends?).

Don't be embarrassed. Your friends at AA know that nobody's perfect and are probably thinking "There but for the grace of God go I." You may feel uncomfortable having to start all over

TWO STRIKES—YOU'RE OUT?

The first time you get out of treatment, you're welcomed back to the world with open arms. "Hey, glad to see you got your life together!" "This is great. Anything I can do to help?" But screw up, and nobody trusts you. Your father won't let you use the car. Your girlfriend dumps you. Someone at work sneers, "You're just a drug addict. You can't leave the stuff alone."

It would be nice if everyone around you realized that relapse is not unusual with the disease of addiction and understood your slip. But, with one or two loyal exceptions, that's not likely. Instead of having others understand your situation, you are going to have to understand theirs. They trusted you to stay sober, and once again you didn't. Not surprisingly, their patience is wearing thin.

The best you can do is level with them. Tell them a relapse wasn't in your plans, but it happened. Tell them that you don't intend this to be a revolving door, that one day at a time, you're going to try very hard to stay sober again—and to regain their trust. Explain that what you've learned from your relapse will help you (but don't make any extravagant promises).

Learn, too, from the attitudes of those around you. They are telling you in the only way they know how that your relapse hurt them as well as you. Maybe their pain coupled with your own will help you to stay clean and sober this time.

WASTED YEARS?

So you had a slip or a relapse after several years of sobriety. You may feel that you blew all that effort. That those years were a waste. But they weren't. During that time your body was free from chemicals, so from the point of view of health, they certainly weren't wasted. And from the point of view of recovery they weren't squandered either. You learned a lot. Your drinking or drugging will never be the same, knowing what you know. It's like ending a bad marriage. If you learn from your mistakes, you can do better next time you walk down the aisle. Learn what led up to this relapse and you'll do better next time too.

again, and may even have to take some ribbing at AA; but mostly you will get a lot of loving support.

Think positive. Anyone can become successfully clean and sober—anyone who is motivated and willing to put in the necessary hard work. This time, that anyone can be you.

30 THE CHALLENGES

None of us knows what tomorrow holds. What we do know is that today is always full of challenges, and if we meet those challenges to the best of our ability—willingly, with honesty and openness—we can improve our chances of a better tomorrow.

Once you have done the work of all three phases of recovery it may seem as though your task is done, you've met the important challenges, you can relax. The future and your Higher Power will take care of the rest. Not so. One day at a time, it will still be necessary to continue to grow in recovery and to enrich your life and the lives of others.

A GUIDE TO THE REST OF YOUR LIFE

If you've done the work of recovery up to now, you probably know the challenges that lie ahead and what you need to do to meet them. One day at a time, you need to:

❖ Remain clean and sober. (Without sobriety, nothing else will have any value.)

❖ Retain your honesty. (It will never lead you astray.)

❖ Continue to learn and to grow. (That's what keeps us young and alive as long as we live.)

❖ Care for yourself, body and soul. (No one can do this as well as you can.)

❖ Nurture your relationships—they'll enrich your life. (But no relationship is harmonious all the time. Each requires constant care and feeding if it is to flourish.)

❖ Hang on to your support group ties—both to keep your own recovery healthy and to help others who are more newly clean and sober. (There may be times when you'll feel that meetings have become as irrelevant as the village blacksmith and you'll be inclined to stop going entirely. But following this inclination—two years into recovery or twenty—could lead you down a slippery slope. On the other hand, becoming as slavishly addicted to the group as you were to chemicals is not a good idea either.)

❖ Work toward making your life and that of others better and better. (But

Guide Lines

❖ Growth in all aspects of recovery—relationships, career, mind, body, and spirit—should continue for the rest of your life.

❖ A major challenge that remains: helping to build a drug-free society. This will help both the community and your recovery.

❖ An awareness of the forces working against efforts to rid society of alcoholism/addiction—from corner pushers to corporate pullers—is vital if we are to overcome them.

❖ Every segment of society—business, religious communities, schools, service organizations—will have to work together to create a new attitude toward substance abuse.

always with the recognition that absolute perfection—though we may strive for it—is an unrealistic and unattainable goal.)

A GUIDE TO MAKING A DIFFERENCE

It sounds like a typical week of daytime soaps and evening "true story" melodrama, but it's all too real. A popular teacher is caught in the crossfire of two drug gangs and later dies. An elderly couple are killed by a drunk driver as they return from a church service. Riding a cocaine high, a bus driver rams an oncoming truck and five people are killed.

A drunken husband savagely beats his wife while his young children watch, helpless and horrified. A child whose parents regularly abuse him takes his anger out on his classmates and teacher, disrupting his fourth-grade class daily. A teenager with a bright future dabbles in drugs, is hooked, drops out of school, is thrown out of his home, and lives precariously on the street. A young woman's persistent drinking during pregnancy results in a newborn bearing the tragic fingerprints of fetal alcohol syndrome.

The cost of alcoholism/addiction in human lives wasted, destroyed, and made miserable is enormous. And it has to be our first concern. But this disease assaults our society in other ways too.

An alcoholic mother who spends her money on booze then shoplifts to get clothes for her children for the new school year. (The department store she "shops" in raises its prices.) When a father's chronic drug use tears his family apart, his pregnant wife goes on welfare, his kids into foster care. (Local welfare costs rise.) A couple of kids with heavy crack habits go on a burglary spree, stealing easily fenced items, and trashing houses as they go. (Everyone's homeowner's insurance in the area goes up.) On any one day, an estimated 20 to 40 percent of U.S. hospital beds are occupied by individuals suffering from the complications of alcohol abuse. (Health costs spiral upward.) A high school buys a metal detector and places armed guards at every entrance to keep dealers, guns, and other weapons out. (Education costs go through the roof and funds for teachers and textbooks are slashed.) The court and prison systems become clogged with the 80 percent of criminals who committed their crimes under the influence or to protect or expand their drug trade. (Local and federal taxes soar again.)

And what of the quality of life? Unsafe streets. Fear. Homelessness. All inextricably intertwined with the use and abuse of chemical substances, legal and illegal. You've heard it all before. The financial costs of alcoholism/addiction—in the tens of billions. The human costs—incalculable. Does alcoholism/addiction affect everyone in our society? You bet it does. Can each of us do something about it? You bet we can. What will happen if we continue to ignore a completely preventable and treatable problem? Let's not find out.

Once you were part of the mess. Now, clean and sober, you can be part of the cleanup. Not alone—you'll need plenty of help, from federal, state, and local governments, families, neighborhoods, houses of faith, law enforcement, parent groups, schools, businesses, service clubs (AARP recently began a major campaign), and health professionals. But you can do your share.

ARE THERE ANY ANSWERS?

Prohibition didn't work in 1919. It just changed saloons into speakeasies, corrupted law enforcers, and made millionaires out of mobsters. Legalizing drugs isn't the way to go, either. Alcohol is again legal and yet it is the most commonly abused drug in this country, destroying more lives than all the illegal substances combined. Hiring more police isn't much of an answer. Our courts and prisons are jammed with drug traders, and still the busy commerce in illegal substances goes on. Nor is blocking entry of drugs into the U.S. a successful solution. We did a great job intercepting shrimp boats loaded with bales of marijuana. This encouraged domestic production (illicit marijuana became the number one cash crop in Georgia) and created a market for cocaine, which is easier to smuggle in. So we solved one problem and created two.

The costly, loudly touted federal war on drugs has failed. Though the use of some drugs is down, with others it's up. High-school students are abusing illegal drugs less and alcohol more.

What *will* work? Changing people's attitudes. As long as drug use is acceptable (or macho, or "in") anywhere, there will be no shortage of customers. As long as kids grow up seeing alcohol as an integral part of life—the way we celebrate, the way we have fun, the way we relax, the way we conduct business—they will accept it as a necessity. As long as we have a society where we think of chemicals as the way to deal with difficulties, immediate gratification as the high road to pleasure, and alcoholism/addiction as "the other guy's problem," there will be a flourishing trade in substances of abuse.

But attitudes can change. They have, in fact, already begun to change. Just as cigarettes gradually went from being sophisticated to socially acceptable to socially tolerable to unacceptable, so the use of alcohol is beginning to lose its glamour and the use of drugs to be frowned upon. But the next steps won't be easy. Those concerned about the effects of smoking on health had to battle the tobacco companies. And those who want to change attitudes toward other substances will have to fight the brewers, distillers, and vintners who spend billions to glamorize their products, as well as the pharmaceutical companies who benefit from increased sales when they push easy pop-a-pill solutions to every problem.

Your goal isn't to become a modern-day prohibitionist. Some people can drink lightly and safely, and they shouldn't have to suffer the evil eye if they choose to imbibe. Your goal is to help move toward a society where there are choices—where not drinking is at least as normal and acceptable as drinking. People should not feel embarrassed and somehow "out of step" when they turn down a beer with the

WHAT ABOUT MY ANONYMITY?

If you are a member of AA or a similar mutual-help group, you are likely to be wondering if you have to adopt an alias (or call yourself "Roger W.") and sport a disguise whenever you're out crusading against the alcohol and drug plague in your community. After all, aren't you supposed to remain anonymous?

Well, "anonymous" doesn't mean that you can't become involved in community efforts under your own name; it means only that you should not talk about your relationship to Alcoholics Anonymous to the press, or on radio or TV. Aside from that, you are totally free not to wear a paper bag over your head while being interviewed, to be yourself, and to become as active and visible as you like in the ongoing struggle to change community attitudes.

pizza, a cocktail at the bar, or wine at dinner, or if they choose straight orange juice at a party or a cola at a ballgame. However, people *should* feel un comfortable when they order that fourth or fifth martini, when they get behind the wheel after consuming alcohol, when they need a drink before lunch, when others begin to notice their drinking habits.

There may be moments when you'll feel like the man (or woman) from La Mancha, tilting at a nuclear power plant. You may doubt that one person can really make a difference. But again and again, little people with big causes have spun the world on its axis. Even if it's only a letter to your legislator or local editor, those on the receiving end know that your letter, phone call, or in-person complaint represents hundreds, maybe thousands of others. If each reader of this book made just one call, wrote just one letter, registered just one grievance, the impact would be considerable.

It's been done before. When customers who drank decaffeinated coffee kept complaining to restaurants when they were served a packet of instant and a cup of hot water, restaurants got the message. Rare today is the eatery, from diner to supper club, that doesn't brew its decaf. Likewise, when the American Heart Association planned a food labeling program that didn't make sense, public outcry forced it to drop the program like a hot pot.

Exactly how you gear your campaign will depend upon you, your lifestyle, your connections. Do a self-inventory. Ask yourself, "How am I linked to society?" Whether it's through your religious life, or work, or community service, you can find a way to make a difference.

BE A ROLE MODEL

Nobody admires the drunk sleeping it off on the sidewalk, or the junkie shooting up in an alley and dining à la carte out of a garbage can. But plenty of drinkers and druggers continue to function (or at least appear to) and serve, for some, as alluring role models. Along with come-on advertising that pictures drinkers enjoying an exciting, sophisticated, romantic, sexually rich lifestyle ("If you've ever been kissed, you already know the feeling of 'X' Cognac"), they give the impression that the way to better living is through chemicals.

Recovering alcoholics/addicts can be powerful antidotes to this Madison Avenue malarkey, as positive role models, demonstrating that it's not only possible to be glamorous, romantic, macho or feminine, and to have fun with a cola in hand, it's easier than when you're sloshing your drink on other people's shoes. Look like a fashion model (male or female) if that's your bent, or like a busy executive or Ivy Leaguer, while you nurse your sparkling water with a twist. Set the mood for romantic dinners with flowers, soft lighting, beautiful music, and bubbling cider. Refresh with alcoholic-free coolers at sporting events, when boating, or while playing softball.* Show you are having as much fun as anyone else at social events (you will probably have more fun watching others making fools of themselves). Throw sober parties that are a blast—with music, dancing, games. Compare experiences with drinking friends about what it's like "the morning after."

BE A LAW-CHANGER

Legislation alone isn't going to change attitudes, but it can make a difference. Two generations ago, children in the South accepted separate restrooms and separate drinking fountains for blacks and whites as the norm. They took it for granted that blacks rode in the back of the bus. Except in documentary films, today's generation has never seen a segregated restroom, drinking fountain, or bus. Many have never even heard of them. Legislation made the difference. Legislation also can make a difference in attitudes toward drinking and drug use. A step in the right direction is the Drug-Free Workplaces law. Another is the passing of stricter laws against drunk driving in many states. All these steps reach their intended goals only if tightly linked to programs for prevention, early intervention, and treatment.

Legislation at the local school board level to clarify school policies—suspension for possession, expulsion for selling or repeated possession, for example—is an important area where much work is still to be done. So is legislation supporting better and more available treatment for alcoholism/addiction. And sober housing for people in recovery, considered by many to be the most effective form of continuing care.

Several parts of the country have already developed models. Oxford House, for example, in the suburbs of Washington, D.C., provides living space with rules against drinking and drug use. Thirty sober residences in Massachussetts house more than 300 recoverees. Los Angeles County has more than twenty very-low-rent sober-living facilities, started by area nonprofit treatment centers. With enough public pressure, on both the Department of Housing and Urban development (to provide rent subsidies and other programs) and the U.S. Department of Justice (to use anti-discrimination laws to overcome the not-in-my-neighborhood syndrome), there could be hundreds more such living facilities constructed and operating around the country.

Another approach to legislation to deal with the problems of alcoholism/addiction has been taken in North Carolina, where a user fee has been levied on alcoholic beverages to help pay for prevention, treatment, and cleaning up of the havoc wrought by abusive use of alcohol.

Support such legislation in any way you can—persuading friends in influential places, writing letters, making phone calls, joining committees. Opposition will be stiff. Powerful, well-funded interests, such as the alcohol lobby (supported by a $1.2 billion ad budget), want their market to expand,

*And stay away from beverages specially labeled "non-alcoholic." Most contain up to 0.5 percent alcohol—not a lot but enough to harm someone in recovery.

SOBERFEST CELEBRATIONS

Soberfest is to alcohol what The Great American Smoke-Out is to smoking. The center of the celebration, which can be sponsored by the local alcoholism/addiction council, the town board, business interests, and treatment centers, is a full day of saturation sobriety for an entire community. This alcoholism/addiction awareness project started in the early 1980s in Statesboro, Georgia. A week of enlightenment and fun culminates in Sober Saturday, when everyone is asked to abstain from alcohol and drugs just for the day,

In fact, Sober Saturday is an eye-opener for a lot of people. When they find they can't stay away from booze for a day or, worse still, experience the shakes and other signs of withdrawal, it makes it tough for them to hold fast to their denial.

not contract. Sometimes it will be subtle. For example, some groups that appear to be promoting "responsible drinking" are simultaneously fighting to preserve the right to advertise beer and wine on radio and TV. Why? Because they are funded at least in part by the liquor industry.* But even uphill battles have been won. This one can be, too.

SUPPORT AN ALCOHOLISM/ADDICTION COUNCIL

If you're a good organizer, start a council. If you're not, join someone who is getting one underway. (Avoid the temptation to be a one-man or one-woman show as you network to get this project started. When you share ownership of an idea with others, they are much more likely to support the concept wholeheartedly.) If you find out that there is already a council in your community, make it your business to set time aside to support it vigorously.

A local alcoholism/addiction council at the city, town, or county level is an organizational fertilizer for grass-roots change. It helps to develop public policy and programs and builds a highly visible forum for the education of the community. It can be used to assess the effectiveness of programs, determine and find funding for new programs as needed, harness the energies of community groups and individuals to participate in them, and provide clout for the forces trying to change attitudes. Some councils have developed programs for schools, provided treatment referral, and even (by providing seed money for a grant proposal) pieced together funding for a community treatment program. Once a program is off the ground, it becomes self-sustaining, and the council moves on to new projects and challenges.

Such a council should be funded locally—possibly by alcoholic beverage taxes and/or donations from organizations, businesses, and individuals. It's wise, however, not to compromise the council by accepting funds from those who produce or sell liquor; there will be corks attached. The council should be composed primarily of peo-

*The Society of Americans for Recovery (SOAR), spearheaded by former Iowa senator Harold Hughes, lobbies against the lobbyists and is not funded by liquor money. For more information, contact the Hughes Foundation, 600 East 14th Street, Des Moines, IA 50316.

ADVERTISING: DISTILLED WISDOM

One study of wine and liquor ads in thirteen national magazines found that succcess and luxury were the principal themes, followed by friendship, relaxation, and pleasure. Drinkers were depicted as wealthy more often than nondrinkers, and as likely to be successful as nondrinkers. So how can booze be bad? Although many adults may see through such blarney, youngsters are often persuaded.

Even the apparent efforts at promoting "responsible" drinking are misleading. To tell youngsters (or anyone else) that it's possible to "know when to say when" or to "think when you drink" ignores the fact that once you've had a drink or two, your brain is anesthetized. Your judgment is no longer sound, your thinking no longer clear.

The fact is that those who *don't* know when to say when do most of the drinking in this country. Only 7 percent of Americans guzzle more than half the liquor, and 30 percent swill over 90 percent. It is at these drinkers that alcohol advertising is aimed, particularly the young ones who have years of drinking ahead of them.

But the danger from advertising is more insidious still. Advertisers, because they spend huge amounts of money and provide the financial underpinnings for radio, television, newspapers, and magazines, wield enormous power. The manipulation goes on behind the scenes, but affects what we hear, see, and read. An article on how alcoholism breaks up families is turned down by a glossy magazine. The mention of smoking as a risk factor for heart disease is dropped from a cover story in another national news weekly. The dangers of both alcohol and tobacco are dropped by nervous editors from a piece on how to improve personal health. If such advertising were banned, we could better trust our eyes and ears. Support for such a ban is another way to change attitudes.

But it's not just the commercials that are delivering a dangerous message. Many TV shows still feature casual drinking: the familiar "I'm tired (upset, bored, sick)—I have to have a drink!" scene. Reasoned protest calls and letters from viewers could help raise scriptwriters' consciousness and change all that.

The alcohol and tobacco industries are quick to cry "infringement of free speech," when their advertising rights are curtailed in any way. But the writers of our Bill of Rights could hardly have imagined that the right of free speech would someday extend to those practicing deception and hawking misinformation for profit.

ple who understand addiction, either through experience or professionally. Good candidates would include recoverees, physicians, school counselors, law enforcement and Employee Assistance Program professionals, and local officials and community leaders. Don't accept representation from anyone who stands to make a profit from the continued consumption of alcoholic beverages.

USE THE POWER OF THE WORD

Preventing a fire makes more sense than waiting to put it out when it has grown to a four-alarmer. In the same way, alcohol/addiction prevention, while in some ways more difficult than treatment, can avert a lot of scorched earth. As a recoveree, you're in a position to tell your story (see page 368) and help others avoid your mistakes. You can also use the written word to influence others—writing to the President, legislators, local or national newspapers or magazines. The Beer Drinkers of America (a drinking constituency created and handsomely subsidized by brewers) and other such groups miss no opportunity to do so, and so should those of us with an alternative point of view.

Don't worry about getting into trouble at AA if your name shows up in the local letters-to-the-editor column. It's your association with AA that needs to remain anonymous, not the fact that you're in recovery. Recovery is something to be proud of. Pass it on.

USE THE POWER OF RELIGION

There is much that houses of worship can do in the battle against the disease of alcoholism/addiction. They can encourage support groups to meet on their premises, help reintegrate recoverees in their midst, offer programming that educates congregants about alcoholism/addiction, provide nonalcoholic options for ceremonies and at social functions, and make it clear that drug abuse or drunkenness will not be tolerated.

As a long-term recoveree, you can take a lead in making this happen. The best way is usually by helping to educate the religious and lay leadership of your congregation. And telling your recovery story or the story of your family's recovery is a good way to begin. This kind of "witnessing" before others in your religious community can be a wonderful opportunity to strengthen your own program, to educate others, and to open the door to recovery for still others.

"I think about God a lot now. But not the way I used to. I used to pray for things, as though God was my servant, my genie, would give me what I want. Now I just ask him to keep me clean, one day at a time."

USE THE POWER OF THE PURSE

Voting with your purse is often as effective as pulling the lever in the voting booth, and it is sometimes more effective. How do you vote with your purse? Don't patronize the restaurant that offers "Buy two drinks, get a third free," or all you can drink for $5.95, or otherwise pushes heavy drinking. Drop in and let the owner or manager know why they've lost your patronage. When selecting magazines to subscribe to, where possible favor those that do not take alcohol or tobacco ads (there aren't many, but the numbers are growing). These publications deserve your support for their refusal to be bought. Let those magazines you're avoiding know the reason why.

USE THE POWER OF THE WORKPLACE

Most of us who are employed outside the home spend at least half our waking hours at the work site. This is often a good place to wage a campaign to change attitudes about alcoholism/addiction, especially if you are in a position of influence as an employer, a manager, or a union representative. Everyone will benefit if you work toward a drug-free workplace, volunteer to assist others in your company's Employee Assistance Program, and help to disseminate information about alcoholism/addiction among coworkers. Simply letting it be known that you, a valued worker, are in recovery will send the message that those with problems should be helped to get treatment rather than being summarily fired, that hiring recoverees is good business, and that the very qualities that keep people sober also make them excellent employees.

If you're an employer or manager, read the information on page 580.

USE THE POWER OF COMMUNITY SERVICE

If volunteerism is a part of your life, the opportunities to spread the word are almost limitless. Whether you work with Little Leaguers or seniors, as a school volunteer or a Rotarian, you can use what you know about alcoholism/addiction to educate others.

YOU'VE COME A LONG WAY

They say at AA that sobriety isn't everything, it's the only thing. And to be sure you don't lose it, they remind you of a pivotal meditation: "God (or my Higher Power), I appreciate your giving me the ability to laugh. But don't ever let me forget when I cried."

The future looks bright now and understandably the bad old days of drinking and drugging are something you'd just as soon forget. But remembering your bottom, the moment that made you realize you'd had enough or that sent you shakily off to your first AA meeting, can strengthen your recovery and help to keep you clean and sober.

Something else worth remembering is a comment heard over and over at the annual homecoming weekends for Willingway alumni. We'll paraphrase: "When I first came here five (or ten or twenty) years ago, I was full of self-pity. I felt like I was a victim with nothing to look forward to but pain and misery. I learned so much in recovery—how to deal with problems instead of drowning them; why I spent so much time lying and drinking and using—that now I can honestly say I'm *glad* alcoholism and drugs messed up my life. It made the rest of my life so much better. Even with all the pain and misery, I wouldn't change that."

The hard work of recovery turns negatives into positives and pain into gain. So maybe you wouldn't recommend that all your friends go out and become alcoholic/addicts in order to improve their lives, but as you reach the end of *The Recovery Book*, you, too, may be starting to appreciate the good that came with the bad of your ordeal. We hope that whatever you've learned will always be a part of your life.

You'll know it's working for you when you can sum it all up the way Dr. John (our all-time favorite optimist) often did: "Recovery means being able to look back at the end of any day of your life—good, bad, even terrible—and say of it, 'How about that? Another sober day. Ain't life great?' "

PART VII

FOR YOUR INFORMATION

RESOURCES: WHERE TO GET HELP

THE REGIONAL ALCOHOL AND DRUG AWARENESS RESOURCES NETWORK

The Regional Alcohol and Drug Awareness Resources (RADAR) Network works in partnership with the National Clearinghouse for Alcohol and Drug Information (NCADI) and consists of state clearinghouses, specialized information centers sponsored by national organizations, and others. Each RADAR Network member offers a variety of information services. Contact the office in your state and, as needed, any specialized center.

ALABAMA
Alabama Dept. of Mental Health/Mental Retardation
Montgomery, AL
(205) 271-9258

ALASKA
Alaska Council on Prevention of Alcohol & Drug Abuse
Anchorage, AK
(907) 349-6602

ARIZONA
Arizona PRC
Tempe, AZ
(602) 965-9666

ARKANSAS
Office on Alcohol and Drug Abuse Prevention
Little Rock, AR
(501) 682-6653

CALIFORNIA
State of California Dept. of Alcohol and Drug Programs
Sacramento, CA
(916) 327-8447

COLORADO
Resource Dept.
Colorado Alcohol & Drug Abuse Division
Denver, CO
(303) 331-8201

CONNECTICUT
Connecticut Clearinghouse
Plainville, CT
(203) 793-9791

DELAWARE
Office of Prevention Resource Clearinghouse
Wilmington, DE
(302) 633-2539

DISTRICT OF COLUMBIA
Washington Area Council on Alcoholism and Drug Abuse
Washington, DC
(202) 682-1700

FLORIDA
Florida Alcohol and Drug Abuse Association
Tallahassee, FL
(904) 878-2196

GEORGIA
Georgia Prevention Resource Center
Atlanta, GA
(404) 894-4204

HAWAII
Coalition for a Drug Free Hawaii
Honolulu, HI
(808) 524-1111

IDAHO
Boise State University College of Health Science
Boise, ID
(208) 385-0577

ILLINOIS
Prevention Resource Center Library
Springfield, IL
(217) 525-3456

INDIANA
Indiana Prevention Resource Center
Bloomington, IN
(812) 855-1237

IOWA
Iowa Substance Abuse Information Center
Cedar Rapids, IA
(319) 398-5133

KANSAS
Kansas Alcohol and Drug Abuse Services
Topeka, KS
(913) 296-3925

KENTUCKY
Drug Information Service Division of Substance Abuse
Frankfort, KY
(502) 564-2880

LOUISIANA
Division of Alcohol and Drug Abuse
Baton Rouge, LA
(504) 342-9352

MAINE
Maine Alcohol and Drug Abuse Clearinghouse
Augusta, ME
(207) 289-2781

MARYLAND
Alcohol/Drug Abuse Administration
Baltimore, MD
(301) 225-6543

MASSACHUSETTS
Massachusetts Information and Referral Service
Cambridge, MA
(617) 445-1500

MICHIGAN
Michigan Substance Abuse and Traffic Safety Information Center
Lansing, MI
(517) 482-9902

MINNESOTA
Minnesota Prevention Resource Center
Anoka, MN
(612) 427-5310

MISSISSIPPI
Mississippi Department of Mental Health
Jackson, MS
(601) 359-1288

MISSOURI
Missouri Division of Alcohol and Drug Abuse
Jefferson City, MO
(314) 751-4942

MONTANA
Chemical Dependency Bureau
Helena, MT
(406) 444-2878

NEBRASKA
Alcoholism and Drug Abuse Council of Nebraska
Lincoln, NE
(402) 474-0930

NEVADA
Bureau of Alcohol and Drug Abuse
Carson City, NV
(702) 885-4790

NEW HAMPSHIRE
New Hampshire Office of Alcohol and Drug Abuse Prevention
Concord, NH
(603) 271-6100

NEW JERSEY
Division of Alcoholism and Drug Abuse
Trenton, NJ
(609) 292-0729

NEW MEXICO
Health and Environment Department/BHSD/ Substance Abuse Bureau
Santa Fe, NM
(505) 827-2601

NEW YORK
Division of Alcoholism and Alcohol Abuse
Albany, NY
(518) 473-3460

Resource Center Narcotic and Drug Research, Inc.
New York, NY
(212) 966-8700, ext. 107

NORTH CAROLINA
North Carolina Alcohol/ Drug Resource Center
Durham, NC
(919) 493-2881

NORTH DAKOTA
North Dakota Prevention Resource Center
Bismarck, ND
(701) 224-3603

OHIO
Ohio Dept. of Alcohol & Drug Addiction Services
Columbus, OH
(614) 466-6379

OKLAHOMA
Oklahoma State Department of Mental Health
Oklahoma City, OK
(405) 271-8755

OREGON
Oregon Drug and Alcohol Information
Portland, OR
(800) 237-7808, ext. 3673

PENNSYLVANIA
Keystone University Research Corporation
Erie, PA
(814) 453-4713

PUERTO RICO
Department of Anti-Addiction Services
Rio Piedras, PR
(809) 763-3133

RHODE ISLAND
Rhode Island Council on Alcoholism and Other Drug Dependence (RICAODD)
Pawtucket, RI
(401) 725-0410

SOUTH CAROLINA
South Carolina Commission on Alcohol and Drug Abuse, Drug Store Information Clearinghouse
Columbia, SC
(803) 734-9559

SOUTH DAKOTA
Dept. of Health, Division of Alcohol and Drug Abuse
Pierre, SD
(605) 773-3123

TENNESSEE
Tennessee Alcohol & Drug Association
Nashville, TN
(615) 244-7066

TEXAS
Texas Commission on Alcohol & Drug Abuse Resource Center
Austin, TX
(512) 867-8700

UTAH
Utah State Division of Substance Abuse
Salt Lake City, UT
(801) 538-3939

VERMONT
Office of Alcohol & Drug Abuse Programs
Waterbury, VT
(802) 241-2178

VIRGINIA
Virginia Dept. of MH/MR/SA
Richmond, VA
(804) 786-3909

VIRGIN ISLANDS
Division of Mental Health Prevention Unit
St. Croix, VI
(809) 773-8443

WASHINGTON
Washington State Substance Abuse Coalition (WSSAC)
Bellevue, WA
(206) 747-9111

WEST VIRGINIA
West Virginia Library Commission
Charleston, WV
(304) 348-2041

WISCONSIN
Wisconsin Clearinghouse
Madison, WI
(608) 263-2797

WYOMING
Wyoming CARE
University of Wyoming
Laramie, WY
(307) 766-4119

FOR SPECIFIC INFORMATION*

AIDS: National AIDS Hot Line: (800) 342-2437; in Spanish, (800) 344-7432; National AIDS Clearinghouse, Rockville, MD; (800) 458-5231.

*At publication, these numbers were current. If you aren't able to reach an organization, the National Institute of Drug Abuse (800) 662-4357, may be able to help.

Al-Anon: (800) 344-2666

Alateen: (800) 344-2666

Alcoholics Anonymous:** AA World Services, 475 Riverside Drive, New York, NY 10115; (212) 870-3400. Phone

**A Twelve-Step program.

for a free catalog of all publications and tapes. To order the Big Book, write to General Service Office at P.O. Box 459, Grand Central Station, New York, NY 10163 or fax your order to (212) 870-3003. There is a minimum order of $10 and a 6 percent shipping and handling charge (no charge on prepaid orders).

Alcoholism: National Council on Alcoholism: (800) NCA-CALL; National Clearinghouse for Alcohol and Drug Information (NCADI); (800) 729-6686.

Anorexia: Anorexic Hotline: (800) 873-8732.

Asians and Chemical Abuse: National Asian Pacific American Families Against Substance Abuse, Inc.,† Los Angeles, CA; (213) 617-8277.

Black Chemical Abuse: Institute on Black Chemical Abuse Resource Center,† Minneapolis, MN; (612) 871-7878.

Canadian Substance Abuse: Canadian Centre on Substance Abuse,† Ottawa, ON; (613) 235-4048.

Children of Alcoholics: National Association for Children of Alcoholics;† (301) 468-0985.

Cocaine Abuse: Hotline: (800) COCAINE; Cocaine Anonymous (CA): ** 6125 Washington Boulevard, Suite 202, Los Angeles, CA 90230, (800) 347-8998; Cocaine Baby Help Line: (800) 638-BABY (2229).

Codependency: Co-Dependents Anonymous (CoDA): ** Phoenix, AZ; (602) 277-7991.

Disabled People and Substance Abuse: Information Center on Substance Abuse Prevention for Persons with Disabilities,† Washington, DC; (202) 783-2900.

Drunk Driving: Mothers Against Drunk Driving (MADD): (800) 438-6233; Students Against Drunk Driving (SADD): (508) 481-3568.

Eating Disorders: Food Addiction Hot Line: (800) 872-0088.

Families Anonymous: ** (800) 736-9805.

Family Issues: National Drug Information Center of Families in Action,† Atlanta, GA; (404) 934-6364.

Indian Chemical Abuse: Indian Health Service,† Colorado River Service, Parker, AZ; (602) 669-2137.

Liver Disease: American Liver Foundation: (800) 223-0179.

Narcotics Anonymous (NA): ** Check your local directory or call (800) 662-4357 for a referral in your area.

Naranon: Call your local NA for referral to this NA equivalent to Al-Alanon.

Overeaters Anonymous (OA): ** (800) 743-8703.

Pill Addicts Anonymous (PAA): ** (215) 372-1128.

Pregnancy and Substance Abuse: the National Association for Perinatal Addiction Research Education (NAPARE): (800) 638-BABY; the National Institute on Drug Abuse Treatment Referral Hotline: (800) 662-4357.

Rational Recovery: (916) 621-4374 or 621-2667 if first number is busy.

Relapse: Relapse Prevention Hot Line: (800) RELAPSE.

Secular Organizations for Sobriety (Save Our Selves; SOS): Box 5, Buffalo, NY 14215-0005, (716) 834-2922.

Sexually Transmitted Diseases: STD Hot Line: (800) 227-8922.

---

†A member of RADAR (see page 566).

Substance Abuse: The National Clearing House for Alcohol and Drug Information, (800) 729-6686; TDD number for hearing impaired: (800) 487-4889 or (301) 230-2867.

Substance Abuse Prevention: Office for Substance Abuse Prevention of the Alcohol, Drug Abuse, and Mental Health Administration of the Public Health Service, P.O. Box 2345, Rockville, MD 20847-2345; (301) 468-2600.

Treatment and Referral: National Institute of Drug Abuse: (800) 662-4357 (call Monday to Friday 9 A.M. to 3 A.M., weekends noon to 3 A.M., except holidays).

Women's Issues: Women for Sobriety, PO Box 618, Quakertown, PA 18591; (215) 536-8026.

BOOKS

At last count there were more than 250 recovery bookstores in the U.S. We asked the owners of two of them (Tom Perrin of Perrin and Treggett Booksellers and Miriam Pollack of Choices) to name books that are either best-sellers for them or deserve to be. The following list is the result.*

About Alcoholics Anonymous

Alcoholics Anonymous (also known as the "Big Book"). Published by and available through AA World Services (see page 568). Also available at special recovery bookstores, in some bookstore chains, and through local AA groups (which can purchase the book at a discount). The Big Book is a compilation of personal histories of AA members starting with the founders; it also includes information on alcoholism, how AA works, on the place of the agnostic in the fellowship, and messages for wives and employers. Also available: a variety of booklets and tapes. Call for 14-page catalog: (212) 870-3400.

*If these books are not available in your local bookstore, check your telephone directory for a local recovery bookstore. If you have any difficulty finding a book, check with Perrin and Treggett Booksellers, 1338 Route 206, Skillman (Rocky Hill), NJ 08558; (609) 497-1122 or (800) 321-7911 or Choices Recovery Bookstore, 220 East 78th Street, New York, NY 10021; (212) 794-3858.

A Program for You (Hazelden)
A guide to the Big Book's design for living.

Getting Better: Inside Alcoholics Anonymous, Nan Robertson (Morrow)
A fascinating, moving, and helpful inside look at AA and the people who make it work.

As Bill Sees It, The AA Way of Life: Selected Writings of AA's Co-founder, Bill W (AA World Services).

Living Sober (AA World Services)
Eighty-eight pages of examples of how AA members throughout the world live and stay sober, one day at a time.

About the Twelve Steps

The Steps We Took, Joe McQ (August House)
A Twelve-Step teacher shares his experiences and hope.

The Little Red Book (Hazelden)
An orthodox how-to guide and intensive study of the Twelve Steps aimed at deepening understanding of recovery as a way of life.

Serenity, Drs. Robert Hemfelt and Richard Fowler (Thomas Nelson)
A companion for Twelve-Step recovery.

On Spiritual Topics

Blessed Are the Addicts, John A. Martin (HarperCollins)
The spiritual side of alcoholism, addiction, and recovery.

I'd Like to Call for Help But I Don't Know the Number, Abraham J. Twerski, M.D. (Pharos)
The search for spirituality in everyday life.

Addiction and Grace, Gerald G. May (HarperCollins)
Love and spirituality in the healing of addictions.

The Sermon on the Mount, Emmet Fox (HarperCollins)
Tapping into the power of prayer as a key to success in life.

On Relapse Prevention

Staying Sober, Terence T. Gorski and Marlene Miller (Herald House/ Independent Press)
A guide to relapse prevention.

On Getting It Together

Stage II Recovery, Ernie Larsen (HarperCollins)
Rebuilding life once abstinence is firmly established.

Overcoming Perfectionism, Ann W. Smith (Health Communications)
One author's key to a balanced recovery.

Organized Serenity, Jann Mitchell (Health Communications)
Practical day-to-day relief from chaos as you learn to manage your time in recovery.

A New Pair of Glasses, Chuck "C" (New-Look)
Taking an undistorted second look at life and yourself.

On Finance

How to Get Out of Debt, Stay Out of Debt, and Live Prosperously, Jerrold Mundis (Bantam)
Negotiating with creditors, collection agencies, and the IRS, the tried and proven Debtors Anonymous way.

For Adult Children of Alcoholics

Adult Children of Alcoholics, Janet Woititz (Health Communications)
The title of this classic says it all.

I Am an Adult Who Grew Up in an Alcoholic Family, Thomas W. Perrin (Crossroad)
An insightful book that doesn't blame the alcoholic for the adult child's troubles.

Healing the Child Within, Charles L. Whitfield, M.D. (Health Communications)
Discovery and recovery for adult children of dysfunctional families.

The Twelve Steps for Adult Children (Recovery Publications)
For anyone who grew up in a dysfunctional environment.

On Codependency

Codependent No More, Melody Beattie (HarperCollins)
Control issues for spouses and others in recovery.

LEGAL ISSUES

Your spouse is having divorce papers drawn up. The judge won't let you have your driver's license back. Your boss has fired you or won't promote you because you once had a drinking problem and he fears that stress could cause a recurrence. Why don't they understand that you're okay now, that alcoholism/addiction is a disease and that you have it under control?

The reason is simple: the world isn't one big AA meeting, and most people in it haven't yet come around to understanding that alcoholism/addiction is as much a disease as hepatitis or tuberculosis. But sick or not you are responsible for any havoc you wrought during active addiction. That means that in sticky legal situations you need sound advice from an experienced attorney. That attorney doesn't have to be in recovery (though it sometimes helps) but he or she should have a thorough understanding of addiction issues, including the job discrimination provisions of the Americans with Disabilities Act (see page 569) and any state laws that apply.

A referral from an AA friend who has gone through a situation similar to yours is the best way to find such a lawyer. For more information on dealing with your legal problems, consult the books listed in the legal issues section of Resources.

On Women and Recovery

I'm Black and I'm Sober, Chaney Allen (CompCare)
A minister's daughter's victory over alcoholism.

Many Roads, One Journey, Charlotte Davis Kasl (HarperCollins)
Advanced recovery from a woman's viewpoint.

On Relationships

Boundaries Where You End and I Begin, Ann Katherine (Parkside)
How to set healthy boundaries and build healthy relationships.

Another Chance, Sharon Wegscheider-Cruse (Science and Behavior Books)
Insights and steps toward recovery for the alcoholic family.

On Non-Alcoholic Drinks

Drinks Without Liquor, Jane Brandt (Workman)
Lively beverages for bashes, beaches, barbecues, and birthdays. Substitute fruit juice concentrate for the heavy doses of sugar called for in some recipes.

On Legal Issues

A Practitioner's Guide to Alcohol and the Law, David Evans (Hazelden)*
Valuable counsel from an attorney specializing in the legal problems of alcoholics and addicts.

Kids, Drugs, and the Law, David Evans (Hazelden)*
What parents need to know about negotiating legal minefields when their children are in trouble.

On Humor in Recovery

The Cat Who Drank Too Much, LeClair Bissell, M.D. and Richard Weatherwax (Hazelden)
A whimsical cartoon-and-text look at alcoholism.

---

*Available from David Evans, Esq., 35 Cold Soil Road, Lawrenceville, NJ 08648 (FAX: 609/844-0241).

For Families

Al-Anon Faces Alcoholism (Al-Anon)**
Professionals in the field and Al-Anon members describe a wide variety of experiences with alcoholism. Includes information on Al-Anon's fellowship, principles, and program.

Courage to Change, One Day at a Time in Al-Anon II (Al-Anon)**
Update of the classic. Splendid collection of insightful daily reflections from friends, lovers, spouses, parents, and children of alcoholics who reveal surprisingly simple things that transformed their lives.[†]

For Teenagers

Turning Yourself Around, Kendall Johnson (Hunter House)
Self-help strategies for troubled teens using behavioral and Twelve Step techniques.

Choices and Consequences, Dick Schaefer (Johnson Institute)
What to do when a teenager becomes a user.

For Children

It Will Never Happen to Me, Claudia Black (Ballantine)
Guidelines and help for children of alcoholics of all ages.

Living with a Parent Who Drinks Too Much, Judith Seixas (Morrow)
Helping middle school children make sense of family alcoholism.

My Dad Loves Me. My Dad Has a Disease, Claudia Black (Mac)
A workbook to help children of alcoholics (to age 14) live with and understand the disease.

**If not available in your bookstore, order directly from Al-Anon Family Services.

My House Is Different, Kathe DiGiovanni (ages 4 to 9) (Hazelden)
The alcoholic family through a child's eyes.

An Elephant in the Living Room, Jill Hastings and Marion Typpo (CompCare)
A workbook for elementary school age children.

I Can Talk About What Hurts, Janet Sinberg and Dennis Daley (Hazelden)
For children in chemically-dependent homes, with a guide for parents to help kids talk about their pain.

The Cat at the Door (and Other Stories to Live by), Ann Mather and Louise Weldon (Hazelden)
A collection of 183 helpful values stories for kids 4 to 8.

The Brown Bottle, Penny Jones (Hazelden)
A poignant fable about a caterpillar who moves into a whiskey bottle and dies there.

The "This I Know" series, P.K. Hallinan (Hazelden)
Playful rhymes and charming stories to teach lessons to troubled children in alcoholic families.

What's Drunk, Mama? (Al-Anon Family Groups)
A read-aloud book for parents and toddlers explaining the disease concept in easily understandable terms.

On Smoking Cessation

Quit and Stay Quit, T.A. Rustin (Hazelden)
An effective personal program for kicking cigarettes out of your life.

A Glossary of Recovery Terms

Every field has a jargon of its own. Recovery is no exception. Becoming familiar with the words and terms used by those who've been there before you will make you both more comfortable and more knowledgeable as you go through your own recovery. Here are the most commonly used, listed alphabetically:

Abstinence syndrome: The group of symptoms that occur when a dependent person abstains from the substance he or she is addicted to; see Withdrawal.

Abuse: The misuse or overuse of a substance (using more than the norm); using a substance in a way different from the way it is generally used, either medically or socially; using any illegal substance (including alcohol if one is underage); continued use of a substance even though it is causing problems in one's life.

ACOA: See Adult Children of Alcoholics.

Addiction: Loss of control and compulsive use of a mood- or mind-altering chemical or chemicals, along with the inability to stop the use in spite of the fact that such use is causing problems in one's life. Having a physical and/or psychological dependence on a substance.

Adult Children of Alcoholics: Adults who grew up in an alcoholic home and were affected by the experience. There are those who believe that such individuals share specific behavioral traits, which frequently adversely affect their adult relationships.

Al-Anon: A Twelve-Step recovery program for family members and friends of alcoholics, including ACOA's.

Alateen: A Twelve-Step recovery program for adolescent children of alcoholics.

Alcoholic: A person with the disease of alcoholism.

Alcoholics Anonymous (AA): The original Twelve-Step recovery program, begun in 1935 by two alcoholics to provide mutual help and support for people who have a desire to stop drinking.

Alcoholism: This is a primary, chronic illness with genetic, psychosocial, and/or environmental factors influencing its development and manifestations. The disease is often progressive and fatal. (Some believe it is *always* progressive.) The alcoholic has either continuous or periodic loss of control over drinking, is preoccupied with alcohol, uses it despite the damage it is doing, and has distorted thinking, most notably denial. The quantity of alcohol consumed is less important than the effect of the drinking on the individual's life and the lives of those around him or her.

HOW PSYCHIATRISTS DEFINE DEPENDENCE

A formal diagnosis of "psychoactive substance dependence" is made if at least three of the following are true:

❖ The substance is taken in larger amounts or over a longer period than the person intended.

❖ There is a persistent desire to stop using the drug and/or unsuccessful efforts to quit.

❖ The person spends a great deal of time trying to obtain the substance (for example, resorts to stealing), taking it, or recovering from its effects.

❖ Using the substance disrupts the person's life and interferes with meeting important social obligations or work activities.

❖ The person continues to use the substance despite knowing that it is causing problems (for example, drinking even though it makes an ulcer worse).

❖ There is marked tolerance: the person keeps needing more and more of the substance to get the desired effect.

❖ There are withdrawal symptoms when the person stops taking the substance.

❖ The substance is taken to avoid the withdrawal symptoms.

Adapted from the *Diagnostic and Statistical Manual of Mental Disorders, III-R* of the American Psychiatric Association.

Antabuse: A medication (disulfiram) that inhibits the metabolism of alcohol. The patient taking Antabuse becomes extremely ill upon taking even a small amount of alcohol.

ASAM: The American Society for Addiction Medicine, the professional organization of addiction specialists.

Big Book: Officially called *Alcoholics Anonymous,* this is the official handbook of AA.

Blackout: A memory lapse while drinking; very common among alcoholics.

Bottom: The term often used to define the level to which the addiction has progressed. The "low-bottom" drunk sinks about as low as one can before getting help. The "high-bottom" quits before material things are lost and life gets really awful. The "middle-bottom" is obviously somewhere in between when going sober.

Chip: A small plastic disk (sometimes called a token) awarded on joining AA and on the completion of twenty-four hours, thirty days, sixty days, ninety days, six months, one year of sobriety, and so on. Each disk is a different color. Some Twelve-Step groups use a different way of marking anniversaries.

Cocaine Anonymous (CA): A Twelve-Step recovery program for those addicted to cocaine.

Codependency: A pattern of behavior in which those who are in a close relationship with an alcoholic/addict become in turn dependent upon that person's chemical dependency. The co-dependent builds his or her needs and life around the dependent person's. The addict is addicted to the drug, but the co-dependent is addicted to the addict. The addict may also be co-dependent.

Cross-addiction: This occurs when an individual who is addicted to one drug substitutes another in the hope of avoiding dependence and then becomes dependent on this drug as well. This can happen with drugs that are very different, such as alcohol and amphetamines.

Cross-talk: A direct response to comments made by another member at an AA meeting. Advice and admonitions are discouraged because each member is supposed to speak from personal experience only.

Denial: The self-deception that prevents alcoholics/addicts from admitting to themselves or to others the destructive nature of their drug use.

Detoxification (detox): Elimination of drugs from the body of a chemically dependent person, with or without the use of other drugs.

Drug dependency: A physical and/or psychological need for a mood-altering substance. Physical dependency is frequently associated with the development of tolerance (you need more to get the same effect) and the presence of symptoms when the drug is withdrawn. Not everyone who becomes physically dependent also loses control and becomes addicted. Some people become psychologically dependent and can lose control without having a physical addiction.

Drug screen: A urine test used to detect those who have been abusing drugs.

Drunkalogue (or drugalogue): A detailed description of one's own drinking (or using) behavior. The term may sometimes be used to describe an AA talk that dwells too much on the good old days and doesn't focus on how things got better and how they are now.

Dry drunk: A person who is sober but is behaving like a drunk.

Enabler: A person close to an alcoholic/addict who unwittingly enables the drinking or drug use behavior by taking over the responsibilities of the user, leaving the addict with little incentive to get well. Enabling behavior includes making excuses for, giving money to, or otherwise "helping" the person.

Enabling: Refers to any behavior direct or indirect, no matter how well-meaning, that allows the alcoholic/addict to continue drinking or using.

Flashback: The reexperience of an event from the past, usually accompanied by a state of fear, terror, or horror. It is often used to describe the recurrence of an hallucination or other drug-related experience when no drug has been used.

God box (or Higher Power box): A container (it can be do-it-yourself cardboard, a child's bank, or a box designed for the purpose and sold at recovery bookstores) that some recoverees use as a receptacle for their troubles. By jotting each problem down and dropping it in the box they turn difficult issues over to their Higher Power in a tangible way.

Half-life: The time it takes for half the concentration of a chemical substance in a person's body to clear from his or her blood. The longer the half-life, the longer the effects of the drug linger.

Home group: The Twelve-Step group that a recoveree chooses to be a member of and whose meetings he or she attends regularly.

Intervention: A carefully planned meeting at which an alcoholic/addict is confronted by family members, friends, and professionals in an effort to break through denial and start the subject on the road to recovery.

Mind-altering drug: Any substance that affects mood or thinking.

Mutual-help groups: Any group of nonprofessionals who meet to help one another deal with a problem, either over the short term (such as a support group for women who experience miscarriage) or the long term (such as Alcoholics Anonymous).

Narcotics Anonymous (NA): A Twelve-Step program for people addicted to drugs other than alcohol or tobacco.

Pigeon: The person sponsored and guided by a veteran member of a Twelve-Step group; also known as a "sponsee" or "baby."

Recoveree. An alcoholic/addict in recovery.

Recovery: The ongoing process of overcoming physical and psychological dependence on mind-altering substances (including alcohol) and learning to live in a state of total abstinence, without the need or desire for those substances. In recovery, one's physical and mental state are modified so that chemical substances are unnecessary for happiness and fulfillment.

Relapse: The return by a person in recovery to the self-prescribed, nonmedical use of any mind-altering drug (including alcohol) and risk of the consequent problems associated with such use. It is often preceded by negative thoughts, distorted perceptions, and even nonspecific physical symptoms.

Self-help groups: See Mutual-help groups.

Serenity Prayer: A nondenominational prayer used at AA meetings.

Slip: A brief return to drinking or drug-use behavior.

Sobriety: A state of mental clarity reached through abstinence from alcohol and other drugs.

Sponsee: The name given to the person who is sponsored by another in a Twelve-Step program; also called a "pigeon."

Sponsor: An individual in a Twelve-Step program who undertakes to guide and serve as mentor to another member. Acting as a sponsor is part of the Twelve-Step recovery process.

Stuffing feelings: This is the term often used to describe the act of keeping feelings smothered or repressed, something often done by alcoholics/addicts, who find it difficult to express feelings.

Tolerance: The need to take an increased amount of a substance in order to achieve a given effect; the amount needed usually continues to escalate.

Treatment for substance abuse: A planned systematic program to help a person become abstinent and remain so, while improving his or her quality of life.

Twelve Steps: The steps taken by the founders of AA as they turned away from alcohol; used today by millions of people attempting to recover from addiction to a wide variety of substances and behaviors.

Twelve Traditions: The guidelines that govern the way Alcoholics Anonymous groups are run.

Withdrawal syndrome: Symptoms that develop when an individual who is physically addicted to alcohol or another drug abstains (intentionally or otherwise) and levels of the drug in the body begin to diminish.

Working the program: Following the basic AA program, including attending meetings, selecting and working with a sponsor, and following the Twelve Steps.

A Note to Physicians

Her lips pursing distastefully, your nurse says, "Mr. Jones is your next patient." You groan inwardly. Not him again. Your reaction is only human—you're not violating your Hippocratic Oath. Of all the patients a family physician sees, the alcoholic/addict is the one who brings the most frustration to a busy practice day.

As doctors we tend to be interested in the areas we know best. Our medical schools routinely train us to recognize exotic conditions that not one patient we see in 10,000 will ever present us with: biliary atresia, say, or the Charcot's joints of late-stage syphilis. Meanwhile, 1 in 6 patients in our waiting room has an alcohol/addiction problem—a condition robbing them, on average, of 15 years of life. But (though this is beginning to change) most medical schools continue to see and hear no evil. They teach us as little about alcoholics and addicts as they do about Aristophanes and Aristotle.

A cycle of ostrich-ism is created. Medical schools (which until recently had little research to teach from) don't teach about alcoholism, so young doctors show little interest in it, so schools don't teach it. So doctors in practice feel inadequate and ill-informed about treating addiction and tend to work as little as possible with patients who have "the problem." So schools don't teach it. So . . .

But slowly our heads are emerging from the sand. Not long ago, *JAMA* published an editorial entitled "Patients Who Drink Too Much: Where Are Their Doctors?" One of the two accompanying articles disclosed that only a small percentage of doctors identify alcohol-related diseases in their patients and issue memorable warnings, *but* doctors who do significantly improve the odds that their patients will recover successfully. The second article concluded that alcoholics who achieve long-term abstinence tremendously reduce their mortality risks as compared to alcoholics who don't.

It's about time we acknowledged that the drinkers and druggers who wind up on Skid Row show up in our offices first, often—and it's up to us to recognize it—at a highly teachable moment. As *JAMA* editorial writer Dr. Thomas L. Delbanco neatly summed up: "Doctors are beginning to take pride in their success stories. After all, as we grapple increasingly with chronic diseases, we encounter few where our intervention can be as pivotal in turning patients away from a progressive, debilitating, and often tragic illness toward a fully healthy life. Alcoholism provides both patient and doctor with that opportunity."

Alcoholism is a disease that causes other diseases—something like 350 of them. No body part or system escapes. Substance abuse (including the well-advertised substance known as tobacco) is responsible for more than half of all needlessly shortened lives in the U.S.

Does quitting make a difference? A recent *JAMA* article concluded that alcoholic men who achieve stable abstinence differ not a whit from nonalcoholic men in mortality experience, but alcoholics who relapse die at a rate 4.96 times that of an age- sex-, and race-matched representative sample. It's not unreasonable to conclude that eliminating alcohol abuse could add more years to life expectancy than curing cancer or heart disease. Some public health authorities—and I don't mean just specialists in addiction medicine—are beginning to see alcoholism/addiction as our number one health problem.

The disease affects not only the patients who are abusing chemical substances but those around them. It's likely that many of your non-addicted patients—spouses, children, siblings, or parents of addicts—are suffering, too. Nationally, 43 out of every 100 do. When nonaddicted family members come in sick, it's important to remember that their physical or emotional presenting symptoms may as likely be caused by a toxic relationship as by a toxic illness.

If Jane Smith's lungs fail, all of her body's linked organs, including her brain, will die. If Jane, mother of three, becomes an alcoholic, a similar ripple effect may destroy her family. In dealing with multiple generations in a family practice, I've found that the pattern of drinking, as well as the addiction itself, seems to be handed down. If dad is a violent and abusive drinker, chances are that Junior will be too. Unless there's appropriate intervention.

So what can you do before your patient's health deteriorates and his or her family disintegrates? A great deal. First, learn to recognize the alcoholic/addict. Learn what the disease is like and what medical and social problems occur in recovery. Then learn how to help him—or her. Reading (or at least skimming) this book, *Alcoholics Anonymous* (generally referred to as the "Big Book"), and attending one or two open AA meetings (you'll find them fascinating) should give you a running start. Additional material aimed at health professionals is available from the National Clearinghouse for Alcohol and Drug Information (for their catalog, write to NCADI Publications, P.O. Box 2345, Rockville, MD 20852).

Most important for you to recognize, as a prescribing physician, is that alcoholism/addiction is still an incurable disease, and that recoverees are at risk any time they use a mood-altering drug (alcohol, antihistamines, benzodiazepines, and so on); some may even be at risk popping aspirins. That risk continues for the rest of their lives. That means that medications should be used only when risk outweighs benefit and under very carefully controlled conditions. Chapter 13 explains safe drug use and non-drug options that should be tried first. American Society of Addiction Medicine (ASAM) can also supply you with guidelines for treating recovering patients.*

How can you make it clear to both your staff and your patients that alcoholism/addiction is a disease, and that doctors can do something about it? For starters, try routinely including questions about alcohol and drug use in your patient histories and placing AA educational pamphlets, the Big Book, and (if you find it as helpful as we've tried to make it) *The Recovery Book* in your waiting room alongside "Ten Cancer Warning Signs" and "What You Should Know About AIDS."

—Al J. Mooney, M.D.

---

*Write to ASAM at 5225 Wisconsin Avenue NW, Washington, D.C. 20015 for a schedule of Category 1 AMA continuing education courses offered to physicians. It's an excellent beginning for acquiring alcoholism/addiction treatment information and could nudge you toward ASAM certification as an addictionist.

A Note to Employers

A subway motorman is drunk and fails to heed a signal. (A train crashes with heavy casualties.) A utility worker turns up for work stoned, and miscalculates. (A fellow employee is seriously injured in a gas blast.) A pilot self-medicates with a drug that hampers his depth perception. (His giant jet's near-miss on landing shakes up his crew and passengers, and the entire airline hierarchy.)

Recognizing that employee impairment by drugs or alcohol places the public at risk, the law requires that utilities, transportation carriers, and other high-risk industries routinely test their employees for these substances. But you don't have to be in a safety-sensitive business to worry about the effects of an employee's substance abuse on your company's reputation, on the safety and welfare of other workers or customers, or on your profit-and-loss statements. You know as well as anyone that billions of dollars a year go down the drug drain—because of missed workdays (substance abusers are absent up to ten times as often as nonusers), accidents (abusers file twice as many workmen's compensation claims and cost two and a half times as much in medical claims), inefficiency and lost business.

With approximately ten people in every hundred estimated to be abusing chemical substances, the odds are good that if you have ten employees, at least one is a catastrophe waiting to happen. Or is gradually happening already. (If you have 1,000 employees, you have 100 time bombs on staff.) You could wait for the explosion, then fire the employee and accept the potentially astronomical financial consequences. Or you could head the blast off before it occurs by identifying employees at risk and giving them the chance to get better before insisting they get out. This second procedure costs a little more initially, but in the long run is much more cost-effective.

It reduces the risk of losses because of worker impairment, allows you to retain experienced employees rather than having to train new ones, and can tremendously improve employee morale. It also gives you a better chance of having a sober employee (since the person being treated is monitored, whereas a new employee may have an equally bad problem that you know nothing about). Another reason firing doesn't make sense: You've put up with deteriorating performance over a period of months or even years. Now when the chance of a handsome payback comes—an exemplary employee—you dump him or her instead. For every dollar invested in treatment, it's estimated there's a $4 return to taxpayers (including you) in reduction of alcohol and drug-related crime, criminal justice costs, and theft.

Before you decide which path to take, you need to learn all you can about the disease known as alcoholism/addiction. You also need to know that the disease is treatable, but not curable. And that an employee who has been treated and is clean and sober is likely to be a better—and safer—employee than one who is still using but hasn't shown any obvious signs of impairment. Yet. Reading this book will give you an intimate picture of what recovery is like and will show why a recovering employee can be a boon to your business.

The Drug-Free Workplace Act may also be a factor in your decision. In order to do business with the federal government or to receive federal grants, companies must comply with this act, which requires that you provide a drug-free workplace* and educate your employees about substance abuse. In high-risk work (nuclear, defense, transportation, utilities) drug testing is mandatory. In most cases, setting up an Employee Assistance Program (EAP) is the best way to accomplish all of this.

Once you've decided that you want to do something to prevent the damage caused by impaired employees, the first step is to draw up a company policy. You will also have to train supervisors and educate employees. For many larger companies, the focus of a substance abuse prevention program is the EAP. For smaller companies, forming a cooperative EAP or joining an existing one is a good route to take. A separate entity from Personnel or Human Resources, an EAP benefits the company by improving the welfare of employees and thus improving job performance. It provides very short-term counseling and help, refers out for longer-term counseling, and supervises outside drug treatment and counseling as well as continuing care to ensure that the employee is working the AA program. In most cases, the union or other employee representatives have imput into the structuring and operation of the EAP. The best EAPs are those which provide other services to employees as well—credit or family counseling, for example—so that visiting the EAP doesn't announce to the world: "I've got an addiction problem." The vast majority of companies who have gone the EAP route find that it works.**

Just as treating substance-abusing employees rather than dismissing them is good business, so is hiring job applicants who are in recovery. The law prohibits your discriminating against these individuals, but that's not the best reason to consider hiring them. Those with experience with such employees know that they not only are good bets, they often make superior workers. First of all, you know that the problem exists and can be on the lookout for signs of relapse. In the general employee population, at least 1 in 10 also has a problem, but you don't know which one and may be much slower to catch on before damage is done. Second, most people in recovery have learned relationship skills allowing them to cope with their lives and their work more effectively and to work better with others. Third, recoverees in the work force tend to self-police. As supervisors, they recognize the problem more quickly in others and are unlikely to tolerantly avert their eyes and "enable." They know the effects such behavior can have on productivity, safety, and general morale. They'll often take steps themselves to guide the offender into AA or treatment.

If you're skeptical, try one or two recovering employees. You're likely to be pleasantly surprised.

—Al J. Mooney, M.D.

*The drugs referred to here in most cases do not include alcohol, although in some industries (such as nuclear and transportation) alcohol testing is becoming mandatory too.

**For more information on setting up a program, call the National Institute on Drug Abuse helpline for managers and CEO's (1-800/843-4971). And send for *An Employer's Guide to Dealing with Substance Abuse,* published by the National Clearinghouse for Alcohol and Drug Information (NCADI, P.O. Box 2345, Rockville, MD 20852; 1-800/729-6686).

INDEX

A

G

N

R

DROP US A LINE

This book is for you. We welcome your suggestions for future editions: Ideas that have helped you (or friends or relations) in recovery. Subjects we've omitted. Problems we may have failed to address. If this book has been helpful, please let us know. If you find flaws, let us know that, too. We look forward to feedback. Write to us at: *The Recovery Book*, c/o Al J. Mooney M.D., 509 Midenhall Way, Cary, NC 27513 or e-mail to: amooney@willingway.com.